PEOPLE of the UPPER CUMBERLAND

PEOPLE
of the
UPPER CUMBERLAND

ACHIEVEMENTS and CONTRADICTIONS

Edited by
MICHAEL E. BIRDWELL
and
W. CALVIN DICKINSON

The University of Tennessee Press • Knoxville

Cloth: 1st printing, 2015.
Paper: 1st printing, 2017.

Library of Congress Cataloging-in-Publication Data

People of the Upper Cumberland : achievements and contradictions / edited by Michael E. Birdwell and W. Calvin Dickinson. — First edition.

pages cm

Includes bibliographical references and index.

ISBN 978-1-62190-371-0

1. Cumberland River Valley (Ky. and Tenn.)—History. 2. Cumberland River Valley (Ky. and Tenn.)—Social life and customs. 3. Cumberland River Valley (Ky. and Tenn.)—Social conditions. 4. Cumberland River Valley (Ky. and Tenn.)—Biography. I. Birdwell, Michael E., 1957- II. Dickinson, William Calvin.

F442.2.P46 2015

976.8'5—dc23

2014037583

CONTENTS

MEDICAL MEN AND WOMEN

AFRICAN AMERICANS AND RACE RELATIONS

ILLUSTRATIONS

ACKNOWLEDGMENTS

Books are not written in a vacuum; they do not miraculously appear fully formed and ready for publication. Writing a book and editing an anthology is a laborious process that requires lots of input, a willingness to take criticism, and an understanding that revising an article is intended to make it better. To all of the authors who helped make this book a reality we owe a debt of gratitude. When compiling the group of people who make a book go from a fledgling idea into reality, there is always that nagging fear—have we left anyone out? Let us say at the outset, that if you had hoped to see your name in print for something you did to assist us and it is not here, we beg your forgiveness. It is not our intention, nor the intention of the authors, to omit anyone who helped this project come into fruition.

Many authors are included to be sure that they name family and close friends first among those who assisted in writing or editing a book. Family and friends did act as sounding boards; they read some of the chapters in various stages of completion; they did offer moral support, and they listened to us blather on about this work as it progressed—often over a good meal or a stiff drink.

The authors want to thank the following people who have worked with us in many ways. Dr. Jeanette Keith provided encouragement, specific suggestions, and was always willing to discuss ideas related to this book. Though she no longer lives in the Upper Cumberland, she remains one of its sagest observers. The editors cannot express enough gratitude to the secretary of the History Department of Tennessee Technological University (TTU), Amy Foster. She assisted us in numerous ways. We want to thank Liz Kassera, who once again agreed to compose the index for us, a thankless task that makes life easier for the reading public. The Reverend Pat Handlson and Carolyn Stumpf of the First Presbyterian Church in Cookeville provided the editors with sanctuary and a place where they could work diligently in peace without fear of interruption.

When defining the region, everyone has an opinion, and most are equally valid in some way. Several people played an important role in helping the editors in their definition, including the academics Dr. Lynwood Montell, Dr. Jeanette Keith, Dr. Troy Smith, Dr. Benita Howells, Dr. Joe Douglas, Dr. Ric Finch, Dr. Roby Cogswell, and Dr. Homer Kemp, the latter who strenuously objects to the fact that the Upper Cumberland is a part of Appalachia. Others who assisted in defining the region were Stuart Carroll and Bobby Fulcher of Tennessee's Department of Environment and Conservation, Paula Stover of the Overton County Heritage Museum, Yvette Clark of TTU's Center of Excellence for Management, Utilization and Protection of Water Resources, and hundreds of other people who voiced their opinions about where it is that they live, work, and play.

Charlene McClain of TTU's Volpe Library is a phenomenal resource. She is like a bloodhound on the trail of a fugitive, and once she got on the scent of some obscure reference we needed, she made it her personal quest to find it. She is a delight to work with and is brimming with ideas for yet another book. Sonya Bowman who oversees Interlibrary Loan at TTU cheerfully tracked down long out of print books and articles. Likewise Mancil Johnson, director of the TTU Archives, is an invaluable resource, and he gave access to many of the scholars who contributed to this book, especially Mary Evins, Laura Clemons, Janey Dudney, and Opless Walker. Their articles could not have been adequately researched or written without Mancil's help. The TTU Archives contain numerous under-utilized collections, such as the Joe L. Evins papers, the Dora Lee Wilder Papers, the T.J. Farr papers, and the Upper Cumberland Medical Society collection, that add to our understanding of the region.

Materials in the various collections available at the Tennessee State Library and Archives (TSLA) provide a treasure trove, and it is easy to get sidetracked and head down some rabbit hole. Darla Brock, Susan Gordon, Carol Roberts, Ralph Sowells, Karina McDaniel, Myers Brown, and Dr. Wayne Moore helped keep us on track. Their enthusiasm for their jobs is infectious and their willingness to assist everyone from researchers to neophytes to seasoned professionals makes it a joy to do research there.

The story of Cordell Hull and John Gore could not have been recounted without the cooperation and assistance of the staff at the Cordell Hull Birthplace Museum in Byrdstown and the Friends of Cordell Hull. Chief among those we owe gratitude is Lana Rossi. Others who provided information and guidance include Kate Hull Ethridge, Ray Tardy, Dorothy Crabtree Harris, Leilabel Officer, Guy Yelton, James Chamberlain, Rose Hart Dale, Will Robbins, and Leon Alligood. Dr. William Brinker and Dr. George Webb of TTU read the article closely and made excellent suggestions for its improvement after the editors had their crack at it.

Research on John Catron began as a fluke when Assistant Public Defender John Nisbet saw Catron's portrait on a largely empty map of famous people from Overton County given out by First National Bank of Livingston. The authors want to thank Millard Vaughn Oakley for publishing and distributing the map that sent them on more than one wild goose chase. Numerous people read, re-read, and read yet again the article on Catron. Because this effort was plowing relatively new ground, many people (in addition to those previously mentioned at TSLA) assisted along the way, including Dr. Jeanette Keith, Dr. Paul Bergeron emeritus professor at the University of Tennessee; Dr. Bobby Lovett of Tennessee State University, Dr. James W. Ely, Jr. of Vanderbilt Law School, Dr. Carol Bucy of Volunteer State Community College, Mark Cheatham of Cumberland University, Ann Toplovich of the Tennessee Historical Society, and Jim Hoobler of the Tennessee State Museum. Members of the Tennessee Bar were prevailed upon for feedback, and they willingly obliged, including Mike Catalano, former Clerk of the Tennessee Supreme Court; Judge Leon Burns; Chancellor Ron Thurman; and, Public Defender David Brady, as well as attorneys Randy Chaffin, Jonathan Young, E.J. Mackie, Mike O'Mara, Donna Simpson, Kay Bradley, and Will Roberson. Paula Stover of the Overton County Heritage Museum cheerfully lent her aid and support of the research. Special thanks go to attorney Jerry Smith of Dickson, Tennessee, and Kristin Wells of TTU. Smith donated funds that made it possible for Nisbet and Birdwell to travel to Washington, D.C., and conduct research about Catron at the Library of Congress and the National Archives. The staffs at the Library of Congress and the National Archives were most helpful and efficient. Gerald York graciously opened his home and provided a great place to stay while in D.C. Diane Mount Nisbet offered her prodigious editing talents to remind the authors that they were writing an article not a book.

Lore surrounding Champ Ferguson is legion. Even so, a number of people graciously shared their research and their knowledge. Chief among those were Dr. Larry Whiteaker emeritus TTU history professor, who collected information on the guerrilla for decades, and Dr. Brian McKnight of the University of Virginia at Wise. Dr. Kent Dollar of TTU and various members the Upper Cumberland Civil War Round Table, including the estimable Jack Hurst, provided insights and criticisms which proved helpful. The cheerful staff of the White County Heritage Museum kept Troy Smith apprised of the community's attitudes toward Ferguson and the person who claimed that Ferguson evaded the gallows and spent a happy life in Texas long after the war ended. David Cross alerted the editors to the historical marker on the Albany, Kentucky, square that denounces Ferguson as a terrorist.

Attorneys and members of law enforcement as well as the family and friends of former moonshiners helped tell a balanced story of willful defiance of the law. The late General Jackson "Jack" Threet started the ball rolling during the numerous interviews with him when working on WCTE's documentary *The Wilder-Davidson Story*. Threet was an unrepentant moonshiner who served his time and continued to make illicit whisky long after bonded liquor was easily obtained. Other people who contributed to telling the story of moonshine in the region include Judge Larry Warner, District Attorney Randy York, Assistant District Attorney Caroline Knight, Assistant District Attorney Tony Craighead, Ivy Gardner, Randy Boston, John Egerton, Dr. Homer Kemp, Dr. E. Morgan Dudney, legendary Kentucky journalist Al Smith Jr., former Putnam County Sheriff Billy G. Smith, Malcolm Williams Jr., Tom Des Jeans of the Big South Fork National River and Recreation Area, Edie Williams, Dr. Minoa Uffleman of Austin Peay State University, the Reverend Caleb Cangelosi, Dr. Jim Jones of the Tennessee Historical Commission, the late attorney Baxter Key Jr., Michael Williams owner of Collier and McKeel Distillery, Dr. Tom Furtsch owner and proprietor of Father Tom's Pub, Bill Landry of WBIR's beloved *The Heartland Series*, Suzanne Russell of Clay County's Moonshine Daze, Dr. Suellen Alfred, Dr. Maggie Phelps, CRMC nurse Marchella Davis, Dr. Hank Mannle, John Clemons, Charlene McClain, and Willie Catherine Davis who reluctantly made shine during the Great Depression.

John Lee provided primary documents concerning Dora Lee Wilder and her medical career, which had not previously been available. William Byrd Young's memoir, which was typed by Janey Dudney's father U.L. "Cricket" Fulmer, formerly existed in only a handful of bound manuscripts. Fortunately, the Bon Air Historical Society in Bon Air, Tennessee digitized and annotated this rare primary document, which is now more widely available. Much gratitude is expressed to Linda Mackie and Don Graham III for making the rare work available. Materials about Alvin York's mother and the Chattanooga Medicine Company were made available by the Sergeant York Patriotic Foundation, and the Chattanooga Public Library, whose staff were gracious and eager to help. Special thanks go to Debbie York in her efforts to preserve the legacy of her great-grandfther. Once again thanks go to the TTU Archives. The T.J. Farr Papers are a bonanza of Upper Cumberland folklore as is the work of his colleague Elzia G. Rogers. Both acted as founding members of the Tennessee Folklore Society in the 1930s. Numerous medical professionals weighed in on the chapters concerning folk and professional medicine in the region. They included Bobby and Jean Davis, Dr. Sam Glasgow, Dr. Chuck Womack, Dr. E. Morgan Dudney, and Dr. Sam Barnes. Several laypersons recounted their personal stories about their medical experiences both good and bad, including Flavious Smith, Bill Smith, Bob Lee Dudney, Sarah Buckner, Callie Melton, Charlie Walker, and Oscar Walker. Randall Clemons and the Granville History Museum provided information and access to images of doctors from Jackson County. Dr. Lee Moore and the Moore family provided pictures of Dr. Tom Moore.

The people of Pleasant Hill, Tennessee, John Buck in particular, made the papers of Dr. May Cravath Wharton available before they were donated to the Tennessee State Library and Archives. The Pleasant Hill community continues to keep Dr. May's legacy alive and well. Thanks to the late Edna Barlow for her memories of the "doctor woman" of the Upper Cumberland.

Native American research was aided significantly by Ben Nance and Sam Smith of the Tennessee Division of Archaeology. Canaan Williams served as a research assistant while working on the essay. Others who contributed their time and their expertise were Dr. Troy Smith and Dr. Joe Douglas. Ward Weems of the Tennessee Department of Conservation and Environment, former head ranger at Old Stone Fort State Park, is a fount of knowledge about Tennessee's Indian past.

While numerous women have already been acknowledged for their contributions to this work, there are still many more who need to be thanked including Charlene Dickinson and Tammy O'Dell. Patsy Williams provided a great deal of information about her mother-in-law Dollie Williams, whose papers the family donated to the Tennessee State Library and Archives. The indefatigable Polly Page provided hours of interviews; she remains a dedicated craftswoman at the age of ninety-five.

Mark Burnett, TTU vice president for student affairs; Dr. Leo McGee, emeritus TTU professor; and Dr. Carl Owens, TTU Professor of Curriculum and Instruction provided information and advice about many of the African Americans discussed in this book. Their insights are much appreciated. Wali Kharif and Lynwood Montell interviewed numerous people who provided stories that would otherwise be lost, including Johnnie Wheeler, Morris Irby, Louise Moody, Robert Evans, Brad Savage, Kayla Buck, Tracey Hackett, Isaac Carver, Ethel Jane Hamilton, and Bea Audrey Isabel. Thanks go to the Cookeville History Museum, Mildred Garrett, and Steve Farley for helping procure images to illustrate "Little Known Voices," and "As Long as Your Money is Green."

Laura Clemons was fortunate to travel to New York to interview J. Robert Bradley, who owes much of his career to Charles Faulkner Bryan. TTU Chemistry professor Barbara Jackson assisted in the Bradley interview. Charles Bryan Jr. read the article and made subtle changes that improved the piece. Mancil Johnson helped in numerous ways from access to materials in the TTU archives to the large collection of photos related to Bryan and Bradley. Bill Zechman, former board member of the Bryan

Symphony Orchestra and volunteer producer and news analyst for WCPI, 91.3 in Bryan's hometown McMinnville, Tennessee provided an insightful interview he recorded with Bryan's widow Edith.

Mary Alice McClellan, Shakey McClellan, Robert Farley, and John Edward Roberts provided invaluable information. They also corrected a number of mistakes in various drafts of the article about John's Place. Steve Farley happily supplied historic photographs. Becky Magura and Amanda Collier of WCTE, Don Dickerson, Karla Clark, Charles Hand, and Russell Clarkson either agreed to be interviewed about John's Place or helped track down leads. Laura Clemons suggested interviewing former Cookeville mayor Bobby Davis, who provided important contextual and factual information. Emeritus TTU professor Dr. David Narrie explained the relationship between John's Place and the TTU Rugby Club. Claudette Stager and Brian Beadles of the Tennessee Historical Commission provided their much appreciated expertise when delving into the history of John's Place. Dr. Reavis Mitchell of Fisk University offered insight concerning John's Place in context with events prior to and during the Civil Rights era, as did our late friend John Egerton, author of the magisterial book *Speak Now Against the Day: The Generation Before the Civil Rights Movement in the South.* Mark Dudney shared an interview he recorded with Shakey McClellan that complemented other interviews with the late proprietor of John's Place. Hal Harder assisted in the research and editing of the article. Numerous people offered personal reminiscences of the heyday of the tavern, including Jenny and Greg Barnes, Mike "Whitey" White, Dave Johnson, Ginna Phillips, Anne Klein, Jim Woodford, Bruce and Alma Anderson, Mike Burduck, Mike Allen, Jack Henry, and Malcolm Rios.

Thanks go to Jeff Roberts, chair of the History Department at TTU, for his support and encouragement during this process that began over five years ago. The Cookeville History Museum, its staff and volunteers including Judy Duke, Pam Philpot, and Joanne White provided information, images, and valued input into this volume.

This project would not have been possible without the encouragement and support of Kerry Webb who recognized the value of this volume. We regret the fact that she left the UT Press to move to another UT Press in Austin, Texas, and wish her the best in her new endeavors. Thomas Wells picked up the torch and ably shepherded this anthology to its completion, and we owe him a sincere debt of gratitude. We also wish to thank Emily C. Huckabay and Pamela G. Strickland for their guidance and copyediting.

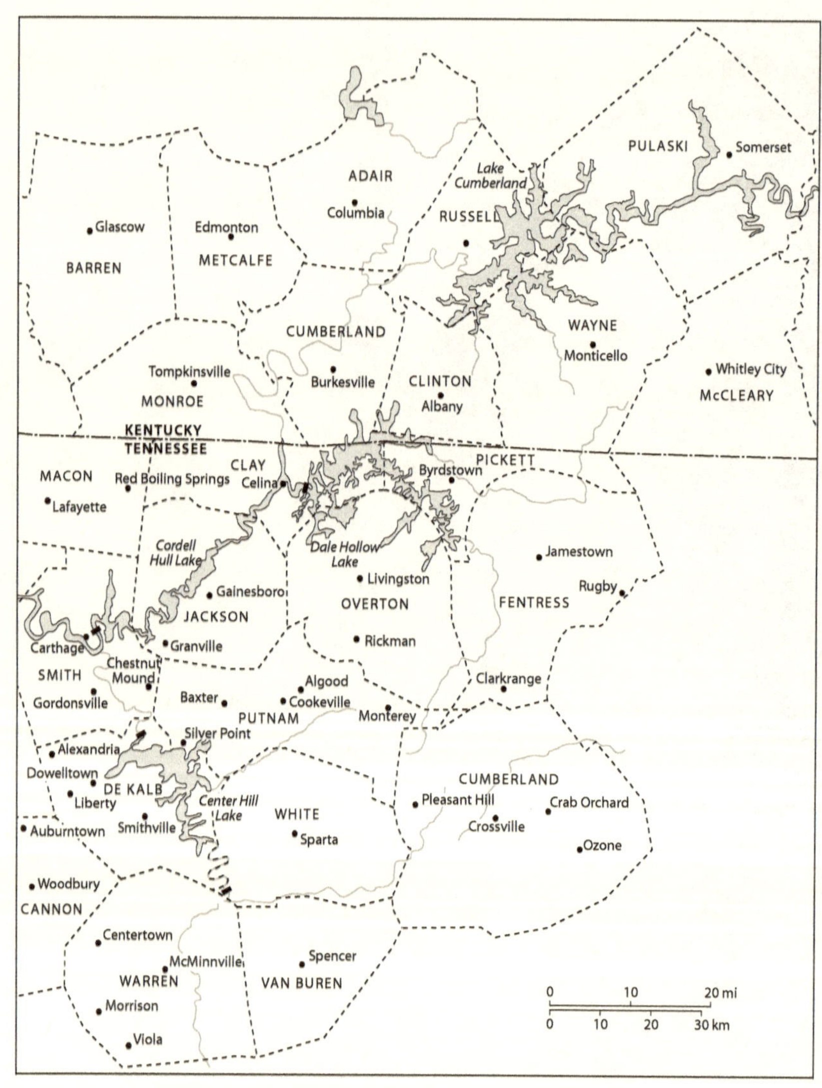

Upper Cumberland Region of Tennessee and Kentucky

INTRODUCTION

Michael E. Birdwell and W. Calvin Dickinson

The Upper Cumberland region of southern Appalachia remains an area that is less researched and less well known than the hills and valleys of Eastern Kentucky, Western North Carolina, East Tennessee, and West Virginia. An area within Southern Appalachia that shares cultural values, idiomatic expressions, foodways, religious rituals, and much more, the Upper Cumberland deserves more scrutiny. As Lynwood Montell has ably demonstrated, the Upper Cumberland is rich in history and culture, and it has only just begun to be seriously investigated. During the past decade citizens in the region have become more aware of the importance of the past and small archives and museums are flourishing, making many documents accessible for the first time. These new repositories are gems on the landscape, and the dedicated people who work at them are eager for scholars, genealogists, students, and others to explore the treasures they have to offer.

The Upper Cumberland Region

The rugged geography and hydrology of the Upper Cumberland of Kentucky and Tennessee shaped not only the landscape, but the people who live there. The Cumberland Plateau's rivers and streams sustain some of the nation's greatest variety of fish and mollusk species; its ravines contain the most diverse flora in all of Southern Appalachia. It is a rugged and beautiful landscape, but much of it is poorly suited to large-scale farming. Atop the Cumberland Plateau the topsoil is so thin many people joke that all they can grow on their farms are rocks. As a result, the few planters who chose to move into the area made their homesteads in the fertile valleys of Warren and White counties. Most people eked out an existence as subsistence farmers who labored at mills, tanneries, potteries, and later as loggers and miners. Those factors meant that slaves were a rarity in the Upper Cumberland, though a number of freed black communities, like Coe Ridge in Kentucky and Free Hills and Free State in Clay County and Jackson County, Tennessee, thrived.

The Cumberland River, which first defined the region, originates with the merging of smaller streams in Harlan County, Kentucky—Poor Fork, Clover Fork, and Martins Fork. As the river flows in its crooked circuitous path other creeks and rivers empty into it, including the Rockcastle River, Laurel River, Buck Creek, and Beaver Creek, in Kentucky. As the river makes its way into Tennessee drainage from the Cumberland Plateau and Eastern Highland Rim flows into it via numerous creeks and springs, that drain the Wolf River, Obey River, Roaring River, and Caney Fork which all make their way into the Cumberland River.[1]

The karst topography of the area is punctuated with caves, sinkholes, deep gorges, and spectacular waterfalls. The forest is primarily deciduous, though in Bledsoe, Fentress, and Van Buren counties in Tennessee, there are large stands of native hemlocks and yellow pines. Because the Upper Cumberland includes the river basin from Burnside, Kentucky, to Carthage, Tennessee, and its many feeder streams, the topography changed dramatically along the river's course in the years before the U.S. Army Corps of Engineers began building dams and impounding reservoirs. From the rugged terrain in the Big South Fork National River and Recreation Area and Daniel Boone National Forest atop the plateau, through its descent onto the Eastern Highland Rim, and finally into the more fertile lands in the river valley, the Upper Cumberland has historically been a difficult place to travel. The impediment of the eastern edge of the Cumberland Plateau proved imposing and forbidding to early settlers as it towered above them at over one thousand feet above the Tennessee River valley. Most tried to find a way around it, and settlement patterns in the Upper Cumberland defied national trends, for it was settled from west to east.[2]

Prior to the completion of the Walton Road in 1801 that connected the Cumberland River to the Clinch River between Carthage to Fort Southwest Point, in Tennessee overland trails were little more than rude paths blazed first by wild game and later improved upon by Native Americans and pioneers. The Walton Road and the Avery Trace that preceded it made overland travel somewhat easier, but roads in the region remained hazardous well into the twentieth century, as several of the essays make clear.

People, no matter where they lived in the Upper Cumberland, depended on the rivers for a variety of things. The advent of the steamboat in 1819 made it easier for people to get their goods to market, and allowed them to purchase finished goods from as far away as Pittsburgh, Pennsylvania, or New Orleans, Louisiana. River traffic and the life surrounding it were not significantly challenged until the railroads began to penetrate the area in earnest in the 1890s. But it was not until the National Highway Transportation Act of 1927 that good roads traversed the area and cars became the dominant means of transportation.

Because many of the people lived in relative isolation until the Civil War and Reconstruction intruded into their lives, old ways continued to linger in many pockets of the region. The people of the Upper Cumberland have historically been men and women of conviction who faced life's challenges stoically. They constitute a proud people who look after their own, and bristle at being called "hillbillies," or other seemingly unflattering epithets.

While many remain suspicious of outsiders—often with good reason—most people who live in the Upper Cumberland are kind, polite, and gracious, but their trust has to be earned. Memories of mistreatment at numerous hands—such as guerrilla fighters during the Civil War, mining companies, large scale lumber operations, owners of sweat shops, and the capriciousness of the federal government that flooded family lands and the graves of loved ones to create Lake Cumberland, Center Hill Lake, Dale Hollow Lake, and the Cordell Hull Reservoir—linger on. Likewise, they remain touchy about how they are depicted in the media, and they are often held up for ridicule. Memory, whether accurate or exaggerated, colors how residents perceive themselves and their region.[3]

The Upper Cumberland is not a unique region any more than the Tug River Valley of Kentucky and West Virginia or Cade's Cove in East Tennessee. It bears many things in common with both places, but it is an area that is rich in history and culture. The Upper Cumberland of Kentucky and Tennessee has produced men and women who gained national and international reputations. Novelist and historian Harriette Simpson Arnow was one of the first scholars to point out the rich diversity of the region. Legendary figure Daniel Boone explored both the Kentucky and Tennessee Upper Cumberland, and named places along the Cumberland River still in use today, including Waterloo and the Roaring River. In addition to Boone, other men and women have left their mark. William Martin of Smith County is reputed to be the first person to call Tennessee the Volunteer State during the War of 1812, though he was later embroiled in a bitter dispute with Andrew Jackson. Cordell Hull of Pickett County, Tennessee, paved the way for the Sixteenth Amendment, won the Nobel Peace Prize and served longer as U.S. Secretary of State than any person in U.S. history. Sergeant Alvin C. York captured the imagination of the nation as the greatest civilian soldier of World War I, but went on to push for progressive causes, championing universal education, good roads, and more in his native Upper Cumberland. Colonel Harlan T. Sanders of Corbin, Kentucky, earned a place in popular culture as he sold his fried chicken, which later became the global enterprise KFC. Basketball legend Neara White of Macon County, Tennessee, pushed the boundaries of what naysayers thought a female athlete could accomplish, while Graeme McGregor

Smith challenged women to do more and not simply live in the shadows of their husbands. Advertiser/author Bruce Barton, who was born in the tiny hamlet of Robbins, Tennessee, wrote the controversial 1920s bestseller *The Man Nobody Knows,* encouraging the development of prosperity theology. Country Music giants Lester Flatt, DeFord Bailey, Uncle Jimmy Thompson, Uncle Dave Macon, Bennie Martin, Dottie West and the Kentucky Headhunters, and less well-known musicians such as Bud Garrett, the Cluster Pluckers, and Ethan Ballinger all hailed from the Upper Cumberland and have influenced or continue to make an impression upon the music industry. Though largely lacking in ethnic diversity, and once touted by local color writers as home to the "purest Anglo-Saxon stock in the nation," the few minorities who moved into the region made a positive, lasting impact on the larger population. This rich tapestry, woven over centuries by hosts of different people, has only just begun to receive the exploration it so richly deserves.

For the purpose of this anthology, most of the essays deal with counties that lie within the Cumberland River watershed, but a few outlying counties are included because they fit within the traditions, history, and culture of the Upper Cumberland region. Counties discussed include Adair, Barren, Casey, Cumberland, Clinton, McCreary, Laurel, Metcalfe, Monroe, Pulaski, Russell, Wayne, and Whitley in Kentucky, and Bledsoe, Cannon, Clay, Cumberland, DeKalb, Fentress, Jackson, Macon, Morgan, Overton, Pickett, Putnam, Scott, Smith, Van Buren, Warren, and White in Tennessee. This volume is more than just a collection of essays about history. It includes essays concerning archaeology, anthropology, pharmacology, medicine, folklore, literature, gender studies, political theory, racial connections, and legal history.

In 2004 the editors produced an anthology, *Rural Life and Culture of the Upper Cumberland*, featuring seventeen articles that focused on its cultural history, with an emphasis on art, literature, film, religion, and material culture found there. Two chapters examined the continuing impact of the Civil War and World War II on the region. That book was not intended to be the final word on the rich history of the Upper Cumberland, nor is this anthology. While compiling the first volume, the editors understood what a treasure trove exists along the upper reaches of the Cumberland River and its tributaries, and this book is a continuation of those efforts.

These essays are intended to complement the research of Harriette Simpson Arnow, acknowledging her pioneering work in chronicling and analyzing the overlooked Upper Cumberland of Appalachia. Others who have contributed significantly to the understanding of the region are Lynwood Montell, Jeanette Keith, Charles Wolfe, Brian McKnight, Douglas

Anderson, Alvin Wirt, and Harry Caudill, in addition to the contributors to this volume. The editors hope that this anthology will inspire further investigations and will lead to a greater recognition and appreciation of the Upper Cumberland.

NOTES

1. When considering the Upper Cumberland one confronts numerous definitions and descriptions of the region. More research has been conducted in the area by geologists, biologists, agronomists, and other scientists than by historians and humanities scholars. For many who live or work in the Upper Cumberland, the region is defined by the drainage area of the upper reaches of the Cumberland River and its many tributaries. Since the river system acted as the first highway system, knowing the river and its numerous pathways proved crucial from its usage by Native Americans up through the early twentieth century. The Cumberland River continues to provide transportation for barges laden with cargo, employment for numerous companies small and large, game fish such as bass, and recreation for locals and tourists alike. While this definition of the Upper Cumberland is useful, it is also problematic. By defining the Upper Cumberland as only those counties whose creeks, rills, streams, and rivers meander their way into the Cumberland River, then only certain sections of some counties lie within the region. Look, for example, at Cumberland and Morgan counties in Tennessee. In the case of Cumberland County, the Obed River in the eastern part of the county empties into the Emory River and finally the Tennessee, while the area known as Grassy Cove in the southern end of the county is where the head waters of the Sequatchie River form, which flows from a cave into the valley and Tennessee River below. Likewise with Morgan County, depending on whether one lives east or west of Frozen Head State Park, the water flows either into the Cumberland River or the Tennessee watershed.
2. Many geologists and biologists define the region more broadly. The Upper Cumberland is honeycombed with caves and sinkholes, and for geologists it is the karst topography that defines the region, and they would include counties that lie beyond the Cumberland watershed. For biologists it is the amazing diversity of flora and fauna that comprise nearly one thousand species of rare plants and vegetation found nowhere else in the United States. These two versions of the Upper Cumberland extend the region beyond the watershed to include such counties as Bledsoe, Morgan, and Scott in Tennessee.
3. Yet another less formal, but in many ways as accurate, is how people identify themselves. There are a number of people who consider themselves citizens of the Upper Cumberland, but live outside the Cumberland River's watershed. For example, people living on the plateau in Rhea County, Tennessee, near the Cumberland County line have a stronger affinity for the Upper Cumberland than do their neighbors in the Sequatchie Valley living in and around Dayton. The same is true of most people who live in Van Buren County south of White County on

the Cumberland Plateau, and even some residents in the northern part of Grundy County. As one old timer remarked, "Just ask people where they go shopping; that'll tell you all you need to know." Well, maybe. It will not tell everything one needs to know, but it is revealing. If people tend to travel to Somerset, Kentucky, or Cookeville or Crossville, Tennessee, to do their routine shopping, they probably identify themselves as citizens of the Upper Cumberland. Another indication of self-identifying with the Upper Cumberland is the number of businesses that use "Upper Cumberland" in their branding and marketing. Yellow Pages reveal scores of businesses such as Upper Cumberland Air Experts, Upper Cumberland Computer Consultants, Upper Cumberland Decorating Center, Upper Cumberland Physicians Center, Upper Cumberland Termite and Pest Control, and so on *ad nauseum.*

REGIONAL OVERVIEW

1

An Enigmatic Tale

American Indians in Tennessee's Upper Cumberland

Randal D. Williams

The story of American Indians in the Upper Cumberland region of Tennessee is not well-known.[1] Due to the region's relative isolation, fewer academic and archaeological investigations have been undertaken in this rugged, predominantly rural area of Tennessee. People who lived there prior to European settlement seemed mysterious and enigmatic to later pioneers. They found Indian artifacts in plowed fields, river and creek bottoms, caves, and rock shelters. Earthen mounds stood silently in river bottoms, abandoned stone enclosures lay scattered throughout the region, and evidence of prior human occupation was everywhere. When Europeans settled in the region, except for a few scattered bands, no large Indian tribes occupied permanent habitation sites. Though the region had been traversed for centuries by Indians who followed animals along ancient pathways and down the Cumberland River and its tributaries, they made numerous camps throughout the region. The area served as a communal hunting ground for several tribes who had little knowledge of the Indians who came before them, adding to the mystery of who the Upper Cumberland's first inhabitants were.[2]

Myths developed about construction of large, earthen mounds settlers found throughout the Ohio and Tennessee Valleys and along the Cumberland River and its tributaries. The myth of a "lost race" of white mound builders arose explaining the existence of mounds and their artifacts, giving credence to what became the entrenched mythos of Mound Builders, deeming American Indians incapable of building such structures.[3] Europeans' interpretation of American Indians of antiquity was decidedly skewed because they believed their culture superior to the "savages" they encountered. Decades passed before scientific researchers started to recognize and understand the artifacts found in the archaeological record of the river valleys of the Midwest and Southeast.[4]

The Upper Cumberland is a region physically characterized by the Cumberland Plateau, the southern segment of the Appalachian Plateaus Province of the Appalachian Highlands, and the Eastern Highland Rim of the Interior Low Plateau Province.[5] The plateau's eastern border is marked by an imposing, one thousand foot escarpment; the western margin of the Cumberland Plateau is irregular and highly dissected due to stream erosion. The Cumberland Plateau is a rugged tableland rising one thousand feet above the surrounding landscape, with mountain peaks rising upwards of three thousand feet. The Cumberland Plateau has influenced human settlement and subsistence patterns since humans first entered the area millennia ago. The Eastern Highland Rim lies immediately west of the Cumberland Plateau, standing one thousand feet above sea level, and soils of the Highland Rim derived from different limestone formations. Numerous springs, creeks, and rivers, chiefly the Cumberland River, water the Cumberland Plateau and Eastern Highland Rim. The term "Upper Cumberland" refers to the navigable portion of the Cumberland River between Carthage, Tennessee, and Burnside, Kentucky. The Cumberland River and its tributaries have been central to life in the Upper Cumberland since the end of the Pleistocene era.

Earliest inhabitants of the Upper Cumberland were bands of nomadic hunter-gatherers known as Paleoindians. It is not known what these people called themselves, what languages they spoke, or the nature of their cosmology. While culturally enigmatic, they left ample evidence behind. Their principal, defining lithic technology involved removal of flakes along the sides of their projectile points, creating channels, or flutes, which gave them a distinctive appearance, commonly referred to as Clovis points.[6] In the Cumberland River Valley, another Paleoindian point, one unique to the Eastern Woodlands, is the Cumberland point, similar to Clovis only narrower and tapered toward the basal end.[7] These fluted points were part of a sophisticated tool kit and apparently indigenous developments, as no antecedent has yet been discovered in Asia or Europe.

The Upper Cumberland was much different climatically in the Late Wisconsin period (ca. 23,000 to 10,500 BCE) and the Early Holocene era (ca. 10,500 to 6500 BCE), than it is today. During the Late Wisconsin—when many believe humans first arrived in the Upper Cumberland—the region was much cooler and covered with coniferous boreal (northern) forest. Large, Ice Age megafauna roamed the region. Remains of extinct species such as mastodon, giant ground sloth, camel, and bison have been located in cave deposits throughout the area. Paleoindians hunted other species, such as peccaries, bears, jaguars, elk, and tapirs that lived in the Upper Cumberland. Remains of a spectacled bear were discovered in the Upper Cumberland in the Grassy Cove Saltpeter cave in Cumberland County. The most diverse fossil fauna ever discovered in Tennessee, and one of the most diverse in all of North America, was found in Robinson Cave, on Maxwell Mountain, in Overton County.[8]

Paleoindians proved adept hunters, pursuing animals of all sizes to supplement their diet. Early regional hunter-gatherers availed themselves to all resources available, both plant and animal. Evidence suggests they hunted primarily with spears, due to the great number of spear points in the archaeological record. Big Clovis and Cumberland points were suited to hunting large animals, but that was probably not their only purpose. Evidence illustrates larger stone blades doubled as knives.

Paleoindians set up camp on ridges or slopes overlooking watering areas where game gathered, allowing hunters elements of observation and surprise. Several Paleolithic campsites and tools found in the Upper Cumberland meet this description, such as the Beaty Swamp area of Overton County, where a ridge overlooks a low-lying swamp that has existed for millennia. Upper Cumberland lake shores and stream banks have revealed the presence of Paleoindian hunters who utilized these resource-rich areas to meet their needs.

Depending on the task at hand, Paleoindians utilized many tools. They employed various types of scrapers and microblades to prepare meat and animal hides. They sewed cloth and repaired garments with bone tools, such as needles and awls. Adept and skilled toolmakers Paleoindians created highly specialized lithic instruments and adapted to their environment.

Dramatic climate change during the Late Wisconsin period (which signaled the end of the Pleistocene era) affected subsistence behavior of Southeastern Paleoindian hunters. Initially spruce-birch-pine boreal forest dominated the region, and hunter-gatherers utilized the resources of their environment; however, by around 10,500 BCE, climate change ushered in the Early Holocene, or Recent, era. [9] Temperatures increased and boreal forests advanced northward as great ice sheets covering the northern part of the continent started to melt. Forests in the highest elevations of the Southern Appalachian Mountains, such as Clingman's Dome in Tennessee, or Mount Mitchell, North Carolina, are remnant boreal forests. The highest Appalachian Mountain elevations are the only environment remaining in the Southeast capable of supporting such forests. When people visit these mountain peaks, they can visualize what the Upper Cumberland must have looked like when Paleoindian hunters existed and followed their nomadic lifestyle.

Virtually nothing is known about Paleoindian social structure.[10] These people were highly adapted to their environment, which indicates a high level of social cooperation, and probably differentiation of roles and duties within the social group. According to Alice B. Kehoe:

> Essentially, Paleoindians were, in global terms, Late Paleolithic people, fully modern anatomically but without agriculture and permanent villages. They lived by hunting, exhibiting high skill in manufacturing weapons and in strategies for moving into range to use their spears, either propelled by hand throw or with the added leverage of the atlatl (spear-thrower board), or thrust directly into the animal. Changing camps to follow game movements and harvest plant foods in season, their habitations sites look meager. Their nomadic life was well adapted not only to surviving on the game of the late Pleistocene, but also adjusting to the tremendous shifts in climate and environments of the terminal Pleistocene. Clovis blades are found throughout the United States, proving the makers' remarkable capacity to enter and exploit new habitat zones, filling the continent with human families.[11]

Future archaeological investigations, improved dating and data gathering techniques, along with advances in genetics and linguistics, may answer fundamental questions about the social structure of Paleoindians, but some answers may lie so far in the remote past to be forever irretrievable.

By 8000 BCE, oak-hickory deciduous hardwood forests recognizable today dominated the Southeast, ushering in the Holocene, replacing the last vestiges of the Ice Age.[12] Paleoindian hunting traditions declined as ice sheets retreated and large, cold-adapted animals became extinct. The Holocene's warmer climate induced vegetal change and a new culture evolved in response. This new tradition, referred to as the Archaic period, was the longest prehistoric period of the Southeast, lasting some seven thousand years, and divided into Early, Middle, and Late phases.[13] An indigenous culture, Archaic tradition most likely developed gradually from earlier Paleoindian cultures, although the exact nature of Archaic cultural development remains shrouded by time.[14]

As Pleistocene megafauna fell extinct, and temperatures rose, human populations of the Upper Cumberland and the greater Southeast adapted. The archaeological record bears this out with new types of projectile points emerging. Gone are fluted Paleoindian Clovis and Cumberland points.

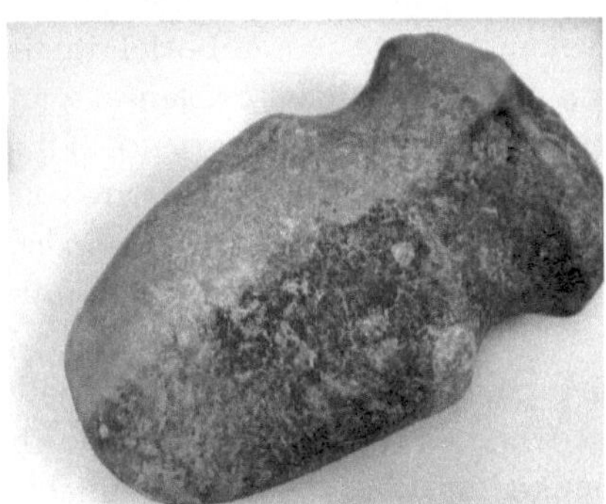

Above: Stone tools and a stone adz head.
Left: Closer view of a stone adz.
Credit: Michael Birdwell.

New game animals and plant resources required different tools, and the highly specialized fluted blades were no longer as effective.

In the Southeast and the Upper Cumberland, stone resources suitable for tool making apparently influenced settlement patterns.[15] Need for high quality flint and chert to produce an expanded tool kit and a higher diversity of projectile points, made quarry sites more important than ever before. Indeed, the Archaic era is marked by widespread changes in projectile styles.[16] Indians used the same quarries for centuries. Archaic people developed polished stone artifacts. Numerous atlatl weights, some highly stylized, called bannerstones or boatstones, exist in their Archaic context. Steatite, or soapstone, vessels and pipes have been found in the region, especially along the Cumberland River. Because the Archaic was the longest prehistoric period more extant Archaic artifactual material exists throughout the Upper Cumberland. Archaic point types ranged from early Archaic Dalton and Hardaway, considered transitional types because they appear soon after the end of the Paleoindian period, to the nearly ubiquitous Early Archaic Kirk Corner-Notched. Hunters used atlatls to propel their spears with great velocity.[17]

Archaic people exploited their resource rich environment. Habitation developed on ridges, stream banks, and lake sides, such as the Penitentiary Branch site in Jackson County, Tennessee, where there was access to food, firewood, and water. Using nuts such as walnuts, hickory nuts, hazelnuts, and acorns, they ground them into a type of flour for bread making.[18] Seeds, roots, berries, fowl, small game, shellfish, and larger browsing animals became staples of the Archaic diet, one much more diverse than their Paleoindian ancestors. Early Archaic people continued to be nomadic. Permanent settlements did not come until later with the advent of a more sedentary, agriculture-based culture after certain plants were domesticated.[19]

By the Middle Archaic, Indians developed more elaborate burial rituals and dedicated cemeteries, indicating a highly ritualized existence, with belief in spirits, gods, and an afterlife. What the religious experience of the Archaic people entailed remains unknown, but it is evident that care was used when burying the dead. Small mound features over grave sites exist, but it was later, during the flowering of the Woodland period, when full-scale mound building commenced.

During the Middle Archaic, people exploited riverine resources in new ways. By 2500 BCE, sea levels were approximately the same as today, which meant river and stream gradients changed, making them more suitable for shallow-water mollusks and different fish species. The Cumberland River Valley contains many shell middens—trash heaps—formed from discarded mollusk shells indicating that riverine resources became staples of the Middle Archaic diet.

As the Archaic period progressed and local populations expanded, natural resources were utilized as never before. Life became more sedentary in resource rich areas. Along with it came different means of processing and transporting goods. During earlier parts of the Archaic, steatite vessels and containers made of plant fibers and organic material represented all that were available. By the latter Archaic period, pottery technology appeared along the coastal plain of South Carolina, circa 2500 BCE.[20] Ceramic technology quickly spread inland, arriving in the Cumberland River Valley shortly thereafter. Trade networks were established with people outside the Cumberland region. These exchange networks followed inland routes and waterways, serving as major arteries for distribution of goods, ideas, and new technologies. The Archaic period, coinciding with the advent of the

Projectile points found during archaeological excavations in the upper Cumberland region. Credit: Michael Birdwell.

Holocene, saw North America's flora and fauna shift into patterns that still exist.[21]

Professionals generally agree that the Woodland period began around 1000 BCE and lasted until roughly 700 CE.[22] As an abundance of new projectile point types represented the main hallmarks of the Archaic period, the Woodland period is known for the development of ceramic technology, or the so-called Container Revolution. According to Charles Hudson, the Woodland period was "probably the most distinctive, the most completely indigenous culture ever to exist in eastern North America."[23] The Woodland period gave rise to full-scale burial mound building, and elaboration of mortuary customs, unlike anything previously. Though pottery and burial mounds began near the end of the late Archaic, they came to fruition during the Woodland. Widespread use of pottery with local variations, and more reliable subsistence agriculture augmented traditional hunting and gathering techniques.

Abundant evidence of Woodland culture exists in the Upper Cumberland. Numerous Woodland period mounds and enclosures remain, though many were destroyed through the years by agricultural practices and construction activity. Areas where prehistoric people settled were advantageous for the same reasons for Europeans. Settlers prized river crossings, springs, fertile bottomland, and elevated ridges since the beginning of human habitation in the region. But Woodland people exploited and shaped their environment unlike any previous culture.

Around two thousand years ago in the Eastern Woodlands, a revolutionary shift in construction began with the building of enormous mounds and other seemingly ceremonial earthworks. Mound building reached its height with Hopewell culture, named for a farm in Ohio where the culture was first described. Hopewell left an indelible mark in the Upper Cumberland. It originated in the earlier Adena complex[24] in the Ohio valley, and was one associated with mound building, elaborate funerary customs, grave goods, and trade networks. Hopewell people expanded and elaborated on this earlier cultural complex. It marked the zenith of the Woodland culture utilizing exotic raw materials such as copper, marine shells, obsidian, grizzly bear teeth, meteoric iron, and creating luxury items for personal adornment throughout the culture. Unique Hopewell artifacts are unlike any previous cultural tradition. Woodland culture produced clay and steatite pipes, including the famous "Blind Wolf" pipe found in Macon County, Tennessee, in 1940. The Hopewell Exchange Zone covered most of the Eastern woodlands, but stretched well beyond, as indicated by exotic materials found in association with Woodland Hopewell sites.[25] While the Cumberland River Valley was well beyond the Hopewell cultural hearth, the influence of this dynamic culture was copied far afield. Hopewell-influenced artifacts have been found throughout Tennessee and the Upper Cumberland.

Why Woodland people created monumental earthworks, what drove them to do so, and what ultimately led to the downfall of their culture is poorly understood. Population increase due to widespread agriculture, and concomitant pressure on natural resources, may have led to the decline of the Woodland culture. New technologies may have influenced their decline, especially as related to weaponry and possible warfare.

The bow and arrow appeared at the end of the Woodland period.[26] Like atlatl technology before it, bows and arrows appeared in different areas of the world at roughly the same time. It is possible that the combination of new weaponry and population pressures led to devastating widespread warfare. Numerous fortified Indian villages from the Woodland period have been identified in several Upper Cumberland locations, with one of the best known near Cherry Creek, in White County, Tennessee.[27]

Woodland culture developed in a time of transition from an exclusively hunting and gathering way of life, to one increasingly based on agriculture.[28] During the Woodland period, agriculture took on a more important role. Through long-term exposure to plants in their environment, and trial-and-error experimentation, Woodland people domesticated a group of plants useful to them in terms of food production and textiles. Goosefoot, sumpweed, knotweed, sunflowers, and maygrass were part of the daily diet. Indians employed a variety of gourds and squashes for food and other purposes.[29] By the close of the period, maize (corn) was introduced from the south, possibly from Mexico. Stable food resources were partly responsible for a more detailed focus on cosmology, time, and seasonal reckoning.[30] For reasons still poorly understood, by the fifth century CE, Woodland culture declined to the point that elaborate earthwork construction and long-distance trade ceased. Within two hundred years, a new and final prehistoric culture emerged in the Southeast, and its affects were felt far and wide, this culture is known as the Mississippian.

The period began around 700 CE along the middle course of the Mississippi River.[31] Considered the climax of prehistory in the Southeast, this period set the stage for historic tribes who encountered Europeans first arriving in North America. Influence of Mississippian culture extended along river systems to virtually every area of the Southeast. When Europeans crossed into the Trans-Appalachian West, into regions such as the Upper Cumberland, they encountered numerous flat-topped, pyramidal mounds, bearing silent witness to those who had once lived in the fertile valleys and bottomland of the Cumberland, Caney Fork, Calfkiller, Collins, Roaring, and other smaller Upper Cumberland streams.[32]

Flat-topped earthen mounds built for ceremonial purposes were the defining architectural feature of the Mississippian tradition. Once numerous throughout the Upper Cumberland, they served as foundations for temples, mortuaries, chief's houses, and other important structures.[33] They differed markedly from conical burial mounds of the Woodland period.[34] Mounds, the focal point of villages, were often protected by palisades and ditches or water-filled moats.

Another seminal development of the Mississippian period was increased reliance on maize agriculture and widespread cultivation of beans in the latter period. Mississippian people relied on cultivation of the "three sisters"—corn, beans, and squash—and they were the first large-scale agriculturalists of the Southeast. They supplemented their food by hunting and gathering, but their primary source of protein and carbohydrates came from agriculture. Mississippian people used simple digging sticks and chert or flint-bladed hoes, augmented by animal bones, as their main farm tools.[35] According to Fagan, "It was the widespread cultivation of maize and beans that helped foster higher population densities, larger food surpluses, and more complex political and social organization in the closing centuries of prehistoric times in eastern North America."[36]

Mississippian culture appeared almost simultaneously across the Southeast. New technologies, food resources, cultural motifs, and ideas spread rapidly along the region's waterways. The Mississippian period can be divided into essentially two phases—Cahokia, or the Cahokian influence (800–1250 CE), and the era of numerous small chiefdoms, which lasted until European contact in 1539, when Hernando De Soto arrived. Climatic conditions may be responsible for some changes in Mississippian culture, as weather patterns shifted making one form of subsistence more necessary than others.

Mississippian people lived in permanent settlements. Dependence on agriculture as their main means of subsistence exposed them to the vagaries and uncertainties of the environment, especially weather patterns and crop disease or failure. Communal granaries, rations, seed stockpiling, reciprocity, and other strategies may have helped individual communities survive difficult times.[37] Communal cooperation implies leadership, coordination, and some type of infrastructure. It is highly likely that a need to coordinate and oversee complex efforts of the community created the basis for a local "Big Man" or chief who directed day-to-day communal activities. Increasingly complex societies require increasingly differentiated leadership. Mississippian elite oversaw a social order more complex than anything previously in the Southeast. Cahokia and sister Mississippian sites equaled any other society in the world.[38]

Mississippian exchange networks linked communities throughout their territory.[39] Exotic materials were traded and cultural motifs were

A stone gorget.
Credit: Michael Birdwell.

fairly uniform throughout the Mississippian sphere of influence. Based on current data, it appears that all members of the community took part in agricultural production, food procurement, and day-to-day tasks of the community.[40] According to Brian Fagan, "Mississippian communities were relatively autonomous, exchanging and producing goods and commodities through age-old ties of kin and reciprocal obligation."[41]

While low level chiefdoms probably held sway over Mississippian society as it became more complex and more highly developed centralized chiefdoms arose, how this process evolved is not understood, and there is little consensus as to what forms these chiefdoms assumed. Indeed, some anthropologists postulate that the whole notion of chiefdoms is "a seventeenth-century European logical construct," unfamiliar to modern Indians.[42] If, as many anthropologists believe, Mississippian culture indeed developed complex chiefdoms, explaining how they arose may be a formidable task.[43]

It would be a mistake to consider Mississippian culture absolutely homogeneous as there were regional differences between Middle Mississippian, South Appalachian Mississippian, and other areas of influence. Different pottery styles indicate local patterns. In the Upper Cumberland, differences in pottery exist in an archaeological context along the various streams of the area, with simpler, sometimes more crude styles found along smaller streams, as opposed to samples found along the Cumberland River. It is almost as if the technique and technology involved in pottery making was less well understood the further away from major population areas.[44] Investigations into the complexity and nature of Mississippian culture will continue into the future.

By the time Hernando De Soto and his conquistadors reached the Southeast in 1539, the Mississippian had passed its apogee. De Soto found Southeastern Indians living much as their ancestors had, but the height and splendor of the civilization had long since waned. De Soto made his way through Florida, South Carolina, and Georgia before arriving in Tennessee in 1540. Although preceded by Cabeza De Vaca and Panfilo De Narvaez by some eleven years, De Soto's expedition into the Southeastern interior marked the beginning of what ultimately signaled the end of a way of life for Southeastern people that had existed for millennia. Driven by a desire to find wealth, De Soto and his men were willing to risk the unknown in order to find it. His exact route through Tennessee remains open to debate, although he may have followed the Hiwassee River into the Great Valley of East Tennessee.[45] There are those, however, who believe De Soto may have crossed the Cumberland Plateau into the Upper Cumberland near present-day Van Buren County, before turning south for Alabama. While De Soto's exact route may be open to debate, one thing is not: his legacy of brutality, disease, and destruction. As the first group of Europeans to enter Tennessee, De Soto's party effectively ended the prehistoric period ushering in an era of profound, culture-altering change throughout the Southeast.[46] Although it would two hundred years before Europeans pushed into Tennessee in earnest, the die was cast, and the life ways of Southeastern Indians forever altered.

Historic Indians encountered by initial white settlers descended from earlier populations, extending back to the Paleoindian period of the Late Pleistocene. Algonquian speaking Shawnee lived along the Cumberland River, with villages probably extending into the Upper Cumberland. They encountered French traders near Nashville as early as 1665.[47] Before British settlers pushed across the Appalachian Mountains, and even for some time afterwards, the Cumberland River was known as the Shawnee River. While Shawnee continued to hunt in the Cumberland area, by the mid-eighteenth century, they had all but been expelled by other Indians, principally the Cherokees and Chickasaws. By the 1790s, the U.S. government only recognized Cherokees and Chickasaws as landowners in Tennessee.

By the time European settlers claimed land in the Upper Cumberland, the area was devoid of any large, permanent habitation sites, although scattered bands of Indians remained in the region. By the late-eighteenth century, the Upper Cumberland was essentially a communal hunting ground utilized by several different tribes. The area's history, rich with evidence of earlier cultures long since passed into the realm of ancient time, eluded everyone. Indians encountered by white settlers had no factual knowledge of the people who formerly lived in the Upper Cumberland. Indians of the historic period created their owns myths and traditions concerning tribal origins and the people who once inhabited the landscape. Cherokee Indians had a myth concerning "moon-eyed" people who lived in the Southeast when ancestral Cherokees first arrived in the region. Other tribes had different origin stories and different traditions concerning those who had once inhabited the land.[48]

According to *Goodspeed's History of White County,* by 1800, when White County was first settled, "a single tribe of Cherokee Indians was found here, the English name of whose chief was Calf Killer, and it was for, or by him, Calf Killer River was probably named..."[49] According to local history and tradition, another band of Cherokee Indians lived in the Cumberland Plateau area of Overton County. These Indians went by the name of Nettle Carrier, in honor of their chief. Albert Hogue claimed, "Nettle Carrier was the last Indian chief to reside in this section, and tradition has it that he lived here until 1799."[50] It is not known how many Indians lived in the Upper Cumberland during initial white settlement. The fact that Indians utilized the land and resources of the Upper Cumberland, and that scattered populations still inhabited the area, created conflict between them and white settlers. Unauthorized settlement of the region led to violent interaction between the two groups in increasingly bitter ways; but the more technologically primitive Indians lost the battle for the ancestral land of the Upper Cumberland.

Millions of acres of land in the Trans-Appalachian West were set aside by the U. S. and state governments as payment for services rendered to those who fought in the American Revolution. These payments took the form of land grants with acreage determined by military rank at the time of service. A private received a section of land, or six hundred and forty acres, while officers received thousands of acres. In theory, granting land as payment for services rendered was equitable, almost egalitarian, and spurred settlement of the vast interior of America. In reality, however, various Indian tribes, who had lived on the land for millennia, already claimed land promised to veterans. Indeed, it was not until 1805 that most of the land comprising the Upper Cumberland was ceded to the United States by the Cherokee in the Third Treaty of Tellico.[51]

The Upper Cumberland was sparsely settled prior to 1806, and most whites who moved into the area squatted illegally on Cherokee land. Ned Cowen of Buffalo Valley, Tennessee, was once such settler. He was among the vanguard of long hunters from Virginia. By the 1780s, Cowen settled several thousand acres of Cherokee land near the Cumberland and Caney Fork Rivers, adjacent to Little Indian Creek in current Putnam County. Cowen hunted between the Upper Cumberland and Middle Cumberland settlements in the Nashville Basin. According to early records, Cowen was killed by Indians sometime prior to 1790.[52] Living on land illegally was apparently a dangerous proposition.

Indians most associated with the Upper Cumberland Cherokees were the largest Indian tribe in the South, with an estimated population of twenty-two thousand.[53] Cherokees claimed all of Middle Tennessee, including the Upper Cumberland. By the time of their final land cession in the nineteenth century, Cherokees lost one hundred twenty-five thousand square miles of land to the United States.[54]

Cherokees spoke an Iroquoian language possibly dating to the Archaic period.[55] According to one theory, Cherokees originated north of their present territory and migrated down the Appalachian Mountains, perhaps forced to do so by other Iroquoian Indians.[56] Many archaeologists disagree, contending that Cherokee culture developed in the Southeast from earlier traditions, and that the Cherokee-Iroquois divergence occurred as long ago as 3800 BCE.[57] According to Cherokee tradition, however, they originated in the East, toward the rising sun, and migrated to the Southeast. Cherokees call themselves, *Tsalagi,* the Principal People, and for hundreds of years, they were, indeed, the principal people of the Southeast.

Cherokees subsisted by hunting, gathering, and agriculture, much like their ancestors. The "three sisters" of native agriculture—corn, beans, and squash—were their primary crops. Agriculture and plant gathering was work primarily performed by women, while men hunted. Cherokee society was matrilineal; women held positions of power and were involved in decision making among the tribe.[58] Women could rise to the rank of *Agehyagusta,* Beloved Woman, and participate in the highest levels of tribal decision making.

The council house, a round structure representing the cosmos, often erected on a mound and containing sacred fire, acted as the focal point of the Cherokee community. Religious ceremonies and important political decisions occurred there. They developed a complex religious system, with celestial deities and animals of the natural order playing central roles in their tribal belief system.[59] The annual Green Corn Ceremony, in which social order and relationships were examined, was the principal religious ceremony. It occurred at the beginning of the corn harvest. A new sacred fire was lit as the old one, representing the past, was extinguished and the new year welcomed after fasting and purification rites were performed.

A trail system used by Indians for millennia traversed the Upper Cumberland. Cherokees utilized these when traveling to and from the region, and later, as tensions between the Indians and white settlers reached a crisis point, trails became war paths. One main trail was the Cumberland Trace, also known as Tollunteeskee's Trail, and later the basis for the Walton Road.[60] Indian paths usually began as game trails, where they tracked animals on their hunts. European settlers followed the same paths, and as more settlers arrived, many trails were expanded and improved becoming the first pioneer roads. In a true sense, these early Indian trails formed the basis for later highways and railroads, such as U.S. Highway 70, U.S. Highway 29, State Route 136, and others throughout the Upper Cumberland.

The Cumberland Trace branched from the Tennessee River, Great Lakes, and Ohio Trail near present-day Rockwood in Roane County. It passed a former Indian town at the Officer Mound site near present-day Algood in Putnam County and from there to the Cumberland River in Jackson County and on to Indian towns around Nashville. According to William Myer, one prong probably led to the "fortified Indian town at the mouth of Dixon's Creek."[61] As white settlement continued, permission was obtained from the Cherokee to open the Walton Road from Kingston to Carthage, essentially following the route of the Cumberland Trace. Other Upper Cumberland trails included the Black Fox, the Nickajack, and the famous Chickamauga Path. These routes linked with others providing passage to all areas of eastern North America, from Canada to the Gulf of Mexico, and from the Atlantic Ocean to the Rocky Mountains. North America was a patchwork of trails allowing human interaction on numerous levels for thousands of years. That interaction included war.

By the late-eighteenth century, Indians in Tennessee had been in contact with European culture for over one hundred years, time enough for affairs of Indians to become inextricably linked with those of the whites. Despite numerous treaties and promises made by the British and the United States, tensions mounted. Though the far-reaching Treaty of Hopewell, signed November 28, 1785, laid out western boundaries for white settlement, unabated encroachment on Indian lands, and various acts of violence, led to a decade of warfare in the Cumberland territory, rendering treaties meaningless.[62]

According to Alvin Wirt, "the Upper Cumberland was the scene of many hostile incidents between white settlers and Indians, few of which were ever recorded on the pages of history. They involved brushes with the border patrol, attacks on travelers crossing the wilderness, and personal encounters."[63] Settlers moving between East and Middle Tennessee, crossing the rugged Cumberland Plateau, were targets of Indians trying to stem the tide of European encroachment. Fort Southwest Point, at the confluence of the Clinch and Tennessee Rivers near the plateau's eastern escarpment, served as a staging area for settlers bound for the Cumberland settlements. Their trip across the Cumberland Plateau, or Cumberland Mountain as it was called at the time, was fraught with danger. Due to ongoing violence a federally garrisoned fort was established at the crossing of the Cumberland River at White's Bend in present-day Jackson County. The post was named Fort Blount in honor of territorial governor, William Blount.[64]

Indian attacks occurring in the Upper Cumberland included the famous raid of Cherokee Chief Hanging Maw upon a camp of surveyors in Smith County, in March 1786. Indians overpowered the team of whites. Indians wounded the surveyors and confiscated their provisions. Defeated Creek received its name in memory of this incident.[65] By 1792, Indian attacks in the Upper Cumberland reached their peak; the years 1792 and 1793 were the bloodiest on record.[66]

Chief John Watts, (also known as Young Tassel) assumed leadership of the breakaway Chickamaugas after the death of Dragging Canoe in 1792.

His fearsome warriors, led by Doublehead, attacked Cumberland settlers on a wide front. At Crab Orchard, they ambushed Captain Samuel Handley's detachment from Fort Southwest Point, deployed by Governor Blount to Nashville. Indians killed three soldiers and captured Handley. The rest of Handley's forty-two man detachment was routed from the field.[67]

In October 1792 Doublehead's men engaged a mounted border patrol of thirty-four men under the command of Captain William Snoddy on the Caney Fork River below Rock Island. After several hours, Doublehead retreated across the Cumberland Plateau toward the Chickamauga towns near Chattanooga. Captain Snoddy lost two men killed and several wounded. Doublehead suffered thirteen dead warriors and numerous wounded.[68] This marked one of the deadliest engagements between Indians and whites in the Upper Cumberland. In 1793, over three hundred people were killed near the Cumberland settlements during the Chickamauga Wars. By 1794, due to military setbacks and political difficulties, Chickamaugan power was broken and the Indian threat to the Upper Cumberland essentially ended.

Cherokee were all but gone from the Upper Cumberland when the Third Treaty of Tellico was formalized in 1805. They primarily lived in their towns in East Tennessee and northern Georgia. As late as 1801 Upper Cumberland pioneer Moses Fisk informed his friend John Wheelock that "there was an account in gazettes of two Indians killed on Cumberland recently by whites. No such thing was done. The Indians are still living, and well."[69] Wheelock apparently planned a Cherokee mission and school in the region, indicating a viable Indian population in the region.[70] The last known incidence of violence in any way associated with Indians occurred in 1807, when an Indian reported to have killed a black man on the Walton Road, was arrested by the Sheriff of Overton County and incarcerated in the Carthage jail.[71]

Due to increasing pressure to cede remaining lands, even though many of them had attempted to integrate into white society, numerous Cherokee sought escape in Arkansas. By 1838, after years of political maneuvering, the Cherokees, except for a small band who escaped to the mountains of North Carolina, were forced to march the infamous Trail of Tears to the Trans-Mississippi West, forever banished from the beloved ancestral homeland. Two routes passed though the Upper Cumberland and witnessed one of the saddest events in American history.[72]

The story of American Indians in Tennessee's Upper Cumberland is an ancient one. How ancient, no one knows. Evidence of human activity stretches back to the Paleoindian period and continues into the historic period. Unanswered questions concerning Indian culture in the Upper

Cumberland gives the story an enigmatic quality; it is a story that continues to unfold. While the main body of the story may have been told, there are chapters left to be written. Many people in the Upper Cumberland have an Indian legacy with ancient DNA flowing through them, while other Indians return to the region for spiritual and cultural reasons. As with all human culture, the story of Indians is ever changing. But one can look to the land of the Upper Cumberland, its rivers, mountains, and forests, and still discern the spirit of its first human beings.

NOTES

1. Original inhabitants of North America will be referred to as American Indians, or simply Indians. Nomenclature related to culture changes often with terms going in and out of fashion. American Indian is a more concrete cultural designation than the ambiguous "Native American." This essay focuses on the Upper Cumberland in Tennessee, but Upper Cumberland counties of Kentucky share a nearly identical cultural and geological history. Terms "white" and "European" are used interchangeably regarding non-Indians. Though Europeans established the dominant culture of the late eighteenth century , African Americans numbered among early settlers of the Upper Cumberland. This essay does not purport to be a complete history of American Indians in the Upper Cumberland, rather a general overview of the subject.
2. See Henry Thompson Malone, *Cherokees of the Old South: A People in Transition* (Athens: University of Georgia Press, 1956), 185; James Adair, *The History of American Indians* (London: E. and C. Dilly, 1775). Adair believed Cherokees were a remnant of the Ten Lost Tribes of Israel. Early settlers attributed construction of numerous stone enclosures to Prince Madoc. Reports of Welsh speaking, blue-eyed Indians persisted into the nineteenth century. While romantic and entertaining, there is no archaeological or DNA evidence to support these legends.
3. Harriette Simpson Arnow, *Seedtime on the Cumberland* (New York: Scribner, 1960), p. 43. Arnow's work contains detailed descriptions of prehistoric and historic Indians of the region. See Brian M. Fagan, *Ancient North America: The Archaeology of a Continent* (London: Thames and Hudson, 1991), pp. 30–33. Moundbuilder myths persisted into the late nineteenth century. Cultural biases played a tremendous role in misinterpretation of Indian culture. In archeology, and for the purposes of this essay, the term "North America" refers to the modern United States and Canada. While Mexico is part of North America, it is considered "Mesoamerica" in anthropological terms, allied culturally with the people of Central America.
4. Modern genetic studies indicate that American Indian populations are descended primarily from four mitochondrial DNA lineages. All four groups have genetic links to modern populations in Siberia and north-central Asia. A fifth group accounts for a small percentage of American Indian DNA, seems to originate in the border area between Europe and Asia. Mitochondrial DNA is a non-nuclear DNA maternally inherited; it is useful in genetic studies because of this unique

inheritance trait. Mitochondrial DNA, since it occurs outside the cell nucleus, is easier to extract from ancient organic material, and easier to analyze than nuclear DNA such as the paternally inherited Y chromosome. For this reason, most genetic studies of ancient American Indians are based on mitochondrial DNA analysis. Dental morphology also plays a key role in identifying Indian origins. Although exceptions exist, most American Indians display incisor shoveling, single-rooted upper first pre-molars and triple-rooted lower first molars. Collectively, these features are known as sinodonty, meaning Chinese-like teeth. Sinodonty only occurs in northern Asia and the Americas. This feature first appeared in the archaeological record of northern Asia some 40,000 BCE, well before the date most mainstream anthropologists accept as the time of man's arrival in North America. For a detailed, non-technical discussion of DNA and its uses in population studies, see Bryan Sykes, *The Seven Daughters of Eve* (New York: W.W. Norton & Co., 2001)

5. For the physiography of the Upper Cumberland see N.M. Fenneman, *Physiography of the Eastern United States* (New York: McGraw Hill, 1938). This seventy-year-old volume remains the standard study of the physical landscape of the Eastern United States. For a concise description of the physiographic regions of Tennessee, see Edward T. Luther, *Our Restless Earth: The Geologic Regions of Tennessee* (Knoxville: University of Tennessee Press, 1977).
6. Charles Hudson, *The Southeastern Indians* (Knoxville: University of Tennessee Press, 1976), p. 39. Hudson's volume is one of the most respected treatments of the subject.
7. For an excellent handbook on Southeastern projectile points and nomenclature see James W. Cambron and David C. Hulse, *Handbook of Alabama Archaeology, Part I Point Types* (Revised Edition, Archaeological Research Foundation of Alabama, 1975).
8. Corgan, 83. For an in-depth discussion of Pleistocene faunal remains in Tennessee see James X. Corgan, *Vertebrate Fossils of Tennessee* (Nashville: Tennessee Department of Environment and Conservation, Division of Geology, Bulletin 77, 1976) and E. Lucy Braun, *Deciduous Forests of Eastern North America* (Philadelphia: Blakiston Co., 1950). Braun provides an excellent natural history of the Pleistocene in eastern North America, showing forest development that would have affected subsistence patterns and strategies in the region.)
9. Fagan, 95.
10. *Ibid.*, 112–114.
11. Alice Beck Kehoe, *America Before the European Invasions* (London: Pearson Education Books, 2002), 15.
12. Fagan, 95.
13. Hudson, 44.
14. *Ibid.*, 45.
15. Kehoe, 29.
16. Fagan, 310.
17. Interestingly, atlatl technology was used by cultures around the world, from Europe to Asia to the Americas. The word atlatl actually comes from the *Nahuatl*

language spoken by the Mexica, or Aztec Indians of Mexico, for whom the country was named by the Spanish.

18. Kehoe, 29. Kehoe offers a concise examination of the Archaic Period, 24–39.
19. Fagan, 319. Little is known about languages of the Archaic people. It is hypothesized that Early Archaic peoples spoke Algonquian-Gulf related languages throughout the Eastern Woodlands, which provided a stable medium for distribution of projectile points over such a large geographical area. The current state of research, however, does not posit any degree of certainty what languages Archaic people may have spoken.
20. *Ibid.*, 335.
21. Kehoe, 39. Because of a more amenable climate and new food resources, human populations increased in size and complexity; life became more diverse agriculturally and materially. Social organization grew more intricate, and life ways gradually evolved into what is known as the Woodland period.
22. Hudson, 55.
23. *Ibid.*
24. *Ibid.*, 369.
25. *Ibid.*, 372.
26. Fagan, 383.
27. For an early description of Tennessee's Indian history, see John Haywood, *Natural and Aboriginal History of Tennessee* (Jackson, Tennessee: McCourt-Mercer Press, 1959). First published in 1823, the volume contains numerous references to prehistoric Upper Cumberland Indian sites. The information is of particular interest because of its discussions of early attempts at archaeology and cultural interpretation of Indian sites across Middle Tennessee. He discusses burial sites, mounds, artifacts, and other empirical data. Haywood, as did many scholars of his era, engages in conjecture as to who the Indians were, their physical characteristics, and whether or not Indians could have been descended from tribes of Eurasia.
28. Hudson, 59.
29. Fagan, 335. Archaeologists later recovered tobacco seeds from Woodland sites, 360.
30. For a discussion of archaeoastronomy in the Upper Cumberland and Cumberland Plateau, see Richard H. Mooney, "Archaeoastronomy in Tennessee: The Moonshadow Site and Indian Sunshrines of the Cumberland Plateau," *Tennessee Anthropologist*, XVIII: 1 (Spring 1992) pp. 33–40. Mooney discusses astronomical observation points on the Cumberland Plateau, including White and Van Buren counties. Sites include petroglyphs and celestial alignment points to mark the winter solstice and vernal equinox. Similar sites have been discovered in Fentress and Putnam counties.
31. Hudson, 77.
32. The height of Mississippian development occurred at Cahokia, near modern Saint Louis, where the Missouri River empties into the Mississippi, the so-called American Bottom area. The largest, most densely populated prehistoric site, Cahokia site covered five and one-half square miles and was arguably the highest cultural

achievement of North America. Cahokia would have rivaled any city in Europe and probably exceeded them in terms of social complexity.

33. *Ibid.*
34. For a discussion of early mound investigations in the Upper Cumberland, see Michael C. Moore and Kevin E. Smith, *Archaeological Expeditions of the Peabody Museum in Middle Tennessee, 1877–1884* (Nashville: Tennessee Department of Environment and Conservation, Division of Archaeology, Research Series No. 16, 2009). It compiles data collected throughout Middle Tennessee by Frederic Ward Putnam and associates, housed at Harvard University's Peabody Museum. Of particular interest are discussions of Upper Cumberland explorations in Jackson County along the Cumberland and Roaring Rivers, carried out in 1878.
35. Hudson, 80.
36. Fagan, 389. Prior to Mississippian reliance on corn, teeth of earlier people had remarkably few cavities, whereas Mississippian teeth are riddled with numerous cavities, lasting evidence of the destructive power of corn sugar. Maize is native to Guatemala's highlands, and how it became a staple in the Southeast remains a mystery. The eastern flint variety grown by Mississippian people is an antecedent of modern, commercially grown corn. While Mississippian Indians continued to cultivate a wide variety of plants, many in use since the Archaic period, importance of maize agriculture in developing Mississippian culture cannot be overstated.
37. Kehoe, 171. She discusses the impact of the Little Ice Age (1550–1850) on agricultural patterns and the culture as a whole.
38. For a detailed description of Cahokian social structure, see Kehoe, 169–178. See Fagan, 394–399. It is important to remember that just as human culture is not static, neither is research designed to seek answers to fundamental questions about human culture.
39. Fagan, 393.
40. *Ibid.*, 394.
41. *Ibid.*
42. Kehoe, 184.
43. Fagan, 103.
44. Many sites have been uncovered throughout the Upper Cumberland, but much remains to be learned. Questions related to religion and language have yet to be answered, as well as specific beliefs related to motifs such as the eye-in-hand and possible similarities between Mexican and Southeastern culture. Southeastern Ceremonial Complex motifs centered on two figures, both of which had winged arms and human bodies. One representation has hawk wings and the other has tobacco-moth wings; both motifs come from Hopewell civilization. A holy dancing man with a spiral conch shell pendant, swastikas, and the cross-in-circle symbol representing the world were common motifs shared by Woodland traditions and those of Mesoamerica.
45. Ronald N. Satz, *Tennessee's Indian Peoples: From White Contact to Removal, 1540–1840* (Knoxville: University of Tennessee Press, 1979), p. 10.
46. Another Indian tribe living in the Upper Cumberland was the Yuchi. They encountered De Soto as he made his way inland in his ill-fated search for riches.

Yuchi were mysterious in that they spoke a language unrelated to any other. Yuchis considered themselves the original inhabitants of the Southeast, "Children of the Sun, a people of significance." They were nearly destroyed by the Cherokees, and ultimately forcibly removed in the 1830s along with other Native American tribes to present-day Oklahoma. See Hudson, 24.

47. Jerry E. Clark, *The Shawnee* (Lexington: University of Press of Kentucky, 1977), 12.
48. See Russell Thornton, *The Cherokees: A Population History* (Lincoln: The University of Nebraska Press, 1990); Walter S. McClain, *History of Putnam County, Tennessee* (Cookeville, Tennessee: Quimby Dyer and Co., 1925), p. 5. Thornton discusses Cherokee origins and cultural history. Numerous New World Indian cultures had legends of other people inhabiting their ancestral homelands at some remote time in the past. Cherokees ascribed features such as stone enclosures and mounds to moon-eyed people, supposedly a light-skinned people who lived underground and were vanquished by original Cherokees. Quetzalcoatl, the feathered serpent god of Mesoamericans is sometimes depicted as a white man.
49. *Goodspeed's Histories of Cannon, Coffee, DeKalb, Warren and White Counties,* Reprint (McMinnville, Tennessee: Ben Lomand Press, 1972), p. 798.
50. Albert R. Hogue, *One Hundred Years in the Cumberland Mountains: Along the Continental Line* (McMinnville, Tennessee: Standard Printing Co., 1939), pp. 9–10.
51. Satz, 73.
52. John Carr, *Early Times in Middle Tennessee* (Nashville: E. Stevenson and F.A. Owen, 1857), p. 12. Carr provides an early history of the Cumberland settlements and Indian warfare related to white settlement. Carr discussed the death of Captain John Hickerson, killed by Indians on Smith's Fork, DeKalb County around 1787. Also see Richard Carlton Fulcher, *1770–1790 Census of the Cumberland Settlements, Davidson, Sumner, and Tennessee Counties* (Brentwood, Tennessee: N.P., 1986).
53. Satz, 11. The Upper Cumberland was most associated with the Overhill Towns of East Tennessee, one of three regions of Cherokee settlement, the others being the Middle Settlements in present-day North Carolina, South Carolina, and Georgia. Overhill referred to Tennessee Cherokee towns on the western side of the Appalachian Mountains and east of the Plateau.
54. Thornton, 12.
55. Fagan, 416.
56. Thornton, 9.
57. *Ibid.*
58. Satz, 19.
59. For an in-depth discussion of Cherokee belief systems see Hudson, 120–183.
60. William E. Myer, *Indian Trails of the Southeast* (Nashville, Tennessee: Blue and Gray Press, 1971), p. 99. This work, originally published in 1925, remains the authority on the subject.
61. *Ibid.,* 100. See also Kevin E. Smith and Emily L. Beahm, "Fortified Town at the Mouth of Dixon Creek" National Register of Historic Places Nomination Form (Murfreesboro: Middle Tennessee State University, 31 January 2010). The form is available at the offices of the Tennessee Historical Commission, Nashville and at the National Register headquarters in Washington, D.C.
62. Satz, 57.

63. Alvin B. Wirt, *The Upper Cumberland of Pioneer Times* (Washington, D.C., Privately Published, 1954), p. 6.
64. A modern recreation of Fort Southwest Point exists at Kingston and is based upon archaeological and historic evidence. For a detailed description of the history of Fort Blount, Indian activity in the Upper Cumberland, and settlement of Middle Tennessee, see Samuel D. Smith and Benjamin C. Nance, *An Archaeological Interpretation of the Site of Fort Blount, A 1790s Territorial Militia and Federal Military Post, Jackson County, Tennessee.* (Nashville: Tennessee Department of Environment and Conservation, Division of Archaeology, Research Series No. 12, 2000), p. 50. Fort Blount was situated at a crossing of the Cumberland River, on a knoll occupied intermittently for millennia. During archaeological investigations, remains of prehistoric hearths and houses were found in association with the remains of Fort Blount.
65. Wirt, 7.
66. John R. Finger, *Tennessee Frontiers: Three Regions in Transition* (Bloomington: Indiana University Press, 2001), pp. 125–151. For an exhaustive account of the violence in the region see John Haywood, *The Civil and Political History of Tennessee From Its Earliest Settlement up to the Year 1796,* Reprint (Nashville: Publishing House of the Methodist Episcopal Church, South, 1891) pp. 271–377.
67. Wirt, 8;
68. *Ibid.*, 9.
69. See Tim Barlow, *The Life and Writings of Moses Fisk* (Collegedale, Tennessee: The College Press, 1980), p. 99. Moses Fisk, an early settler, founded Hilham in Overton County and, with Sampson Williams, founded Fisk Female Academy in 1803, the first school of its kind in Tennessee. A native of Massachusetts Fisk was educated at Dartmouth. By his death in 1840, Fisk owned over thirty thousand acres of land in the Upper Cumberland. His comments on Indians in the Upper Cumberland and their possible origins should not be dismissed today.
70. *Ibid.*, 97.
71. Wirt, 11.
72. For a detailed discussion of Cherokee removal see John Ehle, *Trail of Tears: the Rise and Fall of the Cherokee Nation.* (New York: Anchor Books, 1988); Theda Perdue, *The Cherokee Nation and the Trail of Tears* (New York: Penguin, 2008) and Tim Allen Garrison, *The Legal Ideology of Removal: The Southern Judiciary and the Sovereignty of Native American Nations* (Athens: University of Georgia Press, 2009). For information concerning the Trail of Tears through the Upper Cumberland, see Benjamin C. Nance, *The Trail of Tears in Tennessee: A Study of the Routes Used During the Cherokee Removal of 1838.* (Nashville: Tennessee Department of Environment and Conservation, Division of Archaeology, 2001).

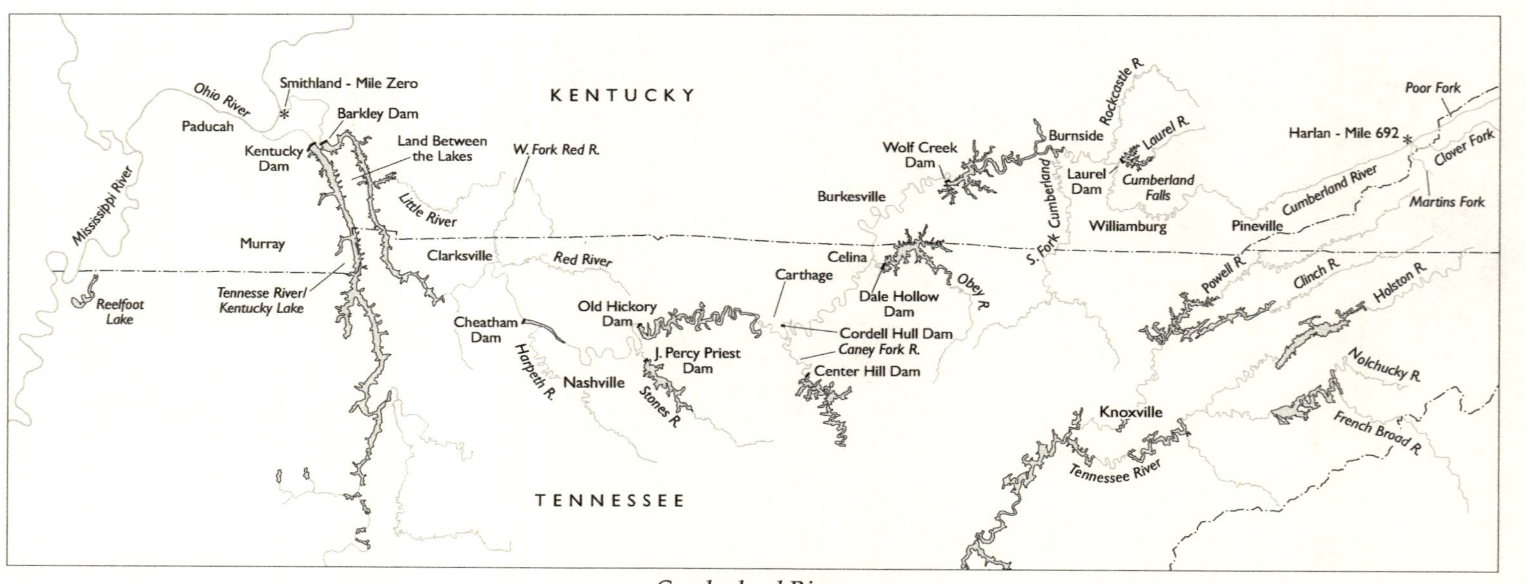

Cumberland River

2

"Hard Way to Make a Living"

Life and Leisure on the Cumberland River

Michael Allen

In *Don't Go Up Kettle Creek,* folklorist Lynwood Montell recounts the harrowing story of Cumberland River log raftsman John Cummings. Floating downstream in the dead of winter, Cummings and his fellow rivermen came upon two stranded Wolf River raftsmen:

> We went to them. One of them was dead, and the other was just barely breathing. We got him out first. Went back and got the other one...The [other rescuers] had a covered wagon there and a big fire; had bed blankets and everything. And we took the live one out. There's one old man there. He said, "I've brought a quart of moonshine whiskey." They just jerked the buttons off the freezing man's clothes and stripped him off. The old man went to bathing him in that whiskey. Had it milk warm, and [the raftsman] was a-breathing pretty good when we took the dead one out.[1]

Boating, in its various incarnations, on the upper reaches of the Cumberland River could be deadly.[2] From the eighteenth through the early twentieth centuries, keelboatmen, flatboatmen, raftsmen, and steamboatmen faced hard work and many dangers as they plied the Cumberland from Nashville, Tennessee, to Burnside, Kentucky. Yet they sailed the river's course with an optimism borne of hope for a better life and firm belief that nature's river was there for them to use and prosper.

Near the Cumberland Gap, where eighteenth century American pioneers first crossed the Appalachian Mountains, the Cumberland River is formed by combination of the Poor Fork, Clover Fork, and Martins Fork rivers. "All three are considerable streams in their own right, rising far back on the western slopes of the Cumberland Mountain watershed," writes James McCague, author of *The Cumberland* in the acclaimed *Rivers of America Series.*

"Thus the Cumberland springs to life full-blown, as it were, and boasts a quite respectable size from the outset."[3]

The first Upper Cumberland rivermen were Cherokee, Shawnee, Iroquois, and other Indians traversing the region. They hunted buffalo, bear, and deer; and they traded along the river as well as an elaborate system of mountain trails.[4] They paddled sleek log canoes which served both peaceful and warlike purposes. Canoes moved families, hunting parties, and cargoes along the river. In wartime they facilitated the rapid movement, attack, and retreat of war parties; on the lower portion of the river (between Carthage and Nashville), Shawnee Indians effectively used canoes to attack European-American flatboatmen in the 1780s–1790s.[5]

In absence of canoes, or of the time to build them, Southeastern Indians used crude craft called "bull boats." They constructed them by forming saplings and tree branches into a circular bowl shape, weaving them together using sap, clay, and mud compounds as sealants. Bull boats were navigated with oars. The bull boat was obviously a stop-gap measure, good for only a few trips or crossings before it needed repair or replacement.[6]

As early as 1761, Euro-American hunters and trappers followed the Indians' existing river routes. Known as "long hunters" they killed wild game for one-to-three years at a time before returning to civilization with hundreds of animal skins. A tale about long hunters Isaac and Abraham Bledsoe provides a clue to the quantities of game these men harvested in a season. Robbed of all their cache by Indians, the forlorn Bledsoe brothers reportedly carved on a tree, "lost 2300 deerskins ruination by god."[7]

Long hunters adapted Indian canoes for their own commercial uses. Enterprising hunters shipped skins, bear oil, salted deer, bear and buffalo meat as far south as Natchez, Mississippi, and New Orleans, Louisiana. In 1766, Philadelphian George Morgan wrote of "twenty large Perrirgous [*sic*] up from New Orleans, killing buffaloe [*sic*] chiefly for tallow." Bragging on the quality of his salted buffalo meat, Morgan wrote, "All ours is [as] good now as the day it was killed."[8]

Intrepid pioneers, determined to carve out a new life, followed the long hunters into the Upper Cumberland to establish homesteads. Due to the imposing barrier of the eastern edge of the Cumberland Plateau, which had only three natural gaps to facilitate movement, much of the Upper Cumberland was settled from west to east.[9] The Cumberland River and its numerous tributaries added another impediment for settlers as they tried to move families and possessions into the region. As a result, several ferries were created out of necessity and a few continue to operate in the twenty-first century. One of the first was established at Fort Blount by Sampson Williams and was known as either the Fort Blount Ferry or the Williamsburg Ferry by travelers along the Avery Trace.

Likewise, William Walton built a road connecting Fort Southwest Point (near Kingston, Tennessee) and Carthage, terminating at the Cumberland River. He owned and operated a ferry that allowed travelers on the Walton Road access to thoroughfares leading to Nashville and the Cumberland Settlements. The Walton Road was commissioned in 1799 by the state of Tennessee. William Walton, William Martin, and Robert Kyle were to establish a new east-west road. Finished in 1801, this highway covered over one hundred miles through the wilderness of the Cumberland Plateau to connect East Tennessee and Middle Tennessee. The new road was more modern than any of the tracks of earlier times. Fifteen feet wide with all stumps removed, it was leveled on the sides of hills and had bridges, causeways, or ferries at the streams. Miles blazed on trees denoted the route. Tolls were fifty cents for four-wheeled carriages, thirty-seven cents for a cart and team, seventy-five cents for a wagon and team, twelve cents for a man and horse, and six cents each for slaves and extra horses. "Stands" (overnight accommodations) along the road provided sleeping arrangements and food for travelers. The Walton Road served the traveling public into the twentieth century, providing the route for railroads and later highways. [10]

As the late eighteenth century progressed, Upper Cumberland settlers and merchant boatmen introduced new and larger river craft already in use on the Lower Cumberland, Ohio, and Mississippi rivers. By 1850, "the Cumberland was considered one of the five major water highways in America."[11] Keelboats, flatboats, and rafts soon dominated the Upper Cumberland River Valley trade and migratory routes until slowly replaced by steamboats and, ultimately, railroads and automobiles.[12]

Keelboats—keels—most closely resembled a large sailboat or small schooner. Sleek, prowed (not flat-bottomed) boats, keels averaged sixty feet in length and eight feet in width. Because they drew only one-to-two feet of water when loaded, keels could run the Cumberland's shallow (shoal) currents in summer, early autumn, and winter. Unlike flatboatmen who could only travel downstream, keelboatmen possessed the equipment and skills to navigate their crafts upstream as well as down.

While keels' sails and rigging resembled sailboats, wind power was only one of several methods boatmen used to propel their craft. Floating downstream, they drifted with the current as the captain manned the large fifteen-to-twenty foot stern oar known as a sweep. Rowing was used mainly for propulsion upstream against the current. If rowing failed, then keelboatmen shouldered their famed poles and literally pushed the boat upstream. Another method to move upstream was hand-winching. Keelboatmen tied a thick, strong hempen rope to an upstream tree. The line emanated from a large wooden capstan on the bow; together the men literally reeled in the line pulling the boat upstream. A more arduous method was for the crew to simply jump into the water, grab the line, and, using sheer muscle-power, pull the keel upstream.

Keelboating on the upper Cumberland River flourished after the founding of Nashborough (Nashville) in 1779. Young Andrew Jackson, who migrated there in 1788 to practice law and manage his plantation, labored part-time as a Cumberland River keelboat builder and merchant navigator. He established a general store, stocking it with goods he shipped from Ohio River ports. Jackson exported goods downstream to Natchez and New Orleans and engaged in the Pittsburgh trade. Most of his commercial river dealings were conducted with his partners at their Clover Bottom shipyard east of Nashville. They constructed one behemoth keel that reportedly carried a ninety-ton cargo. Jackson noted in 1804 that two of his keels, manned by sixteen rivermen, made the journey from the mouth of the Cumberland near Port Isabel (Burnside), Kentucky, to Nashville, consuming "twenty gallons whiskey" during their arduous sixteen-day journey.[13]

The vast majority of pre-steam Upper Cumberland riverboats were flatboats. Known as "arks, broadhorns, and Kentucky boats, the flatboat was simply a large sturdy box with flat sides pitched slightly outward. For long journeys a roof might be added to protect passengers and cargo."[14] Indeed, these ubiquitous flat-bottomed (as opposed to keeled) boats accounted for ninety percent of non-steam commerce and continued to prosper well into the Steam Era and late nineteenth century. One attractive characteristic of flatboats was their low cost and relative ease of construction. For about fifty dollars, even an amateur could fashion a flatboat out of timber felled in the surrounding forest. Many Upper Cumberland flats were built on the Wolf River, near Byrdstown, Tennessee, and as far upstream as Laurel River, below Cumberland Falls in Whitley County, Kentucky. Navigators seeking more seaworthy craft engaged the services of professional boatbuilders. A village in Fentress County, Tennessee—Boatland on the East Fork of the Obey River—earned a reputation as a reliable place to buy sturdy, inexpensive flatboats.[15]

Boxlike craft averaging fifty feet in length and twelve feet in width, flatboats were unadorned and strictly functional. Unlike the sleek keels, flatboats proved extremely difficult to navigate; boatmen steered with a long stern oar and smaller oars on the port, starboard, and bow. Clumsy and unwieldy, flatboats only ran in high water (early spring and late fall) to avoid running aground. Flatboat crewmen soon learned the safest strategy was to reach their destination by running day and night (sometimes as fast as four miles an hour), never landing until journey's end. If and when they made port, the best plan was to steer into a thick stand of submerged willows, cane, or brush to cushion the inevitable collision.

Initially Upper Cumberland flatboat commerce profited little beyond subsistence, but by the mid-1790s farmers were producing surpluses for market. Pork, corn, produce, and tobacco all found their way onto southbound flatboats. Records show scores of Upper Cumberland flatboatmen, including the Cason and Peterman families of Jackson and Clay counties. Down river, Dr. John Bedford kept an elaborate journal record of a trip he made to New Orleans on the *Barge Mary* in 1807. Although flatboat commerce peaked during the decades immediately prior to the Civil War, it continued afterwards. Flatboat commerce was recorded as late as 1880, and it probably existed a decade later.[16]

County histories and oral traditions tell of the Stone, Watson, and Willis families making flatboat trips to New Orleans. John Willis "built a flatboat every year, and loaded it [with] . . . turkeys and wheat and corn . . ." his great-grandson recalled. "[T]hey'd sell all these products in New Orleans and then they'd walk back." Gladys Stone of Celina, Tennessee, told of her husband's grandfather who "made flatboats and put his hogs and what corn he had on hand, and run it to New Orleans."[17]

Unlike the storied New Orleans trekkers, most nineteenth-century Upper Cumberland flatboatmen were bound only for Nashville.[18] As more Americans settled beyond the Appalachians, flatboatmen sailed further southwest and began shorter runs, between Kentucky villages like Burnside and Tennessee River towns of Celina and Carthage. After the invention of the steamboat in 1811, flatboatmen could commute home for cheap deck passage (two-to-three dollar) rates.

After their cargoes were unloaded and sold, flatboatmen dismantled their boats and sold the lumber. Many sidewalks and outbuildings in Ohio and Mississippi valley towns were built of timber salvaged from Upper Cumberland flatboats. Stories abound of "flatboat churches" which, on hot and humid Sundays, began to reek from their waterlogged timbers.

Keel and flatboat cargoes varied. As noted, tobacco and corn were important; sometimes the corn was loaded as meal or, more often, distilled spirits of various description. Hearty fruits and vegetables—such as apples, potatoes, and onions—made excellent cargo because they did not spoil easily in spring and autumn weather. Salted pork was a mainstay, as were animal pelts and dried venison. Tar, turpentine, saltpeter, tallow, beeswax, and hemp all floated south. Sometimes livestock were loaded and shipped on the hoof; chickens sailed in crates. Although human chattel sailed as slave cargo on the Lower Cumberland River, such trade scarcely existed on the upper river and its tributaries.

In high water there was sometimes smooth sailing, but hazards and dangers always lay in wait for intrepid flatboatmen. For starters, the early spring and later fall navigation seasons meant bad weather—freezing rain, sleet, and snow made boating rough business. Although rivermen always tried to run straight through to their intended destinations, fog frequently forced them to make dangerous landings. Despite precautions, boats ran aground on shallow reefs, sandbars, or shoals, whereupon boatmen jumped into ice cold water to muscle the craft back into the current. Other river hazards included boulders, floating debris, and uprooted trees. Some trees, called planters, lay buried underwater in mud. If a flatboat ran over one it could gouge holes into the boat. Swift currents moved some planters above and below water, these were called sawyers. An unsuspecting riverman might steer towards what he believed to be safe water only to see the specter of a rising sawyer ripping a hole into his boat's bow.

Following introduction of the steamboat, a whole new set of hazards immediately appeared. Some slow maneuvering flatboats were run over by steam-belching craft. There was no love lost between flatboatmen and keelboatmen. Ironically, the flatboat's last stand in the late nineteenth century was to serve as a barge towed by a steamer.[19]

Other dangers could take the form of Indians or robbers. Upper Cumberland rivermen who sailed the river's length to the Ohio in the 1790s were caught up in the Shawnee Indian wars. Those sailing as far south as Natchez or New Orleans returned home via an arduous two-hundred-mile overland journey along the Natchez Trace. Whether on horseback or afoot, they trekked from Natchez to Nashville through an "unhealthy country, with bad water," and some sickened and even "died along the way."[20] Others found robbers on the Natchez Trace more troublesome than Indian attacks. Stories of Natchez Trace "land pirates" like Samuel Mason, Micajah Harpe ("Big Harpe" and his brother "Little Harpe"), and John Murrell have been romanticized in oral tradition and print, but these outlaws and other criminals of their ilk existed and practiced their vile trade on the Trace. A flatboatman's profits or wages could end up in saddlebags astride a bandit's pony galloping down the Trace.[21]

Due to increased violence in the Cumberland Settlements between frontiersmen and Indians, settlers asked the territorial governor of the Southwest Territory, William Blount, for protection. A stockade was established in 1794 at the point where Avery Trace (which linked the Eastern and Mero Districts of Tennessee) crossed the Cumberland River. This location at White's Bend in present day Jackson County was commonly referred to as "The Crossing of the Cumberland." Fort Blount was built by the territorial militia at White's Bend of the Cumberland River and garrisoned by federal troops until 1798. The site of the fort became the first seat of Jackson County and was renamed Williamsburg after prominent frontiersman Sampson

Williams (who was instrumental in the establishment of Fort Blount), who operated a ferry and a stand at the site. It represented one of the first river landings in the Upper Cumberland and was an early thriving port.[22]

Thus, a brief look at the history of Cumberland boatmen shows that boating was a hard, exhausting way to make a living. What kind of man was willing to take these risks? What kind of man pursued a career on the river? The answer, in a word, is an entrepreneur. Even the lowliest Upper Cumberland deckhand yearned to get ahead, to make a few dollars to get a start, or enhance a career already begun. The usual Upper Cumberland boatman was a white male, averaging twenty-eight years of age.[23] While Indians, Germans, French, African Americans, and some women, sailed the Cumberland, they represented minorities of men sailing the river north of Carthage, Tennessee. Upper Cumberland rivermen can be divided into four major professional categories—merchant navigators, professional boatmen, farmer flatboatmen, and common deckhands.[24]

The first three groups were older men, in their late twenties and thirties or older. Merchant navigators were businessmen who speculated in Cumberland River goods, built or bought boats to trans-ship cargo, and sometimes piloted the craft themselves. If they could not navigate, they hired a professional boatman to do so for a fee (sometimes they accompanied him; sometimes he was charged with business and navigational chores). A farmer flatboatman represented a seasonal entrepreneur. Late fall and early winter was usually a slow time on the farm, and was perfect for marketing surplus harvest to make a land payment, marry off a daughter, or set up a son with his own farmstead. Deckhands tended to be teen-aged boys in search of adventure, thrilled by the prospect of hard work and a handsome reward. During the decades between the War of 1812 and the Mexican War and the decades immediately following the Civil War, working on the river became a rite of passage for Upper Cumberland youth. A trip to Nashville and points southwest became a substitute for a stint in the army. Many rivermen no doubt took a quick trip on a flatboat, keel, or raft, and then spent the following decades entertaining family and friends with "stretchers" (tall tales) about the glorious days when they sailed the mysterious river below. Using a folk expression of the day, river veterans bragged that they had "seen the elephant," meaning they had traveled far and experienced exotic adventures.[25]

Of course, not all pre-steam rivermen were professional cargo carriers. Thousands of frontier emigrants plied the Upper Cumberland River in flats and keels during the Great Migration of the late eighteenth and early nineteenth centuries. Men, women, and children, with dogs, pigs, cattle, chickens, oxen, mules, and horses traveled up and down the river in search of cheap land and a new chance in life. Commerce was the predominant motive of Upper Cumberland navigators.[26]

These changes paralleled the continued growth of Cumberland River steamboating and the displacement of pre-industrial flats, keels, and rafts with more efficient riverboating technology. In 1811, Nicholas J. Roosevelt steered the *New Orleans* down the Ohio and Mississippi in the first American western rivers steamboat voyage. As he passed the mouth of the Cumberland, the history of Cumberland River steamboating began.[27] Eight years passed before the *General Jackson* arrived in Nashville, Tennessee, in 1819; another decade elapsed before steamers plied as far north as Carthage. But in 1833, E. S. Burge piloted the *Jefferson* to Point Isabel, Kentucky. Because of treacherous shoals directly north of the village, Burnside remained the head of navigation on the Cumberland River for one full century of steamboating.[28]

To understand the technology and design of Upper Cumberland steamboats, one must immediately forget gaudy images from MGM's 1951 feature film *Showboat* or huge modern tourist boats like the *Mississippi Queen* or even the more humble *Delta Queen*. Those boats cater to fantasy and create a false sense of the past. The typical nineteenth century steamboat on the Upper Cumberland was, above all, a workboat; steamers did not sport fancy trappings and luxurious amenities. They were small crafts, with shallow drafts displacing two-to-three feet of water and suitable for navigating lower depths. Smaller crafts were referred to as "chicken stealers," for some long forgotten reason.[29] Powerful boilers made these sleek craft fast and dexterous, but also dangerous. A steamer's average life-span was only five years. They carried a ten-to-twelve man crews, including a captain, pilot, engineer, mate, and deckhands. Although the trade began with several independent operators, larger companies like the Burnside and Burkesville Transportation Company handled most upriver freight, passenger service, and commercial shipping. Nashville's famed Captain Tom Ryman's fleet of over thirty steamers sailed the upper river as well as the entire length of the Cumberland and Tennessee River systems.[30]

Upper Cumberland steamboats ran whenever they could, but peak shipping was the same as for flats, keels, and rafts—the high water of late fall and late spring. Steamboatmen faced danger during fog and freezing temperatures, and from floating and sunken logs, cave-in banks, and shoals. They also faced the added danger of fire. Large black smokestacks bellowed plumes of smoke, and also spit out sparks and burning embers, setting fire to merchandise or parts of the ship if not detected and smothered at once.[31]

The D.H. Pike *1883. Credit: Tennessee State Library and Archives, Byrd Douglas Papers.*

Smaller craft called packets steamed up the river's tributaries along the Caney Fork, Obey, and Obed Rivers. The hull of the first steamboat to sail up the Caney Fork, *Harry Hill,* was built by Sam Caplinger and William Christian near Carthage, and outfitted with its boiler and machinery at Nashville in 1832. On its maiden voyage it sailed from Carthage to Sligo Landing on the Caney Fork. Two packets owned by Amos Livingston Davis before the Civil War—the *Everyday Dick* and *The May Dew*—routinely went as far as Sligo Landing and, on rare occasions when the water was high enough, went all the way to Sparta.[32] Names of some packets reflected their association with the Upper Cumberland region, such as *Burkesville, Burnside, City of Burnside, Caney Fork No. 1, Caney Fork No.2, Celina No. 1, Celina No. 2, Creelsboro, Benton McMillin, Sligo, Sligo No. 2,* and the *Jamestown, Tennessee.* The average Upper Cumberland packet carried roughly three hundred tons of cargo per trip, and the boating season lasted roughly seven months under normal conditions. Cargo ran the gamut from livestock and produce to finished goods. Amanda Bell Hicks of Putnam County recalled that packets delivered all manner of goods to local businessmen "from a toothpick to a casket."[33] Nashville Judge Byrd Douglas, a Civil War veteran and licensed operator who owned "a variety of boats, including towboats and barges, which he piloted along nearly every navigable mile of the Cumberland river,"[34] noted that "packets on the upper river lasted for a century and prolonged the life of steamboat traffic for nearly ten years after that on most other rivers had died a natural death."[35]

Because of the relative isolation of the Upper Cumberland region and its rugged terrain, the area was:

> peculiarly adapted to steamboat transportation. . . From Carthage to Point Isabel many sections would have been completely isolated except for steamboats. It was one of the last frontiers in the Eastern United States, unexcelled in beauty and unadorned by any semblance of modern improvements. Rich in raw materials. . . here was a prize which, when possessed, was destined to remain in the hands of packet owners without any serious competition. Even railroads could not conquer the deep ravines and endless hills of the Cumberland Plateau and find the hidden wealth along the banks of the river. It was not until the arrival of the motor trucks and automobiles that the packets gave up the ghost.[36]

When compared to other western rivers, steamboats came late and stayed later in the Upper Cumberland. By 1850, five or six upriver steamers arrived in Nashville weekly, carrying agricultural produce, raw materials, and passengers, and turning right around to deliver manufactured goods of every description from Nashville warehouses. Upper Cumberland landings proliferated; Burnside, Kentucky, and Carthage, Tennessee, were joined by Butler's Landing, Celina, Gainesboro, and Granville in Tennessee, and Albany, Burkesville, and Creelsboro in Kentucky, in addition to scores more ports. Indeed, by the early twentieth century, there were 121 landings between Burnside and Carthage, and this figure does not include unofficial farmer's landings, where steamers often stopped whenever someone "flagged them down." Mrs. Hugh Kyle of Celina wrote that "People of the Upper Cumberland were perhaps more dependent on steamboats than any other community in the world. Up until very recently it was the only means of transportation for the entire country."[37] Each steamer had a distinctive whistle the pilots sounded as they approached a dock. One old-timer recalled "the way these steamboats would echo up these valleys . . . you'd hear the whistle, then you'd see the boat."[38]

Steamboats played another important role besides transportation for people, raw materials, and finished goods. Each fall the Upper Cumberland rang with the shouts of farmers noisily driving pigs and turkeys to market. Many north-south roads in Upper Cumberland counties had the same name, the Kentucky Stock Road or simply the Kentucky Road. Farmers rounded up their pigs after the crops had been harvested, and before the highly social event of hog-killing time, in order to drive some stock north to Cincinnati. Before the advent of the steamboat, teams drove pork on the hoof overland through Tompkinsville or Somerset and beyond to the abattoirs of Porkopolis. One of the many impediments to such trips was the fact that the pigs often lost weight en route and farmers earned less money as a result. With steamboats farmers only had to drive their pigs to places like Granville, whose population swelled to over ten thousand people during hog season. There pigs were sold to brokers from Nashville, Louisville, and Cincinnati. After the farmer made his deal, he herded pigs into holding pens where they awaited transport on steamboats or barges to be piloted north to Cincinnati to be processed. Many farmers, however, squandered their money in one of the many taverns in Granville, returning home poorer than when they left.[39]

The coming of the Civil War left river commerce on the Upper Cumberland in complete disarray; great hardships resulted from folks' inability to import or export staples via the old river route. While much military history has been written about the role of the Lower Cumberland and Tennessee rivers (and Union General U.S. Grant's "divide and conquer" strategy), the upper river's military history is less well known. This is because the Upper Cumberland did not play a major role in either Union or Confederate action, although plenty of engagements occurred along the river. Confederate General John Hunt Morgan converted steamboats for military purposes near Buffalo Valley along the Caney Fork in Putnam County, which he used to harass Union forces at Carthage. Upriver folk were bitterly divided into Yankee and Confederate sides, and the April 1863 Union attack and sacking of Celina was the most spirited upriver military action. Guerrilla warfare typified fighting in the upper river valley, as Rebel leader Champ Ferguson matched wits against Unionist partisan "Tinker Dave" Beaty and his band. Some rebels sniped at Union gunboats and steamers and even fashioned man-made "snags" to puncture their hulls. But rebel resistance soon fell before the Yankee onslaught. By 1863, fifty or more Union steamboats arrived in Nashville weekly during navigation season, and Union gunboats controlled the river all the way to the head of navigation. Old Columbus in Jackson County was utterly destroyed by Federal troops in a joint landward and riverine expedition in February 1864. The final Rebel humiliation was renaming of the port at Point Isabel, Kentucky, to Burnside, in honor of the erratic Union General Ambrose Burnside.[40]

It took nearly a decade for normal traffic to return to the river after the war. The river had to be cleared of snags and entanglements created by competing military forces, to impede the others' supplies. Normal crop yields and normal traffic returned in tandem, and in 1872 the river bustled once again with regular traffic between Burnside, Kentucky, and Clarksville, Tennessee.[41]

As steamboats came to dominate trade in the Upper Cumberland, opening up a wider world to its residents, entrepreneurs vied for control of commercial enterprises the river offered. James W. Lovell of Dixon Springs in Smith County learned to pilot a steamboat before the Civil War, and after it ended invested in a fleet of boats that served communities from Nashville to Burnside. Unlike the lower Cumberland, the upper river was fiercely competitive, and the only fleet that could rival Lovell's was that of Tom Ryman, who entered the business in 1875.[42]

William Trover (W.T.) Hunter, a second generation Cumberland River steamboat pilot, spent his life on the river. His father, W.A. Hunter, was a pilot during the industry's infancy before the Civil War, and W.T. plied the river until 1915, when steamboats were eclipsed by railroads and automobiles. He recalled that after the river returned to normal:

> Upstream cargoes consisted of groceries, dry goods, farming implements, and general merchandise. . . [while] downstream cargoes were typically grain, stock [primarily pigs or sheep], tobacco, produce, and farm products of all kinds. Also, heavy shipments of lumber, staves, and axe handles. At times it was a common sight to see as much as one million feet of lumber stacked in one yard along the Cumberland River. . . The largest shipment of hogs brought in one single vessel, to my knowledge, was 1500 on the steamer *Dunbar.* The largest number of eggs, 1200 cases; greatest number of coops of chickens, around 600 coops. . . Hogsheads of tobacco frequently weighed as much as 2200 pounds. . . At times shipments were made of from 150 hogsheads from one landing. . . For handling hogs and sheep, each boat carried what was called a screen, which was made of canvas and about three feet high, with a wooden staff paced about every six feet and each staff manned by roustabouts from off the boat, thus making a mobile fence. This screen was placed to an opening of a stock pen and the hogs and sheep were driven to the end of the stage plank on the boat.[43]

During the Steamboat Era (1819–1924) dozens of steamboats sank on the upper reaches of the Cumberland River. The most frequent cause of a shipwreck was crashing into a rock or log and taking on water. Lost steamers included the *John W. Hart, Creelsboro, Patrol, City of Burnside, Henry Harley,* and

The Henry Harley. *Credit: Tennessee State Library and Archives, Byrd Douglas Papers.*

H.G. Hill. "On the morning of April 5, 1897, the steamer John W. Hart struck a hidden obstruction near Granville . . . and sank with her bow against the bank. The stove in the pilot house overturned causing the superstructure to catch fire and burn to the water."[44] One of Tom Ryman's fleet, the *I.T. Rhea,* sank April 6, 1895, near Free State in Jackson County after hitting a rocky bluff abutting the river's shore near Brook's Ferry (site of present day Frank Clement Bridge). Oral tradition blames its sinking on a drunken captain who had recently been jilted by his sweetheart.[45] In the winter of 1899, the *Burnside No. 1* sank between Celina and Burkesville when it hit a bank. A barrel of oil flew off a platform and rolled into a wood stove; a huge fire broke out, killing one crewman.[46]

Steamers hauled just about everything, including the kitchen sink. Tobacco, corn, dry goods, dress materials, shoes, fruit, spirituous liquors, wagons and buggies, pianos, furniture, tools, fertilizer, and Sears and Roebuck parcels all traveled the river. "They carried everything that a farmer would use, or a merchant would sell in country store," recalled pilot Escar O. Coe:

> We made two trips a week. Would leave Burnside on Saturday night, go to Lee's Landing, Tennessee [Nashville], and arrive

> back at Burnside on Wednesday morning. We'd bring egg cases down for people to put eggs in to ship back. . . And bales of wire, roofing, and nails, and all kinds of hardware and groceries shipped to merchants. We'd pick up produce, chickens, eggs, livestock, lumber, staves, and what-have-you that you could load on a boat.[47]

Americans have always been fascinated with steamboat racing; Mark Twain—whose father John Clemens was once the Port Authority of Gainesboro—wrote of the "vast importance" and "consuming excitement" that preceded a race: "Politics and weather were dropped," Twain noted, "and people talked only of the upcoming race."[48] Like Twain's beloved lower Mississippi, the upper stretches of the Cumberland River saw its share of steamboat racing. Claude Hackett remembered, "We had a few steamboat

Samuel Clemons, or Mark Twain, whose writings captured the imagination of life on the rivers. Credit: Mike Allen.

races that burned up all the lard and meat and everything to make more steam. Sometimes they'd adjust the safety valve to where it was dangerous." One momentous upriver race produced this folk song lyric: "The Harley and the Hardison had a race/The Harley threw water in the Hardison's Face." In another folk tradition, a small trophy rotated between the winners on rival steamboats.[49]

Although Congress created the Army Engineers (today's Army Corps of Engineers) in 1824, the vast majority of their dredging and infrastructure work was conducted on the Lower, not the Upper, Cumberland River. In 1834, as more and more residents of the region pressured their representatives, "Congress directed a survey of the upper river from Nashville 'to the highest point on said river susceptible of being made navigable for steamboats.'"[50] Howard Stansbury, the U.S. Civil Engineer, was charged with conducting the survey, and he was impressed by the natural resources of the Upper Cumberland. He recorded twenty-five coal mining operations that employed roughly three hundred men in the area surrounding the Laurel River tributary in Kentucky. Stansbury witnessed one hundred flatboats filled with coal from those mines to be transported to Nashville. Because of that emerging industry, Stansbury reported to his superiors that the Upper Cumberland should be improved at least up to the Laurel River, if not farther.[51]

Steamboat captain William McKnight, who had been employed to oversee improvements on the Lower Cumberland, was hired to work on the Upper Cumberland. He dispatched workers to Carthage, Tennessee, and the mouth of the Laurel River to clear timber and remove snags and boulders. McKnight acquired the *Laurel*, a steam-powered snag boat developed by Captain Henry M. Shreve, to assist in getting rid of snags and rocks. By 1838, one hundred thirty men worked around Carthage, "cutting trees, blasting rocks, and buildings."[52] After the flurry of activity in 1838–1839, serious improvements to navigating the Upper Cumberland ceased until after the Civil War.

In 1888 the Corps resumed its program of building locks and dams to facilitate longer upriver steamboat navigation seasons; state and local governments also subsidized improvements. Colonel M.T. Bryan, a Nashville entrepreneur whose livelihood depended on the river, organized the Cumberland River Improvement Association in 1889 to keep pressure on the federal government to improve navigation and install more locks on the river for even greater traffic. Between 1888 and 1902 seven locks between Carthage and Burnside were completed, though most of their attendant dams were never built. In 1915, "Lock 21," built thirty miles below Burnside, improved navigation to that upriver port.[53]

Log rafting on the Upper Cumberland River warrants a separate and detailed discussion. During the peace and prosperity that followed the Civil War and Reconstruction, a building boom erupted in middle and eastern Tennessee. Around 1872, Upper Cumberland timber became a prime commodity. Once considered too remote to harvest, the advent of narrow gauge railroads and the emergence of log rafting made the timber industry profitable in the Upper Cumberland for the first time. Former subsistence farmers found they could sell their timber for hard currency, if they could get it to market. Each autumn, after their farms' produce was harvested, men began logging the deciduous forests surrounding their farmland. Sounds of double-bitted axes and saws echoed through the woods, followed by the crash of falling timber. Some said it was easier to cut trees in the fall after the sap had retreated. Logs as big as four feet in diameter were sawed into ten-to-fifteen foot lengths. When weather permitted, winter months were dedicated to trimming limbs and branches and preparing logs for their final destination. Once the timber was ready to move, lumbermen hitched teams of oxen or mules to the logs and snaked them to creek and river bottoms to await spring rains. Teams of men sorted logs into "floaters" (light buoyant timber) and "sinkers" (dense hardwoods) and prepared to make a raft.[54]

Raftsmen assembled their vessels—sometimes called "drifts"—in a manner similar to the modern barge tow. They first constructed a number of small rafts— stringers or blocks—and then pieced them together into a larger navigable unit. To secure the logs they strapped and pegged them together with hickory (or other deciduous) saplings and strips (whaling); some hardwoods required metal "chain dogs" instead of wooden pegs.[55] After this arduous task, they proceeded into the challenges and hazards of downstream navigation. A completed raft ranged in size from fifty to two hundred fifty feet in length, and could be composed of as many as two thousand logs or as much as ten-to-twelve thousand board feet of lumber. To guide the raft as the waters rose, sawyers fashioned crude oar locks, in which they secured long poles to steer the craft. Before launching a raft, the crew built a makeshift cabin to provide a modicum of shelter and crude accommodations for sleeping. They shoveled a small amount of dirt on the logs near the cabin and tamped it down, so that they could safely build a fire for cooking and warmth as they made their way down river.[56] As Jesse Rich remembered, "Oak timbers . . . considered . . . too small for saw logs to raft" were hand hewn into cross ties for the expanding railroads in the region. After rafts were constructed five hundred to six hundred crossties were loaded on them as cargo.[57]

Typical log raft during the heyday of the lumber boom. Credit: Michael E. Birdwell Upper Cumberland Collection.

Like flatboatmen, keelboatmen, and steamboatmen, raftsmen sailed mainly in the high water of late winter and spring. Starting out on tributaries—the Obey, Roaring, and Caney Fork Rivers—rafts floated the Cumberland River, whose swift currents swept them on their perilous journey. One Cumberland County, Kentucky, raftsman recalled, "We rafted 'em down the Cumberland to Celina and sold 'em to Kyles [Brothers Lumber Company]. Millard Kyle measured 'em up and gave us our checks and we walked back home then. Yeah, a heap of a-times when you didn't wait for a [steam]boat, you would walk back." Hugh and Millard Kyle were pioneers in an industry that flourished until roughly 1920. The journey to Nashville from busy Upper Cumberland ports like Celina or Byrdstown, Tennessee, normally took five days.[58]

Those men who had money in their pockets and did not fancy the notion of walking home booked passage on steamboats or packets, and they rode back home to the upper reaches of the river. Steamboat pilot W.T. Hunter remembered raftsmen as generally a pleasant, even rambunctious lot. "The raftsman's outfit on going aboard the steamer to go home, would usually consist of his bundle of bedding swung across his back, together with a guitar or fiddle, with frequently a rifle; and in the days of liquor drinking a jug accompanied most of them."[59]

The lively folklore of Upper Cumberland log raftsmen reflects the importance of this work in the history of the Upper Cumberland region of Tennessee. Lumber rafting continued well into the twentieth century. Trips shortened as Upper Cumberland entrepreneurs built their own lumber mills or established "peckerwood" mills in the forest, negating the need for raft construction; by 1900 raftsmen no longer had to travel long distances to reach sawmills.[60] One Upper Cumberland farmer who made his fortune in the lumber boom was "Uncle Billy" Hull of Clay (now Overton) County, Tennessee. A Civil War veteran and moonshiner, Hull turned to log rafting to build a substantial fortune during the postbellum years. He deforested his land (and that of his neighbors), piloting his own rafts to lumber mills in Carthage and Nashville. Specializing in the lucrative hardwood trade, Hull became a wealthy man, transitioning from subsistence farmer to entrepreneur. Indeed, Hull grew successful enough to send his son Cordell to college and to Cumberland Law School in Lebanon, Tennessee. Cordell Hull went on to a storied political career and was the longest serving secretary of state in U.S. history in the Franklin Delano Roosevelt administration.[61]

Another celebrated raft pilot was Cal Hamilton of Celina, Tennessee. An African American employed by the Kyle family, Hamilton earned the grudging respect of his white peers during the age of Jim Crow. His knowledge of the river was unsurpassed and his deftness in handling the unpredictable and difficult craft made the Kyles one of the more successful lumber companies in the Upper Cumberland.[62] Hugh Kyle and Cal Hamilton grew closer over the years and "when it became time for Mr. Kyle to face his final enemy in a Nashville hospital he called Cal to him and said, 'They have doctors and nurses here, but I want you . . . stay with me till it is all over,'" and Hamilton fulfilled his friend's request.[63]

Though largely forgotten, African Americans played a crucial role on the upper reaches of the Cumberland River. While most raftsmen were white, with the exception of men like Cal Hamilton, roustabouts were dominantly black. A crew of roustabouts, twenty to thirty in number depending on the size of the boat, loaded and unloaded cargo, tended animals onboard, and performed any number of physical tasks. Though usually regarded as unskilled labor, roustabouts had to be strong of back and fleet of foot as well as possess a keen knowledge of the workings of a steamboat. They had to learn how to load a boat correctly in order for it to operate at peak capacity and not put undue stress on the boiler. Roustabouts loaded everything destined for markets in the Upper Cumberland from thimbles to pianos. Many suffered abuse by the mates who cussed them with impunity, and Jim Crow laws restricted their movement onboard and on land. W.T. Hunter remembered them fondly, however, and acknowledged their hard work and their loyalty. He criticized their fondness for playing craps, but let them gamble because "you either had to allow them to shoot craps or you did not get any roustabouts."[64]

As the twentieth century progressed, Upper Cumberland steamboating slowly faded away. The last upriver steamer was probably the *Rowena,* a Burnside vessel which sank near Grassy Creek in 1933; the *City of Burnside* and *Celina* met similar fates shortly beforehand. Neither the *Rowena* nor the *Celina* were running under their own steam when they went down; they were being towed downstream by boats fueled by internal combustion engines. The Cumberland Transportation Company had begun using "gasoline powered boats" to haul groceries upriver, and some boats had begun to push or pull cargoes in river barges.[65]

These harbingers of modern towboating never prospered upriver for several reasons, the most important of which revolved around the Army Corps of Engineers. Beginning with the invention of the twin-screw, internal combustion engine-powered pushboat[66] (the universally used term "towboat" is a misnomer), the lower Cumberland River slowly transitioned to diesel-powered boat commerce. This process was furthered by Great Depression public works infrastructure projects under the auspices of the Works Progress Administration (WPA) and Tennessee Valley Authority (TVA); state government and private capital contributed to the internal improvements effort. Like steamers before them, pushboats dotted the Lower Cumberland River, navigating in all seasons via a series of fourteen new and refitted locks and dams constructed by the Army Corps of Engineers.[67]

Pushboats never came upriver because the Corps built and refitted the upriver dams *without* locks. Without modern lockage, diesel pushboats, unlike their low-draft steamboat predecessors, could not navigate the Upper Cumberland. The Corps of Engineers joined other federal and state economic planners in deeming the upriver traffic tangential to modern commerce and designated Nashville, Tennessee, the "head of navigation" on the Cumberland, signaling an end to fleets of boats that formerly recognized Burnside, Kentucky, as the river's headwater port. Slowly, the Upper Cumberland River grew quieter; the sound of steam whistles echoing up the valleys became less and less frequent.[68]

Jesse W. Rich of Pickett County, who rafted logs down the Obey and Cumberland rivers at the turn of the twentieth century remembered the heyday of the river and his fellow rivermen fondly. "Rivermen were tough and hardy men; some of them were rude, uneducated, brave, suffering hardships with their sailor-like stoicism. Some were drinkers and frolickers and pretty reckless, prodigal with their money, yet, in the main, honest and trustworthy, faithful to promises and duty, and often picturesque."[69]

Meanwhile, railroads expanded, penetrating throughout the Upper Cumberland, and so did the quality and quantity of roads built to serve increasing numbers of automobiles and trucks. Although these changes arrived later in the Upper Cumberland than in other parts of America, methods of transport slowly began to dramatically change. Upper Cumberland businessmen and travelers began to turn their backs on the river as they utilized railroads, automobiles, and trucks to travel and ship goods to market.[70] Even though the heyday of the steamboat had ended, some small enterprises continued to thrive in spite of modern highways and automobiles. In some locations, such as Rome, Tennessee, and Tompkinsville, Kentucky, travelers continued to depend on ferries to cross the river where bridges have still yet to be built. By the late nineteenth century, no fewer than forty ferries transported people and products across the river, sometimes dodging steamboats or log rafts. The few that remained harkened back to the rich history of the river, providing not only safe passage from one shore to another, but also a sense of nostalgia for simpler times.[71]

The demise of upper river commercial transportation was, in some ways, a blessing. Just as dams with locks encouraged pushboating, their absence encouraged recreational traffic. Wolf Creek Dam, completed in 1952, not only enhanced flood control and hydroelectric power, it created Lake Cumberland, a 101–mile long reservoir in Kentucky suitable for serious sportsmen and family outings. This 242–foot-high structure, alongside other dams, such as Dale Hollow and Center Hill, created lakes that turned the Upper Cumberland region into a vacationer's paradise.[72] Today aluminum canoes, fishing boats, houseboats, speedboats, and water-skiers dot many recreation sites along the upper reaches of the Cumberland River. Excursion boats often run from Carthage to Granville, Tennessee, locking in at the Cordell Hull Dam and follow a remnant of the watercourse once plied by Indians and frontiersmen. Thus, modern Tennesseans vacation

The Rome Ferry in Smith County. Credit: Tennessee State Library and Archives, Albert Ganier Collection.

and play along the great waterway their ancestors used as a superhighway for two hundred years in canoes, keels, flatboats, rafts, and steamboats.

NOTES

1. Lynwood Montell, *Don't Go Up Kettle Creek: Verbal Legacy of the Upper Cumberland* (Knoxville: University of Tennessee Press, 1983), p. 106.
2. In terms of navigation, the Upper Cumberland River stretches from Burnside, Kentucky to Nashville, Tennessee while the Lower Cumberland River extends from Nashville, Tennessee to Smithland, Kentucky where it merges into the Ohio River.
3. James McCague, *The Cumberland* (New York: Holt McDougal, 1973), p. xiii. While McCague's study is considered the standard on the subject, it is devoid of notes and has a limited bibliography.
4. George E. Webb, "Peaceful Natives: Indians in the Upper Cumberland," *Lend an Ear: Heritage of the Tennessee Upper Cumberland,* Calvin Dickinson, Larry Whiteaker, Leo McGee and Homer D. Kemp, eds. (Lanham, Maryland: University Press of America, 1983), pp. 7, 12, 16–17.
5. John R. Finger, *Tennessee Frontiers: Three Regions in Transition* (Bloomington: Indiana University Press, 2001), p. 92.

6. Michael Allen, *Western Rivermen: Ohio and Mississippi Boatmen on the Myth of the Alligator Horse, 1763–1861* (Baton Rouge: Louisiana State University Press, 1990), p. 59; Leland Baldwin, *The Keelboat Age on the Western Waters* (Pittsburgh: University of Pittsburgh Press, 1941), pp. 39–42.
7. McCague, 36.
8. *Ibid.*, 39. *Pirouge* is the French term for canoe.
9. The three gaps are the Emory Gap, Kimbrough Gap, and Walden Gap.
10. W. Calvin Dickinson, *The Walton Road: A Nineteenth Century Wilderness Highway in Tennessee* (BookSurge Publishing, 2007), pp. XIII-14. U.S. 70N was built adjacent to the road and can be used as a guide to finding the grade of the Walton Road in many places.
11. *Subduing the Cumberland: A History of the "Old" Locks and Dams on the Cumberland River* (Nashville, Tennessee: U.S. Army Corps of Engineers, N.D.), p. 15. Hereafter, *Subduing the Cumberland.* Roughly four hundred steamboats plied the river throughout the 1850s and Nashville was home to thirteen different packet lines.
12. Allen, *Western Rivermen*, 65–66, 144–148.
13. "Account of Expenses," June, 1804 in J.S. Bassett, ed., *Correspondence of Andrew Jackson*, 7 Vols. (Washington, D.C.: USGPO, 1926–1935), pp. 195.
14. Leland Johnson, *Engineers on the Twin Rivers: A History of the U.S. Army Engineers Nashville District, 1769–1978* (Nashville, Tennessee: U.S. Army Corps of Engineers, 1978), pp. 13.
15. Montell, 130–132.
16. James Douglas Anderson Papers, Addition 1 (Nashville: Tennessee State Library and Archives) THS 379, Box 2, Folder 1; John R. Bedford, "A Tour in 1807 Down the Cumberland, Ohio, and Mississippi Rivers from Nashville to New Orleans," *Tennessee History Magazine* 5 (April 1919). p. 63.
17. Montell, 130–132.
18. Allen, *Western Rivermen*, 144–146.
19. This and preceding four paragraphs are based on the author's *Western Rivermen*, 72–78.
20. Dawson A. Phelps, "Travel on the Natchez Trace: A Study of its Economic Aspect," *Journal Mississippi History*, 15 (July 1953), pp. 155–64.
21. S. Wilkerson, "The Commerce of the West," *American Pioneer* 2 (March 1843), pp. 163–64; Allen, *Western Rivermen, 1763–1861*, 78–85; James L. Penick Jr. "John A. Murrell: A Legend of the Old Southwest." *Tennessee Historical Quarterly* 48:3 (1989). pp. 174–183; see also James L. Penick Jr., *The Great Western Land Pirate: John A. Murrell in Legend and History* (Columbia: University of Missouri Press, 1981). Michael E. Birdwell, "Cumberland Tales: Terror in Tennessee: John Murrell, The Great Western Land Pirate," *Herald-Citizen* (August 11, 2013): C-4. John Murrell spent his last days on earth in the Upper Cumberland. After his release from the Tennessee state prison, Murrell took up residence on the White County-Van Buren County line and worked as a carpenter and blacksmith. He joined the Methodist Church in Sparta where he was a member in good standing. His nefarious reputation preceded him, however; people still relate tales of horror about the man now buried in the Nine Mile community of Bledsoe County. According to legend, as reported

by Caroline Knight, he was buried face down so that on the day of judgment he would be staring into the pit of hell.

22. Samuel D. Smith and Benjamin J. Nance. *An Archaeological Interpretation of the Site of Fort Blount, A 1790s Territorial Militia and Federal Military Post, Jackson County, Tennessee.* Research Series No. 12. (Nashville: Tennessee Department of Environment and Conservation, Division of Archaeology, 2000), pp. 4–6. Smith's Bend was named in honor of Revolutionary War veteran Samuel Smith, who received a land grant and took up residence in the area. For a while the area was known as Williamsburg or Smithland. One of Smith's slaves was the hanged in the first public execution in Jackson County history.
23. Michael Allen, "The Riverman as Jacksonian Man," *Western Historical Quarterly* 21 (August 1990), pp. 305–320.
24. My categorizations are based in part on those of Harry N. Schreiber, "The Ohio Flatboat Trade: Some Reconsiderations," David M. Ellis, ed., *The Frontier in American Development: Essays in Honor of Paul Wallace Gates* (Ithaca, New York: Cornell University Press, 1970), pp. 277–298.
25. Allen, *Western Rivermen*, 94–102.
26. *Ibid.*, 3, 35.
27. Byrd Douglas, *Steamboating on the Cumberland* (Nashville, Tennessee: Parthenon Publishing, 1961), pp. 132–161.
28. Montell, 132–133; Douglas, 35.
29. Douglas Anderson, "Old Times on the Upper Cumberland: Steamboat Excitement," *Nashville Banner* (April 4, 1925).
30. Louis C. Hunter, *Steamboats on Western Rivers: An Economic and Technological History* (Cambridge, Massachusetts: Harvard University Press, 1949); Eric F. Haites, James Make, and Gary M. Walton, *Western River Transportation: The Era of Internal Development, 1810–1860* (Baltimore, Maryland: Johns Hopkins University Press, 1975). Montell, 146.
31. Douglas, 41.
32. Monroe Seals, *History of White County, Tennessee.* (Sparta, Tennessee: Civitan Club, 1935). p. 42.
33. Interview with Amanda Bell Hicks, Double Springs, Tennessee, August 2, 1983.
34. Byrd Douglas Family Papers,1819–1968 (Nashville: Tennessee State Library and Archives) MF 1547. Hereafter Byrd Douglas Papers.
35. Douglas, 35, 57, 58, 62. According to W. T. Hunter boats leaving Nashville at 5:00 p.m. usually reached Carthage the next day around noon, then on to Celina the next day arriving about noon, steaming on to Burkesville sometime that night and arriving at Burnside sometime the next afternoon.
36. *Ibid.*, 59.
37. Douglas Anderson, "Old Times on the Upper Cumberland: One Landing, Three Rivers," *Nashville Banner* (September 19, 1925).
38. Montell, 139.
39. Interview with Rufus Barlow (Cookeville, Tennessee, August 8, 1987); interview with Haskell Smith (Cookeville, Tennessee, March 3, 1977); Eddie Reasoner, *Once Upon A River* (Nashville: Nash-Angeles Productions, 1996).

40. Larry Whitaker, "'The Enemy is My Brother': The Civil War in the Upper Cumberland," *Lend An Ear: Heritage of the Tennessee Upper Cumberland,* W. Calvin Dickinson, Larry Whiteaker, Homer D. Kemp and Leo McGee, eds., (Lanham, Maryland: University Press of America,1983), pp. 33–43; McCague, *The Cumberland,* 175–76, 161–81. For a more detailed discussion of the war in the region see: James B. Jones Jr., "Fevers Ran High: The Civil War in the Upper Cumberland," *Rural Life and Culture in the Upper Cumberland,* Michael E. Birdwell and W. Calvin Dickinson, eds. (Lexington: University Press of Kentucky, 2004), pp. 73–104 and Brian McKnight, *Confederate Outlaw: Champ Ferguson and the Civil War in Appalachia* (Baton Rouge: Louisiana State University Press, 2011).
41. Joseph B. Killebrew, *Resources of Tennessee* (Nashville, Tennessee: Tavel and Eastman, 1874), pp. 622–624; 775–779.
42. Douglas, 189, 214. Tom Ryman became a legendary steamboat entrepreneur. Until his conversion to Methodism by the Reverend Sam Jones, Ryman's steamboats were floating dens of vice. Afterward, he quit serving alcohol on his fleet and forbade gambling. He built the Union Gospel Tabernacle to act as a venue for church conventions in Nashville, and the auditorium was named "Jones Hall." Later known as the Ryman Auditorium, the venerable building was home to the Grand Ole Opry and remains one of the great concert stages in America.
43. Cumberland [River] Recollections of Captain W. T. Hunter (Nashville: Tennessee State Library and Archives, Byrd Douglas Papers, Box 5, Folder 150, pp. 1–2.
44. *Ibid.*, 6.
45. Montell, 160; Douglas, 341. In fact a sudden storm blew the *I.T. Rhea* into the bluff.
46. Montell, 160–161.
47. *Ibid.*
48. Mark Twain, *Life on the Mississippi* (1874 Reprint New York: 1986), p. 139.
49. Montell, 153.
50. Johnson, 65.
51. *Ibid.*, 65–66. Stansbury suggested the creation of wing dams be built perpendicular to the current to force water into regular channels whose depth could be moderated as needed to support regular steamboat traffic as far as the Big South Fork.
52. *Subduing the Cumberland,* 14.
53. Michael C. Robinson, *History of Navigation of the Ohio River Basin,* National Waterways Study NWS-83-5 (Washington, D.C.: USGPO, 1983). p. 33; Anne Paine, "Cumberland Once Busy . . . Colorful," *Nashville Tennessean,* January 27, 1985. p. 2; Douglas, 221; *Subduing the Cumberland,* 46–47.
54. Steven A. Schulman, "Reminiscence of Logging on the Cumberland," *Kentucky Folklore Record,* 18 (1972), pp. 96–98; Schulman, Steven A. "The Lumber Industry of the Upper Cumberland River Valley." *Tennessee Historical Quarterly* 32 (1973), pp. 255–64.
55. Chain dogs were two large metal spikes welded to a length of logging chain of varying lengths from as little as six inches to as much as three or more feet. Nashville lumber mills often provided loggers chain dogs free of charge as a means of luring business their way. Jesse W. Rich, *Cutting, Rafting and Running Logs Down the Obey River, 1880–1920.* (Self-Published, 1972), p. 8.

56. Schulman, "Reminiscence of Logging," 96–98; Steven A. Schulman, "Rafting Logs on the Upper Cumberland River," *Pioneer American* 6:1 (1974), pp. 14–24; Rich, 9.
57. Rich, 16–17.
58. *Ibid.*, 22; Rich, 4. Other major logging concerns on the Upper Cumberland River were operate by Captain A.C. Dale, Pleasant (Pleas) and Hobart (Hob) Harrison, Mounce Gore, J.D. Hatcher, and George Birdwell. Douglas Anderson reported that at the height of log rafting on the Caney Fork roughly four hundred rafts were piloted down river each season from December to April. See Douglas Anderson, "Old Times on the Upper Cumberland: Celina to Caney Fork," *Nashville Banner* (June 27, 1925).
59. Recollections of W.T. Hunter, 3.
60. Keith, 86–87. A peckerwood mill was a small portable sawmill that could be placed on a narrow gauge rail car and taken to the area where lumber was being harvested. It could be cut into board feet on the spot and delivered to planing mills for finishing. Such mobility expanded the logging industry in the Upper Cumberland, making men in the timber industry less dependent on the river and its seasonal conditions.
61. Cordell Hull, *The Memoirs of Cordell Hull*, Vol. 1 (New York: Macmillan, 1948), pp. 19–21. Hull's brothers rafted logs as well, but they did not pursue careers in law or politics.
62. Douglas, 237.
63. Douglas Anderson, "Old Times on the Upper Cumberland: Mrs. Kyle's Story," *Nashville Banner* (July 25, 1925).
64. Recollections of W.T. Hunter, 4, 8. He said that unless roustabouts were unloading cargo, they were confined to the boat until it returned to Nashville.
65. Douglas, 145–146, 160–61; McCague, *The Cumberland*, 204; Jeanette Keith, *Country People of the New South: Tennessee's Upper Cumberland* (Chapel Hill: University of North Carolina Press, 1995), pp. 23–24; Schulman, "Rafting Logs," 16.
66. George P. Parkinson Jr. and Brooks F. McCabe Jr., "Charles Ward and the *James V. Rumsey:* Regional Innovation in Steam Technology on the Western Rivers," *West Virginia History* 39 (January-April, 1978), pp. 143–180.
67. Robinson, 28–33; McCague, 206–7.
68. *Ibid.*, 46–47; Paine, 2.
69. Rich, 21.
70. Keith, 77–89 (railroads) and 100–117 (automobiles).
71. Among the recorded historic ferries were: Albany Ferry, Allen's Ferry, Barksdale Ferry, Bender's Ferry, Bennett Ferry, Black's Ferry, Boatland Ferry, Brook's Ferry, Buffalo Valley Ferry, Butler's Ferry, Celina Ferry, Clifton Ferry, Cumberland River Ferry, Denny Ferry, Dillon Ferry, Doyle Ferry, Eastport Ferry, Eddy's Ferry, Fort Blount/Williamsburg Ferry, Fancher's Ferry, Frank's Ferry, Franklin Ferry, Gainesboro Ferry, Gate's Ferry, Granville Ferry, Greenmoss Ferry, Harrison Ferry, Hick's Ferry, Highland Ferry, Hodge Ferry, Holliman's Ferry, Hunt's Ferry, Love's Ferry, McElroy Ferry, McMillan's Ferry, Old Bailiff Ferry, Pin Hook Ferry, River Hill Ferry, Rome Ferry, Sligo Ferry, Walton Ferry, and Winfrey's Ferry.
72. Robinson, 46–47.

3

"A Woman's Work is Never Done"

Women's Achievements in the Upper Cumberland

Ann Toplovich

The history of women in the Upper Cumberland is a story of labor, rather than leisure. The old English proverb, "A man's work lasts till set of sun, a woman's work is never done," captures these women's lives. American Indian women controlled and farmed the land until European folkways transferred those chores to men. Female pioneers from Atlantic colonies into the Upper Cumberland continued to provide food, clothing, and comfort to their families. With the changing economy in the 1800s, women participated in production of goods for markets. During the onslaught of Civil War, they fought and sacrificed. Moving toward and through the twentieth century, women took on public work and community service.[1]

"A Woman's Work is Never Done," a seventeenth century English song, enumerates the tasks of a married woman: rising early to clean the house, making the fire, fixing her husband's breakfast, dressing and feeding the children, suckling the baby (who "doth gnaw and bite, and sorely me molest"), preparing dinner over the fire, knitting, spinning, washing, sewing, making beds, waiting on her husband at supper, putting the children to bed, getting up in the night to nurse, and sometimes serving her husband's needs.[2] An Upper Cumberland woman would add to the list of tasks: planting and tending the kitchen garden, putting up food for the winter, and helping in the fields. No wonder that an eighteenth century song added the lyric, "And Happy She whose Strength holds out to the End of its rays."[3] At least one tombstone in Tennessee has an epitaph taken from the verse Mark 14:8 in the New Testament, "She hath done what she could."

Few Native Americans lived in the Upper Cumberland when white settlers first arrived in the 1780s—a few of them accompanied by slaves.[4] White women moved with their families first into the Smith and Jackson County area along the Cumberland River, then up its smaller tributaries and creeks—the Caney Fork, Roaring River, the Obey, and others—into counties like Putnam, Overton, and Clay in Tennessee and Clinton, Wayne,

A woman's work is never done. Credit: Michael E. Birdwell.

and Pulaski in Kentucky. Later they settled in areas opened by the road from the Holston settlements in East Tennessee to the Nashville Basin, or the Old Kentucky Road that ran from Maysville, Kentucky, to Huntsville, Alabama, along the eastern edge of the Cumberland Plateau.[5]

Sarah Jones Walton was one of the first women known by name in the Upper Cumberland. In 1785, at age twenty-two, she and her husband William moved from North Carolina and settled on the Cumberland River opposite the mouth of the Caney Fork near present day Carthage. She had seven children—four sons and three daughters. William Walton was a partner in building the Walton Road about 1800. Using part of the Avery Trace, the road extended west from Fort Southwest Point (Kingston, Tennessee) through Kimbrough's Gap onto the Cumberland Plateau and Highland Rim, descending to a terminus on the Cumberland River at Carthage, where the Walton family operated a ferry and tavern on this important route.[6]

Travelers such as the French botanist and explorer Andre Michaux and future president Andrew Jackson stayed with Sarah Walton as they traveled the Walton Road.[7] She witnessed flatboats, keelboats, and the advent of steamboats in the 1820s as commerce increased on the river. Many travelers on the Walton Road and the Cumberland River sought respite at her

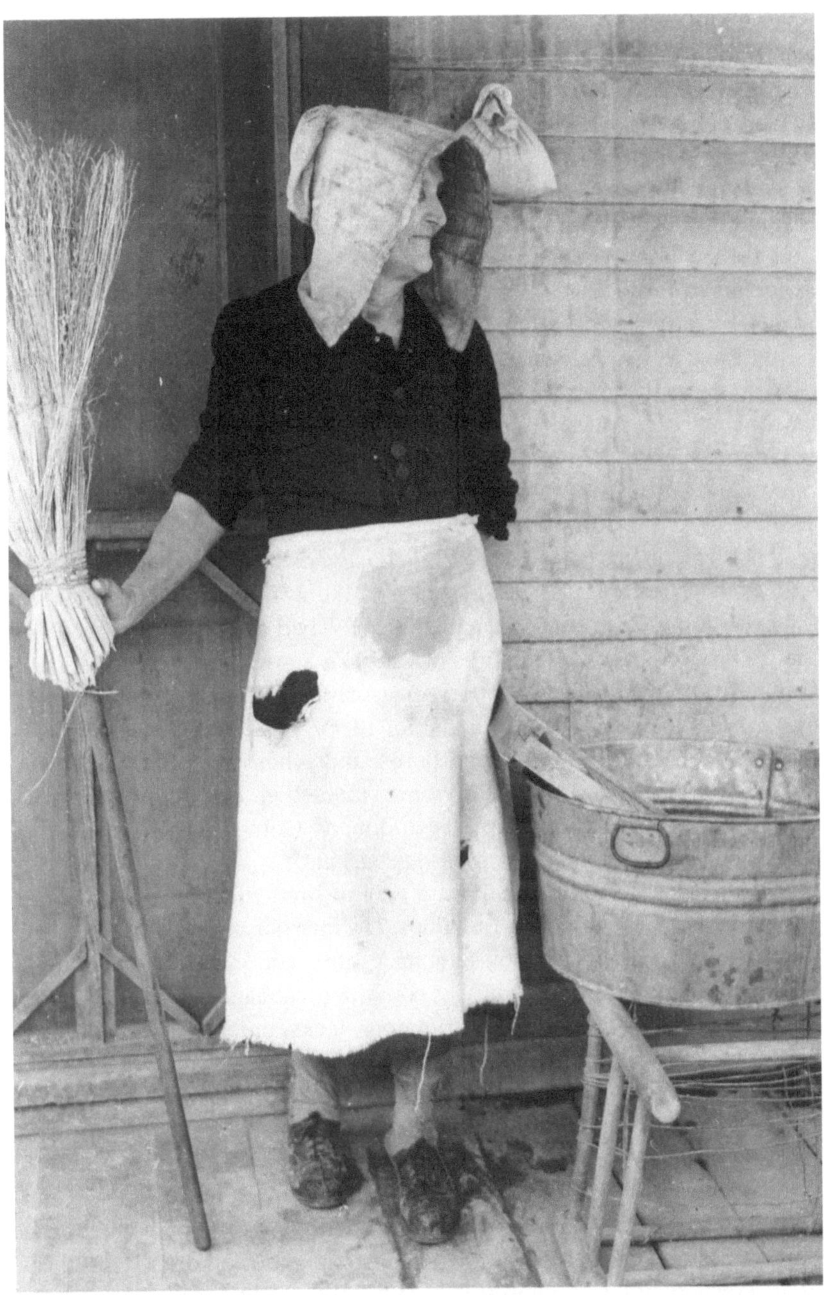

Farm wife in Pall Mall, Tennessee, 1939. Credit: Albert Ganier Collection, Tennessee State Library and Archives.

tavern. Meanwhile Carthage grew into "a flourishing post town" of seven hundred in 1834, with thirteen stores, three taverns in addition to her own, a printing office, carpenters, lawyers, doctors, blacksmiths, tailors, a hatter, two academies, a steam mill, and one church. Sarah Walton died in 1841 at age seventy-eight.[8]

Walton and other Upper Cumberland farm women—like their sisters throughout the southern back country—faced a constant round of chores. Life at their homesteads was bustling, noisy, and crowded. Women were expected to provide all food and clothing for the family and any farm workers. Cultivated fields and the wild lands around them provided virtually everything the family needed to survive. While mercantile stores stocked items the farm could not provide—such as salt, cane sugar, coffee, tea, or sewing supplies—most lay several miles (or even days) distant and cost more than most frontiersmen could afford. People developed sophisticated handicrafts. Inventive out of necessity, folks made what they needed as they needed it. Almost everything in the early days of Upper Cumberland settlement was handmade. While husbands fashioned bedsteads with wood hewn onsite and augured holes in them to lace hempen ropes for the bed's foundation, women made all of the bed clothes, which included mattress ticks often stuffed with corn shucks, straw, moss, or goose down. Gourds were invaluable as dippers, measuring devices, storage containers, and more. A variety of gourds fashioned for specific purposes hung in most kitchens holding salt, dried herbs, and other necessities. Hollowed out logs served as washtubs, and women made their own soap. They wove chair bottoms from wooden splints, and many women earned a wide reputation for the quality of their split-oak baskets.

Subsistence farming remained a way of life for many women in the Upper Cumberland well into the 1900s. The farm sustained the family and produced most of its vegetables, fruits, grains, and meats for the table. A woman's kitchen garden typically contained cabbages, carrots, turnips, mustard greens, beets, radishes, potatoes, leeks, onions, shallots, chives, garlic, cucumber, okra, squash, collard greens, green beans, peas, gourds, tomatoes, pumpkins, mint, and parsnips. During most of the growing season, more than seven months each year, women preserved foods through canning or pickling. The quality of these products was a special point of pride. When county fairs came into vogue, beginning in the Upper Cumberland town of Alexandria in 1856, women competed with each other putting prized jams, jellies, pickles, and baked goods on display. Blue ribbons adorned jars of the winners, making the proud woman the envy of her peers.

Settlers usually established small orchards, planting peach, apple, and pear trees; in addition to providing dried fruit and preserves, a portion of the harvest was turned into brandy and cider. Wild foods also appeared in the larder; collecting mushrooms, blackberries, and nuts were sometimes occasions for social outings, while sugar maples were tapped for syrup. Wild greens such as watercress, poke sallet, and dandelion were welcome additions to the diet in spring and considered a healthy tonic to remove winter's toxins from the blood.

Although women might prepare deer, rabbit, squirrel, duck, fish, and other wild game for meals, the majority of the family's protein was raised on the farm. Women tended to livestock not used as work animals. They preserved and prepared meat after the first hard frost signaled hog killing in the fall. Pork was the most commonly eaten meat because pigs reproduced more rapidly, grew more quickly than cattle or sheep, and could forage for themselves. No part of the pig was wasted. Tenderloins, brains, and delicate parts of the animal were eaten immediately, while other cuts were cured with brine, smoke, or sugar. Even the intestines, carefully cleaned, were used as sausage casing or prepared in African American communities as "chitlins."

Upper Cumberland farms often included sheep, and some folk enjoyed eating lamb or mutton, although the wool was more highly prized. The fowl yard contained chickens, guineas, turkeys, and geese; their feathers were used for stuffing pillows and mattress ticks. Cattle were more important for the dairy than the smokehouse; beef was more difficult and costly to salt cure than pork. Spring houses acted as refrigerators and were filled with butter and cheeses made by the farm wife and her daughters.

When a beef was killed, most of the animal was used and women rendered tallow from the fat. Beeswax was a luxury for candles, while tallow was more readily available; candle-dipping was considered a special skill. Rendered pork fat—lard—was an essential ingredient for the kitchen and the household. Farmers used it to lubricate machinery and keep leather supple among other uses. Most food consumed contained lard. It made biscuits light and fluffy, while acting as a flavor enhancer and binder in pie crusts. Melted in cast iron skillets, lard provided oil for frying chicken, pork chops, squash, okra, apples, and the like. Lard was added to Dutch ovens filled with beans or other vegetables for taste and to keep the concoction from sticking together. Lard was also an essential ingredient in ointments and lotions in the days before medical doctors appeared on the scene.

Fat was necessary for making soap, along with lye and potash. Great quantities of soap were made at a time, using large cast iron kettles in the house's work yard. Although today people think of soap as primarily for bathing, it was first developed and used to remove the lanolin from sheep's wool, for this natural grease interfered with dyeing wool. Lye was also used to make hominy. Lye was placed in water for cooking dried field corn. Without this process it was difficult for humans to digest the dried corn kernels.

Corn was important in the early Upper Cumberland diet and was served in a number of ways. Although corn was eaten fresh from the field during its roasting ears stage, the great majority was harvested in the fall after the kernels had hardened and could be easily stored in corn cribs. Dried corn was ground into meal and primarily consumed as cornbread or cornmeal mush. A common farm breakfast utilized day-old cornbread crumbled into a bowl and covered with buttermilk or clabbered milk. Many in the family—including women and children—washed the concoction down with a glass of whisky made in the family's still.[9]

A time-consuming task for women was providing clothes for the family. Women made counterpanes and quilts for all farm residents and guests. Spinning and weaving wool and linen cloth from a farm's sheep and flax plants consumed a great amount of women's time. Sheep had to be sheared and the wool carded before spinning it into thread and putting it onto a loom. Workers used hackles, a wicked looking device, to shred the flax stalks and make it pliable enough to spin into thread. Women recycled many products, turning "tow" sacks or flour sacks into clothes, table cloths, napkins, or other things. As they could afford the expense, women first supplemented and later replaced their own homespun product with bolts of cloth bought at stores. But linsey-woolsey and other homemade fabrics continued to be worn by many people in the Upper Cumberland into the twentieth century.

By the age of five or six, girls joined their mothers in producing food and performing the numerous daily tasks on the farm—milking cows, carrying water from the spring or the well, cleaning house, and more. If education occurred at all it took place in homes where a parent or sibling had the skills, teaching a girl the rudiments of reading, writing, and enough arithmetic to manage household accounts. As in most agrarian societies, advanced education for girls was seen as non-essential, even frivolous. As historian Jeanette Keith observed, "By law, custom, and religion, fathers dominated Upper Cumberland families. Patriarchy as a labor system operated undisguised by the sentimentalities of middle-class notions of women's sphere or the nurturance of children. . . A man did not 'support' his wife and children; they supported him . . . did not the Bible itself enjoin the submission of women and children to the head of the house?"[10]

As the Upper Cumberland back country attracted more settlers, some unusual opportunities emerged for women. In 1795, Dartmouth-educated idealist Moses Fisk arrived from Massachusetts to claim ninety thousand acres of land as a partner in the Cumberland Association. He moved to the region because of its central location when the western border of the United States extended only to the Mississippi River. As one of his tasks, he surveyed the aforementioned Walton Road (1799–1801). In 1805, Fisk established Hilham in Overton County with the assistance of Sampson Williams of Jackson County. Although then a bachelor, Fisk is credited with founding the Fisk Female Academy at Hilham that same year. The academy has been called the first female college west of the Alleghenies, though it only operated one year. It established an important precedent that women were worthy of education and should not be denied. After Fisk married in 1813, he and his wife had seven daughters and two sons; the town of Celina, Kentucky, was named for his eldest child, a daughter. He insisted on education for his wife Nancy and his daughters.[11]

Overton County continued in the 1800s as a locus for education in the Upper Cumberland. One such educated woman was Mary Catherine "Molly" Sproul. Born at Boatland in Fentress County in 1835, Sproul attended Maryville Female Institute in the 1850s and was teaching in Livingston, Tennessee, when the Civil War began. Sproul came from a Unionist family in a predominantly Confederate town, and the wartime journal she kept remains a significant source on life in the Upper Cumberland during the nation's upheaval.[12]

Sproul was especially interested in the politics of the day and in the arguments for preserving the Union. Early in the war, secessionist families removed their children from her school, much to her dismay. She told her class in late 1860 that pro-Union speech should be honored: "My God! Are you going to prohibit the freedom of speech in this free, enlightened, and blood bought land?"[13] She confided in her memoirs, "I sometimes thought I would say nothing as it did not become ladies to dabble in politics."[14] But after C.J. Allison withdrew his children from her school because of her father's "duplicitous" vote against secession, she wrote him saying:

> Sir, I am glad you have discontinued your children from my school if what you communicated be the cause: Sir I am a poor girl, I have to teach school for my own sustenance, but Sir, before I would relinquish my principles for the sake of yours, or anybody's patronage, I would spin tow [linen] for ten cents per week. I never have been, I am not now, neither will I ever be, a tool for any party, sect or association... I am glad, thrice happy

> today, Mr. Allison [that] the vote of my dear Father [for the Union] was recorded—doubtless twas recorded too in Heaven. It was you, Mr. Allison, [who] exhibited "duplicity" of heart for when you cast your vote Sir to break asunder the ties which held us together as a mighty nation of free and happy people, you violated that compact framed by our revolutionary Sires. You Sir, cast your vote to sever the chain linked by a Washington, you have disregarded the state that gave you birth, and your children will cry out treason against you, your children's children will weep and wail yet, at the duplicity of heart practiced by the Grandfather. Mark my predictions, Sir. Yours very independently, M.K. Sproul[15]

The Upper Cumberland was bitterly divided during the war, and noncombatants suffered disproportionately from their counterparts in occupied Knoxville or Nashville. Forage raids and conscript sweeps deprived families of their farm stores, fathers, and sons. The spirited Sproul wrote about life on the home front and detailed the violence of Confederate Champ Ferguson and other Rebel guerrillas against Union sympathizers. Confederate General John Hunt Morgan's soldiers stole her family's horses in 1862. Depredations caused great hardships to Union women of the region, toiling away in the absence of their men at war: "I have known hundreds of Union ladies whose feeble Strength forbade laborious exercise, but through sheer necessity have been compelled to plow and hoe to make bread for the little sufferers around her and ere She reaped the fruits of her toil She must see it dragged away from her by the defenders of 'Southern Rights.'"[16]

In 1863, General Morgan "and his Robbers" passed through again, this time confiscating Sproul's mare.[17] Other Confederate troops traversed the area via the Old Kentucky Road, a route they used to avoid Federal detection. She provided detailed commentary on Union and Confederate sympathizers and their actions that she witnessed. As the situation worsened she was forced to flee her home. A refugee in Kentucky in 1865, Sproul looked forward to her return to Overton County. Sproul's little-known memoir is especially rich in descriptions of Civil War's impact on women and their families in the Upper Cumberland.[18]

After the war Sproul married Union veteran Bailey Bowden of Fentress County. One of her grandsons was Governor Albert Houston (A.H.) Roberts, who was instrumental in Tennessee ratifying the Nineteenth Amendment, which granted American women the right to vote in 1920.

Though Harry Burn of Niota, Tennessee, is renowned as the man responsible for women in the United States being granted the right to vote, two men from the Upper Cumberland deserve recognition for their work in making it possible for women to gain the franchise. Overton County native A.H. Roberts jeopardized his political future by defending women's right to vote, and Roberts failed to win re-election in the aftermath of Nineteenth Amendment vote. Equally important was the Chief Justice of the Tennessee Supreme Court Dick Latta (D.L.) Lansden of Cookeville, Tennessee. At the request of the Attorney General Frank M. Thompson, Lansden issued writs of *certiori* and *supersedeas* granting Governor Roberts permission to promptly "certify and send to the Capitol of the Nation Tennessee's ratification of the Nineteenth Amendment."[19] A.H. Roberts' strong, outspoken grandmother probably influenced his opinion about women's role in politics. Sproul died in Livingston in 1926; one can assume that she voted in every election she could.

World War I and the absence of men in military service required women to enter public work as part of the war effort—Tennessee women in 1916 were asked to voluntarily register at drafting places, specifying their line of work and training. Some Upper Cumberland women boarded a train daily bound for the DuPont plant at Old Hickory to manufacture gun cotton for the war effort.[20] Others moved temporarily to the mill village adjacent to the plant for the duration of the war. As Keith observed, "In all, the war years in the Upper Cumberland worked an incomplete revolution."[21]

In the 1920s, subsistence farming persisted, and in this lies some of the exceptionalism of the Upper Cumberland. The University of Tennessee conducted an economic survey of the area in 1924. In Overton County, "farm families sold little, bought less, and ate what they produced at home." In Pickett County, ninety-seven percent of households had gardens: "The ordinary garden was considered as of paramount importance in the life of practically all the visited families."[22] Women's work remained essential to putting food on the table.

The emergence of women like Mary Catherine Sproul disrupted the norm of the Upper Cumberland's gender roles, where the region's culture, especially through its churches, still presented "the ideal of a modest, quiet, homebound wife."[23] The Disciples of Christ exercised a strong influence in the region, and its official publication, the *Gospel Advocate,* carried a sermon in 1892 warning, "An education that leads a woman to the ballot box, or even to as sacred a place as the pulpit, is a sin in the eyes of God."[24] The nascent Church of Christ split from the Disciples of Christ in part because the Disciples allowed women to pursue a public role in the church. *Gospel*

Advocate editor David Lipscomb wrote in the 1890s, "The habit of women preaching originated in the same hotbed with easy divorce, free love, and the repugnance to child bearing."[25]

Old attitudes died hard. Women winning the right to vote became a focus for fears that the traditional gender roles would soon be gone. A man writing to the *Carthage Courier* in April 1920 joked that votes for women would bring a "New Dispensation:" where women would be the ones holding elected office, doing jobs like stringing telephone lines, and generally behave like men, while area husbands would be tending house and babies.[26] His cynical prediction later came true, with women performing capably in all of the jobs he feared while juggling the roles of wife and mother with great dexterity.

Due to new labor saving machines for the home and farm, women could more efficiently complete their labors at home, allowing some to enter the public work force. Manufacturing provided new opportunities for women. Shortly after the creation of the Roane Iron Company, which employed men from the Upper Cumberland, the Harriman Hosiery Mill was established, and many ironworkers' wives and daughters found employment there. Soon other "shirt" factories sprouted up in most small towns, like Sparta, Livingston, and Cookeville, specifically targeting women.[27] Circumstances seemed to favor change in the region's roles for women more than men. Considered capable workers who rarely caused trouble, women worked diligently in factories often in less than ideal conditions. Many facilities lacked air conditioning or windows, and women forged ahead with little complaint. By the mid-to-late 1960s many women had been elevated to family bread winner. New jobs in textile work, furniture factories, or teaching were more suited to women and more mobile. Despite the earlier bias against schooling girls, women were becoming better educated than men, and more likely to complete the eighth grade.[28] A common joke in the area that underscores the diligent, hard work of Upper Cumberland women was:

> "Well mister what do you do?"
> "I'm a go getter."
> "What does that mean?"
> "I take my wife to work and then I go get her."[29]

Thousands of Upper Cumberland women's names have been lost to history. Newspaper articles rarely printed a woman's given name, for they were generally referred to by their husband's name with the title "Mrs." placed before it. In Overton County's Okalona Cemetery, and no doubt in others throughout the region, one crudely fashioned marker simply claims the spot to be where the "Wife of" a certain male resident was laid to rest. In spite of these oversights, a number of women made significant contributions to the Upper Cumberland. Ruth Morgan Reeves of Putnam County, Tennessee, challenged four men for the office of Registrar of Deeds in 1934 and handily won the election. Two years later Kate Bradford Stockton of Clarkrange in Fentress County became the first woman in Tennessee

Poet laureate of Tennessee Clara Cox Epperson of Algood in Putnam County. Credit: Clara Cox Epperson Papers, Tennessee State Library and Archives.

history to run in a gubernatorial election.[30] Though she lost, her bold platform demanded equal rights for women and offered some fresh ideas to tackle the ongoing economic depression. In 1972 Annell Hickey of White County, shattered another gender barrier and was the first woman to be elected sheriff in Tennessee.

Clara Cox Epperson may have been the most successful poet of the Upper Cumberland region in the last decade of the nineteenth century and the first decades of the twentieth. Born in Gainesboro, Tennessee, on the Cumberland River in 1869, her family was prominent in the region, and Clara's parents encouraged her education and interest in fine arts. She graduated from the Nashville College for Young Ladies in 1887, and earned a Master of Arts degree four years later, studying under Dr. G.F. Price, president of the school. Prior to her marriage to John A. Epperson, she taught school in Gainesboro.

Her publications were numerous and varied. She wrote children's stories, short stories, and essays, and she collected her mother's memories of the Civil War which she published in a series of articles. She chaired the Book Lover's Club of Cookeville, which led to the creation of its first public library in 1923, which was later renamed in her honor. Interested in American history and her family's role in it, Epperson was the organizing regent for the Walton Road Chapter of the Daughters of the American Revolution.[31]

Although predominantly a poet, she wrote and published many prose essays in newspapers and journals. She published poetry in *International Poetry Magazine, Progressive Teacher, Southern Woman's Magazine, Tennessee Club Woman, Bridge World, Christian Herald, Will Carleton Magazine, Life, Progressive Farmer,* and *Bob Taylor Magazine.* Engaging in one of the few avenues that a woman at that time could use for recognition, Clara was a member of prominent clubs, including the Tennessee Woman's Press and Author's Club, League of American Pen Women, and Tennessee Federation of Women's Clubs. In 1934 Epperson was named poet laureate by the Federation, replacing the venerable Will Allen Dromgoole, and Epperson held that honor until her own death in 1937. She died in Cookeville at the home of her daughter.[32]

Among the women who left an indelible mark was Graeme McGregor Smith, who was named Putnam County, Tennessee's "Woman of the Century," in 1995. Smith married native Cookevillian Rutledge Smith and the two made a formidable pair. Rutledge was fond of saying about his wife, "She is an old battle axe. Peace disturbs her mind."[33] Together they coedited the *Putnam Press* and played a significant role in acquiring many of the volumes that led to the creation of the first public library in the county due to Graeme's role as chair of the Book Lovers Club in 1922.

The indefatigable Graeme McGregor Smith, of whom her husband said, "Peace disturbs her mind." Credit: Rutledge and Graeme Smith Collection, Tennessee State and Library Archives.

She joined or led any number of clubs and civic groups, including the League of Southern Writers and the Tennessee Federation of Women's Clubs. Graeme believed in hard work tempered with a degree of altruism. She embraced causes and pursued them like a terrier, from acquiring livestock for Baxter Seminary to getting a portrait of Rachel Jackson in the White House. Her daughter Eudora "Dollie" Smith Williams believed her mother's greatest accomplishment was helping establish the Parent Teacher Association.[34]

During World War I, Rutledge Smith was in charge of the draft for the Southeast region of the United States as well as civilian mobilization, and Graeme enthusiastically supported him. Proud and patriotic, Graeme was a regent in the Daughters of the American Revolution, a member of the Daughters of the War of 1812, and the United Daughters of the Confederacy. Rutledge once remarked, "She never met a war she did not like." Graeme was unflappable during the Great War and organized women to write letters to soldiers, make bandages, help local families whose sons or husbands had gone to war. She hosted bond rallies, volunteered with the Red Cross, and presided over dinner parties for departing soldiers from the Upper Cumberland. She kept records on every Tennessean who served in the war, no matter what capacity they served in, adding her own personal assessment of many of them. Once soldiers started being deployed overseas, she continued to update her files. She noted whether or not they saw combat or were wounded or killed. Her keen interest in the well being of all of Tennessee's soldiers is remarkable. She noted that George Ashburn, a member of the First Marine Division from Clarkrange, was not only the first Tennessean, but the first American to be wounded in combat on December 3, 1917. He died of his wounds on January 21, 1918.[35] Her grandson Al Smith Jr. recalled, "Graeme was a club woman. She was a regent or president of the daughters of almost any carnage you can remember about your American history. . . Her favorite wars were those in which we spilt all the blood on American soil."[36]

During the flu pandemic of 1917–1918 Graeme, her daughter Dollie, and the pastor's wife from the First Presbyterian Church, Mrs. A.J. Coile, tended the sick and led a campaign entitled "Don't Be Afraid of the Flu!" They encouraged people to wear masks, practice good hygiene, and cover their mouths when they coughed or sneezed. After the pandemic passed, a Cookeville minister, "Brother Seward," introduced her to his thankful congregation saying, "There were two women who made history in the world—one was Mary the mother of Jesus—the other was Mrs. Rutledge Smith."[37]

Interestingly, and uncharacteristically, Graeme McGregor Smith lobbied against votes for women. She argued that politics was a rough and tumble game that would coarsen females, leading to loose morals and questionable behavior. When women gained the right to vote, she was the first woman in Putnam County to register and vote. When challenged about her reversal, her grandson Albert said she remarked: "Well, if women now have the right to vote, they need someone to show them how to use it properly."[38]

Her daughter Dollie emulated her mother and broke down a number of gender barriers in the early twentieth century. Dollie's parents built the first tennis court in Cookeville on the grounds of their home, and she soon became a gifted player. When she enrolled at Vanderbilt she wanted to play collegiately, but was denied. She persisted and became a tennis champion on the new women's team. Dollie also lettered in basketball. After graduation she established a summer camp for girls near New Orleans, but later moved that camp to Putnam County, Tennessee, near Monterey. That camp continues to thrive and attracts young women from around the United States, who are taught self-reliance, critical thinking skills, team work, and to appreciate and conserve the natural beauty the Upper Cumberland has to offer.[39]

The appreciation of nature was shared by many women who toiled on the region's farms. The land's natural beauty and its hardships deeply marked the consciousness of Harriette Simpson Arnow. Raised in the hills above the Cumberland River at Burnside, Kentucky, Arnow provided a voice, in her novels and historical writing, for the region's women and the changes the mid-twentieth century wrought in their lives.

Harriette Simpson was born in Wayne County, Kentucky, in 1908. Her parents Mollie Jean Denney and Elias Simpson were rural school teachers, but Mollie Jean left teaching to raise her six children while her father became a bookkeeper in Burnside to support the family. Simpson fondly remembered her Upper Cumberland childhood, the beautiful flowers and the vegetables she tended in the garden, time to read, and wonderful storytellers among her family. Simpson's desire to retell their stories inspired her writing career. As a young girl, her mother told her that if she would learn to milk a cow new to the farm, she could have the extra money to buy a used typewriter.[40]

In 1926, after two years of college at Berea, Simpson, who was only eighteen, accepted a teaching position at a remote country school in Pulaski County. After arriving at the nearest train station, she rode eight miles into the hills on a mule. She boarded in a log house near the school, which had an enrollment of fourteen pupils. Simpson loved the rugged beauty of the country and the life of the people: "I remember molasses stiroffs and music parties and a rousing charivari—mostly shotgun blasts—for a wedding."[41] But she was also impressed by the poverty of these women so far from town: "Birth, illness, and death all took place in the home and were attended to by neighbors. There was no shortage of food but money was scarce. Unlike people around Burnside, these people had no outlet for their extra butter, eggs, or milk. The closest market was miles away and over very difficult terrain."[42]

Simpson taught a second year near her family home in Burnside, left briefly to complete her BA at the University of Louisville, and then took a teaching position at Somerset in Pulaski County. She moved back to Louisville in 1931, but quit teaching in early 1930s to work on her writing, supporting herself in Cincinnati as waitress. Simpson used her teaching experience in the Upper Cumberland for the plot of her first novel, *Mountain Path,* published in 1936.

In March 1939 Simpson married journalist Harold Arnow, and the country-loving couple moved to an abandoned farm on the Big South Fork of the Cumberland; they called their log house "Submarginal Manor."[43] Harriette delivered her first child there in December 1939, a stillborn infant. Because farming was not enough to support the family Harriette Arnow returned to teaching in 1940. Her daughter Marcella was born in 1941, and the remoteness of their home and distance from doctors began to wear on the couple.

Arnow's writing continued to focus primarily on the Upper Cumberland, with the novels *Hunter's Horn* in 1949 and the best seller *The Dollmaker* in 1954. Her heavily researched histories of early life in the region, *Seedtime on the Cumberland* (1960) and *Flowering on the Cumberland* (1963), remain unsurpassed, and are standard sources of information about the Upper Cumberland.[44]

Arnow's novels dealt sympathetically, but realistically, with the Upper Cumberland women she grew up with and worked among. She recognized that life was hard for both genders, "Men and women were yoke-mates, pulling together."[45] Her hill women had few available options to escape from the grinding struggle for existence other than leave everything they knew and loved behind in an effort to create a new identity beyond the region. In *Hunter's Horn,* Lureenie Cramer almost escapes from the community at Little Smokey Creek to a new life with her husband in Cincinnati, but had to return to the country. Unable to sustain the work of supporting her children during her husband's absence in the city, she fell ill. Facing death, she said she had rather "go out like a cedar bush in a brush fire than wear out slow like a doorsill." Sue Annie Tiller, a farm wife and mother caring for Cramer, responded in regional dialect, "Child, th world cain't git along without doorsills to walk on; that's why th good God made women; but it's allus seemed to me that all women, when they die, they ought to go to heaven; they never have nothing much down here but hell."[46]

Arnow captured the plight of women forced to leave the Upper Cumberland for jobs in the North in her masterpiece, *The Dollmaker.* Gertie Nevels was a determined farmwife who had been saving money for fifteen years from her sale of eggs, black walnuts, and molasses to buy the Tipton Place. She took rightful pride in her work for her family:

> The hominy making, the gathering of walnuts, and their other regular chores in the clear, sharp weather had given them all good appetites. Gertie, sitting at the foot of the table with a lard

> bucket of sweet milk on one side of her, buttermilk on the other, a great platter of hot smoking cornbread in front, and other bowls and platters within easy reach, was kept busy filling glasses with milk, buttering bread, and dishing out new hominy fried in lard and seasoned with sweet milk and black pepper. It was good with the shuck beans, baked sweet potatoes, cucumber pickles, and green tomato ketchup. Gertie served it up with pride, for everything, even the meal in the bread, was a product of her farming.[47]

But Gertie sacrificed her dream of owning a farm and used the long-saved money to take her family to Detroit, where her husband Clovis found war work and wanted his family to join him. Gertie learned to substitute an understanding and appreciation for people in crowded Detroit for the relationship with nature that had sustained her in the hills.

As Arnow scholar Martha Billips Turner observed, "By the time she wrote *The Dollmaker,* Arnow saw the life of the self-sufficient Kentucky subsistence farmer as primarily a thing of the past; in her view, the need for cash had driven the people from the land and had made wage-oriented jobs outside the mountains increasingly attractive."[48] Arnow left the region forever, and she was buried in Michigan after her death in 1986. She could not foresee that many of the children and grandchildren of her generation would return to the Upper Cumberland by the end of the century as they retired from factory jobs.[49]

As the 1960s and 1970s unfolded, traditional ways were ebbing away. Modern conveniences, proliferation of strip malls, ease of travel due to the interstates, and television made old crafts—once necessary for survival—obsolete. Quilts, split oak baskets, gourds, corn shuck dolls, and the like seemed quaint. Yet, in spite of such attitudes a craft revival emerged in the mid-1960s, and what were once considered crude homemade objects gained a new respect. The quest for authentic crafts elevated former utilitarian objects to the level of high art. Many Upper Cumberland women were shocked and thrilled to discover that quilts handed down from one generation to another could earn hundreds of dollars. The interest in local crafts led in part to the creation of the Tennessee Arts Commission and the Joe L. Evins Appalachian Center for Craft near Center Hill Lake.

The 1960–1970s craft renaissance marked the second time in the twentieth century that Upper Cumberland handiwork proved lucrative. During the Great Depression a subsidiary New Deal agency attached to the Works Progress Administration (WPA), the Federal Arts Project, encouraged a return to traditional crafts that had long since disappeared in many parts of the country. At Pleasant Hill Academy in Cumberland County, Tennessee, local craftsmen, artisans, and instructors taught woodworking, pottery, chair making and a number of other traditional crafts to high school students. Many went on to be professional craftsmen and luthiers. One of those students was Polly Page.

Intent on keeping traditional crafts alive, Page built a studio and continued to teach the techniques she learned from her instructors. A renowned and beloved wood carver, Polly Page's traditional dolls, animals, nativity scenes, and depictions of Upper Cumberland denizens have been displayed in museums and sold to collectors worldwide. Her signature dolls are her Uncle Pink and Aunt Ginny articulated dolls based on an old couple from her childhood who lived in the Browntown community. She

Legendary doll maker Polly Page of Pleasant Hill, Tennessee, with her Jack and Pink dolls. Credit: Hal Harder of Moose Creek Media.

carves each one individually, sews their clothes, dresses them, and carves the livestock, farm implements, and other accouterments of rural life in the Upper Cumberland.

In 1984 Harriette Simpson Arnow's *The Dollmaker* was made into a television drama starring Jane Fonda as Gertie Nevels and the late Levon Helm, famed drummer for The Band, playing her husband Clovis. Dolly Parton, who befriended Fonda during the filming of *Nine to Five*, encouraged her to spend time in the Upper Cumberland while preparing for her characterization of Gertie. Parton and Fonda traveled to Pleasant Hill, Tennessee, to meet Polly Page; they learned how to carve for the movie, and the film featured several pieces of Page's, which remain popular collector's items.[50]

On the political scene Anna Belle Clement O'Brien of Cumberland County, Tennessee, embarked on a successful career in the Upper Cumberland, acting as an example for many women who followed her in public service. Politics came naturally to her. As a young woman she worked in the gubernatorial campaign of her older brother Frank Clement, who served as Tennessee governor from 1953 to 1959 and again from 1963 to 1967. Her career in public service began in 1955 as an assistant to future Governor Buford Ellington, commissioner of the state Department of Agriculture in her brother's administration. When Ellington became governor, she served as his executive assistant. Upon her brother's re-election in 1962, Anna Belle was appointed the first female chief of staff to the governor in Tennessee history.

"Miss Anna Belle," as most people referred to her, was known for saying, "Politics is a beautiful word to me." To improve the lives of regular people was her first priority. She believed "politics made children with handicaps walk, made education more accessible to everyone, gave people with mental illness a better life, and helped working people, seniors and children."[51]

In 1974, O'Brien ran for and won election to the Tennessee House of Representatives, and in 1976 she won election to the Tennessee Senate becoming only the second woman to win a seat in the state Senate. Miss Anne Belle was the first woman to chair a committee when she was appointed to the Senate Transportation and Senate Education committees. After a battle with breast cancer O'Brien led the effort to pass legislation mandating insurance coverage of mammograms. She authored the landmark Tennessee Living Will Law, and she sponsored numerous pieces of legislation concerned with quality of life issues.

Though she never ran for nor held elective office, Pauline Gore left her own indelible mark on the political landscape of the Upper Cumberland if not the nation. When she enrolled in the Vanderbilt Law School in 1933, she joined only three other women in a class dominated by men. Not born to privilege, she worked her way through law school as a waitress at a café in the Andrew Jackson Hotel where she met her future husband, Albert Gore of Jackson County, Tennessee. The tenth woman to earn a law degree from Vanderbilt, she practiced briefly in Arkansas and was one of the first women to specialize in oil and gas law. She returned to Tennessee in 1937 to wed Gore. The couple moved to a farm near Carthage, while Albert acted as superintendent of Smith County Schools.

An amateur fiddle player with political aspirations, Pauline acted as Albert's closest political advisor when he served as a U.S. congressman and senator. An avid New Dealer, Gore's career reflected his desire to improve the lives of average Americans. His wife, who admired Eleanor Roosevelt, looked to the first lady as a role model for the wife of a civil servant. Her legal training and southern charm made Pauline Gore a shrewd political ally. When Albert decided to challenge Tennessee's most powerful senator Kenneth McKellar, chairman of the Senate Appropriations Committee, few people believed Gore had a chance. Pauline is often credited with orchestrating his successful defeat of Boss Ed Crump's last stalwart. McKellar's campaign slogan, "The thinking feller votes for McKellar," was trumped by Pauline's phrase, "Think some more, vote for Gore."[52]

It was during one of her husband's most courageous stands that the counsel of Pauline Gore helped Albert remain resolute. After the *Brown v. Board of Education of Topeka, Kansas* ruling was handed down in 1954 demanding the end of segregated schools, most southern politicians in Washington, D.C., reacted angrily. The Declaration of Constitutional Principles, better known as the Southern Manifesto, was a racist diatribe that pledged to defy integration. Albert Gore, along with Tennessee's other senator, Estes Kefauver, refused to sign the document, opening them up to bitter criticism that threatened both their political careers.[53]

As Albert Gore Sr. gained more authority and respect through sponsorship of such legislation as the Interstate Highways Act, Pauline remained his most important advisor. She managed each of his campaigns for reelection. Though they spent several months each year in Washington, the Gores always considered the Upper Cumberland to be their home, and they tried to instill the importance of place in their children Kristin and Al Jr.

Albert lost his Senate seat due to his stance against the war in Vietnam in 1970. Realizing that her husband's days as a politician were over, Pauline returned to an active law practice. When her son Al Jr. decided to run for Congress representing the Upper Cumberland, Pauline's endorsement proved persuasive. Later when he served as vice president under Bill

Clinton, Pauline Gore continued to offer sound advice to her son. In 1999 her alma mater named her its distinguished alumna, making her the first female recipient of such an honor at Vanderbilt. Pauline Gore remained active in public life until her death at age ninety-two.[54]

Whether it was toiling as a mother, gardener, craft maker, teacher, factory worker, cook, writer, editor, club woman, or politician, women through out the Upper Cumberland of Kentucky and Tennessee acted as help mates and trailblazers.[55] Although many changes came to the Upper Cumberland throughout the 1900s, for most women many of the old ways continued. They continued to tend gardens and cook, although many worked for wages away from home. For some a basic education remained sufficient to navigate the modern world. Church remained an important institution both for their personal spiritually and for their community as a whole. Life still centered on taking care of husbands and children. For most Upper Cumberland women little things made the work worthwhile. With their husbands they created a network of small farms and small towns that forged the economy and society of the region. They left a mark on the material culture of the region through their quilts, crafts, and other utilitarian objects now cherished as high art. The story of women is one of work, but also of satisfaction for their accomplishments throughout their lives. While many women in the Upper Cumberland gained equality in political and professional roles, they carried with them the legacy of traditional roles rooted in the home and family.

NOTES

1. The people of the Upper Cumberland were exceptionally independent. For a discussion of public work by women, that is, working for someone else to earn a paycheck, see Jeannette Keith, *Country People in the New South: Tennessee's Upper Cumberland* (Chapel Hill, 1995), pp. 188–191. Keith's chapter "Families and Communities" provides a great deal about women's lives in the region.
2. William Chappell and George Alexander, *The Ballad and Popular Music of Olden Time: A History of the Ancient Songs, Ballads, and the Dance Tunes of England, With Numerous Anecdotes and Entire Ballads, Also a Short Account of the Minstrels.* Vol. 2 (London: Chappell and Co., N.D.), p. 558.
3. Quoted in Diary of Martha Moore Ballard (November 26, 1795), available at http://dohistory.org/diary/1795/11/17951123_txt.html?d=17951126
4. One group was the Calf Killer band of Cherokee in White County in the eponymous river valley. Cherokee primarily lived in villages of southeast Tennessee or intermarried with Euroamerican settlers. Upper Cumberland subsistence farming made slavery uneconomical for the region, and the African American population was far lower than in other parts of the state. Many left the area after

the Civil War, although freed black settlements, such as Free Hill in Clay County, persisted into the twentieth century.

5. The 1788 road from East Tennessee's Holston settlements to the Cumberland settlements at Nashville is called by various names, including the Avery Trace.
6. "William Walton," in Robert M. McBride and Dan M. Robison, *Biographical Directory of the Tennessee General Assembly, Vol. 1, 1796–1861* (Nashville: Tennessee Historical Commission, 1975), p. 759; W. Calvin Dickinson, *The Walton Road: A Nineteenth Century Wilderness Highway in Tennessee* (BookSurge Publishing, 2007), pp. 5–14; John R. Finger, *Tennessee Frontiers: Three Regions in Transition* (Bloomington: University of Indiana Press, 2001), pp. 121, 196–197.
7. Sarah Walton and her family lived in fear during the Cherokee raids on the Cumberland Settlements in 1792–1793, the bloodiest years on the frontier. John R. Finger, *Tennessee Frontiers: Three Regions in Transition* (Bloomington: Indiana University Press, 2001), pp. 38–46; John Haywood, *The Civil and Political History of the State of Tennessee from its Settlement up to the Year 1796* (Nashville: W.H. Haywood, 1823), pp. 262–292; J.G.M. Ramsey, *Annals of Tennessee to the End of the Eighteenth Century* (Charleston, South Carolina: John Russell, 1853), pp. 558–596; Samuel Cole Williams, *Early Travels in the Tennessee Country, 1540–1800* (Johnson City: Watauga Press, 1928), pp. 269, 518; Andre Michaux, "Journal of Andre Michaux, 1793–1796," *Philosophical Society Proceedings* (1889), pp. 91–101, 114–140; Reuben Gold Thwaites, ed., *Travels West of the Alleghenies: Made in 1793–1796 by Andre Michaux, in 1802 by F.A. Michaux, and in 1803 by Thaddeus Mason Harris, M.A.* (Cleveland, Ohio: Arthur H. Clark, Co., 1904).
8. Eastin Morris, *The Tennessee Gazetteer* (1834; Reprint. Nashville, 1971), p. 127.
9. Harriette Simpson Arnow, *Flowering of the Cumberland* (New York: Macmillan, 1963), pp. 271–282. Dried corn was also used to feed farm animals like chickens or pigs.
10. Keith, 27. Many young women found their husbands at public gatherings such as church, and courtship usually took place at their parents' homes in the 1800s. Most married before age eighteen and bore six children. As in many agrarian cultures, women gave birth to children roughly every two years until menopause. Infant mortality rates were high and 40 percent of the women experienced the death of at least one child. See Keith, 31–37.
11. Timothy J. Barlow, *The Life and Writings of Moses Fiske* (Collegedale: College Press, 1980). Fisk's other daughters were Perilla, Sarah, Zeda Anne, Ardelia, Elana, and Elanda.
12. Mary Catherine Sproul's journals were published by her granddaughter Helen Roberts Gayden in 1944 and by the Tennessee Historical Society; see Albert W. Schroeder Jr., ed., "Writings of a Tennessee Unionist, Part 1," *Tennessee Historical Quarterly* (September 1960), pp. 244–272, and Shroeder, ed., "Writings of a Tennessee Unionist, Concluded," *Tennessee Historical Quarterly* (September 1960), pp. 344–361.
13. Schroeder Jr., ed., "Writings of a Tennessee Unionist, Part 1," 246.
14. *Ibid.*, 247.

15. *Ibid.*, 249–250.
16. *Ibid.*, 266.
17. Schroeder Jr., ed., "Writings of a Tennessee Unionist, Concluded," 344.
18. Of equal interest and from the southern perspective is the diary of Amanda McDowell of White County, Tennessee (*Fiddles in the Cumberland*), who had one brother in the Confederate army and one in the Union army.
19. "Memorial to Chief Justice D.L. Lansden, Supreme Court of Tennessee, February 12, 1925: Remarks of Hon. K.T. McConnico," *Reports of Cases Argued and Determined in the Supreme Court of Tennessee, 1924*, Vol. 150, Frank M. Thompson ed., (Columbia, Missouri: R.W. Stephens Publishing Co., 1925), p. 713. The Supreme Court later rubber stamped Lansden's historic decision. Lansden was born and raised in White County and practiced law throughout the region. He served as Chancellor of the Fourth District until he won a spot on the State Supreme Court in 1911. He is buried in the Cookeville City Cemetery.
20. Deborah McConnell, "Lou Cretia Owen and the Old Hickory Munitions Plant During World War I," *Tennessee Historical Quarterly* (Summer 1999), pp. 128–139.
21. Keith, 169.
22. *Ibid.*, 176.
23. Keith, 37.
24. Quoted in Keith, 37.
25. Quoted in Keith, 49. Many Upper Cumberland congregations joined Lipscomb's conservative Church of Christ revolt in 1906.
26. "The New Dispensation," *Carthage Courier*, (Carthage, TN) April 8, 1920, quoted in Keith, 187–188.
27. W. Calvin Dickinson and Patrick D. Reagan, "Business, Labor, and the Blue Eagle: The Harriman Hosiery Mill Strike, 1933–1934," *Tennessee Historical Quarterly* LV:3 (Fall 1996), pp. 240–256.
28. Keith, 189–190.
29. As related by park ranger Stuart Carroll (Fall Creek Falls State Park, Alliance of the Cumberlands annual meeting, February 18, 2010).
30. W. Calvin Dickinson, "Radical Hillbillies: Socialism in Tennessee," *Rural Life and Culture of the Upper Cumberland* (Lexington: University Press of Kentucky, 2004), pp. 211–226.
31. Mary Jean Delozier, *Putnam County, Tennessee, 1850–1970* (Cookeville, Tennessee: McQuiddy Publishing, 1979), pp. 189–90.
32. Clara Cox Epperson (1869–1937) Papers (Nashville: Tennessee State Library and Archives, Acc. No. 1991.238), Boxes 1 and 2.
33. Interview with Dollie Williams, Monterey, Tennessee, 1997; Interview with Malcolm and Patsy Williams, Cookeville, Tennessee, August 24, 2012; Al Smith, *Wordsmith: My Life in Journalism* (Louisville, Kentucky: Pied Type Press, 2011), pp. 38–39, 43.
34. *Ibid.*
35. Rutledge Smith (1870–1962) and Graeme McGregor (1875–1949) Papers. Nashville: Tennessee State Library and Archives, Tennessee Historical Society Collections,

THS RG 893, Military Records Files. Smith's assessment that George Ashburn was the first American to be wounded is not actually accurate, for several men went to Canada or to Europe to enlist before the U.S. entered the war.

36. Al Smith Jr., "Graeme Gives a Party," 41. Unpublished manuscript in the Dollie Smith Williams papers owned by Malcolm Williams, Monterey, Tennessee.
37. Mary Jane Pardue, "Graeme McGregor Smith: Nomination for Putnam County's 'Outstanding Woman,'" (Cookeville, Tennessee: Putnam County Commission, December 13, 1995), p. 3.
38. Interview with Albert Smith Jr. (Cookeville, Tennessee, September 29, 2003). "Dollie" Smith Williams told a similar version of the story with a number of embellishments.
39. Interview with Malcolm and Patsy Williams, Cookeville, Tennessee, August 24, 2012.
40. Wilton Eckley, *Harriette Arnow* (New York: Twayne Publishers, 1974), p. 7.
41. Quoted in Eckley, 34.
42. *Ibid.*
43. *Ibid.*, 41.
44. Harold Arnow landed a job in the war industry at Detroit in 1944. With regret, Harriette stayed behind to sell the family's livestock and then followed, moving to a wartime housing development. There she found a crowded, hectic world filled with hill people who had moved North for work, newly arrived immigrants, and native Yankees. After the war, the Arnows remained in Michigan, settling on a small country property near Ann Arbor. Detroit neighborhoods populated by people from the Upper Cumberland and points east were often referred to as "Little Appalachia."
45. Quoted in Eckley; Arnow to the *Detroit Free Press* (1958), 125.
46. Harriette Simpson Arnow, *Hunter's Horn* (New York: Macmillan, 1949), p. 372.
47. Harriette Simpson Arnow, *The Dollmaker* (New York: Macmillan, 1954), p. 97.
48. Martha Billips Turner, "The Demise of Mountain Life: Harriette Simpson Arnow's Analysis," (1991), *Border States On-Line Journal of the Kentucky-Tennessee American Studies Association*, http://spider.georgetowncollege.edu/htallant/border/bs8/turner.htm
49. A good example is the village of Granville in Jackson County, Tennessee. It essentially lost all of its citizens to northern migration during the 1940s. By the late 1990s people who moved to Detroit, Michigan, Muncie, Indiana, and other towns for work, returned to their home to retire.
50. Interview with Polly Page, Pleasant Hill, Tennessee (May 9, 2011). When Fonda arrived at Page's studio, "she wouldn't try to carve wood. She used a potato," she scoffed. Though Fonda delivered a convincing, sympathetic portrait of Gertie Nevels, she never convinced Polly Page that she was an actual dollmaker. Adapted for television by theatre veteran Hume Cronyn, the production was generally faithful to the spirit of the book.
51. R. Neal, "Annabelle Clement O'Brien," *Knoxville News* (September 1, 2009). Anna Belle also said, "Politics got me a good husband," and she married Charles O'Brien, a state senator and widower from Memphis at a reception in 1964. After

they wed they moved to Cumberland County. He later served as Chief Justice of the Tennessee Supreme Court.

52. Albert Gore Sr., *Let The Glory Out: My South and Its Politics* (Athens, Georgia: Hill Street Press, 2000.), pp. IX, 79.
53. *Ibid.*, 100–111. Nineteen southern senators and eighty-two southern congressmen signed the document.
54. "Pauline Gore, Outstanding Alumnus," *Vanderbilt Register* (March 15–21, 1999).
55. By the 1940s local high schools had girls' teams, and an elite group of athletes could play professionally on Amateur Athletic Union (AAU) teams. Nera Dyson White was born in Macon County on November 15, 1935 and played basketball for Macon County High School, where she was designated the most valuable player for her high school district in 1954. She joined the Nashville Business College team in1954 and was an All-American for the first time in 1955. She led the team to ten AAU national championships, with eight of those in consecutive years from 1962 to 1969. According to several accounts White, a dominating center, possessed both incredible quickness and an uncanny sense of the court. She was also one of the first women to dunk the ball. Her biography in the Naismith Memorial National Basketball Hall of Fame calls her the pioneer of modern women's basketball. White was named an AAU All-American a record fifteen times. She also competed successfully in international tournaments and was named most valuable player at the 1957 World Games in Rio de Janeiro, Brazil. A fierce competitor, she played women's softball in the summer and was selected for the All-World team twice. She was also a member of the National Women's Basketball Hall of Fame and in 2000 was ranked seventh in *Sports Illustrated* listing of the fifty greatest sports figures in Tennessee history. Her hometown of Lafayette named the high school's Nera White Gymnasium in her honor. See Steve Marntz, "A Good Life Regretted," *The Sporting News* (March 4, 1996).

POLITICIANS AND POLITICS

4

Republican Redoubt

The Politics of Kentucky's Upper Cumberland

Al Cross and David Cross

Kentucky's Upper Cumberland region was a birthplace of the commonwealth's Republican Party and has remained one of the major strongholds for the Grand Old Party (GOP) for more than a century, in a state that has largely been run by Democrats. The reasons for the phenomenon date to the Civil War. This hill country was dominated by Union Democrats and was not dependent on slavery, and when former Confederates took over the state Democratic Party after the war, the region turned Republican.[1] In the eight counties that are indisputably part of Kentucky's Upper Cumberland, more than two of every three voters is a registered Republican. Voters in Kentucky must register with a political party by December 31 of each year in order to vote in that party's primary election the following May. Kentucky does not allow crossover voting. On June 27, 2014, the eight counties had 78,785 Republicans (68.6 percent), 30,202 Democrats and 5,844 independents or members of other parties. Statewide, Republicans were only 38.6 percent of total registrants. Including the marginal counties of Barren and Casey, the ten-county ratio is much the same: 98,171 Republicans (63.3 percent), 49,067 Democrats and 7,835 others.[2]

The region's loyalty to the Grand Old Party has put it at odds with a state that joined the losing side after the Civil War. In the great disruption during and after the war, the Bluegrass State went Democratic while Kentucky's Upper Cumberland became the major stronghold of the new Republican Party. The region thus joined a side that has lost more than it has won in state elections. But in federal elections, Kentucky has often gone Republican, and the region has produced some notable Republican federal officials—most notably two from Somerset, Senator John Sherman Cooper and Congressman Harold "Hal" Rogers, who became chairman of the House Appropriations Committee after the 2010 elections.

In state politics, the Upper Cumberland has produced four Kentucky governors: Thomas E. Bramlette, a Union Democrat during and after the Civil War; Preston H. Leslie, a Democrat during the postwar realignment;

and Edwin P. Morrow, a Republican whose family was instrumental in founding the Republican Party in Kentucky soon after the war. Republican governor Louie B. Nunn hailed from Barren County and used the Upper Cumberland as his major base of support. When he took office in 1967 he was the first Republican to be elected governor since Simeon Willis in 1943. Another was not elected until 2003.

The postwar realignment remained constant in most of Kentucky for more than a century, especially in places like the Upper Cumberland, which had little in-migration. But one of the region's most interesting political figures was Dr. W. Godfrey Hunter, a native of northern Ireland who settled in the region at the end of the war.[3] Hunter served as a doctor in the Union army during the war. He later represented two vastly different Kentucky districts in Congress, became a Republican Party leader, and formalized the use of the log cabin to symbolize it as the party of Abraham Lincoln, who was born in a Kentucky log cabin.

On the local level, the region has produced many interesting political characters, including school superintendents who have often exercised most of the local political patronage available in this Republican territory within a Democratic state. One founded a political dynasty that had few rivals anywhere for its power and tenure, and extended its influence all the way to Washington.

Kentucky's Union-oriented Civil War governor was the first major political leader to emerge from the Upper Cumberland. Thomas Elliott Bramlette was born January 3, 1817, in a part of Cumberland County that became Clinton County in 1836. Bramlette opened a law practice in Albany in 1837, served in the Kentucky House in the 1840s, and was appointed the commonwealth's attorney in 1848. In 1850, he resigned and moved to Adair County, where in 1852 he lost a race for Congress by thirty-five votes, but in 1856 he was elected circuit judge for a large district. During the Civil War, Bramlette became a major general in the U.S. Army, U.S. Attorney for the Commonwealth of Kentucky, and then governor.

When war broke out, Governor Beriah Magoffin, who believed that states had the right to secede, tried to keep Kentucky neutral. That policy soon crumbled, but even before it did, Bramlette and other Unionists formed regiments. In the Upper Cumberland, slavery was not a major economic factor because most farms were small, and the land too infertile to support a plantation economy. The exceptions were Barren County, which was 24 percent black, and Cumberland at 20 percent. The Appalachian foothill counties of Clinton, Russell, Wayne, and Pulaski all had less than 10 percent. Free blacks were scarce in Kentucky. Only Barren County and Bramlette's home, Adair County, had more than two thousand slaves.

For Kentuckians early in the war, slavery was secondary to preservation of the Union, a cause Henry Clay and others had burned into the political mind set of Kentuckians. Through October 1863, more than half of military-eligible men in Upper Cumberland counties fought as Union soldiers, except Clinton and Wayne counties. Enlistment in those Tennessee border counties lagged, in all probability not because Confederate sympathy prevailed, but because there was so much Confederate sentiment and guerrilla activity that it discouraged Union enlistment. Union Captain John Tuttle noted that Union sympathy in Clinton was strong when the war began, and Bramlette spoke in Albany to enlist volunteers for both his regiment and Colonel Frank Wolford's.[4]

During 1862, Kentuckians' sentiment began to turn against Union forces because of their violation of civil liberties, their harboring of runaway slaves, and President Lincoln's Emancipation Proclamation. Several commanders of Kentucky federal units resigned their commissions. Bramlette was among them, but reportedly because of a dispute about which unit he was to command. Upon his resignation in 1863, Lincoln named him U.S. attorney for Kentucky, and when former Whig Joshua Fry Bell resigned the Union Democrats' nomination for governor, the party committee chose Bramlette. In an election marred by widespread interference from Union forces, Bramlette defeated the candidate of the "Regular" or "Peace" Democrats, former Whig Charles Wickliffe, by 68,422 to 17,503.

While many Union Democrats and their newspapers virtually matched the opposition's criticism of Lincoln, Bramlette sounded a more moderate tone, especially upon taking office. That soon changed. When the Union Army began recruiting African Americans, Bramlette went to Washington and secured an agreement that blacks would not be recruited in Kentucky unless the state failed to meet its quota of recruits. Soon there was a new Union commander in Kentucky, Major General Stephen Burbridge, who started enlisting blacks to fill the Union ranks. Bramlette was livid, and in 1864 he supported General George B. McClellan for president against Lincoln, who during the campaign suspended the writ of *habeas corpus* in Kentucky.[5]

Lincoln's order, and Burbridge's harsh treatment of Kentuckians under martial law, turned the commonwealth into a police state. Burbridge continued the military interference in elections, and his troops executed Confederate sympathizers in reprisal for raids by guerrillas, earning him the nickname "Butcher Burbridge." His moves outraged Bramlette and his lieutenant governor, Richard Jacob, who had not only raised troops for the Union, but had been wounded in battle. Bramlette authorized Colonel Frank "Old Wolf" Wolford, commander of the 1st Kentucky Cavalry, who

Congressman Harold Dallas "Hal" Rogers. Credit: Official U.S. House of Representatives photo.

had been discharged from the army for his harsh criticism of the policy concerning black troops, to raise a regiment answerable only to him and Bramlette.[6] Burbridge jailed Wolford, reputed captor of the infamous Confederate raider and fellow Kentuckian John Hunt Morgan, for sedition.

Immediately after the 1864 presidential election, Burbridge banished Wolford and Jacob to the Confederacy for alleged sedition. Lincoln reversed the order and removed Burbridge from command, but the die had been cast by a long line of federal insults. After the war, Kentucky joined the losing side.[7]

Amid the turmoil Bramlette tried to steer a middle course. At one point in 1864, a Union spy reported to the secretary of war that the governor "knows his people are disloyal, so he qualified his Unionism."[8] Bramlette urged the General to steer a middle course when he could. He urged the General Assembly to ratify the Thirteenth Amendment abolishing slavery, but the legislature defeated it, in part because slave owners were not to be compensated.

Bramlette pardoned most former Confederates under indictment. He said that was done for the sake of peace, but his action "released many unsavory characters who would be a source of violence in the coming decade and that the war made many good men do bad things."[9] While Bramlette reflected the state's strong racism on most issues, he nominated a Republican as state treasurer (though the legislature refused to confirm him), encouraged immigration into the state, and was largely responsible for the creation at Lexington of a state Agricultural and Mechanical College, which became the University of Kentucky.

Resentment over federal policies in the highly confused political situation that existed after the war caused Bramlette's Union Democrats, then called Conservatives, to lose control of the Democratic Party to former Confederates. Bramlette and his allies tried to appeal to former Union soldiers, but in the gubernatorial and legislative elections of 1867 they finished a poor third, and he was passed over for nomination to a U.S. Senate seat. Bramlette, who had moved to Louisville when he became U.S. attorney, practiced law there until his death on January 12, 1875.

Kentucky did not allow governors to succeed themselves between 1800 and 1999. In 1871, its new governor was another son of the Upper Cumberland, Preston Hopkins Leslie, born March 8, 1819 in a part of Wayne County that became part of Clinton County. Like Bramlette, who started his public career as a crossroads postmaster at Elliot's Crossroads, Leslie served as postmaster at the crossroads of Paoli.[10]

Leslie was orphaned and moved to Monroe County, where he practiced law and farmed, and served in the state House and Senate, first as a Whig and then as a Democrat. Though he did not serve in the war he was a Confederate sympathizer, which proved to be a political plus in postwar Kentucky. He returned to the state Senate in 1867, after an absence of twelve years, and Leslie was elected Senate president in 1869. He became governor in early 1871 when Governor John Stevenson was elected to the U.S. Senate, and easily defeated Republican nominee John Marshall Harlan, 126,089 to 89,083, for a full term.

During his campaign, Leslie moved closer to the more progressive views of *Louisville Courier-Journal* editor Henry Watterson, who was becoming a nationally recognized Democratic force. With Leslie's support, the legislature allowed African Americans to testify in court, and passed a law to rein in the activities of the Ku Klux Klan. Leslie declined to veto a bill authorizing construction of the Cincinnati Southern Railroad, which brought Kentucky's Upper Cumberland its first rail service. He may be known best, however, as the devout Baptist governor who prohibited alcohol at state functions.

After leaving office, Leslie lived and practiced law in the Barren County seat of Glasgow, and he served as circuit judge for six years. He lost his judicial re-election bid by four votes to Republican Commonwealth's Attorney Dulaney Carr, who, like Leslie, who was born in Clinton County and lived in Barren County. In 1887, on recommendation of his 1871 political adversary John Marshall Harlan, then a Supreme Court justice, Democratic President Grover Cleveland named Leslie territorial governor of Montana.[11]

He encountered many political problems, which were exacerbated by his continued stand for temperance, and Republican President Benjamin Harrison removed him from office in 1889. After Cleveland defeated Harrison in an 1892 rematch, he named Leslie U.S. attorney for Montana, which had become a state in 1889. Leslie held the job from 1894 to 1898 and later served as president of the state bar association until his death on February 7, 1907. He was buried in the Montana state capital of Helena.

Postwar Realignment

Kentucky's postwar turn to the South did not include the Upper Cumberland, where the demise of slavery had little impact. Small farmers of the Upper Cumberland had little in common with the slave owners and little sympathy for their losses. It was generally poor country, populated by poor people.

A major factor in making Kentucky's Upper Cumberland Republican was Confederate guerrilla activity, particularly that of the notorious Champ Ferguson, who caused many families to forsake the Democratic ticket. For most of the war and years afterward, the border counties were plagued by bandits and guerrillas such as Ferguson, who was hanged in Nashville as a war criminal soon after the war.[12] Many hated Lincoln, but they hated Ferguson more.

The paramount consideration for political leaders in Kentucky's Upper Cumberland was practicality. People of the region had been Union supporters. Now the conservative Bourbon faction that controlled the state Democratic Party "waved the bloody shirt" and made an effort to exclude Union supporters from state government. The Bramlette-led Union Democrats soon realized they were unappreciated and unelectable.

Thus, in the late 1860s, the current alignment of Kentucky politics jelled, as former Union soldiers and Republican Radicals were joined by moderates such as Thomas Z. Morrow of Pulaski County, J.A. Brents of Clinton, Silas Adams of Casey, and Dulaney Carr of Clinton.[13] The Republican Party's first candidate for governor of Kentucky was a former Union colonel from the Upper Cumberland, Sidney M. Barnes of Somerset. He ran a poor second in the three-way 1867 election, during which he endured harassment by the Ku Klux Klan. He lost a race for Congress in 1868, and at age fifty he moved to Arkansas, saying he was "disgusted with Kentucky politics and thoroughly tired of the whole situation."[14]

Other Republicans persevered, led in part by Morrow, a Somerset lawyer who had edited a Democratic newspaper before the war. The party mounted credible, though unsuccessful, campaigns with John Marshall Harlan in 1871 and 1875. Morrow was the gubernatorial nominee in 1883, state party chairman in 1884, and circuit judge for much of the Upper Cumberland from 1886 to 1903. His brother-in-law, William O. Bradley of Lancaster, was elected the state's first Republican governor in 1895, and his son, Edwin P. Morrow, was elected governor in 1919. The Upper Cumberland's growing Republican allegiance was demonstrated by presidential election results. In 1868, Monroe County joined Pulaski in the Republican column, and in 1872, President Ulysses S. Grant was the choice of every Upper Cumberland county except Barren, where the Union general lost by less than one percentage point.[15]

One vivid illustration of the region's change in allegiance soon after the war was Clinton County, which voted firmly Democratic in the special election for governor in 1868 but staunchly Republican in 1871, when the Democratic nominee and acting governor was none other than its native son, Preston Leslie. Other counties showed similar shifts during the period. They would still vote for Democrats if they were Union men, but such men were getting nowhere in the Kentucky Democratic Party, so they were becoming Republicans.

In the next three presidential elections, Casey, Adair, and Russell counties went Democratic, perhaps influenced by Wolford, who had switched allegiances after being disciplined by President Lincoln. In 1888, by the time he lost re-election to Congress, the region's only Democratic counties were Barren and Wayne. By 1892, Wayne was added to the Republican column, and the political alignment of the Upper Cumberland had been set. A region that had cast a mere handful of votes for Lincoln was now firmly ensconced in his political party.

About the time the Civil War ended, a northern Irish immigrant who had served in the Union army settled in the Cumberland River town of Burkesville, seat of Cumberland County. By 1874, Whiteside Godfrey Hunter was in the state House and by 1887 he was in Congress. Hunter was instrumental in making the Republican Party competitive statewide, and he was one of the most interesting characters in Kentucky politics in the fifty years following the war, but he has been largely lost to history.[16]

W. Godfrey Hunter was drawn to Cumberland County by his fascination with the new oil industry. He came from Pennsylvania, where Edwin Drake drilled what many consider the first commercial oil well in 1859, the year after Hunter immigrated, and he moved to the Kentucky county that was the site of a huge, albeit accidental, oil well in 1829. Hunter, who had studied medicine in Philadelphia, called himself a surgeon and soon married Sue Alexander, who came from a prominent local family. Though his in-laws were Democrats, Hunter aligned himself with the Republican Party and was appointed postmaster of Burkesville by President Grant. He went to the legislature from the Clinton-Cumberland county district in 1872.[17]

Republicans were few in Frankfort, and Hunter was soon recognized as a capable and canny politician, earning the nickname "Gumshoe,"[18] which may have come from his rubber shoes, purportedly the first in Cumberland County, or his secretive nature, or both. He made the first of several races for Congress in 1878, and ultimately was elected three times, twice in a district in which Cumberland was at or near the eastern edge.

The most prominent and interesting stage of Hunter's career began in 1895, when he was chairman of the State Republican Executive Committee while serving in Congress. With widespread illiteracy and the advent of secret ballots, the General Assembly required political parties to select illustrations to appear at the top of each party's ticket. Hunter chose the log cabin, associated at the time with Lincoln, and it remains the official ballot device of the Kentucky Republican Party.

Hunter developed a plan that involved spending substantial amounts of money for the election of William O. Bradley of Lancaster as Kentucky's first Republican governor. Though Bradley won, he and Hunter soon fell out, for reasons that remain vague. Hunter then sought the U.S. Senate seat occupied by Democrat J.C.S. Blackburn of Versailles, whose term was scheduled to expire in 1897. Three factors complicated Blackburn's chances for re-election by the General Assembly: a Republican governor, a legislature divided among Republicans and free-silver and hard-money Democrats, and Blackburn's support for 1896 Democratic presidential nominee William Jennings Bryan and Bryan's policy promoting the free coinage of silver.

With 138 legislators, it took seventy votes for any candidate to be elected senator. Some Democrats refused to support Blackburn, and some Republicans, including some close to Bradley, would not back Hunter. Ballot after ballot was cast, each time Hunter was within a vote or two of victory. Hunter had flip-flopped on the silver issue, however, and his credibility was so damaged that he withdrew from the race. Meanwhile, eligibility of some legislators had been challenged, and when an effort was made to oust two Republican senators, chaos erupted. Most members were said to be carrying weapons, and each party stationed armed guards at the chamber entrances. Bradley called out the state militia and the legislature adjourned, with fewer than forty bills passed and no senator elected.[19]

Hunter re-entered the battle, but seemed to go out of his way to feud with Bradley, openly speaking against the governor as a potential vice-presidential candidate for William McKinley. While Hunter campaigned against Bradley, perhaps in search of anti-silver Democratic votes, John Rhea vied with Hunter and defeated him for Congress in November 1896.

Nevertheless Hunter was reinvigorated and determined, and was the leading Republican candidate at a special session called by Bradley to decide the Senate seat in early 1897. Hunter again came within a single vote of victory. Blackburn refused to withdraw, and finally an exhausted Hunter demurred from the battle. After 112 ballots W.J. Deboe, became Kentucky's first Republican senator.[20]

Hunter's withdrawal was accompanied by rumors of bribery, and he and several others at Frankfort were indicted on charges of conspiring to pay five thousand dollars for the votes of three legislators. Asserting his innocence, he and all other defendants were acquitted. Exhausted and likely broke, Hunter accepted McKinley's appointment as minister to Honduras and Guatemala. Controversy followed him there, both regarding his own actions as well as a Guatemala City gunfight that resulted in the death of another American at the hand of Hunter's son.

Hunter returned to Burkesville in 1903, where he was elected to Congress to fill a vacancy in a southeastern Kentucky district into which Cumberland County had been relocated. There were many lawsuits in various counties over the nomination, and ultimately the House decided in Hunter's favor. He was not nominated for a full term, and left Burkesville for Somerset, where he founded the Somerset Water, Light and Traction Co. He secured a presidential appointment as collector of revenue for Kentucky for his son Willie, and focused his attention on silver mines in Mexico and other grandiose schemes, none of which bore much lasting fruit. In 1915 at age seventy-four, Hunter sought the governorship, but deferred to Edwin P. Morrow of Somerset, and in return Willie Hunter became the Republican nominee for state treasurer. Both lost by narrow margins. Godfrey Hunter died in Louisville in 1917, nearly penniless. His fifty years in Kentucky politics are largely forgotten.[21]

Ed Morrow's 1915 race for governor was one of the most colorful in a state known for colorful politics. Morrow, U.S. attorney for the eastern half of Kentucky in 1910–1913, ran against Democrat A.O. Stanley, a Western Kentucky congressman. They were great friends, traveled together, sometimes sleeping in the same bed and drinking from the same whisky bottle. One hot day, as Morrow was speaking, the weather and the bourbon Stanley had consumed caused him to vomit, in full view of the crowd. When it came his turn, Stanley said, more or less, "This just proves what I have been saying all over Kentucky: Ed Morrow plain makes me sick to my stomach."[22]

Morrow lost the election by only 471 votes out of nearly four hundred forty thousand, but a contest would have been decided by the Democrat-controlled legislature, and he politely bowed out. That earned him much good will, and in 1919 he defeated Governor James D. Black, who had ascended to the office when Stanley took a U.S. Senate seat, by more than forty thousand votes.[23]

Morrow was the first Republican governor to have an allied legislature, thanks to a Democratic defector in the Senate and the tie-breaking vote of his lieutenant governor. He reorganized state government, initiated the fifth state gasoline tax in the United States, and started a meaningful road program, as highways were putting an end to the steamboats that still plied the upper Cumberland River and its tributaries. He failed in a bid to make Kentucky's judicial elections nonpartisan, an idea that was finally adopted in 1975.

A progressive Republican who supported women's suffrage and wanted to end racial violence, Morrow received national attention for sending the National Guard to protect an African American, William Lockett, on trial for murder in Lexington in 1920. When a mob charged the courthouse, the troops fired, killing six and wounding as many as fifty. It marked the first time that a Southern governor used military force to uphold civil rights, though it should be noted that Stanley had personally confronted and dispersed a similar mob in Murray as governor in 1917.[24]

In 1927, when Stanley supported an old factional foe for governor, Morrow ridiculed him. A few years later, when they both held appointive posts in Washington, they met on the street, and Stanley refused to acknowledge Morrow. Upset, Morrow confronted Stanley: "Owsley, we have been friends for fifty years. We campaigned against each other, but always remained friends. We slept in the same bed and drank from the same whiskey bottle. What have I done that is so terrible that you can't forgive me?" Stanley, red-faced, turned and replied, "Morrow, for all of those years we campaigned against each other, you were lying about me. But in the 1927 governor's race, you told the truth and, by God, I resent it!"[25] Morrow lost a race for Congress in 1934 and died in 1935.

In 1923, the last year of Morrow's governorship, a young man from his hometown of Somerset was voted most likely to succeed at Yale University. John Sherman Cooper went on to Harvard Law School, but had to quit because his dying father, once the wealthiest man in town, had suffered severe business reverses. Young Cooper sold the family's mansion and spent the next twenty-five years paying off his father's debts and sending his six siblings to college.[26]

Cooper was elected state representative in 1927 and county judge in 1929, just in time to see his county hit hard by the Great Depression. During his eight years in the office, which was both judicial and administrative, he provided relief to many destitute people and developed a sense of compassion that guided him for the rest of his political career.

Cooper lost the 1939 Republican primary for governor and continued to practice law until enlisting in the army during World War II. While he assisted in the restoration of the Bavarian judicial system after the war, he was elected circuit judge for Pulaski, Rockcastle, Wayne, and Clinton counties. Cooper was judge for less than a year because Republicans nominated him for a U.S. Senate seat that former Governor Albert Benjamin "Happy" Chandler, had resigned to become commissioner of baseball. A Republican wave in the 1946 elections sent Cooper to Washington, but in his first vote he crossed party leaders and told them he would vote as he saw fit. He exhibited the same independent streak for the rest of his career.

John Sherman Cooper. Credit: Centre College.

Cooper won passage of nearly full price supports for tobacco, the main cash crop of the Upper Cumberland, but when he sought a full term in 1948 the presence of Democratic Senator Alben Barkley on President Harry Truman's ticket for vice president largely ordained his defeat by Democrat Virgil Chapman. Truman appointed Cooper a delegate to the United Nations in 1949, and he was an alternate delegate in 1950–1951.

Chapman died in 1952, and Cooper regained his Senate seat in that fall's election, but in 1954, Barkley won it back. It was widely believed that only Barkley could have defeated Cooper, who had developed a loyal following across the state. But Barkley died in 1956, and Cooper won yet another special election. In the interim, he served as ambassador to India.

Cooper won full terms in 1960 and 1966, setting electoral records for statewide Republican candidates.[27] He was in some ways the most liberal Republican in the Senate. He supported the 1964 Civil Rights Act despite his constituents' opposition, and fought to limit U.S. military activity in Indochina. Earlier, he was one of the first Republicans to criticize the red-baiting tactics of Wisconsin Senator Joe McCarthy during the Cold War witch hunts.

Though he was called "the global Kentuckian,"[28] Cooper kept his fences mended back home. In his final term he worked with Senator Howard Baker Jr. of Scott County, Tennessee, to create a national recreation area on the Big South Fork of the Cumberland River.[29] Cooper served on the Warren Commission, which investigated the assassination of his good friend, President John F. Kennedy. After retiring from the Senate, he was the first U.S. ambassador to East Germany and later practiced law in Washington, D.C.

When Cooper retired in 1972, he was succeeded by Democrat Walter Darlington "Dee" Huddleston, who lived in Elizabethtown in Central Kentucky but was born in Burkesville, the son of a Methodist minister. Huddleston lost the seat to Republican candidate Mitch McConnell in 1984, who at this writing was the Senate Minority Leader.

To reach the Senate, Huddleston defeated former governor Louie B. Nunn, who was from the Barrens region just northwest of the Upper Cumberland, but relied on it for his political success. After narrowly losing the governorship in 1963, he won it in 1967, the only Republican elected to the office between 1943 and 2003. Nunn was sometimes called "Kentucky's version of Lyndon Johnson"—a larger-than-life character with a huge heart, a big frame, and a bigger ego, who was craftier than any of his contemporaries and used all the available tools to work his will.[30]

Nunn ran on a "no-new-tax" pledge, but once in office faced a hard choice. He could raise taxes or cut programs and give up hope of carving out the sort of record he had envisioned for himself, which included

Senator Albert Benjamin Chandler. Library of Congress.

granting some overdue favors to his Upper Cumberland constituents. He chose the former, getting the Democratic-controlled legislature to raise the sales tax from 3 percent to 5 percent, and that probably kept him from winning another election. Even so, Nunn ushered in improvements in education, mental health, and roads, including the four-lane Cumberland Parkway that bisects the Upper Cumberland from Glasgow to Somerset. His name was added to it before his death in February 2004.

McConnell said that the most consequential Republican to ever serve in state government at Frankfort was Burkesville lawyer David L. Williams, who bore some resemblance to Nunn in his physical presence and political skills. Williams, a legislator since 1985, engineered the GOP's first takeover of the state Senate in 1999, and became its president in 2000. He lost the 2011 race for governor to Democratic incumbent Steve Breshear, who then rid himself of his nemesis in 2012 by appointing Williams to a vacancy on the circuit judgeship for Clinton, Cumberland, and Monroe counties.

In 2014 McConnell was Kentucky's most prominent Republican and the U.S. Senate minority leader,[31] but the dean of the state congressional delegation was Harold "Hal" Rogers of Somerset, first elected in southeastern

Kentucky's Fifth District in 1980. He made an unsuccessful race for lieutenant governor in 1979 with Louie Nunn atop the ticket, and gained a district-wide organization that helped him win the eleven-candidate GOP primary, which was tantamount to election. He rose through the ranks of the U.S. House Appropriations Committee and became chairman after the 2010 elections, but only by swearing off budget earmarks, a tool he had used to funnel tens of millions in federal funds to the Fifth District, the nation's most rural and one of its poorest.

Powerful, Varied, and Colorful Characters

The most prominent Republican from the most powerful Republican county in the mid-twentieth century was Judge Roscoe C. Tartar, the brother of John Sherman Cooper's mother. Though Tarter did not always support the same candidate as his nephew, he served several terms as Pulaski County judge, once sat in the legislature, and was first elected circuit judge in 1927. He lost the seat in 1933, but got it back when his nephew went to the Senate and Tarter remained on the bench until his death in 1968. Nunn, governor at the time, said he got a call from Somerset lawyer Lawrence Hail, telling him that Tartar had died and asking Nunn if he, Hail, could take his place. Nunn said that he told Hail, "Lawrence, that's all right with me—but you better check with the undertaker."[32]

Other notable political figures from the Upper Cumberland region have included Judge James Garnett and Judge Rollin Hurt of Adair County; Judge Morris Montgomery, Judge Jimmy Weddle and Senator E.C. Moore of Casey; state House Speaker Bobby Richardson of Barren; Wendell Butler of Metcalfe, who was state senator, commissioner of agriculture and superintendent of public instruction; and Lilburn Phelps of Russell, who served in the legislature and was U.S. District Court clerk.

One of the region's most colorful political figures never held office, but not from lack of trying. Jamestown lawyer Silas Sullivan, more noted for his oratory than his integrity or legal skills, ran in eleven Republican primaries for offices ranging from lieutenant governor to Russell County attorney, ending in 1957. People flocked to hear him speak, and before one address to the legislature he said he had "a set of lungs like a Norwegian jackass," but he never came close in an election. In one of his last races, his young, fair-haired opponent for county attorney harangued Sullivan on his inability to be elected, telling voters they should vote for someone who could win in November. Sullivan replied that all his opponents had either vast sums of money or impeccable character, and "I'll have you know that little yellow-haired fellow has neither."[33]

The chairman of Nunn's successful campaign for governor was Erbon Powers "Tom" Sawyer, son of James Garfield "Jim" Sawyer, a Clinton County native who served as Metcalfe County sheriff from 1934–1937. Tom Sawyer moved from Glasgow to Louisville, was elected county attorney of Jefferson County and was appointed Jefferson County judge (a largely administrative post) by Nunn after Judge Marlow Cook's election to the Senate in 1968.[34]

One of Jim Sawyer's daughters married Dr. W.C. Mann, a native of the Creelsboro area on the Cumberland River in Russell County who moved to Cumberland County and served in the state House and Senate; the other married Monroe County native Cass Walden, who also served in both chambers. Walden was best known as the long-sitting circuit judge for Barren and Metcalfe counties from 1964 until his retirement in 1983, being elected as a Republican in a Democratic district when judicial races were partisan. His network of storytelling lawyers and other friends was memorialized by noted author Calvin Trillin in a 1984 *New Yorker* article, "Telling a Kentucky Story."

One of Walden's mentors was James C. Carter Sr., whose family showed how far the family ties and patronage politics of the Upper Cumberland can go. For more than one hundred years the Carters represented the main political force in Monroe County, where the river flows from Kentucky into Tennessee. In the history of Kentucky, no Republican county has ever been dominated by one family to the extent that the Carters have dominated Monroe. Perhaps only the eastern coalfield's Breathitt County, heavily Democratic and dominated by the Turner clan, could rival Monroe County as a family bastion.

Monroe is one of the poorest, most isolated, and most Republican counties in Kentucky. It has no federal highway; never had a railroad; and its only river landing was at the eastern end of the county, far from the county seat of Tompkinsville. To this day there is not a complete, modern road route to the town. In such places politics is an important source of jobs, and the Carter family dispensed patronage and dominated Monroe County for the greater part of the twentieth century.

The family patriarch was Washington "Wash" Carter, who was elected county school superintendent in 1905. He obtained a license to practice law and began the manipulations and orchestrations that would mark the history of the Carter family for the next century. Wash Carter was instrumental in the election of his brother, James C. Carter, as circuit judge for Metcalfe, Monroe, Cumberland, Adair, Barren, Russell, and Casey counties from 1909 to 1945, even though Monroe was at the far end of the district. His son, J.C. Carter Jr., "Young Jimmy," succeeded him, serving until his retirement in 1983. In 1975, Columbia lawyer Robert Hutchison Jr., beat Carter in the Democratic primary, but lost the Republican primary in the last year of partisan judicial elections in Kentucky. The Carters agreed that the judge would resign on July 1, 1979, and that they would support Hutchison for appointment to the vacancy and election to the unexpired term or he would withdraw, and he did. In a remarkable documentation, Judge Carter memorialized the deal in a letter to Hutchison, and an accompanying endorsement letter was signed by the Commonwealth's Attorney Paul Carter, County Attorney Abe Carter, County Judge Doug Carter, and Congressman Tim Lee Carter. The judge did not resign.[35]

"Old Jimmy" Carter's political influence expanded through his sons. Abe Parker Carter was elected sheriff in 1937, county judge in 1941, and county attorney in 1945, the office he held until his death in 1984. Before rising to the bench, Young Jimmy was elected mayor of Tompkinsville and state representative from the Metcalfe-Monroe district.

Tim Lee Carter reelection bid poster. Credit: David Cross collection.

The third son, Tim Lee Carter, took three successive Tompkinsville High School basketball teams to the State Tournament, established a large medical practice, and became school board chairman. When Eugene Siler Sr. of Williamsburg retired from Congress in 1964, Carter won the Fifth District seat in a crowded Republican primary. Running from the westernmost county in the district, which stretched to the Virginia border, Carter dominated the western counties, won handily, and served until 1980. His Somerset office was headed for years by Doris Petercheff, who stayed on with Rogers, and was for years one of the district's most influential political operatives.

Even before Tim Lee Carter went to Washington, Carter influence did not end at the county line. Pearl Carter Pace, a daughter of Old Jimmy, was elected sheriff of adjacent Cumberland County in 1937, when her husband Stanley was term-limited. "Mrs. Pearl," as she was known, was the first woman ever elected sheriff in Kentucky for a full term in her own right, and she served as Kentucky's Republican national committeewoman for several years. Her son-in-law, M.C. "Doc" Keen, served two terms as Cumberland County sheriff.

The Carter domination did not stop with Old Jimmy's children. Nephew Paul Carter, son of Wash, succeeded Young Jimmy as commonwealth attorney and served until 1983. Doug Carter, son of Earl, served three terms as county judge and several terms as county attorney, holding that office when he died in 2008. Doug's brother Windell was mayor of Tompkinsville and a school board member. Their nephew Louis Lee Carter was elected Property Valuation Administrator (PVA or tax commissioner) and at this writing remained so.

Several other Carters held offices both elective and appointive. Dr. Jimmy Carter, son of Abe, was school board chairman, and his brother Jack ran the local Agricultural Stabilization and Conservation Service office of the U.S. Department of Agriculture for years. The most important appointed position, or sometimes any position, in counties such as Monroe was the position of county school superintendent, and Darrell Carter, son of Washington Carter held that post from 1952–1980. He was one of several superintendents in the Upper Cumberland to enjoy a long tenure.

With the retirements of Tim Lee, Young Jimmy, Abe, and Paul Carter, the family's domination waned. The Carters began feuding among themselves with a faction led by Windell Carter opposing Dr. Jimmy Carter in school board races. That period of disharmony, coupled with a lack of younger Carters to fill the offices that required a law degree, resulted in fewer Carter names on the doors of elective offices. Nevertheless they remain the stoutest political faction in Monroe County, and Lewis Darrell

Carter was school superintendent at this writing. It was State Representative James Comer (grandson of Harlin Comer, who led anti-Carter forces in the 1980s), who has become the best-known Monroe County politician. After serving in the state House, he was elected state agriculture commissioner in 2011 (the Republican's only statewide winner in the election) and has announced his intention to run for governor in 2015.

The Carter legacy is a matter of opinion. Some say they have been great benefactors, but others say they have held the county back from progress in their desire to maintain control. In 2011–2012, student test scores were relatively low, at the 41st percentile statewide, but in 2012–2013 rose to the 85th percentile, meaning that only fifteen percent of school districts in the state scored higher.[36]

The Carters' early domination of the Twenty-Ninth Judicial District led one young Russell County lawyer, dissatisfied with practicing under Carter rule, to go to great lengths to have Russell removed from the circuit. After serving in the State House from the Casey-Russell district, Terill A. Wilson won a state Senate seat in 1949, defeating four-term incumbent W.C. Farmer of Clinton County in the Republican primary in Clinton, Cumberland, Wayne, Russell, and Monroe counties. Wilson persuaded the legislature to create a new Fortieth Judicial Circuit composed of Russell, Clinton, and Wayne, with the cooperation of leaders in the other counties, which were in a district dominated by Pulaski. The Democratic governor appointed Democrats circuit judge and commonwealth attorney, but in 1951 they were defeated by Wilson and James A. Hicks of Albany. Wilson thus followed the example of Breathitt County's Ervine Turner, who won a circuit judgeship he helped create.

Wilson and Hicks formed an alliance that year that went largely unchallenged in the district for eighteen years. In 1969 Hicks defeated incumbent W.C. Mann for the state Senate, but Wilson lost the judgeship to Jamestown attorney Kenton Cooper. In 1975 Wilson co-managed the successful campaign of his brother, Jamestown attorney Leonard Wilson, against Cooper, who was later elected to the state Court of Appeals. Leonard Wilson, former Russell County attorney and state representative, served on the bench until 1983. His son, Robert L. "Bobby" Wilson, later served as district and circuit judge until his death in 2003.

Hicks was succeeded as commonwealth's attorney by Eddie C. Lovelace of Albany, another major courtroom and political force in the region, losing in the crowded race for Congress in 1980 in an eleven-way primary.[37] Lovelace was elected Clinton County attorney in 1965, and has held office since, served as the commonwealth's attorney from 1970–1991 and circuit judge from 1992 to 2012.[38]

Political machines such as the Carters' were notorious for playing games with election laws, and some counties in the Upper Cumberland remain hotbeds of vote buying, as indicated by the large percentages of absentee votes—the easiest kind for the buyer to verify. In the local primary elections of 2006, Kentuckians cast 4.6 percent of their votes by absentee; the percentage was higher in every Upper Cumberland county except Pulaski and Barren, and was 16 percent in Monroe and 13 percent in Cumberland and Clinton. In 2006 and 2010, when local offices were on the ballot, Kentuckians cast 4.6 percent of their votes by absentee; the percentage was higher in almost every Upper Cumberland county. In the 2006 general election, Clinton's absentee share neared 15 percent and Monroe's surpassed 21 percent. That year, a major federal investigation resulted in the conviction of the Monroe judge-executive and others on charges of conspiracy to buy votes. In the 2010 elections, its absentees plummeted to 6.9 percent and Clinton's fell to 10.3 percent. There is a tradition of "floaters" going back to the earliest days of voting. Buying votes, though not as prevalent as in the past in most counties, has become more sophisticated. Historically the African American population in Kentucky's Upper Cumberland supported Republican candidates. Blacks have occasionally held

A somber John Sherman Cooper at the end of his congressional career. Credit: David Cross collection.

local office, and their degree of accomplishment in that area is notable considering their limited number in the region.

The area's two most notable black politicians have been Luska J. Twyman of Glasgow and O.M. Travis of Monticello. Twyman, a Republican, was the principal at the segregated Ralph Bunche School in Glasgow and later served as mayor, a nonpartisan office, from 1968 to 1985. Travis, a native of Clinton County, was a leader in education and civil rights in the area and served in various state appointive positions. He was the first African American on the State Board of Education, appointed by Republican Governor Simeon Willis in the mid-1940s. He was a delegate to the Republican National Convention in 1960. African Americans have served on several city councils in the region, and Republican Judd Anders was elected magistrate in Cumberland County district that had only a handful of black voters.

The last half-century has brought Kentucky's Upper Cumberland closer to the state's political mainstream, where it was before the Civil War. It remains a Republican redoubt in a state with majority-Democratic voter registration, but the state has trended Republican and the region has again produced significant political leaders—and more than its share of colorful characters.

NOTES

1. Many mountainous counties to the east did likewise, but turned Democratic in the 1930s because of Franklin D. Roosevelt's New Deal policies and the influence of the United Mine Workers.
2. Kentucky State Board of Elections, https://vr.sos.ky.gov/stats/voterstatscounty.pdf
3. Northern Ireland did not yet exist as a political entity when Dr. Hunter migrated to the Upper Cumberland.
4. In the June 1861 election, the Union candidate for Congress in most of the counties won them over a States' Rights candidate by a ratio of 4.7 to 1.
5. Ross A. Webb, "Thomas Elliott Bramlette," *Kentucky's Governors*, Lowell Harrison, ed., (Lexington: University Press of Kentucky, second edition, 2004), p. 79. For more about Burbridge see Bryan S. Bush, *The Butcher Burbridge* (New York: Acclaim Press, 2008).
6. Though Wolford was a native of Adair County and lived his final years there, at that time he resided in Casey County.
7. McClellan got 70 percent of the vote in Kentucky and 76 percent in the Upper Cumberland region.
8. E. Merton Coulter, *The Civil War and Readjustment in Kentucky* (Chapel Hill: University of North Carolina Press, 1926), p. 210.
9. Webb, *Kentucky Governors*, 81.

10. Paoli is now known as Peolia.
11. John Marshall Harlan, the GOP nominee for governor in 1875, was appointed to the U.S. Supreme Court in 1877 by Rutherford B. Hayes. He is best remembered for his stinging and prescient descent in the 1896 case *Plessy v. Ferguson*, which legitimized segregation.
12. Champ Ferguson, a Clinton County, Kentucky, native, operated out of White County, Tennessee, during the war. He is remembered with a historical marker at the Clinton County Courthouse in Albany with the blunt, but accurate, title "Civil War Terrorist." See Brian McKnight, *Confederate Outlaw: Champ Ferguson and the Civil War in Appalachia* (Baton Rouge: Louisiana State University Press, 2011) and Troy D. Smith's article "A Legacy of Blood: Champ Ferguson," in this volume.
13. J.A. Brents helped fashion the collective memory of Champ Ferguson and his brother Jim who served in the Union army in his book, *The Patriots and Guerrillas of East Tennessee and Kentucky; The Sufferings of the Patriots; Also the Experiences of the Author as an Officer in the Union Army* (New York: Henry Dexter, 1863).
14. Anne Marshall, *Creating a Confederate Kentucky: The Lost Cause and Civil War Memory in a Border State* (Chapel Hill: University of North Carolina Press, 2010), p. 46. Morrow, Adams, Carr, and Brents all served as Union officers. All but Morrow served under Colonel Wolford who remained a Democrat.
15. Willard Rouse Jillson, *Edwin P. Morrow, Kentuckian: A Contemporaneous Biographical Sketch*, (Louisville, Kentucky: G.T. Dearing Printing Co., 1921), pp. 22–23.
16. Sources disagree about where Hunter was born. Some say near Belfast, others place his birth in Londonderry.
17. Nancy Buchanan, "W. Godfrey Hunter," (Bowling Green, Kentucky: Unpublished paper written for Frances Richards, Western Kentucky State College, 1960).
18. Joseph William Wells, *History of Cumberland County* (Standard Printing Co., 1947), p. 304.
19. See Hambleton Tapp and James C. Klotter, *Kentucky: Decades of Discord, 1865–1900* (Frankfort: Kentucky Historical Society, 2008), pp. 356–359; and Franklin Circuit Court records in Frankfort, Kentucky. The *New York Times* covered Kentucky politics rather thoroughly during the period and provides an excellent insight into the issues and key figures of Hunter's day.
20. Jasper B. Shannon and Ruth McQuown, *Presidential Politics in Kentucky, 1824–1948* (Lexington: University Press of Kentucky, 1950).
21. David M. Cross, Unpublished Manuscript, (Albany, Kentucky, 2011).
22. Lowell Harrison and James Klotter, *A New History of Kentucky* (Lexington: University Press of Kentucky, 1997), p. 268.
23. James Klotter. *Kentucky: Portrait in Paradox, 1900–1950* (Frankfort: Kentucky Historical Society, 1996), p. 227.
24. *Ibid.*, 233. General J.M. DeWeese deployed over one thousand troops to Lexington to protect Lockett, who had been accused of raping and murdering a ten-year-old girl. It should be pointed out that a number of racially charged incidents, including riots, took place in 1919 and 1920.
25. *Ibid.*, 69; Author's correspondence with Franklin Circuit Judge Philip J. Shepherd, Frankfort, March 16, 2011, quoting his former law associate, the late Edward F. Prichard Jr., Frankfort, who was in Washington during that era.

26. Albin Krebs, "John Sherman Cooper Dies at 89," *New York Times* (February 23, 1991).
27. Cooper garnered 483,305 votes in 1966 to John Y. Brown Sr.'s 266,079, defeating his opponent by a margin of 217,726.
28. Robert Schulman, *John Sherman Cooper, The Global Kentuckian* (Lexington: University Press of Kentucky, 1976).
29. The property comprising the Big South Fork National River and Recreation Area formerly belonged to the Stearns Coal and Lumber Company and straddles the Kentucky-Tennessee Upper Cumberland. The land abuts Daniel Boone National Forest in Kentucky and Pickett State Park and Forest in Tennessee.
30. Al Cross, *Louisville Courier Journal,* February 8, 2004, p. D-1.
31. McConnell brokered a deal with Senate Majority Leader Harry Reid to end the government's first shut down since 1996 in 2013 amidst growing frustration among Americans with the U.S. Congress.
32. David Cross dinner conversation with Louie B. Nunn, 2002.
33. Judge Leonard Wilson interview with David Cross, 1983.
34. Sawyer was running for a full term when he died in an auto accident in 1969. By that time his daughter, Glasgow native Diane Sawyer, had begun her television career.
35. A copy of the letter is in the possession of David M. Cross, Albany, Kentucky.
36. For Monroe County school data see: http://applications.education.ky.gov/SRC/ProfileByDistrict.aspx
37. The race had a number of strong candidates with solid records in the realm of public service. In order of finish after Rogers, the candidates were Tom Emberton of Edmonton, a 1971 candidate for governor; state senator Gene Huff of London; state senator John D. Rogers (no relation to the winner) of Somerset; state representatives Raymond Overstreet of Liberty and Elmer Patrick of Williamsburg; and four minor candidates.
38. His district was redrawn to comprise Clinton, Cumberland, and Monroe. In a final irony, Terill Wilson last held court in Monroe, as a special judge in an election-fraud case in the 1980s.

5

Sons of the Cumberland

Early Careers of Cordell Hull and John Gore

Mark Dudney

Cordell Hull (1871–1955) remains the most prominent statesman the Upper Cumberland has produced. U.S. secretary of state longer than anyone in U.S. history, he was a Democratic Congressman, U.S. senator, an architect of the United Nations, and recipient of the 1945 Nobel Peace Prize. John Gore (1878–1939), though less well-known, was an intriguing political figure in his own right. A Republican trial lawyer and politician in a Democratic district, his native ability and statewide political leadership propelled him to the federal bench as the inaugural judge for the Middle District of Tennessee. How these men made the unlikely journey from backwoods country boys to positions of honor and responsibility is worthy of investigation and emulation.

Born in the same decade, Cordell Hull and John Gore shared many of the characteristics of their time and place. Their forebears were Scots-Irish who moved into the Upper Cumberland in the early nineteenth century. Their home "was a rugged area encompassing the watershed of the Cumberland River north of Carthage, Tennessee, including the Caney Fork, Obey, Wolf and Roaring Rivers."[1] Pursuing traditional activities of the Tennessee frontier, their families engaged in subsistence farming, small businesses, logging, and moonshining. Both Cordell Hull and John Gore came from large families (each had four siblings) and learned the value of hard work.

Hull and Gore were well educated, which was unusual for people growing up in rural post-Civil War Tennessee. They each studied with private tutors, attended public schools in the days before mandatory public education, and enrolled in private academies, pursuing a classical education that included Latin, Greek, rhetoric, history, literature, mathematics, and other subjects. Both proved to be adept students who were encouraged to continue their education beyond the rudimentary knowledge typical throughout the region. Although Hull and Gore pursued diverse interests and training, they shared a common interest in law and government which steered them toward their life-long careers. In a staunchly Democratic region, Hull became an active party stalwart, eventually chairing the National Democratic Party before becoming secretary of state under President Franklin Delano Roosevelt. Gore, on the other hand, fell under the influence of a prominent Union veteran in Gainesboro, Tennessee, and he rejected the party of his father and friends to become an influential leader in the Republican Party. Early in their lives, both men were drawn to governmental issues on the local and national level, and each considered the legal profession the logical introduction into a career in public service.[2]

A political prodigy in his teenage years in Clay County, Cordell Hull was fascinated with local government and current affairs. He learned the machinery of politics from Congressman Benton McMillin,[3] who was born and raised in Monroe County, Kentucky. When the congressman canvassed Celina during one of his reelection campaigns in 1888, Hull seized the opportunity to enter the political arena. He saved enough money to rent a team of horses and a buggy from a Celina livery to drive the congressman across the district. He chauffeured McMillin for seven days, asking him questions and studying his moves and speeches on the stump. Hull admired McMillin's intellect, his command of facts, and his campaigning ability. Hull fondly remembered, "I learned many of my political lessons then and later at Benton McMillin's feet."[4]

The summer of 1890 proved important in Hull's political life. The Clay County Democratic Party met at the courthouse in Celina to reorganize its county committee. Eighteen- year-old Hull sat on a back bench when John Hampton, a leading farmer and Confederate veteran, nominated him for chairman of the executive committee. Hull was elected before he could react. His new office required him to organize rank and file Democrats; Hull rode horseback throughout the county visiting voting precincts and talking to hundreds of voters.[5]

From age sixteen to nineteen, Hull's legal education coincided with his raft pilot training during the post-Civil War logging boom that brought hard cash and employment to the region. Hull never claimed to acquire the skill as a log raftsman that his father or his brother Senadius (Nade) achieved, but he became an adequate Cumberland River raft pilot.[6] His father William "Uncle Billy" Hull paid him the same wage as other hands and Cordell spent most of his earnings on secondhand law books. He carried them wherever he went, reading them whenever time permitted. During the fall of 1887 he read law with Celina attorney John H. McMillin, a brother of Joseph S. and Benton McMillin. By 1890 the McMillins not only aided in his legal career, but encouraged him to be more involved in local politics.[7]

In January 1891, Hull entered the senior class at Cumberland Law School in Lebanon, Tennessee, after passing a rigorous entrance exam; his ten months there constituted his formal legal education.[8] While in law school Hull formed a partnership with M.C. Sidwell, a Celina attorney with an established law practice. He worked with Sidwell for one year and then launched his own practice in Celina. He described his approach to practicing law: "As clients came to me, I took their cases if they had an honest basis for contest. If the case was bad or seriously doubtful I so advised the client frankly. Rather than accept his case and take it to trial, I counseled him to compromise if he could."[9]

Cordell Hull's political ambitions are illustrated by the fact that he ran for the state legislature in 1892, despite the fact that he was only twenty years old, ineligible to hold office or even vote. He won the Democratic nomination for representative for Clay, Fentress, Overton, and Pickett counties.[10] Carrying all four counties in the primary, he defeated his Republican opponent in the general election, reaching the age of maturity one month before the November election. In 1894, Hull was re-nominated, running without opposition; he won a second term.[11] A diligent public servant, he impressed people with his work ethic and continued to practice law in Celina and Nashville when the legislature was not in session. Hull declined the nomination for a third term and returned to Celina to practice law full-time.[12]

The Spanish-American War interrupted Hull's private practice. Both Cordell Hull and John Gore volunteered for military service. Hull was twenty-six and Gore twenty. Gore was rejected due to defective eyesight. When the War Department called for creation of a new infantry regiment Hull immediately raised a company of volunteers from Clay and adjoining counties, organizing Company H of the 4th Regiment, Tennessee Volunteer Infantry. Because of his rudimentary military training at Cumberland University, Hull was commissioned captain. He personally secured the enlistment of nearly every man in Company H. They were raftsmen from the upper Cumberland River, mountaineers, farmers, and coal miners.[13]

The 4th mustered into the service of the United States at Knoxville during the first two weeks of July 1898. Most of the 1,375 men had no military experience, including the officers. They arrived in Cuba after the war ended and served garrison duty until May 1899. Essentially Hull's task was "to cooperate with the Cubans in getting a suitable local government restored and operating."[14] During his service in Cuba, Hull began smoking cigars and developed a reputation as a savvy poker player, routinely filling his pockets with his fellow soldiers' money. His poker face served him well years later as congressman and secretary of state. Fondly remembering his time in uniform, the Cuban occupation gave Hull a broader world view, strengthened his leadership skills, and elevated his understanding of human nature.[15]

Meanwhile John Gore read law under Judge Bancroft Murray in Gainesboro.[16] Considered one of the top trial lawyers in Tennessee, Murray maintained an extensive practice throughout the Upper Cumberland. Like Hull, Gore demonstrated political leadership early and served as chair of the Jackson County Republican Executive Committee at age eighteen.[17] Thriving during his apprenticeship with the Murray firm, Gore earned his license to practice law in 1899 at age twenty-one. His admission to the bar coincided with Hull's return to private practice. Intent on broadening his law practice, Hull left Celina in 1901 and moved to Gainesboro to partner with John Gore.[18] On December 5, 1901, the *Gainesboro Sentinel* published the following announcement:

> Captain Cordell Hull of Celina will shortly move to Gainesboro to locate. Mr. Hull is a lawyer and young man of excellent character. He has formed a partnership with J. J. Gore, and they will occupy the office recently vacated by G. B. Murray and Son. To Captain Hull we extend a hearty welcome and hope that he may find Gainesboro a pleasant and profitable place to reside. For the firm of Hull and Gore, or whatever it may be, we predict success, for with two such worthy young men working together nothing short of success will be their lot. Here's to you, boys.[19]

Although Hull was a staunch Democrat and Gore an equally faithful Republican, their political differences did not strain their relationship. Hull admired Gore, describing him as "popular and possessing excellent native ability, a most agreeable personality and a wide acquaintance."[20] Both men enjoyed reputations for zealously serving the underprivileged and working long hours for their clientele. "We began industriously, to say the least," Hull recalled. "Each night we worked until midnight or even two in the morning. We acquired a very good practice extending to a number of counties."[21]

The legal setting for their fledgling law partnership was the old Fifth Judicial District of Tennessee. The Fifth was the largest Tennessee circuit, crossing the territory from Pickett, Fentress, Cumberland, and White counties on the east, to Jackson, Clay, Overton, Putnam, DeKalb, Macon, Trousdale, and Smith in the center and west. Roads in the district remained abysmal and travel proved tedious and tiring.[22] Lawyers, judges, and clerks rode circuit together, boarding at local hotels for days at a time, conducting

Republican John Jordan Gore, aspiring attorney and political operative. Credit: Mark Dudney Collection.

their business in the mountain and river towns. Members of the bar broke bread together and swapped stories and drinks at the end of the day. Terms of court drew large crowds and provided entertainment for the masses as well as the dispensing of justice.[23] Hotel operators "would always try to have fresh green beans for the court crowd."[24]

A country law practice consisted of real estate matters, wills, litigation, and court-appointed criminal work. Civil cases reflected the agricultural economy, consisting mainly of quarrels between farmers and merchants, clouded land titles, and boundary disputes. Criminal cases were often the product of alcohol-fueled violence. Long-time Crossville Clerk and Master C.G. Black remembered criminal dockets of the district at the beginning of the twentieth century. "In those days, the offenses were matters of fist and skull."[25]

While Hull and Gore built their law practice, they enjoyed the social life Gainesboro offered. Although tall and handsome, Hull was shy and spoke with a pronounced lisp. He bashfully courted several local women.[26] A date generally consisted of going to church or a church-sponsored social. At one such church date, Hull arrived late and was embarrassed when the entire congregation turned around and took note. One onlooker commented that "Hull had his hands in his pockets up to his elbows and his face was red as blood."[27]

Hull and Gore's partnership, though successful, was short-lived. In 1903, Judge W. T. Smith of Sparta resigned from the bench and Governor James Frazier appointed Hull to fill the unexpired term. Hull initially declined. "I was genuinely interested in my private practice, and besides I was not sure I was fully capable of handling large personal injury and other complicated cases in the railroad and mining section of the circuit."[28] Smith prevailed on Hull and he accepted the job. One of the youngest judges in the Volunteer State's history, Hull maintained his residence in Gainesboro, the geographical center of the circuit. The river town lay within a single day's drive, albeit a long, hard journey by surrey through the mountains, from each town where he held court.

The job of a circuit-riding judge suited Cordell Hull, but he found the task that confronted him overwhelming. Hull conducted a one-to-two week term of court every four months in each county within the circuit. Most of the swollen dockets were at least one year behind when he assumed the bench. Holding his first term in Sparta, Hull presided over ten murder trials among other cases under review. Hull held extra sessions of court whenever he could, working exhausting hours. As a result, his court convened fifty-two weeks a year. "I had to work night and day to clear up the dockets," he noted.[29]

Presiding over criminal dockets was no small task. Drunkenness and violence pervaded the court dockets, as well as petty crimes and larceny. By all accounts, Hull was a no-nonsense judge. Though fair, he was firm and "made short shrift of law violators, especially if they were chronic."[30] He also kept lawyers in line, which was no small feat, for many liked to test his mettle, engage in histrionics, and indulge in elaborate performances to play on the emotions of juries.[31] Hull's tenure as judge was met with wide approval by most people in the district, except for the lawless element, who sometimes threatened him. Undaunted, Hull remembered, "I traveled by myself over that mountain country, covering long distances scores of times and at all hours of the night, but I never carried a pistol."[32]

Having filled Judge Smith's unexpired term, Hull was unanimously elected judge in 1904. Hull appointed Carthage lawyer L.A. Ligon attorney general pro-tem in the August term of 1904. After plowing through the docket for six days straight, Ligon remembered, "I was fully convinced of the judge's driving capacity when it came to down-right work."[33] Hull's friend and personal attorney, H.B. "Brad" McGinness of Carthage, echoed Ligon, saying "it seemed never to occur to Judge Hull to suspend work."[34] Hull's diligence paid off. Although he served as circuit judge less than four years, he earned the respect of the people of the Upper Cumberland, who put their faith in him politically for decades to come. Hull was pleased that

Circuit-riding Judge Cordell Hull was known for his fairness and efficiency. Credit: Cordell Hull Birthplace Museum.

many continued to call him "Judge" long after he retired as U.S. secretary of state. He considered his time on the bench "the largest single factor in my getting to Congress."[35]

A natural trial lawyer, John Gore was good-natured, quick-witted and hard-working; he maintained an active private practice in the Upper Cumberland for twenty years before assuming the federal bench. Democratic friends praised him, but expressed disappointment that he was on the other side, saying "politically Gore belonged to the Republican Party, but by inheritance and environment and by every token he should naturally have been a Democrat."[36] Active statewide in Republican politics, Gore was a talented, respected politician. During President Theodore Roosevelt's administration, Gore served as postmaster of Gainesboro before being appointed surveyor and collector of customs for the port of Nashville. Soon after a steamboat was named for him, which proved a dubious honor, for the craft capsized the moment it was launched. Gore served as surveyor of customs from 1907 to 1910, before returning to his law practice in Gainesboro.[37]

Gore's term as surveyor proved fortuitous and he became a formidable force in state politics thereafter.[38] In 1914 he ran for the state Senate, representing Clay, Fentress, Jackson, Overton, Pickett, and Putnam counties.[39] Gore defeated Procter Pile of Pall Mall, Tennessee. Pile's home county of Fentress had been dominated by Republican politics since the Civil War. A contemporary legislative biography of Gore noted:

> Although a member of the minority party of the Senate of the Fifty-Ninth General Assembly, every Senator on the "other side" loves and respects John Jordan Gore, Republican, of Gainesboro, Jackson County. He stands firm for his people and his party. His friends as well as his enemies know where to find him on any question. Therein lies the secret of the regard and respect he holds of his fellow senators.[40]

John Gore served only one term in the legislature, choosing not to run for re-election; he returned to his legal career. He moved his practice to Cookeville in 1920 to form a partnership with Worth Bryant of the Putnam County bar. During the presidential election of 1920, Gore simultaneously served as chairman of the Republican executive committees for Jackson County and the state of Tennessee. In 1921 Gore managed the successful gubernatorial campaign of Alf Taylor, the last Republican governor elected in Tennessee for almost half a century. When Congress authorized a new federal trial court for Tennessee's Middle District in 1922, President Warren G. Harding rewarded Gore, appointing him the first federal trial judge of the new district on March 2, 1923. Several Upper Cumberland newspapers expressed their congratulations and support.[41] Commentary from Cookeville's *The Upper Cumberland News* stated, in part: "The people of the Upper Cumberland section have supported him in his aspirations, regardless of political affiliations, and his appointment is a victory for them, one and all. The Upper Cumberland country never produced a more sincere, nor a more popular citizen than Judge John J. Gore, whom we delight to see honored as he so justly deserves."[42] *The Carthage Courier* sang Gore's praises, stating, "He is a good lawyer, a good citizen and he will make a good federal judge."[43]

Clara Cox Epperson, a noted writer, activist, and poet laureate of Tennessee in 1934, swelled with hometown pride at Gore's appointment. She wrote a glowing assessment of him in *The Jackson County Sentinel*. Epperson reflected on the number of talented people who rose to prominence from

Gainesboro and the Upper Cumberland. She mused that the rugged hills were a source of strength and inspiration to ambitious young men like Hull and Gore, who dreamt of higher things. Epperson wrote, "I thought of the many men of power—who went from the little town of Gainesboro, nestled among the green clad hills of Jackson County, out into the world to win success for themselves and honor for their hometown . . ."[44]

John Gore was forty-five when he took the oath of office on March 10, 1923. For the swearing-in ceremony, he used the Bible his mother gave him as a boy. Realizing the weighty responsibility before him, he inscribed and signed a pledge to her on the flyleaf. Gore humbly promised to do his duty to the best of his ability and temper justice with mercy. Gore soon presided over questions of corporate and constitutional law which were largely new to him. His country law practice had not prepared him adequately for the task before him. Gore was not a learned judge, nor did he pretend to be, but was "a man of good common sense."[45] A patient listener to competing arguments of opposing counsel, especially in more complex litigation, Gore possessed a keen sense of fairness and evolved into a just, careful, and impartial judge. Observers were impressed that Judge Gore retained as clerk of the court at Nashville H.M. Doak, a Democratic appointee and Confederate veteran. When court was in session he resided in Nashville at the Hermitage Hotel, commuting to his home on Roaring River when possible.[46]

In 1925, the Middle District became involved in a dispute regarding the venue of the upcoming Scopes Monkey Trial. John T. Scopes' defense attorneys—Arthur Garfield Hays and Dudley Field Malone of the American Civil Liberties Union—asked Judge Gore for a federal injunction to halt the pending state criminal prosecution against their client. The defense attempted to get the case transferred to federal court, arguing that the Butler Act, which banned the teaching of evolution in public schools, was unconstitutional, and in violation of the basic principles of academic freedom. They feared that the case would pit science against religion if it were heard in state court, rather than address the real issues the Butler Act raised. They expressed concern that the state court would limit its decision solely to whether Scopes had violated state law. Judge Gore rejected their motion on grounds that, as a federal judge, he had no authority to prevent legitimate state officials from acting as authorized by state law. Gore refused to grant the injunction and guaranteed the case be tried under state jurisdiction in Dayton, Tennessee.[47]

A confirmed bachelor, Gore enjoyed a social drink, particularly the homemade kind distilled in his native Upper Cumberland. In 1932, after H.M. Doak's service ended, Gore appointed Republican Elijah Lee Dudney to succeed him. Dudney, a Jackson County native and World War I veteran, served as clerk of the Middle District Court for the remainder of Gore's tenure.[48] As two middle-aged bachelors, Gore and Dudney enjoyed the social life of Nashville and resort towns like Red Boiling Springs during the 1930s.

Gore earned a reputation for geniality and wit. His years on the bench were flavored with humor and anecdote. One story related a defendant from Gore's home county appearing before him on a charge of selling moonshine. The man pled not guilty, and denied ever having anything to do with illegal liquor. Stunned by this pronouncement, Gore said, "Are you going to stand there and say that to me, when I've bought ten gallons of the stuff from you, myself?"[49]

Gore's puckish sense of humor was illustrated when a newly-appointed Republican postmaster in Gainesboro asked him what to do about packages he was unable to deliver. He gravely explained that such packages had to be held for at least two weeks to give the addressed parties full opportunity to collect them. Gore immediately bought a large slab of Limburger cheese and mailed it to a fictitious person in Gainesboro. Before the two weeks expired, the postmaster nearly suffocated and the post office received few customers.[50]

John W. Hilldrop told a story demonstrating Gore's true nature. He picked a man up and gave him a ride on his way to court one morning. The passenger, not knowing who Gore was, explained that he had walked all night to face "that tough old judge" on an illicit distilling charge. The poor, ragged man said he was determined to tell the truth and carried a small bundle of clean clothes to wear in jail. When the defendant appeared in court, Gore fined him one cent. He then gave the man the money not only to pay the fine, but to eat and buy transportation home.[51] Dorothy Crabtree, daughter of Vernon Crabtree, caretaker of Judge Gore's Roaring River farm, remembered Gore essentially as a second grandfather. She fondly recalled that Judge Gore gladly paid for her art lessons.[52]

Some modern conservatives would approve of Gore's philosophy of judicial restraint, even though he sometimes made exceptions. He believed that every law, good or bad, should be enforced to the letter. "If a law is good," he used to say, "then it would be to the benefit of society to enforce. If it was bad, on the other hand, enforcement would quickly reveal its deficiencies."[53]

Gore's most notable case involved the constitutionality the Tennessee Valley Authority (TVA). In 1936, nineteen southern utility corporations sued to enjoin the TVA from building generating facilities and selling electric power. They contended that the act creating TVA unlawfully empowered the federal government to engage in business, unfairly competing with private enterprise. The government contended that the purpose in creating the TVA was improvement of navigation and flood control, and that the production and sale of electricity was merely incidental. When Gore initially granted the injunction, he was excoriated by New Deal proponents in Congress, who called for his impeachment.[54]

Gore's decision played a role in the enactment of the Judiciary Reform Act of 1937, part of Franklin Roosevelt's controversial "court-packing" plan. It forbade issuance of an injunction by any district court suspending enforcement of any act of Congress upon constitutional grounds, unless approved by a specifically convened three-judge panel. Accordingly, Judge Gore, District Judge John D. Martin, and Sixth Circuit Court of Appeals Judge Florence Allen were designated to try the case in Chattanooga's new federal courthouse. The ensuing trial attracted national attention and lasted nearly two months, with over one thousand exhibits offered into evidence. In January 1938, the panel handed down its decision. Gore and his fellow judges ruled that the federal government, in selling electricity created at dams lawfully erected, was not unconstitutionally entering into private business. TVA, therefore, conducted legitimate federal services and appropriately disposed of its property. The ruling signaled the green light for TVA's rural electrification program. Judge Gore was in poor health at the time of the TVA litigation and the stress of the long trial took its toll. On February 21, 1939, after holding court until late in the afternoon, Judge Gore died of heart failure in his room at the Hermitage Hotel. At age sixty-one, he had served sixteen years on the federal bench.[55]

Cordell Hull's first election to the Fourth District Congressional seat in 1906 proved one of the hardest political fights of his career. Facing a heated Democratic primary, opponents accused him of moving from town to town in the region for political purposes. Hull responded to the criticism stating, "I thought enough of the people in each county to move into their midst, be one of them and cast my lot with them, while my critics had not." Hull narrowly won the primary by fifteen votes. He defeated his Republican opponent in the general election and faced no opposition within the Democratic Party for the seat for the next twenty years.[56]

After election to Congress, Hull established residency at Carthage, staying at his father's house when in Tennessee. When he moved to Washington, D.C., Hull engaged Carthage lawyer H.B. McGinness to act as his private secretary. McGinness served one term with Hull before returning to Carthage to resume his law practice.[57] Thereafter, he worked as Hull's private attorney and his political representative in the district. In 1910, Hull hired Miss Will Harris of Livingston as his secretary. At the time, Harris

Democrat Cordell Hull early in his political career. Credit: Mark Dudney Collection.

served as legal secretary to Livingston lawyer and future Tennessee Governor Albert Houston Roberts. Hull recognized the young woman's intellect and ability and asked Roberts' permission to hire her. Roberts said, "I hated to lose her, but felt that I couldn't say no."[58] Harris loyally and capably worked for Hull nearly four decades in Washington, throughout his years in Congress and as secretary of state. An expert in dictation and transcription, Harris could literally say she "wrote the Atlantic Charter."[59]

Hull determined early in life that he wanted to serve the national interest, as well as his constituents in Tennessee's Fourth District. He diligently studied monetary and tax policies and was recognized by his peers as an expert in these fields. He served eleven terms in the U.S. House of Representatives, from 1907–1921 and from 1923–1931. A member of the powerful Ways and Means Committee for eighteen years, Hull led national efforts to lower tariffs and tear down trade barriers. His first, and only electoral defeat, came during the Harding Landslide of 1920. Republican Wynne Clouse beat him by approximately three hundred votes. Hull noted the irony that his former law partner John J. Gore was chair of the State Republican Committee, and led the campaign effort against him. "At heart he wanted to see me win," Hull wrote wistfully. His friendly rival, Gore simply followed the political advice that Hull had given him several times when they were law partners: "In regular elections where I am a candidate, with a Republican opponent, it is only fair that you should vote the Party ticket. Otherwise you might be in for serious attack in the event that you should seek political honors yourself in the future."[60]

Following his campaign loss, Hull served as chair of the Democratic National Committee for two years. When he recaptured the Fourth District seat, Hull faced an uphill battle in the Republican-controlled Congress of the 1920s. By 1929, he considered retiring from public life. When Senator Lawrence Tyson of Knoxville died in office, however, Hull ran for the next full term as U.S. senator from Tennessee. Hull won the primary and defeated Republican Paul Divine in the general election.[61] He served in the U.S. Senate from 1931 to 1933, before accepting President Roosevelt's offer to serve as his secretary of state.[62] Hull's record as secretary of state is well known. He served almost twelve years, the longest tenure in American history. He promoted Roosevelt's Good Neighbor Policy with South and Central

Hotel proprietor and Gainesboro fixture Aunt Polly Williams. Credit: Tennessee State Library and Archives.

America, negotiated international reciprocal trade agreements and advocated American rearmament. After America entered World War II, Hull immediately took steps to ensure such a cataclysm could not easily happen again. His proposal of a new world organization dedicated to security and peace resulted in the creation of the United Nations. President Roosevelt nominated Hull, the "Father of the United Nations" for the 1945 Nobel Prize for Peace, describing him as "the one person in all the world who has done his most to make this great plan for peace an effective fact."[63]

Hull's personal life was more prosaic. He did not marry Frances Witz until he was forty-six. The couple had no children and their lives revolved around his career. When Frances died in 1954, Hull's niece Katherine Hull Eldridge lived with her ailing uncle. He died July 23, 1955 and was buried in the National Cathedral in Washington, D.C. At age eighty-three, Hull devoted nearly four decades of his life to national service.[64]

John Gore, a lifelong member of the minority party, enjoyed enormous popularity with people of all political stripes and built a solid record as a federal judge. The two men could not have been more different in their personalities and their politics. Hull was famously reserved. Gore, by contrast was the more natural politician and raconteur.[65] Hull believed in the transformative power of government, while Gore an arch conservative was wary of government intervention. As a member of Congress and proponent of the New Deal, Hull helped usher in the modern regulatory state. As a federal judge enjoining the TVA, Gore's ruling briefly impeded it.

In spite of their obvious differences, Hull and Gore shared many similarities. Both were consumed by an interest in law and politics from an early age. Both served as chair of their county executive political committees at eighteen. Hull married late in life, while Gore remained a bachelor. Neither man had children. Both embodied the concept of the Citizen Lawyer. They embraced the Jeffersonian ideal that lawyers should be more than excellent legal practitioners; they should be good citizens and lead by example. Though the two men often disagreed they remained lifelong friends.[66]

In some ways, both men's life journeys remained tied to the Cumberland River. Although he lived in Washington most of his adult life, Cordell Hull maintained the family home in Carthage as his Tennessee residence. As secretary of state he displayed a large landscape painting in his office depicting the confluence of the Caney Fork and Cumberland Rivers.[67] Likewise Gore's roots ran deep in his Roaring River farm in Jackson County. He never bought a home in Nashville, opting instead to reside at the Hermitage Hotel. When Gore died, he was laid to rest in his family's cemetery on Roaring River, a tributary of the Cumberland.

NOTES

1. W. Calvin Dickinson, Michael E. Birdwell and Homer D. Kemp, *Upper Cumberland Historic Architecture.* (Franklin, Tennessee. Hillsboro Press, 2002), 1.
2. While it has become a standard trope in the Gore story that he was lured into politics by a Union veteran, the author has been unable to find the name of that veteran who has been lost to posterity.
3. Benton McMillin, was a native of the Kentucky Upper Cumberland who adopted the Tennessee Upper Cumberland as his home. He practiced law and political ambitions led McMillin to the U.S. Congress representing the Fourth District of Tennessee from 1879–1899. He left Congress to run for governor of Tennessee and served in that capacity from 1899–1903. In his last political post he served as ambassador to Guatemala from 1919 until 1922, when he returned to Tennessee and returned to private business.
4. Cordell Hull, *The Memoirs of Cordell Hull,* Vol. 1 (New York: Macmillan, 1948), p. 26.
5. *Ibid.,* 24.
6. *Ibid.,* 21. Taking turns with other raftsmen, Hull piloted night and day, learning "every crook and turn in the river, every island, every towhead, every 'hard pull,' and every bad place."
7. *Ibid.,* 19. During the spring of 1890, Hull read law at Nashville in the firm of Pitts and Meeks. His practical experience as a farm hand, logger, and clerk in his father's store boosted his reputation as a hard worker.
8. *Ibid.,* 27. Hull graduated and was admitted to the bar at age nineteen. Although state law required applicants to be twenty-one, a peculiar exception permitted Cumberland graduates to be licensed earlier.
9. *Ibid.*
10. Harold B. Hinton, *Cordell Hull: A Biography* (New York: Doubleday, Doran and Co., 1942), p. 43.
11. Hull, 30.
12. *Ibid.,* 29, 33.
13. *Ibid.,* 34; Hinton 61–69.
14. Hull, 34.
15. *Ibid.,* 36.
16. "Our Picture Series No. 6: George Bancroft Murray," *Jackson County Sentinel,* (Gainesboro, Tennessee) February 2, 1899, p. 1. John Porry Murray, Bancroft's father, served as a state trial judge, a Tennessee Representative in the Confederate Congress and later a delegate to the Democratic National Convention in 1876.
17. "Judge John J. Gore Dies After Heart Attack," *Nashville Tennessean,* February 22, 1939, p. 2.
18. Hull, 37.
19. Hinton, 74.
20. Hull, 37.
21. *Ibid.,* 38.

22. L.A. Ligon, "Hull Was Little Known When Appointed Judge at 32," *Carthage Courier,* (Carthage, Tennessee) May 2, 1940, p. 1. The Fifth District was formerly known as the Mountain District; today it is composed of the Thirteenth and Fifteenth Judicial District's.
23. Hinton, 75.
24. Interview with Leilabel Officer and Rose Hart Dale (Livingston, Tennessee, October 8, 1995). Their aunt, "Miss Will" Harris, rode the Fifth Circuit as a court reporter and later worked for Hull.
25. Hinton, 77.
26. Interview with Kate Hull Ethridge (Byrdstown, Tennessee: Cordell Hull Folk Festival, October 1, 1995).
27. Interview with Ray Tardy (Gainesboro, Tennessee: Anderson & Haile Drug Store, September 15, 1995). Tardy's mother was Hull's date. Since he was late and the church was packed, Hull had to sit in the Amen corner, up front for all to see.
28. Hull, 38.
29. *Ibid.*, 38–39.
30. *Ibid.*, 39.
31. James N. Cox, "Hull Beat Cox Out of Girl; Lost Her to Kentuckian," *Carthage Courier,* (Carthage, TN) May 2, 1940, p. 42.
32. Hull, 39.
33. Ligon, 1.
34. H.B. McGinness, "Hull's Outstanding Trait is his Plain, Simple Manner," *Carthage Courier,* (Carthage, Tennessee) May 2, 1940, p. 32.
35. Hull, 40–42.
36. John W. Green, *Law and Lawyers: Sketches of the Federal Judges of Tennessee* (Jackson, Tennessee: McCowat-Mercer Press, 1950), p. 74.
37. "Judge John Gore Dies After Heart Attack," 2.
38. Morgan Blake, *Lawmakers and Public Men of Tennessee* (Nashville, Tennessee: Eagle Printing Co., 1915), p. 49.
39. *Ibid.* Proctor Pile was the brother of Pastor Rosier Pile the mentor and friend of Sergeant Alvin C. York. Though Pile and his constituents were and are active in the Republican Party, York was a lifelong Democrat after his service in World War I. He became a political force in his own right, and though he never ran for public office, he helped shape state politics for years.
40. Blake, 49.
41. "Judge Gore Dies After Heart Attack," 1; www.ca6.uscourts.gov "History of Tennessee District Courts." The Judicial Act of September 14, 1922, authorized a Judge for the Middle District of Tennessee.
42. *The Upper Cumberland News,* (March 8, 1923), 1.
43. *Carthage Courier,* (March 8, 1923), 1.
44. "Noted Lady Pays Tribute to Judge Gore and Gainesboro," *Jackson County Sentinel, (Carthage, Tennessee)* March 8, 1923, p. 1; *A Pictorial History of Jackson County, Tennessee,* (Paducah, Kentucky: Turner Publishing Company, 2001), pp. 86, 151.

45. Charles G. Neese and Thomas A. Wiseman Jr., *Pen Sketches of the History and Judges of the Federal Court at Nashville, Tennessee: February 17, 1797 to February 17, 1988* (N.P: N.D.), p. 45.
46. Green, 71; Telephone Interview with Wayne Crabtree, February 20, 2009. Gore left management of the farm to his friend Vernon Crabtree, whose family moved onto the property in January, 1929.
47. "Scopes Fails to get Federal Injunction; State Trial Friday," *New York Times,* July 7, 1925, p. 1. Editor's note: Transcripts of the Scopes Trial make it clear that the bill was poorly written, for it says that it is unlawful to teach that man descended from a "lower order of animals." John Washington Butler, the bill's author, failed to understand basic biological taxonomy, and the fact that man is a member of the order Primate was surely lost on him.
48. "Deaths: Elijah Lee Dudney," *Jackson County Sentinel,* (Gainesboro, Tennessee) November 22, 1956, p. 2; Interview with Bob Lee Dudney, Free State, Tennessee (January 28, 1989).
49. Interview with Bob Lee Dudney (Free State, Tennessee, March 27, 1991).
50. "Judge John J. Gore Dies After Heart Attack," *Nashville Tennessean,* February 22, 1939, p. 2.
51. "Portrait Unveiling Recalls Kindness of Judge Gore," *Nashville Tennessean,* December 18, 1951, p. 2.
52. Telephone interview with Dorothy Crabtree Harris (February 18, 2009).
53. "Judge John J. Gore Dies After Heart Attack," *Nashville Tennessean,* February 22, 1939, p. 2.
54. *Ibid.,* 1–2.
55. Green, 73. On the first day of the case, Judge Allen led her two colleagues through what she thought was the courtroom door. Finding herself in a restroom, she wheeled and led them up and down several corridors, until Judge Gore dryly remarked, "Is there a courtroom in this house?" See "TVA Clear," *Time,* (January 31, 1938), 2; Judiciary Reform Act 50 Stat. 751 (1937).
56. Hull, 43.
57. *Ibid.,* 47; Interviews with attorneys Guy Yelton and James Chamberlain (Lafayette, Tennessee, October 8, 2002). McGinness later achieved near-legendary status as a lawyer in Middle Tennessee.
58. Interview with Leilabel Officer and Rose Hart Dale, Livingston, Tennessee (November 8, 1995).
59. *Ibid.*
60. Hull, 46, 106; www.cordellhullmuseum.com/history Hull gladly endorsed his friend and former law partner's ascension to the federal bench as Judge of the Middle District of Tennessee.
61. Hinton, 195; Hull, 106, 113, 124, and 134.
62. Hull, 158. Hull had helped steer the Democratic Party toward Roosevelt in the Presidential election of 1932.
63. Cordell Hull Museum, Byrdstown, Tennessee: Copy of letter from FDR to Cordell Hull on display at the site. The original is among the papers housed at the Cordell Hull Birthplace Museum.

64. Interview with Kate Hull Ethridge (Byrdstown, Tennessee, October 1, 1995).
65. "Aunt Polly Williams at Hotel," *Carthage Courier, (Carthage, Tennessee)* (April 14, 1924).
66. www.law.wm.edu/about/wmcitizenlawyer. When Gore died, Cordell Hull telegraphed condolences to Gore's sisters: "Mrs. Hull and I feel a deep sense of personal loss in the death of your brother and our friend of many years. Judge Gore was a leader at the bar, a leader in civic affairs and a widely recognized force for good in his section of the country." See "Gore Funeral Planned Today," *Nashville Tennessean*, February 23, 1939, p. 2.
67. Hull, 168.

6

"Moderation in All Things"

Joe L. Evins's Middle of the Road Politics for Progress, People, and Public Service

Mary A. Evins

Joe L. Evins, U.S. congressman 1947 to 1977 from Middle Tennessee's Upper Cumberland congressional district, was a political moderate. Although Evins has been characterized in the present day as having been a southern conservative,[1] the conceptual and philosophical distance between the designations moderate and conservative is loaded with current connotation and historic imagery. In truth his politics ran the gamut from very progressive to restrained by his southern rural constituency, but his own personal disgust for the Dixiecrats, McCarthyites, John Birchers, and racists of his era sets him apart from the true conservatives of his day and of the present day. The principles in which he believed, and the public actions by which his district knew him, were explicitly based on the Jeffersonian republicanism, Jacksonian democracy, and Lincolnesque magnanimity that inspired his public service and were the basis of his value system. Wilsonian progressivism and FDR's New Deal policies were the mother's milk of his own political development. To broad-brush Joe L. Evins with the moniker "conservative" generalizes him through facile stereotype or historic dustiness. He would be saddened and surprised by such a label, as his daily standard throughout his entire adult life was "moderation in all things."[2]

To remember him more fully, details of Congressman Evins' career in support of a balanced interpretation of his political legacy are presented to highlight his more progressive credentials. No lack of bias is suggested; the author is his daughter, and framing of historic legacy is inherent in the relationship. However, the subject is intimately known, the perspective is unique, and many details are first-hand knowledge.

An analytical history of Joe L. Evins has yet to be written. The biography Joe L. Evins authorized by Susan B. Graves, *Evins of Tennessee,* is somewhat useful.[3] Frequently cited, it is unfortunately riddled with factual errors and unedited. A later biography was undertaken, but never completed.[4] Fuller study of the region's positions within state and national contexts of the times and Evins' contributions to state, regional, and national sociopolitical and socioeconomic mosaics will inevitably be forthcoming. The present chapter is intended to provide a brief summary of his personal and professional history and to examine some of his perspectives, positions, and actions during his career.[5]

A staunch Democrat, Joe L. Evins served in the U.S. House of Representatives in the decades immediately following World War II, from 1947 to 1977. He represented Middle Tennessee for thirty years beginning in the "G.I. Joe" Eightieth Congress. He joined the class of young veterans, welcomed home as heroes who immediately jumped into a different kind of melee—public service—by running for elected office in their respective home districts. Joe L. Evins was the quintessential G.I. Joe: "He Helped Us Over There—Let's Help Him Here" read one of his first campaign posters.[6] Evins stepped down after his fifteenth term. He went to Washington under Harry S. Truman and left with Gerald R. Ford.

Born and reared in DeKalb County, Joe L. Evins[7] was a product of the Tennessee Upper Cumberland. His father, James Edgar Evins, was the eldest of a large farm family that continued to reside on the hilly, hardscrabble land his Irish forbears chopped out of the forest in the early 1800s. He lived in the clapboard home that enveloped an original two-story chestnut log cabin Edgar's immigrant great-grandparents[8] had built on the tableland at the top of Snow's Hill by the 1840s.[9] Joe L. Evins' grandfather, William Sellars Evins, was a farmer and father of eight. A boy during the Civil War, W.S. Evins lived in that crowded multi-generational log cabin with a house full of brothers and sisters. By age fifteen in 1870, an African American boy his own age named Jake Smith lived and worked with and for the family.[10] The Evins family were strong Democrats; they recalled protecting their few possessions from renegades and bushwhackers during and after the Civil War.

Joe Evins' mother, Myrtie Ola Goodson, came from a Smithville family. The Goodsons formerly farmed in southern DeKalb County. Myrtie's father, Andrew Jackson Goodson, a lawyer who moved to Smithville to earn a living, married into the prestigious Webb family. He served as DeKalb County school superintendent in the 1880s, was U.S. Deputy Marshal under President Benjamin Harrison for four years, and then was Smithville postmaster for thirteen years from 1894 to 1907.[11] He built a make-a-statement brick home at the turn of the century three blocks from the courthouse, in a community where—at the time—most houses were modest clapboard and some still made of log. He was a public servant throughout most of his life.

Edgar and Myrtie married in 1907 and had two sons. Edgar taught in a one-room school house in DeKalb County for eight years, farmed with his father, and became a justice of the peace (JP) in 1905 at age twenty-three. He engaged in business, selling coffee as an itinerant St. Louis Coffee salesman. He opened two general stores, which Myrtie operated in his absence. A rural entrepreneur, Edgar was a contractor who built city blocks in Smithville; ran a flour mill, a hotel, and a restaurant; and started banks throughout the county. Due to his diverse interests and investments he became, by small town standards, prosperous.[12]

Edgar Evins leveraged his business involvements into political access. As a JP he served on the county court. President Woodrow Wilson appointed him to the DeKalb County Draft Board during World War I and he sold War Savings Stamps.[13] Edgar chaired the court's building committee and supervised construction of the new DeKalb County courthouse in 1925.[14] Involved with the Democratic leadership in Nashville, he often traveled to Washington, D.C., to visit political friends who were Tennessee's movers and shakers in the nation's capital, such as Congressmen Cordell Hull and Ewin L. Davis. In 1934 Edgar Evins was elected to one term in the Tennessee State Senate and a decade later, in 1944, elected again for one term.[15] By 1937 he was mayor of Smithville and served in that capacity continually (even while in the State Senate) until 1953, when he resigned due to illness. On the state's Democratic Executive Committee for years, Edgar was a Tennessee delegate to the Democratic National Convention in 1940 and 1944, renominating Franklin Delano Roosevelt each time. During World War II, Edgar chaired the DeKalb County Draft Board.

In this expressly political milieu, Joe L. Evins grew up. Whereas Joe's older brother was drawn to his parents' business interests, the younger son went to Vanderbilt, majored in history, and studied and practiced law, following his father into politics. At thirteen Joe Evins was taken for the first time to Washington, on one of his father's trips to meet the Tennessee congressional delegation.[16] Evins always affirmed that he was smitten by D.C. during that first trip and it influenced his future career choices.

Joe's expanded experiences beyond rural Middle Tennessee had begun even earlier, however. As a sick child with tuberculosis, he was placed in a children's sanitarium in Texas for three months.[17] His parents built a screened-in sleeping porch upstairs at their home in Smithville so he could breathe the night air to improve his lungs.

In a further desire to travel and see the broader world, after high school graduation Evins and a friend traveled to New York City for the first time; they landed jobs on a freighter and worked their way to Europe and back in the summer of 1929. College in Nashville followed, where Evins became the Vanderbilt football team manager,[18] traveling with the team and collecting laundry in his fraternity house to help pay bills. Immediately after college he studied law at Cumberland University in Lebanon, Tennessee, then he returned to Smithville to practice briefly.

Although Joe Evins enjoyed the law, what he really wanted was to work in Washington, so he applied to the Federal Trade Commission (FTC), seeking an appointment from Judge Ewin L. Davis of Tennessee, then Chairman of the FTC. Evins was hired in 1934, but stationed at the FTC's Chicago office.[19] He determined to be a successful Federal Trade attorney, while hoping to be transferred to FTC headquarters on the Potomac. He investigated and prosecuted business and industry abuses—false advertising, price fixing, price discrimination, and antitrust violations—across the Midwest and nationally, experiencing firsthand the necessity for federal regulatory oversight of business.[20] After four years in Chicago the reassignment to Washington came through in 1938.[21] Evins and his wife, Ann Smartt of Warren County, Tennessee, moved to Washington and lived there until 1943.[22] He was appointed attorney to the FTC (1934–1939) and assistant secretary of the FTC (1940–1942). The Evinses' two eldest daughters were born in Washington during the FTC years.[23]

In 1939, Evins joined the U.S. Army Reserves. After Pearl Harbor Evins reported for active duty in the spring of 1942. He was assigned to the Judge Advocate General (JAG) Corps of the U.S. Army operating within the greater Washington area. By fall of 1943 Captain Evins was sent to England in the European Theater of Operations (ETO); by summer 1944 he was promoted to major and deployed to Paris after the liberation of France. During the war Evins' cases primarily concerned courts martial.[24]

Immediately following his release from active duty Evins returned home to his family in Smithville in November of 1945, spending his time "eating and sleeping" with plans of "hanging up a shingle to let . . . the folks of Tennessee know that a person who once thought he was a good country lawyer is again open for business." Only a few months later, however, he was running for Congress in his home district.[25]

The political landscape in Tennessee in 1946 included Kenneth McKellar and Tom Stewart as Tennessee's two U.S. senators.[26] Tennessee then occupied ten seats in the House of Representative. B. Carroll Reece, Estes Kefauver, Albert Gore Sr., Percy Priest, Tom Murray, Jere Cooper, and Clifford Davis were among the Volunteer State's luminaries when Evins returned from France. His home district at the time was Tennessee's Fifth Congressional District. Congressman Harold Earthman was the freshman representative from Murfreesboro, who had run for Congressman Jim

Young Joe L. Evins. Credit: Joe L. Evins Papers, Tennessee Tech University Archives.

McCord's seat when McCord stepped down to run for governor in 1944. Evins determined to challenge Earthman in the Democratic primary in 1946, in a campaign that proved the most aggressive of any of his fifteen bids for public office.

Evins and his family—his well-connected state senator father and his well-respected father-in-law, Circuit Court Judge Robert White Smartt of Warren County—moved into full political mode during that first election. The family made every possible personal connection to businesses, clubs, organizations, farmers, veterans, political officials, businessmen, teachers, and ministers; blanketed the district with ads, flyers, fans, posters, and newspaper releases; gave speeches throughout the district; and addressed potential opponents individually, who dropped out to support Joe in a team-of-rivals approach that netted Evins close lifelong friendships. That first campaign was, however, noteworthy for diatribes and mudslinging on both sides. It was explicitly political, harsh against the incumbent, and not particularly affable, as Evins' campaign ads referred to him. With fifty-eight percent of the vote, Evins won that first primary on August 1, 1946. He ran unopposed in the general election in November.[27] Following the 1950 census, congressional districts were reconfigured and Evins' district was renamed the Fourth Congressional District. Although county composition within the Fourth District shifted two additional times during his years in Congress, in subsequent legislative reapportionments and remappings, and with substantial realignment each decade, his district continued to be the Fourth Congressional District throughout the remainder of his tenure.[28]

After that first heated election, later ones had the benefit of established networks and were less confrontational and more genial, especially as Evins' congressional seniority and years of service increased. Political clout that came with committee chairmanships and Washington power functioned at home to fend off potential opponents in advance of elections, as did working the district to extinguish fires before they started.[29] Edgar Evins directly influenced his son's politics and political behavior; the younger Evins absorbed the lessons, skills, and direct connections within Tennessee politics from his father, as well as from his father-in-law, Judge Smartt.

Edgar Evins died in 1954. Joe once commented to a relative that a person never completely grows up and becomes fully his own man until his father passes away. That truism must have influenced the younger Evins' public actions.[30] No longer circumscribed by his dad's political persona and harder-nosed tactics, Joe Evins became his own man and treated people in his own manner. Whereas Edgar was known as an acerbic, tough personality, Joe had a winning personality and was known for "a kind word with a smile," whose naturally "pleasant ways attracted" people easily.[31]

When Joe L. Evins arrived in Washington in January 1947, he entered a freshman class composed of many World War II veterans. Among the vets who entered the House of Representatives as freshmen that year were John F. Kennedy, Richard M. Nixon, Carl Albert, Omar Burleson, and Dixiecrats John Bell Williams and Otto Passman. Though Democrat Harry Truman was president, both houses of Congress were controlled by a Republican "do-nothing" majority aided by a coalition of conservatives who bridged party lines.

Evins' interests, political focus, and personal philosophies evolved and matured over his thirty years in the House, reflective of the changing times and politics in which he lived. He entered the House on the domestic platform of benefits for veterans, increased agricultural appropriations, rural electrification for remote corners of his district, improved schools, and federal funding for education. Internationally he favored continuation of Cordell Hull's reciprocal trade agreements and in halting communist expansion. Americans must "steer clear of national selfishness," he wrote; we must not "draw into ourselves and become selfish either as an individual or a nation" and must "assum[e] the proper attitude towards our responsibilities of world leadership."[32]

Evins' first committee assignment fittingly placed him on the Committee on Veterans' Affairs, which he found personally meaningful.[33] By his second term he was appointed to the Select Committee on Small Business and soon chaired its Subcommittee on Federal Regulatory Agencies. Utilizing his past experience with the FTC he believed a critical function of Congress was to act as a watchdog to monitor and check excesses in business and in federal agencies. Later he chaired Subcommittee No. 1 that directly oversaw the federal Small Business Administration. From 1963 on he chaired the full House Committee on Small Business for the remainder of his Congressional career.[34]

Evins aspired for a seat on the Committee on Appropriations. He quickly saw that "[s]ome committees—the Appropriations Committee, for example—have achieved such high respect that their decisions are seldom seriously questioned and are difficult to overturn when they are questioned" because the committee's expertise influenced successful passage of its legislation.[35] "After my election to the House in 1946 I made it a point to observe . . . where the true sources of power existed in Congress—and it became obvious to me that the appropriations committees were the key to the assuring the success or failure of most programs . . . for the nation . . . [because] without funding, no program or project can be initiated and advanced to construction."[36] By 1953—at the beginning of his fourth term and after six years in Congress—he earned an Appropriations Committee appointment and relinquished his seat on Veterans Affairs. He was placed on two powerful subcommittees. One was the Appropriations Subcommittee on Independent Offices, which appropriated the federal budgets for the Federal Communications Commission (FCC), Interstate Commerce Commission (ICC), Securities and Exchange Commission (SEC), General Services Administration (GSA), Veterans Affairs (VA), and Federal Aviation Administration (FAA), as well as many more federal agencies, including the Public Housing Administration (later Housing and Urban Development [HUD]) and later agencies such as the National Aeronautics and Space Administration (NASA).[37] The other was the Appropriations Subcommittee on Public Works that oversaw and funded the Atomic Energy Commission (AEC), the U.S. Army Corps of Engineers, water services of the Department of the Interior such as the Bureau of Reclamation, and many regional power administrations, including TVA. Independent Offices was, to him, a more prestigious subcommittee, but Public Works was more important to him regionally because it dealt with federal agencies immediately affecting Tennesseans and their daily lives.[38]

At the behest of the House speaker, Evins also served on the House Ethics Committee for several years. The Ethics Committee examined issues of personal conduct by congressmen and conflicts of interest. It established a mechanism for ongoing internal housecleaning, to hold members accountable and provide constituents assurance of internal quality controls. Evins' selection to the committee indicated the regard with which his colleagues held him, as a member whose "unassailable personal life" was above reproach. His squeaky-clean record and discomfort with other lawmakers' peccadilloes were widely attested, even by his detractors.[39]

In terms of historic legacy, political perception now is primarily framed around a politician's positions on two pivotal themes during the era when Evins sat in Congress: race and the war in Vietnam. By no one's evaluation of history could Evins be construed as ahead of his time on race. He was not. He grew up in the era of white and male preeminence. That being said he kept maturing into a broader acceptance of a genuinely diverse America; he changed as society changed. He did not lead in the new vision. Neither was he a racist, Dixiecrat, nor "neobourbon." He was proud of the fact that Tennessee, a border state, had been "last in, first out" of the Confederacy and was distinctly different from the Deep South. He abhorred the bigotry and classism that the entrenched Deep South vigorously defended. Even so, he voted with them on occasion.[40]

Congressman Joe L. Evins at his desk in Washington, D.C. Credit: Joe L. Evins Papers, Tennessee Tech University Archives.

Evins voted against the 1964 Civil Rights bill, as did liberal Tennessee Democratic Senator Albert Gore Sr. and Senator Herb Walters. In 1965 Evins supported the Voting Rights bill, as did Senator Gore and Senator Ross Bass.[41] Earlier, during Eisenhower's presidency, neither Evins nor any of the Tennessee Democratic House members voted "Aye" on the Civil Rights Acts of 1957 and 1960. Senators Estes Kefauver and Gore, along with Nashville Congressman Percy Priest, were the only Democratic members of the Tennessee delegation who refused to sign the Southern Manifesto in 1956. All three were re-elected, although Priest and Kefauver died in office not long thereafter.

Evins' acquiescence to the Southern Manifesto is subject to debate. In publications of the full manifesto and its signatories the name Joe L. Evins is missing; he has even been explicitly identified as a non-signer.[42] Conversely, he is discussed as, indeed, having signed it.[43] As difficult as it is to read, the manifesto as released was actually a watered-down document that underwent multiple rewrites to persuade southern moderates to endorse it.[44] Apparently Evins signed at the eleventh hour and declared that doing so was irrelevant.[45] He endured both the drubbing that the *Tennessean* rightly gave him for his lack of courage and the letters of appreciation he received from state conservatives for his "wise" decision.[46] Evins, though an admirer of Kefauver's political courage, did not venture far ahead of the values of his constituents. "He's no Kefauver," it was said of him. "He's cautious." Even so he was recognized as "more liberal than his district."[47] Evins may have been one of those who shrank at signing the manifesto, but whose pragmatism in so doing permitted his re-election. His votes on race through the years did not deviate much from that pattern.[48]

Joe Evins fully backed President Lyndon B. Johnson's mission in Vietnam and kept faith with President Richard M. Nixon and U.S. Secretary of State Henry Kissinger's efforts to develop an exit strategy. Evins was heartsick about the war draining funds from domestic projects he valued, the bombing and devastation in Southeast Asia, and the loss of American lives. Even so the errors of appeasement and fear of global communism weighed heavily, and convinced him to stay the course defending America's military objectives in Vietnam. While eager to see the conflict over and the troops safely back home, he did not campaign openly to that end like his colleague Gore who suffered political repercussions due to his stance against the war.[49]

Like President Johnson, Evins believed the best aspect of national service was being in the position to support domestic programs that more equitably distributed power and access, dispersed federal dollars to those in need, and provided better opportunities for millions of Americans. In 1965

Joe L. Evins with the Appalachian Regional Commission. Credit: Joe L. Evins Papers, Tennessee Tech University Archives.

alone, Evins supported Great Society programs and voted for the Hospital Insurance Program for the Aged under the Social Security Act creating Medicare, the new Immigration and Nationality Act, and D.C. Home Rule, in addition to the Voting Rights Act. He wrote that year,

> [T]he administration of justice requires that the letter of the law must be combined with the spirit of the law. In the Congress, we are now writing many new laws. . . in the economic and social spheres. . . . We—the Congress, our country, the American people—are engaged in a continuing effort to bring the spirit of justice, of fairness, into the rules of law by which [we] must live together and labor together. . .enab[ling] us to be compassionate, to be helpful, to give people a fair chance.[50]

Perhaps if a single dominant stereotype has stuck to the image of Evins it is that of a southern congressman who funneled federally funded projects to his state and district. And that image would be true. Evins was certainly a pork-barrel congressman whose earmarks brought jobs to his area. Detractors deemed his rural Middle Tennessee constituency "by far one of the most pampered districts in the country."[51] Evins was not embarrassed by that perception. He honestly thought that was his job, and he delivered. A member of the Tennessee General Assembly said that every county in the state wanted to be in Evins' district.[52] He unabashedly channeled monies directly into his own home town and home county through War on Poverty programs such as Model Cities and the Appalachian Regional Commission, localized opportunities for development that were deemed excesses of congressional "parochialism" by some.[53] Because of his ability to deliver federally financed programs to his district, he was considered unbeatable.[54] LBJ recognized that Evins' achievements for his district meant quality of life improvements such that "[g]enerations of Americans yet unborn will benefit from the labors of this man."[55] While Evins earned a reputation for bringing large projects to Tennessee, smaller meat-and-potatoes enterprises peppered throughout rural communities over the course of his thirty years in Washington were the projects that made him most proud.[56]

> [T]he Fourth District and the State of Tennessee—since Joe L. Evins reached his influential position in the House—have seen giant dams begin to rise —have seen Post Offices built or modernized in every county, have seen a flow of Federal assistance for a great variety of projects—libraries, airports, sewage and water facilities, watershed projects, streets, health centers, hospitals, and national guard armories, among others.[57]

At the time of his retirement, Evins compiled a summary overview of his achievements over thirty years. He called these "solid investments in America that yield rich dividends in benefits to our people."[58] Political activist Ralph Nader's organization wrote pejoratively that "he's a real dollars-and-cents type politician" whose "accomplishments could best be tabulated on an adding machine."[59] Evins' constituents appreciated his efforts on their behalf.

Relationships between Evins and his constituents were personal.[60] Authentic and unpretentious, he liked people and campaigned face to face. He held his hat in his hand, knocked on doors, then sat and visited in people's living rooms. When he went calling he often carted along his family; he believed "short visits make long friends." His old style campaigning took him into every little community, all the byways, towns, and county seats, with lots of hand shaking, visits to hardware stores and barber shops, and hanging around the courthouse square. He believed in asking each individual for his or her vote and "pressing the flesh." There was no artifice of folksiness. He never drove a pickup truck nor wore a plaid flannel shirt to promote a good-old-boy image. Quite the opposite, he always wore a shirt and tie—and his signature up-curled fedora, with a white cotton handkerchief, a buckeye, and a pocketknife in his pocket. He believed respectable people dressed properly, and that constituents expected their congressman to look dignified. He was genuinely egalitarian and honestly a people person. He drew his energy from Tennesseans, especially rural Middle Tennesseans. He created friendships wherever he traveled and remembered everyone he met, even years later. Making people know they were important was sincere for him and was his hallmark, which endeared him to his voters.

Evins whittled with folks around the courthouse square and talked politics; it was an easy way to be together. He truly loved to whittle. It calmed him. He whittled at home in the side yard sitting by himself in his lawn chair, thinking. He took pleasure in the way the cedar shavings curled from the bottom of his knife. He never made anything; he was not a craftsman. He simply liked whittling and carried sticks of Tennessee cedar with him; he kept them in his desk, in his chest of drawers at home, and in his Dopp Kit. He whittled on sticks folks offered him or would pass around his own cedar and invite others to whittle with him.

Evins taught his children from their earliest years how to properly shake hands. He considered a good strong handshake an outward manifestation of a person's character and inner fortitude. He was put off by a tepid, fishy handshake. He instructed his family to introduce themselves to every individual. "Hello, I'm Joe L. Evins. Good to meet you." "I'm Joe L. Evins. Glad to make your acquaintance." "I'm Joe L. Evins. Good to see you again." He believed it was the polite, gracious, and right thing to do when you meet or re-meet someone; never presume anyone knows your name, don't put him on the spot, help him out, put him at ease. The response hopefully would be that the person would then supply his own name. If Evins had any pet peeve it was when people would withhold their names to test him: "You remember me, don't you, Joe?" and then wait to see if Evins could conjure up a name. He typically could, as he had an inherent gift of being exceptionally good at people's names. When on occasion he did not immediately remember, Evins was upset with himself and quite embarrassed.

Evins believed his job demanded open accessibility. People knocked on the front door of his home in Smithville daily, unannounced, with no appointment. All were welcome. He was always dressed in a shirt and tie ready to receive guests when at home. A tray with ice water, iced tea, or lemonade was always offered. The living room was kept straight and the front porch swept, ready for callers.[61]

A dedicated letter writer, Evins answered almost every letter personally. He had fine secretaries who took rapid dictation, but he personally penned numerous letters with his heavy fountain pen with its wide nib.

Keeping in written contact to show appreciation was a strong value to him. He even wrote thank you notes for thank you notes he received. Whether away or at home, Evins kept up a brisk correspondence.[62]

As a person who personally tried to live a life of moderation, he advocated tolerance and compromise. He knew an effective statesman had to be flexible in order to get things done in Washington. A history major in college, he spoke frequently about the great compromises of U.S. history, in the writing of the Constitution and with major pieces of legislation. He railed against obstructionists. He would grow impatient and "get the thumps" when do-nothing congressmen with no forward-thinking ideas acted only to block legislation. Anything was possible with a willingness to discuss and compromise, and to speak with a civil tongue. Evins honored the tradition of graciousness and gentility that characterized congressional process during his time. The ability to disagree vehemently with an esteemed colleague but shake hands and converse courteously was important to him.[63]

His moderation was expressed in his own demeanor. His vocabulary was reasoned, not harsh. Off-color jokes made him uncomfortable, and friends' disrespect of their wives personally disturbed him. Loyalty was of primary importance to him. Yet he did not like appearing to be a prude. At parties in Washington he would nurse a drink through the evening. "The Evins [*sic*] are good honorable people who have not been seduced by Washington society" and "Joe isn't on the cocktail circuit," were comments from the time.[64]

Evins' Church of Christ background influenced his behavior. He never missed church on Sundays and took communion weekly, although he did not always love church. Evins considered some ministers, as with obstructionist politicians, dour and not uplifting. He wanted sermons with inspiring messages, not merely lists of sins. He preferred enlightenment over diatribe. He took notes during negative sermons with suggestions for the preacher about how to elevate the dialogue and provide ideas for personal betterment. More than likely his regular ministers gritted their teeth when they saw Brother Joe writing during the lesson. Evins' faith was ecumenical, respecting all religions; he certainly did not hold to any exclusivity of his denomination. He enjoyed worshiping with other churches and did so on a regular basis. But the Church of Christ was his home church and he remained loyal to it.[65]

Quite frankly, Evins' true faith was in the Democratic Party. "Do unto others" and "suffer the little children to come unto me" were philosophies he thought should be fundamental tenets of good government.[66] He credited his party with standing for the arc of the moral universe that bends towards justice. He understood that progress towards wider access to equality was what America is all about and the Democratic Party represented the means toward that end. He always said, "The more you learn, the more you study, the more you open yourself to new ideas, the more broad-minded Democrat you become." He also said Democrats were proud of being Democrats and would readily tell you so, but "Independents are really Republicans, just too embarrassed to say so."

Evins felt very strongly about the importance of the separation of church and state. He interpreted the *Engel v. Vitale* 1962 Supreme Court decision to his constituents saying that the Court had not "ruled out prayer in the public schools" but instead had ruled to "protect the free exercise of religion and preserve the principle of the separation of church and state."[67] He would be disconcerted by the present-day injection of fundamentalist religion into the political arena.[68] He aspired to modesty in his religious faith, that his expression of it be humble and not used for show to gain political credibility. Religious fearmongering surfaced during the 1960 presidential election. Few stories showcase Evins' progressivism better than when he took on conservative forces in Tennessee and the country by addressing it within his own church.

Joe and Ann Evins attended the Democratic convention in Los Angeles in the summer of 1960, fully supporting fellow southerner Lyndon Baines Johnson as the nominee. When they returned a week later, however, both wore Kennedy buttons. Kennedy's Catholicism was a sticking point in the South, especially among fundamentalist Christians. Although Evins was broad minded and ecumenical, his denomination was known for strict construction of the Bible and narrow interpretation of many issues of the day. Evins' mother cast Catholics in unflattering light, so he understood the mind set and culture in which those prejudices thrived. Southern churches were bulwarks of protectionism against trumped-up fears that the Vatican was exercising undue influence over a Catholic president, a papal puppet dictating American policy.

The weekend of October 9, 1960, the Evinses were visiting their eldest daughter Joanna at Vanderbilt University. They picked her up to attend Sunday worship service at Hillsboro Church of Christ, home pulpit of one of the church's most preeminent and respected ministers, Batsell Barrett Baxter. Unwittingly, they walked into a service in which Baxter denounced Catholicism for press coverage. News cameras recorded Baxter and reactions to his sermon for a Chet Huntley NBC news program to air on national television. Evins later learned that Brother Baxter had been preaching a series of sermons about the spread of the Catholic Church and presumably of the dangers inherent in Senator Kennedy's bid for the White House. Evins regarded the service as blatantly political and a set-up. He refused to let the moment pass. The Evins family sat on a back pew when they arrived. After the sermon, before a final hymn and closing prayer, Evins walked along a side aisle to the front pew and sat beside Baxter. Having served in the House of Representatives for over a decade, Evins was known in Nashville, particularly in the Church of Christ community. He quietly asked Baxter for permission to address the congregation and the minister acceded.

Unfortunately, what Evins said in rebuttal to Baxter's sermon was not recorded. Family narrative says Evins told the congregation he appreciated Brother Baxter and valued his wisdom and spiritual guidance, but on this particular issue Evins wanted to point out that he knew Jack Kennedy well, having been friends with him for fourteen years. Not once had Kennedy's religious affiliation inappropriately influenced his actions as a public servant. Separation of church and state was a founding principle that Kennedy highly valued, and Evins could personally confirm. Evins reminded the congregation that people of faith must defend the Christian value of tolerance. The role of the church was to sustain faith and offer hope, he argued, not to dictate negative politics nor incite fear. Evins thanked the congregants and stepped down. What was caught on tape were Evins' comments exiting the sanctuary. The incident was later reported in the national news.[69]

Responses poured into Evins' office from all over the country. Reactions were fairly evenly split. Some irate Americans accused him of being a communist, a papist, and a sinner. Others condemned him to hell, saying he committed a "betrayal of the Church," an "indiscretion," and an "outrageous action." Others sent him unexpected statements of approval:

> I am proud for the stand you took Sunday morning at Hillsboro.
>
> I was proud to be a Tennessean when I read . . . your words [which were] the words of a true Christian who comprehends the plain teachings of the Bible on the question of tolerance.
>
> [I want to] congratulate you on your courage to speak up against prejudice and bigotry.
>
> [O]ur more intelligent southern leaders take a very forward position.
>
> We don't believe many people want to go to worship and find they are attending a "Republican Rally."
>
> I think you did just what you should have done.
>
> [W]hen you run for re-election we will work that much harder for you.
>
> The country needs more men of your caliber.
>
> Thanks again Mr. Evins for your stand on the religious issue.[70]

Beyond separation of church and state, Evins considered the federal government critical to the well being of the nation. He appreciated the complexity of the American governmental framework and the system of checks and balances established by the Founders.[71] He believed with conviction that a great nation looks out for the country as a whole, and takes care of its own, each person contributing to the common good through civic and economic participation. "No one likes to pay taxes," he would say, "but we do it—honestly, with right heart—because it's the right thing to do. It's the great national honor system."

The role of government to regulate business was a function that promoted domestic tranquility. Evins was both pro-business and pro-regulation. A strong advocate and friend of thriving business, he opposed "the oppression of vested interests," differentiating "between business and brigandage." He fought for a nation that valued the working man, "the common man's dignity," and endorsed regulations that kept competition open rather than an economy manipulated by "the privilege of the mighty financiers."[72] Evins shared the Small Business Committee's disgust of economic power in the hands of the few manipulated by Wall Street. He recoiled at concentrated power that schemed, wore down ordinary men and women, and operated by the laws of the jungle. He materially loathed corporate callousness.[73] For Evins small business meant opening competition widely, helping regular Americans start their own enterprise by preserving a fair and just playing field for entrepreneurship.[74] He termed small business "the seedbed of our American free enterprise system" and fought "to preserve, promote and perpetuate our American competitive free enterprise."[75] He felt strongly that regulatory controls established during the New Deal needed to be maintained and rigorously enforced for competition to thrive in an open, creative business environment and to protect average Americans from the avarice of securities brokers and the investment industry. That so much of the regulatory framework has been eviscerated in subsequent years would have distressed him.

As for business development, Evins enthusiastically sought industries looking for healthy, hard-working communities in which to plant new roots. He labored intentionally to bring companies to Middle Tennessee. In the 1960s, with its focus on urban renewal and inner city development, Evins continually reminded Capitol Hill and the White House that developing diversified economies in rural communities generated incentives for Americans in the countryside to remain there and construct futures in their home towns, while stemming the flow of population into urban centers by families looking for employment. Evins believed that building up rural America benefitted cities. Toward that objective, in addition to bringing federal projects and federal dollars to Tennessee, Evins was instrumental in fostering platforms for new business start-ups and intervening to get outside businesses and industries into the area.[76]

On leaving Congress in 1976, the final wisdom Evins imparted to his colleagues on the Hill was to maintain strong regulatory oversight not only of corporate excesses but also of federal agencies that exceed their congressional and presidential mandates and forget their original principles and objectives.

> Oversight is a major responsibility of the Congress, not only to insure that agencies carry out Congressional intent but also to make sure the Federal bureaucracy does not go beyond the authority granted to it by Congress. . . .There is no corner of the Federal bureaucracy that should be safe from inquiry or from the hot breath of congressional committee hearings and investigations. Congress must continue to be the watchdog of the people—to serve the public interest.[77]

He cited painful wrongdoings by public officials who should have been above reproach, conflicts of interest, sweetheart deals with contracts that should never have been awarded, and excessive expansion of power by

Joe L. Evins celebrates twenty-five years in Congress. Credit: Joe L. Evins Papers, Tennessee Tech University Archives.

boards, commissions, departments, and bureaus that should have been, and must continue to be, reined in, regulated, and watched like a hawk. He included the TVA in that assessment. As much as he valued and appreciated the work of TVA he was adamant that it must not be allowed to operate with impunity. Congress must hold the agencies to the highest standards, to which Congress must hold itself as well.[78]

Evins was not ahead of his time, he was of it. Progress for rural Tennessee, opportunities and protections that benefitted the little guy, and the honor of public service were his guideposts. He was not a frontrunner on social issues, but continued to learn. By his own value system he was open to change, and social changes allowed him to live more truly aligned with his own ideals and principles. He had the heart of a servant and mind of a student. By his own philosophy he espoused forward thinking put into action. His love of Tennessee and Tennesseans informed all his accomplishments. He was of their culture and saw people as good. He deplored reactionaries, naysayers, rightwingers, and those who blocked progress. He was hardly a liberal, but he was most assuredly not a conservative. He was a purposeful political moderate who aspired to moderation in all things.[79]

A public figure's historic legacy represents the interplay of political record, productivity, personal ethics, and interpersonal human dynamics. Evins was a progressive rural southern Democrat who brought good programs home to his counties, contributed to elevating the local standard of living across thirty years, and represented his region very well. He had the common touch, was valued and respected by the people of Middle Tennessee, and he in turn cherished the Upper Cumberland with the friends and neighbors he cared about most. When he retired from Congress in 1976, he returned to Smithville and to "the good people of Middle Tennessee" for the remainder of his days.

Evins believed in the work of the United States Congress and was pleased to have represented Tennessee in Congress for three decades. He deemed Congress, "the branch of our government closest to the people," the great "bulwark of our democratic system."[80] He saw Congress as the national mediator, the voice of average Americans speaking to the preserves of the advantaged. "Congress stands in the middle, endeavoring to serve," he wrote.[81] He could have written those words about himself, because he too stood in the middle and endeavored to serve.

NOTES

1. Carroll Van West, "Joseph Landon Evins, 1910-1984," *Tennessee Encyclopedia of History and Culture* (Nashville: Rutledge Hill Press, 1998), pp. 294-295.
2. Joe L. Evins invoked the old phrase "moderation in all things" multiple times almost every day of his life, throughout his congressional career and to the end of his life; see moderation statement in *Congressional Record,* 91st Congress, 2d session (October 1, 1970), pp. 3640-45; Harry Clor, *On Moderation: Defending an Ancient Virtue in a Modern World* (Waco, Texas: Baylor University Press, 2008).
3. Susan B. Graves, *Evins of Tennessee: Twenty-five Years in Congress* (New York: Popular Library, 1971).
4. G. Frank Burns, unpublished manuscript, c. 1987, about Congressman Evins, in the Joe L. Evins Collection, Tennessee Technological University Archives, Record Group 1. Hereafter JLE Collection.
5. For assistance with research and for the wealth of material in its holdings, sincere thanks are due to the University Archives of Volpe Library, Tennessee Technological University (TTU), which houses the Joe L. Evins congressional collection and personal papers. Evins' papers helped establish the TTU Archives. Personal appreciation is especially expressed to University Archivist Mancil Johnson, for his knowledge, generosity of time, unfailing helpfulness, and graciousness, always. His work on the JLE Collection has made its materials available for research. In 2008 Carolyn Powell, then a graduate student in public history at Middle Tennessee State University, produced a documentary about the congressman in cooperation with the archives. Powell's thesis points to the richness of the JLE Collection and may encourage other researchers to delve more deeply into its resources.
6. 1946 campaign poster, flat files, Drawer 5, JLE Collection. JLE's last election was in 1974.
7. Born October 24, 1910, DeKalb County, Tennessee; died March 31, 1984, Vanderbilt Hospital, Nashville.
8. The family name was originally Navin; the core letters "vin" seem to have transferred from JLE's great-great grandfather's Irish last name into Evins, which he came to use in the United States.
9. No Evins household is entered in the 1840 DeKalb County census, but the family appears in the 1850 census. See Joe L. Evins, *The Evins Family: A Genealogical Study* (Washington, D.C.: Joe L. Evins, 1938), p. 10. The original log cabin, built by JLE's great-great grandfather and later sheathed in white clapboard, was the farmhouse JLE's grandparents lived in through the 1930s, and JLE preserved through his lifetime. It was sold by its inheritor after JLE's death in 1984. Not until the house was torn down in 1994 was its log core visible. The original pioneer cabin, built of massive chestnut logs, with window frames pinned by eight-inch chestnut pegs, provides structural evidence that the Evinses settled in the Upper Cumberland by the early 1800s.
10. According to family history Jake Smith moved around the country, working in the North for years at a time, but he tended to return to the Evins home, where he lived until his death at ninety-three in 1949. He is buried with the Evins family in Town Cemetery in Smithville. In the 1870 census Jacob Smith is listed as

a fourteen-year-old black laborer living in the household of Dr. John A. Evins, father of William Sellars Evins.

11. Thomas Gray Webb, *A Bicentennial History of DeKalb County, Tennessee* (Smithville, Tennessee: Bradley Printing Co., 1995), p. 13; "A.J. Goodson, Postmaster," *Smithville Review* (May 20, 1901) and Smithville, Tennessee, Postmasters, Microfilm M841 *Record of Appointment of Postmasters, 1832–September 30, 1971,* National Archives. Copies on file in Thomas G. Webb Genealogy Room, Justin Potter Library, Smithville, Tennessee.
12. Myrtie Goodson Evins, a businesswoman in her own right, had been a clerk at the Smithville post office in her teens and was an admirable partner in, and force behind, Edgar's financial success. Edgar launched a bus company between Smithville and the train station in Watertown in 1920. The bus company expanded its routes and added a petroleum business to supply its gasoline. Both companies eventually sold, and Edgar's grandsons later turned their roadside properties into the Cracker Barrel restaurant chain.
13. Evins, *Family,* 14; Thomas G. Webb, *DeKalb County* (Memphis: Memphis State University Press, 1986), p. 86.
14. Evins, *Family,* 19; Webb, *A Bicentennial History,* 7.
15. Evins, *Family,* 18. Cordell Hull was a Pickett County native residing in Carthage, while Ewin L. Davis was from Tullahoma.
16. Graves, *Evins of Tennessee,* 17.
17. Box 732, File 6, Military Record, Report of Physical Exam, JLE Collection.
18. "Broadcast—January 25–26, 1947," Box 437, File 3, Speeches by Evins, JLE Collection.
19. Graves, *Evins of Tennessee,* 40. Chairman Davis had formerly represented Tennessee in the U.S. House of Representatives.
20. Box 731, File 6, FTC Correspondence, File 7, FTC Material, File 11, FTC Cases, JLE Collection.
21. Box 731, File 6, Correspondence with Judge Ewin L. Davis, JLE Collection.
22. Evins and Smartt married in 1935.
23. Box 454, File 2, Evins Biographical Sketch; Box 731, File 6, FTC Correspondence, JLE Collection. The Evinses' third daughter, the author, was born in Washington during the congressional years.
24. Box 731, File 6, FTC Correspondence, File 20, Joe L. Evins Orders; Box 732, File 6, Military Record; Box 733, Files 4–6, Legal Cases from JAG Corps, JLE Collection. Summer 1945 after VE day, Evins was moved to JAG operations at Versailles. Brigadier General E.C. McNeil, Assistant Judge Advocate General and the general under whom Evins worked as Board of Review officer for the JAG ETO, wrote all his ETO officers in mid-May of 1945 that the war had provided "a thorough and comprehensive trial of practical application" of the nation's "system of military justice" and that JAG attorneys had had an unusual opportunity to observe the operation of the system through intensive actual experience . . . [and so Gen. McNeil's JAG officers were] invited . . . to communicate . . . a frank critique of the system of military justice based upon your actual observation and experience with your recommendations for changes, whether fundamental, substantive, or procedural. . . .

It was after this memo on the need for a reevaluation of military justice procedure that certain JAG officers, including Evins, were removed from Paris to Versailles. What went on in Versailles during the summer of 1945, presumably in preparation for the Nuremberg trials, is not to be found in any of Evins' otherwise comprehensive JAG files. Evins continued in the ETO until fall 1945, was released from active duty and back in Tennessee by November 1945, but was not discharged from the Army until 1946. In February of 1946 General McNeil wrote to him of members of their ETO JAG Office who were then in Nuremburg. In October of 1946 Major General Thomas H. Green, The Judge Advocate General in Washington, also wrote to Major Evins stating that "the shortage of trained judge advocates has become critical, particularly in the European Theater" and asked if Evins "would be interested in returning to active duty . . . for service in Europe. . . . " He was told his family could join him overseas. One of Evins' former colleagues wrote from "Dachau Detachment" in November 1947: "This is quite an experience here Joe. I am defending 52 former S.S. officers all accused of murder...a rough and tough outfit. . . ." Evins was not part of the post-war legal cleanup in Europe and did not take up General Green on his offer of a new JAG posting to Europe. At the time of his receipt of the JAG redeployment invitation, barely home at year, Joe L. Evins had been involved for months in a heated race for the United States House of Representatives, had already won a hard-fought primary, and by November secured the general election. He was headed back to Washington, D.C., with his family. E.C. McNeil, letter May 16, 1945, to All Judge Advocate Officers, Box 731, File 20; E.C. McNeil, letters Feb. 7 and Feb. 18, 1946, to Major Joe L. Evins, Smithville, Tennessee, Box 733, File 3; Thomas H. Green, letter Oct. 7, 1946, to Major Joe L. Evins, Smithville, Tennessee, Box 733, File 3; Chick O'Connor, letter Nov. 15, 1946, Box 733, File 3, JLE Collection.

25. Joe L. Evins, letter Nov. 10, 1945, to Brigadier General E.C. McNeil, Saint Cloud, France, Box 733, File 3; "Evins Makes Opening Speech on WSM," Box 454, File 4, Evins Advertisements, JLE Collection.
26. Kenneth McKellar chaired the Senate Appropriations Committee and was a force to be reckoned with. He was the inspiration for Senator Seabright Cooley in Alan Drury's *Advise and Consent* and in part for the *Looney Tunes* cartoon character Foghorn Leghorn. Tom Stewart gained national attention as the prosecutor in the Scope's Trial.
27. Boxes 452–454, 1946 Campaign; Boxes 454–459, Evins Clippings and Election Returns, JLE Collection. These boxes contain voluminous materials associated with the first congressional campaign. In his fifteen elections to the House, he ran unopposed in the Democratic primary in eleven elections, winning his four opposed primaries by 58 percent (1946), 84 percent (1950), 79 percent (1952), and 84 percent (1964). He had Republican opposition five times and won those elections by 88 percent (1962), 90 percent (1966), 76 percent (1968), 83 percent (1970), and 81 percent (1972). In no election was there ever Democratic and Republican opposition in the same election cycle; opponents challenged him in either the August party primary or in the November general election, but never in both. After the first campaign, Evins' only other serious challenges, when his vote margins fell below 80 percent, were in the 1952 primary and the 1968 general election. His

victory percentage dropped in 1952 with redistricting; two primary opponents were favorite sons in their respective counties, and Dwight D. Eisenhower took the White House. It dropped again with redistricting and the Richard M. Nixon presidential election in 1968.

28. His district had four different county structures over thirty years, having at one time or another encompassed thirty-one of Tennessee's ninety-six counties: the Fifth District of eleven counties in middle and southern Tennessee, 1946–1952; the Fourth District of twenty-three counties from the Kentucky line to the Alabama line and pushing the district more to the east, 1952–1968; the Fourth District of twenty-one counties, losing the southernmost counties and shifting the northern sector farther into eastern Tennessee, 1968–1972; and the Fourth District at the time of his retirement, of twenty-five counties, again stretching from Kentucky to Alabama and tacking back into a more classic Middle Tennessee district, losing the most northeastern counties, 1972–1976. Campaign files 453–5, 457–5, 463–5, 469–1, 466–7, JLE Collection.
29. See for example Robert L. Keele, letter to J. Edgar Evins, Dec. 20, 1949, Box 720, File 7, Correspondence with James Edgar Evins, JLE Collection.
30. Diemer Smartt to Mary A. Evins, personal communication, April 3, 1984.
31. Kate S. James, first woman Registrar in DeKalb County, "Joe L. Evins Receives the Endorsement of His Home Folks, Here's What They Say," Box 454, File 4, Evins Advertisements, JLE Collection.
32. Joe L. Evins, "Address before Maryville College Alumni, Washington, D.C., June 6, 1947," p. 8, Box 437, File 3, Speeches by Evins, JLE Collection.
33. Boxes 569–573, JLE Collection.
34. Boxes 555–561; Box 561, Files 2–3, Small Business Correspondence; Boxes 561–569, JLE Collection. During most of JLE's years in Congress the House Small Business Committee was a Select Committee; it became a permanent standing committee in 1975.
35. Joe L. Evins, *Understanding Congress* (New York: Clarkson N. Potter, Inc., 1963), 199–200.
36. Joe L. Evins, "On Serving 30 Years in Congress," 1976 Capitol Comments by Evins, Box 737, File 2, JLE Collection.
37. Boxes 496–519, 521–525, JLE Collection.
38. Boxes 496–519, 525–554, JLE Collection. For several years in the 1960s and into the early 1970s, Evins chaired both the Independent Offices and Public Works Subcommittees of the House Appropriations Committee *and* the House Small Business Committee and beginning in 1965 the House Patronage Committee, an internal committee appointed by the Speaker to allocate patronage jobs on Capitol Hill such as elevator operators, mail room clerks, police, pages, and doormen. See Box 520 for records of Patronage Committee, JLE Collection.
39. Box 520 for records of Ethics Committee, JLE Collection; Luther J. Carter, "Rep. Joe Evins: NSF and NASA Get a New Master of Finance," *Science* 155: 3764 (Feb. 17, 1967), p. 810; Anne Millet, "Joe L. Evins, Democratic Representative from Tennessee," Ralph Nader Congress Project, "Citizens Look at Congress" (August 1972), pp. 9–10, Box 467, File 6, JLE Collection.
40. See Numan V. Bartley, *The Rise of Massive Resistance: Race and Politics in the South in the 1950's* (Baton Rouge: Louisiana State University Press, 1969).

41. Governor Frank Clement appointed Walters to the U.S. Senate after the untimely death of Estes Kefauver. Ross Bass replaced Walters.
42. Brent J. Aucoin, "The Southern Manifesto and Southern Opposition to Desegregation," *Arkansas Historical Quarterly* 55: 2 (Summer 1996), p. 193; "Court's Ruling on Schools Called Abuse of Judiciary," *Nashville Tennessean*, March 13, 1956, p. 5.
43. Tony Badger, "Southerners Who Refused to Sign the Southern Manifesto," *Historical Journal* 42: 2 (June 1999), p. 526; "Three Above Expediency," *Nashville Tennessean*, March 14, 1956, p. 10.
44. Aucoin, "Manifesto and Southern Opposition."
45. Badger, "Southerners Who Refused," 526; "Three Above Expediency," 10.
46. *Ibid.*; Bill Litchford, letter to Evins, June 6, 1956, Box 475, File 9, JLE Collection.
47. Carter, "New Master of Finance," 808; Joe L. Evins, Endorsement of Kefauver speech at Kefauver rally, Bethesda, Maryland, April 30, 1952, Box 475, File 9, JLE Collection; Dewey W. Grantham, "Tennessee and Twentieth-Century American Politics," *Tennessee History: The Land, the People, and the Culture*, Carroll Van West, ed. (Knoxville: University of Tennessee Press, 1998), p. 219.
48. Grantham, "Tennessee and Twentieth-Century American Politics," 221; Badger, "Southerners Who Refused," 526.
49. Carter, "New Master of Finance," 808; "Three Above Expediency," 10.
50. Joe L. Evins, "Family Reunion July 1965," pp. 8–9, Box 719, File 8, JLE Collection. In 1965 Evins also voted for the Public Works and Economic Development Act and the Appalachian Regional Development Act. In 1964 Evins headed LBJ's presidential campaign in Tennessee and brought in the state's electoral votes for Johnson.
51. Millett, "Democratic Representative," 1.
52. *Ibid.*, 2.
53. Bernard H. Ross and Myron A. Levine, *Urban Politics: Cities and Suburbs in a Global Age*, 8th ed. (Armonk, New York: M.E. Sharpe, 2012), p. 277; Sean J. Savage, *JFK, LBJ, and the Democratic Party* (Albany: State University of New York Press, 2004), p. 138.
54. Carter, "New Master of Finance," 810.
55. Lyndon B. Johnson, Introduction, in Graves' *Evins of Tennessee*, 7. Monies for projects through TVA, Corps of Engineers, Arnold Engineering Development Center and Tennessee Space Institute in Tullahoma, and the Atomic Energy Commission at Oak Ridge were big-ticket operations that demonstrated Evins' Washington clout.
56. Evins, "On Serving 30 Years in Congress."
57. "Joe Evins—Legend in His Own Time," *Cookeville Citizen* (Cookeville, Tennessee), October 18, 1966, p. 9, Box 811, JLE Collection.
58. Joe L. Evins, "The Committee That Makes Things Move," in "On Serving 30 Years in Congress," 1976, Capitol Comments by Evins, Box 737, File 2, JLE Collection. He itemized the hundreds of reservoirs, waterways, fish hatcheries, dams (seven of them), breeder reactors, test facilities, electrification projects, buildings, bridges, highways, airports, libraries, schools, training facilities, and the like that he steered through Congress, for Tennessee and the nation.
59. Millet, "Democratic Representative," 2.
60. See comments throughout scrapbook, Box 811, JLE Collection.
61. Evins told his daughters not to walk through the living room in hair curlers when there were guests; that was another pet peeve. In addition to dropping by, people

phoned him at home at all hours. His name was always in the phone directory, both the house in Smithville and the house in Washington. It was not uncommon for constituents whom he barely knew to call him in Washington in the wee hours of the morning from jail, drunk, asking him to make bail. He usually did. He would speak to the sheriff, promising to send a personal check in the morning if the sheriff released the constituent on good behavior.

62. "[B]usy as we get…we must not neglect writing," he penned to his parents and in-laws one Sunday from his office in Washington. His frequent reminders to his daughters included admonitions for increased letter writing and thank you notes. His daughter Joanna remembers his final tutorial to her, from his hospital bed, was that she respond speedily—since he was not physically able—to the thoughtful people who had sent him cards. Only a few hours before he passed away he dictated to her a thank you note for Speaker Tip O'Neill who had sent him a get-well message. See Joe L. Evins, letter to Edgar and Myrtie Evins and Judge Robert Smartt and Mrs. Alma Smartt, Sunday, Jan. 18, 1948, Box 722, File 6, Personal Family Correspondence, JLE Collection.
63. Evins, *Understanding Congress,* 129–130.
64. Carter, "New Master of Finance," 810.
65. He was particularly fond of small rural churches, African American churches, and demonstrative evangelical congregations. The Evinses never failed to attend Sunday services when on the road to Washington or Tennessee. The family always drove between the two destinations, a two-day trip before Interstate construction, or took the train between Knoxville and D.C.'s Union Station, because Evins never flew after WWII if he could avoid it.
66. Randall Balmer, "Jesus is Not a Republican," *Chronicle of Higher Education* 52: 42 (June 23, 2006), pp. B6-B9.
67. Evins, *Understanding Congress,* 262.
68. Randall Balmer, *Thy Kingdom Come: How the Religious Right Distorts the Faith and Threatens America* (Cambridge, Massachusetts; Basic Books, 2006), *God in the White House: How Faith Shaped the Presidency From John F. Kennedy to George W. Bush* (New York: Harper Collins, 2008).
69. James Talley, "Evins Mounts Pulpit, Answers Political Sermon: NBC Films Baxter Attack on Catholic Church But Not Reply," *Nashville Tennessean* (October 11, 1960), pp. 1–2; "Evins Rebuts Anti-Catholic Talk in Pulpit," *Washington Star* (October 11, 1960), p, C7; "Evins Defends JFK in Pulpit," *Knoxville News Sentinel* (October 12, 1960), p. 14; "Sermon Reply Scored: Representative is Chided for Rebuttal Given in Church," *New York Times* (October 21, 1960), p. 14; Carroll Kilpatrick "South's Political Battle Rages in Many Pulpits," *Washington Post* (October 24, 1960), pp. A1, A10; all in Box 477, File 4, Hillsboro Church of Christ Affair, JLE Collection.
70. Box 477, File 4, Hillsboro Church of Christ Affair, JLE Collection.
71. Evins, *Understanding Congress,* 281–290.
72. Joe L. Evins, "Pre-Jackson Birthday Speech," pp. 5–7, Doc. 30, Box 437, File 5, JLE Collection.
73. Evins, *Understanding Congress,* 291.

74. Dale Vineyard, "Congressional Committees on Small Business," *Midwest Journal of Political Science* 10: 3 (August 1966), p. 369.
75. Joe L. Evins, "Working for Small Business," in "On Serving 30 Years in Congress," 1976, Capitol Comments by Evins, Box 737, File 2, JLE Collection; Evins, *Understanding Congress*, 245.
76. Carter, "New Master of Finance," 810.
77. Joe L. Evins, "Parting Advice: Maintain Oversight," in "On Serving 30 Years in Congress," 1976, Capitol Comments by Evins, Box 737, File 2, JLE Collection.
78. *Ibid.*; James Branscome, "Destroy to Save? Power to Move Mountains," *Environment* 17: 6 (Sept. 1975); see also S. David Freeman, "The Nine Lives of TVA," *Environment* 27: 3 (April 1985); Brad Schrade and Anne Paine, "TVA Board Meets Behind Veil of Secrecy" and "Agency Created to be Run with Little Oversight," *Tennessean* (June 12, 2009), pp. 1A, 4A.
79. A Star Named Joe," *Tennessean Magazine*, October 16, 1966, p. 22, Box 811, JLE Collection.
80. Evins, *Understanding Congress*, 267.
81. *Ibid.*, 297.

LAWYERS AND LAW BREAKERS

7

"One of the Best-Hated Men of His Day"

John Catron, the Upper Cumberland's First Supreme Court Justice

Michael E. Birdwell and John B. Nisbet III

John Catron strode among the giants of his day, interacting with such luminaries as Andrew Jackson, James K. Polk, Thomas Hart Benton, Felix Grundy, Ephraim Foster, Hugh Lawson White, John Bell, John C. Breckenridge, David Crockett, Abraham Lincoln, and many others. A frontiersman cum Supreme Court Justice (on both the state and federal bench), Catron dispensed the law with empathy for the dispossessed, the poor, and those who had no public champion. Though he usually avoided the trappings of politics, on at least two critical occasions he caved-in to the will of special interests to devastating effects. A rough-hewn product of the Upper Cumberland of Kentucky and Tennessee, John Catron was a figure to be reckoned with in his day. From his humble beginnings he married well, wedding the cousin of James K. Polk's wife Sarah Childress, Matilda Childress, who introduced Catron to a more elite circle.

Justice John Catron handed down opinions that continue to have far-reaching implications to this day. He challenged the wisdom of allowing corporations the same rights as citizens under the law. Perhaps because he had no heir, Catron advocated property rights for women long before it became commonplace. His attitudes toward slavery stood diametrically opposed to most of his contemporary southerners. Though himself a slave owner, Catron argued that African Americans were human beings who held implicit rights. He advocated the same for Native Americans, until he reversed himself for political reasons. Perhaps it is because he was involved in cases that remain controversial, such as *The State v. Foreman,* which provided a rationale for Cherokee Removal, or his concurring opinion in *Dred Scott v. Sandford* based on a very narrow technicality—that he has been generally written out of history in recent years.[1]

"A Johanine Triumvary were master-builders of the broad foundations of Tennessee jurisprudence. They were John Overton, John Haywood, and

John Catron—*and the greatest of these was Catron.*" With these words Dean of the University of Tennessee Law School Henry Hulbert Ingersoll introduced Catron to early twentieth-century readers of legal history.[2] Lawyer and scholar Joshua W. Caldwell argued a decade earlier that opinions penned by Catron were "undoubtedly the most learned in our reports. . . [and] invaluable to the student of history as well as the lawyer."[3] Historian Theodore Brown Jr. observed that while Catron sat on the Tennessee Supreme Court he "authored nearly 350 signed opinions. . . more than any of his colleagues."[4] Henry S. Foote, writing in 1876, proclaimed that "John Catron is a name which will long be venerated by all American patriots,"[5] while Tennessee attorney John Hallum argued that "Justice Catron. . . was the ablest land jurist on the Supreme Bench of the United States, and rendered more aid in settling western titles than any other Federal Judge."[6] Yet John Catron, whom many scholars have dismissed as either unimportant or peripheral to history, served as the first Chief Justice of the Tennessee Supreme Court and was the only Tennessean on the U.S. Supreme Court (1837–1865) before Howells Edmund Jackson assumed the bench in 1893.[7]

Catron's early years remain cloaked in obscurity. Disagreement about his place of birth—Pennsylvania or Virginia—and the date of his nativity—as early as 1779 or as late as 1786—cloud what little is known of his life before the Catron family moved to the Upper Cumberland. His father Peter, a German immigrant, fought in the Revolution and moved his family west after the war. Settling first in Wayne County, Kentucky, in the Big South Fork region around 1804, the Catrons later moved to the more fertile soil of White County, Tennessee, where the future justice toiled, farming, driving hogs to market along the Kentucky Road, and working with horses.[8]

In his "Biographical Letter," published in 1854, Catron admitted that his education was meager. He announced that he had been "flogged through the common schools of Western Virginia and Kentucky," taking advantage "of such academies as the western country afforded, humble enough in all conscience where little else but Latin and the lower mathematics was added to the common school training."[9] Describing frontier schools as crude one-room affairs usually led by a clergyman, Catron noted that students primarily learned by rote and were not encouraged to think.[10] He attributed much of his instruction to Presbyterian minister James Witherspoon, a man he considered preoccupied with "dead languages."[11] Wanting to focus more intently on English than on Latin, which "all lawyers forgot very soon," Witherspoon accommodated Catron.[12] Though books were scarce in the Upper Cumberland, Catron "read everything that came to hand as it came."[13] Literature he cherished most included works of

William Shakespeare, Alexander Pope, and Lawrence Sterne's rambunctious, bawdy, picaresque novel *Tristram Shandy* which, like his snuff box, he often hid because he enjoyed it too much.[14]

Acknowledging his scholarship was haphazard and unfocused, Catron's "course of reading and study [was left] almost exclusively on [my] own judgment, unguided by a single man of reading and matured scholarship."[15] In an attempt to silence his critics who considered him rough, uncultured, and boorish, Catron argued that if placed in his shoes, "few [of them] would have done better, or judged more wisely, and thousands would have done worse."[16] Even so, he did not believe his "labors [had been] wasted on this first confused effort."[17] A serious student, he read at least one hundred pages per day, assiduously taking notes, then abridging the day's efforts for easier recollection. "With this confused mass of self-taught knowledge," he confessed, "I commenced to read law in April 1812," in the office of George Washington Gibbs at Sparta, Tennessee.[18]

Both he and Gibbs volunteered for the Tennessee militia in 1813. They mustered at Sparta in the Second Regiment under Colonel William Pillow and John H. Anderson, and they were dispatched to the Natchez expedition. After a few months fighting near Talladega, at Tallusatchee and Fort Strother, soldiers braved the frigid waters of Coosa and were disappointed to find no provisions at Fort Strother. Catron mustered out in November 1813, due to sickness as a result of the campaign. His brief stint in uniform proved significant, however, and influenced the rest of his life.[19] Contrary to many claims, John Catron did not fight valiantly with Andrew Jackson, William Carroll, and John Coffee at the Battle of New Orleans, for he was at home in Sparta diligently practicing law.[20]

Upon leaving the military, Catron and Gibbs returned to Sparta and Catron continued his study of the law. In 1815 Catron gained admission to the bar and began his law practice at Monroe, the county seat of Overton County; from there he roved all over the Third Judicial District trying cases. Commonly referred to as The Mountain District, it encompassed the Cumberland Plateau and Eastern Highland Rim to the east and extended west to Gallatin and the state capitol at Cannonsburg (now Murfreesboro). The largest judicial district in the Volunteer State, it included Franklin, Jackson, Overton, Smith, Sumner, Warren, and White counties. Its topography and limited number of good roads made transportation difficult; it was no small task to go from one trial location to another in a timely fashion.[21]

While studying law Catron befriended Attorney General Isaac Thomas, who took the fledgling under his wing. Thomas entered politics in 1815, securing a seat as a representative in the Fourteenth U.S. Congress.

Presumably due to his influence, the legislature replaced Thomas with Catron, who served as attorney general for the Mountain District for a two-year term. As district attorney, Catron prosecuted cases ranging from petty crimes to capital offenses.[22]

Riding circuit proved arduous work. Catron "had to fight the battle, single and alone, and to work day and night. No man worked much harder, I think; my circuit judge was an excellent criminal lawyer . . . [who] always stood firmly by the state and leaned *strongly* against the culprit."[23] Less polished in the courtroom, and sometimes guilty of "blundering in my law, if not bad grammar," Catron prevailed through sheer bluster and force of personality.[24] Conscientious, he labored diligently to live up to his personal expectations of the prosecutor's office. His contemporary Judge Josephus Conn Guild observed that, contrary to claims of critics who derided Catron as an incompetent, illiterate buffoon, Catron excelled as "a laborious student, careful, pains-taking in the examination of authorities and the preparation of his cases, and never appearing in a cause on the spur of the moment."[25]

For numerous reasons attorneys and judges rode the judicial circuit together in a pack moving from one venue to another, discussing upcoming cases, sharing yarns, imbibing whisky, and forging bonds of friendship or loathing. Travel usually occurred on Sunday, and members of the bar rented rooms at a local tavern for a week of court proceedings before heading to the next venue. Catron noted:

> Each man was well appointed, carried pistols and holsters, and a negro waiter with a large portmanteau behind him. All went on horseback. The pistols were carried, not to shoot thieves or robbers, but to fight each other, if by any chance a quarrel was hatched up, furnishing an occasion for a duel, then a very favorite amusement and liberally indulged in—and the attorney-general for the circuit was expected to be, and always was, prepared for such a contingency.[26]

Once lawyers arrived at an appointed destination, they generally had a good time. Attorneys and judges "made as free with whisky punch and empty bottles as did our Irish brethren at a Galway assize . . . nor were games at cards overlooked."[27] Catron did his share of drinking and gambling, though he later wrote opinions criticizing both when their abuse proved self-destructive.

Because few people on the Upper Cumberland frontier had money, clients bartered for an attorney's services. Some paid their lawyers and their preachers with home-distilled whisky or peach brandy. Others offered salt-cured hams, handicrafts, and gunpowder, or agreed to provide manual labor for their counselors for a specific duration of time. As Joshua Caldwell noted, "In the good old days, fees were not large, and as money was a scarce commodity, payment was often made in produce and livestock. It was not uncommon for lawyers to carry branding irons to mark the cattle they received for fees."[28]

Catron's success stemmed from his willingness to do the requisite homework. While important to know how the law applied to specific cases, he took pride in knowing things opposing counsel failed to discover. Rather than simply depose witnesses and read legal briefs, Catron insisted on going to "see the land surveyed, and the corner trees blocked," or personally visit the "workshop, steamboat, or counting house to see how the thing is done." He prided himself in speaking the common language of the working class, and enjoyed ribald stories. Armed with practical information gleaned on-site, Catron claimed he could "beat a dozen of his equals in capacity, crammed with law to the throat."[29] A former laborer, he believed the "experience of everyday life" trumped any deficiencies he had as a trial lawyer.[30]

Catron earned a reputation as a lawyer who filed bills of exception to great effect. In both criminal and civil cases, he developed a knack for reviewing court proceedings to ferret out a rationale for retrying cases. While court was in session Catron took laborious notes, filing bills of exception shortly after the judge banged his gavel finalizing a case. That ability, acknowledged by his colleagues, played a significant role in Catron's elevation to the state's superior court.[31]

Apparently Catron's relationship with Andrew Jackson matured during his days as a prosecutor, and they crossed paths often. Even so, Catron—who became a life-long friend of the general—did not fear him. In the ongoing dispute between Catron's friend Colonel William Martin of Dixon Springs in Smith County and Andrew Jackson over attempted mutinies in the ranks in 1813, Catron stood by his friend from the Upper Cumberland. Jackson severed his ties with Martin, and accused him of conspiracy and publicly maligned the colonel for years afterward. Martin published a letter Catron wrote him saying, "It would be with extreme regret that I should hear those friends of mine charged with the blackest of crimes of which they are certainly innocent. They were the most efficient troops to their number I ever saw or would ever hope to see. I cannot help believing. . . General Jackson had no better friend in the army than yourself."[32] Remarkably, Catron remained friends with both men, who loathed each other.

Jackson encouraged him to move to Nashville, and in the late fall of 1818 Catron took up residence there though he continued to own property in White County and elsewhere in the Upper Cumberland.[33] No longer a prosecutor, Catron defended clients in criminal cases, but spent the bulk of his time in chancery court. Due to the Panic of 1819, court dockets were overwhelmed with bankruptcies, foreclosures, and issues related to the economic downturn. By year's end Catron claimed: "I had more business than I could do in the town itself, and rarely left it."[34] Carving out a niche at the Nashville bar, he focused on perfecting land titles, while fighting for the property rights of the less fortunate. Like frontier politician David Crockett, he championed "enforcing the seven years act of limitations in real actions," so that people could rightfully own property they had improved.[35]

Admitting he lacked the theatricality and poise of his peers, Catron was not a polished orator, as witnesses observed. "As to my mode of speaking at the bar, I have no very exact recollection. It was not methodical, [it was] tolerably fluent, sometimes stormy, and often sarcastic, which habit cost me dear on one or two occasions."[36] Judge Guild, who knew Catron well, wrote an oft-quoted description of him. He claimed Catron was:

> as bold and as rough as the hills he traversed in his circuit. . . He was a harsh, unpleasant speaker with a squeaking, unmelodious voice, and his gestures were like those of a man engaged in a fight; but there was a continued flow of hard, practical sense, while his argument was so enforced by homely illustrations, that his speeches were not only interesting, but frequently convincing. He generally left a black eye before he came out of the battle.[37]

Though Catron was clearly a man of ability who strove to improve himself, other factors played an important role in his success. When riding circuit Catron often appeared at court in the state capitol at Cannonsburg. At some point the rising lawyer met the wealthy and well-connected Matilda Childress, granddaughter of James Robertson (the so-called "Father of Middle Tennessee") and first cousin of Sarah Childress, wife of James K. Polk. How they met and began to woo is lost to history; the two made an unusual pair. His contemporaries noted that Catron was gruff, tall, and stocky, with a full head of black bushy hair and the bearing of a mountain man. Childress, by contrast, clad in the fashion of the day with her hair piled up on her head and long ringlets framing her delicate features, was elegant and at ease in polite society. Childress opened doors for the ambitious Catron, who welcomed the cachet the Childress name afforded him.

On Thursday, January 25, 1821, the couple married, forging an alliance that suited them well for the rest of their lives. In the parlance of the Upper Cumberland, John Catron had "done good [*sic*]," and "married up," changing his station in life and his standing in the community.[38] Attorney John Darby said that Catron "took the world easy and never elbowed or pushed himself for promotion. But his wife in this was his opposite, was all energy and full of ambition for the husband she idolized, and she generally had her way."[39]

Catron's close connections with the political establishment in Tennessee by necessity turned him into a political animal. As Supreme Court scholar Carl B. Swisher observed:

> Catron never became so interested in law as to lose interest in contemporary politics. He continued political correspondence with Andrew Jackson until the latter's death in 1845. He was a close advisor of James K. Polk both before and during his presidency, and was similarly close to James Buchanan. He was a

Matilda Childress Catron. Credit: Tennessee State Museum.

> go-betweener with respect to members of Congress and the Supreme Court where legislation affecting the judiciary was involved, and on circuit he was a kind of news carrier about happenings in Washington. He was the complete opposite of the cloistered oracle of the law.[40]

Tennessee's legislature elected John Catron to the Supreme Court of Errors and Appeals as an Associate Justice in 1824, to fill the vacancy created when Judge William L. Brown resigned. Legal scholar and former Tennessee Governor Albert S. Marks maintained that the legislature chose him because of Catron's extensive knowledge of property law.[41] The General Assembly wanted him to break an impasse concerning real property and title claims stemming in part from the Panic of 1819. At the heart of the issue was enforcement of the aforementioned seven years statute of limitations regarding land grants and titles. Several people across the state had staked out claims and improved land they believed they rightfully owned. An unscrupulous land speculator, Patrick Darby, filed a series of lawsuits that threatened to deprive them of their land and their money. Darby's actions infuriated Catron, and he told several legislators where he stood on the matter, resulting in his election to the superior court. He forged an alliance with Judge John Haywood; they broke the deadlock and forced Darby out of the state, a result which "gave repose to the people and the country."[42]

In addition to Haywood, Catron joined Robert Whyte and Jacob Peck on the superior bench. Though Catron found an ally in Haywood, he and Peck disagreed over the disposition of numerous cases. At that time judges served at the whim of the legislature, and were subject to the vagaries of shifting political winds.[43] Appellate Court judges rode across the entire state to hear myriad cases both civil and criminal throughout all the state's judicial districts. They faced a number of difficulties, not least of which were terrible roads, limited hotel accommodations, and inclement weather. Those hardships were compounded by the fact that when they convened at Knoxville, Carthage, or Nashville to hear cases, the judges were often handed a stack of hand-written briefs by the clerk, and no counsel stood before them to argue the earlier ruling.[44] So the "Court seems to have been left to hunt out for itself, the grounds of error for appeal."[45]

From 1821 to 1827, the appellate court fulfilled the duties of chancery court, hearing cases concerning equity issues. In 1825, Catron served as Chancellor for the first Chancery Court conducted in West Tennessee at Jackson.[46] Under Catron's influence, Sparta, his former hometown, replaced Carthage on the circuit in 1824, after he ascended to the high court. Catron used the time in Sparta to oversee his land holdings in White County and renew acquaintances with old friends in addition to settling court cases. Joshua Caldwell noted that though "Judge Catron was not an educated man. He broadened very much after he was made a judge, and by diligent application acquired a very wide learning."[47]

As a judge, Catron's station in life improved substantially. His contacts among the Volunteer State's elite provided opportunities both financially and culturally.[48] Critics like Samuel Hervey Laughlin of Warren County, accused him of getting above his station. He claimed Catron put on airs, dressed ostentatiously, and was embarrassed when confronted by former friends from the Upper Cumberland. Catron ignored Laughlin's slurs and kept the alcoholic newspaper editor's *Nashville Daily Union* afloat. Catron repeatedly loaned the ingrate Laughlin money, and wrote guest editorials and other articles for his paper.[49]

Catron dispensed justice as he saw fit. Because he "was never a candidate for any political place, nor held any office," he was beholden to no one. He delivered opinions based on the intrinsic merits of each case. Historian Edmund C. Gass noted that Catron's written opinions, "while lacking in literary quality, reflect the simple and pragmatic philosophy of the frontier."[50] Catron's decisions reflected attitudes and concerns of the people he knew best—simple hard-working folk who struggled to keep kith and kin together. Like most citizens of the Upper Cumberland and his ally Andrew Jackson, Catron was wary of big banks, corporations, and other such organizations.[51] Henry S. Foote observed that many of Catron's opinions were "replete with suggestions of a moral cast, and have reference to the suppression of social crime."[52] Theodore Brown Jr. noted that Catron's opinions "occasionally revealed glimpses of remarkable native intelligence, if not brilliance." At other times, however, they betrayed his partisan political leanings, "the prevailing moral standards and principles of the time, often relying upon moral principles when the law failed him."[53]

Judge Catron confessed that "with the floating masses I had nothing in common: I punished many of them for crimes, and always severely. They feared and disliked me."[54] Equally firm with gentry and social elites, he stated: "Among the great masses of property-owners, thousands have been alienated by decisions adverse to their interests."[55] Judge Catron, the expert on title law, made hard decisions where lesser men would have acquiesced to the influence of the wealthy and powerful. His ethos had its consequences. As he acknowledged, "a judge may have great cogency and influence. . . but if he be a stern and unquailing official, it is not in human nature that he should be a popular man; so at least has been my experience." Walter Chandler observed Catron "was unmoved by the political dangers of just but unpopular rulings."[56] With his penchant for sarcasm, refusal to bow to outside influences, and inflexible political affiliations, Catron counted few people as his true friends. Albert S. Marks observed "Judge Catron was a most intense partisan, and was one of the best-hated men of his day."[57]

Inconsistency and contradiction permeate several of Catron's opinions, if not his life. More than once he reversed himself, taking positions directly opposite earlier rulings. Whether these reversals stemmed from a personal desire to correct perceived past mistakes, or from a willingness to forsake precedent to render a decision he believed appropriate, remains open to debate. In some instances, (e.g. *The State v. Foreman*) Catron appears to endorse the general sentiments of average Americans, delivering an opinion then regarded popular. On other occasions he embodies Walt Whitman's declaration, "Do I contradict myself? Very well, then I contradict myself, (I am large, I contain multitudes)."[58] What seems to be forgotten or overlooked is the fact that most people change over time, and often recoil at past behavior. Catron, who came from relative obscurity and poverty, amassed broad experience that allowed him to operate in various social, cultural, and political circles. In some ways (e.g. his attitude toward property rights and fear of corporations) he never left the Upper Cumberland; whereas, in others (e.g. his role as a power broker in state and national politics) Catron walked among the giants of his day, influencing lives of poor and rich alike. Critics regularly pointed out his shortcomings, yet Catron carried on as he saw fit.

A brief examination of some of Judge Catron's decisions illustrate not only his attitudes about certain crimes, but also his belief in what the law should do. His intense loyalty to Andrew Jackson, however, sometimes caused politics to replace discretion. Catron's career sheds light on issues of his day and public attitudes toward them. Unafraid of criticism or scorn, Catron handed down decisions he deemed appropriate, no matter how unpopular they were. He judged hundreds of criminal cases in his long career; many established precedents that continue to influence state and federal laws.

Though no stranger to dueling or the violence that passed for entertainment on the frontier, Judge Catron despised the practice. He rubbed elbows with people who proudly engaged in duels as a means of upholding their honor, settling personal scores, or enhancing their reputations. As Albert S. Marks observed "Duelling [*sic*] was common in Tennessee; and Judge Catron himself, when a lawyer riding the circuit, carried a brace of duelling-pistols [*sic*] as a part of his outfit, and never declined a challenge to use them. But he thoroughly reprehended the practice. . ."[59] For Catron to take legal action against dueling and condemn it in *Smith v. State* (1829)[60] made him the subject of ridicule in some quarters. "I was scorched with many a racy sarcasm," he wrote, "such as, that a sinner who had carried the blank challenges in the crown of his hat and slept with his pistols under his head, was a very proper man to turn saint and lecturer, to put down a vice he so well understood in all its bearings."[61]

In a nutshell *Smith* involved two lawyers who decided to duel over an issue and settle it to their satisfaction. Since dueling was illegal in Tennessee they traveled to Kentucky to shoot each other. Though Smith returned home triumphant he was immediately tried for murder in Tennessee. Although acquitted, he lost his law license. Smith appealed; Catron considered him not only unfit to be a member of the bar, but guilty of murder. Catron stated that death by duel has "always has been murder, punishable with death, without the benefit of clergy."[62] With venom, Catron railed against the practice: "Let it be once understood that the bar of Tennessee *dare* not fight, and it will be deemed cowardly to challenge a member of it; and this court solemnly warns every lawyer, that if he violates the laws made to suppress duelling [*sic*], we will strike him from the rolls of the court, upon the fact being made know to us."[63] It did not matter where the duel took place, only that it happened. Catron concurred with revoking Smith's law license. His ruling influenced future legislation, for "the Constitutional Convention of 1834 followed in his [Catron's] footsteps, and deprived a participant in a duel of the right to hold any office of profit or trust in the State."[64]

Another case involved a man named Brooks, convicted of being "in the constant habit and practice of haunting and frequenting bawdy houses . . . to the common nuisance and damage of the people."[65] Catron pointed out that common law required the prosecution to state explicitly in its indictment and prove at trial that Brooks knew the places he visited were houses of prostitution.[66] Chiding the prosecution, Catron stated: "If the defendant did not *know* the character of the houses, he committed no offense."[67] He argued what is now settled law—an indictment must allege all the elements of an offense. In *Brooks* the crime of frequenting houses of ill repute required proof he had acted "open and notoriously," but the indictment failed to contain these essential elements of the crime.[68]

Perhaps Judge Catron's most famous and influential criminal case in Tennessee was *Grainger v. The State* (1830).[69] It focused on the concept of self-defense; in both 1830 and in the present, one may resort to violence if a "person has a reasonable belief that there is an imminent danger" and the danger "is real, or honestly believed [by the person] to be real at the time" and "the belief of danger is founded upon reasonable grounds."[70] Grainger, after imbibing with two gentlemen at a tavern, started home only to be accosted by a former drinking companion named Broach. Fleeing to a neighbor's house, Grainger tried to get in for his safety, but the neighbor, a man named Rainey, refused to open the door. Afraid for his life, Grainger pulled his gun and killed Broach. Catron found Grainger "was much alarmed, and with good cause... he could not get away ... [He] used all the means in his power to escape from an overbearing bully... He shot only to protect his person from threatened violence. . ."[71] Catron's ruling has been the source of controversy over the years. Critics, like his contemporary Hugh Lawson White, claimed the ruling allowed wholesale murder without consequences, and made a travesty of the law. Closer reading shows that Catron's opinion, though less than artfully written, is appropriately juridical.

In another murder case, Catron found the defendant killed without premeditation. In *Mitchell v. State*, Jesse Mitchell stood accused of murdering a man named Wilson. Prosecutors presented evidence that Wilson was surveying land his employer recently purchased. "While walking the land, Wilson came upon Mitchell ploughing a field. An argument broke out 'and after some harsh language,' Mitchell. . . got an axe, returned and gave deceased a blow upon the head, of which he died."[72] The jury found Mitchell guilty of first degree murder. On appeal, Catron overturned the conviction. He held that to find:

> To have authorized this [a capital verdict], the slaying must have been premeditated, that is, conceived in the mind, and intended by Mitchell to be executed beforehand. Did he deliberately act upon pre-determination; or, did he act upon a sudden impulse of passion, disconnected with any previous design to kill? If the former state of mind induced the act, then it was murder in the first degree; if the latter, murder in the second.

Catron ruled it a crime of impulse and ordered a new trial, insisting Mitchell be tried for second degree murder.[73] The judge identified a specific legal point: a premeditated act must be "conceived in the mind, and intended. . . to be executed beforehand." [74]

Catron's attitudes toward Native Americans rank among his most problematic. Initially a man who regarded Indians with dignity and worthy of the full protection of the law, he reversed previous opinions for what appear to be purely political reasons. Starting with his opinion in *Cornet v. Winton's Lessee* in July 1826, Judge Catron recognized Tennessee Cherokees' right to own property. In *Cornet*, Catron decided who possessed the better legal title to real property. The case centered on a land grant issued by North Carolina ceding Cherokee lands in Tennessee. A jury denied

Cherokee claims of ownership.[75] North Carolina, Catron concluded, did not have the authority to issue a land grant, citing an 1819 treaty with Cherokees.[76] Catron charged "North Carolina had no right to take it [possession of the land] from the Indians . . . The Cherokee are, in point of fact, a conquered people, with acknowledged rights; which rights, I am proud to say, have for the last thirty years been respected. . ."[77]

In the 1830 case *McConnell and Mayfield v. Mousepaine's Lessee*, frontiersmen McConnell and Mayfield moved onto property claimed by Mousepaine, a Cherokee. They cleared and fenced land, and possibly erected structures. Catron relied on treaties negotiated in 1817 and 1819, between the United States and the Cherokee, stating that taken "together, they vest in each head of an Indian family residing on the ceded territory, six hundred and forty acres" as long as the Cherokee filed his claim with the Cherokee agent by January 1, 1820.[78] Catron reasoned that by registering, Mousepaine "became and was a naturalized citizen of the United States" and registry vested title to Mousepaine.[79] Catron ruled that no action by either the United States or Tennessee's governments "could divest this vested right."[80]

That same month, July 1830, the state Supreme Court heard *Blair v Pathkiller's Lessee*. The trial court found in favor of Pathkiller, a Cherokee. On appeal Blair's attorney, Hugh Lawson White, argued that "the government of the United States had no power, by virtue of any treaty, to cede to individuals the property of a Sovereign State of the Union [Tennessee]."[81] Addressing the question directly, Catron concluded that because of acts of 1789 and 1806, North Carolina had no legal claim to the land, for the Cherokees transferred title to the "United States, as grantees of the treaty of 1819."[82] Rejecting the General Assembly's attempts to override or modify the 1817 and 1819 treaties, Catron stated that "the United States alone, by the Treaty of Holston, had the right to extinguish the Indian title."[83] Remarkably, Catron ruled that, by their lawful possession of land, Tennessee's Cherokee were citizens of the United States.[84]

Sadly, in 1835 Catron expressed the direct opposite view of the Cherokee Nation's legal status in *The State v. Foreman*. Catron upheld the State Legislature's attempts to pass laws applicable to certain crimes occurring in and on Tennessee Cherokee lands, involving only Cherokees.[85] James Foreman was indicted for murdering John Walker; both men were Cherokee and the killing occurred on Cherokee land. Foreman's defense counsel moved to dismiss the case for lack of jurisdiction and the trial court agreed. The State appealed.[86]

The real issue *The State v. Foreman* decided was whether Tennessee, by an act of the General Assembly, extended its jurisdiction to cover the crimes of murder, rape, and larceny that occurred in Cherokee territory in Tennessee. At the beginning of his rambling opinion, Catron declared the 1833 act extending jurisdiction over the Cherokee did not "conflict with either the treaties or laws of the United States."[87] He tried to justify his position over the next fifty pages. His opinion challenged the U.S. Supreme Court's rulings in *Cherokee Nation v. Georgia* and *Worcester v. Georgia.* In *Foremen* Catron offered President Jackson an opportunity to revisit *Worcester v. Georgia* if negotiations with the Cherokee failed. It eventually led to Cherokee removal in Tennessee, leading to the infamous Trail of Tears.[88]

When it came to slaves, John Catron differed markedly from many of his peers in Tennessee, and he was certainly more humane than most in the deeper South. According to the U.S. Census, Catron owned six slaves in 1830, five slaves in 1840, ten slaves in 1850 and fourteen slaves in 1860.[89] While on the state Supreme Court Catron wrote a number of opinions concerning slavery and consistently found negroes (both slave and free) to be human beings, not mere chattel, and said they should be treated as such. In *Loftin v. Espy* (1833), a case involving whether or not a slave could be seized to pay a master's debt, Catron wrote:

> Nothing can be much more abhorrent to these poor people, or to the feelings of every benevolent individual, than to see a large family of slaves sold at sheriff's sale. . . . To treat them as other domestic animals would be to declare, that, as a people, we had, in reference to this class, sunk all feeling of humanity, and that the slave was not elevated in his sensibilities over the lower classes of animals, which are allowed to have none worthy of the protection of man.[90]

In a similar vein, Catron's opinion in *Harris v. Clarissa* (1834) considered the rights of slaves and revealed his compassion for them. Clarissa, a slave, was freed by her master's will when she turned twenty-five. Her master's heirs contested the will. Catron wrote that not only was Clarissa free, but her three children born before she was twenty-five were free as well.[91] Catron adopted North Carolina's rule "of nature pertaining to human beings, in declaring that the condition of the mother should be that of the child."[92] Catron wrote that Clarissa had "a present right to freedom" and she "took a vested and undoubted right to freedom" from her owner's will.[93] Catron continued, saying that "[t]he children born of Clarissa in the state of Tennessee come into existence impressed with the *rights* our laws confer."[94] In *Fishers Negroes v. Dabbs* (1834), another case involving slaves manumitted by their master's will, Catron wrote that slaves enjoyed "every natural right" afforded to other free Americans.[95]

As John Catron continued his career on the bench in Tennessee, he earned the grudging respect of his peers. Though often harsh in and out of the courtroom, he was fair except when it came to his issues challenging his loyalty to Andrew Jackson. Henry H. Ingersoll, when examining Catron's legal career in Tennessee, found much to praise. He declared:

> Catron's influence upon the jurisprudence and morality of the state of Tennessee by his twelve years of judicial service amongst a pioneer population when institutions were being molded, social habits being formed, and a constitution for the state was being formulated, under which it attained its greatest prosperity and its highest judicial fame, was such as entitle him to the first rank among the citizens and lawyers whom our people and profession delight to enshrine in their Hall of Fame.[96]

In 1831 the legislature created a new position of Chief Justice of the Supreme Court of Tennessee, and elected John Catron to be the first judge to hold the office. As Chief Justice Catron locked horns with the legislature, demanding that the judges be better paid and their dockets lightened. Due to poor traveling conditions, judges were tremendously overburdened and swift justice was non-existent. In an effort to get their attention and address problems facing the court, Catron lambasted the legislature in a letter tendering his resignation. That letter provided Governor William Carroll, who empathized with the judges, with ammunition he needed to amend the judiciary in Tennessee.[97] This eventually led to the Constitutional Convention of 1834, which addressed some issues Catron raised; it also guaranteed his ouster. Irascible, stubborn, and never one to back down from a fight, Catron's partisan political leanings led to his removal from the Supreme Court. The revised Constitution reduced the Supreme Court from four justices to three.

By the end of Andrew Jackson's second term as President his popularity in the Volunteer State reached an all-time low. The Whig Party in Tennessee, which stood for everything Jackson hated, filled its ranks with Old Hickory's enemies and courted his friends and family, including his nephew Andrew Jackson Donelson. While many abandoned Jackson, Catron remained a staunch and loyal ally. In doing so Catron lost political capital in the Volunteer State and gained a host of new enemies.[98]

Conflicting stories attempt to explain or debunk how Catron landed on the Supreme Court of the United States. The Judiciary Act of 1836 increased the number of justices on the court from seven to nine, creating two vacancies on the bench. Detractors argued that the reason Catron was chosen for the nation's high court was because his well-heeled wife prevailed upon President Jackson to give her husband the position.[99] Carl B. Swisher rejected such a story, though he agreed that it would not have been out of character for Matilda to act in such a fashion. Rather, Swisher argued that Catron made his first appearance before the Supreme Court in January 1837, and argued two cases before Chief Justice Roger B. Taney and the associate justices. Catron was in Washington and took advantage of the moment. "He was ambitious and aggressive and by no means inclined to hold himself back. In the disparaging words of Justice [John] McLean, he was 'full of himself.' He did not require a wife's intercession."[100]

Others argue that his appointment stemmed from Catron's willingness to reverse himself in *The State v. Foreman*. To those critics *Foreman* represented a craven attempt to curry favor with Andrew Jackson by duplicitous support of Indian removal.[101]

These arguments ignore the fact that Catron had been a loyal member of Jackson's cadre for decades. He faithfully canvassed for Jackson and other Democrats in local, state, and national elections. As Joshua Caldwell observed, "From 1820 to 1828 the efforts of political leaders of Tennessee were concentrated in the single effort to elect Jackson president, and William B. Lewis, John Catron and John Overton, who were at the head of the movement, displayed a capacity for political management that has never been surpassed."[102] An outspoken defender of Jackson during the Bank War, he wrote widely circulated editorials demanding the bank's destruction. During the Nullification Crisis Catron staunchly supported Jackson's appeal for a Force Bill.[103] He sustained Jacksonian policies while on the state Supreme Court, and was a party stalwart. Catron was campaign chairman for Martin Van Buren in Tennessee to succeed Jackson against the Volunteer State's own native son Hugh Lawson White. Catron reveled in excoriating the Whigs, whom he regarded as traitors to the state and nation. Notwithstanding the fact that Catron understood property issues better than his peers, all of these factors must have played a part in his appointment. Expansionist policies of Jackson and recent establishment of the Republic of Texas by former Tennessean Sam Houston and his compatriots created a need for judges intimately familiar with property law, and according to Walter Chandler, Catron's "knowledge of land laws was uncanny."[104]

So, for whatever reason, on March 3, 1837, Andrew Jackson recommended John Catron for one of the new positions on the U.S. Supreme Court on his last day in office. Five days later the Senate confirmed his nomination by a vote of twenty-eight to fifteen, making him the first Tennessean to sit on the highest court in the land. He served on the federal

Justice John Catron early in his legal career. Credit: U.S. Supreme Court Historical Society.

bench for the twenty-eight years, making him the only Tennessean on the U.S. Supreme Court before the Civil War, working ably under nine presidents.[105] A man who never got over his humble origins nor forgot the days he rode circuit in the Mountain District, John Catron succeeded far beyond his aspirations. He wrote that "when the incidents of [my early life] were narrated, they would only prove what Campbell says of Lord Mansfield—that when he came up from Scotland to Westminster School on a Highland pony, the chances were a billion to one against his ever being Chief Justice: I can safely say, that quite as many chances stood in my way of being a Supreme Judge."[106] The rough-hewn product of the Upper Cumberland matured into a seasoned justice who earned the respect of people beyond his home. The *Daily National Intelligencer*, published in the U.S. capital, praised Catron as "one of the most original and remarkable men that ever sat on the bench of the Supreme Court. With legal abilities rarely attained, a facility in the investigation of a subject which nothing but a powerful memory and a quick perception can apply, and an accuracy of judgment that a strong common sense can alone secure, he has a style of expression entirely his own, and which will be recognized in all his opinions."[107]

Once on the U.S. Supreme Court, John Catron's duties did not begin on the first Monday in October and end with the court delivering its opinions the following spring. In those days Supreme Court justices rode a circuit just like local judges in Tennessee. Catron was assigned to the newly created Eighth Circuit, composed of Kentucky, Missouri, and Tennessee. He presided in each of these states until 1863, when the district was reorganized and he was transferred to the Sixth Circuit, composed of Arkansas, Kentucky, Louisiana, Ohio, Tennessee, and Texas.[108]

Riding federal circuit Catron learned the intricacies of bankruptcy law and became an expert on the subject. Exhibiting empathy for those plunged into the humiliation and despair of losing their material possessions and social standing in their communities, "he treated bankruptcy as a misfortune and not a crime."[109] Well versed in homesteading laws, he agreed with Whig stalwart David Crockett that in a land so vast and so empty, even the poorest among them should be allowed to own property in order to sustain a living. Catron immersed himself in the laws of the disparate states in the circuit, and "border controversies were peculiarly within his grasp."[110]

As a justice on both the state and federal benches, Catron grew impatient with lawyers who stood before him unprepared. "I insist on thorough legal training and constant study; but object, whether it comes from the bar or bench, to piles of references and figures, formidable as a treasury report, gathered from the index, and having no value in the particular case; and which parade of authorities reminds one of two grains of wheat smothered under two bushels of chaff; such being the plain condition of the little law that is applicable."[111]

Catron opposed corporations, viewing them as a threat to the common man and a way for moneyed interests to amass power and corrupt governments. By 1854, John Catron had his fill of corporations as evidenced in his dissent in a case involving two railroad companies. He forcefully stated "that a corporation is not a citizen;" furthermore "I view this assumption of citizenship for a corporation as a mere evasion of the limits prescribed to the United States courts by the Constitution."[112] Five months later Catron continued to be wary of the power wielded by corporations. When considering "the vast amount of property, power and exclusive benefits, prejudicial to other classes of society. . . vested in and held by these numerous bodies of associated wealth, I cannot but feel the grave importance of being called upon to sanction the conclusion that they [corporations] hold their rights of franchise and property. . . and stand above the state government creating them."[113]

As a U.S. Supreme Court justice, Catron wrote two unanimous opinions concerning property rights of Indians. In *Marsh v. Brooks*, Catron settled a title dispute between "half-breeds" of the Sac and Fox tribes. Writing the unanimous opinion, and citing his own findings in *Cornet*, Catron ruled that "The Act of 1834 vests the ultimate title remaining to the United States in the half-breeds of the Sac and Fox tribes; thereby giving them a perfect fee-simple."[114] Ten years later, Catron wrote a second unanimous opinion in *Doe ex dem Mann and Hannah v. Wilson*.[115] Catron used the same principles he deployed in *Marsh v. Brooks, Pathkiller's Lessee* and *Cornet*. In fact, he cited his opinions in *Pathkiller's Lessee* and *Cornet* in his *Wilson* ruling.[116] Catron concluded that, by entering into a treaty with the United States, the Pottowattomie Nation ceded its lands in Indiana, Illinois, and the Michigan Territory.[117] As in other treaties, the 1832 treaty made reservations to certain individuals. Catron concluded that the title vested in Mann and Hannah through the Indians' reservation was superior to the title Wilson claimed.

Catron heard numerous cases involving African Americans, most famously *Dred Scott v. Sandford*, the most controversial antebellum Supreme Court ruling. Though he came to the same conclusion as Chief Justice Roger B. Taney, Catron based his decision on a completely different argument. Scholar Don Fehrenbacher asserts that the constitutional question in *Dred Scott* "was whether Congress had the power, exercised in the Missouri Compromise, to prohibit slavery in the territories."[118] If this was the question to be answered, John Catron's concurrence answered the question succinctly—"no!" His opinion focused solely on the constitutionality of the Missouri Compromise and its attempt to limit rights of citizens living in the new territory. Catron deemed the Missouri Compromise unconstitutional: "My opinion is, that the third article of the treaty of 1803, ceding Louisiana to the United States, stands protected by the Constitution and cannot be repealed by Congress."[119] Catron held treaties sacrosanct. In his estimation, the Missouri Compromise violated the U.S. Constitution's privileges and immunities provision.[120]

Having stated in *Fisher's Negroes* and elsewhere that slaves had rights and could become citizens, Catron refused to accept the logic of Chief Justice Taney's majority opinion in *Dred Scott*. He could not, however, dissent because as a slave owner he did not want to limit his right to take his property—including slaves—to other states or U.S. territories. *The New York Times* pointedly asked the question: "Can a Negro be a citizen of the United States?" In doing so they examined the attitudes of the Supreme Court justices on the issue and concluded that "the Court stands thus: Three in the affirmative [including Catron], three in the negative and three silent."[121]

While the *Dred Scott* decision was pending, Catron wrote President-Elect James Buchanan several times about it.[122] In these letters, which to day appear to be an ethical breach, he urged Buchanan to write Justice

Robert C. Grier and persuade him to vote with the majority.[123] Catron advised Buchanan on the eve of his inauguration about what he could expect from the court concerning *Dred Scott* and what the president-elect might reasonably say about it. The *Dred Scott* decision created a firestorm, and was a central feature in debates between Stephen Douglas and Abraham Lincoln when they ran for the U.S. Senate in Illinois. Though Lincoln lost the election, that race placed him in the national spotlight, setting the stage for his presidential candidacy. *Dred Scott* heightened anxieties about the fate of slavery, and while southerners applauded the decision, the country moved closer to the brink of war.[124]

When not in Washington, D.C., or riding circuit, Catron spent his time at his home in Nashville or other places in Tennessee. He owned an interest in a ferry in Smith County near Carthage and his wife had a summer home constructed in Tullahoma. The Catrons spent a great deal of time in the Upper Cumberland, as the judge oversaw his various business interests.[125]

When Lincoln won the 1860 election by a plurality South Carolina urged slave holding states to secede. On February 9, 1861 voters in the Volunteer State faced the possibility of Tennessee's withdrawal from the Union, less than a month before Lincoln was sworn in as the sixteenth president of the United States. Though a slave owner John Catron was a staunch unionist and lobbied against secession, urging friends and associates to remain calm and not act rashly. Tennesseans voted overwhelmingly to remain in the United States. Rational behavior was short lived.

Between February and June, Governor Isham Green Harris and his allies urged Tennesseans to reconsider and staged another vote. In the intervening period pro-secessionists resorted to terror tactics. They intimidated unionists, made violent threats, and damaged private property. In some cases they actually beat people up and even tarred and feathered a few who opposed secession. Their targets included Judge Catron. In spite of his efforts to preserve the union, Tennessee seceded on June 8, 1861.[126]

When the U.S. Supreme Court session adjourned in 1861, Catron left Washington City and returned to Nashville. He came home to a city in a frenzy. Catron intended to hold federal court in the state capitol before traveling to circuit court in Frankfort, Kentucky, and St. Louis, Missouri. Because his outspoken stance against the Confederacy was well known, Catron's life was in danger. Not only that, many old friends like Judge Josephus Conn Guild and State Supreme Court associate justice Alfred Osborne Pope (A.O.P.) Nicholson staunchly supported the Rebel cause.[127] With his life imperiled Catron "was warned by the United States Marshall that his life would be in danger if he persisted in his plans to hold Circuit Court in Nashville. A committee soon called upon him and advised him

Justice John Catron became a seasoned and respected justice who staunchly supported the Union. Credit: Tennessee State Library and Archives.

to resign from his seat on the Supreme Court or leave Tennessee within 24 hours."[128] Catron fled Nashville, leaving "behind his ailing wife, who subsequently joined him in Louisville, Kentucky, and an estate valued at more than $100,000."[129]

Fleeing the state unsettled Catron and he struggled to come to grips with his loss of personal property, friends, and colleagues. He wrote President Lincoln about his flight from Nashville and his refugee status in Louisville, Kentucky:

> I came here from Nashville to procure a residence–intending to return, & send my furniture, & bring my wife & servants–but I had left just a week when Mrs. Catron, & her attendants were sent after me by her alarmed friends–leaving 4 Slaves behind–and every other species of property except her clothes, & those of her attendants. Then, I was notified of the act of May, passed at Richmond, forfeiting the goods, & lands of such who were even in Ky, as did acts prejudicial to the Confederacy.

> Mr. Benjamin's instructions published here yesterday, may, & I think will, sweep mine in Nashville, worth over a $100.000. It covers my income on Houses & Stocks–nor do I expect, or hope for any charity, as I have to punish for Treason & will.[130]

In spite of the situation, Catron informed Lincoln that he held circuit courts in Kentucky, at Covington and Louisville in September and October, and at Frankfort at the end of October.

While holding circuit court in Missouri in July 1861, Catron weighed in on secession, deeming that those who intentionally left the Union and waged war against the United States committed treason. In his charge to the Grand Jury Catron defined treason carefully and deliberately. "When war exists all who are in league with the general conspiracy and perform any of the various and essential military parts of prosecuting it are guilty of treason." In his estimation a person did not have to actually engage in combat to be guilty. "[A] commissary who is at a distance from the scene of active military operations and who may never have been present at any hostile assemblage or even seen the Rebels camp . . . may by furnishing

John Catron. Credit: Tennessee State Library and Archives.

supplies to the traitorous forces be as guilty as if he had been in battle with arms in his hands."[131] For Catron anyone who supported the Confederate cause committed treason.

Catron returned to Nashville in 1863 to resume his circuit court duties as a Supreme Court Justice in the federally occupied state capital. While the war waged beyond Nashville, Catron was estranged in his adopted city. His hometown of Sparta changed hands seven times during the war, and citizens of White County were deeply divided. The notorious Confederate guerrilla Champ Ferguson of Clinton County, Kentucky, made White County his base of operations. The Upper Cumberland of Tennessee and Kentucky witnessed a war that truly pitted brothers against brothers. The war and the privations Catron and his wife suffered broke his spirit and his health. Though bitterly disappointed that the nation warred upon itself, he lived to see the Union preserved. When Fort Sumter was retaken by federal forces Catron was invited to join other dignitaries in a ceremony to commemorate the event and raise the United States flag to fly over the fortress. Catron was too sick to attend, but it no doubt gave him some small comfort. Judge John Catron died peacefully in his Nashville home on May 30, 1865.[132]

Justice John Catron, who once loomed over the landscape, has faded into obscurity. Docents working at the U.S. Supreme Court in Washington, D.C. stare vacantly when asked questions about him. Likewise most Americans have never heard of the man buried in a crypt at Mount Olivet Cemetery in Nashville; but his influence lingers. The man whose values were forged in the Upper Cumberland championed causes that continue to resonate from property rights, racial and gender equality, fear of corporate greed, and concerns about gun violence, to a belief in basic dignity for all mankind.

NOTES

1. George S. Yerger, ed., *The State v. Foreman* (Knoxville, July 1835), *Tennessee Reports of Cases Argued and Determined in the Supreme Court of Tennessee,* Vol. VIII (Columbia, Missouri: E. W. Stephens Publishing Co., 1912), pp. 171–248. Hereafter Yerger, *State v. Foreman. Dred Scott v. Sandford* 60 U.S. 393, 407; 15 L. Ed. 691, 702.
2. Henry Hulbert Ingersoll, "John Catron, 1781–1865," *Great American Lawyers; The Lives and Influence of Judges and Lawyers Who have Acquired Permanent National Reputations and have Developed Jurisprudence of the United States: A History of the Legal Profession in America,* William Draper Lewis, ed. (Philadelphia, Pennsylvania: John C. Winston Company, 1907), p. 241, emphasis added. Ingersoll's essay is fascinating and frustrating; it provides significant insights into Catron's career, but is utterly devoid of citations. His prose is decidedly purple: "the writer welcomes

this opportunity to place a stone upon the Catron Cairn," or "John Catron attained manhood on the western slope of the Cumberland Plateau and was thus a sample product of middle Appalachia, where grow the largest men on average on the globe," p. 242.

3. Joshua W. Caldwell, *Sketches of the Bench and Bar of Tennessee* (Knoxville, Tennessee: Ogden Brothers & Co. Printers, 1898), pp. 90-91.
4. Theodore Brown Jr., "The Formative Period in the History of the Supreme Court in Tennessee, 1796–1835," *A History of the Tennessee Supreme Court,* John Ely, ed. (Knoxville: University of Tennessee Press, 2002), p. 21.
5. Henry S. Foote, *The Bench and Bar of the South and Southwest* (St. Louis, Missouri: Soule, Thomas and Wentworth, 1876), 145.
6. John Hallum, *The Diary of an Old Lawyer: Scenes Behind the Curtain* (Nashville, Tennessee: Southwestern Publishing House, 1895), p. 350.
7. Tennesseans who have served on the U.S. Supreme Court in addition to Catron are Howell Edmunds Jackson (1893–1895), Horace Lurton (1910-1914), James Clark McReynolds (1914–1941), Edward Terry Stanford (1923–1970), and Abe Fortas (1965–1969).
8. Ingersoll, 244–245; Dunlap "Judge Catron," 172; Clare Cushman, ed., "John Catron, 1837–1865," *The Supreme Court Justices: Illustrated Biographies, 1789–1993* (Washington, D.C.: Supreme Court Historical Society, 1993), pp. 126–127. Ingersoll claimed Catron purposely obfuscated the details of his early life.
9. John Catron, "Biographical Letter from Justice Catron, of the Supreme Court of the United States," *Portraits of Eminent Americans Now Living; Including President [Franklin] Pierce and His Cabinet with Biographical and Historical Memoirs of Their Lives and Actions,* John Livingston, ed. (London, U.K.: Sampson Low, Son, and Company, 1854), p. 73; hereafter Catron, "Biographical Letter." Upon his death the *Nashville Daily Union,* reprinted Catron's "Biographical Letter," in its entirety. See *Nashville Daily Union* (Thursday, June 1, 1865), pp. 1–2.
10. *Ibid.*
11. *Ibid.*
12. *Ibid.* They used *Murray's Grammar* as their text for English usage.
13. Catron, "Biographical Letter," 73. A voracious reader he devoured works by Henry Fielding, Tobias Smollett, Oliver Goldsmith, David Hume, Thomas Paine, Edward Gibbon, Alexander Pope, and more recent works by Washington Irving.
14. *Ibid.* Catron claimed the "matchless humor" of Washington Irving "stood me in hand many times before juries, who got into the dangerous mood of an inclination to cry, when the clear interest of my client was that they should laugh."
15. *Ibid.*, 74–75.
16. *Ibid.*, 75.
17. *Ibid.*
18. *Ibid.*, 75. George W. Gibbs became a noted attorney later moving to Nashville and a successful practice. Famed White County Confederate general and industrialist George Gibbs Dibrell was named in honor of George Washington Gibbs.
19. John Catron Papers, 1826–1865 (Nashville: Tennessee State Library and Archives [TSLA], Small Collections, S-8, Folder 1, Ac. No. 79).

20. Numerous authors make the claim. See Joshua W. Caldwell, *Sketches of the Bench and Bar of Tennessee* (Knoxville, Tennessee: Ogden Brothers & Co. Printers, 1898), p. 86; Albert S. Marks, "The Supreme Court of Tennessee," *The Green Bag: An Entertaining Magazine for Lawyers* 5 (1893), p. 126; Cushman, "John Catron, 1837–1865," 127 Walter Chandler, "The Centenary of Associate Justice John Catron of the United States Supreme Court," *Tennessee Law Review*, 15 (December 1937–June 1938), p. 33; Tom Kanon, "Regimental Histories of Tennessee Units During the War of 1812," TSLA http://www.tennessee.gov/tsla/history/military/1812reg.htm Many of Jackson's troops suffered from malnutrition, dysentery, and malaria; Catron's limited service was not unusual. For the Creek War and problems facing Jackson's troops see Robert Remini, *Andrew Jackson and His Indian Wars* (New York: Penguin, 2002). It is assumed that Catron made his first acquaintance with Andrew Jackson during the Creek War.
21. Chandler, 33. In 2011 that district included aforementioned counties plus current day counties of Bedford, Cannon, Clay, Cumberland, DeKalb, Fentress, Grundy, Macon, Marion, Morgan, Putnam, Sequatchie, Scott, Trousdale, Van Buren, and Wilson.
22. Catron, "Biographical Letter," 75; Chandler, 33. Several authors argue Catron acquired Thomas's practice, but provide no evidence to support their claim. See Josephus Conn Guild, *Old Times in Tennessee with Historical, Personal, and Political Scraps and Sketches* (Nashville: Tavel, Eastman & Howell, 1878), pp. 113–115, for an example of a lawyer's courtroom education.
23. Catron, "Biographical Letter," 75–76. Emphasis is in the original.
24. *Ibid.*, 76.
25. Josephus Conn Guild, "Construing the Statutes of Limitation of 1715 and 1796—How Judge John Catron got on the Supreme Bench of Tennessee," in *Old Times in Tennessee*, 459. Guild was a prominent and prosperous judge in Gallatin, Tennessee.
26. Catron, "Biographical Letter," 76.
27. *Ibid.*
28. Joshua W. Caldwell, *Sketches of the Bench and Bar of Tennessee* (Knoxville, Tennessee: Ogden Brothers & Co. Printers, 1898), pp. 74; Guild, *Old Times in Tennessee*, 113–115.
29. Catron, "Biographical Letter," 79. Catron had a wicked sense of humor and his contemporaries commented on his withering use of sarcasm.
30. Timothy Huebner, "John Catron, Jacksonian Jurisprudence, and the Expansion of the South," *The Southern Judicial Tradition: State Judges and Sectional Distinctiveness, 1790–1890* (Athens: University of Georgia Press, 1999), p. 44.
31. John Catron, "Biographical Letter," 76. Bills of Exception are the current equivalent of providing necessary evidence to secure a new trial for a case previously adjudicated.
32. William Martin, *The Self Vindication of Colonel William Martin Against Certain Charges and Aspersions Made Against him by Gen. Andrew Jackson and Others in Relation to Sundry Transactions in the Campaign Against the Creek Indians in the Year 1813* (Nashville, Tennessee: John S. Simpson, 1829), p. 28.

33. *Ibid.*, 76–77; Henry S. Foote, *Bench and Bar of the South and Southwest* (St. Louis, Missouri: Soule, Thomas and Wentworth, 1876), p. 145.
34. Catron, "Biographical Letter," 77. Tennessee has the oldest chancery court system in the United States.
35. *Ibid.*, 76–77. In both the state legislature and the U.S. Congress, Crockett pushed for squatters' rights for settlers and a homestead bill that eventually became law after his death. See James R. Boylston and Allan J. Wiener, *David Crockett in Congress: The Rise and Fall of the Poor Man's Friend* (New York: Bright Sky Press, 2009), pp. 27–42, 327.
36. *Ibid.*, 77–78.
37. Guild, "Construing the Statutes of Limitation of 1715 and 1796—How Judge John Catron got on the Supreme Bench of Tennessee," *Old Times in Tennessee*, pp. 459–460.
38. Catron Papers, TSLA, Folders 1–4; see also *Nashville Gazette* (Saturday January 27, 1821); James Robertson was one of the founders of Nashville.
39. John Hallum, "Appointment of Judge Catron to the Supreme Bench of the United States," *The Diary of an Old Lawyer: Scenes Behind the Curtain* (Nashville, Tennessee: Southwestern Publishing House, 1895), p. 106. Catron made savvy business investments during his career. Catron and his brother owned an iron foundry and sold it for a handsome profit.
40. Carl B. Swisher, *History of the Supreme Court of the United States.* Vol 5. (New York: Macmillan, 1974), p. 64.
41. Albert S. Marks, "The Supreme Court of Tennessee." *Green Bag* 5 (1893), pp. 120–128.
42. In October, 1824 the number of judges was increased to five, and added John Catron and Hugh Lawson White to the state Supreme Court. Robert H. White, *Messages of the Governors of Tennessee, 1821–1835*, Vol. 2 (Nashville: Tennessee Historical Commission, 1952), pp. 68–69 (Hereafter White, *Messages of the Governors*); Marks, 127–128; Guild, 460-461.
43. William L. Frierson, "Some Incidents in the History of Tennessee's Court of Last Resort," *Proceedings of the Nineteenth Annual Meeting of the Bar Association of Tennessee Held at Lookout Mountain, Tennessee, July 18, 19, and 20, 1900* (Memphis: Paul & Neibert Printers and Publishers, 1900), p. 149.
44. White, *Messages of the Governors*, 69–70.
45. Ingersoll, 253.
46. Chandler, 35.
47. Caldwell, 115; Albert S. Marks, 126.
48. In 1827 John Catron, his brother George and Lucius J. Polk bought the Buffalo Iron Works, which George operated. A profitable venture, John Catron owned a portion until 1844 when Dr. E. W. Napier bought him out. See Dawson A. Phelps and John T. Willett, "Iron Works Along the Natchez Trace," *Tennessee Historical Quarterly* 12:1 (March 1953), pp. 309–322.
49. Samuel Hervey Laughlin Papers, 1796–1850 (Nashville: TSLA, THS 8)
50. Edmund C. Gass, "The Constitutional Opinions of Justice John Catron," *East Tennessee Society Publications* 8 (1936), p. 54.
51. *Ibid.*, 55. In 1829 Catron wrote a series of editorials in the *Nashville Republican* excoriating the Bank of the United States, and called for closing its branch in

Nashville. In the Bank War he was a staunch ally of Jackson and commentator for his cause.

52. Henry S. Foote, *The Bench and Bar of the South and Southwest* (St. Louis, Missouri: Soule, Thomas, and Wentworth, 1876), p. 146. Foote said Catron was "never able to supply the deficiencies of his early education," and was apparent in decisions that lacked a "graceful and polished style," 146.
53. Theodore Brown Jr., "The Formative Period in the History of the Supreme Court in Tennessee, 1796–1835," *A History of the Tennessee Supreme Court*, John Ely, ed. (Knoxville: University of Tennessee Press, 2002), p. 23.
54. Catron, "Biographical Letter," 78.
55. *Ibid.*, 78.
56. Chandler, "Catron Centenary," 41.
57. Marks, 128.
58. Walt Whitman, "Song of Myself," *Leaves of Grass* (Boston, Massachusetts: Small, Maynard & Co., 1904), p. 78.
59. Marks, 126. Catron was friends or associated with people who fought duels including Andrew Jackson, Thomas Hart Benton, Sam Houston, and many more.
60. George S. Yerger, *Calvin M. Smith v. the State of Tennessee* (Nashville, January, 1829), *Tennessee Reports of Cases Argued and Determined in the Supreme Court of Tennessee*, Vol. I (St. Louis, Missouri: G. I Jones and Co., 1876), pp. 207–220.
61. Catron, "Biographical Letter," 77.
62. *Smith v. State*, 232. The italicization of the word dare occurs in the original document.
63. *Ibid.* 234.
64. Marks, 126; Chandler, 35–38; Ingersoll, 250-251; 1834 Tennessee Constitution, Article IX, Section 3.
65. *Brooks v The State of Tennessee*, 2 Yerger 482 (Cooper, ed.), 10 Tenn. 426 (Nashville, TN Jan. 1831), pp. 482, 426.
66. *Ibid.*, 483, 427. At that time in Tennessee virtually all crimes were common law infractions, because the Tennessee General Assembly had only codified a few crimes.
67. *Ibid.*
68. *Ibid.*, 483, 427. This remains the situation in Tennessee, an indictment or affidavit of complaint/warrant, must contain all essential elements of the crime charged. *State v. Smith* (Tenn. Cr. App., 612 S.W. 2d 493; Nashville, Tennessee, November 25, 1980), pp. 493–498.
69. *Grainger v. The State*, 5 Yerger (Cooper, ed.) 458, 13 Tenn. 377 (Jackson March 1830). Catron was chief justice of the Tennessee Supreme Court when he delivered the ruling. For another description of the case see: Guild, *Old Times in Tennessee*, 361–365.
70. The common law concept of self-defense stated in Grainger is now codified in Tennessee Code Annotated § 39–11–611 (2010).
71. *Ibid.*, 461, 379. Further discussion of *Grainger* is the subject of an article in progress. In the Upper Cumberland, *Grainger* is sometimes referred to as the "he needed killing" defense.
72. *Mitchell v State*, 13 Tenn. 340; 5 Yerger 340 (Cooper, ed.) (Sparta, Tennessee 1833), pp. 279–289, 340–341. In the antebellum era all murder cases were capital cases.

73. *Ibid.*
74. *Ibid.* This is no longer true in Tennessee. Under current statute, premeditation is an act committed after the exercise of reflection and judgment; "intent to kill must have been formed prior to the act itself. It is not necessary that the purpose to kill pre-exist in the mind of the accused for any definite period of time." See Tennessee Code Annotated § 39–13–202 (d) (2010). Recent cases have held, with substantial criticism, that premeditation can be formed in an instant. See *Tennessee v. Brown,* 836 S.W.2d 530 (Knoxville, Tennessee, 1992).
75. *Cornet v Winton's Lessee,* 2 Yerger 143, 10 Tenn. 129 (Knoxville, Tennessee, July 1826), 143, 129.
76. *Ibid.*, 148–149, 134.
77. *Ibid.*, 149–150, 134–135.
78. *McConnell and Mayfield v. Mousepaine's Lessee,* 2 Yerger 436, 10 Tenn., 387 (Knoxville, Tennessee, July 1830), pp. 438–439, 388.
79. *Ibid.* Emphasis added.
80. *Ibid.* Alabama courts proved less concerned about Native American property rights. That is the subject of an article in progress.
81. *Blair v. Pathkiller' Lessee,* 2 Yerger 406, 10 Tenn. 361 (Knoxville, Tennessee, July 1830). Hugh Lawson White was a son of James White, founder of Knoxville. During his career he served on the Tennessee Supreme Court, as a U.S. senator, was chairman of the Committee on Indian Affairs, and was president pro-tempore of the Senate. He split with Jackson over Van Buren and the Bank War, becoming a prominent Whig, who ran unsuccessfully for president in 1836. White carried Tennessee and Georgia in the election
82. *Ibid.*, 412, 365.
83. *Ibid.*, 413, 366. Although rejecting the General Assembly's ability to extinguish rights of the Cherokee Nation, Catron laid the theoretical groundwork for his intellectual about-face in *The State v. Foreman.*
84. *Ibid* at 422, 374. This statement foreshadows Catron's opinion in *Dred Scott v. Sandford.* Native Americans did not become U.S. citizens until 1924.
85. *The State v. Foreman,* 8 Yerger 256, 16 Tenn. 171 (Cooper, ed.) (Knoxville, Tennessee July 1835). For a thorough discussion of *Foreman v. State* (with some minor misstatements and misinterpretations) including the fate of James Foreman see Tim Alan Garrison, *The Legal Ideology of Removal: The Southern Judiciary and the Sovereignty of Native American Nations* (Athens: University of Georgia Press, 2009), pp. 198–233. Garrison's treatment of *Foreman* is a thorough analysis of the *Foreman* decision. See Sidney L. Harding, *Crow Dog's Case* (New York: Cambridge University Press, 1994), p. 43, footnote 72.
86. *The State v. Foreman,* 8 Yerger at 256, 16 Tenn.,171. Meigs's digest states that "the case may be read with profit by any one [*sic*] who desires to acquaint himself with the history and progress of legislation in reference to the Indian tribes, the former masters of the county."
87. *The State v. Foreman,* 8 Yerger 256, 16 Tenn. 171 (Cooper, ed.) (Knoxville, Tennessee, July 1835), pp. 258, 172.
88. See for example George S. Yerger. *Cornet v. Winston's Lessee* (Knoxville, July 1826), *Tennessee Reports of Cases Argued and Determined in the Supreme Court of Tennessee,*

Vol. 2, (St. Louis, Missouri: G.I. Jones and Co., 1876), pp. 129–149. When the federal Indian Removal Act of 1830 was passed, (introduced in the U.S. House and Senate by Tennesseans John Bell and Hugh Lawson White), the Tennessee General Assembly passed legislation that was at issue in the *Foreman* decision. (See the *Public Acts of the General Assembly of Tennessee, 1833:* 10.) Catron upheld the constitutionality of this act under the Ninth Amendment.

89. *1830 Census of the United States www.censusrecords.com; 1840 Census of the United States* www.censusrecords.com; *1850 Census of the United States,* "Slave Schedule, September 6, 1850," (Washington: Government Printing Office, 1853), p. 641. Jim Hoobler,"Sally Thomas 1787–1850," *Civicscope Nashville,* http://www.civicscope.org/nashville-tn/SallyThomas. John Hope Franklin and Loren Schweninger, *In Search of the Promised Land: A Slave Family in the Old South* (New York: Oxford University Press, 2006), p. 14. Nashville African American oral tradition maintains John Catron had a son, James Thomas, through a relationship with a slave Sally Thomas. In his autobiography, James Thomas claims Catron as his father; there is documentation that Catron acted as trustee in a land transaction involving one of his slaves, Willis Hickman, and James Thomas and loaned James Thomas six hundred dollars to complete the deal. Theodore Brown Jr., stated, "There appears to be no surviving corroborating evidence to support this claim" in James Thomas's autobiography. See Theodore Brown Jr., "The Formative Period in the History of the Supreme Court of Tennessee 1796–1835," in *A History of the Tennessee Supreme Court,* James W. Ely Jr., ed. (Knoxville: The University of Tennessee Press, 2002), p. 380. For more on slaves and the law in Tennessee, see Arthur F. Howington, *What Sayeth the Law? The Treatment of Slaves and Free Blacks in the State and Local Courts of Tennessee* (New York: Garland, 1986).
90. *Loftin v. Espy,* 4Yerger 84, 12 Tenn. 68 (Cooper, ed., Jackson, Tennessee 1833), pp. 92, 75.
91. *Harris v. Clarissa,* 6 Yerg 227, 14 Tenn. 153 (Cooper, ed., Nashville, Tennessee 1834).
92. *Ibid.,* 245, 166.
93. *Ibid.,* 243, 164.
94. *Ibid.,* emphasis added.
95. *Fishers Negroes v. Dabbs,* 6 Yerg 120, 14 Tenn. 78 (Cooper, ed., Nashville, Tennessee, 1834), pp. , 106. A key aspect of Catron's decision in *Fisher's Negroes* was that the Tennessee judiciary possessed "an independent power, and, where it has jurisdiction, sovereign power, just as much as the legislature itself." Catron empathized with the plight of slaves, but to modern readers some of his words appear especially harsh. Even though slaves could be manumitted, Catron noted in *Fisher's* Negroes that slaves freed in Tennessee had to be deported to Liberia.
96. Ingersoll, 263.
97. John Catron, "Letter to the Judiciary Committee," reprinted in Robert H. White, ed., *Messages of the Governors of Tennessee, 1821–1835,* Vol. II (Nashville: Tennessee Historical Commission, 1952), pp. 353–354.
98. Huebner, 64–65. Among the Tennesseans who joined the Whigs were Davy Crockett and John Bell. Catron and Martin Van Buren later parted ways due to their diametrically opposed views on slavery. By 1844 Van Buren curried favor with the Barnburners in the Democratic Party who favored abolition.

99. "How a Wife Made a Supreme Judge; Mrs. Catron Gets the Appointment from Andrew Jackson," *New York Times* (May 10, 1896), p. 29; Joshua W. Caldwell, *Bench and Bar,* 87; John Hallum, "Appointment of Judge Catron to the Supreme Bench of the United States," *The Diary of an Old Lawyer: Scenes Behind the Curtain* (Nashville, Tennessee: Southwestern Publishing House, 1895), pp. 106–108.
100. Swisher, 63.
101. Edmund C. Gass, "The Constitutional Opinions of Justice John Catron," *East Tennessee Historical Society Publications* 8 (1936), pp. 55–58.
102. Joshua W. Caldwell, *Studies in the Constitutional History of Tennessee,* 2nd. Ed. (Cincinnati, Ohio: Robert Clark Co., 1907), pp. 233.
103. Paul H. Bergeron, "Tennessee's Response to the Nullification Crisis," *The Journal of Southern History* 39: 1 (February 1973), pp. 33–34, 41–42. Usually a state's rights advocate, Catron opposed South Carolina's initial unwillingness to compromise, opting for secession rather than serious negotiation.
104. Chandler, 42. Chandler argued that Catron interpreted laws and applied them to "make each settler safe in his landed rights," and safeguard them against predatory speculators. He praised Catron, "be it said to his credit that he was consistently in the minority on the Supreme Court when the gigantic land frauds . . . were being perpetrated on the courts," 42–43.
105. Chandler, 32, 42. He notes that Catron was the "only Justice ever nominated by one President. . . and confirmed on that nomination in the term of another Chief Executive. . ." 32. Jackson recommended John McKinley of Alabama for the other seat on the Supreme Court. The second Tennessean on the bench was Howell E. Jackson who served from 1893–1895.
106. Catron, "Biographical Letter," 73.
107. "Judge Catron," *National Daily Intelligencer* (March 17, 1852).
108. Chandler, 42. Creating the new district from states currently at war with the United States displayed a belief that the Union would soon be restored. These courts were the intermediate courts in the federal judicial system. At the lowest level was the district court, presided over by a district court judge appointed by the president. Appeals from district courts went to the appropriate circuit court presided over by a U.S. Supreme Court justice. Appeals from the various circuit courts were argued before the U.S. Supreme Court.
109. Chandler, 43.
110. *Ibid.*
111. Catron, "Biographical Letter," 79. While on the federal bench Catron was a staunch supporter of the Ninth Amendment, generally invoking it in cases regarding the Commerce Clause of the Constitution. As such he was "vigorous champion of the police power of the states." Even so, he was a committed unionist to his dying day.
112. *The Northern Indiana Railroad Company, et al v The Michigan Central Railroad Company,* 249. Andrew Jackson shared the same sentiment and supposedly said that corporations had neither "a body to kick nor a soul to damn." Quoted in David S. Reynolds, *Waking Giant: America in the Age of Jackson* (New York: Harper Perennial, 2008). If he were alive, Catron would probably take issue with the U.S.

Supreme Court's decision in *Citizens United v. Federal Election Commission* 558 US 50, 130 S. Ct. 976 (2010).

113. *Ohio Life Insurance and Trust Co. v. Debolt*, 57 U.S. 416,; 14 L. Ed. 997; 16 Howard 416 (Washington City, May 24, 1854) p. 441.
114. *Marsh, Lee and Delavan v Brooks, et al*, 49 U.S. 223; 12 L. Ed. 1056; 8 Howard, 223 (Washington, D.C. Feb.1850), pp. 232–233. "Fee-simple" means one has complete ownership of the land and no other claims by anyone or any government to the land, on or below the surface.
115. *Doe ex dem Mann and Hannah v. Wilson*, 64 U.S. 457; 16 L. Ed. 584; 23 HOW 457 (Washington, D.C. May 4, 1860).
116. *Ibid.*, 463.
117. *Ibid.*, 461.
118. Don E. Fehrenbacher, *The Dred Scott Case* (New York: Oxford University Press, 1978), p. 102.
119. *Dred Scot v Sandford, 60 U.S. 393, 407; 15 L. Ed. 691, 702; 19 Howard 393 (1857),* The U.S. Supreme Court read opinions in *Dred Scott* case March 6, 1857, two days after Buchanan's inauguration.
120. Catron held treaties sacrosanct except when it came to Native American rights in *The State v. Foreman,* which is inconsistent with his other opinions. *Dred Scott,* XX.
121. "What the Dred Scott Case Decided," *New York Times,* July 16, 1857.
122. Philip Auchampaugh "James Buchanan, the Court and the Dred Scott Case," *Tennessee Historical Magazine* vol. IX, No. 4 (January 1926; issued Oct. 1928), pp. 233–238. Justice Curtis wrote his uncle about the deliberations of the *Dred Scott* case. Benjamin R. Curtis to Ticknor, April 8, 1856, Benjamin R. Curtis, *Memoir of Benjamin Robbins Curtis* (Boston: Little, Brown, 1879), pp. 179–180. Incredibly, Justice Curtis's brother George was one of Dred Scott's defense attorneys, and the Supreme Court justice refused to recuse himself from the case.
123. *Ibid.*
124. *Ibid.*
125. *John Catron v. Warren Moore,* 41 Tenn. 358; 1860. Catron considered the home in Tullahoma to be his wife's personal property, and he had to defend her right in the Tennessee Supreme Court.
126. James B. Jones Jr., "'The Reign of Terror of the Safety Committee has Passed Away Forever': A History of the Committees of Safety and Vigilance in West and Middle Tennessee, 1860–1862," *West Tennessee Historical Society Papers* LXIII (2009), pp. 1–28; Derek Frisby, "The Vortex to Secession: West Tennessee and the Rush to War," *Sister States/Enemy States: The Civil War in Kentucky and Tennessee,* Kent Dollar, Larry Whiteaker, and Calvin Dickinson, eds. (Lexington: University Press of Kentucky, 2009), pp. 46–71.
127. Brian D. McKnight, *Confederate Outlaw: Champ Ferguson and the Civil War in Appalachia* (Baton Rouge: Louisiana State University Press, 2011), pp. 164–172. When the war ended Guild acted as Champ Ferguson's attorney in his war crimes trial. After the federal army occupied Nashville A.O.P. Nicholson refused to sign the oath of allegiance to the United States. Military Governor Andrew Johnson had him arrested and deported from the Volunteer State.

128. Harry Phillips, "The Courts," in *History of the Sixth Circuit* (Bicentennial Committee of the Judicial Conference of the United States 1976), p. 52.
129. Cushman, "John Catron, 1837–1865," 130. "From Nashville: Judge Catron, of the Supreme Court, was Last Week Expelled from Nashville by the Vigilance Committee, because of his Refusal to Resign his Judgeship. He was Obliged to Leave his Wife in Nashville on Account of her Sickness." *New York Times* (August 14, 1861); "Southern News Through Louisville," *New York Times*, August 2, 1861. H.K. Stevenson wrote the *Nashville Union* saying "Judge Catron will not undertake to hold Federal Court in Nashville again, no matter what may occur."
130. John Catron to Abraham Lincoln, Wednesday, October 09, 1861 "Abraham Lincoln Papers," Library of Congress Washington, D.C. Transcribed and Annotated by the Lincoln Studies Center, Knox College. Galesburg, Illinois. "Law Reports . . . Supreme Court–Chambers. A Missouri Judge on Treason. Charge of Judge Catron," *New York Times*, July 15, 1861.
131. "Law Reports: A Missouri Judge on Treason—The Charge of Judge Catron," *New York Times*, July 15, 1861, p. 6.
132. McKnight, 115–139; "Fort Sumter: Departure of the *Arago*—The Old Flag on Board," *New York Times*, April 10, 1865, p. 5. Champ's brother Jim fought for with Union forces. Catron's old friend Josephus Conn Guild acted as Champ Ferguson's attorney during the guerrilla's murder trial in Nashville.

8

A Legacy of Blood

The Legend of Champ Ferguson

Troy D. Smith

On October 20, 1865, Confederate guerrilla Champ Ferguson ascended a scaffold in the Nashville penitentiary yard. He had been charged with twenty-three specifications of murder, many involving multiple killings, for a total of fifty-three alleged victims. In a highly publicized trial, he had been convicted on twenty-one of those counts. It is impossible to gauge how many lives Ferguson actually took during the war, but the number was substantial, as historian Brian D. McKnight stated, "Perhaps no other single participant in the Civil War could claim a bloodier career."[1]

Ferguson defended his actions in a statement to the press:

> I was a Southern Man at the start. I am yet, and will die a Rebel. I believe I was right in all I did. I don't think I have done anything wrong at anytime. I committed my deeds in a cool and deliberate manner. I have killed a good many men, of course; I don't deny that, but I never killed a man whom I did not know was seeking my life. . . I repeat that I die a Rebel out and out, and my last request is that my body be removed to White County, Tennessee, and be buried in good Rebel soil. . .[2]

The scaffold's trap door opened beneath Ferguson's feet a few minutes before noon, and he made a two-foot drop into eternity. Though his war, his career, and his life were over, Champ Ferguson's hold on the cultural imagination of the Upper Cumberland was only beginning. Journalists from the *Nashville Dispatch* reported that, after they had witnessed his execution, "we found a rumor in circulation that Champ had been pardoned or had his sentence commuted at the last moment. Many persons believed it, and it was the general impression that he would not be hung [*sic*], but have his sentence changed to imprisonment for life." Even after reports of the hanging, some people refused to believe Ferguson was dead, and rumors circulated—in some quarters up to the present day—that his execution had been staged, and that the notorious guerrilla had been secretly released to begin a new life in the West.[3]

Champ Ferguson was born in Clinton County, in the Kentucky Upper Cumberland on November 29, 1861. He was named after his grandfather, who "was sometimes called Champion."[4] Ferguson spent most of his life as a farmer, and was well-known along the Tennessee-Kentucky border of the Upper Cumberland region. He was regarded as a man who loved horses and liked his liquor. Several of his contemporaries, who were admittedly not impartial, described his pre-war reputation: He was "a bully, a ruffian, and daredevil kind of fellow," and was "known as a gambling, rowdyish, drinking, fighting, quarrelsome man. He seemed to always be in hot water."[5]

Ferguson turned a significant corner in 1858, and the hot water he was accustomed to experiencing reached a boiling point. He attended a camp meeting in Fentress County, Tennessee, (probably more for the attendant social activities than the religious ones) and ran afoul of some personal enemies—Floyd and Alexander Evans—with whom he had been involved in a financial dispute. They had sworn out a warrant for Ferguson, claiming he had been stealing horses from them to recover a debt they owed him. A brawl ensued, and in the melee Ferguson stabbed two men, one of them fatally. The deceased was Jim Reed, a constable from Jamestown, Tennessee—and a relative of the Evans brothers who had accused Ferguson of horse theft. Ferguson claimed that he simply acted in self-defense.[6]

Ferguson was subsequently arrested and released on bail. He was represented by a young lawyer, Scott Bledsoe, who after the war began raised a band of Confederate partisans. When Tennessee voted to secede, Ferguson was awaiting trial for the murder of Reed. With war close on the horizon, there was little time to devote to pending judicial actions. The trial was all but forgotten, and Ferguson declared his sympathies for the Confederacy. He later claimed that he had been "induced to join the army on the promise that all prosecution in that case would be abandoned."[7] This is a credible explanation for his political stand, considering that the overwhelming majority of people in his home county, including his own relatives, remained loyal to the Union.

The Upper Cumberland was bitterly divided during the Civil War. The northeastern counties along the Kentucky-Tennessee border tended to be primarily pro-Union while those in the southwest were pro-Confederate, but every community was split to some extent. Although the region saw few large-scale military actions, the conflict was bloody and disruptive nonetheless. Roaming bands of partisans, representing each side, but often

General John Hunt Morgan. Credit: Tennessee State Library and Archives.

little more than opportunistic outlaws, raided and robbed at will. Courts and local governments were brought to a standstill. Farmers found themselves victimized by one side or the other, and sometimes by both. Idle speculation about an individual's affiliations could lead to their homes being raided and their lives threatened or ended. Many locals found it wise to relocate, or at least to find a good hiding place for their stock and themselves in the event of an attack.

Numerous guerrilla leaders operated in the Upper Cumberland on both sides of the conflict, including Fentress County's "Tinker" Dave Beatty and his Union Scouts, as well as Boney Pruitt and Rufus Dowdy. Prominent Confederate guerrillas included Pomp Kersey, Captain John Francis, Colonel John M. Hughs, and Colonel Oliver Hamilton. None, however, could match Champ Ferguson's brutal reputation. Some in the Upper Cumberland regarded him an opportunistic thug, while others viewed him as a hero, largely dependent on their own political loyalties.[8]

Guerrillas from both sides showed little mercy to their enemies, and their tactics did not follow military rules of engagement. An individual known, or even suspected, to support the opposition might be hunted down and callously dispatched within sight of their families. Ferguson himself gave an apt description of the situation:

> We were having a sort of miscellaneous war, up there, through Fentress county, Tennessee, and Clinton county, Kentucky, and all through that region. Every man was in danger of his life; if I hadn't kill[ed] my neighbor, he would have killed me. Each of us had from 20 to 30 proscribed enemies, and it was regarded as legitimate to kill them at any time, at any place, under any circumstances.[9]

Ferguson proved early on that he was, indeed, willing to kill under any circumstances. On November 1, 1861 he visited the home of fellow Clinton County native William Frogg. Ferguson had heard the man was seen near Camp Dick Robinson, a recruiting site in Kentucky for the pro-Union Home Guard.[10] He also claimed to have heard that Frogg planned to kill him. Frogg had, in fact, recently joined the 12th Kentucky Infantry (Union), a detail he probably did not choose to share with his unexpected visitor. Frogg lay in bed with measles; his five-month-old baby lay in a crib in the same room.

Frogg's wife was on the front porch peeling apples when she saw Ferguson and his two comrades approach. She offered him an apple, and he curtly declined—"I have been eating apples," he said, before he went inside to confront her husband while his companions waited outside. Frogg protested that he was sick, and Ferguson replied, "I reckon you caught the measles at Camp Dick Robinson." He shot the sick man twice. Like many of his killings, Ferguson considered it justified. If Frogg had recovered from his illness, he would only have come after Ferguson to give him the same treatment. Ferguson viewed his own actions as preemptive self-defense. "I took time by the forelock, as people say," he explained.[11]

Frogg's murder established a pattern Ferguson would follow throughout the war. A month after killing Frogg, he targeted one of his own oldest acquaintances, Reuben Wood. Ferguson confronted Wood at his home, in front of his children. "Don't you beg, and don't you dodge," he told the older man. When Wood protested that he had babysat Ferguson when he was a child, the guerrilla replied, "You have always treated me like a gentleman, but you have been to Camp Dick Robinson, and I intend to kill you." He was true to his word, although Wood put up a fierce fight.[12]

On April 1, 1862, Ferguson encountered sixteen-year-old Fount Zachery in Fentress County. The youth surrendered his shotgun, but Ferguson shot him anyway, then proceeded to stab him with a Bowie knife as he lay on the ground. The guerrilla excused his actions by claiming he had orders to kill any armed men he found in the area. Zachery was the first of four males in his family to die at the hands of Champ Ferguson.[13]

A few months later Ferguson shot Washington Tabor in the head and stomach. As the man lay on the ground writhing in agony Ferguson's men persuaded him to put the old man out of his misery. Ferguson put his pistol to the man's head and blew his brains out. Ferguson suspected Tabor of killing some of his comrades and deserving to die. Having no quarrel with the men who rode with Tabor, Ferguson let them go. He told one of them, George Thrasher, "I'm not in favor of killing you, Thrasher, you have never been bushwhacking or stealing horses. . . I have killed old Wash Tabor, a damned good Christian, and I don't reckon he minds dying."[14]

Ferguson eventually moved his family from the heavily pro-Union Clinton County, Kentucky, to the much more Confederate-friendly White County, Tennessee, where he bought a farm on the Calfkiller River a few miles north of Sparta. Soon afterwards, Ferguson joined several other local partisans to serve as guides for John Hunt Morgan's scouting expedition into Kentucky. Ferguson caught the attention of Morgan's second in command and brother-in-law, Major Basil Duke:

Champ Ferguson, taken while on trial in Nashville, surrounded by his guards. Credit: Tennessee State Library and Archives.

> At Sparta, Champe [*sic*] Ferguson reported himself as a guide and I, for the first time, saw him, although I had often heard of him before. He had the reputation of never giving quarter, and, no doubt, deserved it (when upon his own private expeditions), although when with Morgan he attempted no interference with prisoners... he was a man of strong sense, although totally uneducated, and of the intense will and energy, which, in men of his stamp and mode of life, have such a tendency to develope [*sic*] into ferocity, when they are in the least injured or opposed. [15]

Later in the war Ferguson served in a similar capacity under the command of General Joseph Wheeler, then under that of General John C. Breckinridge in Southwest Virginia. During the latter period Ferguson was involved in one of his most notorious atrocities. He fought in the Battle of Saltville on October 2, 1864, which ended in a Union retreat. Witnesses later testified that the morning after the battle they had seen Ferguson among the Tennesseans who mercilessly killed a number of wounded Union soldiers, especially black ones and the whites who had served with them. A few days later Ferguson entered the hospital where surviving prisoners had been taken, apparently looking for someone in particular. He killed two more wounded black soldiers, almost as an afterthought, then killed Lieutenant Elza Smith—a Union soldier and relative of Ferguson's wife—in his bed.[16]

Ferguson, who was taken into custody at the end of the war, expected to be paroled as other partisans had been. Instead he was arrested and taken to Nashville to stand trial as a guerrilla and a murderer. Ferguson's defense that he had acted as a soldier under the orders of superior officers did not sway the military court. The tribunal denied that he had ever officially joined the Confederate Army, but instead claimed he had acted as an independent citizen in carrying out his killings.

Three weeks after the death of Champ Ferguson, the federal government also executed the Swiss-born commander of the infamous Confederate prison camp in Andersonville, Georgia, having found him guilty of eleven counts of murdering prisoners. Heinrich Hartmann Wirz, by then known as Henry Wirz, has remained infamous ever since, and he has often been referred to by both amateur and professional historians as the only Confederate executed for war crimes. While this may be technically accurate, since the ambiguity of Ferguson's official status within the Confederate military was a factor in his own conviction, some historians would nonetheless include Ferguson's name beside Wirz's. The Andersonville commandant and the Upper Cumberland guerrilla's trials were both sensational events, covered by the national press, and the verdicts were indictments—not only of the individuals—but of the Confederacy, providing avatars on whom the government and an outraged public could exact symbolic revenge as well as mete out literal justice.

Unlike Wirz, however, Ferguson seems to have generally faded from the national consciousness until recent decades. Throughout the twentieth century, the guerrilla was little known outside his home region except to some historians, military specialists, and folklorists. Within that Upper Cumberland region, however, his memory grew to mythological proportions. Seeds of his legend had already sprouted during the years of his activity and flourished in subsequent generations. While it is true that encyclopedias did not list Ferguson alongside Wirz as a war criminal, it is equally true that no one repeated romanticized myths about Wirz's motivations or fate. Ferguson's wartime nemesis "Tinker" Dave Beatty has also remained alive in Upper Cumberland memory, albeit primarily as a counterweight to Ferguson in terror, but Beatty's exploits have not become the stuff of legend.

This author was born and raised in Champ Ferguson's adopted hometown of Sparta, Tennessee, and can testify that in the 1970s Ferguson was a strong presence, not just in local history, but in folktales and popular lore. Older relatives regaled me as a child with stories of our local guerrilla's ferocity, framed as Southern patriotism, and his tragic martyrdom. Such tales were strong threads in the Lost Cause tapestry woven, generation by generation, in our community, as surely as were the annual screenings of *Gone with the Wind* (MGM 1939) at Oldham's Theater on the town square.

One part of the legend, discussed earlier, first took hold on the very day of Ferguson's execution, when Nashville reporters encountered rumors that he had been secretly pardoned and released. While one might assume that the actual killing of Ferguson, witnessed by hundreds of onlookers, and his subsequent burial would lay those rumors to rest; they did not. In 1886 a *Nashville Banner* reporter wrote that he had been told by "a man from the mountains" that the execution had been an elaborate hoax, with a different condemned criminal hanged in Ferguson's stead, after the condemned man had paid fifteen thousand dollars for his freedom.[17]

A different, and more detailed, alternate history was presented in a 1909 Fentress County *Gazette* article. In that version, a life-sized doll was hanged at the Nashville penitentiary and then buried in Ferguson's White County grave. The article included information gleaned from an Oklahoma man who claimed to be Ferguson's son; the author later reported that Ferguson was alive and well in Mississippi.[18]

In the afterword of the 1995 edition of his father's biography of Ferguson, Thurman Sensing Jr. recounted a story he had read in a Cookeville, Tennessee, newspaper detailing the guerrilla's escape from death.

This version involved the complicity of a sympathetic U.S. military, a specially constructed gallows, federal troops purposely obstructing the crowd's view, and the live Ferguson being placed in his casket only to hop out once the funeral procession slipped away from prying eyes and embarking on a new life in Oklahoma with his family.[19]

None of these stories can be supported by evidence, beyond the hearsay testimony of a handful of very dubious witnesses. That has not prevented their dissemination in the Upper Cumberland. Many citizens of the area with an interest in Ferguson and his legend are willing to entertain the possibility that, like Jesse James and Billy the Kid, their semi-mythic hero surmounted even death. As recently as 2012, the White County Heritage Museum received a couple of visits from an elderly gentleman with Oklahoma roots who claimed to be descended from a child fathered by Ferguson with a Native American lover. While hiding out in Oklahoma after his escape from execution, Ferguson engaged in a tryst while waiting for his wife and child to join him from Tennessee.[20]

While the end of Ferguson's bloody career has become the subject of fable, its beginning has spawned even more fantasy. Tall tales about the guerrilla's motivations abounded even during the Civil War. While evidence indicates that Ferguson was an opportunistic criminal, his admirers have long ascribed nobler, or at least more romantic, reasons for his violent actions toward his enemies. These have usually involved revenge, turning Ferguson's career into a series of vendettas against those who had deeply wronged his family.

One of the most enduring of those myths centers on Ferguson's little son, three years old at the beginning of the conflict. In one version the boy is shot and killed in crossfire during a skirmish, but the most commonly told story proved even more incendiary. Allegedly, the little boy was standing on his family's front porch when he saw a column of soldiers approaching. With childish excitement, he waved the Confederate flag vigorously as they passed. Unfortunately, they were Union soldiers, not Rebels. They were so incensed by the sight of their enemy's flag that they shot the little boy dead. This legend saw print several times after the war; one version, in a 1909 issue of *Confederate Veteran*, described Ferguson's reaction: "O anguish! How that father's heart bled! His spirit welled up like the indomitable will of the primitive Norseman. In a moment of frenzy he said that the death of his baby would cost the "bluecoats" a hundred lives. And it did. One hundred and twenty is believed to be the number he put to death."[21]

The main problem with this story is that Ferguson did not have a son, of any age, at the beginning of the Civil War. His only living child was a daughter. He once had a son, by a previous marriage. That child died in an epidemic when he was three years old, about sixteen years earlier. Nonetheless, the story held enormous symbolic power and longevity, as demonstrated by the many times it has been recounted on the page, and the innumerable times it has been repeated orally. In the spring of 2012, this author accompanied several other historians, including Brian McKnight, Michael Birdwell, and Larry Whiteaker, on a tour of Ferguson's gravesite and the former location of his house by the Calfkiller River. A couple of local citizens were on hand to provide access to the private property that had once been Ferguson's farm. One of them was surprised and disappointed to learn that the story of Ferguson's flag-waving son was untrue.

A second legend about Ferguson's motives has even more standing in the cultural memory of the Upper Cumberland. This one does not mention a non-existent son, but includes the rest of Ferguson's family. This story, which has probably been repeated more often than the apocryphal tale about the shooting of Ferguson's young son, involves an outrage committed against Ferguson's wife and daughter by his enemies. There are many versions; some claim that the assailants were regular Union soldiers, others say they were Home Guards or Jayhawkers, while others involve a combination of predatory Yankees. The attackers usually number at least eleven, though some versions claim as many as sixteen.

Whatever its constitution, the group of Unionists allegedly visited Ferguson's home while he was away (in one iteration, he was in a nearby cave trying to decide whether or not to go to war). The assailants forced Ferguson's wife and teen-aged daughter to strip naked and cook them a meal while nude; the unfortunate women were then forced to walk up and down the road in shame and display their nakedness to the world. In at least one version soldiers drive them with a whip. Some versions specify that they were raped; in fact, it was sometimes reported that they were raped and murdered, while their house burned down around their dead bodies.[22]

In the various tales, Ferguson returned to his home—or in some cases, the smoking ashes that remained of it—and discovered the horrible crime. In accounts where the family survived, he learns the identity of their attackers. In every version, he swears terrible revenge. The names of men Ferguson brutally killed during the course of the war often appear on lists of his family's violators; his treatment of them, therefore, is presented as the justifiable rage of a vengeful husband and father.[23]

The story was disseminated and repeated by Ferguson apologists while he was an active guerrilla. In fact, a soldier who served under General John Hunt Morgan's command, John Weatherred, claimed in his diary that Ferguson himself referenced the tale. When Morgan's men were dismayed by the sight of Ferguson cutting the throat of the wounded Union guerrilla Elam Huddleston, Ferguson offered an excuse for his brutality, as recorded by Weatherred: "We were very mad that he did this; but he explained that Capt. Elam Huddleston had burned his house and outraged his wife and daughter a few months before this and he had sworn revenge against him and his men who were there at the outrage."[24]

If Weatherred's account is accurate, Ferguson did not hesitate to use the growing legend to his advantage. It is the only written report, however, of the guerrilla claiming that his family had been violated. In his biography of Ferguson, Brian McKnight has suggested that internal inconsistencies in Weatherred's undated diary indicate that it was written many years after the fact, and that the author may have inadvertently presented the popular story as a personal memory.[25] Such speculation notwithstanding, it is a fact that not only did Ferguson never repeat the story to anyone who might record it, but when pressed on the question by reporters during his trial Champ Ferguson adamantly refuted it:

> We have repeatedly heard it stated that Lieut. Smith, who was killed at Saltville in the hospital, went to Ferguson's house with his company, and offered Mrs. Ferguson and her young daughter the most outrageous insults. This, it was said, led Champ to kill him. We asked him if it was so. He said that the story was absurd, that Lieut. [Elza] Smith was a relative of his first wife, and that his family were never insulted or mistreated by Federals during the war; but they robbed her, like everybody else, of all she had to eat, which was a slight failing on both sides. . . Champ denies the killing of Smith or the massacre at Saltville, and claimed alibi.[26]

Later, Ferguson admitted killing Smith, but expressed no regret at having done so, as Smith had been merciless to Ferguson's comrades-in-arms. There had also been testimony suggesting Smith may have killed Ferguson's friend and fellow guerrilla leader Oliver Hamilton. At no time, however, did Ferguson offer up the sexual assault of his family as justification for his wartime actions—not during his defense at trial, nor in his final statement to the press. Verifying, or at least claiming to verify, that such an outrage occurred could potentially have been very helpful to Ferguson. It is reasonable to assume he would have done so had there been a shred of truth, or even credibility, to it.

Nonetheless, the story of the Union band's alleged attack on Ferguson's family has maintained traction in the cultural memory of the infamous guerrilla. Ferguson's admirers and defenders in the Upper Cumberland reverently repeat it, as if it were gospel. The story of the assault against the Ferguson women's staying power in the public mind has probably been reinforced by Thurman Sensing's 1940 biography of Ferguson, which for decades was the only book devoted to the guerrilla and avidly sought out by those interested in his story, remaining in print for most of that time.

Sensing was for many years the research director, and one of the leaders, of the Southern States Industrial Council (SSIC). A group composed of right-wing businessmen SSIC was known for "trumpeting the twin goals of economic growth and racial retrenchment." Sensing wrote widely in support of the group's platform opposing civil rights and the welfare state, contributing articles not only to SSIC publications, but also to such venues as the Libertarian journal *The Freeman*. Sensing was not only a defender of traditional Southern racist hierarchies, he was also an apologist for the "Confederate martyr" Ferguson. His biography, although filled with helpful references to primary documents, was ultimately a celebration of Ferguson as a Southern hero.[27]

Sensing noted Ferguson's repudiation of the assault story, but added, "We cannot afford to give this statement too much weight." He observed that Ferguson initially denied killing Smith, then later changed his story. Therefore, in Sensing's view, he may have been dissembling when he said there had been no attack on his family. Such an assault, after all, would have been the worst injury Ferguson's enemies could inflict on him—and hating him as they did, would have proved hard to resist.[28]

Sensing then engaged in an impressive effort at logical acrobatics—citing the fact that Ferguson just mentioned the assault on his family once, and then spoke only to deny it, as evidence that it must therefore be true.[29] Sensing opined, "One might also point out that it would be contrary to mountaineer code or custom either to admit that such a thing had happened or to discuss it afterward… It would be nothing at which to be astonished that the matter should never again be referred to by Champ Ferguson or admitted when referred to by another."[30]

In his discussion of Smith's murder, Sensing repeatedly implied that the victim was the last member of the group who assaulted Ferguson's wife and daughter, and thus the final object of Ferguson's revenge. He speculated that Smith was actually an alias for Ferguson's pro-Union brother, Jim—an unverifiable assertion that, Sensing admits, may be only "a wild suspicion,"[31] but which he repeated in his later book. For decades, Sensing's work was the only biography of Ferguson. The volume's unprofessional claims helped reinforce mythology under the guise of history for generations, bearing as it did the imprimatur of the Vanderbilt University Press.

In 1999 this author, at the time a historical novelist, but not yet a professional historian, set about the task of writing a fictionalized version of Ferguson's story. I made use of resources readily available, including documents at the Tennessee state archives, to research the subject as thoroughly as I could. This resulted in another, simultaneous project: a history article for *Civil War Times Illustrated.* In the article I made clear the ahistorical nature of the alleged outrage on Ferguson's family. In the novel, however, I chose to follow the advice of the editor Dutton Peabody in John Ford's *The Man Who Shot Liberty Valance* (Paramount, 1962): when fact becomes legend, print the legend. After all, the legend makes for much better drama in this case. I included an introduction which clearly stated the fictional nature of my work, and referred readers to my *Civil War Times* article for a more accurate portrayal of events.[32]

Nonetheless, I had occasion years later to regret that decision. Invited to speak at a meeting of Sons of Confederate Veterans in Crossville, Tennessee, I used the forum to try to shed light on some common misconceptions about the war. One member in attendance told me that my novel about Ferguson, *Good Rebel Soil,* had enraged him due to my inclusion of the "family assault" legend. He had been trying for years to disabuse people of that myth, he said, then I came along and reinforced it. Having earned a bachelor's degree, then a doctorate, in history since the first publication of the novel, I was abashed. As a novelist, however, my sole defense remained unchanged: It made for a darn good story.

And that may explain why it spread so rapidly and widely during Ferguson's lifetime, echoed through the generations afterward, and in fact became a part of common American memory about the Civil War. The efficacy of a good narrative, coupled with the justification affixed to grisly events by the attachment of a story that stokes moral outrage, make for a powerful, resonant thread in popular culture.

The Champ Ferguson revenge legends may have started while he was still alive and wreaking havoc, but it was in the post-war period, when the Lost Cause narrative was being expounded by Confederate veterans and their supporters, that they began to be disseminated widely, beginning with Basil Duke's *History of Morgan's Cavalry* in 1867.[33] Lost Cause apologists wove a counterfactual narrative in which all Confederates had been noble and misunderstood, doomed to failure by forces beyond their control, fighting—not to ensure the continued enslavement of human beings—but solely to defend their homes, their honor, and the safety of their women.

It is no surprise, then, that the Champ Ferguson legends which proved so long-lived involved unprovoked attacks on his family by evil Unionists. The bullet-riddled body of the three-year old boy, Rebel flag still clutched in his little fingers, is an image that drips with symbolism. The wife, and perhaps even more the teen daughter, stripped naked, raped, and sometimes murdered and immolated are perhaps even more incendiary imagery. Ferguson stalks through these narratives—not as a brutal criminal—but as a wronged Scottish Highlander or an enraged latter day Norseman, seeking a bloody revenge that is not only harsh justice, but a vindication of the purity of the Southern (white) people whose homes had been so ignominiously invaded.

That sort of Lost Cause imagery was especially effective in formerly Confederate regions, but also proved successful in reframing memory of the War throughout the country. The 1915 D.W. Griffith film *Birth of a Nation,* based on Thomas Dixon's novel *The Clansman,* which glorified the Ku Klux Klan during Reconstruction as the protectors of Southern white womanhood, was not only popular in the South,[34] it was a nationwide hit praised by President Woodrow Wilson. It was so successful in its message that it helped spur a renaissance of the Klan in the 1920s. The idea of using terror to carry out revenge for Yankee depredations against Southern women struck a very resonant national chord. The noble Southern man's otherwise barbaric actions are not only rendered understandable, they are applauded and approved.[35]

Historian Brian McKnight has pointed to the possible influence of the Champ Ferguson legend on the fictional western *The Outlaw Josey Wales.* The novel was written by Asa Earl Carter, under the pseudonym Forrest Carter (his pen name was based on Nathan Bedford Forrest, Confederate general and founder of the Ku Klux Klan). Carter was originally from northern Alabama, and may well have been familiar with the Champ Ferguson mythology. He was also a white supremacist, a speech writer for Alabama Governor George Wallace, and a contemporary of Thurman Sensing. In fact, he wrote the words Wallace famously spoke decrying civil rights: "Segregation now! Segregation tomorrow! Segregation forever!"[36]

In 1973 Carter wrote the novel *The Rebel Outlaw Josey Wales,* which was later renamed *Gone to Texas* and released as the film *The Outlaw Josey Wales,* directed by and starring Clint Eastwood in 1976. The eponymous character, McKnight suggests convincingly, is a composite of Ferguson and several Missouri Confederate guerrillas including Jesse James and Bloody Bill Anderson. James and Anderson were rumored to have had female relatives who were killed by Yankees; Anderson in particular was allegedly fueled by rage, and was known for scalping his enemies. Like Ferguson, Jesse James attempted to surrender to Union forces; he was shot and almost killed.[37]

In the Warner Bros. film, Josey Wales is a simple Missouri farmer whose homestead is attacked by Kansas Redlegs. They burn his cabin with his wife and child inside, leading Wales to swear revenge on Yankees—he rides with William Clark Quantrill until the end of the war. Wales refuses to surrender with the rest of his band, and he witnesses their betrayal and execution by their Union enemies.

Despite the Missouri setting, there are far more parallels between Josey Wales and the stories about Ferguson than James or the other Quantrill followers. Wales suffered both Ferguson's revenge catalysts; the murder of a little boy and the burning of his whole family in their home. Like Wales, Ferguson declined to surrender when his men did; when he attempted to do so, he was betrayed.

On the run and a wanted man, a motley group of refugees gravitate toward Josey Wales for their survival. He tries desperately to free himself from them because they remind him of his personal loss. When it is clear that they will not leave him, Wales instructs the character Laura Lee in terms evocative of the rhetoric associated with Ferguson. Wales tells her, "Now remember, when things look bad and it looks like you're not going to make it, then you gotta get mean, plumb mad-dog mean. 'Cause if you lose your head and give up then you neither live nor win—that's just the way it is."[38]

The film fails to provide sufficient background detail given in the novel: Josey Wales may have become a Rebel because of the 1858 Redleg attack on his Missouri home, but he had only moved his family to the Ozarks the year before. Wales had been born and raised in the Tennessee mountains. Carter mentions more than once in the narrative that his protagonist lived by a Mountain Code which demanded revenge for transgressions, and naturally preferred mountains to flatlands. The narrator explains that "Josey Wales was conceived of the Highland Code, born of the Tennessee mountain feud, and washed in the blood of the Missouri."[39]

The following passage is just one of many examples that seem much closer to a description of Champ Ferguson than Jesse James:

> There was, in truth, no place for Josey Wales to go. The fierce mountain clan code would have deemed it a sin for him to take up life. His loyalty was there, in the grave with his wife and baby. His obligation was to the feud. And despite the cool cunning he had learned, the animal quickness and the deliberate arts of killing with pistol and knife, beneath it all there still rose the black rage of the mountain man... He only felt the feeling of generations of the code handed down from the Welsh and Scot clans and burned into his being.[40]

Josey Wales, as portrayed by Eastwood, represented the ultimate embodiment of the noble, valorized Confederate guerrilla. Reluctant to fight until the Yankees forced him to by invading his home and attacking his family—this romanticized figure, Josey Wales, became a representative for the South in general. Wales, in effect, represented the man Ferguson apologists wanted their guerrilla hero to be.

Eastwood's biographer, Richard Schickel, when examining the director/star of *The Outlaw Josey Wales* and his tenuous connection to its tainted creator made an observation that perfectly fits the Champ Ferguson myth, "This is America, where memories are short and re-invention a national pasttime."[41] The Ferguson persona in the modern apologist's mind is an image of a man wronged by outside forces that imposed themselves on his innocent life, and that in order to reclaim his manhood he must avenge his past. *The Outlaw Josey Wales,* by contrast is ultimately a story of reconciliation, and the futility of vengeance. Eastwood told Schickel, "at the time I felt that it was a statement that mankind has to find a better solution than just battling themselves into the ground."[42] Schickel agreed, noting that "In *Josey Wales,* obsession is portrayed as dehumanizing, the force. . . that has robbed this hero of everything he holds dear, and from which he desperately runs."[43] While Josey Wales Confederate turned vigilante may have its origins in the Ferguson saga, the film version humanizes Wales through humor, something sorely lacking in the exploits of the Upper Cumberland guerrilla.

It is worth noting that in Hollywood westerns it has consistently been the Confederate veteran, deprived of a home by carpetbaggers, who becomes the itinerant paladin of the plains, the outlaw and the gunslinger, while the Yankee veteran assumes the role of lawman authority figure.[44] Henry Fonda and Tyrone Power presented a romantic view of Frank and Jesses James in 1939 and 1940, in the Twentieth Century Fox films *Jesse James* and *The Return of Frank James;* James Stewart's morally conflicted bounty hunter Howard Kemp tries to raise enough money to regain the ranch stolen from him by corrupt Yankees while he was at war in *The Naked Spur* (MGM, 1953), while Alan Ladd's John Chandler returns home from the Civil War to find his house burned, his wife dead, and his son traumatized in *The Proud Rebel* (MGM, 1958).

One of the most enduring Rebel gunfighters appeared in John Ford's classic 1956 MGM film *The Searchers.* John Wayne plays Ethan Edwards, a Texan who returns home several years after the Civil War. Like Ferguson he had refused to surrender and instead fought as a mercenary in Mexico; it is implied that his past included even more unsavory elements. His brother's family, including the sister-in-law Edwards secretly loved, are killed by

Indians; Edwards and his adopted nephew spend years searching for the young niece who had been abducted by the raiders. Edwards is a complex character, and the viewer is left wondering until the climax whether he plans to rescue the girl or kill her because she has been sullied. In Ethan Edwards audiences sympathized with the seething Unreconstructed Confederate who suffered the tragic loss of family, and acted as the ultimate defender/avenger of White Womanhood (even if, the viewer is led to believe, he may have to kill her to defend her.)[45]

These themes were crystallized in Josey Wales. If Ferguson did in fact influence Asa Earl "Forrest" Carter's creation, through that character his footprint has been extended onto the larger canvas of American culture and twenty-first century editions of the Lost Cause Hero. The vengeful Rebel has gone from a common trope to a virtual stereotype embodied in Eastwood's memorable anti-hero.

The 2006 film *Seraphim Falls,* written and directed by David Von Ancken, tells the story of Confederate Colonel Carver (Liam Neeson) and his vengeful hunt. The colonel, returning home because the war was over, had been detained for questioning by Union forces. The Union commander, Gideon (Pierce Brosnan), ordered the colonel's barn burned; it spread to the house, which burned down around the colonel's wife and children. Most of the film centers around the colonel's attempts to find the Yankee and get revenge. Gideon is consumed by guilt, but nothing he does can assuage the implacable engine of vengeance that Carver has become. Echoes of Wales, and Ferguson, are obvious.

In 2011 AMC launched the western series *Hell on Wheels* about construction of the transcontinental railroad. The protagonist, Cullen Bohannon (played by Tennessean Anson Mount), is a former Confederate captain whose wife and son were brutally murdered by a group of Union soldiers, and their bodies left in their home that burns down around them. He has been systematically hunting the Yankee terrorists down and murdering them, and the last two men on his list are working on the railroad. Much like Eastwood's Josey Wales, Mount portrays Bohannon as a formerly gentle man who has grown hard in his quest for vengeance. The opening sequence of the series shows Bohannon, posing as a priest, murdering one of the Yankees as the man kneels in a confessional booth. Later, in the railroad camp, Bohannon meets a kindly minister who urges him to get on his knees and pray for forgiveness. He refuses to do so, explaining that he does not deserve it. Later, he learns that the minister has sins of his own—he rode with John Brown in Kansas, murdering pro-slavery men. Bohannon angrily taunts the preacher, saying, "We hanged his sorry ass!" Wartime hatred, it seems, will die slowly (if at all) in this series, and is highly resistant to faith, forgiveness, and contrition.[46]

In an interesting twist on the same theme, in the late 1970s and 1980s British author Terry Harknett (under the pen name George S. Gilman) wrote a series of western novels about a former Union captain known as Edge who was on a mission of vengeance. Union soldiers under his command during the war had been a band of misanthropic cutthroats. Resentful of their captain's efforts to keep them under control and prevent them from raping and murdering civilians, at war's end they go to his ranch and kill his family. Even though the hero of this series was a Northerner and the author an Englishman, it was still understood that it is the Yankees who are the rapists and pillagers in any Civil War scenario.[47] One is reminded of the scene in *Gone with the Wind* when Yankees arrive at Tara—not to free the slaves—but to try to rape Scarlett O'Hara.

The emotional appeal of the "noble Southron [*sic*] seeking revenge" theme helps explain why Ferguson (much like Jesse James in some quarters) is still so well regarded by many people in Sparta, Tennessee, and other parts of the Upper Cumberland. Since the release of McKnight's biography of Ferguson, I have heard much rumbling in White County about the negative portrayal their hero received in that book. One elderly lady (and faithful member of the United Daughters of the Confederacy) chastised me at a book signing, complaining about both my novel and McKnight's biography, proclaiming us shameful for putting Ferguson in a bad light—after all, as she said, he had been the only force protecting Sparta from the vicious Yankees.

I had felt some trepidation when I first started writing the novel *Good Rebel Soil*, anticipating the reaction I might receive in Champ's (and my) hometown. I feared that White County natives would resent the brutal side of Ferguson's nature that I tried to portray frankly. At the same time, citizens of some neighboring counties that had been pro-Union continue to harbor ill will toward the memory of the Confederate raider, and I expected some of them to be angry about the parts where I showed the character's gentler nature. This dichotomy in the Upper Cumberland where Ferguson's reputation is concerned, dependent on the degree of Union or Confederate sentiment citizens' ancestors had, is aptly illustrated in two historical markers that stand roughly sixty miles apart.

Near Ferguson's birthplace in Albany, Kentucky, one finds this marker erected in the town square in 1964:

> CIVIL WAR TERRORIST
> CHAMP FERGUSON BORN HERE IN 1821. GUERRILLA LEADER WITH CONFEDERATE LEANING, BUT ATTACKED SUPPORTERS OF BOTH SIDES THROUGHOUT THE WAR IN SOUTHERN KY., TENN. OVER 100 MURDERS ASCRIBED TO FERGUSON ALONE. HUNTED BY BOTH CSA

> and USA. Taken after end of war, convicted by US Army Court, Nashville, and hanged Oct. 20, 1865. Buried at home in White County, Tennessee.

Meanwhile, at Ferguson's burial place in a quiet cemetery near the Calfkiller River in White County, a few miles from Sparta, Tennessee, this marker was erected in 1975 by the Sons of Confederate Veterans:

> cap't champ ferguson
> (Confederate Guerrilla)
> Gen'l Morgan's Cavalry was joined at Sparta, June 1862, by Champ Ferguson, as guide for Morgan's invasion into Kentucky. Cap't Ferguson, and his co-fighters, were the only protection the people of the Cumberland and Hickory Valley area had against the Federal guerillas during the Civil War.
>
> Ferguson was hanged by the Federals, in Nashville, but by his request, buried here in White County.

Those two signs display a broad range of opinion. Both signs vividly display attitudes that continue to exist and no doubt will well into the future. It is always worth pointing out that Federal guerillas were the only protection Fentress County, Tennessee, and southern Kentucky had against Champ Ferguson.

For reasons outlined above, I was anxious about how readers with such a wide range of opinions about the subject matter would react to my novel. I was quite surprised. Those who admired Ferguson, mostly from Sparta, generally expressed approval of my portrayal of him: "I showed his gentler side, and that he wasn't all bad."[48] Readers who had previously regarded Ferguson as a thug, on the other hand, also expressed approval: I had shown just how vicious he really was. No one's opinion seemed to have changed, and everyone saw in my narrative what they had expected to see about Ferguson, about their home region, and ultimately about themselves. It is much the same reaction, I imagine, that many of them have when they read history books.

Champ Ferguson, as with his fellow Rebel vengeance seekers, and with the Lost Cause narrative of the South in general, continues to seduce the storytellers and stymie the historians. The legend, once in print, does not become fact; convincing the public of that, however, can sometimes seem like the true Lost Cause.

NOTES

1. Brian McKnight, *Confederate Outlaw: Champ Ferguson and the Civil War in Appalachia* (Baton Rouge: Louisiana State University Press, 2011), p. 1.
2. "Execution of Champ Ferguson–Scene at the Scaffold–His Full Confession." *Nashville Dispatch* (October 21, 1865) p. 5
3. *Ibid.*, 2
4. "Champ Ferguson. A Personal Interview with the Rebel Chieftain–What He Thinks and Says." *Nashville Dispatch*, (Nashville, Tennessee) August 19, 1865.
5. Thurman Sensing, *Champ Ferguson: Confederate Guerrilla* (Nashville, Tennessee: Vanderbilt University Press, 1940), p. 3; Major John A. Brents, *The Patriots and Guerillas of East Tennessee and Kentucky: The Sufferings of Patriots, Also the Experiences of the Author as an Officer in the Union Army, Including Sketches of Noted Guerillas and Distinguished Patriots* (New York: Henry Dexter Publishers, 1863), p. 21.
6. McKnight, 21–23.
7. *Nashville Daily Press and Times*, (Nashville, Tennessee) July 13, 1885; *Nashville Dispatch*, August 19, 1865; McKnight, 23–24, 40, 60, 65, 74, 77, 140, 192.
8. The latter assessment would only grow over time, especially in White County, Tennessee, which served as his base of operations during the war and became his final resting place.
9. "Execution of Champ Ferguson," *Nashville Union*, (Nashville, Tennessee) October 21, 1865.
10. In the summer of 1861, the U.S. War Department established a military district in Kentucky and Tennessee under command of Brigadier General Robert Anderson. He was ordered to organize the first Union training camp south of the Ohio River. After conferring with prominent loyal citizens of adjoining counties Anderson located the camp in Garrard County, Kentucky, on the farm of Richard "Dick" Robinson, six miles from Lancaster at the crossroads between Danville and Nicholasville. See "The Story of Camp Dick Robinson," *Louisville Courier-Journal* (1895).
11. Troy D. Smith, "Don't You Beg and Don't You Dodge," *Civil War Times Illustrated* 40:6 (December 2001), 41–43; McKnight, pp. 44–45; *Nashville Union* (October 21, 1865).
12. Miss Elizabeth Wood Testimony, August 4, 1865; Robert W. Wood Testimony, August 5, 1865. Cited in McKnight, 46.
13. Sensing, 98–100; McKnight, 70.
14. George D. Thrasher Testimony, July 29, 1865, cited in McKnight, 102; Smith, "Don't You Beg," 45–46.
15. Basil Duke, *History of Morgan's Cavalry* (Cincinnati, Ohio: Miami Printing and Company, 1867), p. 182.
16. McKnight, 150–52; Sensing, 177–87; "Dr. Murfree Meets Champ Ferguson," *Rutherford County Historical Society Newsletter* (Winter 1973), pp. 15–19.
17. "Champ Ferguson—the Noted Rebel Guerrilla Chieftain and His Execution in Nashville." *Nashville Banner* (October 16, 1886).
18. Fentress County *Gazette*, March 4, 1909; Nicholas Stayton Miles, "I Do Not Want to Be Buried in Such Soil as This: The Life and Times of Confederate Guerrilla Champ Ferguson," pp. 89–90; both cited in McKnight, 222.
19. Sensing, 257.

20. Museum staff informed me of the gentleman's visits, but said he was "shy" and reluctant to talk to historians.
21. Bromfield L. Ridley, "Champ Ferguson," *Confederate Veteran,* 7:10 (October 1899), p. 442. Ridley graduated from Cumberland Law School at Lebanon and served as Chancellor of Overton County and the Mountain District prior to the war. After Tennessee seceded Ridley rose to the rank of Lieutenant General on A.P. Stewart's staff. Ridley was quite familiar with the Upper Cumberland and the stories surrounding Champ Ferguson. He later published *Battles and Sketches of the Army of Tennessee* (Mexico, Missouri: Missouri Printing and Publishing Company, 1906).
22. E. G. Rogers, *Memorable Historical Accounts of White County and Area* (Collegedale, Tennessee: The College Press, 1972), pp. 53.
23. J. P. Austin, *The Blue and the Gray: Sketches of a Portion of the Unwritten History of the Great American Civil War* (Atlanta, Georgia: Franklin Printing and Publishing, 1899), p. 90.
24. Diary of John Weatherred, quoted in McKnight, 181.
25. McKnight, 181.
26. "Champ Ferguson. A Personal Interview with the Rebel Chieftain—What He Thinks and Says." *Nashville Dispatch,* August 19, 1865.
27. Jason Morgan Ward, *Defending White Democracy: The Making of a Segregationist Movement and the Remaking of Racial Politics, 1936–1965* (Chapel Hill: University of North Carolina Press, 2011), pp. 96–98; Thurman Sensing, "The Fallacy of the Minimum Wage," *The Freeman: Ideas on Liberty* 10: 5 (May 1960), p. 9.
28. Sensing, *Champ Ferguson,* 37–38.
29. Sensing was apparently unaware of Weatherred's diary.
30. Sensing, *Champ Ferguson,* 37.
31. *Ibid.,* 37, 187–88. James Ferguson, who fought under the command of Colonel Frank Wolford of the 1st Kentucky Cavalry was killed in 1863 in Lancaster County, Kentucky by Confederate guerrillas.
32. Troy D. Smith, "Don't You Beg and Don't You Dodge," *Civil War Times Illustrated* 40:6 (December 2001), pp. 40–46, 72–73; Troy D. Smith, *Good Rebel Soil: The Champ Ferguson Story* (New York: Writer's Club Press, 2002). Dutton Peabody was played by Edmund O'Brien.
33. J. D. Hale and John A. Brents wrote extensively about Ferguson during the Civil War, and much of their material has contributed to the guerrilla's legend as well as his history; however, they were not seeking to romanticize or apologize for Ferguson, on the contrary, they sought to excoriate him. Not surprisingly, then, their accounts do not include any fanciful excuses for his behavior, other than his own depravity and personal interests. See Major John A. Brents, *The Patriots and Guerillas of East Tennessee and Kentucky;* J. D. Hale, *Champ Ferguson: A Sketch of the War in East Tennessee Detailing Some of the Leading Spirits of the Rebellion,* Cincinnati, Ohio: Privately printed, 1862.
34. Thomas Dixon, an ordained Southern Baptist minister from North Carolina published the novel in 1905 as a part of his Reconstruction Trilogy that included the incendiary *The Leopard's Spots* and *The Traitor.*
35. David Wark (D.W.) Griffith grew up in rural Kentucky. His father Jacob "Jake" Griffith joined the 1st Kentucky Cavalry (Confederate) and fought at Shiloh,

Stones River, Chattanooga, and other battles rising to the rank of colonel. For much of the war he served under the command of General Nathan Bedford Forrest. Griffith grew up hearing stirring tales of his father's exploits and believed wholeheartedly in the myth of the Lost Cause. See Richard Schickel, *D.W. Griffith: An America Life* (New York: Limelight Editions, 2004), pp. 20–31.

36. Allen Barra, "The Education of Little Fraud: How Did a Racist Speechwriter for George Wallace Turn into a 'Cherokee' Sage and Author of a Revered Multicultural Text? The Weird Tale of Asa ('Forrest') Carter," *Salon* (December 20, 2001). http://www.salon.com/2001/12/20/carter_6/

    Carter who was also a virulent anti-Semite and a notorious drunk, parted ways with George Wallace because the governor became too liberal in his views regarding race.

37. According to Richard Schickel Clint Eastwood's production company, Malpaso, received an unsolicited copy of *The Rebel Outlaw: Josey Wales* "bearing the imprint of a publishing firm in Gant, Alabama that no one had ever heard of." Normally such things were returned to sender within twenty-four hours, but one of Eastwood's staff, Bob Daley, read it and convinced his boss to option it immediately. Eastwood confided in Schickel that the Josey Wales character resonated with him because the character was an outsider like him. Eastwood was not yet held in esteem by Hollywood's elite in 1976 and considered to be a modest talent at best. See Richard Schickel, *Clint Eastwood: A Biography* (New York: Alfred A. Knopf, 1996), pp. 318–19, 335–38.
38. *The Outlaw Josey Wales* (Los Angeles, California: Warner Bros. DVD, 2011).
39. Forrest Carter, *Josey Wales: Two Novels* (Albuquerque: University of New Mexico Press, 1989), pp. 5, 58, 248–49. This volume includes the original text of the Delacorte Press editions of *Gone to Texas* and *The Vengeance Trail of Josey Wales.*
40. *Ibid.,* 10–11.
41. Schickel, *Clint Eastwood,* 322.
42. *Ibid.,* 324.
43. *Ibid.,* 333.
44. Robert B. Ray, *A Certain Tendency of the Hollywood Cinema, 1930–1980* (New Jersey: Princeton University Press, 1985), pp. 70–88; Philip French, *Westerns: Aspects of a Movie Genre* (London: Carcanet Press, 2005), pp. 30–46, 206–10.
45. Natalie Wood played the niece abducted by Indians who really had no desire to be rescued adding another layer of complexity to a film that asked who the real savages were in the history of Manifest Destiny. John Ford ably directed what many consider to be his Western masterpiece and John Wayne's most effective turn as an actor.
46. David Von Ancken, writer-director of *Seraphim Falls,* directed the pilot of *Hell on Wheels* as well as several other episodes. He currently serves as the executive producer of the series in addition to his directing duties.
47. George S. Gilman, *Edge: The Loner* (New York: Pinnacle Books, 1972.) Harknett/Gilman wrote sixty-one Edge novels between 1972 and 1989.
48. The elderly lady at the book signing described earlier was a notable exception.

9

"There's a Lot of Nourishment in an Acre of Corn"

Upper Cumberland Moonshine

Michael E. Birdwell

Whisky production in the Upper Cumberland of Kentucky and Tennessee began shortly after the first Europeans settled in the region. Born of Scots-Irish descent, intrepid pioneers learned from their forebears how to turn grains into *uisce* or whisky, which means "water of life" in Gaelic.[1] For them, many of whom were proud Presbyterians with a strong work ethic, whisky production was a noble profession. Often more lucrative than the back breaking work of clearing land to eke out an agrarian existence, liquor was as essential to life on the frontier as salt. Whisky production and consumption bore no stigma of sin nor degeneration. Distilling counted among the first industries established in the plateau regions of Kentucky and Tennessee, the others being gristmilling, saltpeter mining, and gunpowder mills. According to folklore the first person to distill whisky in Kentucky was Baptist minister Elijah Craig in 1789, though existing records credit Evan Williams with establishing the initial distilling operation. Whisky, like salt, acted as currency on the Cumberland frontier, and it was utilitarian as well as profitable. Frontier folk had little or no use for currency, but could take comfort in swapping good triple-run whisky for a mule, tools, or other commodities needed for survival. Christian congregations often paid their preachers with whisky, brandy, or applejack. Frontier "doctors" administered whisky both orally and topically when treating patients. They created concoctions of herbs, fruits, roots, and other ingredients with whisky or peach brandy to create medicines for treatment of specific ailments. Doctors claimed their liquor-laced remedies warded off chills or cooled down fevers.[2]

Whisky acted as not only a social lubricant, but as a necessity. Often when spring rains poured down in torrents, privies overflowed, sending human waste into streams and rivers, and contaminating wells. Likewise fresh manure flowed into rills and cisterns, spoiling drinking water. To quench one's thirst with water often proved deadly, due to frequent outbreaks of cholera and other water borne diseases. Whisky, by contrast, saved lives. It acted as a "disinfectant, a tranquilizer, and a medicine for countless ills."[3] Although some churches condemned consumption of alcohol as a sin, "corn liquor from a moonshiner was readily available for medicinal purposes." Almost every home in the Upper Cumberland kept corn liquor on hand in case of emergencies; most homes also had a supply of "blueberry, blackberry, cherry, and peach wine" as well.[4]

Over time, however, tax collectors, social reformers, and outsiders demonized the practice, leading to the creation of a subculture steeped in myth, tradition, romance, and adventure. Production of legal whisky and its illegal counterpart—moonshine— went hand-in-glove in the history of the Upper Cumberland. Hills, hollers, and caves provided not only locations adjacent to spring water, but also places to hide when making illicit whisky. During the post-Civil War era outsiders' zealotry to modernize the mountaineer sometimes resulted in a battle of wits that degenerated into armed conflict. The image of the moonshiner changed over time, depending on who told the story and their personal attitude toward alcohol. Stories of tragedy intermingle with tales of joy when examining the history and impact of distilling spirits in the Upper Cumberland.

Moonshine, the illicit distillation of sprits, gained prominence in America with the onset of the Civil War. The federal government established the Office of Internal Revenue in 1862, imposing excise taxes on whisky and tobacco as a means of helping finance the Union army.[5] Tax on whisky depended upon its proof; the higher the proof the higher the tax.[6] When the war ended, federal taxes not only remained in place, but were raised from twenty cents to two dollars per gallon; but the tax was reduced to fifty cents in 1868.[7] After the war, Congress mandated creation of the Revenue Bureau of the Treasury Department. It was in 1876, under Commissioner Green B. Raum, that the bureau created a police force to hunt down moonshiners and enforce tax law without regard to state lines. The bureau increased the whisky tax an additional one dollar and ten cents per gallon in 1894, an exorbitant cost at the time, which "encouraged drinkers to buy untaxed liquor from moonshiners."[8] The new excise damaged the profits of legal distilleries, and emboldened those willing to take the risk to circumvent the law. Commissioner Raum used every weapon available to launch "Raum's War," which raged from 1878 to 1881 at a cost of roughly three hundred thousand dollars, but yielded two and a half million dollars in tax revenue.[9] George Atkinson, a loyal agent of Raum's, lamented that the Revenue Bureau's lack of respect was a direct result of the "want of nerve, and laziness of the bench of the Federal Courts. The low, worthless, and truckling newspapers has encouraged violators of the law." Not only that, "wicked demagoguery of aspiring politicians has led those engaged in crime to believe they would eventually get immunity and go off scot-free."[10]

For Upper Cumberland distillers various attitudes helped them justify willful defiance of the law. For ex-Confederates, revenue agents represented another invasion by ruthless Yankees who were intent on destroying their way of life. Union veterans-turned-moonshiners fought the law as assiduously as their Rebel counterparts, finding the law onerous and unreasonable. Others maintained that only state laws applied when distilling and distributing alcohol; therefore, federal agents overstepped their authority. Some claimed the prohibition law unconstitutional and an infringement on their rights. Pious moonshiners argued that God Almighty abhorred tax collectors, considering them an abomination and anathema. The *New Testament,* they observed, considered tax collectors the worst among sinners. They, by contrast, were modest God-fearing men simply trying to provide for their family. Thus, as revenuers adopted more aggressive measures to search for moonshiners and destroy their stills, distillers responded in kind. Both sides resorted to violence with often disastrous results.[11] A common phrase uttered by those who enforced the law and those who chose to break it was, "Where there's smoke there's bound to be whisky."[12]

Newspapers in Kentucky, Tennessee, and even *The New York Times* covered stories about moonshine and violence with an almost pathological curiosity. Often referring to illegal operations as "wildcats" or "wildcatting," reporters filled column inches with news of raids by revenuers, shoot outs, and impenitent moonshiners sentenced to federal prisons. Raum's revenue agents conducted raids that lasted weeks on end in some cases. One revenuer complained, "Jackson County [Tennessee] is apparently invincible. My raiders can march through the country and receive the fire of the enemy from every hill top . . . but the nature of the ground is such that no arrests of the armed violators can be made. . . . I am convinced that nothing can conquer Jackson but to camp a strong force in that county to remain there for months."[13]

Revenuers proved more successful in Putnam County, Tennessee, where they destroyed five stills, impounded numerous tools, corn, sugar, and other items needed for whisky production. The raid led to several arrests in the Monterey area in 1878.[14] Meanwhile, a number of citizens of Overton County endorsed moonshine raids, leading to a general escalation of violence. They issued a petition to the Quarterly Court demanding that order be restored, not just in Overton County, but Jackson and Putnam counties as well.[15]

Federal judges who heard alcohol-related cases often sided with the moonshiner. Between 1870 and 1903, judges heard over five thousand cases in Kentucky and Tennessee. In February 1873, Judge Connally Trigg held federal court in Knoxville, presiding over five hundred cases concerning moonshine—only six resulted in guilty verdicts. Many district judges simply did not consider moonshining a serious criminal offense. U.S. Secretary of State Cordell Hull, whose father operated a still in Bunkum Cave in Pickett County, Tennessee, expressed the attitudes of most Upper Cumberland residents, saying that people attached no stigma to whisky production. Hull wrote, "Everyone in our section looked upon the tax as an outrage, an infringement of human rights, popular rights, and everything else."[16] With such sentiments being widespread, it should come as no surprise that Tennessee ranked third in the number of violators of the despised whisky tax behind North Carolina and Georgia in 1879.[17]

Federal Judge Bland Ballard earned a reputation of lenience concerning moonshiners. An indicted man from Cumberland County, Kentucky, stood before him accused of manufacturing untaxed liquor. The prosecutor demanded the maximum sentence, but the judge disagreed. Finding the moonshiner guilty, Ballard sentenced him to sixty days in jail and fined him one hundred dollars. Appreciative, the convict exclaimed, "Judge, if I ever make any more moonshine whisky, I'll send you a keg of it." Several months later the justice received a package containing a five gallon cask of "superior moonshine whisky" accompanied by a thank you note from the lapsed distiller.[18]

The moonshine wars were particularly violent in 1878. Revenuers captured or destroyed 1,258 stills, made 2,990 arrests, and twenty-three revenue agents fell dead or wounded nationwide. Forty-six percent of those arrests took place in Tennessee, most of them in the Upper Cumberland. Tennessee ranked the second most violent state during the Whisky War. Unknown numbers of moonshiners and runners were killed and wounded that year.[19] As violence increased, many mountaineers sought numerous methods of resistance. People sympathetic to law enforcement were intimidated by threats of violence or property damage. In some cases informants were beaten, their barns burned, and their livestock stolen or killed.[20] Adding to the violence of 1878 was a new stratagem on Raum's part—enlisting the aid of the U.S. military and special posses to assist revenue agents. This created resentment on the part of civilian and soldier alike. Civilians refused to see themselves as enemy combatants and introducing soldiers into the situation only made matters worse, rekindling flames of resentment that smoldered during and after the Civil War. Even General William Tecumseh Sherman, who made war on civilians with impunity during the

Uncle Billy Hull. Credit: Michael E. Birdwell Upper Cumberland Collection.

Civil War, questioned the logic of Raum's strategy and feared the kind of justice his men would receive in mountain courts. Moonshiners in Alabama, Kentucky, and Tennessee took up arms against the U.S. military to protect their livelihood.[21]

A three-day pitched battle took place nine miles north of Cookeville, Tennessee, on the Overton County border in a region known as "Little Putnam," and "Waterloo." The affray, commonly referred to as either "The Siege of Waterloo" or "The Peek Fight," lasted from August 23–25, 1878, and was "one of the severest battles ever fought between Government officers and moonshiners."[22] The area known as Little Putnam was reputed to be a veritable "paradise of moonshiners."[23] Deputy Internal Revenue Collector James M. Davis, "one of the most noted and daring revenue officers who ever served the government of the United States,"[24] along with Joe Spears and Lee Ayers, led a party of revenue agents in search of moonshiner Campbell Morgan of Gainesboro, Tennessee. George W. Atkinson claimed that Morgan's infamous reputation "next to [Major Lewis] Redmond of South Carolina [was] the most notorious moonshiner in America."[25] Joining the band of revenue agents were Captain S.D. Mather, a commissioner of the federal circuit court, as well as Robert Brown, Robert Rawls, C.E. Tippin, J.M. Phillips, Felix Young, Pres Smith, Milton Howe, and Charles "Charlie" W. Strain. Their hunting proved successful on their first day. That morning the revenuers took some illicit distillers by surprise and "cut up Brown & Bradley's brandy distillery, within three miles of where the fight occurred."[26] Unfortunately for them, destruction of the illegal operation emboldened Morgan's men.

After searching the vicinity for more illicit operations in the vicinity, the revenuers sought lodging at the home of elderly John Peek—who was reputed to be 102 years old—on the Overton County line adjacent to Spring Creek around six that evening. The old man demurred because two neighbors were visiting him, and he lacked adequate space or provisions to comfortably house the posse. Peek suggested they make camp at the Barnes residence roughly a mile distant. Several men dismounted, tied their horses, and put feed bags on their animals in spite of Peek's protestations.

Meanwhile, James M. Davis, Winchester rifle in hand, accidentally flushed out a covey of quail which caught him off guard, revealed his position to moonshiners making their way down an adjacent hillside toward them. Recovering his composure, he shouldered his rifle to shoot the birds when he spotted the armed men. Davis and J.M. Phillips—who was unarmed—attempted to jump a split rail fence and take cover in Peek's cornfield. Campbell Morgan's men opened fire, shooting Phillips in the left side of his chest, the bullet passing through his body. Phillips "cried out in great pain, 'Oh, Lordy and then came a responsive echo from the wildcat man, 'Oh yes, God d–m you!' With that between twenty and thirty of them showed themselves and regular firing was commenced, lasting forty-five minutes."[27] Davis tried to return fire but "his rifle burst and he had to rush to the house for another gun."[28]

Phillips writhed in agony as the fight raged on about him. He begged for mercy and safe quarter, but the moonshiners refused to yield, and continued to advance within roughly fifty feet of the revenuers. Captain Mather responded to Phillips's plea for help, and ran into a hail of bullets and dragged the wounded deputy to Peek's home as hot lead whizzed around them. The rest of the posse ran for cover, joining them in Peek's house against the old man's will. As Charles Tippins dashed toward the two-story log structure, he was shot through the nose and covered in blood as he fell onto the porch.[29]

Pres Smith suffered injuries as well, being shot thrice through the left arm. "Smith confronted six of the enemy at one time, stood out in the open field and cursed them, and told them to come out from behind the trees and fight like men." Staggering and bleeding profusely, Mather asked Smith to surrender his gun to him and seek shelter in Peek's home. Smith refused, saying "he would fight until he fell."[30]

In the melee, posse member Rawls ran the wrong way toward Morgan's men, who shot the hat off his head. When he turned to run the other way and moonshiners shot the stock of his rifle.[31] He rushed toward Peek's home, and made it to safety without any bodily injury.

At roughly seven, Davis ordered Lee L. Ayers and Charlie Strain to proceed at once to Cookeville and telegraph Collector William Woodcock in Nashville. "For God's sake," Davis said, "tell Woodcock to send me 100 men as quick as possible. Go there or kill your horses in the attempt." Leaving their weapons and ammunition behind, Ayers and Strain "made a hasty exit. When we got a half a mile distant we heard firing, as if heavy skirmishing was in progress, and then came single shots at intervals. We heard nothing from them after taking leave, and they may have fought their way out or been killed," Ayers later reported to his boss in Nashville uncertain of the fate of his comrades or Morgan's men.[32]

The remainder of the posse shouldered their weapons and fired in the direction of Morgan's army of moonshiners, providing covering fire for Ayers and Strain. The men successfully eluded their enemies, and made their way to Cookeville. Ayers informed Woodcock, "Our ammunition is short. Get all the men you can. I will try to get some horses here. The place of attack is nine miles north of Cookeville, Overton County."[33]

Upon receipt of the telegram, Woodcock responded with his own wire, inquiring how many men were needed and about the seriousness of the situation. Ayers reported that his attempt to gather horses had failed, and that at least three of Davis's men were seriously wounded. He told Woodcock that he would board the next train to Nashville and report to him in person. Meanwhile, Woodcock contacted Commissioner Raum in Washington, to apprise him of the situation. Raum authorized the Collector to "employ as many men as you deem necessary," to quell the whisky rebellion and "enforce revenue laws in Overton County."[34]

As darkness descended on the first day of the siege, Campbell Morgan's men, roughly fifty in number, surrounded Peek's homestead. They covered the path to the creek so that Deputy Collector Davis's posse could not fetch water for themselves or their horses. After the revenuers assessed their damage, Davis realized that he had only seven men left "fit for duty." Peek's son and his two neighbors, "Mr. Hurley and Mr. Eldridge," did their best to tend to the wounded.[35]

On the morning of the second day, James Peek ventured out of the house to recover some of the horses and get water. Morgan's men immediately fired on him and Peek retreated to his father's house empty handed. Later in the day Campbell Morgan allowed Dr. J.P. Martin of Cookeville to tend to the wounded revenuers and return home unmolested. During the night sympathetic citizens had joined Morgan, providing ammunition, food, and encouragement to rid the region of federal busy bodies. Moonshiners and revenue agents shot at each other throughout the day. Well-provisioned, Morgan's men intended to make the posse waste its ammunition.[36] Commissioner Mather reported that "it seemed as if there were a thousand men around and about us judging from. . . the yells of demon moonshiners, and the balls were pouring into the walls of our block-house. The night that followed was pandemonium itself."[37] Meanwhile Morgan's men erected barricades on surrounding roads, making rescue more difficult. Morgan warned those trapped in the house not to attempt to go to the spring and collect water. Mather complained bitterly, "the whole country had joined the moonshiners, or were in sympathy with them."[38]

In the meantime, Ayers and Strain arrived in Nashville and met with Woodcock. The collector contacted Governor James D. Porter Jr., asking for his assistance. The governor issued twenty breech loading rifles and twenty rounds of cartridges per weapon to Woodcock, as well as placing twenty able bodied men from Nashville under the command of the Internal Revenue. Though the number was far fewer than Davis requested, other reinforcements were gathering in Cookeville. The twenty men in Nashville departed the Capital City and headed out toward the Upper Cumberland at nine on the morning of the 24th, hoping to arrive on the scene by midnight.[39]

Moonshiners fired on Peek's place in regular intervals, roughly every ten minutes throughout the day. Poorly provisioned, Davis ordered his men to "shoot sparingly." Rain began falling around ten in the morning and Davis ordered federal agents to capture water running off the roof. In doing so, they put their lives in danger; Mather reported that gunfire increased precipitously during the downfall. Continuous shots could be heard for miles, and a delegation of curious citizens arrived at Morgan's barricade from Livingston, wanting to know what was going on. Morgan told them that they had infamous revenuer James M. Davis surrounded and they intended to burn him out if he did not surrender soon. Citizens suggested a parlay with Davis, and Morgan allowed them and two moonshiners to approach Peek's home under a flag of truce. Morgan sent word explaining why he rounded up area moonshiners to besiege the revenuers. He had it on good authority that "Capt. Davis intended to kill him on sight," and he feared for his life. Asking for clemency, Morgan's men told Davis that he would disperse the militia of moonshiners if he promised not to murder him. He agreed to surrender to any other officer except Davis and "do everything in his power to correct the evil ways of his neighborhood and this would be his last resistance to United States authority."[40]

Reinforcements arrived from Cookeville, led by Major J.C. Freeze and Elijah Terry, to assist the revenuers at about the same time Morgan surrendered. His men were allowed to disperse without arrest. Escorted to Cookeville under armed guard, Morgan later stood trial in federal district court in Nashville. Fined and sentenced to jail, he served his time and then, incredibly, joined Commissioner Raum's agents as a deputy U.S. marshal. He earned a reputation as an effective and fair agent who arrested former associates.[41] "He and Capt. Davis are now sworn friends. . . Davis says Morgan is as true a man as he ever knew, and he would be willing to trust him in any emergency."[42]

A reporter for *The New York Times*, contemptuous of moonshiners, tarred them all with the same brush. "These 'moonshiners' are illiterate and ignorant. They scarcely ever read a book or a newspaper, and know very little of what is going on in the world. If they were better informed they would not break the law." He described their dress and their demeanor with condescension and held no sympathy for their plight, nor did he try to understand why the men and women who filed in to federal court chose to make illicit liquor. "During the sitting of the court held by Judge Baxter they filled the large courtroom almost to suffocation, while the corridors and all approaches to the room were crowded with men from the mountains. . ."[43] Men, primarily from the Cumberland Plateau, filled the federal courthouse in 1880; Commissioner Raum offered amnesty if they agreed to enter a guilty plea. Violators of the agreement faced the maximum penalty available. The reporter considered the notion of amnesty a foolish policy that would embolden the moonshiners to flaunt the law.[44]

The author acknowledged that some federal judges empathized with the moonshiners and held similar views concerning the law, saying "the law has been administered by federal court in a way as to make it a farce. When men were sentenced to prison by the court it was in a half-apologetic way, and the imprisonment in many instances was merely nominal. In some counties prisoners–so called–were allowed to carry the keys of jails in their pockets and to go out when they chose. . ."[45]

For most convicted moonshiners the sentence resulted in one year or less in a federal facility for doing something they did not consider a crime.

Ironically moonshiners, who might on occasion fire upon revenue agents or local deputies, were regarded as model prisoners by their jailers. A grudging respect developed over the years. When summoned to court, reputable moonshiners always arrived on time if not early to learn their fate. After passing sentence, judges often asked them how long it would take them to get their affairs in order before being sent to serve their prison sentence. On the day they were to report, illicit distillers usually showed up hours ahead of time so that no one could accuse them of shirking their responsibilities. There were numerous exceptions, however; Frank Whittaker of Putnam County, Tennessee, landed a four year sentence as well as a heavy fine because he wounded Deputy Marshall Tom Price when trying to protect his still.[46]

Due to the persistent attitude that the tax was unjust and revenue agents extralegal entities, several federal agents found themselves under indictment for a variety of crimes. Among the crimes they stood accused were making arbitrary arrests, committing "murder, assault, carrying a concealed weapon, or trespassing."[47] They faced hostility on the local level from judges and juries, which caused federal agents to seek a change of venue.[48]

The U.S. Supreme Court weighed in on the situation in the case *Tennessee v. Davis*, supporting the need for a change of venue in certain circumstances. On August 29, 1878, the fore-mentioned revenue agent James M. Davis was indicted for "wilfully, premeditatedly [*sic*], deliberately, and of his malice aforethought killing one J.B. Haynes" of Grundy County in the South Cumberland.[49] Davis's attorney, James A. Warder, filed a petition for change of venue, arguing that his client could not possibly get a fair trial in Grundy County. He also argued that Davis did not commit murder, but fired in self-defense against at least six men who guarded a still. In carrying out his duties as an agent of the U.S. Government, Warder maintained that the case should be held in a federal court rather than in a local venue hostile to federal regulation of Internal Revenue. In a lengthy opinion justices of the U.S. Supreme Court agreed with Davis and his attorney, granting a change of venue to the U.S. district court at Nashville. Acquitted by federal authorities, Davis went back to work hunting down wildcatters.[50]

Two moonshiners, William Cagle and James Curtis, were hauled into federal court in 1899, creating quite a stir. Revenue agents arrested them on the Cumberland Plateau forty miles north of Chattanooga in Bledsoe County, where they poured out three thousand gallons of moonshine and destroyed the seventy gallon capacity still. What confounded the federal authorities was the fact that Cagle and Curtis were outstanding members of their community. "The arrests of the men created great excitement in the vicinity owing to their prominence," *The New York Times* reported.[51] A successful businessman, Cagle was worth thirty thousand dollars (that is equivalent to $763,403.82 in 2009 dollars), and owned a percentage of four gristmills. He clearly did not need the money that his side venture in distilling provided, but engaged in the practice just the same. For Cagle and Curtis, operating the still was an open act of willful defiance against an unjust law that needed to be reconsidered if not repealed outright. "He has never been arrested before and is a prominent church worker. He is an Elder in the Methodist Church and Superintendent of the local Sunday School." *The New York Times* reporter added, somewhat incredulously, "He does not deny his guilt." With the inherent implication that Cagle, a man of respect and an upstanding member of Upper Cumberland society, did not consider what he was doing to be either a crime nor a violation of his Christian faith.[52]

One could argue that by 1900 revenue agents actually performed a much needed public service in the Upper Cumberland. Representing an armed outside threat to the region, and despised by former Yankee and Rebel alike, revenuers provided a common enemy that brought former combatants together in a common cause. Though many historians argue that the wounds of the Civil War began to heal when former Unionists and Confederates came together during the Spanish-American War, that process began earlier in the Upper Cumberland in a more personal conflict. Embattled with tax collectors since the end of the Civil War, moonshiners and their families set aside old scores to fight their new enemy the Internal (or as many called it "Infernal") Revenue Service. Most now preferred to argue over party politics, while taking their aggression out on the tax men.

As the Local Color School of writers descended upon the Appalachians, they distorted or romanticized people who lived there. For some writers they represented the purest strain of Anglo Saxon stock, and were noble, independent, and self-sufficient. For others they were uncivilized, incestuous, and violent throwbacks who threatened civility and the Judeao-Christian ethic. A writer for the *Literary Digest* took umbrage with both depictions. "It is declared unfair to blame them as a class for what a few of the most reckless ones do, for every region has its ruffians."[53] The author argued that while the person living on the East Coast might take offense at some of their behavior and "disapprove of their irregular methods of distilling," they operated on partial information.[54] The writer argued that "these people do not think they are violating any moral law" when they run whisky, and that the Internal Revenue Service stood in the way of their making an honest living.[55]

The aforementioned uncredited writer noted that when mountaineers needed protection from the law, for whatever reason, it rarely arrived.

Moonshiners, therefore, had little use for the law, protecting family and property by themselves out of necessity. Federal agents searching for local distilling operations were "a mere invader—he was no better than a pirate, and fit to be shot on sight as such vermin."[56] Government agents eschewed respect for property rights, destroying not only copper pot stills, but most of the other sad provisions the moonshiner owned.

Travelers who stopped at homes in the Upper Cumberland were often struck by how genuine and hospitable the folk were, no matter how poor. When industrialists started buying up property and mineral rights in the region, common folk continued to be courteous and welcoming. The relatively rapid change from an agrarian lifestyle dictated by the rhythms of the seasons to an industrial economy proved incredibly disruptive. Selling mineral rights, instead of improving their lot, usually forced mountaineers off the land they thought they owned into the downward spiral of life in a company coal, lumber, or textile towns, where the barter economy no longer held sway and workers were paid in scrip rather than hard cash. In such an atmosphere, moonshining offered a way for the formerly independent farmer to acquire legal tender through illegal means.[57]

Many outsiders, however, consumed by Progressive Era reforms, concluded that alcohol production and consumption were the primary source of all of society's ills. One writer noted that the people of the Cumberland Mountains were the most gracious and generous he had ever encountered. "They will divide the last ration the have with a stranger, even tho he be a revenue officer."[58] Most mountaineers, wanting to be good hosts, offered their guests their best peach brandy or moonshine whisky. As a result the "hospitable distiller is immediately eligible for a prolonged course in entertaining at the Government's exclusive hotel, the Atlanta Penitentiary."[59]

In the late nineteenth and early twentieth centuries social reformers targeted alcohol as the source of most human failings. Abuse of alcohol cost people jobs, ruined marriages, and led to widespread disrespect for the law and created a tacit acceptance of violence. Both Kentucky and Tennessee, states with a reputation for producing fine sipping whiskies and brandies, fell under the gaze of reformers. In 1903 *The Putnam County Herald* commented that "Last Thursday saw the final closing of Putnam County's only saloon, and we hope for a better condition of affairs as a result."[60] By 1907 many counties in both states had gone "dry," while Kentucky continued to operate 253 distilleries. By that year eighty-seven counties in Kentucky prohibited alcohol consumption, though Louisville "escaped the wave of reform." A *New York Times* reporter wrote that this "seems strange to us of the North who have been taught to look upon the South as the land of the julep and the cobbler and to regard every southern gentleman as an accredited judge on the merits of whisky."[61] For a farmer cum moonshiner, distilling alcohol made perfect sense. In the era directly following the Civil War a wagon load of corn yielded on average ten dollars, whereas a wagon filled with moonshine average done hundred fifty dollars, making it possible for him to better provide for his family.[62]

On the eve of nationwide Prohibition, journalists and reformers looked for new ways to further demonize alcohol, mountaineers, and the Appalachian South. A reporter for *Scientific American* fumed, "Ever since our entry into the great war Moonshine Land . . . has become a hotbed of slackers and deserters. Over and over again the government officers, while they have been trying to raid illicit distilleries, have found in the same neighborhood deserters and slackers for whom Uncle Sam has been looking, in some cases, for months. . ."[63] By 1916 "all of the old moonshine states

Melvin Long with his still, Clay County. Michael E. Birdwell Upper Cumberland Collection. Credit: Tennessee State Library and Archives.

Two men swig moonshine made in Clay County. Michael E. Birdwell Upper Cumberland Collection. Credit: Tennessee State Library and Archives.

except Kentucky and Missouri were dry, and blockaders enjoyed a vastly expanded market and unprecedented profits."[64]

As World War I wound down, the assault against moonshine increased. Between June 1 and November, 1918, federal agents seized or destroyed more than five hundred stills in the mountainous regions of Alabama, North Carolina, and Tennessee. Roughly fifty thousand gallons of whisky spilled into the woods and caves as federal agents attacked stills with everything from axes to dynamite. Shots rang out in the Cumberland Mountains between moonshiners and revenue agents, and the numbers of dead hovered around sixty while nearly two hundred were wounded during those months. Revenuers rounded up two hundred men for prosecution in Tennessee, demonizing them in the press with names like, "slacker," "deserter," and "Bolshevik." During their raids, feds seized copper pipe, corn meal, and more than thirty thousand pounds of sugar in those six months.[65]

While Theodore Price and Richard Spillane acknowledged that Local Color writers romanticized moonshiners, often depicting them as victims of rapacious industrialists, they called for a reassessment of that stereotype. "There is no romance in moonshining to-day. It is commercial, demoralizing, and . . . far more threatening than ever before."[66] To combat these people who avoided the World War to wage their own campaign against proper American values, Commissioner Daniel Roper, on June 17, 1918 organized a special moonshine unit known as the Flying Squadron. Headquartered at Nashville, agents from the Flying Squadron made routine raids into Clay, DeKalb, Fentress, Jackson, Macon, Overton, Pickett, Putnam, Smith, and White counties. In Roper's view, not only did those shiftless moonshiners undermine mountain morality with their illicit whisky, they did so with impunity and scoffed at the notion of paying taxes. As the journalists noted, "There is always reluctance to pay taxes. Few persons paid them with good grace." But responsible, patriotic citizens tithed a portion of their hard earned money to the federal government for the betterment of all concerned.[67]

Some tactics employed by the federal government, however, actually encouraged a black market in commercially produced whisky and moonshine. In 1887, the federal government placed an excise tax on legal whisky at one dollar per gallon, roughly equivalent to $23.67 in 2008. During the First World War the tax was raised to eight dollars per gallon (roughly $133.21 in taxes) beyond the regular price of the liquor in 1917. Under such onerous conditions a number of legal distilleries were forced to close their doors or produce a different product. Moonshiners, however, reaped unprecedented profits, encouraging some less scrupulous, less talented people to engage in the enterprise.[68]

Another irony centered on the fact that the U.S. military responded to America's entry into the war in a paternalistic way. Wanting to keep soldiers pure and away from immorality, the army in its inestimable wisdom chose to locate most of the training camps as far away from urban areas as possible. They placed new camps in the South because most of that region was dry before 1917. "Every precaution seemed to be taken to safeguard the men from temptation, and yet in a short period after the establishment of the camps. . . liquor was pouring in."[69] In some areas moonshiners had agents in the camps, in other cases mountain boys who either enlisted or answered the draft brought their distilling skills with them. Just as the army tried to shield soldiers from prostitution and failed, it also provided little deterrent for any soldier who really wanted a drink.[70]

Weighing in on the debate, Rollin Lynde Hartt noted a double standard. He remarked, "Personally, I detest moonshine. . . but respect moonshiners. Middle-Westerners turn corn into hog to make it portable; with the same object a very limited class of mountaineers turn corn into whisky."[71] He observed that "even feudists and moonshiners go to church," and that these were good people trying to make the most of difficult times.[72]

At this time when people of the Cumberland were being demonized William Aspenwall Bradley stood up in their defense. He argued, "Less is really known about the Cumberlands than about any other corner of the country. The reason is that those who have done the writing have only a slight, or else a very narrow and often limited knowledge of their subject. Often. . . none at all first hand."[73] He went so far as to call the region "The Balkans of America."[74]

Prohibition did little to stem the tide of illegal alcohol production or consumption. During the so-called Roaring Twenties, novelists like F. Scott Fitzgerald and Ernest Hemingway wrote novels and short stories awash in booze. Hollywood played its part in criticizing the Noble Experiment, depicting flappers whooping it up while drinking bathtub gin. Meanwhile newspapers filled hundreds of column inches with stories about the Al Capone Gang, rum runners off the Atlantic Coast, and moonshiners in the Appalachian hills of Kentucky and Tennessee, flaunting an unpopular law with impunity. As journalists flocked to the Canadian Border and the Florida Keys to follow stories about the illicit liquor industry, they also returned to the Cumberland Mountains. One, Stephen Sennet, was surprised to find out the long pedigree of the liquor trade. Not only was it not a recent phenomenon, but it embodied a tradition passed down from generation to generation. Sennet empathized with folks eking out a living. "Poverty of a nature hard for urbanites to visualize is there. Yet, they will deprive themselves of the necessities of life to comfort a stranger and make a brave show of hospitality." Some of that hospitality often flowed from the mouth of a crock jar with a corn cob stopper.[75]

As Prohibition became the law of the land, enforcement proved incredibly difficult. In Chicago and elsewhere gang warfare emerged as organized crime stepped in to take over the illegal liquor industry. Al Capone created a network of bootleggers who smuggled bonded whisky into the United States from Canada and rum from islands throughout the Gulf of Mexico. Rum runner Joseph P. Kennedy made so much money from illegal importation of spirits that he bought respectability for his family and a place at the table among Hollywood moguls. In spite of the fact that much of the illegal liquor trade was centered in New York, Chicago, and New Orleans, journalists often focused their gaze on the mountainous section of Alabama, Georgia, Kentucky, North Carolina, and Tennessee.

Harry Burn, best known as the Tennessee legislator who cast the ballot that ratified the Nineteenth Amendment and granted women the right to vote, bristled with disgust at the spectacle outside media made of the Appalachian South. Kentucky, Tennessee, and West Virginia were routinely parodied in northern newspapers and magazines. Reporters stereotyped the region as a population of slack-jawed, raw-boned, ill-clad, barefoot, Bible-thumping, whisky-swilling, incestuous, illiterate, and lazy people who violated laws with impunity. Burn lamented a commonly held opinion of Cumberland mountaineers, "It is to be regretted that the authors of recent articles did not feel inclined to sign them."[76] Taking issue with the Local Color School, Yellow Journalism, and general outside bias against the Mountain South, Burn argued that rather than criticizing the mountaineer, reporters should be more responsible. Journalists purposely omitted discussion of respected leaders who served on the local, state, and even national level, such as Cordell Hull, Alvin York, and John Sherman Cooper. He implored reporters to find positive things to say about the region and to endorse nationwide public education.

John J. Gore, a native of Jackson County and former law partner with Cordell Hull, was appointed the first federal judge in the newly created Middle Tennessee District in 1922 by President Warren G. Harding. Though nationwide Prohibition was the law of the land, both men flaunted it with impunity. While trucks arrived at the White House from Canada laden with spirits, Gore received his whisky from longtime friends and moonshiners. Federal judges in those days wielded a great deal more discretion than current judges. Instead of mandatory minimum sentences, judges weighed each case on its specific merits, and they were granted a great deal of latitude based upon mitigating factors. As such, Judge Gore tended to show leniency to the illicit distillers who stood before him for judgment.

Stories about Gore and his time on the federal bench dispensing justice to moonshiners are legion. One oft repeated story concerns two different moonshiners who appeared before his bench on the same day. When the first man stood before him, Gore demanded that the bailiff bring him a sample of the accused's product. The judge took the mason jar and shook it, checking the bead of the whisky. He then poured out a thin line on his desk, lit a match, and set it aflame. The alcohol burned with a blue flame. Gore announced that he could find no fault with the man or his product; he was simply trying to supplement his meager income. He charged the man a small fine and sent him home with a warning. The other accused moonshiner stepped forward, and the same procedure ensued. When he lit the other man's whisky it created an orange flame. Gore turned red with rage announcing, "This man is a menace! He is manufacturing poison and is a threat to the community!" and then sentenced him to the maximum penalty available under the law."[77]

On another occasion Gore visited a moonshiner on a snowy evening in the late 1920s. He purchased a couple of gallons of whisky in individual pint jars. Arriving at his home as the snow piled up, he left the two gallons of hooch in a cardboard box on his back porch. The following morning Gore went out onto the porch to retrieve some firewood, and noticed that all of the jars had frozen and burst. In a rage he called the Jackson County sheriff and demanded that he arrest the moonshiner. When he appeared in Gore's court he was found guilty and sentenced to the maximum penalty.[78]

During the Great Depression it was not unusual for women to assist their husbands, fathers, or brothers in manufacturing white lightning. The author was shocked when his ninety-four year-old grandmother, Willie Catherine Davis, confessed that she made moonshine during that decade. "Honey, times were tough, and we needed some more money to get by. I ran off batches in the late fall or early winter. I was real careful and made a good product. After I'd made thirty gallons or so, we dismantled the still and hid it until the next year." When asked if she ever worried about being caught or losing her inventory, she chuckled and said, "Lord, no! I hid my jars underneath the floorboards of the Taft Church of Christ because nobody would ever think to look there."[79]

Successfully prosecuting moonshiners often proved difficult for a number of reasons. Local families alerted friends and neighbors who distilled without a license when strangers entered the region. Many distillers found ways of co-opting revenue agents through bribery, sexual favors, or blackmail. Moonshiners developed a number of ways of dispensing their product without being directly associated with it. A common tactic involved a buyer leaving money in an agreed location, and the distiller hiding his whisky where the buyer knew to pick it up.

Moonshiners usually carried a hammer or hatchet and matches with him. After running a batch, the moonshiner loaded his wagon with whisky and covered it with straw, protecting the Mason jars from breakage and easy detection. Hammer and matches provided "Plan B," should he be stopped by revenuers. If it appeared his product might be detected or seized, he broke a jar, lit a match and dropped it in the wagon, sending the evidence up in flames.[80]

Former West Virginia moonshiner Francis Pridemore, who was familiar with moonshiners in the Upper Cumberland of Kentucky and Tennessee, ran his last batch in 1916. He said that when he made white liquor, "Moonshine was not a business; it was a gesture of defiance."[81] When World War I erupted he and other moonshiners, either out of patriotism or demonization by the media, quit distilling. He fought in Europe, returning to find a relative operating his old still. Due to Prohibition attitudes toward moonshining changed, revolving around the thirst of a population deprived of its liquid vice. When Pridemore ran moonshine he made sure his liquor was at least triple-run, free from impurities, tested, tasted, and the product of personal pride. By 1923 quality of moonshine throughout West Virginia, Tennessee, and Kentucky fell prey to easy profit. He

Jack Threet. Michael E. Birdwell Upper Cumberland Collection.

lamented that "moonshining, once a gentleman's avocation—like golf—is now—like golf—a business. . ."[82] As new moonshiners adopted the craft and industrialized it, they cut corners, cared more for money, and took on airs of the *nouveau riche.* "Taking it by and large," he confessed, "I would far rather work for them than for the coal companies." Nationwide Prohibition did something he had not thought possible, for it brought hard cash into the hands of families in Southern Appalachia for the first time, letting them profit from the fruits of their labors. Later critics of the moonshine industry echoed Pridemore's sentiments that the new generation of manufacturers sacrificed quality for mere money. Some unscrupulous distillers in the 1950s, however, did more than simply sacrifice quality, they endangered lives.

One curious and repetitive factor concerning moonshine revolved around election cycles. During federal elections raids by revenue agents increased dramatically, as politicians promised to get tough on criminal behavior.[83] Interestingly, in many local elections for sheriff, local law enforcement agents often curtailed their activity, wanting to win the votes of moonshiners, bootleggers, and their families.[84]

Longtime moonshiner General Jackson "Jack" Threet of Twinton, Tennessee, told the author that once a year the sheriff of Fentress County informally rounded up all the moonshiners in the county. They met at an inconspicuous location, and the law enforcement officer informed them that federal agents were on their way into the region.

> He'd look at each one of us and say, "Boys its time to draw straws." Somebody would give him a broom and he'd break off a bristle as he called everybody's name. Then he'd size them up so they all looked about the same size, and give each of us a turn. Anybody who'd just got out of the federal pokey was exempt, and didn't have to draw no straw. After everyone had their straw we had to present them to the group. There were usually three short straws, and those people stepped forward. Then the sheriff would tell them to get their affairs in order, and told them when to expect to be raided.
>
> We had a common brotherhood. And when someone was raided, with knowledge beforehand or not, the other moonshiners took care of the family of them what's went to jail. They were good people and the sheriff didn't want no trouble. Hell, he was one of our best customers, as was most of the judges and doctors and businessmen in the county.[85]

Moonshining continued to fill the dockets of federal courts after World War II, even though legal whisky was more widely available, comprising most of the cases to come before the district courts in Tennessee, Georgia, North Carolina, and Alabama.[86] During the 1950s moonshine production returned to the front pages of newspapers in a new phase of the alcohol debate. Television shows presented American husbands coming home to the suburbs where housewives dripping pearls kissed their husbands and handed him a drink when he entered the door. In the booze-soaked fifties the South lagged behind the rest of the country in liberalizing its liquor laws. Soldiers who fought in World War II returned to the America of the baby boom, suburbs, and conspicuous consumption. Southern veterans returned to a South that professed to be dry, but in reality never had been. Wanting a drink they had to depend upon bootleggers who sold liquor at highly inflated prices. Loyal Durand Jr. estimated that the monthly production of white lightning in the Cumberland Plateau area to be roughly twenty-five thousand gallons per month in 1955 alone.[87] In April of that year one hundred forty stills were seized or destroyed by local and federal officials. Tennessee's illicit distillers, especially from Jackson County in the Upper Cumberland and Cocke County in far eastern Tennessee, earned a reputation for the quality of their product and runners exported Tennessee moonshine (presumably to relatives or friends) in Michigan, Ohio, and Illinois.[88]

Though many moonshiners prided themselves in producing triple-run liquor in copper stills, less scrupulous distillers cut corners. During the mid-1950s and early 1960s billboards dotted the region declaring: "Moonshine Kills." Some shiners were veterans of World War II or the Korean War, and they learned how to make whisky in the service rather than from experienced distillers. Showing little concern about the quality of their product, disreputable distillers in that era made it easier for politicians, preachers, and social reformers to demonize white lightning. They usually ran the whisky only once rather than the preferred triple-distilled product. Boosting the sugar content, they ran batches with a higher alcohol content and harsher disposition that burned all the way down one's throat. One moonshiner bitterly complained, "It's only them [*sic*] bastards that use [car/truck] radiators and steel pots and steel mash barrels. . . they're the ones that make poison whisky."[89] During that time frame the federal government reported that fewer than 10 percent of the new moonshiners distilled from copper rigs. Use of automotive radiators introduced a broad variety of lethal impurities into their product. Ethylene glycol, a major ingredient in antifreeze, is a colorless, odorless, sweet tasting chemical that causes intoxication. An overdose could cause brain damage, but also negatively affected the liver, kidneys, and lungs. Poisoning altered body chemistry, and could cause profound shock, organ failure, and death. As little as one hundred twenty milliliters of ethylene glycol could kill an average-sized man. While one of the disorders suffered by people who drank bad moonshine in the 1930s was jake leg (or jackleg), an often temporary paralysis that made people walk with an exaggerated gait accompanied by a limp; it did not kill.[90] Some people who persisted in drinking poisoned moonshine experienced total paralysis. In the 1950s and 1960s adulterated moonshine often included the addition of Aqua Velva, wood alcohol, and other contaminants that resulted in blindness in many cases. A myth emerged that all a person needed to do in order to drink tainted moonshine safely was "to strain it through a loaf of white bread."[91] Less scrupulous distillers added detergent to their whisky to make it appear to bead like good moonshine.[92] In addition to poisonous chemicals, moonshiners who represented a real public menace, dumped lye, poison ivy and the carcasses of dead animals into the mash to speed the fermentation process along. Federal authorities found "dead rats, squirrels, snakes, raccoons, opossums and even pigs in seized mash barrels and boxes."[93]

During the late 1960s, due in part to the negative stigma attached to moon-shining because of adulterated whisky and its deleterious effects, illicit distilling fell into sharp decline.[94] Many people argue, however, that moonshining declined because marijuana production increased sharply. Though marijuana usage had a long history in America before the 1960s and 1970s, it was never mainstream. Sam Houston used marijuana while living among the Cherokee, and in the late nineteenth and early twentieth centuries cannabis was associated with African Americans and jazz music. The Counter Culture embraced marijuana out of open rebellion against their parents, choosing it over alcohol. Additionally many soldiers drafted into the Vietnam Conflict were introduced to the drug, and the army reflected the division in mainstream America. Regular army personnel preferred to drink whisky and beer and were referred to as "Juicers," while draftees who smoked marijuana were known as "Heads."

The Upper Cumberland of Kentucky and Tennessee proved to be ideal locations to grow marijuana. An ironic twist to this story is that during the Depression and World War II farmers in both states learned how to grow and cultivate hemp, the nonintoxicating sibling to marijuana. Armed with knowledge of the plant, numerous former moonshiners and their families dropped making corn liquor in favor of producing "Mary Jane." These men and women used some of the same hills and hollers where their ancestors cooked shine to grow cannabis. Attitudes toward marijuana production were just as ambivalent as those held toward production of white whisky.[95]

In the late 1990s and early 2000s a new era of moonshining emerged. Most recent distillers defy stereotypes with the exception of legendary moonshiners like the late Marvin "Popcorn" Sutton, whose "likker" could be found throughout the mountain South. The new breed tended to be college-educated, well-employed, and they flew easily beneath the radar. Large copper stills tucked away in the backwoods were no longer the norm. Fueled in part by legislation that made home brewing beer legal, some argued that the same should be true of whisky. Impatient that the law refused to catch up with the times, a few men and women hunted down moonshine recipes and learned to distill small batches for personal consumption, rather than for retail sale.[96]

This new breed, which also tended to be environmentally aware, intended to make high quality spirits in the best conditions. Many of them already brewed beer or made wine, and enlarged upon that knowledge.

A reproduction of a still at Short Mountain Distillery. Credit: Michael E. Birdwell, Upper Cumberland Collection.

Armed with first-class equipment, not car radiators and rusty barrels, the new breed made stills from Pyrex or bought apparatuses custom-made by artisans. Websites and internet chat rooms made it possible for like-minded people to discuss home-distilling, share recipes, and explore the arcana of corn whisky. For example, "Mr. Distiller," of "Mile High Distilling" in Lakewood, Colorado, provides a cornucopia of products, advice, and a variety of stills that can be purchased online. People can buy specially manufactured milk cans converted for the production of whisky, miniature pot stills, and even the Mr. Distiller Counter Top Distillation Unit, and much, much more.[97]

New interest in moonshine led to the creation of "Boutique Moonshine," high quality whisky, free from impurities and without the exaggerated alcohol content of liquor made in the 1950s and 1960s. Reducing the alcohol levels to a more drinkable 40 to 48 percent, new illicit distillers prefer to make sipping liquors. Willing to experiment with the product, many infuse their brews with fruit extracts and spices, creating liqueurs of superior quality. A recent distiller in Cookeville, an engineering graduate from Tennessee Technological University, perfected a recipe in high demand in the Upper Cumberland. "Apple Pie" moonshine hit the region in the mid 2000s and continues to be a popular commodity. People drank it at parties, sporting events, and even wedding receptions. A number of different *nouveau*-moonshiners throughout Kentucky, North Carolina, and Tennessee distilled versions of it, but the "Pie Man" took it to a new level. Quart jars of the amber liquid were referred to as "slices." Folks who imbibed made comments like, "it really tastes like a slice of apple pie, not like moonshine or apple juice at all." One person remarked, "Oh My God! This is amazing. I can even taste the crust!" While an exaggerated assessment of the spirit, Apple Pie was ubiquitous at social gatherings, and was soon available legally through a number of boutique distillers. Though of reduced alcoholic content, it still packed a wallop. Because it was so smooth and easy to consume, more than one person overstepped the legal limit for consumption. The Pie Man could not keep up with demand, and in 2009 he ran his last batch, distributing them to friends for the holidays. Now, a slice of pie, if it can be found, can run up to sixty dollars.[98]

In addition to fear of being caught for making Apple Pie, another trend convinced the Pie Man to leave the business. A handful of Southern Appalachian states listened to folks who wanted to make white whisky and do so legally. North Carolina, Virginia, Kentucky, and Tennessee passed legislation allowing for the manufacture of legal moonshine. Legal distillers, who either have no will or lack the resources to compete with large scale operations like Jack Daniel, George Dickel, Wild Turkey, Makers Mark and others were granted the right to produce small batch liquor for an expanding niche market. These operators create an alternative to larger distillers with high quality products that retain the mystique and romance of moonshine. They also want to reclaim the tradition while dispelling the stigma associated with white lightning, created in response to the unscrupulous distillers of the 1950s and 1960s. After the legislation passed in Tennessee in 2009, Hank Williams Jr. announced his intentions of partnering with J&M Concepts to distill and market "Popcorn Sutton's Tennessee White Whiskey," using one of Sutton's favorite recipes.[99] Since 2009 a number of boutique distilleries have opened in Tennessee including Collier & McKeel, Corsair, Short Mountain Distillery, and most recently the Chattanooga Whisky Company. As the craving for craft distilling increases there will no doubt be several new distilleries opening for business.

Moonshine production in Appalachia appears to have gone full circle. Beginning as a noble profession transplanted across the mountains from the British Isles by the Ulster Scots, it went through a number of hardships. First attacked by Second Great Awakening pastors and social reformers, it went underground during and immediately after the Civil War. Criminalized by the federal government, revenue agents scoured the region searching for violators. Stereotyped, ridiculed, and demonized by the Local Color School of writers and outside journalists, moonshiners were depicted as an endemic threat to the security of the nation. Nationwide Prohibition improved attitudes toward illicit distillers, as more people joined their cause, chaffing at the notion that the government could legislate morality. Moonshiners respect proved short-lived, for unscrupulous manufacturers posed a real and legitimate threat to health in the 1950s and 1960s, and the stigma lasted over a decade. Slowly the moonshiner has regained respectability, and is once again engaged in a family tradition.

NOTES

1. The Irish version of the Gaelic word *isusquebaugh,* whereas *uisce* is Scottish. Irish distillers spell the spirit "whiskey," while economical Scots dispense with the "e" spelling it "whisky." The Scots spelling is preferred by the author. See Bruce E. Stewart, *Moonshiners and Prohibitionists: The Battle Over Alcohol in Southwestern Appalachia* (Lexington: University Press of Kentucky, 2011), pp. 9–17. The Scots-Irish are also referred to as Ulster Scots.
2. David W. Maurer, *Kentucky Moonshine* (Lexington: University Press of Kentucky, 2003), p. 19. Famed Methodist circuit rider and the first Bishop in the United States, Francis Asbury, railed against the production and consumption of alcohol in his journals and sermons. He often complained bitterly about being paid with liquor for his services rather than some other commodity.
3. Edie Brown Williams, "Cumberland Tales: William Tyler: Judge, Jury and Executioner," Cookeville *Herald-Citizen, (Cookeville, Tennessee)* (March 8, 2009), p. C-9. Moonshine was also used as a disinfectant and a cleaning solvent.
4. Leigh Capshaw, *Dixie University: Dixie College—A Historical Vignette* (Cookeville, Tennessee: Self-published, 1989), p. 2; Stewart, 29.
5. Patricia E. Brake, *Justice in the Valley: A Bicentennial Perspective of the United States District Court for the Eastern District of Tennessee* (Franklin, Tennessee: Hillsboro Press, 1998), p. 58.
6. Wendell Rawls Jr., "Some Hard, Cold Facts about Moonshine Whisky," *Nashville Tennessean* (November 4, 1971), p. B-1. According to Rawls old-time moonshiners measured the proof with equal parts whisky and gunpowder. If the mixture failed to burn it was too weak; if it burned too brightly the whisky was too hot. Only a clear-blue flame proved the concoction to be just right.
7. Wilbur R. Miller, "The Revenue: Federal Law Enforcement in the Mountain South, 1870–1900," *Journal of Southern History* 55: 2 (May 1989), p. 197.
8. Miller, 198.
9. Miller, 204–206; Brake, 60; Maurer, 20.
10. George W. Atkinson, *After the Moonshiners by one of the Raiders: A Book of Thrilling yet Truthful Narratives* (Wheeling, West Virginia: Frew and Campbell Steam Book and Job Printers, 1881), p. 30.
11. Personal Interview with Jack Threet, (Twinton, Tennessee, October 9, 1988); Miller, 200; Brake, 58–62.

12. Quoted in Joseph Earl Dabney, *Mountain Spirits: A Chronicle of Corn Whiskey from King James's Ulster Plantation to America's Appalachians and the Moonshine Life* (Asheville, North Carolina: Bright Mountain Books, 1974), p. 51.
13. "The Tennessee Moonshine Raids," *New York Times*, October 15, 1878, p. 1. By 1878 Adolph Ochs of Chattanooga owned *The New York Times*, and many otherwise local stories found their way into the newspaper of record.
14. "Five Distilleries Destroyed; One Day's Work of a Deputy Collector's Party in Tennessee, *New York*, October 17, 1878, p. 1.
15. "Moonshiners Hide Out; Citizens of Overton Moving for the Suppression of Illicit Distilleries; The County Court Issues a Proclamation that Means Business," *Nashville Daily American* (October 26, 1878), pp. 3–4.
16. Brake, 58; Maurer, 50; Cordell Hull, *Memoirs of Cordell Hull*, Vol. 1. (Washington, D.C.: Hodder and Stoughton, 1948), p. 5. It should be noted that Hull was an expert on tax law, and was the primary author of the text of the Sixteenth Amendment that resulted in the federal income tax. Interestingly, George Atkinson reported that caves, though they might provide an excellent water source, were the easiest operations to raid because revenue agents could block their entrance, preventing the distiller's escape.
17. Brake, 60.
18. Atkinson, *After the Moonshiners*, 157–158.
19. Louanne Seagraves Love, "Murder, Mayhem and Moonshiners in the Upper Cumberland: The Assassination of Deputy U.S. Marshal Henry Seagraves," *The Upper Cumberland Researcher* 25:2 (Summer 2010), pp. 23–26; Miller 201.
20. Miller, 202.
21. Miller, 206. The tactic backfired in many areas leading to greater resentment of the military and the federal government.
22. Atkinson, *After the Moonshiners*, 44; Walter S. McClain, *History of Putnam County, Tennessee* (Cookeville, Tennessee: Quimby Dyer and Co., 1925), pp. 37–38. Atkinson did not participate in the raid; he related the account based upon the reports filed by Captain S.D. Mather and the testimony of James Davis.
23. Henry M. Wiltse, *The Moonshiners* (Chattanooga, Tennessee: Chattanooga *Times* Publishing Co., 1895), pp. 60; Atkinson, *After the Moonshiners*, 43; Atkinson reported that significant moonshining activity occurred at Bloomington (Springs), Buffalo Valley, Blackburn Springs, and other areas in the Cookeville vicinity. Among those who ran shine were the Blaylock, Jared, Maddox, and Riggs families. See "The Sad Fate of Eliza Bleylock [*sic*]," *Harper's Weekly* (March 5, 1881) reprinted in Atkinson, 196–209.
24. James M. Davis was a tenacious, well-respected revenue agent from the region who was the subject of Chapters XI and XII of Atkinson's book. Davis killed several men during the course of his career, and suffered a fractured skull in a raid between Cookeville and Monterey. See Atkinson, 89–103. See also T.P. Crutcher, M.D., *Spurrier with the Wildcats and Moonshiners* (Nashville, Tennessee: University Press, 1892), pp. 60–63.
25. Atkinson, 43–44. Confederate veteran and son of a Presbyterian minister, Morgan operated a number of stills throughout the Upper Cumberland of Kentucky and Tennessee.

26. War in Tennessee: Encouraged by the Condition of Things in South Carolina, The Illicit Distillers in Tennessee Make Armed Resistance to the Revenue Officers." *Chicago, Illinois, Inter Ocean*. (August 26, 1878), p. 5.
27. "War in Tennessee."
28. Atkinson, 44.
29. *Ibid.*, "War in Tennessee."
30. "War in Tennessee."
31. Atkinson, 44–45.
32. "War in Tennessee"
33. "War in Tennessee."
34. *Ibid.*
35. Atkinson, 45.
36. *Ibid.*, 46
37. Quoted in *Ibid.*
38. *Ibid.*, 47.
39. "War in Tennessee.
40. *Ibid.*, 46–48; McClain, 37–38.
41. Atkinson presented a colorful portrait of Campbell Morgan in Chapter XIV, entitled "Campbell Morgan, Sachem of the Moonshiners of the Cumberland Mountains," 105–111.
42. Atkinson, 107. Davis was murdered during a raid near McMinnville, Tennessee, in 1882. By the time of his arrest he was credited with more than three thousand arrests. Davis assisted Atkinson in raids throughout the Upper Cumberland of Kentucky and Tennessee. Some of their most tense situations occurred in Breathitt, Cumberland, and Pulaski counties in Kentucky and Fentress, Jackson, Overton, and Scott counties in Tennessee. See also Crutcher, 63.
43. "Moonshine in Tennessee: How the Illicit Distillers thrive in the South; A Few Gallons of Whisky Produced During the Year—the Farce Which has been Enacted in the Federal Courts—an Illiterate Crowd who are Trying to Make a Living by Breaking the Law, *New York Times*, February 2, 1880.
44. *Ibid.*
45. *Ibid.*
46. "Local Happenings," *Putnam County Herald* (April 26, 1903), p. 1; interviews with numerous moonshiners (who desire to remain nameless) between 1989 and 2006.
47. Miller, 202–203.
48. *Ibid.*, 203; Maurer, 50. Patricia Brake said that a number of politicians ran for Congress promising to repeal the tax. As Miller points out, however, "the whisky tax became the largest domestic source of revenue," by 1900. Both political parties recognized its significance in raising money to fund the government. It is ironic, therefore, that the nation adopted Prohibition and politicians from both parties endorsed it. See page 214.
49. *Tennessee v. Davis*, 100 U.S. 257; 24 L. Ed. 648 (Washington, D.C.: March 1, 1880), p. 1; Atkinson, 95–103.
50. *Tennessee v. Davis.* The opinion runs twenty-nine pages. Citizens of Grundy County empathized with Haynes and wanted to avenge what they deemed his murder. Grundy County, in the Cumberland, has a long history of criminal

behavior. During the late 1970s Tracy City was home to several car theft rings and ranked number one in chop shops across the country.

51. "Moonshiners in Tennessee: A Prominent Churchman Captured for Making Illicit Whisky," *The New York Times*, July 23, 1899.
52. *Ibid.* When Tennessee went dry in 1909 Lem Motlow, the proprietor of Jack Daniel's Distillery in Moore County defiantly challenged the law, arguing that it was unconstitutional and made it impossible for him to make a decent living. Indicted and found guilty for illicit distilling, the state seized three hundred and seventy-five gallons of whisky; he appealed to the state Supreme Court. The court upheld his conviction and fined him two hundred and fifty dollars and sentenced him to ninety days in jail. (Moonshining amounted to a misdemeanor with maximum penalties being eleven months and twenty-nine days in jail and a one thousand dollar fine.) What is ironic is that the court upheld the right of doctors and some industries to import from other states alcohol if it was over 188 proof, but forbade Tennessee distillers from making it. See: *Motlow v. State* (Tennessee State Supreme Court, December Term, 1911), pp. 557–594. Justice Neil wrote the majority opinion with Justice Green dissenting.
53. "A Defense of the Mountaineer," *Literary Digest* 44 (April 20,1912), p. 800; Ben Ray Redman, "In Moonshine Land," *The New York Times*, June 19, 1921.
54. "A Defense of the Mountaineer," 800.
55. *Ibid.*
56. *Ibid.*, 801.
57. Ronald Eller, *Miners, Millhands, and Mountaineers: Industrialization of the Appalachian South, 1880–1930* (Knoxville: University of Tennessee Press, 1982) pp. 161–198 *passim*; Miller, 198–199. Many industrialists moving into Kentucky, Tennessee, and West Virginia considered themselves superior in every way, and fervently endorsed prohibition for the citizens of the Upper Cumberland while hypocritically defending their own right to drink alcohol. For lengthy discussions about the development of the mountaineer stereotype see: Altina Waller, *Feud: Hatfields, McCoys, and Social Change in Appalachia, 1860–1900* (Chapel Hill: University of North Carolina Press, 1988); J.W. Williamson, *Hillbillyland: What the Movies Did to the Mountains and What the Mountains Did to the Movies* (Chapel Hill: University of North Carolina Press, 1995); and Anthony Harkin, *Hillbilly: A Cultural History of an American Icon* (New York: Oxford University Press, 2005).
58. "On a Still-hunt for Stills," *Literary Digest* 59 (October 7, 1916), pp. 915, 917.
59. "A Raid on Moonshiners," *Literary Digest* 44 (May 4, 1912), pp. 957–960.
60. "Local Happenings," *Putnam County Herald* (April 29, 1903), p. 1.
61. "Prohibition in Kentucky," *The New York Times*, August 5, 1907. Reformers urged politicians to move toward moderation in the dispensing of legal alcohol in Tennessee in 1831. Legislators passed a law requiring saloon owners to procure a license to sell alcohol. The price of the license was prohibitive for some and the records they were required to keep, forced many of them out of the legal business of dispensing spirits.
62. Brake, 57.

63. "Moonshine Land, Where Slackers and Deserters are Finding Refuge," *Scientific American* 86: 2222 (August 3, 1918), p. 68.
64. Miller, 216.
65. Theodore H. Price and Richard Spillane, "The Commissioner of Internal Revenue as a Policeman: His Work in the Suppression of the Traffic in Moonshine Whisky, 'Dope,' and Counterfeit Butter," *The Outlook* 120 (November 27, 1918), p. 498.
66. *Ibid.*
67. *Ibid.*
68. *Ibid.*, 503.
69. *Ibid.* Realists, the two journalists doubted that Prohibition would change America for the better. "Prohibition does not altogether prohibit," they noted. They argued that even though legislation was passed to make all liquor traffic illegal, the nation lacked the police and the will to enforce it.
70. David M. Kennedy, *Over Here: The First World War and American Society* (New York: Oxford, 1980), pp. 185–187, 364–365.
71. Rollin Lynde Hartt, "Mountaineers: Our Own Lost Tribes," *Century* 95 (January 1918), p. 400.
72. *Ibid.*
73. William Aspenwall Bradley, "The Folk Culture of the Kentucky Cumberlands," *The Dial* 64 (January 31, 1918), p. 95.
74. *Ibid.*, 98.
75. Stephen Sennet, "Along the Road in the Cumberlands," *The Mentor* 15 (July 1927), pp. 15–19. He also notes that "There is so much misinformation about the Cumberland Mountaineers. . . They have been maligned and poorly used," p. 17.
76. Harry T. Burn, "Tennessee is not a Hooch Paradise: Legislator Resents Articles Depicting State as National Habitat of the Moonshiner; Natives Like Other Folk and of Pure Anglo-Saxon Descent, He Says---Sterling-Towner Bill's Provisions Needed," *The New York Times* (May 21, 1922).
77. Story related by Dr. Homer Kemp, (Cookeville, Tennessee, May 14, 1998).
78. *Ibid.*
79. Interview with Willie Catherine Davis (Cookeville, Tennessee, 2004). The author appeared in an episode of CMT's series *Most Shocking*, "Moonshine Madness," which his grandmother saw, prompting her to tell this curious episode in family lore.
80. Interview with Randy York, District Attorney for the Thirteenth Judicial District of Tennessee," (Cookeville, Tennessee, February 16, 2010); Threet interview; Miller, 202.
81. Francis Pridemore, "How Doth the Busy Moonshiner! A One-time Operator of a West Virginia Still Ironically Considers a Growing Industry Which has Brought Affluence to Impoverished Communities," *North American Review* 228:1 (July, 1929), p. 13.
82. *Ibid.*, 1914.
83. Prohibition led to strange bedfellows. When the subject became part of the political dialogue in the 1932 presidential election, a chorus of opposition against the

repeal of the Volstead Act filled the radio airwaves and print media across the country. On the one hand, churchmen and social reformers argued that it would lead to widespread crime and depravity. On the other hand, moonshiners and bootleggers feared legalizing beer, wine, and spirits would send them back into abject poverty.

84. William Aspenwall Bradley, "Hobnobbing with Hillbillies," *Harpers* 133:787 (December 1915), pp. 91–103.
85. Jack Threet interview. The largesse Threet discussed showed up repeatedly in other instances throughout the Upper Cumberland. Threet made moonshine for decades in the coal mining region of Fentress, Overton, and Putnam counties, and the author interviewed him dozens of times between 1988 and 1991. He often boasted, "I can make whisky out of anything." While that may have been so, he also made some horrific booze, among the worst being his tomato shine. He did make fine peach brandy. The article "On a Still-hunt for Stills," told of a similar situation where a moonshiner was serving a year-long sentence in the federal penitentiary. While his wife had little to eat in her house beyond cornmeal, neighbors looked after her in his absence. Rawls's article substantiated Threet's claim, saying that sheriffs and deputies often alerted moonshiners that feds intended to raid the area. In some cases they only went through the motions of destroying stills, leaving them to be reassembled.
86. Brake, 57.
87. Loyal Durand Jr., "Mountain Moonshining in East Tennessee," *Geographical Review* 46:2 (April 1956), 168. It was estimated that in 1955 over one and a half million gallons of moonshine were distilled in Tennessee. In Cookeville, Tennessee, in the 1950s and 1960s, the local cab company ran the bootlegging business. Very few people in the region needed a cab, unless they wanted to buy a drink.
88. *Ibid.*
89. Rawls, B-1.
90. Maurer, 21. Jake leg was not often the result of moonshine whisky, being cut with one hundred forty proof Jamaican Ginger extract with triorthocresylphosphate phosphate, (TOCP) to mask the alcoholic content from authorities. Originally considered harmless TOCP attacked the central nervous system, temporarily or permanently paralyzing those who imbibed. Jake was the nickname of Jamaican Ginger. The walk it caused is reminiscent of the Monty Python sketch, "Bureau of Silly Walks."
91. Threet interview; Rawls, B-1.
92. Rawls, B-1.
93. Rawls, B-3.
94. Even so, Tennessee ranked second in moonshine production in 1970, with Georgia taking top billing.
95. During the early and mid-2000s a threat emerged in the region as insidious as the adulterated moonshine that impaired the lives of thousands. The Upper Cumberland became a haven for the production and distribution of methamphetamine. It menaced the region and destroyed lives. For a good overview of the problem see Todd Jarrell's Emmy winning documentary, *Crank: Darkness on the Edge of Town*, produced by PBS affiliate WCTE (Cookeville, Tennessee: 2006).

96. Michelle Tsai, "Why is Moonshine Against the Law? You Can Make Your Own Wine and Beer, Can't You?" *Slate* (October 18, 2007) http://www.slate.com/articles/news_and_politics/explainer/2007/10/why_is_moonshine_against_the_law.html. Interviews with people who wish to remain nameless. The legislation allowing home brewing possible also spawned the growth and competition of micro breweries across the United States. Similar legislation allowed persons to make wine at home, also stimulating the U.S. wine industry.
97. State District Attorney Randy York informed me about the Mr. Distiller website, but would not admit that it is monitored by law enforcement authorities. People shopping at Mr. Distiller can buy any component for constructing a high-quality still, plus yeasts, malts, and other ingredients. They even offer wooden barrels for aging the product. See www.milehidistilling.com.
98. Interview with the Pie Man's brother-in-law and other people who wish to remain nameless. Interestingly Apple Pie moonshine appeared in two episodes of the second season of *Justified* on FX. The first episode to feature apple pie, "Brother's Keeper," aired April 6, 2011 and the second episode, "Bloody Harlan," was broadcast on May 4, 2011. The show is set in Harlan County, Kentucky, and other environs in and around the Kentucky Upper Cumberland.
99. Fran Daniel, "This Isn't Your Grandaddy's Likker: Distillery Makes Catdaddy Carolina Moonshine and It's Legal," *Winston-Salem Journal* (June 17, 2006); "Moonshine Quietly Gets a 21st Century Makeover: Sherman Owen's Moonshine Odyssey Started at 19 When he set out to Distill 'Ultra-Clean' Vodka, *West Virginia Gazette* (April 4, 2010); Lissa Sims, "Local Distillers Bring New Respectability to an Age-old Illicit Kentucky Tradition," *Smiley Pete Publishing* (November 3, 2010); "East Tennessee Hooch Goes Legit in Nashville: Hank Jr. Backs Legendary Recipe," *Nashville Tennessean* (November 12, 2010). Former Tennessee legislator Mike Williams of Franklin played a key role in getting the law passed allowing small batch operations. The bill was sponsored by State Representative Joe Carr of Lascassas, Tennessee. Williams' distillery, Collier and McKeel, began selling its white liquor in May, 2011.

MEDICAL MEN AND WOMEN

10

To Find a Cure

The Practice of Folk Medicine in the Upper Cumberland

Opless Walker

The Upper Cumberland Region lies inside the boundaries of a vast geological area known as Appalachia.[1] Recognized as one of the most botanically diverse regions of the world, Appalachia is home to over two thousand five hundred plant species, of which some eleven hundred have been utilized for their medicinal properties. Following the Civil War, Appalachia became the primary source of crude drugs in the United States, providing the basic ingredients for patent medicines and precursors to Big Pharmaceuticals (Big Pharma) such as Eli Lilly.[2] Folk medicine emerged in the Upper Cumberland out of necessity and pioneers learned the efficacy of plants and minerals through trial and error or interaction with Native Americans who shared their knowledge with the settlers. Over decades tried-and-true remedies evolved alongside some outrageous concoctions that did more harm than good. In the years before the establishment of professional doctors and medical schools, citizens got by on their knowledge of native plants and potions derived from them. As the medical industry grew into a true profession, the knowledge of local healers and their folk remedies fell into decline. The medical profession tended to dismiss homeopathic remedies in favor of medicines manufactured by multinational conglomerates. In recent years, with numerous medicines recalled for debilitating side effects or removed from the market outright, the ingredients employed in folk medicine have witnessed a resurgence. While both prescribed medicines and some folk remedies have tremendous drawbacks, they each have something to offer the person in need of treatment. Both have had good reason to be wary of the other when claiming to cure certain ailments with dubious results, from baldness, miracle weight-loss cures, diabetes, cancer, and many more. Some of the touted folk cures seem ludicrous at best today, while others continue to advance the abilities of modern medicine to effect new treatments with fewer side effects and greater efficacy.

Native American inhabitants and European settlers made their home in the Upper Cumberland of Kentucky and Tennessee in the midst of a natural supply of medicinal plants that had a broad healing potential if the correct plant could be found for a given infirmity. The Cherokee held an unwavering trust in the abundant natural medicines of the forest and field. They believed that "even the grasses and the weeds had healing power if only the 'spirit' would reveal their power to the medicine man."[3] Although the Native Americans practiced folk medicine long before the arrival of the Europeans, folk medicine was enhanced by the addition of European cures unknown to the natives of North America. By the eighteenth century Native Americans learned how to apply the medicines of the Old World, as well as being introduced to Scots-Irish folk customs and medical practices.[4]

Cherokee influence upon folk medicine in the Upper Cumberland, although not significant to the population as a whole, was nevertheless important to individuals related to or associated with Cherokees in the region. There were two main direct sources of Cherokee medicine: Chief Nettle Carrier lived in the area of Overton County now known as Alpine, Tennessee, and Cherokees who escaped the Trail of Tears in the 1838 removal and settled north of Monterey, Tennessee. Several descendants of the Monterey Cherokee moved to Doyle, Tennessee, in White County around 1900, while others made their way back to the Cherokee Reservation in North Carolina. Cherokee and their descendants resided in Overton and Putnam Counties during all of the nineteenth century.[5] The most celebrated Cherokee resident was Chief Nettle Carrier, who was quite knowledgeable about the healing plants in the Upper Cumberland. Living east of Monterey, Tennessee, was Chief Pathkiller who enjoyed a reputation as a man of substance. Chief Black Fox hunted in the Upper Cumberland, and made contact with several regional residents; however, none of his descendants are known to have lived in the area. Chief Pathkiller's daughter Nelly Pathkiller shared her father's herbal medicine knowledge with others in the Upper Cumberland.[6]

Although the Cherokee practiced shamanism, there existed a Native American belief that each tree, shrub, and herb, down even to the grasses and mosses, could furnish a cure for diseases if only mankind could harness their curative factors. How reliable was Cherokee medicine? James Mooney (1861–1921), an American anthropologist who lived for several years among the Cherokee, observed the healing potential of the top twenty herbs (known as the principal plants) used by the Cherokee. Mooney observed:

> Concerning the medical properties of plants, we find that five plants, or 25% of the whole number, are correctly used; twelve, or 60 percent, are presumably either worthless or incorrectly used, and three plants, or 15 percent, are so used that it is difficult to

> say whether they are of any benefit or not. Granting that two of these three produce good results as used by the Indians, we should have 35 percent or about one-third of the whole as the proportion actually possessing medical virtues, while the remaining two-thirds are inert, if not positively injurious. It is not probable that a larger number of examples would change the proportion to any appreciable extent. A number of herbs used in connection with these principal plants may probably be set down as worthless.[7]

With advancements in analytical chemistry and clinical observations, it is now possible to prove or disprove the medicinal attributes of principal Cherokee plants. Several compendia serve as authoritative sources of rigorous clinical testing; however, sufficient data is found in the well-respected *PDR (Physician's Desk Reference) for Herbal Medicine.*[8] The following table summarizes comparisons between twenty main Cherokee plants and their efficacy according to the herbal medicine *PDR*.

The health of Native Americans in the eighteenth and nineteenth centuries must surely be credited in some degree to their living outdoors in a less polluted atmosphere than that currently found in the Upper Cumberland. Their highly active lifestyle cannot be overlooked when regarding the health of the Native Americans. Health practices of the Cherokee depended primarily on ritualistic medicine, which if responsible for a cure at all, was due to psychosomatics. Regardless of the lack of efficacy of most of their herbal remedies, the Cherokee Medicine Man enjoyed great respect from most of the Upper Cumberland's citizenry. Almost every carnival traveling through Upper Cumberland villages in the years prior to the 1960s included an Indian medicine man, whether fake or genuine. Many folks purchased the fifty-cent or one dollar bottle of cure-all medicine hawked by the sideshow performer.

Professional doctors have acknowledged Native American contributions to medicine through the use of mayapple and charcoal. Allopathic (regular) physicians utilize podophyllin from mayapple for the removal of warts. The chemotherapeutic drug known as etoposide (podophyllotoxin) is derived from mayapple. Charcoal scrapings from burned wood and bone were utilized to treat upset stomach by the Cherokee. Activated charcoal continues to be sold in drugstores, and charcoal is used in hospitals around the world in management of ingested poisons.

There was a time when all medicine was folk medicine; ideological divisions did not exist. The first attempt to standardize medications based on safety and efficacy occurred in 1820, to develop a highly diversified list of so-called cures to treat any number of maladies. Eleven physicians met

Principal Plant	Cherokee Use	PDR Statement	Effectiveness
Snakeroot	Snake bites, fever, coughs	expectorant, antibacterial	possibly
Beggar's Lice	improves memory	not listed	unproven
Wild Senna	fever	cathartic	possibly
Life Everlasting	colds	cramps, diarrhea	possibly
Vetch	upset stomach, cramps, back pain	not listed	unproven
Catgut	energy enhancer	not listed	unproven
Milkweed	skin eruptions, purgative	purgative	very effective
Skullcap	diarrhea, breast pains	not listed	unproven
Maidenhair Fern	rheumatism, chills	expectorant	possibly
Wild Alum	thrush, mouth ulcers	not listed	unproven
Indian Physic	tonic	blood purifier	effective
Liverwort	coughs	diarrhea	possibly
Tassel Flower	cuts, bruises	not listed	unknown
Ginseng	headache	tonic	effective
Meadow Rue	diarrhea	not listed	unknown
Lady's Slipper	worms	irritant	possibly
Cone Flower	anti-inflammatory	anti-inflammatory	effective
Solomon's Seal	boils	steroid	effective
Queen of the Meadow	diuretic	diuretic	effective
Shield Fern	skin protectant, rheumatism	not listed	unknown

in Washington, D.C., and organized the United States Pharmacopeia (USP) in that year. Of the hundreds of medications from which to choose, they selected 217 drugs that became the foundation of medical regimens for all legitimate physicians thereafter. Since no sophisticated analytical laboratories existed, the eleven physicians developed their list based on observation and opinion. Founding the USP marked the beginning of the distinction between "accepted" medication and "unaccepted" medications in the United States. Herbs and minerals rejected by the USP delegates as official regimens in the treatment of various ailments were ostracized from the accepted medical practice. Creation of the USP marked the beginning of tensions between the practitioners of folk medicine and the professional medical community.

Individuals who continued to depend upon herbs and minerals not listed in the USP were considered unprofessional and shunned by the established medical community of physicians. Later, the founding of the American Medical Association (AMA) at Philadelphia in 1847 polarized medical therapy in American. From its very beginning, the AMA promoted medical education reforms that favored its own preferred style of medical practice, thus declaring their mode of medical treatment as the only legitimate one. As a result of the dominance of the AMA, state licensing examinations began to favor allopathy (conventional medicine as sanctioned by the AMA), and the AMA's control over licensing boards eventually brought the pluralistic system of medical care in the United States to an end.[9] From the late 1800s through the 1940s—a period of health reform in America—an attitude of intolerance towards folk medicine prevailed within the medical and nursing professions. Until recently few efforts were made to conduct objective, dispassionate research on the topic.

For people in the Upper Cumberland few regular doctors (a term locals used to describe professional physicians) lived among them, and medical care was scarce until the twentieth century. A sick person who sought medical assistance did not care where or what source the treatment was as long as it was available and reliable. Illness often struck quickly; but the ability to procure professional help took time, if available at all.

Reliability, accessibility, availability, and affordability of healthcare were paramount in the decision making process of individuals needing medical attention for themselves or their family members. In 1910, ninety years after the eleven doctors met in Washington, D.C., to establish the United States Pharmacopeia, studies revealed that only fifty percent of the professionally prescribed medicine actually established a cure of the disease for which it was intended.[10]

Until practices were standardized and college courses made more rigorous physicians were poorly trained, acquiring their medical knowledge through an apprenticeship under the guidance of a doctor. Few attended a medical school, others simply read medical books and declared themselves to be doctors. According to a survey conducted in East Tennessee in 1850, there were 201 physicians serving a population of 164,000. Thirty-five of them graduated from a medical school, while forty-two doctors attended a course of medical lectures, but did not graduate. Ninety-five were self-taught (known as "book doctors"), twenty-five were classified as botanical doctors, and two practiced homeopathy. More respected physicians read medical books under a tutor at a medical college, and/or served a two-year apprenticeship with an established physician. Several Upper Cumberland physicians trained at Transylvania University in Lexington, Kentucky.[11]

Medical care from regular doctors could not be guaranteed in the days of bad roads and horses and buggies. Weather, time, distance, other conditions, and personal circumstances often deterred a doctor from making house calls. A good example of the extent to which some inhabitants of the Upper Cumberland region went to insure medical assistance is that of Charlie Walker, who lived on Bee Tree Ridge in Overton County, Tennessee. Bee Tree Ridge was incredibly remote, accessible only by horse, mule, or on foot. In order to entice doctors to come to his home when needed, Charlie built a one-room guest house behind his small home. Although other guests spent nights in the structure, it was intended for doctors. The Walker family insured good food and overnight lodging for any physician who came to their aid.[12]

Ironically, the American Civil War solidified use of folk medicine in the Upper Cumberland. In early 1861 medicines and medical supplies were declared contraband in the South by the Lincoln administration, and all states belonging to the Confederacy were cut off from dependable sources of medicine. The Northern blockade of the South included, in order of importance: first guns and ammunition; second, clothing and footwear; and third, drugs and chemicals.[13] Physicians in the Upper Cumberland were forced to revert to folk medicine, since they had no access to pharmaceutical distributors in the North. For the first time since 1820, medical doctors and those depending on medicine relied on innovation and traditional Appalachian folk remedies. Medicinal preparations formulated during the Civil War proved so successful that they continued to influence the art of healing in the Upper Cumberland through the decade of the 1950s.

Examples of cures originating in the Civil War include: tincture of monkshood, when applied directly to the skin to relieve surface pain, served as an external anesthetic and pokeberry combined with sarsaparilla root, sassafras, and prickly ash were consumed as a tea or in solution with whisky as an analgesic to treat headaches and other pains. Poultices—compounds made from a variety of ingredients including such things as onions, garlic, pokeroot, celery, pepper, dogwood bark, parsley, and sage—were applied topically for any number of maladies and were often found satisfactory.

For such ailments as cough, croup, and asthma, sufferers consumed lobelia tea or homemade cough syrups using white whisky, peppermint, horehound candy, lemon juice, and honey. Cough syrup was made from various ingredients. Horehound herb was steeped in hot water, was strained, and sugar was added, then the mixture was boiled down into a thick syrup. A teaspoonful or two a couple of times a day was reputed to cure any cough. A cold-water dressing with a decoction of red oak bark was applied to some wounds for the disinfectant properties of the oak bark.[15]

Other medical practices of Upper Cumberland inhabitants created during the Civil War continued on for two to three generations. Folk remedies from the Upper Cumberland were compiled, cataloged, and described by Tennessee Polytechnic Institute (TPI) Professor T.J. Farr, one of the founders of the Tennessee Folklore Society. Dr. Farr cataloged a number of ingredients that did have some degree of medical value, many of which were also employed by licensed physicians in the Upper Cumberland. They included, alum, asafetida, blood root, baking soda, balm of Gilead, borax, castor oil, catnip, copperas, Epsom salts, fennel, flax seed, ginseng, honey, horse radish, mayapple, mint, molasses, mullein, nutmeg, vinegar, peach pits, pennyroyal, pumpkin seeds, sage, sulfur, turpentine, queen of the meadow, turpentine, and witch hazel. Most inhabitants of the Upper Cumberland kept many of these ingredients on hand for both preventative medicine and as home cures they depended on for generations.[16] Farr's papers provide insight into the understanding of the medical efficacy of certain plants and herbs by some, while also revealing a great deal of superstition regarding the mysteries of healing the sick. His research demonstrated that while many may have been excellent treatments for specific ailments, others had no restorative properties at all.[17]

Farr's papers list hundreds of so-called cures, and what follows are examples that recur repeatedly in his collection of treatments for a variety of ailments. Minor cuts and abrasions were covered by a teaspoonful of sugar containing a drop or two of coal oil (kerosene) or turpentine and bound up with a clean rag. If the cut was deep and bleeding copiously, it was filled with chimney soot, and then bandaged tightly. Most people maintained a rag bag hanging on the kitchen wall containing well-washed white rags for bandaging emergencies. If no rags were handy, people were instructed to stuff the wound with cobwebs to stem the bleeding.[18]

Wilted jimson weed was bound to bruises and held in place as long as needed for the bruise fade away. Other cures for bruises included immersing the affected area in buttermilk or soaking it in a stream with cold-running water.

If a person suffered a puncture wound from a nail or other sharp object stuck into the body, a piece of an old wool rag was thrown on live embers to generate thick smoke. The wound was held over the smoke for as long as the individual could tolerate it. Then sugar and coal oil and/or turpentine were applied to the puncture, and it was tightly bound with a clean rag.

Nose bleeds were common and were a source of considerable fear. The sight of blood coming streaming down a person's face produced considerable anxiety. Several remedies exist among the Farr Papers for treating a nose bleed. If available, cold water or crushed ice was placed on the forehead and the back of the neck. One remedy called for a dime to be placed under the upper lip while the person pressed hard on the lip. If a dime were unavailable small rolls of a brown paper sack were put under the upper lip. If the nosebleed did not stop in a reasonable time, a person of faith was summoned. A verse from the *King James Bible*—Ezekiel 16:6—was recited aloud over and over again until the bleeding stopped. Some faith healers reputedly had the ability to stop nose bleeds at a distance; they needed only the name and location of the afflicted person. Often, a necklace of red corn and a piece of paper inscribed with the Lord's Prayer was worn around the neck of the bleeder to stop and prevent further nosebleeds.[19]

Burns, depending on their severity, were covered with heavy cream fresh from the spring house, or the meat of a fresh pumpkin was scraped and bound to the burn using a clean white rag from the kitchen rag bag. If these remedies failed to work satisfactorily, a person who "was born after his/her father had died" was sought for the cure. Such an individual was believed to have the power to "blow the fire out of burns." These same people cured "the thrush" by blowing into the mouth of the ailing person. Of all the remedies for burns, application of scrapings from an Irish potato seemed to work best.[20]

For earache sufferers warm tobacco smoke was blown into the affected ear to cure it. If earaches occurred in the summertime, the head of a "Bessie" bug was pinched off, and a drop of blood was placed in the ear. If a person suffered from night terrors, night sweats, or insomnia, healers instructed them to place a Bible beneath the bed before they tried to go to sleep.

Rags soaked in cold water were placed on victims of headaches. Pressure was often applied equally against each temple or a drop of camphor was rubbed on each temple and on the forehead. This mixture was sparingly used, since camphor gum was often hard to get. Myriad tea concoctions were used for numerous treatments with varying degrees of success.

Sassafras tea was used to treat chills and fevers. Old-timers believed that sassafras tea taken in February would ward off chills and fevers later in the year. Catnip tea supposedly cured the colic. Boneset tea was used to treat ague (a fever accompanied with chills). Sage grass tea was believed to breakout the measles. A tea made from pine bark, life everlasting, burdock root, and molasses reputedly soothed sore throats associated with colds and flu. Women drank pennyroyal tea to relieve menstrual cramps, and it was believed that large doses caused spontaneous abortions.[21]

Common afflictions such as boils, carbuncles, corns, and skin eruptions were often very painful. The aim of treatment was to draw the boil to a head. Warm cornbread crumbs mixed with unsalted butter as a poultice was often used. Some used slices of fat meat directly applied to the boil, which most sufferers detested. The thin membrane inside an eggshell was sometimes the sought after remedy. A favorite treatment for boils was a poultice made from flour and milk cooked down into a thick roux and applied while it was still hot-to-warm.

Diarrhea, often referred to as flux or "the summer complaint," could be deadly to a small child. A tea made from blackberry root was used and dosed out one teaspoonful at a time. The most effective cure for the flux, some people vowed, was cabbage soup made with rusty bacon. Callie Myers Melton, a former student of Dr. Farr, said that her mother often remarked that, "It takes money to buy good whiskey and ride the train."[22]

Head colds, sinus infections, and catarrh (inflammation of the mucous membranes resulting most often in sinus drainage) were treated in numerous ways, many of them to no or ill effect. Rabbit tobacco, common in the Upper Cumberland, (also known as sweet everlasting and white sweet balsam) was often smoked if tobacco were unavailable. Its reputed healing powers soothed the throat and helped relieve sinus pains. Others relied on various poultices applied to the chest, made from camphor, mustard, turpentine, and other such ingredients. Some relied on spices, citrus peels, and aromatic herbs placed in boiling water to create a healing steam that wafted into their mouth and nostrils. To treat a sore throat that often accompanied coughs and colds, mutton tallow was rubbed on the throat and covered by a wool sock.[23]

A salve made from peeled buckeyes cooked down in lard was applied frequently to the inflamed area surrounding hemorrhoids. Whereas kidney problems were treated with a tea made from butterfly weed roots. It was consumed daily until the problem abated.

To remove pain and swelling from sore eyes, an Irish potato was cut into slices roughly an inch thick, and placed over the eyes, holding the potatoes in place with a clean bandana to "draw the fire out."[24]

Seeds from vermifuge plants were gathered and carefully preserved throughout the winter. In the spring, the seeds were mixed with molasses and given to a person suffering from worms. Callie Myers Melton claimed this unorthodox remedy proved highly effective.[25]

Many reputed remedies clearly had no medicinal value whatsoever, and such remedies probably put the patient in greater danger. A few defy all sense of logic. In order to cure whooping cough, a curious remedy instructed mothers to smother three minnows to death in a baby's mouth before the child reached its first birthday. Another curious cure claimed that in order to cure measles, the patient should drink a tea made from sheep manure poured into an old shoe. To comfort a teething baby, mothers were instructed to rub the infant's sore gums with warm rabbit brains wrapped in a soft cloth. Carrying a buckeye in one's pocket supposedly warded off pain, while an onion in the pocket insured epileptics that they would not fall prey to paroxysms. Sucking the wick of a kerosene lamp reportedly cured colds and opened nasal passages.[26]

The author experienced the ministrations of a respected folk medicine "expert" as a child, when he contracted chicken pox at age six. Loggan Waddles (1857–1955), a citizen of Monterey, Tennessee, lived in a tiny four-room shanty behind the First Baptist Church and practiced folk medicine. The Waddles family had no electricity, procured water from a well, utilized an outdoor toilet, and maintained a yard full of chickens and roosters. With a small garden, the Waddles family subsisted. "Logg" (pronounced with a long "ō") was known as a master of herbal decoctions and external preparations. He was also known for ritualistic therapies as well. Instead of going to one of Monterey's three physicians, to treat the chickenpox the author's mother took him to see Logg. When he emerged onto the porch, Logg looked the child over from head to foot, and instructed him to lie down along the threshold of the front room door. With assurance that the boy would not move, Logg, his wife, and the child's mother went around the house and opened the kitchen door. Frightful sounds filled the air as multiple chickens were herded through the house towards the exit and over the author's body. In order for the cure to be effective it was necessary for the chickens to run through the house—for some reason known only to Waddles. Although sixty years have passed since that experience, the author can still see and feel the chickens as they flew in a panicked state over his face and chest. Did it cure him? Probably not.[27]

Many other children were taken to Waddles for the same chicken pox cure as well as for other healing remedies. Logg was known as an individual who had inherited the ability to blow into the mouth of a child with thrush (pronounce "trash" in southern vernacular) for the purpose of curing the condition. This author's three-year-old brother B.C. Walker was taken to Waddles and held by him as Waddles blew deep into the toddler's mouth, supposedly curing the lad.[28]

In addition to folk remedies, hot springs were utilized by conventional physicians and folk medicine dependents alike, across the United States and Europe. Since the larger culture touted the benefits of a mineral bath or the internal effects of mineral water in which minerals and spas abounded. As early as 1840, the waters in Salt Lick Creek in Macon County, Tennessee, were believed to have curative properties. The settlement became a mineral water resort and later took the name of Red Boiling Springs, Tennessee. Fifteen years after the Civil War ended, Red Boiling Springs became a popular resort for "taking the waters." That phrase implied more than just drinking mineral water; rather the entire concept of drinking, inhaling mineral vapors, and bathing in the waters was expressed. Faith in the healing factors of mineral water was so prevalent that many famous persons visited Red Boiling Springs. Hotel registers included names of judges, mayors, lawyers, heads of industry and business, famous musicians and singers, governors and even one President of the United States—Woodrow Wilson. There were five different healing waters at Red Boiling Springs, and medical doctors were on hand to prescribe treatments which worked for a particular ailment.[29] The five waters were:

> **Red Water**—So named because it turned a silver coin red, this water was taken internally as well as utilized as a steam or tub bath. Red Water was supposed to be effective in urinary tract diseases and various skin conditions. Consumed in sufficient quantity and over an extended period of time, Red Water was said to have the ability to dissolve kidney stones. The flavor of Red Water was lightly sulfurous and easily tolerated by most visitors.
>
> **Black Water**—This water turned a silver coin black, hence its name. Black Water was taken internally for three basic infirmities: diseases of the digestive tract, to provide energy to individuals suffering from exhaustion, and to treat insomnia. Black Water was also utilized as a steam and tub bath. The taste of this water was not for the faint-of-heart; Black Water was very-strongly sulfur flavored and only those with an acquired taste could stomach it.
>
> **Freestone Water**—So named because this water was free from trace minerals. Freestone Water was an internal and external cleanser. Doctors often prescribed Freestone Water when the

desire was to flush the stomach, intestinal tract, and the kidneys. This water was preferred by many due to the foul taste of all the others.

White Water—Minerals in this water acted as an antacid. Patients drank White Water for dyspepsia. Reports are that this water was highly effective in treating stomach ailments.

Famed Double and Twist Water—Reserved mostly for mineral baths, this water when consumed internally often gave the person intestinal cramps and diarrhea. Utilized for chronic constipation, Double and Twist was advertised as the "only water of its kind in the United States."[30]

Eventually, the remoteness of Red Boiling Springs and the loss of confidence in mineral waters added to the causes of the resort's decline. There were other, less visited sites, which offered mineral water for ingestion. This author remembers an animated advertisement located on the south side of old Highway 70N just east of Carthage, Tennessee. The sign, depicting an individual raising a glass of mineral water to his mouth, advertised sulfur or mineral water for consumption. Many travelers along Highway 70N drove the short distance to the source to purchase a gallon jug of the restorative water.

In addition to treatment from sulfur and mineral waters true herbal cures were as near as the farmer's vegetable garden, but were thought of simply as a food source to give energy and a feeling of satiety rather than as a medicinal preventative or cure. Benefits of fruits, berries, nuts, and vegetables were looked upon equally by fork medicine practitioners and physicians practicing conventional medicine.[31]

Examples of medicinal fruits, berries, nuts, and vegetables of the Upper Cumberland are:

Apples that act as gastrointestinal tract stabilizers during bouts of diarrhea. Pectin in apples binds carcinogens of the intestinal tract, thus decreasing the risk of colon cancer. Apples reduce cholesterol and combat arteriosclerosis. **Cherries** act as a blood cleanser. They contain anthocyanin, a chemical known to inhibit tumor growth. **Grapes** boost the immune system and have anti-tumor, anti-cancer, and antioxidant properties. They stabilize capillary walls, thus inhibiting edema, and contain powerful proanthocyanidins. **Peaches** promote heart health, aid digestion, and combat obesity. **Pears** lower blood pressure and promote healthy kidney function.

Blackberries are rich in fiber (5.3 percent), vitamins, and minerals; they contain flavonoids that nourish the retina of the eyes, thus improving vision. They are a potent antioxidant protectant against cardiac disease and cancer. **Raspberries,** one of nature's antibiotics, protect the kidney and liver. Raspberries detoxify the body. **Strawberries** contain potent antioxidants and protect against cardiac disease and cancer. **Nuts,** high energy foods, reduce bad cholesterol and elevation of healthy cholesterol (HDL). They are a rich protein source for building muscle tissue and help promote healthy heart function. **Cabbage,** known as the "poor man's medicine," protects the mucous membranes of the stomach. It has multiple properties including anti-ulcer, anti-cancer, prevention of bladder cancer, treatment of asthma, and is useful as a treatment for gout. Sauerkraut is the most powerful form of cabbage. **Pumpkin**, one of the most medicinal fruits of the garden, reduces cholesterol absorption from the intestinal tract, while protecting the heart. Pumpkin treats inflammation of the kidneys, indigestion, acid stomach, and has anticarcinogenic properties. High beta carotene levels make pumpkin a perfect food for improved eye health. Interestingly, pumpkin seeds were an official medicine from 1865–1936. Known as Pepo, pumpkin seeds are effective in the prevention of prostatic hypertrophy. In addition, pumpkin seeds are effective in removing intestinal parasites from humans.

By far the most medicinal vegetable in Upper Cumberland gardens is the **onion**. Now known to contain the antimicrobial chemical thiosulphinate, onions are effective against E. coli, decreasing lipids in the blood, decreasing blood pressure, inhibiting blood clotting; are anti-asthmatic, anti-allergic, and a therapy for fevers and colds. Onion soup, especially cooked in milk, provides a good mucolytic (breaks up the mucous present during congestion). **Carrots** protect against many cancers, especially cancers of the lung, bladder, and ovaries. They can prevent and heal many gastrointestinal infections.

In the twentieth century with more money available, families could take advantage of readily available store-bought patent medicines, and could rely less on botanicals and ritualistic medical cures. Faith in patent medicines was such that most homes in the Upper Cumberland maintained a pharmacy to treat any problem with the exception of those ailments considered beyond the potency of the pills, syrups, and salves available in local

Various medicinal bottles from the period.

drugstores without a doctor's prescription. Fancy labels, containers, and assurances of efficacy from the manufacturer or distributor of the patent medicines and personal testimonials, proved most convincing to the consumer. Examples of trusted medicines found in many homes in the 1940s included **Cloverine Salve,** which earned the *Good Housekeeping* Seal of Approval. Text on the small container touted it as a treatment for burns, cuts, sores, ulcers, chapped lips, face and hands, common sore throat, chafes, galls, nasal catarrh, itching piles, sunburn, and tired, sore, and aching feet. The label boasted: "Discovered by a physician and used by people of refinement."[32]

The **Black Salve** of the households in the Upper Cumberland during the 1930s and 1940s contained ammonium bituminosulfonate—a product obtained from the distillation of sulfur-rich oil shale. Known as a "drawing slave," it lived up to its reputation. Having antimicrobial properties the salve was used to treat infections and to "draw out" splinters, stingers, and thorns.

Saint Joseph and Bayer **Aspirin,** acetasalicylic acid derived from willow bark, was used for fevers, headaches, and toothaches when dissolved

Cloverine Salve white petroleum jelly. Credit: Opless Walker collection.

in the hollow of the infected tooth. It was used to treat any number of ailments, and powdered aspirin packets of BC Powder were a staple in homes and businesses. Aspirin or aspirin powder provided relief from insect bites and stings when dissolved on the affected area. It also has anti-fungal qualities as well as some use in the treatment of acne.

Vick's Salve (or Vick's Vap-O-Rub) and its cheaper knock-off **Soltice** (manufactured by the Chattanooga Medicine Company) was used for congestion from colds. Small amounts were placed in the nasal passages, swallowed for sore throat, or applied directly to the throat, then covered by a warm cloth. In severe colds and flu the entire chest was rubbed with Vick's Salve and covered with a warm cloth. This was a very effective treatment for cold symptoms. Containing camphor and menthol, congestion could be cleared by breathing the mixture when placed in hot, steaming water.

Rock Candy, crystalline table sugar, when mixed with whisky, was believed to be a cure or prevention of many illnesses. Some families faithfully used this mixture daily. Sugar that looked like rock crystals took on a medicinal property in the opinion of many. Some families of the Upper Cumberland learned how to make it for themselves. A simple recipe is:

3 cups water
6 cups granulated sugar
Cotton string
Jar
Stick or pencil

Cut a cotton string long enough to be wound around a stick placed across the top of a jar. Dangle the string inside the jar to within one inch of the bottom. Wet the string and roll it in granulated sugar, and allow it to dry. Boil the water and add the sugar slowly while stirring. Continue until all the sugar is dissolved and thin syrup is formed. Tie a small weight to the end of the string having the dried sugar and insert the string—tied to a pencil or stick—into the empty jar. Once the syrup is cooled, pour it into the jar. Cover the top of the jar with a cloth and set aside in dim light or a dark area where the jar will not be disturbed. Sugar crystals begin forming within four hours. Allow the rock candy to grow until it is the size desired.

Medicine may be dissolved in the syrup prior to pouring the syrup into the jar. In that manner, the rock candy will have a true medicinal attribute.

Castor oil provided an extremely effective laxative for every member of the household, at a time when many people suffered from "locked bowels." For a variety of reasons from the lack of refrigeration to the lack of variety in the average diet, many people suffered from chronic constipation. Castor oil, with its distinct odor and taste, provided the key that opened relief to many a sufferer.

Turpentine was used for external treatments of poison vine and insect bites or bee stings. A common ritual that took place every spring was lining the family up across the front porch and giving each member a teaspoonful of sugar upon which two or three drops of turpentine was added. The purpose was to poison stomach or intestinal worms accumulated during the winter months so they could be removed from the body using the castor oil as a laxative.

Often used as an anesthetic and antimicrobial substance, **camphor** aided in clearing nasal tissues and helping patients breathe with more ease. Small amounts were placed near a person's nose (most often a pouch hanging around the neck) to ward off germs that might be inhaled. Camphor is an active ingredient in Vick's Vap-O-Rub/Soltice.

Asafetida, most commonly used as a digestive aid, was a favorite remedy for coughs, bronchitis, and cold symptoms. For internal use asafetida was dissolved in whisky. This author's mother placed asafetida near his nose when nauseated to keep him from vomiting. The effects were always contrary to the desired outcome; the smell always made the author regurgitate.

Lard was an official medicine selected by the United States Pharmacopeia (USP) in 1820, and it was considered such until 1950. Every family had access to commercial lard, or they rendered their own during the hog-killing season. Lard is known as an emollient, a substance that softens and soothes the skin, correcting dryness and scaling of the skin. It was also applied to burns and used to treat numerous other skin conditions.

A plentiful and inexpensive compound, **salt** was used as a gargle for sore throats, mouthwash for oral sores, and as a soak for skin conditions. A small container of salt was often placed near the bedside to be utilized during the night when a cough or sinus drainage was a problem; swallowing a pinch of salt temporarily relieved a cough. No one at the time knew the dangers of salt increasing the user's blood pressure.

One of the most trusted medicines for family use was **Peruvian balsam.** When ingested it was anti-parasitic, mild laxative, a decongestant, and an expectorant to remove phlegm from a congested chest. Externally Peruvian balsam was antibacterial, antifungal, and speeded healing of cuts and insect bites.

Considering the history of medicine in America, it is now possible to compare the benefits and shortcomings of both folk medicine and conventional medicine. Folk medicine, so often criticized by conventional

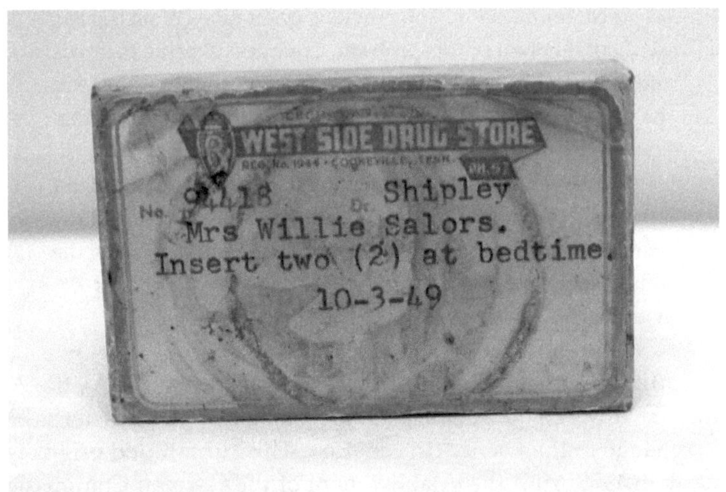

West Side Drug Store prescription box, 1949. Credit: Opless Walker collection.

medicine practitioners, has proven to have many desirable attributes with less adverse reactions and side effects than conventional medicine. An article published in the *Journal of the American Medical Association* (*JAMA*) leaves no doubt that conventional medicine is aware of a serious problem in the current method of medical practice. The report showed that there are one hundred and six thousand annual deaths from adverse effects of medications used when a patient dies as a direct result of treatments by a physician, whether it is from misdiagnosis of the ailment or from adverse drug reactions used to treat the illness. Drug reactions are the most common cause, with medical errors being the third leading cause of death in the United States. This explains why the World Health Organization (WHO) estimates that 80 percent of the world's population utilizes herbal medicines for some aspect of primary health care.[33] A statement in *Folk Medical Lexicon of South Central Appalachia* expressed the prevailing attitude of the Upper Cumberland citizens from the very beginning:

> Medical professionals of late have become increasingly aware of what the great majority of their patients have known all along: that the efficacy of healing is critically related to the health care provider's ability to communicate effectively with a patient. Indeed, some physicians view the public's growing dissatisfaction with modern, scientific medicine and the corresponding rise in popularity of other, alternative medical belief systems (e.g., herbalism, reflexology, homeopathy, and chiropractic) not as a failure of the paradigm of scientific medicine, but more as a failure in communication. The previous generations of physicians were not ignorant of this problem. Countless articles, manuals and books on medical interviewing have been published over the years, but there remains a persistent inability or unwillingness on the part of what is alleged to be the majority of physicians to converse, to listen, to try to understand, to learn about a patient's life world, the natural history of the illness and the search for help, and about the circumstances under which the illness arose and the meaning to the individual of his or her symptoms of illness.[34]

The attitude of the Food and Drug Administration (FDA), the AMA, and the USP towards the botanicals represented by folk medicine is beginning to change in the twenty-first century. This turnaround originated in Germany in 1978, with the establishment of the German Commission E. This group of renowned medical experts developed a list of botanicals that were both efficacious and safe. In 1998 their findings resulted in the publication of the *Physician's Desk Reference (PDR) for Herbal Medicine* in the United States. The late Dr. Varro Tyler, a well-known professor of pharmacognosy at Purdue University, stated in his foreword to the Commission E report, ". . . safety data were reviewed by the Commissioners according to a 'doctrine of absolute proof' and efficacy according to a 'doctrine of reasonable certainty.'"[35] In addition, studies performed in renowned institutes of learning, such as the *Harvard Lycopene Study*, verify the medicinal efficacy of many fruits, vegetables, and botanicals. The efficacy and safety of many of the botanical remedies used in folk medicine by the Upper Cumberland people have now been verified.

A statement by David Heber, MD, PhD, Professor of Medicine and Public Health, David Geffen School of Medicine at UCLA, taken from the *Foreword* of the *PDR for Herbal Medicines*, Fourth Edition, is worth noting: "In view of their [herbal medicines] preventive benefits and potential lack of toxicity when properly used, I view these botanicals as the medicines of the twenty-first century and predict they will ultimately be used for the prevention and treatment of many modern chronic diseases of aging."

NOTES

1. Editors' note: Dr. Opless Walker is a renowned pharmacologist. He acts as head pharmacist at the Cookeville Regional Medical Center and is a proponent of better health through natural substances.
2. Anthony Cavender, *Folk Medicine in Southern Appalachia* (Chapel Hill: University of North Carolina Press, 2003), p. 59. Eli Lilly traveled across Tennessee during the Civil War as a member of General John T. Wilder's Lightning Brigade. He recognized the healing potential of native plants in the Upper Cumberland region and had them shipped to his factory in Indiana. The Chattanooga Medicine Company, founded in 1879 by Zeboim Cartter Patten, used herbs and minerals from the Cumberland Plateau to create its patent medicines such as Black Draught and Wine of Cardui.
3. Robert J. Conley, *Cherokee Medicine Man: The Life and Work of a Modern-Day Healer* (Norman: University of Oklahoma Press, 2007), p. 18.
4. Thurman Wilkins, *Cherokee Tragedy* (Norman: University of Oklahoma Press, 1989), p. 6; William George Black, *Folk-Medicine: A Chapter in the History of Culture* (London, England: Elliot Stock, 1883), pp, 178–203. See also: Azariah Shelton, *Shelton's American Medicine: Or Improvement in Uniting His new Steam System and the old Practice of Medicine: In Which Doctors' Terms are Explained, and the Complaints of Men, Women and Children, are Treated in a Satisfactory manner; And Remedies Suited to all Climates, Constitutions and Circumstances of the American People; The Valuable Practice and Preparations of Dr. Isaac Wright, of Tennessee, are Fully Developed in This*

work; It Also Contains a Plain Description of the Whole Human frame: With General Rules for Preserving Health Without the use of Medicines; And a Choice Collection of Roots and Plants, not Explained in any Other Book; and the Practice is Made Perfectly Safe, Simple and Convenient to all Capacities, with but Little Expense (Madisonville, Tennessee: Henderson and Johnson, 1834).

5. Oral traditions of Buckner and Swallows families concerning the history of Standing Stone, Tennessee (now Monterey). Alex Buckner's family had Cherokee friends who escaped the Trail of Tears. Several Renegade Cherokee families sought refuge in the vicinities of eastern Putnam County and southern Overton County. Sarah Buckner (1866–1955) spoke of "her friends the Cherokee" who taught her herbal medicine. Sarah indicated that the Cherokee (ca. 1900) left the area with some going to North Carolina and others moving to Doyle, Tennessee. This fact was confirmed in 1981 when descendants (now living in North Carolina) of the Doyle, Tennessee, family attended a meeting of the Eastern Cherokee and the Cherokee of Oklahoma in the Multipurpose Room of Roaden University Center at TTU.
6. The author's mother and maternal grandparents knew the Cherokee who lived north of Monterey.
7. James Mooney, "Myths of the Cherokee and Sacred Formulas of the Cherokee," *Nineteenth Annual Report of the Bureau of American Ethnology 1897–98* Part I. (1900) and "The Sacred Formulas of the Cherokees," *Seventh Annual Report of the Bureau of Ethnology to the Secretary of the Smithsonian Institution, 1885–1886,* (Washington, D.C.: Government Printing Office, Washington, 1891), pp. 323–329.
8. David Heber, *PDR for Herbal Medicines Fourth Edition* (Montvale, New Jersey: Thomson Healthcare. 2007).
9. H.S. Berliner "A Larger Perspective on the Flexner Report," *International Journal of Health Service* 5 (1975), pp. 573–592.
10. Cavender, 24–27.
11. *Ibid.*
12. Charlie Walker was the author's grandfather. He often reflected upon the hardships of raising a family in Overton County, Tennessee. One of his infant daughters became ill and passed away without access to a doctor. Charlie dug the infant's grave, and he is listed as the "Undertaker" on the child's death certificate. He serves as a good example of an individual who did all he could to insure that the doctor's orders were carried out. Once he rode his mule to a general store in Overton County to purchase prescribed medication for his daughter; when he arrived he discovered that the drug cost fifteen cents. Having no money Charlie asked the clerk to charge it to his account, but the clerk refused. Stepping off the porch of the store, he saw a dime and a nickel lying in the dirt. He promptly picked up the money, bought the medicine and administered it to his sick child.
13. Mary Louise Marshall, "Medicine in the Confederacy," (New Orleans: 44th Annual Meeting of the Medical Library Association, New Orleans, May 7–9, 1942).
14. A tincture is a medicinal extract dissolved in alcohol.
15. *Ibid.*
16. "Folk Remedies," T.J. Farr Papers, RG 59 (Cookeville, Tennessee: Tennessee Technological University Archives), Box 9, Folders 6 and 7. Hereafter Farr Papers.

17. *Ibid*. Farr's informants were all identified, and included such people as Bob Lee Dudney, J.B. Gaither, W.J. Lee, Frank C. Pharris, Willis Burk, Velma Thompson, and Sid Sutton.
18. *Ibid,* Folder 6.
19. *Ibid.*
20. *Ibid.* Folder 7.
21. Farr Papers, Box 9, Folders 6 and 7.
22. Callie Myers Melton, *Folklore of the Upper Cumberland* (N.P., 2004), p. 16. Camphor was made by shaving a small block of camphor gum and dissolving the shavings in moonshine.
23. *Ibid.*
24. *Ibid.*
25. Melton, 17.
26. Farr Papers, Box 9, Folder 7; E.G. Rogers, *Early Folk Medical Practices in Tennessee* (Murfreesboro, Tennessee: Midsouth Publishing, 1941), pp. 30-34, 55–63.
27. Chicken pox is known to be self-limiting, with healing taking place within a twenty-day period. Allowing chickens to fly over a child could have very well induced histoplasmosis and/or salmonella in the youngster.
28. Oscar L. Walker (1908–1996), father of the author, practiced a mixture of herbal and ritualistic medicine. At age seven warts appeared on both of the author's hands. Oscar took his son outdoors, and told him to look away while he "did something." He later confessed that he had gone to seven different trees to collect leaves from each. Twisting and smashing the seven leaves together, he rubbed the mixture on the warts, then took the leaves off and placed them under a rock after telling the child to not look. If the leaves were moved, the remedy would be ineffective. This author has never understood how and why the cure was successful; however, the warts went away within two weeks from the date of the leaf rubbing.
29. Jeanette Keith, "Good Times: Vacationing at Red Boiling Springs," *Rural Life and Culture of the Upper Cumberland,* Michael E. Birdwell and W. Calvin Dickinson, eds. (Lexington: University Press of Kentucky, 2004), pp. 178–195; Jim Bellar, *Red Boiling Springs: The Tradition Lives* (Lafayette, Tennessee: Macon County Times Publishing Co., 1981).
30. *Ibid.*
31. George D. Pamplona-Roger, *Foods and Their Healing Power* (Hagerstown, Maryland: Review and Herald Publishing Association, 2004).
32. First marketed in the 1890s, Cloverine Salve is still available.
33. Barbara Starfield, "Medical Errors-A Leading Cause of Death," *Journal of the American Medical Association* 284:4 (July 26, 2000).
34. *A Folk Medical Lexicon of South Central Appalachia,* Miscellaneous Paper No. 1, History of Medicine Society of Appalachia, 1900.
35. Blumenthal, Busse, Goldberg, Gruenwald, Hall, Klein, Riggins & Rister, eds. *The Complete German Commission E Monographs: Therapeutic Guide to Herbal Medicines* (Austin: The Austin Botanical Council in Cooperation with Integrative Medicine Communications, 1988), Foreword.

11

Battling Ignorance and Superstition

Early Upper Cumberland Medical Professionals

Janey Dudney and W. Calvin Dickinson

Early Upper Cumberland medical history is in large part a direct result of the area's geography. There were no macadamized roads, only a series of trails of varied quality, and no reliable means of convenient communication, which was exacerbated by the fact that people lived in scattered, low populated areas. In the nineteenth and early twentieth centuries most doctors' offices were in their homes, but they routinely made house calls. "The story of those adventurous years can only be hinted at here. There were day and night calls in all weathers; swollen streams that must be forded on horseback or muleback; canyons too steep and rocky for even a mule to find footing. Patients were brought in from long distances on extemporized stretchers. . ."[1] Intrepid doctors, far from railroads and main thoroughfares, traveled so-called highways that deteriorated into virtual hog-wallows after "frog choking" storms.[2] University of Chicago sociologist S.S. MacClintock described the roads in 1901, saying:

> The roads are along or through the streams. It is no uncommon thing to cross and recross a stream a dozen times in a few miles, and, as there are no bridges, it has to be done by fording. . . The roads are rough to an almost incredible degree. They are not graded at all, and seldom worked. Loose rock and large boulders and deep ruts are abundant. It doesn't take long to shake a wagon to pieces, and, of course, the loads are light, 1,200 to 1,500 pounds being considered a fair load for a two-horse team. Sometimes the roads are so narrow in places that it is impossible for two teams to pass each other. I know of one case in which the wheels had to be taken off of the inner wagon, which was then turned upon its side, so that the other one might pass.[3]

Later, when rudimentary roads were improved, they traveled by horse and buggy in a somewhat greater degree of comfort. It could take several hours to get to a patient needing attention. If that person was very ill the doctor often stayed in their home for two or three days, until the patient was well enough for the physician to resume his normal practice. During his time at the invalid's side, unfortunately, he was unavailable for others who needed his services. On the positive side of this situation, doctors on horseback had time to "think, philosophize and meditate over unusual symptoms as he rode from house to house over muddy roads, through rain, sleet, snow and storm and winding mountain trails."[4] Most country doctors in the Upper Cumberland of Kentucky and Tennessee spent as much time away from their offices as they did in them. Incidentally, the cost of a house call was $1.00 per mile traveled. Delivering a baby cost $5.00.[5]

In a time when specialists were nonexistent, country doctors had to be medical polymaths. They did it all, practicing internal medicine, obstetrics, general surgery, eye, ear, nose, and throat medicine as well as orthopedics. Because there were no hospitals babies were delivered at home, usually without prenatal care, and doctors often performed surgeries on the kitchen table in the patient's home. Because of the scattered population and poor traveling conditions, doctors were in high demand. While every community had one or more doctors, their numbers were often inadequate

Rough Road. Credit: Tennessee State Library and Archives, Department of Education Files, Fentress County.

to service the enormous case loads. Many ignorant or unscrupulous doctors practiced without ever attending medical school. A "physician" simply registered his practice with the county clerk and started treating patients; he was a doctor because he said he was.[6]

The practice of medicine in the Upper Cumberland evolved from the practice of primitive techniques to highly sophisticated advances in treatment and medical technology in a relatively short period of time. In the early part of the twentieth century there were no hospitals, no medical schools in the immediate region, and little formal training for physicians. Doctors faced serious medical problems from endemic tuberculosis to injuries resulting from accidents associated with farming, logging, coal mining, and other hazardous occupations in the region. Country doctors set bones, sewed up gaping wounds, amputated limbs, delivered babies, and much more, often for little or no compensation.[7]

In a fascinating article concerning "The History of Medicine on Bon Air Mountain," Dr. W.J. Breeding offered evidence that the development of the highly successful coal mining industry was closely associated with advances in medical practice on the mountain.[8] Dr. William Byrd Young, an 1888 graduate and valedictorian of the Medical Department of the University of Tennessee at Nashville, was employed as physician and surgeon of Bon Air Coal and Iron Company on the Cumberland Plateau in White County. According to Dr. Breeding, Dr. Young's office became a sort of medical center. A training program under a "real" doctor was available for interested would-be physicians merely by showing up and requesting it. It provided hands-on training in real-world situations as they emerged in the mining community. In exchange for bed and board, a young man could carry water from the mountain spring, perform other menial tasks, and learn, in a short time, to dispense cough syrups and headache powders to the miners and their family members. The novice physician, immediately introduced as "our new doctor," had the assurance that he would, usually within two or three weeks, enter the field of active practice, depending, of course, on his ability to recognize and prescribe the available nostrums and tonics.[9]

First day curriculum included instructions in "tooth pulling." (If doctors were scarce, imagine the lack of dentists.) At that time there was only one remedy for a toothache, prompt extraction. The average country doctor possessed one pair of rusty tooth forceps or "twisters," kept over the front door for use in emergencies. As proof of his advanced skills, Dr. Young had three pairs of "bright, shiny forceps, one for uppers, one for lowers, and one for roots." Dr. Breeding's description of the procedure defies paraphrase and is therefore included in full.

> The patient was asked to locate the offending tooth, grasp the chair rounds and fix himself firmly as far as possible toward the root of the tooth. The slogan was "Lay on McDuff and damned be he who cries, hold on enough." When something popped and an appraisal made of results it was found that one or more of five results were apparent: (1) It had been crushed and the soft parts lacerated and mangled; (3) [*sic*] it had reluctantly come away with an attached piece of alveolar process (part of the jaw containing the tooth sockets); (4) we had unwittingly pulled the wrong tooth; or (5) the forceps had slipped off. The first expression from the trembling and bleeding victim was, "Did you get it, Dock [*sic*]?"[10]

Devotees of sedation dentistry, rejoice. Having been instructed in these and other procedures, the newly-minted "doctor" was sent out into the mining community with a little leather bag "carrying medicines of which he knew nothing, to deposit in willing human bodies of which he knew less."[11]

In an address given at a meeting of the White County Medical Society at Bon Air on August 9, 1928, Dr. Young declared that men became doctors "by reason of circumstances."[12] The Civil War created a serious need for the development of doctors for service in the armies. If a man had talent for nursing the sick and could stand the sight of copious quantities of blood, he was selected for hospital service. If hospital attendants were bright they often developed into physicians and continued to follow that career after the war was over.[13]

Prior to 1892, there was no knowledge or understanding of germs or bacteria or the necessity of hand washing before surgeries. The concept of sterile technique was foreign and the importance of proper sanitation measures simply dismissed. Immunizations were unavailable and epidemics of typhoid, diphtheria, malaria, dysentery, cholera, and tuberculosis wiped out whole families and devastated entire communities because people refused to believe that these diseases were contagious. Before significant improvements in communication and transportation, most children were born at home. If doctors were unavailable, neighbors assisted in the delivery. Because of unsanitary conditions, lack of sterile instruments, and ignorance, both the mother and the child were at risk. Many women died in childbirth and the mortality rate for infants was a sad but accepted part of life.[14] Conditions under which licensed doctors tried to practice and patients tried to survive led to the realization of a desperate need for further education and training.[15]

Although many instances and examples of change may be cited, one remarkable story graphically illustrates the advances in medical practice in the last century. In 1924, fourteen-year-old Bob Lee Dudney, who lived in the Free State community of Jackson County, suffered an appendicitis attack. It was not uncommon for patients to die from this condition because of misguided treatment using laxatives to relieve abdominal pain. Dr. C.E. Reeves of Gainesboro was called, but wisely did nothing for two or three days. Unfortunately the appendix ruptured, and the young boy, in his own words, "began to drift into a dream-like state." Dr. Reeves contacted Dr. W.A. Bryan, a well-known surgeon in Nashville, and persuaded him to come to the home in Free State and perform the necessary surgery. Other local doctors strongly opposed the surgery and advised against it.[16]

Dr. Bryan sent detailed instructions for preparing the room where the surgery was to take place. These included thoroughly cleaning the room by using bread made from wheat flour to wipe the ceiling, walls and floor to ensure that all dust was removed. Eight days after the initial onset of illness, Dr. Bryan, Dr. C.C. Core, and two nurses left Nashville in a Model T Ford and drove to Gallatin, Hartsville, and Carthage and on to Highway 85 to Brooks Ferry located one mile from the Dudney home. They arrived at dusk, technically too late to operate the ferry which was supposed to cease taking travelers across the river at sundown. "Uncle" Ben Meadows, the ferry pilot, knew the situation and chose to disobey the law. He ferried the Model T and its passengers across the river, and they went immediately to the Dudney residence.[17]

An old, homemade walnut kitchen table became the operating table. As there was no electricity, a gasoline mantle lamp borrowed from the nearby church provided light. Dr. Reeves administered the anesthetic (ether) and the operation, although lengthy, was successful. After the surgery, the doctors and nurses were treated to a sumptuous country supper that had been prepared earlier. According to Bob Lee's account, he soon woke up and felt better immediately.

The doctors returned to Nashville the next day, but left one nurse, Miss Effie Lowe, to care for the patient. Because of infection from a drainage tube, recovery was slower than hoped for, but ultimately all was well. Lowe remained with the patient for twenty-three days. Total cost for all services: Dr. Bryan, Dr. Core, one nurse, $325.00; Miss Lowe, twenty-three days, $148.45; Dr. C.E. Reeves, three house calls, $9.00, for a total of $482.45. The ferry man, "Uncle" Ben Meadows, made no charge. Bob Lee Dudney lived another eighty years and the walnut kitchen table is still in use in the same house in Free State.[18]

Upper Cumberland doctors not only battled the elements as they trekked across the countryside treating patients who suffered from any number of maladies, they also combatted superstition, ignorance, and tradition. Pauline Myers, a public health nurse in the Kentucky Upper Cumberland, graphically illustrated beliefs and ideas encountered by doctors and nurses in the backwoods. She observed that parents of children with cleft palates, scoliosis, physiological defects, "crippled through infantile paralysis, tuberculosis, or the insidious inroads of inherited blood taints," accepted a commonly held notion that "God made him like that. We can't fight the will of God."[19] Attitudes prevailed that children born with congenital disorders were a living testament to the sins of the parents, and they were intended to be constant reminder of their indiscretions. Any attempt to rectify their child's wretched condition was tantamount to blasphemy.

Myers presented a specific case concerning an adolescent female whose elbow joints never fully developed, and the difficulties encountered while trying to determine if her condition was treatable. Denizens from more remote corners of the region eyed x-rays with dubious curiosity. Myers wrote that she "chartered a mule" and carried in her saddlebags before and after images of children who had been treated successfully, greatly improving their self-esteem and their quality of life.[20] The unidentified family remained skeptical, but allowed the child to be x-rayed and examined by a doctor in far-off Louisville, who determined that a series of surgeries might give the teenager use of her arms for the first time. Myers observed that this was "a story without an ending," because the family "watches in dread for the manifestation of the first wrath of the Almighty on those who try to overcome his will."[21] Fear and distrust of modern approaches to health care not only threatened beliefs that originated on the frontier, it represented yet another invasion of the region which included Civil War armies, coal magnates, and other outside business ventures.

In addition to superstition and entrenched ideas disregarding science, doctors also had to undo damage caused by folk remedies and area "healers" who conjured cures that often did more harm than good. These shamans advocated a number of interesting, if not bizarre, treatments. If a baby suffered teething pains healers recommended tying a mole's foot around the child's neck. To remove warts, rub the area with a dishrag and bury the scrap cloth. If stung by a wasp or a bee one needed to chew tobacco and tie a wet wad of it around the inflamed area. Many nostrums involved mixing any number of things with alcohol, including King Leo Peppermint sticks, honey, horehound candy, ginseng, rose hips, tea laurel, coffee beans, and more. One remedy widely accepted for congestion was a paste made from camphor and mustard rubbed onto the chest. "Housewives brewed sassafras tea to improve the blood, made poultices of slippery elm bark and dried calamus root for colic, applied yellowroot for sore mouths, and advised drinking blackberry juice for diarrhea."[22] To cure a cold they had a variety of cures, most commonly a brew with heady doses of moonshine. Other cold remedies included the use of "pennyroyal, ratsvein, and boneset. . .[and] mullein leaves."[23] Some used leeches to aid in healing wounds. Healers prescribed ingesting turpentine to treat worms, golden seal to cure ulcers, and ginseng to relieve the pain of arthritis. Many people claimed that catnip, horsemint, elderberries, as well as black and blue cohosh when correctly prescribed could cure a plethora of maladies. Some of the aforementioned remedies actually had beneficial effects.[24] Other folk remedies that people swore by were based solely on superstition and had no medicinal value whatsoever. To stop hemorrhaging one needed to put an axe under the bed of the bleeder. Putting a lock of the sufferer's hair in a hole in a tree cured asthma. To rid a foot from a troublesome corn "cut it with a blade that has been used to shave the dead." Rubbing a goiter with a toad would make it disappear. Passing a baby over and under a mule nine times cured whooping cough. Wearing earrings soothed sore eyes. [25]

Emeritus professor at Tennessee Technological University, Flavious Smith, recalled a few home remedies that his parents and grandparents employed when he was growing up at Seven Springs in Putnam County. After coming down with the croup his grandfather, John Bradley Smith, treated him with "skunk oil." A farmer who trapped game in the winter, Smith caught a skunk in one of his traps, killed it, skinned it, and as he prepared the pelt, he scraped the fat and boiled it in a special pan. Once the fat cooked down, he mixed it with a variety of herbs, making a tea for Flavious to drink. While he cannot testify to the efficacy of the concoction, he never came down with the croup again. His mother, Avo Thomas Smith, also made her own version of a hot poultice from a mixture of water and corn meal heated in a skillet. Once warm enough, she emptied it into a cloth sack and placed it on the chest of the sick person. His father, Haskell "Hack" Smith, applied kerosene mixed with rose salve to cuts, and tied them off with a rag. He used kerosene to relieve the itch of chigger bites. Hack believed that crushed leaves and stems of wild forget-me-nots rubbed on skin that came in contact with poison ivy would cure it. When growing up, Flavious only saw a doctor twice until he was twelve. In the first instance his brother Hulon's appendix ruptured and his parents contacted Dr. J. Fred Terry. He arrived on foot because the roads to the Smith home were so bad that he had to walk the last mile. Had Dr. Terry not been notified, Hulon would have died. The second visit from the doctor occurred after a mule kicked Flavious and cut his leg above the ankle to the bone. They treated it with kerosene and rose salve to no effect. As days passed, the wound became infected and Flavious drifted in and out of consciousness. Dr. Terry saved his leg and his life.[26]

Doctors and patients alike relied upon patent medicines to treat various conditions. Common patent medicines were developed by Eli Lily, Lydia Pinkham, the Chattanooga Medicine Company, and others in the post-Civil War era and touted to cure anything and everything. Traveling salesmen typically had among their wares any number of bottled panaceas. Across the Upper Cumberland of Kentucky and Tennessee three reliable products graced the shelves of most drug cabinets: Castor oil, Black Draught, and Wine of Cardui. Castor oil appeared to be the common cure-all before aspirin arrived on the scene. It was administered both topically and orally, and was often mixed with other ingredients. Black Draught and Wine of Cardui were manufactured much closer to home at the southern end of the Cumberland Plateau in Chattanooga, Tennessee.[27]

Due to the diet of the region in the late nineteenth and early twentieth centuries, everybody suffered from varieties of ailments referred to as "gastric distress," especially constipation. Former Union soldiers from John T. Wilder's "Lightning Brigade," Zeboim "Zip" Cartter Patten and H.T. Payne, joined their old commander, taking up residence in Chattanooga after the war. Patten and Payne worked for one of their comrades in the Indiana Cavalry, Eli Lily, providing him with medicinal plants found on the Cumberland Plateau which he transformed into patent medicines. In 1879 Patten decided to go into direct competition, forming the Chattanooga Medicine Company (CMC). Using his knowledge of medicinal plants gained while gathering them for Eli Lily, with the help of friends who acted as human guinea pigs, Patten bought the formula from a local healer for Black Draught, a laxative with four active ingredients instead of one. Black Draught quickly caught on, insuring the success of the company.[28]

"Drummers," traveling salesmen employed by the CMC, roamed all over the Upper Cumberland of Tennessee and Kentucky with the miracle cure for constipation. They also sought testimonials. When Sergeant Alvin C. York returned to Fentress County in 1919, Mrs. H. Lee Grimm of CMC approached him for a testimonial and he flatly refused. Having turned down over a million dollars in endorsements, he was not about to sell his name to a patent medicine company. Unfortunately, his mother, Mary York, agreed to participate in an ad campaign testifying about the relief she received after a dose of Black Draught. She claimed that the laxative not only loosened her bowels, "It is splendid for torpid liver, sour stomach, headaches and such."[29] Mother York also endorsed Wine of Cardui, a

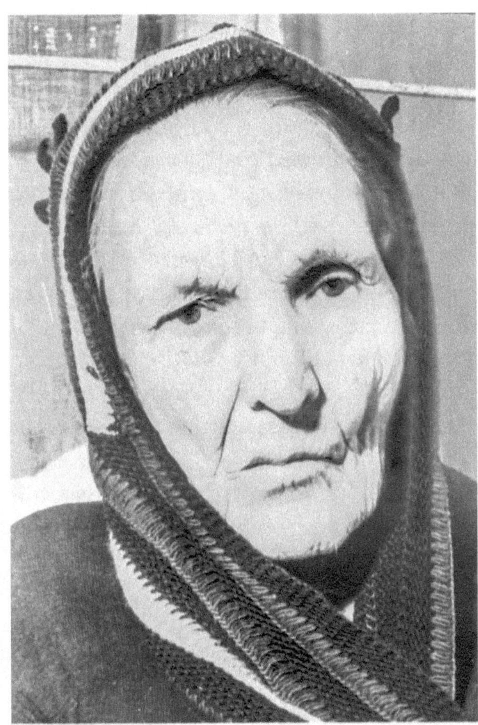

Mother York. Credit: Sergeant York Patriotic Foundation.

concoction made from *carduus benedictus*, golden seal, *viburnum prunifolium*, and copious quantities of alcohol marketed for the treatment of "women's ailments." Mother York said that after she drank two or three bottles she was completely cured. When Tennessee went dry in 1909, sales of Wine of Cardui went through the roof, becoming a "temperance tipple." Even men, it seemed, suffered from women's ailments during Prohibition.[30]

Dr. Thurman Shipley, who practiced medicine in the region for fifty-two years, recalled conditions that exacerbated good health. Houses in the area lacked many modern conveniences. Central heat and air conditioning were nonexistent. Most homes had no screens, and in the summer windows and doors stood wide open while flies darted in and out landing on everything. They contaminated food and spread disease. Likewise, refrigeration was unheard of and people often ate tainted food, which sat out on kitchen tables uncovered for hours at a time. Electricity was slow to come to the region; power lines did not arrive in Lancing, Tennessee, in Morgan County until 1951.[31]

Shipley remembered that conditions improved markedly when the Works Progress Administration (WPA) programs provided education, employment, and leadership to the area. Mocked by detractors in the region as the "We Piddle Around," WPA employees built roads, sidewalks, post offices, and government buildings. They collected oral history interviews from local residents. WPA also employed local artists and craftsmen to create public art for the community to enjoy. The WPA did much more, but from a medical stand point, WPA workers built fly-proof pit toilets on concrete foundations, designed to keep fecal matter and parasites from leaching into ground water or flow into streams. Fly-proof toilets "broke the cycle of the main source of food and water contamination," while the education programs showed "people how to protect their springs and wells from surface water sometimes laden with disease germs and intestinal parasites."[32]

Of course, there were medical societies in more metropolitan areas, but because of the geographical constraints, lack of state highways and relative isolation, it was difficult, if not impossible, for doctors in the Upper Cumberland to attend meetings held in Nashville, Tennessee, or Lexington, Kentucky. But forward-looking physicians saw the need for localized medical societies where rural doctors could meet, discuss treatment options and learn about new advances in medicine.

The first attempt to organize a medical society for the Upper Cumberland took place in Celina, Tennessee, October 27, 1890, but failed to bear fruit.[33] In 1894, Dr. Wilson Tallyrand (W.T.) McColgan of Arcot in Clay County contacted Dr. W.B. Young of Sparta and asked him to write every doctor in the area in hopes of establishing an Upper Cumberland Medical Society. Its inaugural meeting was held in October, 1894 in Cookeville at the county courthouse. Even though only six physicians attended, officers were elected and plans made for the next annual meeting.[34] Dr. McColgan was elected president, and Dr. W.J. Breeding, who rode forty miles on horseback to attend, was elected secretary. The second meeting proved more successful. Every physician in the ten counties that composed the district was contacted and encouraged to participate. At the meeting held on May 7, 1895, fifty attended. Convening at the Methodist Church in Cookeville, the conclave was covered by the press, and attended by curious lay people. Among those who attended were Cookeville native Rutledge Smith, vice president of the Tennessee Central Railroad and publisher of the *Putnam Press*. He wrote a number of stories about the event as well as synopses of presentations.[35]

While Dr. W.T. McColgan is considered the father of the Upper Cumberland Medical Society, his son James Tallyrand (J.T.) McColgan, also a physician, played a crucial role in the organization's creation. A Confederate veteran who joined the army at age fifteen, J.T. distinguished himself at the battles of Mill Springs and Shiloh.[36] After the war, he enrolled in the University of Nashville Medical School, later graduating from New Orleans Medical College. J.T. McColgan also operated a printing press and began to publish and edit a weekly medical journal, *The Country Doctor.* The first edition was published January 29, 1890. At that time, there were only seven weekly medical journals in the United States and *The Country Doctor* was the only one published in the South. A one-year subscription cost one dollar. The twelfth issue of *The Country Doctor* suggested creation of a medical society in the Cumberland region, promising the full support of the journal. In 1896 the weekly became a monthly publication and was printed in Sparta by the Favorite Publishing Company. Dr. William B. Young assumed the duties of editor and Dr. Sam Brown (S.B.) Fowler was associate editor. Due to financial problems, the journal ceased publication in 1899.[37]

The Upper Cumberland Medical Society included doctors from Kentucky and Tennessee. The society continued to meet for "social, scientific, and literary reasons" for over one hundred years at various sites in the area.[38] Early meetings were held in churches, private homes, and later

Dr. W.B. Young. Credit: Janey Dudney.

gatherings met at hotels. When doctors arrived at their destination the hosting town greeted the guests with enthusiasm. Annual meetings generally lasted two days, with formal presentations in the daytime and entertainments of varying types at night.[39] The Donoho Hotel in Red Boiling Springs and Fall Creek Falls State Park became favorite meeting places.[40] At the 1898 meeting in Carthage in May, Judge John R. Aust addressed the assembled group of physicians, saying "I think doctors are all good men. They are great men and useful men without doubt, who season pottage, or expel the gout, whose sciences keep life in, and keeps death out."[41] Dr. W.B. Young considered the judge's comments a call to action to combat ignorance and disease throughout the Upper Cumberland. Doctors needed to be professional, empathetic, and to keep abreast of the latest breakthroughs in medical science.[42]

Doctors who practiced at the turn of the century included Society members like Samuel Denton, who grew up in the Onward community in White County, Tennessee, studied rudimentary medicine under Professor William Newton Billingsley and then went on to Vanderbilt Medical School. Receiving his degree in 1890 he moved to Buffalo Valley on the Caney Fork River in western Putnam County. He roved all over the region, first on horseback and later in a Model T. When looking back over his career, he wrote a cousin on March 6, 1930 saying, "I have felt the finish of poverty and the winter blasts and summer's heat, and sleepless nights of anguish that the mother might die tonight and leave a batch of orphans—or mother's darling might die and leave her broken hearted."[43] Like other doctors in the Upper Cumberland, they forged ahead in hard times. The floods of 1927 and 1929 wiped out homes and businesses of whole communities throughout the region. Those tragedies coupled with the Great Depression added unforeseen problems. Patients who had no money to pay him, nor hope of employment during that dark period, offered eggs, milk, or other items in exchange for his services; he treated many grateful people for free.[44]

Dora Lee Wilder was the first woman to receive a license to practice medicine in Tennessee. She and Dr. May Wharton, who engaged in medicine in Cumberland County, were pioneering female doctors in the state.[45] Dr. Wilder recognized her unique status in a speech and emphasized the work of other women in the field of medicine. She recognized the first female to receive an MD in the United States, Dr. Elizabeth Blackwell in 1849. Wilder proudly associated herself with this pioneer; she noted that they both came from the Asheville, North Carolina region. Dr. Wilder testified that this male dominated profession presented a challenge for a woman because of gender prejudice. "It is not a flowery pathway to bread and butter,

Dora Lee Wilder. Credit: John Lee Collection, Tennessee Tech University Archives.

but a thorny one, a way that must be trod with dignity and silence. But the trail has been blazed into the plain of success, and we have pitched our tents to stay."[46] She and Dr. Wharton were up to the task, as their inspiring stories detail. Wilder's interesting life has always been overshadowed by the fame of her husband, U.S. Army General John T. Wilder.

Dora Ethel Lee had been born in 1877 (or 1878) in Buncombe County, North Carolina.[47] Attending Asheville Female College for three years, by 1900 she had acquired enough education to be listed in the census as a nurse. In 1901 a letter from Dr. Sterne's Sanatorium for Nervous Diseases in Indianapolis endorsed her "for any position in the nursing world." Dora trained and worked as a nurse in the sanatorium for six weeks, where she was "devoted."[48] Between 1902 and 1905 she attended the Medical College of Indiana with three other women. After she married John Wilder, Dora enrolled in the Tennessee Medical College in Knoxville. In 1906, she took medical exams in Knoxville and completed her medical degree, interning at the Knoxville General Hospital.[49]

The couple married at Lake Toxaway in 1904, a newly developed resort in western North Carolina about fifty miles south of Dora's childhood home.[50] Despite the vast age gap between John and Dora, a deep and abiding affection developed between the two.[51] Returning to Knoxville, John and Dora lived in Wilder's large two-story home, Cherry Hill.[52] In 1910,

John Wilder resigned his position as customs agent in Knoxville, and the couple moved permanently to his home in Monterey, Tennessee.[53]

Some stories of Dr. Wilder's occasional medical practice were mentioned in a newspaper column by folklorist Elzia Guy (E.G.) Rogers. He noted the case of a Tennessee Central Railroad employee with a "severe arm injury" that she treated to good effect. Dr. Wilder once amputated the leg of a railroad worker at the Imperial Hotel. The man had been involved in a train wreck outside Monterey, and Dr. Wilder was summoned from the dinner table to operate. Local citizens observed the surgery through the basement windows. John Wilder "persuaded" her "to discontinue medical practice" after some time.[54]

Dora Wilder was always interested and vigilant about the state of medicine in Monterey and the Upper Cumberland. When a young man expressed an interest in medicine, Dr. Wilder promised to assist him in attending medical school if he agreed to return to Monterey to practice. He held up his end of the bargain; Dr. Theodore Crane engaged in medicine there for many years. On at least one occasion a fraudulent "doctor" practiced medicine in Monterey, diagnosing a woman's pregnancy as a tumor, and accidently killing the fetus. Dr. Wilder investigated; she discovered the man had no medical education or license, and persuaded him to discontinue his practice and leave town.[55]

Dr. Wilder attended meetings of the Upper Cumberland Medical Society and the Tennessee Medical Association, where she delivered papers on medical subjects. In 1911 Wilder was vice president of the Upper Cumberland Medical Society, and her name was listed at meetings in 1912, 1914, 1915, 1916, and 1917. In 1911 Dr. Wilder presented a lecture on "Preventable Blindness" at the meeting. In 1915 she read a paper on "Twilight Sleep in Labor," and invited the society to meet in Monterey in 1916. The society met in the assembly room of the Imperial Hotel. Dr. Wilder read a paper entitled "Should a Tubercular Mother Nurse her Child?" The next year the society met in Cookeville; Dr. Wilder gave a paper on "Infantile Paralysis."[56]

In an undated speech presented in Cookeville at the invitation of Graeme McGregor Smith,[57] Dr. Wilder discussed the care of children, a subject that was obviously of great interest to her. Saying that she "could talk hours and days on" the subject, she declared that "it's the mother's duty to keep her child healthy." Teeth are "most important" for proper care. "Care at home must be supplemented by care at school." Eye problems are caused at birth "by neglect," by "contagios [*sic*] diseases contracted at school," and by "poor lighting. . . Blindness can be prevented in 80% of the cases." She urged mothers to "Feed your children properly, pure milk, wholesome food, clothe them correctly . . . protect them from disease, avoid pacifiers."[58]

Tuberculosis (TB) treatment was a particular topic of interest to Dr. Wilder. At the turn of the century TB was the leading cause of death in the United States; for a time Putnam County, Tennessee had more cases that any other in the nation. Dr. Wilder read a paper in Nashville at the annual meeting of the Tennessee Medical Association in 1909, entitled "The State Sanitarium in the Prevention and Cure of Tuberculosis." She declared it was the "duty" of the state to "protect its citizens," and she listed states with tuberculosis hospitals. The paper "aroused such interest by her portrayal of the existing conditions in this state and the need of a sanitarium that the resolution later offered was carried by an unanimous vote." The resolution suggested a committee of three to seek forty thousand dollars from the legislature to erect a state sanitarium to treat tuberculosis.[59] The hospital opened thirty-one years later in 1941.

The 1910 issue of the *Southern Medical Journal* published Dr. Wilder's four-page article "The Cure of Tuberculosis by the General Practioner [*sic*]." In the essay she referred to "those of us who are especially interested in the treatment of the disease," and she noted that "it is now admitted everywhere by the ordinarily intelligent that tuberculosis is a curable, preventable disease." Dr. Robert Koch had determined the cause of the disease in 1882, and "an almost inexhaustible supply of literature upon the subject" showed "the curability of the disease. . . An early diagnosis is necessary," and "the modern graduate should have no difficulty in making a diagnosis." Some cases could be treated in "a well built, well placed, well conducted sanatorium, but most patients would be "obliged to remain at home and do the best they can there." For the home patient she prescribed the "cardinal remedies" of "air, food, rest and mind." These are

> God given remedies that we can always get. . . All patients should be required to sleep outdoors. . . Make it possible for your patient to stay in bed all the time. . . The chief articles of diet are milk, eggs, fresh meat and pure olive oil. . . If you encourage your patient in the belief that he is improving, soon the mental state is showing in actual weight. . . You will find that with the patient resting in the open air medicines are rarely needed. The cough and toxic symptoms quickly subside.[60]

These were the same treatments used by Dr. May Wharton at her tuberculosis clinic. Later, at the Upper Cumberland Medical Association meeting in Cookeville Dr. Wilder read a paper on "The Home Cure of Tuberculosis."

The hospital in Monterey was Officer Sanatorium, owned and operated by Dr. William Carson (W.C.) Officer. It specialized in the treatment of tuberculosis. Officer built and operated the hospital from 1925 to his death in 1935.[61] A newspaper article indicated that

> Dr. Officer has made a life study of tuberculosis, . . . and has surrounded himself and his offices with the very best in modern equipment. The patients' rooms are large and each one so situated as to get a maximum of fresh air and sunshine. . . . His Sanitorium [*sic*] is practically filled with patients and many more come and go at intervals for diagnosis and treatment."

Although Dr. Wilder expressed an interest in tuberculosis there is no evidence that she was associated with Dr. Officer or his hospital.[62]

At the 1912 meeting of the Upper Cumberland Medical Society Dr. Wilder suggested that a state public health department be established. She declared that "public health has become a national problem."[63] Dr. W.C. Officer appointed her chair of a committee to investigate the possibility and feasibility of such an office.[64] The state took no immediate action; it was 1923 before the state created a Department of Public Health. In the meantime the membership of the Upper Cumberland Medical Society resolved to create "a department of Public Health with a chairman whose duty it shall be to concentrate the force of our membership and use it for the benefit of public health." Dr. Wilder was appointed "chairman of the Health Department,"[65] but it was an office in name only.

In February of 1919 Dora married P.B. (Percy Berkeley) Smith, an official with the Tennessee Central Railroad, at St. Paul's Episcopal Church in Chattanooga.[66] Smith had often stayed at the Imperial Hotel, where he became a close friend of the Wilders, and he and Dora continued to operate the establishment.[67] Dr. Wilder died on July 29, 1963 at age eighty-seven. Her funeral was an Episcopal service at Goff Funeral Home in Monterey. Before the service an old woman approached the family and asked to view the body. With her was a middle-aged daughter, obviously mentally and physically afflicted. The mother commented, "I wanted you to see the woman that saved your life."[68]

Meanwhile the Upper Cumberland Medical Society continued to grow and prosper. Its annual meetings attracted highly respected, well-known physicians, not only from Nashville and Knoxville, but included guest speakers and visiting doctors from Kentucky, North Carolina, Texas, New Mexico, Ohio, Virginia, New York, and Alabama. Topics of discussion and papers presented reflected advances in medicine found in new procedures in obstetrics, surgery, geriatrics, diabetes, pediatrics, pulmonary diseases, and public health issues. Sessions remained open to the public, and often drew curious crowds from throughout the Upper Cumberland. Annual meetings provided an opportunity for professionals and lay people to interact in positive ways outside of a doctor's office or a hospital. It was encouraging to learn from reading the minutes of the 1950 meeting at Red Boiling Springs, that in a discussion of medical and scientific advances, it was agreed that the "dominant theme in any treatment, any surgical technique, any therapy by drugs, the comfort and consideration of the patient has absolute priority."[69]

Unfortunately as transportation, communication and specialization advanced, there was less interest in and need for a localized medical society. Doctors continued to see the benefit of sharing information about the latest medical discoveries, new techniques for treatment, and social interaction, but they chose to attend larger conventions around the United States. The last meeting of the Upper Cumberland Medical Society, the 111th, convened in 2005 at the J.T. Moore Education Center of the Cookeville Regional Medical Center. Only eleven members attended; they agreed that it was time to close that chapter in the medical history of the region. Upon its dissolution, the Upper Cumberland Medical Society ranked as the second oldest medical association in the history of the United States.[70]

No history of medical practice in the Upper Cumberland would be complete without including two of the best-known and most loved and respected physicians of their time. Dr. J. Thomas Moore of Algood and Dr. Luther M. Freeman of Granville were contemporaries and had similar experiences in their practice. Both graduated from the University of Tennessee Medical School in Nashville, Dr. Moore in 1899 and Dr. Freeman in 1905. Practicing in small rural areas as typical horse and buggy doctors, they made house calls, charged little, and dealt with illnesses for which there were no known cures. In an interview published in the *Nashville Tennessean* in 1971, Dr. Freeman's daughter, Eliza Freeman Thompson said she remembered her father leaving on horseback to make house calls, "His derby hat on, his beard flowing, his saddlebag packed with quinine and calomel, digitalis and laudanum and a few surgical instruments." She recalled him coming home with his feet frozen to the stirrups after riding through the creek and being unable to dismount until her mother thawed the stirrups.[71] Dr. Freeman practiced medicine until shortly before his death at the age of ninety-four in 1973. He was also Granville's longest serving postmaster, and his tiny office has been preserved and remains a popular attraction at the annual Granville Heritage Celebration.

Dr. Moore, fondly known as Dr. Tom, published memoirs in 1957, recounting his experiences and noting changes and advances in medicine which he witnessed during his time: immunizations, antibiotics, x-rays as

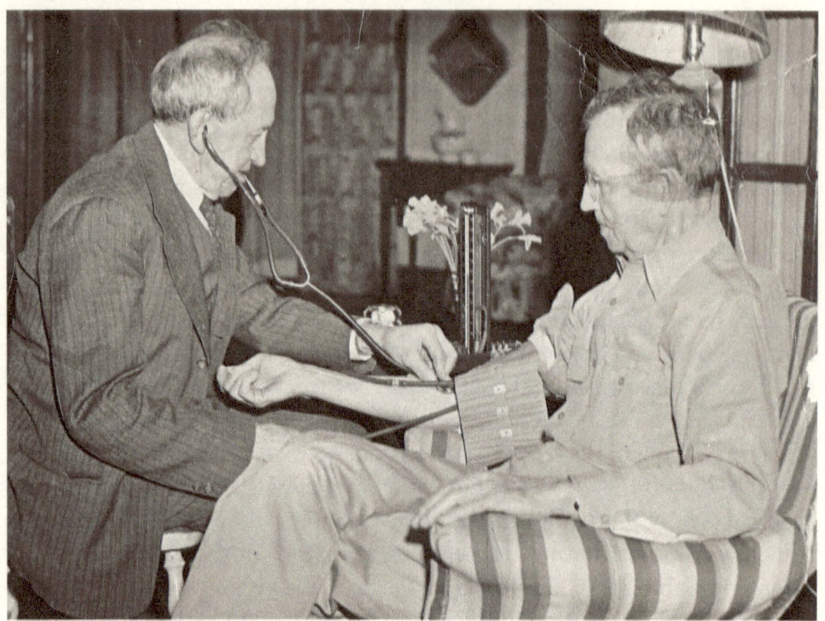

Dr. Tom Moore Sr. Credit: Dr. Lee Moore.

a diagnostic tool, insulin used to treat diabetes, and the introduction of the miracle drug, aspirin. His partner, Dr. W.A. Howard, built a hospital in Cookeville in 1921, where doctors from across the region saw patients.[72] Both Dr. Moore and Dr. Freeman were faithful members and supporters of the Upper Cumberland Medical Society, serving as officers and Dr. Freeman served as its secretary for over fifty years. Cooperation and sharing new information was an essential part of medical practice in the Upper Cumberland, but there was also good-natured competition among these hard-working physicians.

At a meeting of the Putnam County Medical Society held at Livingston in the early 1960s, Dr. Charles Everett (C.E.) Reeves of Gainesboro, said that he guessed he had delivered five thousand babies, which prompted Dr. Tom Moore of Algood to declare that he had delivered seven thousand babies. After the meeting adjourned, Dr. Reeves informed his traveling companions that "Tom Moore is a damn liar." Dr. Reeves said later, "don't ever tell your story first."[73]

Doctors in the Upper Cumberland of Kentucky and Tennessee left an indelible mark. In the years immediately after the Civil War they faced any number of hardships that no longer confront physicians today. Medical personnel risked their lives to heal their patients, often with nothing to show for it monetarily. Tales of doctors making house calls at all hours of the day and night through hazardous conditions were commonplace. Facing treacherous, almost impassible roads, packs of dogs roaming the woods, and horses sinking up to their chests in mud during the flood seasons and much more stood in the paths of a post-bellum doctor, but the intrepid physician carried on regardless. As people of the region began to put more value on college-educated, licensed practitioners of medicine, their status began to climb. Doctors became respected civic leaders throughout the Upper Cumberland. They worked with local politicians and bureaucrats to promote better education and better hygiene to improve the basic quality of life, not just for their patients, but for the entire citizenry. They led the charge for the establishment of public health departments and more clinics and hospitals, to more completely serve the growing population. Appreciative patients responded in a number of ways, from giving the doctors all manner of gifts including fresh eggs, a fully cured ham straight from the farm, homemade quilts, pies, cakes, jams, and much more. The gift that truly showed how much they cared, was when patients named their children in honor of the doctor who faithfully served the family.

It is not possible to name every doctor of the Upper Cumberland who worked tirelessly and selflessly to care for their patients and who enjoyed the love and loyalty of those they treated. But it is certain that most families in the area have favorite stories about the family doctor who came when he was called. Advances in care and technology may have revolutionized the practice of medicine, but the early pioneers will not soon be forgotten.

NOTES

1. Dora Read Goodale, "Forty Miles from a Hospital—In U.S.A.," *Missionary Review of the World* 60 (December 1937), p. 578.
2. *Ibid.*
3. S.S. MacClintock, "The Kentucky Mountains and Their Feuds; I: The People and Their Country." *American Journal of Sociology* 7:1 (July 1901), p. 13.
4. Dr. William Byrd (W.B.) Young, "Our Family Tree," (Bon Air, Tennessee: Unpublished Manuscript, ca. 1935), p. 97.
5. *Ibid.*, 98. See also May Cravath Wharton, *Dr. Woman of the Cumberlands* (Pleasant Hill, Tennessee: Uplands, 1953); "William Bedford Buck Diary, Jackson County, TN," *Upper Cumberland Researcher* 29:1 (Spring 2004), p. 21.
6. J. Thomas Moore, *Dr. Tom: Memoirs of Dr. John Thomas Moore* (Nashville, Tennessee: Parthenon Press, 1957), p. 192.
7. Laura E. Clemons, *The People's Hospital: A History of Cookeville Regional Medical Center, 1950–2010* (Cookeville, Tennessee: The Foundation of the Cookeville Regional Medical Center, 2010), pp. 6–7.

8. Roberts-Moneyham Upper Cumberland Medical Society Collection (Cookeville, Tennessee: Tennessee Technological University Archives), RG 60, File 43–1. Hereafter Upper Cumberland Medical Society Collection. For more about the coal mines at Bon Air see Betty S. Huehls, "Life in the Coal Towns of White County, Tennessee, 1882–1936," (Cookeville: Tennessee Technological University, Unpublished Master's Thesis, 1983).
9. *Ibid.*
10. *Ibid.* There is no number 2 in the list of instructions about pulling teeth in the original document.
11. *Ibid.*
12. *Ibid.* The apprenticeship system for doctors was known as a "preceptorship." See Dr. John B. Thompson, "Med Schools 'Flower' in the Late 1800s," *Nashville Tennessean* (November 29, 1976), p. 15.
13. See Ira Rutkow, *Bleeding Blue and Gray: Civil War Surgery and the Evolution of American Medicine* (New York: Random House, 2005), Frank R. Freeman, *Gangrene and Glory: Medical Care during the American Civil War* (Champagne-Urbana, Illinois: University of Illinois Press, 2001) and Horace Herndon Cunningham, *Doctors in Gray: The Confederate Medical Service* (Baton Rouge, Louisiana: Louisiana State University Press, 1993).
14. Lynwood Montell related a story of a woman who gave birth in a squalid environment. She gave birth on filthy sheets covered in blood, amniotic fluid, urine, and feces, with her new child awash in the filth. Meanwhile her husband sat beside her rebuilding a carburetor. See Lynwood Montell, *Tales from Kentucky Doctors* (Lexington: University Press of Kentucky, 2008), pp. 74–75. Montell said that in the early twentieth century it was common to clean a newborn baby with a mixture of lard and salt.
15. Clemons, 2–8. Joseph Lister discovered germ theory in 1865 and recognized their role in sepsis. His work built upon that of Louis Pasteur and led him to use carbolic acid to clean wounds in 1869. Lister became the major proponent of hygiene, and the necessity of a sterile environment in conducting surgery and other medical procedures. Such practices took a long time to be accepted in the Upper Cumberland.
16. Robert Lee Dudney "Personal Account," (Free State, Tennessee: Unpublished reminiscence of his brush with death).
17. The ferry operated at what is now the Frank G. Clement Bridge crossing the Cumberland River.
18. Dudney reminiscence.
19. Pauline N. Myers, "Fighting the Will of God in the Kentucky Mountains," *Hygeia* (June, 1930), p. 539.
20. *Ibid.*, 540. Myers confessed that when she and the mule returned to town disenchanted, "I am never a speed maniac when it comes to mules," 541.
21. *Ibid.*, 541.
22. Mary Jean DeLozier, *Putnam County, Tennessee, 1850–1970* (Nashville, Tennessee: McQuiddy Printing Co., 1979), p. 203.
23. Ken, Wahler, Angela Wahler, and Salissa Wahler, "'Bad Roads and Blue Cohosh,' An Oral History of the Obed River Region, Tennessee and McCreary Count

Kentucky," (Wartburg, Tennessee: Unpublished Manuscript at the Obed National Scenic River, National Parks Services, n.d.), p. 6.

24. *Ibid.*
25. Esther Sharp Sanderson, *County Scott and its Mountain Folk* (Nashville, Tennessee: Blue and Gray Press, 1958), pp. 168–169.
26. Flavious Joseph Smith Sr., *Enduring Memories: Growing up in Dry Valley, the Heart of the Upper Cumberland* (Cookeville, Tennessee: Self Published, 1984), pp. 59, 67–68. Flavious was chair of the Physical Education Department at Tech throughout the 1970s and 1980s.
27. Detractors of patent medicines, and they were legion, considered the makers to be charlatans profiting off the misery of others. Decried as "snake oil salesmen" and worse, many were a potential threat to the well-being of sick people. Most simply concocted elixirs composed mainly of alcohol. When aspirin arrived it was widely prescribed for dozens of uses. Lynwood Montell reported that some doctors even used aspirin as a suppository; see page 78.
28. Thomas D. Clark, "The Farmer and His Almanac," 1–3; and "Dr. Irvin Grote's Talk to Chattanooga Historical Association, 4/25/71," 1–5 (Chattanooga, Tennessee: Bicentennial Library, Historical Collection Clipping File—Chattanooga Medicine Company).
29. Black Draught advertisement (Pall Mall, Tennessee: Sergeant Alvin C. York Papers) Chattanooga Medicine Files, Box 1, Folder 1, October 28, 1919. York's mother's testimonial led to his first of many lawsuits and a clarification from CMC that he had nothing to do with the endorsement.
30. Clark, 5; Grote, 4. Patent medicines fell under the scrutiny of the federal government, first with the Pure Food and Drug Act in 1906, and later in the 1960s as organizations like the American Medical Association and Pharmaceutical placed pressure on legislatures to create legislation to limit or abolish their consumption. When legislation made narcotics illegal except by prescription, several people shuddered when they could no longer buy things like Paregoric over the counter.
31. Mary Jo Denton, "Dr. Thurman Shipley Remembers the Early Twentieth Century," *Herald-Citizen* (March 30, 1989); Wahler, 8. Electricity did exist in places like Cookeville and Sparta due to power generated by the Tennessee Electric Power Company (TEPCO) in the late 1910s. Power plants at Burgess Falls (on the Caney Fork in Putnam County) and the Great Falls Dam (at the junction of the Caney Fork and Collins rivers on the border of Warren and White counties) provided electricity for hundreds of homes before the advent of TVA. Both are now state parks—Burgess Falls State Park and Rock Island State Park.
32. *Ibid.*
33. Upper Cumberland Medical Society Papers, Folder 1. Though the society failed to form, potential officers were elected. The first president pro-tem was Dr. C.K. Haggard of Burkesville, Kentucky.
34. *Ibid.* Doctors who attended were: William Tallyrand McColgan, William B. Young, John Martin, W.J. Breeding, Sam Denton, and J.L. Jones. Arcot was a small community near Celina, Tennessee.
35. Lee R. Minton, "An Early History of the Upper Cumberland Medical Society," *Journal of the Tennessee Medical Association* 65:2 (February, 1972), p. 110. During

World War I Rutledge Smith was appointed by Secretary of War Newton Baker to oversee the draft in the Southeast Region of the United States. He was also in charge of civilian mobilization and was the only person in the United States. to assume oversight of both. He reportedly ran the cleanest draft in the country. See William J. Breen, *Uncle Sam At Home: Civilian Mobilization, Wartime Federalism and the Council of National Defense* (West Port, Connecticut, Greenwood Press, 1984). The society's third meeting convened at Bloomington, Kentucky.

36. *Ibid.*
37. Minton, 109; Moore, 168. In January of that same year, 1899, the Jackson County Medical Association organized in Gainesboro.
38. Minton, 109.
39. Louise Davis, "Doctors Versus 'God's Will,'" *Nashville, Tennessean* (June 13, 1971).
40. Upper Cumberland Medical Society Collection, File 43–1. Between 1934 and 1944 the Society met at Red Boiling Springs every year except 1942 and 1944 when members met at Cookeville and Livingston.
41. Dr. W.B. Young, "A Review of the Organization of the Early History of the Upper Cumberland Medical Society," Upper Cumberland Medical Society Papers, Box 43, Folder 60.
42. "Constitution of the Upper Cumberland Medical Society," Upper Cumberland Medical Society Papers, Box 43, Folder 60.
43. Quoted in James L. Fletcher, "Story of a Country Doctor and Banker," *Smith County Historical Society* 19:2 (Spring 2002), p. 39.
44. *Ibid.*, 39–41.
45. A contemporary history asserted she was "the first woman to pass the medical examination in the state of Tennessee." Will T. Hale and Dixon Merritt, *A History of Tennessee and Tennesseans: The Leaders and Representative Men in Commerce, Industry and Modern Activities*, Vol. 6 (Chicago and New York: Lewis Publishing, 1913), 1612. See May Cravath Wharton, *Doctor Woman of the Cumberlands* (Pleasant Hill, Tennessee: Uplands, 1953). She practiced medicine at Pleasant Hill from 1917–1946 and is the subject of another essay in this anthology.
46. Dr. Dora Lee Wilder, "The Woman in the Field of Medicine," (Cookeville, Tennessee: Tennessee Technological University Archives, unpublished typewritten speech mss., N.D.)
47. The 1880 census listed her as age three.
48. Letter to Miss Dora Lee from Albert Sterne (December 11, 1901), John Lee Jr. Papers, Brentwood, Tennessee. Hereafter, John Lee Jr. Papers.
49. John Lee Jr. Papers. Few women attended medical schools at that time, and the printed school forms use only the words "Mr.," and "his." Dora's brother Plato also graduated from medical college, the Nashville School of Medicine, later Vanderbilt School of Medicine.
50. Built in the mountains on Toxaway Lake, the resort opened in 1903 and attracted wealthy persons such as Henry Ford, Harvey Firestone, and Thomas Edison. No record of the Wilder-Lee wedding could be found, but considering the general's wealth, it was probably a lavish affair.
51. Personal interview with John Lee Jr. (Brentwood, Tennessee, February 18, 2010). John Lee Jr. saw numerous affectionate letters between Dora and the general.

52. This house, listed on the National Register of Historic Places, is located at 2027 Riverside Drive in Knoxville. The nomination form is available at the Tennessee Historical Commission in Nashville.
53. Wilder had other houses around the state in Rockwood, Chattanooga, Knoxville, and Johnson City. The Wilders did vacation in Florida every year as long as the general was healthy.
54. Elzia Guy (E.G.) Rogers, "Lore and Legend of the Upper Cumberlands: Dora Lee Wilder Pioneer Surgeon," *Cookeville Herald* (January 28, 1964). The "mountain men" allowed Dr. Wilder to deliver babies because she was a woman. She worried and complained that men often waited too long to bring their wives to her. Email from John Lee Jr. (May 12, 2010).
55. Email from John Lee Jr. (February 21, 2010).
56. Papers of John Lee Jr.; Upper Cumberland Medical Society Papers. After her husband's death in 1917 she quit attending the meetings.
57. Graeme McGregor Smith was the wife of Rutledge Smith and involved in numerous civic clubs and progressive causes.
58. Dora Lee Wilder, "The Physical Child Makes a Mental Man," Upper Cumberland Medical Society Papers.
59. *Knoxville Daily Journal and Tribune* (April 15, 1909); *Nashville Banner* (April 15, 1909).
60. Dora Lee Wilder, "The Cure of Tuberculosis by the General Practioner [*sic*]," *Southern Medical Journal* (1910)
61. Before he built the sanitarium Dr. Officer and Dr. Alva Johnson operated St. Raphael Mission in Monterey. This was an Episcopalian training facility and hospital. The first hospital in Putnam County, it opened in 1914 and closed in 1943. See Laura Clemons, *The People's Hospital: A History of the Cookeville Regional Medical Center* (Cookeville, Tennessee: Foundation at Cookeville Regional Medical Center, 2011), p. 3.
62. "Officer's Sanatorium," *Putnam County Herald* (March 28, 1928). No evidence was found indicating that Dr. Wilder in Monterey and Dr. Wharton in Pleasant Hill communicated about treatment of tuberculosis. Dr. Wharton was not a member of the Upper Cumberland Medical Society.
63. "Society and Women," *Knoxville Daily Journal and Tribune* (April 15, 1909),
64. Minutes of the Upper Cumberland Medical Society, Upper Cumberland Medical Society Papers, Box 45 (May 28–29, 1912), p. 65.
65. *Ibid;* Clemons, 6. Putnam County did not have a health department until 1942. For more about its creation and its history see Jewell Nolen, *The History, Development, and Services of the Putnam County Health Department* (Cookeville, Tennessee: Putnam County Health Department Cooperating with the Putnam County Court, 1965).
66. Dr. Wilder was also courted by the president of another railroad after General Wilder died. The railroad leader made his private railcar available to Dora for travel. Email from John Lee, Jr. (March 22, 2010); *Chattanooga Daily Times* (February 25, 1919).
67. P.B. Smith came from a prominent Wisconsin family, but was asocial and a stutterer. He was "very energetic, practical and frugal." Smith was a pallbearer at the general's funeral. At his Monterey farm he raised Percheron horses. Important to

Dora in her later life was genealogy. She became a member and a participant in the Daughters of the American Revolution in 1928, claiming membership through her Revolutionary ancestor James Lee. Dora was initiated into the Bonny Kate Chapter in Knoxville, and she served as registrar for the chapter. Email from John Lee Jr. (March 22, 2010).

68. *Ibid.* Her death certificate listed her occupation as "housewife." Evidently her medical degree and career were long behind her and forgotten.
69. Upper Cumberland Medical Association Papers, File 43–3; Minton, 109–112. One early particularly memorable meeting mentioned in several accounts was held at Celina. Dr. Sam B. Fowler of Gainesboro invited all Society members to convene at Gainesboro and then be conducted by him up the Cumberland River to Celina. Doctors arrived on horseback and by buggy, leaving their animals at Dr. Fowler's farm, and boarded the riverboat where they were greeted with "most cordial" hospitality. Dr. Fowler's son Samuel Benjamin Fowler, followed in his father's footsteps and was the first physician in the South to successfully perform a bloodless hip joint amputation using the Wyatt Method.
70. The Medical Society of New Jersey is the nation's oldest organization of physicians, and dates back to 1766.
71. Upper Cumberland Medical Society Papers, File 43–3.
72. The first hospital in Tennessee's Upper Cumberland opened in 1837 at Livingston. Operated by Dr. William M. Brown and Dr. Herman B. Nevans, and sponsored by the Women's Board of Missions of the Disciples of Christ, Lady Ann Hospital was established in the former girl's dormitory of Livingston Academy. The second hospital in the region, also church-sponsored, was St. Raphael Mission, founded by the Episcopal Church at Monterey in 1914. Dr. W.C. Officer and Dr. Alva Johnson ran the facility until it closed in 1943. See Clemons, 3; Robert L. and Mary Eldridge, *Overton County, Tennessee: Bicentennial Echoes of the History of Overton County, 1976* (Livingston, Tennessee: Self-published, 1976).
73. Story related to the author by Dr. E. Morgan Dudney (Free State, Tennessee, October 8, 2009).

12

"To Help Bring Health to This Mountain"

Dr. May Cravath Wharton

W. Calvin Dickinson

Dr. May Wharton devoted her life and her talent to improving the medical health of residents in the rural village of Pleasant Hill and the surrounding area of Cumberland County, Tennessee; however, her efforts had more far-reaching effects. She established the first hospital in the county; she established one of the first tuberculosis clinics in the region; and she eventually engineered the building of the first modern hospital in Crossville. Her career represented an important component of the medical and regional history of the Cumberland Plateau area of Tennessee during the first half of the twentieth century.

Pleasant Hill in western Cumberland County was an early nineteenth century settlement, beginning as early as 1819 with the building of a log house by Lewis Whitaker. Other families, mostly from North Carolina, joined the Whitakers. The Civil War almost destroyed the community, leaving only three houses standing between Crossville and Pleasant Hill. In the postwar period several new families, mostly from the North, moved to Pleasant Hill. A.A. Hubbard and M.L. Abbot established a nursery business, and Hubbard built the largest house in the community, which later became the Pleasant Hill Academy principal's house. Extensive orchards were planted by several new settlers. By 1886 Pleasant Hill had established a school, a post office, and a store. The *Crossville Times* described the settlement in 1886: "It has fine farm houses, barns, a neat school house, store and post office. . . . We have four sawmills and two gristmills."[1] In 1917 Dr. Wharton described it as "a rural village. Some 2 dozen houses & 2 simple country stores."[2]

The most significant development in Pleasant Hill was the interest of the American Missionary Association (AMA) in the community. The AMA was founded in the first half of the nineteenth century as a Protestant abolitionist group. With the vision of promoting Christian values, the organization worked to eliminate slavery, educate blacks, and promote racial equality. Most closely associated with the Congregational Church, the AMA broadened its educational efforts and established more than five hundred segregated schools for blacks and whites in the South.

The Amos Wightman family came to Pleasant Hill from Illinois in 1868, having lived in an Illinois town with an AMA school. Wightman bought land around Pleasant Hill and became one of the most prosperous settlers in the area. Interested in education for their children, Helen Wightman wrote several letters to the AMA about a school for Pleasant Hill. Then in 1883 she traveled to Boston, Massachusetts by train to visit the AMA and ask for a school. In 1884 AMA sent Mary Santley as a teacher to Pleasant Hill. After an appeal from her, AMA sent the Reverend Benjamin Dodge, his family, and another teacher, Hannan Lord. Reverend Dodge led an effort to raise money and built several buildings. A boarding school was established, and high school as well as elementary curriculum was offered. Students worked on the school farm and other facilities in order to pay at least part of their tuition. Pleasant Hill became a popular educational institution for students who had few other opportunities.

The Reverend Edwin R. Wharton came to Pleasant Hill in 1917 as the new principal. An architect, Wharton improved the buildings that already existed at the academy. The original building [Woodbury Hall], whose exterior resembled a church, was erected in 1887. Pioneer Hall, originally a dormitory for boys and girls, was completed and occupied in 1889. Wheeler Hall for girls was built in 1889. In 1896 Dodge Hall was constructed for boys. Wharton reconstructed the assembly room of Woodbury Hall, building a stage with dressing rooms behind. Pioneer Hall was remodeled and "finished very attractively,"[3] with additions of offices, a music studio, and a mechanical drawing classroom. He also rebuilt Dodge Cottage, the principal's house. But Wharton "didn't want to be an architect. He wanted to be a minister."[4]

May Cravath Wharton joined her husband at Pleasant Hill in 1917. Born on a farm in Minnesota, May had attended Carleton College in Minnesota and the University of South Dakota. She studied in Europe and earned her medical degree at the University of Michigan in 1905.[5] Personal characteristics described at the end of her life included "delightfully dry humor," "debonair gaiety," "subtle sense of the ironic," "joy of living," and "genuine humility."[6] A student from the 1940s described her as "pleasant," "generous," "helpful," and "positive."[7]

May met and married Edwin Wharton in Atlanta, Georgia, where she had established a medical practice. Her description of Wharton was: "not very young, not very tall, with a face that crinkled all over with kindly

Dr. May and Edwin Wharton doing the rounds in a horse and buggy. Credit: Michael E. Birdwell Upper Cumberland Collection.

smiles and keen humor."[8] She remembered that "beauty entered into all our relationships."[9] The couple lived and worked in Ohio and New Hampshire for several years before accepting positions at Pleasant Hill Academy.

The move to Pleasant Hill was described by Dr. Wharton:

> One day a leader from the American Missionary Society came to visit us. . . Not long afterward we received a letter from him, offering my husband the place of principal of an academy at Pleasant Hill, Tennessee and suggesting to me the great need of medical work in the mountains. . . this was call just after our own hearts. It haunted us day and night till finally there seemed nothing to do but answer the call.[10]

Dr. Wharton traveled to Crossville by train to join her husband in Pleasant Hill. Her first impression of the area was not flattering. "Crossville was a flat little town with one main street on which [stood] a few stores, the courthouse and the bank."[11]

John Frey and his "ancient Ford" met her at the railroad station. "Just what kind of a conveyance I was expecting, I do not know, but I was hardly prepared for the dilapidated Model T Ford with flapping curtains that drew up at the depot for me."[12] Her description of the ride to Pleasant Hill was frightening:

> We careened into the ditch and slithered along until I thought we would certainly turn over. . . . he pulled the car up on the other side of the ditch, and it bounded into the woods. 'The mud ain't deep in here as 'tis in the road. . . . I'm trying the woods road now.' . . . We zigzagged between stumps and trees, and bounced over rocks. . . . Trees loomed before us, rocks popped up, now on this side, now on that.[13]

Arriving at Pleasant Hill after the harrowing ride, her first impressions of the village were not positive. "My heart sank from all the experiences of the day." Following a happy reunion with her husband, she was shown to a "dark and dingy" room where the couple was to live until the principal's cottage could be prepared.[14]

Edwin and May Wharton enjoyed only a short time living and working together in Pleasant Hill. In 1920, after a period of sickness, Edwin died. His death certificate, signed by his wife, indicated "acute gastritis" as the major cause of death, and "chronic nephritis" as secondary cause. The death certificate indicated that Dr. Wharton attended him from November 11–19, and she was with him when he died at three in the morning on the 19th. May Wharton briefly mentioned his death in her writings. In her notebook she stoically referred to his demise as "my recent shock and loss."[15]

Dr. Wharton seriously considered leaving Tennessee immediately after Edwin died. A simply but powerful petition from the local residents changed her mind. "The people here wants you to stay here as their Dr. . . . We feel that we cannot do without you. . . That [petition] was all I needed to make me decide to throw the rest of my life into the effort to help bring health to the mountain."[16]

In addition to acting as physician for the Pleasant Hill area, Dr. May taught science and math classes and acted as physician to the students and faculty at the school. One student, recalling his experiences at the school, commented that Dr. May or her assistant went to the academy building each morning to attend to the medical needs of the students.[17] She found the students handsome: "fine-cut faces, beautiful to look at, eager intelligent eyes;" but she was appalled at the ignorance of the students in the 1920s. "They had never learned to read intelligently. . . . Most had only 3 mo. [months] schooling a year."[18]

May Wharton's first task as the school doctor was to give physical examinations to the students. Most had never been examined or treated by a doctor, and most had never been to a dentist. She faced a medical catalog of chronic problems among the students—poor eyesight, infected tonsils, hernias, badly set fractures, rickets, rheumatic fever, tuberculosis. Several

Dr. May Cravath Wharton. Credit: Pleasant Hill Historical Society.

cases of measles and one case of typhoid were some of her first medical emergencies. "There was scarcely a sound body among them."[19] After some opposition to inoculation, Dr. Wharton immunized the students. Then she contracted with a dentist and an optician in Crossville to examine and treat the students at a group rate.

The school did not escape the nationwide flu epidemic of 1918 despite its isolated location. Eventually forty-five of the fifty female students, six teachers, and all but about six boys were in bed with the fever. Miss Elizabeth Fletcher, Wharton's assistant, was invaluable in her service, sparing the doctor many tiring tasks. None of the students or staff died from this plague, which killed half a million nationwide. One or two persons in the surrounding countryside died of influenza. Ten years later there was another "bad epidemic of influenza raging" in the Pleasant Hill area.[20]

In addition to her school duties, Dr. Wharton served as medical doctor to the population of the rural area west of Crossville. "It began to seep out into the hills that there was some kind of a doctor woman at the school."[21] Several physicians lived and practiced in Crossville, but they rarely ventured into the countryside outside the town, and the rural population could not come into town because of poor roads and lack of money. Crossville doctors charged one dollar per mile to visit patients outside town, and most people could not pay such costs. One person told Dr. Wharton, "Since most people handle less than a hundred dollars in actual cash in a year, they cannot even think of calling a doctor. They cure themselves with herbs and simples or they die."[22] Some pitifully explained: "We haven't got no money. . . . We could get along without a doctor."[23]

Family members would come to Pleasant Hill begging Dr. Wharton to travel to their home and render medical aid. Entreaties such as "Mammy's about to wink out. She can't get nary a breath;" and "Come as quick as ye kin—Carries misery has started. Better be quick" tugged at the heart of the doctor; and she always responded.[24]

Dr. Wharton's medical practice in the Pleasant Hill area was demanding and dangerous. The roads were poor, or non-existent, so she often had to ride horse or even walk long distances to see patients. In 1921 she was given a Ford. "Although a car was useless on our roads in winter, . . . in summer when the roads were dry we could get around much more quickly."[25]

Late one night a boy came running into Pleasant Hill seeking the doctor. Although her associates begged her not to go—"a very hard two mile walk from here"—Dr. Wharton decided to struggle through the slow rain in her rubber boots and raincoat to see the patient. Downhill to a creek, across a slippery thirty-foot log, back up the hill, and half a mile over a cow path brought May Wharton and nurse Alice Adshead to a small cabin. A mother of four children had a severe case of flu. After treating the woman and her children, Dr. Wharton and Miss Adshead left at three in the morning to walk back.[26]

Another case also illustrates the difficulties and dangers Dr. Wharton encountered:

> Tuesday was blazing hot. . . Dr. Wharton found. . . a summons to a little girl across the Caney Fork River, who had "split her foot open with an axe." Such a call means adventures in a region where the rocky bed of a stream, now dry, goes by the name of a "road." In this case it meant traveling part of this road afoot, leaving the disabled car in its tracks. Loaded with medicine bags, it was a hard pull. It meant a damaged car, due to rocks too big to get around or to climb, a broken brake, a borrowed mule and chain, a searching party from the hospital.[27]

Another problem Dr. Wharton encountered practicing medicine on the Cumberland Plateau is illustrated by the following story. Called to deliver a baby several miles into the country, she set out alone in her car in a heavy

"Driving up the creek bed." Tennessee State Library and Archives Folklife Collection.

fog. Unable to see more than a few feet, she drove the car into a hole at a bridge about a mile and a half from the patient's house. Walking to a nearby home she appealed for assistance. Unable to free the car the doctor and one man walked to the patient's log house. The baby had already arrived but the mother needed surgical repair. As Dr. Wharton prepared to treat the woman her husband entered the room and demanded, "What you aimin' to do to my woman. . . . I'll have no stitches tuck in my woman."[28] Dr. Wharton had to pack her bags and leave.

Homes Dr. Wharton visited were often primitive log structures. She described one such house:

> The mud chinking had fallen out of most of the cracks between the logs. The door was very low. I had to stoop over to enter. . . There was a rough fireplace and above it the mantle on which stood a few precious items of household comfort—a box of snuff—a bottle of syrup of pepsin—a few needles stuck into the

> wall—an old valentine and a lamp. Back on the dark corner of the room was a bed and around the fireplace a few mountain chairs.[29]

Word about the woman doctor who could work miracles spread throughout the Upper Cumberland. Though most of Dr. May's medical treatments occurred in Cumberland County, her reputation as a healer spread far and wide. William Stewart of Double Springs in Putnam County, Tennessee, met her numerous times when he worked as a brakeman for the Tennessee Central railroad before becoming a master brick mason employed by Scott and Smoot builders of Cookeville. William's daughter, Alma Stewart Birdwell, was pregnant with her first child in 1925, and delivered her son William Edward prematurely. The tiny infant weighed only two pounds and two ounces. Infant mortality rates were high in the rural Upper Cumberland and preemies rarely lived very long at that time. Determined to save his grandchild, Stewart phoned Pleasant Hill and told the person on the other end of the line to send Dr. Wharton to Double Springs on the next available train because without her "little Billy Edward will surely die." Stewart drove to the Double Springs depot roughly two miles away and waited for the doctor. After what seemed an eternity the train arrived and Dr. Wharton hopped off carrying a large contraption. It was a chicken incubator. William "Bill Ed" Birdwell spent the first weeks of his existence in the incubator while Dr. May stayed at the Stewart home over a week. As the baby grew to normal size she continued to look in on him. He lived to be eighty years old. Birdwell's story is a testament to the ingenuity and devotion of Dr. Wharton to her patients and the people of the region.[30]

Dr. Wharton's first medical facility at Pleasant Hill school was a room in the boys' dormitory. She had only the medical supplies that she had brought and the meager stock in the school's medicine cabinet. Her assistant was Elizabeth Fletcher, the art teacher at Pleasant Hill.

A recruit from Amherst, Massachusetts, Fletcher was one of the first persons May Wharton met at the academy, and Fletcher would become a most valuable companion and assistant to Wharton during her service at Pleasant Hill. As will be noted later, Fletcher used her Amherst connections to raise money on numerous occasions for the school.

Dr. Wharton encountered many cases of tuberculosis in Cumberland County. In the early twentieth century Tennessee led the nation in number of cases, and neighboring Putnam County for a time led in the number of deaths. Dr. Wharton went to North Carolina Sanatorium for training in treating the disease. There she met Alice "Adsie" Adshead, who worked as a nurse in an adjoining facility, and the two became friends. Adshead was a native of England who graduated from Provincial Hospital in Toronto. A

Elizabeth Fletcher.
Credit: Pleasant Hill Historical Society.

Alice Adshead.
Credit: Pleasant Hill Historical Society.

correspondence ensued, and in 1921 Adshead joined the Pleasant Hill staff as a nurse. Dr. Wharton described Adsie: "She had a heart-warming smile, pretty red hair, and a seemingly boundless supply of energy."[31]

Adshead joined Wharton and Fletcher in converting a small house with no running water into a hospital. It was a poorly built two-story structure with two rooms and a kitchen downstairs and three small rooms upstairs. Dr. Wharton made the kitchen her office. The other two downstairs rooms were for reception, examination, and treatment. The three upstairs rooms were for patients, furnished with two second-hand beds from a Nashville army surplus store. Opening the facility in August of 1921, Dr. Wharton called the building "Sannex"–sanatorium annex. She was excited, "with heart & minds full of visions."[32]

Tragedy soon struck the school. One night in December, 1921 fire broke out on the third floor of Dodge Hall. The fire spread quickly through the brick structure because of high winds, and the boys sleeping in the building were wakened; all escaped except Gordon Roberts on the third floor. Carried out of the burning building, he was hurried to Sannex. Dr. Wharton labored seven hours to dress the burns the first time, replacing the bandages each day. Roberts struggled for three weeks before dying. Dr. Wharton lamented, "It was impossible for him to recover."[33]

An early patient at Sannex, Bill had a "pain in the stummick [*sic*]"—an ulcer.[34] He was a patient for ninety days, lying on his back consuming a bland diet. Bill's expenses were almost

> $300, and he could not pay. His proposition was, "You need a man for a lot of jobs."[35] Bill turned out to be worth much more than $300. He was a handyman, but did much more. He became the buggy driver, and later the automobile driver, for the doctor. Sometimes he even assisted in medical treatment. Often timid, mountain people talk to Bill more easily about their problems than they would to the doctor.

In 1922 Dr. Wharton built her first true hospital, Uplands Sanatorium. "Up from the lowlands" was the meaning of the name.[36] The Frey family donated twelve acres of land for the facility. Dr. Wharton contributed more than three hundred dollars. She made a trip to New England and Ohio, returning with two thousand dollars. An anonymous donor from Ohio sent six hundred dollars. Elizabeth Fletcher wrote her brother, a librarian at Amherst, who sent her a list of alumni. Letters appealing for financial donations went out, and the response was gratifying. As will be noted several times, Fletcher could work wonders with her letters of solicitation. She was the corresponding secretary for the board of directors, and she wrote thousands of letters to solicit funds for Uplands. The 1932 board minutes noted that she averaged a hundred letters a month.[37]

The hospital cost six thousand dollars. It was a fifteen-bed structure with two wards, four single rooms, and an office on the first floor. The kitchen and dining room were in the basement. Electricity produced by a gasoline engine provided lights and water. "The building was a model of neatness and convenience and is so arranged that there is not a foot of waste space. . . . The outlook for the future is most promising."[38] Other hospitals in the area included Chamberlain Memorial in Rockwood in 1917, Howard Hospital in Cookeville in 1921, and a White County clinic in 1925.

Uplands was dedicated in June "to the glory of God and the welfare of his children." Dr. Wharton began "in a day or two to keep regular office hours to which people trekked in from the hills and hollows, bringing with them samples of most of the ills that man is heir to."[39] In 1922 Uplands treated fourteen patients. Ten years later the hospital was treating almost a hundred patients, as well as conducting hundreds of home visits and office patients.[40]

One generous relative who helped Dr. Wharton meet the expenses of her medical practice was her brother, William Cravath, a lawyer in New Jersey. Although he thought Wharton was wasting her life on the Cumberland Plateau, he began early in her practice sending twenty-five dollars a month. He sent a generous check each Christmas and he contributed to financing various projects. After Uplands opened Cravath's wife was a patient in the hospital. She was visiting May and became sick from a chronic ailment. In thankfulness for her medical treatment she offered to buy the Frey farm and its nice farmhouse for her sister-in-law. She would pay half the price if Pleasant Hill could raise the other half. Elizabeth Fletcher worked her magic again, writing letters to friends in New England. A few months later enough money had been pledged to match the sister-in-law's bequest. Two hundred acres and several buildings were purchased. Naming the old farmhouse "The Homestead," Dr. Wharton claimed it for herself, Elizabeth Fletcher, and Alice Adshead. Later the basement of the farmhouse was developed into rooms for obstetrical use.

In 1936 Dr. Wharton finally had her own private newly-built home, which she named "Yonside"—"the other side of the hill." Wharton drew the plans for the house. The location was the side of a hill, and the plans accommodated the site and its trees. "The house climbs the hillside."[41] Built of stone and lumber salvaged from the site, the interior wood was mostly chestnut. There was no lock on the house, and the large iron door latches and hinges were handcrafted. Two handmade iron chandeliers decorated the rooms.

With expansion of the facilities there was a need to expand the staff beyond Dr. Wharton and Elizabeth Fletcher. First Adsie Adshead joined, and Bill became the handyman. Then Dora Read Goodale became director of occupational therapy. A poet of some widespread fame, Goodale never accepted a salary for her work at Uplands, and she made "substantial contributions" to the hospital.[42] In 1933 Dr. Margaret Kesler became the second medical doctor to join the staff. She earned her degree at Vanderbilt Medical School and worked in the outpatient clinic there for three years before coming to Uplands.

The first surgery at Uplands was performed by Dr. William Boyce, a Knoxville surgeon. He amputated a boy's leg in an abandoned schoolhouse which had been cleaned by girls from Adshead's home nursing class. By 1927 Dr. Wharton wanted to make surgery a regular part of treatment at

Uplands. The modern paved Memphis-to-Bristol highway had been completed and travel east and west from Pleasant Hill was faster and easier. Crossville was now only a thirty minute drive; Knoxville, at eighty-five miles, was now only a one day trip.

Rockwood, thirty-five miles east, was the home of Dr. Thomas H. Phillips, whom Dr. Wharton persuaded to act as Uplands staff surgeon. He traveled the new highway to Pleasant Hill every Thursday. One day on this journey a falling tree struck the front of his car; after the tree was removed he motored on to Uplands for surgery. One night he slept in the operating room at Uplands because ten inches of snow had fallen while he was operating in the clinic. Sometimes he would extract fifteen or twenty tonsils in one morning of a "tonsil clinic." One busy day involved two ruptured appendixes, two abdominal cases, and a gall bladder case. Gunshot wounds, gall bladder extractions, stab wounds, and highway accidents were all treated by Dr. Phillips and Dr. Wharton. One boy showed up with his entrails encased in a pillow case after a knife fight. In 1933 Dr. Phillips performed nineteen major operations. The year before only two patients had died, one of cancer and one of tuberculosis. Seventy-three patients had "left entirely well."[43]

Dr. Phillips soon requested an operating room, and the three women—Wharton, Adshead, and Fletcher—started to make plans and figure costs that very night. Fletcher and Goodale wrote letters; Wharton made a trip to New England and Ohio; soon the money had been promised and collected. In 1935 the surgery annex was constructed at Uplands. It consisted of an operating room on the upper floor and a surgical ward below. An elevator connected the two floors.

By 1936 the medical facilities at Pleasant Hill were valued at forty-five thousand dollars. The annual budget of twenty thousand left an operational deficit, but this was the "first time in years the hospital is practically without debt." Gifts had increased 85 percent over a two year period.[44]

The staff by this time had grown to twenty. A new medical doctor, Dr. Aza Z. Hall joined the staff, coming from private practice in Colorado. In 1935 the hospital handled 146 cases, performed twenty-four major operations, and extracted thirty tonsils.[45] Patients were treated from such distant cities as Chicago, Philadelphia, Greensboro, North Carolina, Detroit, Chattanooga, Nashville, Knoxville, and Cookeville.[46]

By 1937 Uplands needed someone to handle the increasingly complicated business matters of the hospital. J. Frank Meisamer accepted the position as business manager; and his wife joined the staff as head nurse. Frank had been paymaster for five Marshall Field's cotton mills, and Frances was an experienced anesthetist. Later Meisamer's responsibilities and his title changed; he was made superintendent of Uplands. In preparation for the new hospital, after World War II Meisamer went to Chicago to attend a ten-day training session at the Hospital Administrators Conference.[47] Meisamer served Uplands until his retirement in 1961.

In addition to medical services at Pleasant Hill, Dr. Wharton and her associates taught health classes to plateau residents as well as students at the academy. She started an examination and treatment out-clinic at Toddtown (Pilot Knob) in 1932. Later clinics were established at Burgesstown, Ravenscroft, Big Lick, Mayland, Neverfail, Genesis, and Ozone. "The mountaineer families come to these clinics from miles around, sometimes riding double on mule back; often on foot with babies in their arms." Mother and baby clinics were held once a month to examine children younger than seven. Birth control clinics were also conducted.[48]

Dr. Wharton frequently made fund-raising and publicity trips to northern states. In 1941 an extended tour involved speaking engagements in New Jersey, New York, Boston, and Hartford, Connecticut. In 1942 she spent "five strenuous weeks" in New England and Pittsburgh, making twenty-five talks, "sometimes speaking two or three times a day."[49] All this in addition to managing the facilities at Pleasant Hill and making house calls in the entire region.

Occasionally Dr. Wharton took vacations. Her brother Will provided the money, with Elizabeth Fletcher, Dora Goodale, or Alice Adshead was her companion. She enjoyed cruises on the Caribbean, tours in Europe, and one round-the-world adventure. She attended a medical convention in Mexico City in 1935. Other staff persons also took adventurous trips. Elizabeth Fletcher traveled to Turkey alone in 1930 to visit her sister. Alice Adshead visited her sister in Toronto in 1935.

The next expansion at Uplands was a separate building for tuberculosis patients. Van Dyck Sanatorium, financed largely by E.M. Van Dyck of Brooklyn, New York, was a thirty-bed structure built in 1938. It was furnished by donations from Crossville merchants and other donors. This new facility filled up quickly because only Tennessee's four largest cities had beds for tuberculous patients. Dr. Stewart managed the new facility, and the state provided free chest clinics and pneumothorax treatment. Dr. W.C. Officer had operated a tuberculosis sanitarium in nearby Monterey (Putnam County) between 1925 and 1935. The state tuberculosis hospital finally opened in Davidson County in 1941.[50]

Charlie Brown, from Hilham in Overton County, was a patient at Van Dyck in 1941. His mother and two of his siblings had already died of tuberculosis (TB). A local doctor told Charlie that Uplands was his only chance for survival. Because his family could not pay for treatment at Van Dyck, his sister, who had just graduated from high school, went to Pleasant Hill with him to care for patients and pay for his treatment. For two years Charlie and his sister Leiron lived at Uplands. Charlie received the customary treatment for TB, including pneumothorax. This was a very painful procedure which included collapsing one lung for rest and healing. In 1943 they returned to Hilham with the hope that Charlie had recovered. With relapse he had soon returned to Uplands. Finally in 1945, with four years at Van Dyck and with treatment by Dr. Hollow Johnson in Nashville, Charlie returned home to a normal life with wife, family, and agricultural pursuits.[51]

By 1940 Uplands was treating over three hundred patients annually in the facilities. Donations amounted to over thirteen thousand dollars annually, and seventeen thousand dollars was collected for patient services. Uplands performed free and uncollectible services that year worth almost ten thousand dollars.[52] A report detailing the situation gave an encouraging picture of the facility. "Uplands owned 235 acres with two main hospital buildings--Cumberland General with 18 beds, and Van Dyck Sanatorium with 30 beds. The staff consisted of three resident doctors, three nurses and eight assistants." According to the report Uplands served approximately six hundred square miles "of mountainous territory."[53]

The 1940s witnessed the culmination of Dr. Wharton's dreams about modern medicine for the Cumberland Plateau. The need for additional space had always been in the mind and in the dreams of Dr. Wharton. As early as 1930 she had "discussed the need of a health center in this region."[54] In 1941 she drew a crude sketch of a new hospital facility for Pleasant Hill. But a disturbing thought interrupted her planning. Should the new building be constructed in Pleasant Hill—or should it be built in Crossville, a more urban environment with better road connections? At the next Uplands board of directors meeting she presented the new idea to the board members. Everyone was enthusiastic, even U.S. public health officials in Washington. "You folks are doing something down in Tennessee that has never been done before. . . . it will represent a bold but logical step in the evolution of medical care in rural America."[55]

Then the Japanese attacked the U.S. naval base at Pearl Harbor. World War II caused delay in enacting the plans for building the hospital in Crossville, but funds could be raised. Dr. Wharton reported to the board of directors in 1942 that the project had not been abandoned, "altho the war had hampered the raising of funds."[56] Money was plentiful in Cumberland County with a prosperous economy and war industries. So Dr. Wharton and her friends proceeded with fund-raising. M.E. Dorton, president of the First National Bank of Crossville, accepted the chairmanship of the board and director of the fund drive. "Friends of Uplands, who had contributed heavily before, again pledged large sums. By this time Uplands had accrued a mailing list of fifty-three hundred names. In 1945, 361 persons made donations for the New Hospital Fund and four hundred sixty gave for the general operating fund."[57]

Dr. Wharton made tours to the north to raise funds for the hospital. On one trip she visited Connecticut and Massachusetts. Several months later she scheduled meetings and conferences at Mayo Clinic, New York City, and Washington, D.C.[58] Her brother William Cravath donated ten thousand dollars, a "magnificent sum;" and George D. Olds donated one thousand dollars. Dr. Margaret Olds pledged thirty-five dollars a month, "her entire salary as intern."[59] Crossville pledged generously, as did Cumberland County and the State of Tennessee.

One problem which became urgent during the war was the scarcity of personnel. A report to the board of directors in October of 1943 complained that "it had been necessary to turn patients away at times, not because of lack of beds, but simply because there were not workers enough to care for them."[60] In January of 1944 the board complained that "operating the hospital for the past six months has been very trying, . . . from the labor side."[61] In that year Van Dyck TB hospital "was constantly full with several on the waiting list."[62] Dr. Wharton reported that Dr. Hall had left Uplands, and that "nurses are also urgently needed."[63] But in the same meeting she reported a letter from a Dr. Robert Metcalfe of Mayo Clinic. The letter suggested the possibility that "we should come to your area to work"[64] Dr. Metcalfe arrived in October of 1945 to become medical director of the hospital.

When the war ended scarcity of building materials delayed construction again; but the cost estimate of two hundred thousand dollars had been almost completely pledged. In the spring of 1945 the board met with an architect, Charles McCauley of Birmingham, Alabama, and approved plans that he had drawn for the new hospital. Later that year they purchased ten acres from A.L. Garrison for the site of the structure.[65] In 1948 construction began, but the lifting of wartime price ceilings increased the cost of building to four hundred fifty thousand dollars. Hill-Burton Act hospital building fund loans provided the additional money, but again the cost estimate had increased—to seven hundred fifty thousand dollars. The State of Tennessee now filled the financial void, providing one-third of the entire cost of construction.

Cumberland Medical Center in Crossville was dedicated in March of 1950. Built of stone, brick, and glass on a hilltop just south of town, the new facility was outstanding. Two operating rooms and a delivery room, a lab and x-ray room, kitchen, administrative offices, waiting room, and twenty-eight patient rooms with fifty beds made up the modern facility. Cookeville, in neighboring Putnam County, opened a new hospital in 1950 using Hill-Burton grants. A fifty-bed hospital in Jackson County also opened in 1950.

Dr. Metcalfe was chief administrator of the new hospital. Moving from Pleasant Hill, he put together the staff of doctors who would use Cumberland Medical Center. Until this time Uplands in Pleasant Hill had been the only hospital in Cumberland County. Now all hospital services were moved to Cumberland Medical Center in Crossville. Only the Van Dyck TB facility remained open in Pleasant Hill. But Dr. Wharton was not finished with her work in Cumberland County. May Cravath Wharton Nursing Home opened in 1957, a thirty bed building with assembly room, dining room, and terrace. Cottages were constructed on the beautiful spacious grounds of Uplands, and retired persons moved to Pleasant Hill to occupy the structures. Some retirees built their own homes in the retirement village.

In 1946 Dr. Wharton concluded that "the time has now come at 73 years for me to retire from active duty."[66] She owned "a little cabana at Sunset Beach" in St. Petersburg, Florida, and she hoped sojourns there would add "to the possibilities of enjoyment through the sunset years."[67]

She was honored in her last years for monumental work and achievement in Cumberland County. In 1954 the Tennessee Tuberculosis Association lauded her "in recognition of outstanding service in the field of tuberculosis control." In 1956 the Tennessee Medical Association named her "Outstanding General Practitioner of the Year." The University of Chattanooga awarded her an honorary degree "in recognition of high personal attainments and many services to the citizens of Tennessee."[68]

Writing her Christmas letter in the last year of her life, Dr. Wharton reminisced "What changes . . . from the early days when I came to bring medical care to a lonely mountain area."[69] Before the letter was sent May Wharton died. After a two-year period of failing health Wharton was "physically frail for many months" and "was quite sick for many weeks."[70] She died on November 19, 1959 at age 86. Funeral services were held at the Pleasant Hill Community Church with burial following in Pleasant Hill cemetery. Her death certificate, signed by Dr. Metcalfe, listed no cause of death.

Dr. Wharton had lost her husband early in their marriage. She had no natural children. She never acquired material wealth. She never accepted "a penny of salary" for her service at Uplands, and she "made frequent contributions from her slender personal income."[71] An indenture had been established in New York for her in 1929. When it was terminated at her death it had a principal of $109,658. From this indenture she left ten thousand dollars plus a monthly stipend to Alice Adshead. Dr. Robert Metcalfe, Frank Meisamer, Frances Meisamer, Dr. Margaret Stewart, and Dr. Asa Hall each received two thousand dollars. The church received seventy-five hundred dollars.[72]

Dr. Wharton adopted the mountain folk of Cumberland County and later all the citizens of the area, devoting herself unselfishly to the health and general well-being of everyone. Her work as a doctor, teacher, fund-raiser, builder, and administrator was beneficial not only to the residents of Pleasant Hill and Cumberland County, but was significant in the medical history of the region and the state.

NOTES

1. June, 1886.
2. May Cravath Wharton, "Notebook IV," (Nashville: Tennessee State Library and Archives (TSLA), Pleasant Hill Collection) and MF. 1812, Pleasant Hill Academy Records, (1908–1961) Amistad Research Center, 4 reels. It should be noted that Notebook IV has no pagination. Page numbers from that source unfortunately do not exist.
3. Emma Florence Dodge, *Souvenir History of Pleasant Hill Academy* (Privately Printed, 1924), p. 39.
4. Wharton, "Notebook III," 89.
5. Dr. Wharton's medical education was better than most Tennessee doctors in the early twentieth century. The first medical school in Tennessee was the privately operated Memphis Medical College founded in 1846. The Medical Department of the University of Nashville opened in 1851. The competing Nashville Medical College opened in 1877, but was purchased by the University of Tennessee and transferred to Memphis in 1911. A medical college in Knoxville admitted female students in 1904. Vanderbilt Medical College, created in 1874, was the most prestigious medical school in the Volunteer State. By 1910 there were nine medical schools in Tennessee, including Meharry Medical School in Nashville which was the only training facility for African American physicians in the South at the time of its founding.
6. Dr. Metcalfe at May Cravath Wharton's funeral (Nashville: TSLA, Pleasant Hill Collection, Folder 7).
7. Personal interview with Thomas Keane (Pleasant Hill, Tennessee, September 25, 2008).
8. May Cravath Wharton, *Doctor Woman of the Cumberlands* (Pleasant Hill, Tennessee: Uplands, 1953), p. 25.
9. Wharton, "Notebook III," 78.

10. *Ibid.*, 88–89.
11. *Ibid.*, 92.
12. *Ibid.*
13. *Doctor Woman*, 13.
14. Wharton, "Notebook III," 94.
15. Wharton, "Notebook IV."
16. *Doctor Woman*, 95. Fifty heads of local families signed the petition. She professed on the same page, "I resolved that mothers should be saved; and that the little children should be given a fair start in life; that pneumonia, pellagra, diabetes, anemia, and all the rest should not go on and on until no medical skill could cure them. . ."
17. Keane Interview.
18. Wharton, "Notebook III, Part IV, Chapter III, 'The School.'"
19. *Doctor Woman*, 34.
20. *History of Uplands: Cumberland Mountain Sanatorium, Pleasant Hill, Tennessee, 1920–1946* (N.P.: N.D.), p. 7. Hereafter *History of Uplands.*
21. *Ibid.*, III.
22. *Doctor Woman*, 33.
23. Wharton, "Notebook III."
24. *History of Uplands*, 10; Wharton "Notebook III."
25. *Doctor Woman*, 110.
26. *Ibid.*, 41.
27. *History of Uplands*, 24–25.
28. *Doctor Woman*, 178.
29. Wharton, "Notebook III," 106–107.
30. As related by Edna Stewart Barlow (Double Springs, Tennessee, July 7, 2003). Edna was Alma's sister and raised Bill after her sibling died when he was nine-years-old. John William Birdwell abandoned his children after Alma's death. Alma endured two more difficult childbirths, and she did not survive the final one. Her youngest child, Louise, contracted tuberculosis as a youngster and spent several years in sanatoria at Pleasant Hill and Nashville. Edna said that after her nephew/son was large enough to remove from the incubator, he was still tiny, and was often pinned to a pillow and covered with a down-filled quilt.
31. Pleasant Hill Historical Society of the Cumberlands, *History by the Page, 1976–2007*, II: p. 2. Hereafter, *History by the Page.*
32. Wharton, "Notebook IV."
33. *Ibid.*
34. *Doctor Woman*, 101.
35. *Ibid.*, 107.
36. *Ibid.*, 131.
37. "Organizational Meeting Minutes, Uplands Sanatorium, 1922–1925," (Nashville: TSLA, Unpublished Minutes in the Pleasant Hill Collection, October 8, 1932), p. 25.
38. *History of Uplands*, 6. Chattanooga, Knoxville, and Nashville all had hospitals in 1922.

39. *Doctor Woman*, 131–134.
40. *Ibid.*, 8.
41. *History by the Page*, I: 1.
42. Margaret Prosser, "Uplands: Cumberland Mountain Hospital and Health Services," (Nashville: TSLA, Unpublished Report in the Pleasant Hill Collection, 1940), p. 8.
43. *History of Uplands*, 10.
44. "Minutes," (Nashville: TSLA, Pleasant Hill Collection, July 13, 1936), 65.
45. *Ibid.*, (July 12, 1935), 54.
46. *History of Uplands*, 11; "Minutes," (July 13, 1934), 45.
47. "Minutes," (October 13, 1944).
48. *Ibid.*, (July 15, 1938), 80-81.
49. *Ibid.*, (January 8, 1943), 168.
50. Laura Clemons, *The People's Hospital: A History of Cookeville Regional Medical Center, 1950–2010* (Cookeville, Tennessee: The Foundation of the Cookeville Regional Medical Center, 2010), pp. 6–7.
51. Edie Brown Williams, "Uplands: An Untold Story," (Cookeville: TTU Archives, Unpublished Manuscript).
52. "Minutes," (July 11, 1941), 125.
53. Posser.
54. "Minutes," (June 2, 1930), 12.
55. *Doctor Woman*, 195.
56. "Minutes," (July 10, 1942), 143.
57. *Ibid.*, 228.
58. *Ibid.*, (January 2, 1945), 217.
59. *Ibid.*, (October, 1943), 190
60. *Ibid.*, (January 14, 1944), 196.
61. *Ibid.*, (October 13, 1944), 211.
62. *Ibid.*, (July 14, 1944), 204.
63. *History of Uplands*, 26.
64. "Minutes," (March 16, 1945), 221, and (May 24, 1945), 223.
65. Pleasant Hill Collection, Folder 4, 304.
66. *Ibid.*, 305.
67. *Crossville Chronicle* (November 20, 1959).
68. Pleasant Hill Collection, Folder 2 (Nashville: TSLA).
69. "Metcalfe Eulogy of May Cravath Wharton" Pleasant Hill Collection, Folder 7.
70. Prosser, 8.
71. *Ibid.*
72. Pleasant Hill Collection, Folder 2.

McCLELLANS CAFE
Coca-Cola
ED'S PL
EAKS • COUNTRY HAM
OPEN

AFRICAN AMERICANS AND RACE RELATIONS

13

Little Known Voices

African American Contributions to the Upper Cumberland

Wali R. Kharif

Examination of the life histories of Upper Cumberland African Americans proved as varied as the personalities involved. Their stories illustrate how men and women who have been otherwise ignored, made a significant impact in the region, regardless of their racial or societal status. A few African Americans stood out as local legends to both black and white residents of the Upper Cumberland. These include former slaves, politicians and government employees, soldiers, ministers, educators, professional athletes, and entertainers. Their stories also reflect changing attitudes about race from the days of slavery to the Civil Rights Movement and beyond. Though most of these people remain unknown outside the Upper Cumberland of Kentucky and Tennessee they made significant contributions to their communities.[1]

Jane "Granny" Bedford (Monroe County, Kentucky), Fountaine "Uncle Fount" Clark (Metcalfe County, Kentucky), and Robinson Crusoe Buck (Putnam County, Tennessee) were former slaves who became legends in the region. Jane Bedford, called "Granny" by African Americans and "Aunt" by whites, was born on May 10, 1840. She was a slave of Bennett Bedford, a large landowner along the Cumberland River. Bedford lived most of her life in the Mt. Gilead-Strodetown area of north central Monroe County, along the headwaters of East Fork Creek. The mother of four, she smoked a pipe throughout her life. A great-granddaughter, Louise Bailey Moody of Forkton, Kentucky, described her as a nice old lady who customarily wore clothing which the younger generation considered "funny looking." She wore a big black bonnet and long flowing dresses. According to Moody: "And speaking of that old black dress and bonnet, that's what she was buried in. That's what she wanted, and that's the way Aunt Minnie, her daughter, had her fixed [prepared for burial]."[2]

A renowned storyteller, Jane Bedford enjoyed sharing local history. She is fondly remembered as a midwife, and for the number of mothers and babies she nursed in the community and for miles around. Bedford died at her Forkton residence on September 2, 1944. The fact that she was buried in a grave, though unmarked, in the nearby white cemetery at Mt. Gilead Cemetery, speaks well of how local whites regarded her and her gifts. She lived to be 104 years old.

Another former slave who left an impression on the Upper Cumberland was Fountaine Clark, called "Uncle Fount" by local blacks and whites. He was born February 18, 1853 or 1855, depending on which source is correct—the Metcalfe County Cemetery Records or the Federal Census of 1870. Although Clark was born a slave, he earned the reputation of one of the most trusted members of society in southern Metcalfe County, Kentucky. He was highly respected and well known in the Summer Shade area and was fondly remembered by older people there.

Joshua Johnson wrote in "Uncle Fount and His Four In Hand" that Clark learned to drive a horse-drawn wagon at the age of 10. That turned out to be the lifetime occupation of Clark, who was remembered as "a fairly big man with a big [loud] voice." Clark ran errands for the whole town. According to Johnson,

> Uncle Fount served the people of Summer Shade as a transporter of goods, a mail carrier, and a banker. Prior to 1900, when there was no bank in Summer Shade, Fount was entrusted to carry the money of local white merchants to the bank in Glasgow. He also picked up drugs from Glasgow pharmacists and transported them to physicians in Summer Shade. It is said that although Fount was uneducated, he learned to code all items so that his deliveries could be made without error. For example, one person's order might have a corner turned down; or perhaps a little of a corner torn off for another person's order. Messages and packages were always promptly and properly delivered. . . [He became] the most highly respected black man that ever lived in the Summer Shade vicinity. His integrity was unquestionable.[3]

Clark and his wife Mary owned a small farm on the southeast edge of Summer Shade. They lived in a two-story structure, with a one-story addition attached to the rear. In addition to his profession as a deliveryman, Clark earned a reputation as a skilled carpenter. Along with his two carpenter brothers, George Robert and Thomas J., Clark was credited with erecting many of the older residential structures in Summer Shade.

Clark died on February 17, 1937, one day short of his eighty-fourth birthday. The closing words of an obituary that appeared in a local newspaper

Robinson Crusoe Buck. Credit: Cookeville History Museum.

summed up Clark's life as follows: "With his passing, goes a landmark of pioneer days. Tho' he lived in days of slavery, he had acquired quite a fortune and the high esteem of all who knew him, and all hearts are saddened that this faithful servant has passed from the walks of life, and that the echo of his wagon wheels will be heard no more."[4]

On the Tennessee side of the Upper Cumberland, former slave Robinson Crusoe Buck left quite an impression. Buck, who went by his middle name, had plenty of recollections, many of which he shared with others in the area. Buck often told stories about his master, Abraham Buck, an early white settler of Putnam County, who owned a plantation located northwest of Cookeville. One of Buck's favorite memories was how he personally, when about 20 years old, took care of his master, a Confederate sympathizer, when Union soldiers entered and occupied that area during the Civil War.[5]

Crusoe Buck remained with his master after the slaves had been freed. Once the Civil War had ended, Buck's master gave him four hundred acres of plantation land believed to be located in Putnam County, Tennessee. He lived near Algood, east of Cookeville, for several years before moving to Livingston, located in adjacent Overton County. Buck possessed the ability to lay his hands on people as a means of healing them of various diseases. Area residents, both black and white, attested to and sought his healing services.

A high point in Buck's life occurred in 1936, when he went to Washington, D.C., to visit with President Franklin D. Roosevelt and Secretary of State Cordell Hull, native son of adjacent Pickett County. During that visit Buck was presented with two large-framed portraits of FDR and Hull, which he prized. He was often photographed holding those images. On his return trip to Tennessee, Buck passed through Richmond, Virginia, where he saw the slave block on which, according to family tradition, his mother was sold as a slave.

James B. Hunter of the Overton County Historical Society had this to say about Buck:

> Crusoe had a charming grace about him. His conversation was like poetry. After the Civil War, he refused freedom and took care of his master, whose health was broken by the war. He never considered himself free until his master died. He became a successful businessman, and was friends with several governors of Tennessee. He was a guest of Franklin D. Roosevelt for a week at the White House. He was a close friend of Cordell Hull, Secretary of State. Crusoe lived to be 110 years old and had the distinction of being the oldest Black Democrat. He was born in 1845 and died in 1955.[6]

Buck's popularity is indicated when in May, 1953 he participated in a local rodeo and parade sponsored by the Cookeville Jaycees. The more than twenty thousand spectators viewed a parade that day featuring twelve bands and numerous floats, headed by the 109-year-old Buck riding in a car flanked by Governor Frank Clement and Lieutenant Governor Jared Maddux, mounted on white horses.[7]

In addition to former slaves leaving their mark in the region, some African Americans made lasting impressions in politics and government service. In the era following the *Brown Decision*, John Lee McClellan, Johnnie Wheeler, and Robert Evans pioneered in public service. John Lee McClellan, born June 15, 1913 (died July 19, 1973), was a leading Putnam County black businessman and politician. He was the second of Albert and Fannie Roland McClellan's six children. A combat veteran of World War II, John married Mary Alice Peake of Algood and was active in the Masonic Lodge,

American Legion, and Jaycees. McClellan owned and operated the Hooker Funeral Home in Algood, and John's Place, a popular tavern in Cookeville frequented by local blacks and whites. His father had operated a business at the same location for fifty years.[8]

McClellan is often described as an intelligent man who helped bridge the racial gap between blacks and whites in Putnam County. In 1972 he was elected to the Putnam County Court representing the Tenth District, becoming the first African American on the Putnam County Court, forerunner of the county commission. In that capacity, he served as the county's first black justice of the peace. He also served on the court's Fiscal Review Committee.

In making his announcement to run for county court clerk, McClellan commented:

> I want to say just a word about race relations. I was born and raised in Putnam County, and live on the same spot where my father was born. We have always tried to be good citizens and respectful of all people, black and white. And my friends and my father's friends before me were just friends. Not black, not white, just friends. And when I am elected, that is the way I intend to treat everyone, as an important person, a member of the community. . ."

Soon after he was elected, McClellan became ill and was diagnosed with cancer. He died on July 19, 1973.[9]

Another Putnam County politician was Johnnie Wheeler, one of six daughters born in Huntsville, Alabama, to Arlene and Johnnie Sales. She attended school in Huntsville and received certificates to teach and train teachers from various states. She moved to Cookeville in 1975, when her husband James Wheeler, an employee of GTE telephone company, was transferred to Cookeville.

It did not take long for Johnnie Wheeler to become involved in her new community and in local politics. Wheeler was a social activist in every sense of the word. She worked with the Cookeville Rescue Mission, served on the boards of Genesis House, Habitat for Humanity, and the Victims Offense Reconciliation Program. Wheeler directed local childcare programs, trained substance abuse counselors, conducted public relations work for Citizens Involved With Change, served as vice president for Alliance Against Domestic Violence, and as president of the Cookeville Jaycees. Wheeler was active with Character Counts, a program at the Upper Cumberland Human Resource Agency in Cookeville. She worked with schools to promote character education as well as with Juvenile Court judges on a program for juvenile offenders called "Crossroad: This Is Your Life, You Manage It."[10]

African Americans in the Upper Cumberland contributed to the region as public servants. Robert Evans was a long-time director of the Cordell Hull Head Start Program. Born in the White County neighborhood of Mt. Gilead, located between Doyle and Sparta, he was a sharecropper's son. Evans first went to school in Sparta, White County, then attended school in Lebanon for a period of time. After his parents purchased a farm in the Stonewall community of Smith County, he enrolled in Smith County schools for black children at New Middleton and Carthage. After attending the Colored Junior High School in Carthage, Evans returned to Lebanon to attend high school.

He quit school for a while and went to work, raising tobacco to support himself and to pay for his younger brother to go to school in Lebanon. After completing his high school education, he enlisted in the U.S. Air Force. After his discharge Evans spent some time as an artist, before landing a federal position with the Head Start Program. He also worked on location as an artist for Columbia Pictures.

While he dealt with occasional acts of bigotry—pranks by local whites at Head Start training, which was often held in state parks, and refusal of local merchants to cater to blacks and white sympathizers—Evans praised Macon County residents. He commented in a meaningful manner, "People say that Macon County is notorious for its opposition to black people, but would you believe that they've never shown that to me? I came here in 1972, and I have never seen the bad side of the white people here."[11] Evans worked with the Cordell Hull Head Start program, which served Macon, Smith, Jackson and Clay counties for many years after first joining the agency as an equal opportunity officer.

Upper Cumberland African Americans also served the country in the military. They performed in many different capacities on the home front, whether working in war plants, maintaining homes, or attending school during war years. Black soldiers experienced the same racial discrimination as black civilians in the larger society. Most were never welcomed as equals by their white counterparts. Thus, black soldiers were subjected to segregation and dissimilar combat units, separate training academies, and separate camp facilities until President Harry S. Truman integrated the military in 1948. Some, like Isaac Carver, were World War II veterans.

Isaac Carver had already experienced segregation before he entered the U.S. Army. After graduating from the all-black Darwin High School in Cookeville in 1938, the year of the school's first graduation, Carver moved

Isaac Carver. Credit: Mildred Garrett.

to Milan, Tennessee, seeking better opportunities. He got a job at the Proctor and Gamble plant in Milan, but soon lost his position there, given that black Americans had far more difficulty maintaining jobs during the Great Depression era in the South. After returning home to Cookeville, he received his draft notice for induction into the military. Carver reported to Camp Shelby, Mississippi, for basic training. He considered Mississippi to be the worst state in which a black soldier could be stationed. He referred to his time spent there as being a member of the "Jim Crow Army."

Racial violence was the norm on military bases, and Camp Shelby was no exception. Carver recalled the times when he and other black soldiers engaged in fights with white soldiers, simply because the blacks were unable to handle the racial prejudice frequently manifested by whites. The situation at Camp Shelby was so bad that many black soldiers asked to be transferred, but were always refused by the U.S. War Department.

From Camp Shelby, Carver was transferred to Camp Davis, North Carolina, where his training lasted eight weeks. There, he experienced racial segregation and racist episodes just like those endured at Camp Shelby. Carver and his unit, the 333rd Field Artillery, were sent to Camp Cameron, New Jersey, where they awaited transport overseas to New Hamilton,

England. While abroad, Carver experienced some discrimination, but nothing as bad as that he previously encountered in the southern training camps. He believed that less discrimination in England was due to the fact that the British were delighted that America fought with them against a common enemy, Adolf Hitler and his Nazi regime.[12]

In England, the social freedom black soldiers enjoyed caused racial friction with white American soldiers, especially when stationed in the same locale. Carver noted that American policy purposely segregated black and white soldiers, to prevent the eruption of racial violence in England, due to the frequency of racially motivated episodes on military bases in the United States. In addition to racial tension was sexual anxiety. Black soldiers could interact with white women in England to a greater degree than they could in the United States. That fact angered many white soldiers, especially southerners who could not stand the sight of black men with white women. "Me and a few black soldiers would beat up white soldiers for calling us 'monkeys' because they were mad at us for talking to white girls," Carver recalled.[13] Sadly, it was common for racial violence to break out in little pubs throughout England where black and white soldiers gathered. In sharp contrast with white Americans, British soldiers often sided with black soldiers in potentially violent situations. Interestingly enough, for the first time in the lives of white American soldiers, they experienced the same kind of discrimination by the English people that blacks endured in America.[14]

Many African Americans in the Upper Cumberland were prominent in the field of ministry. One of the most respected names in black ministerial circles in the Upper Cumberland is that of the Reverend Walter R. Munday (November 20, 1906–September 10, 1996), who led a congregation for twenty-two years, from 1936–1957, in Somerset, Kentucky. After that, he was pastor of St. John's African Methodist Episcopal (AME) Church in Monticello until he retired in 1983. While in Monticello, he also preached part-time for a church in Campbellsville. Bill Mardis described him as a person who "has a passion for making friends. His friendly attitude and sincerity have made him one of the most popular and respected men in Somerset."[15]

Reverend Munday was born in Richmond, Kentucky, on November 20, 1906. He attended all-black Richmond High School on East Main Street. A hard worker, Munday landed his first job at the age of nine. Thrifty, he saved the money he earned cleaning houses and performing janitorial service. When he graduated from high school he had nine hundred dollars in the bank, a sizable amount savings for the Depression Era. He used this money to help defray expenses associated with enrolling at Wilberforce

University, an affiliate of the AME Church located near Xenia, Ohio. During his five years there, Munday earned a Bachelor of Divinity Degree from Payne Theological Seminary and a Bachelor of Arts from Wilberforce. This prepared Munday for his role as minister in the AME Church.

Reverend Munday graduated from Wilberforce in 1933 and returned to Richmond. There he led the congregation at St. Paul's. That same year he wedded Delmar Merritt. As an AME minister, Munday served at the pleasure of the Conference. In 1935, the Conference sent him to the Davis Chapel Church on North Main Street in Somerset, Kentucky. He ministered that church until 1957, and continued to live in Somerset afterward.

During the Depression, black economic opportunities in Somerset were bleak. With most of his church members earning subsistence wages, the church could barely pay the preacher for his services. Rather than ask for more money, after praying on the matter, Reverend Munday secured a janitorial position at a local hair salon to augment his earnings.

Munday worked for many people in Somerset and made many close friends. Those who knew him claimed that he vowed "to make a new friend each day." Some were local politicians, such as Circuit Judge R.C. Tarter and lawyer John Sherman Cooper, who later became a U.S. senator. Others were businessmen like Dick Williams, president of the First National Bank of Somerset, Kentucky. Munday attributed improved race relations to courageous men like John F. Kennedy and Martin Luther King Jr., both of whom he described "as gifts from God."[16]

Following a stroke in 1986, Munday was admitted to the Midtown Care Home in Somerset. According to David Baxter, "With one leg amputated, and moving about in a wheelchair, he continued to preach for nursing home inmates on Sundays, and made frequent visits to their rooms for song and prayer."[17] The beloved Reverend Munday died September 10, 1996. Journalist Bob Sears observed, "Though he served as pastor of Davis Chapel A.M.E., Rev. Munday ministered to the entire community, black or white. . . . Brother Munday's life's work is done but his memory will live on."[18]

Among Munday's noted local accomplishments was serving as a stalwart in the Pulaski County Republican Party. He also served as president of the Pulaski County Ministerial Association, and he was its only African American member. Reverend Munday was honored for his lifetime of public and ministerial service on February 28, 1993 by the Black Heritage Association in Somerset, Kentucky.

On the Tennessee side of the Upper Cumberland, an outstanding minister was the Reverend Leroy Jackson. Reverend Jackson was born to Louis and Elizabeth Newton Jackson on December 29, 1890 in Natchez,

Mississippi. In his early adult years Reverend Jackson worked in various towns as a waiter and railroad employee. He became a student at the American Baptist Theological Seminary in Nashville in 1940. While at seminary, Jackson drove weekly to Granville, Tennessee, in southwestern Jackson County, where he pastored a church for four years. According to a biographical obituary published in the *Cookeville Herald-Citizen*, December 9, 1993, it was in Granville where he met his wife Maggie Brooks. The couple had seven children.

Following his pastoral services in the Granville area, Jackson served as minister for three-and-a-half years at a church in Gainesboro. He moved to Cookeville in the mid-1940s where, with the help of the First Baptist Church, he established the Trinity Baptist Church in a log house on West Broad Street. Trinity was the only black Baptist Church in Cookeville. Reverend Jackson led this small but important church for forty-five years, retiring in 1990 as he neared his one hundredth birthday.

In addition to providing spiritual guidance, Jackson was a leading social activist in the Upper Cumberland. When the all-black Darwin School burned in 1963, Jackson was a strong advocate for school desegregation. He sent his children to the historically all-white Central High School, rather than the make-shift black schools in Cookeville, which were created following the destruction of the Darwin School. Throughout the early years of racial integration, Jackson was called upon by various white churches to talk about race relations and how integration would affect the youth of that era. Jackson died December 7, 1993, twenty days short of his 103rd birthday.[19]

There were prominent African American educators in the Upper Cumberland. In Tennessee, Isaac H. Bohanon was the last principal of the aforementioned Darwin High School, Cookeville's segregated all-black school. He was born in 1916 and was raised in Algood, Putnam County, by his parents Isaac Taylor Bohanon and Mary Elizabeth Marchbanks Bohanon.

Bohanon graduated in the first senior class at Darwin High School in 1938. He enrolled at Tennessee Agricultural & Industrial University (later Tennessee State University in Nashville), where he attended school one day and worked the next for a period of three-and-one-half years. Bohanon's college career in Nashville was interrupted when he was drafted into the U.S. Army in the early 1940s. Upon discharge from the army at the close of World War II, he re-entered Tennessee State, where he completed his bachelor's degree and later obtained a master's degree in teacher education. Bohanon returned to Darwin High School as an English and social studies teacher in 1946, and became the school's principal in 1952. He also served as an athletic coach for many years. He was principal at Darwin when it was destroyed by a fire on January 7, 1963. Following school desegregation that same year, Bohanon taught history at Putnam County Senior High School in Cookeville until his retirement in 1978.

When asked to describe the greatest accomplishment during his professional years, Bohanon stated, glowingly, "The best thing that ever happened to me was becoming a school principal, then teaching classes at a racially integrated school in which ninety-five percent of the students were white." His wife, Amanda, also an educator, taught math and algebra at various schools, including Turner High School, Carthage. In Putnam County she taught at Darwin High School, Putnam County Junior and Senior high schools, and Sycamore Elementary School. Isaac and Amanda Bohanon served as grand marshals of the Thirty-first Annual Cookeville Christmas Parade, December 16, 1997.[20]

William Twyman of Metcalfe County, Kentucky, contributed to education in the region. Born in 1949, he served the Kentucky education system as a teacher, assistant principal, and principal during his years as an educator. In 1993, he was honored with the Milken Education Award for his outstanding career as an educator.

Twyman, the son of William Morris and Mary Lillian Garnett Twyman, was born in Echo, a small community situated along the Barren-Metcalfe County border. While games and self-made toys were an integral part of Tywman's childhood, his favorite pastime was reading. He read the Bible in its entirety by the time he was 10 or 11. "I am religious," he stated, "but that was a book to read and it was available."[21]

William Twyman attended Old Blue Springs School, a rural one-room all-black school, during his first eight years of education. Attending this school involved a two-mile daily walk, regardless of the weather. Treading across fields, following paths, going under and over fences, and through gates en route to school provided William ample room for adventures.

Twyman entered high school in 1962, the year that Metcalfe County schools integrated. It was a challenge to Twyman, being one of only thirty blacks in a school attended by six hundred whites. "When I went to Metcalfe County High School, I knew that I was going to have to work hard," he commented. "All of the black students felt that we had to work tremendously hard just to keep up."[22]

Twyman's cousin Luska Twyman greatly influenced his decision to seek a career in education. The latter, who served as principal of Ralph Bunche High School in Glasgow, was elected mayor of Glasgow in 1963, becoming Kentucky's first black mayor. The elder Twyman was a highly respected and successful black man. Next to William's parents, Luska Twyman was a model who became the single greatest influence in William's life.

William Twyman began his career as a science teacher at Metcalfe County High, the same high school he attended in the early sixties. During his first year of teaching he met his wife Lou Frances Stockton. They married in 1972 and had four children. Later, he taught in the Glasgow school system before becoming principal of the black Ralph Bunche Elementary School. In November, 1993, Twyman received the prestigious Milken Education Award, which included a twenty-five thousand dollar honorarium.[23]

Some African Americans in the Upper Cumberland contributed to education by breaking barriers. At age 46, Leona Lusk Officer of Sparta was the first African American to enroll as a student at Tennessee Technological University in Cookeville. Tennessee Tech was the last of the Tennessee Board of Regents schools to desegregate. She was formally admitted on January 3, 1964, for the winter quarter. During that school term, Tech admitted 4,327 students, but Officer was the only black person in the group. School officials kept her enrollment "low key," but her admission was supported and arranged by Dr. Charles Golden, superintendent of City Schools in White County. Golden, who later served as dean of Extended Services at Tennessee Tech, strongly encouraged school officials to accept Officer, a Sparta teacher who had been commuting from Sparta to Nashville in pursuit of teacher education certification.

She was admitted to Tennessee Tech when Dr. Golden impressed upon the school officials that it was neither safe, fair, nor feasible for Officer to commute the lengthy distance from Sparta to Nashville, when Tech was so close. Without delay, she was admitted to Tech. On August 28, 1965, at age 47 Officer graduated with a B.S. in Curriculum and Instruction, and became the first African American to graduate from Tennessee Technological University in Cookeville.[24]

The Upper Cumberland had its share of African American sports heroes. Baseball was popular in the region. In the western DeKalb County, Tennessee, town of Liberty, blacks had played organized baseball games from the 1880s. The most outstanding baseball player from DeKalb County, and one of the best from the Upper South was Robert Lee Griffith, recognized as one of the greatest pitchers to ever play in the professional Negro Baseball Leagues.

Griffith was born in Liberty on October 1, 1912 to Robert "Bob" and Eunice Baker Griffith. A well-respected stone mason, Bob later accepted a job with Overall Bros. as a truck driver, a position for which he earned one dollar a day. His son Robert Lee Griffith, who was 6'5" and weighed 225–250 pounds in his prime years, went by the name of "Big Grif" throughout his baseball career. Griffith fired the ball with lightning-like speed, so it is said, and he could make the ball rise, drop, or curve at his masterful command.

Of the twenty-five or so black families in Liberty at the turn of the century, the Griffith family name was prominent in baseball. Along with Big Grif was his first cousin, Frank Griffith, also a pitcher. In the 1920s, both were members of the Smithville Tigers, a team that played black baseball teams from Carthage, Cookeville, Gordonsville, Granville, McMinnville, Mt. Juliet, Sparta, and Watertown among others. They traveled from town to town in old trucks, paying their own expenses. Requests for contributions to help defray costs of transportation, balls, and uniforms never resulted in enough money to meet expenses.

During his baseball years in the 1920s–1930s, DeKalb County had no high school for black students; thus Big Grif attended a black high school in Lebanon, the Wilson County Training School, from which he graduated on May 18, 1933. While there, he boarded with a local family during the school year. Upon completion of high school, he married Christie Hunt and moved to Nashville to attend Tennessee A & I. In Nashville, he continued his baseball career as a member of the Nashville Elite Giants, a member of the Old Negro Leagues. Griffith's fast ball brought him victory after victory, and he left Nashville to play for the Elite Giants in Columbus, Washington, and Baltimore. Within a few years, he was pitching for the Philadelphia Stars. Griffith was named to the All-Stars in 1936 and, according to DeKalb County historian Thomas G. Webb, was recognized in the *Biographical Encyclopedia of the Negro Baseball League* as "one of the brightest prospects in black baseball."[25]

When World War II erupted, Big Grif exchanged his baseball uniform for that of a soldier. Corporal Griffith fought in the European theater until the end of the war, at which time he traded his military uniform for one issued by the Kansas City Monarchs. He played for the Monarchs for a brief period of time, then joined The Newark Eagles, a team that won the Negro World Championship in 1946.

Big Grif was lured away from the Eagles by the Philadelphia Stars, and subsequently by the New York Black Yankees. Both teams were affiliated with the National Black Baseball Association. During baseball's off-season in the United States, Griffith and other notables such as Satchel Paige played exhibition games in Canada, Cuba, Puerto Rica, Venezuela, and various other South American countries, showing off their prowess and skill. On September 23, 1948, Big Grif pitched for the North American All-Stars against Cuba's All-Stars in Havana. After winning that game, Big Grif played during the winter season as a member of the Venezuelan

Magellanas, a team that won the 1949–1950 championship of the Caribbean Winter League.[26]

Big Grif terminated his contract with the New York Black Yankees in the early 1950s when he chose to pitch for the Indianapolis Clowns. He remained with the Clowns until 1953, then retired from his legendary baseball career. He continued to reside in Indiana, where he worked as a city, county, and state security guard until he retired from public service about 1976. Robert Lee Griffith died from a blood clot, November 8, 1977, at the Veterans Hospital in Indianapolis. His body was returned home and he was buried in Salem Cemetery in Liberty, DeKalb County, the place of his birth. In death, Big Grif was not far away from the old dusty baseball diamond where he learned to play the game that brought fame to himself, his family, and to Liberty.[27]

Another famed black baseball star from DeKalb County, influenced perhaps by Big Grif, was Greg Tubbs. The latter graduated from DeKalb County High School in 1980, then played baseball for Austin-Peay State University, where he was named to the All-Time Ohio Valley Conference baseball team. Tubbs was drafted by the Atlanta Braves in 1984, then subsequently played for some of the Braves' Class A affiliates. He later played for the Cincinnati Reds and other major league teams. He finally served as a recruiter for the New York Mets.[28]

The Upper Cumberland also had its share of African American entertainers. Robert "Bud" Garrett was viewed as the leading blues musician and singer in the Upper Cumberland region. He was also renowned for his ability to make flint marbles for use in competitive marble games like Roley Hole. A life-long resident of the black Free Hill community in Clay County, Bud Garrett was born on January 28, 1916, to John Tom Garrett, a tobacco farmer, and his wife Adeline Hamilton Garrett. In adulthood Garrett owned his own junkyard business; ran a taxi service at various times; delivered ice; operated a restaurant and juke joint; served as a car, truck, and small equipment mechanic; worked for a live bait company; drove a school bus for many years; made flint marbles for personal play purposes and for sale; and served as a notary public. In his later years, Garrett spent most of his time working on cars and entertaining customers and visitors with his marble-making skills, performing blues music, and story-telling.

He learned how to play Roley Hole and make flint marbles from his father. Garrett stated about his father:

> He would take a piece of flint to the field with him every day. He would file a little of it away every day until he got it round. Then

> he would put it in a rounded-out form [a carved-out hole] made of sandstone and put it in a creek where the water would keep turning the marble over and over. The whole process might take a year and a half, but he would come up with a smooth round marble. On the other hand, there might come a flood and [the marble would wash away. Then] he would have to start over.[29]

Garrett's ability to make marbles came from his childhood years. The same can be said of his blues music career. He learned to play the blues in Free Hill when he was big enough to hold a guitar. He commented to Jonathan Newton, "My daddy put the guitar in my hands and I haven't put it down since."[30]

Writing about Garrett's music talents, Elizabeth Peterson and Tom Rankin concluded:

> Bud began playing guitar as a young boy and he recalls Blind Lemon Jefferson's 'Black Snake Moan' and the common fiddle tune 'Boil That Cabbage Down' as two of the first songs he heard as a child. Both songs are also emblematic of his musical influences; he absorbed as much from the fiddle and banjo tunes and minstrel songs played at square dances for blacks and whites in the area as he did from the blues he heard in juke joints and on the radio.[31]

Garrett learned his musical style from his older brother and family relations. His professional music career began in 1943 at local dance halls and honky tonks in the Upper Cumberland of Kentucky and Tennessee. He recorded a number of songs on a variety of labels, including Excello. Among his more popular were "Quit My Drinkin'" and "Do Remember." Writing in the *Tennessee Folklore Society Bulletin*, Anne Romaine observed that Garrett "adopted well-loved mountain songs such as 'Old Joe Clark' to his own blues and ragtime style." Though he never recorded a full album of his music, Garrett appeared on several anthology LPs.[32]

Garrett performed before regional and national audiences. According to Romaine, "Bud was one of the great Tennessee blues singers, having performed all over the South in clubs, bars, colleges, and community centers. He performed with the Southern Grassroots Music Tour and the Tennessee Crossroads Days in Nashville. He also performed in the 1982 World's Fair and the Smithsonian Folklife Festival as well as the Tennessee State Parks Folklife Festivals, the Fisk University Folklife Festival, and others."[33] Petersen and Rankin argue that Garrett's blues repertoire in the 1980s consisted primarily of post-war rhythm and blues standards by bluesmen such as T-Bone Walker and Little Milton, and country standards by Merle Haggard and Don Williams "which he often reworks into a slow 12– or 16–bar blues. . . ."[34]

Although Garrett continued to play and sing for audiences as far away as Ohio well into the 1980s, his Free Hill home remained his first love. It was there that he maintained his junkyard, with its derelict buildings and rusted tire rims. It was where he daily greeted people, both black and white, from all walks of life, who came to buy, sell, or just socialize. Garrett was truly a rich man in his attitudes about life and his fellow human beings.[35]

Garrett died of a massive heart attack, November 24, 1987, while playing marbles at the Bud Garrett Marble Yard in Free Hill. Survived by his wife Edith Garrett and his children, Garrett was buried in the Free Hill Cemetery three days later. His own composition written in the 1960s, "I Got A Place In Free Hill," continues to be played and sung by his friends who treasured his leadership, friendship, musical, and marble playing skills. Garrett may be gone, but he is not far away from his home in Free Hill.[36]

Since the Civil Rights Revolution of the sixties, which ushered in more positive race relations and the inclusion of minorities to a greater extent in social, economic, and political arenas, African Americans in the Upper Cumberland have become more visible in local government and entertainment. Future generations will be able to evaluate the effectiveness of African American contributors, such as Curtis Hayes, who first was elected a city alderman, and in 2006 elected the first black mayor of Livingston, Tennessee. Located in Overton County, Livingston had only sixty African Americans in its population of four thousand in 2006.[37]

Future generations will have to assess the achievements of Scotty Roberts, who is believed to be the first African American to establish a subdivision in Putnam County. Scotty Roberts' internationally famous blues musician and singer cousin Roy Roberts of Overton County has entertained audiences around the world. Following his success outside the region, Roberts has come back and performed at local fundraisers to advance causes, such as promoting Cookeville's public television station WCTE which serves the Upper Cumberland of Tennessee and Kentucky.[38]

African Americans have contributed to the overall growth and development of the Upper Cumberland. Their contributions are often overlooked because, in most instances, they do not write their histories and do not dominate the social-economic-political scene. The magnitude of their contributions must be measured within the context of their opportunities to contribute. As America and the South become more open and inclusive, future generations will share the merits of hitherto little known contributors.

NOTES

1. Detailed examination of the African American experience in the Upper Cumberland is contained in Wali R. Kharif and Lynwood Montell's, *Reminisces and Reflections: African Americans in the Kentucky-Tennessee Upper Cumberland Since the Civil War* (London, Kentucky: Janze Publications 2005). Hereafter Kharif and Montell.
2. Louise Moody, Forkton, Monroe County, Kentucky, Interview with author, June 12, 1996.
3. Joshua Johnson, "Uncle Fount and His Four in Hand," in Linda Branstetter, Kay Harbison, Rita McMurtrey, *Trails of Metcalfe County's Past*, Vol. 1 (Summer Shade: Summer Shade Elementary School, 1991), pp. 11–12.
4. *Ibid.*, 12.
5. Though no major battles occurred in Putnam County, several skirmishes took place and the area changed hands multiple times during the course of the war. For more about the Civil War in the Upper Cumberland see James B. Jones Jr., "Fevers Ran High: The Civil War in the Upper Cumberland," *Rural Life and Culture of the Upper Cumberland*, Michael E. Birdwell and W. Calvin Dickinson, eds. (Lexington: University Press of Kentucky, 2004).
6. Quoted in Kharif and Montell, 59, 266.
7. Mary Jean DeLozier, *Putnam County, Tennessee, 1850–1970* (Nashville: McQuiddy Publishing, 1979), p. 281. Jared Maddux, a native of Cookeville was a circuit judge before becoming lieutenant governor.
8. For more about John Lee McClellan see "We Don't Care What Color You Are as Long as Your Money is Green," in this anthology.
9. *Putnam County Light*, (Cookeville, TN) November 2, 1995, p. 4. He left behind a widow, Mary Alice Peake McClellan, and four children, Shirley, John Jr., Marcio Robert, and Willie Margaret Booker. Mary Alice was his third wife.
10. Kelly Thompson, "Johnnie Wheeler . . ., The First Black Person Elected to A County Office," *Putnam County Light* (October 29, 1995), p. 5–A.
11. Robert Evans, Interview with author, Lafayette, Tennessee (July 13, 1994).
12. To refuse to accept the local laws would mean jail, often a beating, or even death. Carver never permitted himself to be placed in situations that might lead to violence or jail, but many of his friends did.
13. Information obtained from an essay written by Brad Savage, a student of Michael Birdwell's at Tennessee Technological University, Cookeville. Savage cited several sources about military history in compiling his essay, including books written by Russell A. Buchanan, Mary P. Motley, Philip McGuire, Walter White, and Neil A. Wynn. The bulk of Savage's information was provided by Isaac Carver during a tape-recorded interview, July 9, 1997.
14. *Ibid.*

15. Bill Mardis, "Rev. Munday Left His Seminary Sermon At Home," *Louisville Courier-Journal*, February 27, 1933, p. A-1.
16. *Ibid.*
17. David Baxter, "Reverend Walter R. Munday" (Bowling Green: Western Kentucky University, Folklife Archives, Kentucky Library, Unpublished Manuscript, April, 1992.
18. Bob Sears, "Gentle Man of Dignity Left His Mark on Family, Community," *Pulaski News Journal*, (Somerset, KY) September 19, 1996.
19. Information about Reverend Jackson was provided by Tennessee Tech history student, Kayce Buck, who interviewed him during the spring term, 1991. See also Don Foy, "Rev. Leroy Jackson . . . Dies at 102," Cookeville *Herald Citizen* (December 9, 1993), p. 1; and Mary Hopson, comp., *Siftings From Putnam County, Tennessee: Towns, Communities, People* (Cookeville, Tennessee: Diversified Graphics, 1991), p. 285.
20. Transcript of Jeanne C. Potter Interview with Isaac Bohannon (February 14, 1991), pp. 1–6; Tracey Hackett, "Long-time Teachers Head Parade," Cookeville *Herald-Citizen* (November 30, 1997), pp. 1, 16. During that stint, he met and married Amanda. Bohanon and Amanda, had one son, Charles Taylor Bohanon, who enrolled as a senior in Central High School, Cookeville, when it first integrated in 1963. That year, Charles played basketball for Central High, later renamed Cookeville High. As the only black player at Central, he was sometimes advised by the coach and others not go to certain towns in the area to play basketball against all-white teams.
21. William Twyman, Interviewed by Debbie Reece (October, 1996). From that interview Reece wrote the initial version of Twyman's life history
22. *Ibid.*
23. *Ibid.*
24. Dr. Charles Golden, Interview with Author (Cookeville, May 21, 1990). See also DeLozier, 326. The Leona Lusk Officer Black Cultural Center at TTU was created to honor Lusk's memory and contributions to education in the Upper Cumberland.
25. Thomas G. Webb, *A Bicentennial History of DeKalb County, Tennessee* (Smithville, Tennessee: Bradley Printing Co, 1995).
26. Information gleaned from newspaper articles by Stony Merriman and Craig LaFevre published in the *Smithville Review*, circa 1985 and December 29, 1999, Section B, 1, 2.
27. Thomas G. Webb, "Town's Black Community Highly Respected," *Smithville Review*, (September 17, 1997), pp. 12–13. Louise Phillips, daughter of Big Grif, Smithville, interviewed June 12, 1997. Big Grif had two daughters, Louise (Mrs. Walter) Phillips, and Minnie (Mrs. William) Hurd, and two sons, William "Big Grif Jr.," and John Griffith. All total, Big Grif had sixteen grandchildren and eight great-grandchildren
28. Thomas G. Webb, *op.cit.*, 154.
29. Anne Romaine, "In Memoriam: Robert 'Bud' Garrett (1916–1987)," *Tennessee Folklore Society Bulletin*, LIII: 1 (1988), pp. 27–28.

30. Jonathan Newton, "Junk Yard Blues," in photo-journalism Mountain Workshop booklet *Celina* (Bowling Green: Western Kentucky University, 1985), pp. 32–35.
31. Elizabeth Peterson and Tom Rankin, "Free Hill: A Sound Portrait of a Rural African American Community," *Tennessee Folklore Society Bulletin* (1985), pp. 13–15.
32. Romaine, 28.
33. *Ibid.*, 27.
34. Peterson and Rankin, 14.
35. Kharif and Montell, *Reminisces and Reflections*, 98–99, 113, 115, 209.
36. *Ibid.* See also Elizabeth Peterson, "Trickster and Trader: Portrait of An Afro-American Entrepreneur," (Bloomington: Indiana University, Unpublished Doctoral Dissertation, 1990). Additional information supplied by Jane Garrett Taylor of Indianapolis, Indiana, and Garrett's sister, Ethel Jane Hamilton of Celina, Tennessee, with assistance from Bea Audrey Isabel, Principal of Warren Elementary School, Bowling Green, Kentucky, June 25, 2000.
37. *Cookeville Herald-Citizen*, (Cookeville, TN) June 23, 2006 and May 20, 2008.
38. *Cookeville Herald-Citizen*, (Cookeville, TN) December 26, 2007. Cookeville is the smallest town in the United States to have its own PBS station, and it creates excellent, award-winning original programming. Todd Jarrell's documentary, *Crank: Darkness on the Edge of Town* won an Emmy for its graphic depiction of methamphetamine addiction in the Upper Cumberland.

14

Sorrow Songs

How Music Made Brothers of J. Robert Bradley and Charles Faulkner Bryan

Laura Clemons

It was hot in the church that night in August 1938. Parishioners had flung open the windows and doors of St. Mary's Baptist Church in McMinnville, Tennessee, to catch any breeze that might wind its way up the hillside, and the lights attracted moths and hard-shell night bugs that dusted ladies' hats, dodged their fans and clattered onto the podium where a young man played piano.[1] The church was packed. A touring Baptist entourage had come to town for a week-long revival. The meeting had been amply promoted, and people came in from all around this small rural community on the Southern edge of the Tennessee-Kentucky Upper Cumberland region. Revivals had little trouble filling the house during the Depression.[2]

Charles and Edith Bryan, the only white people in attendance, waited along with the rest of the crowd for J. Robert Bradley, a young but much-touted baritone, to take the stage. Musicians themselves, the Bryans were on summer break from their teaching jobs in Cookeville, higher up on the Highland Rim of the Cumberland Plateau.[3] J. Robert Bradley entered and walked over to the piano. Although he was just eighteen years old, his stage presence was immense. He stood tall, shoulders thrown back, chest high, his hands folded formally across his stomach. A stocky, dark-skinned man, he was missing one eye from a childhood accident.[4] When Bradley opened his mouth to sing, the richest, fullest, most naturally endowed voice Bryan ever heard poured out, and he nearly jumped to his feet, exhilarated. Edith had to grab his arm to keep him in the pew. "I have never heard a voice like that," he told her.[5]

As the program ended, the couple worked their way to the front of the sanctuary to introduce themselves to Bradley. Bryan desperately wanted to get to know the singer, and he had a proposition to make. Bryan complimented Bradley's big and powerful voice, but cautioned him that it would never last a lifetime of performance. Vocal exercises could help protect him

Charles and Edith Bryan. Credit: Charles Faulkner Bryan collection, Tennessee Tech Archives.

and even improve his technique. Bryan offered to begin lessons the next morning.[6]

Bradley did not know what to make of the situation. Here he was, in the middle of a black church in the rural South, when a white man—a complete stranger only a few years older than himself—offered him advice about something he thought he had already mastered. Bradley knew he could sing; it was the one skill people had bragged on since he was a youngster growing up in Memphis. Because he was already employed as a church performer touring the South, he saw no point in interrupting his career, stopping long enough to go back to the classroom.[7]

But there was something about this earnest young man, who looked up into Bradley's eyes with both confidence and admiration, that gave Bradley pause. Bryan said he was a classically trained musician and that he was head of the music division at the college in Cookeville. His voice, with its genteel Southern accent, was distinguished. And there was an air of refinement about Edith Bryan, who stood quietly at her husband's side.[8] When Bradley was just a boy, a little girl named Pearl lived nearby who spoke in a voice far different from the uneducated urban tones of his Memphis neighborhood. From the minute he set eyes on her, Bradley wanted to grow up to be just like that—a cultivated person who stood out from the rest.[9]

Bryan asked if Bradley would meet him at the church at nine the next morning for his first lesson. Bradley arrived at eight. And thus began a seventeen-year relationship between these two men that would bridge the gap between black and white, professional and amateur, a small college auditorium and the most celebrated concert halls of New York and London. Most of all, this relationship was about trust and an even stronger emotion; for the rest of his long life, Bradley maintained that the Bryans had loved him—not only for his amazing natural gift of song, but for himself, as a brother. Throughout a lifetime split between suffering and jubilation, he never forgot that.[10]

J. Robert Bradley and Charles Faulkner Bryan occupied a transitional niche in American music. They began their careers in the 1930s, at least a decade before folk music influenced nearly every musical genre in the United States. The golden age of gospel, one of the sacred branches of folk music, was on the near horizon, and the protest music of the 1960s, with its roots in both sacred and secular folk music, lay a little farther up the road.[11] But while Bryan and Bradley were coming up, it is doubtful that anyone saw that major shift in popular music coming. Folk songs in all their mutations were still largely confined to churches and front porches. Bryan and Bradley helped change that.[12]

Bradley was part of a new wave of singers performing hymns written specifically for African American Baptists who, along with their Methodist brethren, had become uncomfortable with the primitive exuberance of the Pentecostal and Holiness churches, where hymns were accompanied by shouts and foot-stomping. Songwriters and music leaders of the National Baptist Convention insisted on a more refined approach to praise. When Bradley strode onto stages outside the church, as he and his fellow gospel singers increasingly did, he brought to both black and white spirituals a certain respectability that the larger public quickly came to appreciate—and which quickly assimilated into the mainstream.[13]

For his part, Charles Faulkner Bryan was among a handful of American composers whose enthusiasm for folk music showed up in his compositions, his classrooms, and his concert and recital programs. He relished every variety of folk song, regardless of origin or tradition—these songs he had grown up with in the Upper Cumberland—and he was intent on restoring this music to the plane of popularity it once had enjoyed. And the way he began that quest was by collecting it—rescuing it, really—from the isolated pockets where it had languished, thus contributing to the folk music revival. It is likely that the Bryans chose to attend the St. Mary's revival in McMinnville as much to collect hymns and spirituals as to enjoy a musical religious experience.[14]

Charles Faulkner Bryan. Credit: Charles Faulkner Bryan collection, Tennessee Tech Archives.

Both Bryan and Bradley shared one other major musical aesthetic. They interpreted the vernacular through the classical form. The way Bradley sang "Amazing Grace," for instance, differed significantly from the way Mahalia Jackson performed it. Bradley delivered lyrics formally, while Jackson sang them with abandon. The same with Bryan—his interpretation of a folk song was more akin to what Americans came to expect from the classic smoothness of Burl Ives than from the less-studied Woody Guthrie. They had so much in common, these two native Tennessee musicians, that the one glaring difference—their race—never seemed to be of consequence.

The son of a stevedore and a cook, John Robert Lee Bradley was born in 1920 in one of the poorest neighborhoods of Memphis, Tennessee, a small community called Pinch, near the riverfront where African slaves were once auctioned. His father, John, hauled cotton bales from docks to barges and back again; a heavy drinker, gambler and ladies' man, John died when Robert was seven or eight years old. His mother, Lela, depended on her eldest son to help feed the family, which grew to three with the birth of his little brother, Van. Robert rummaged through alleys behind restaurants, looking for food he could sell or take home; he became an expert at catching crawfish from the banks of the Mississippi, where he escaped when school frustrated and bored him, which it generally did. He could lie on the riverbank for hours, watching the clouds go by while singing, always singing.[15]

It was one such day in 1933, when there was no food in the house, and Lela asked her son for help, that he sang in front of a large crowd for the first time. Just thirteen years old, Robert was on his way home with a bucket full of crawfish when he heard the unmistakable sounds of a professional church choir drifting out over the city streets. He followed the sound, mesmerized, barefoot, muddy, carrying his pail of crawfish, all the way to the city auditorium, where a huge crowd had gathered for a meeting of the National Baptist Convention—the nation's largest black denomination. He wandered right up to the stage, and when one of the women singers protested, the music director, Miss Lucie Eddie Campbell, hushed her, beckoned Robert to the piano, wiped the mud off his face and asked if he knew the words to her hymn "Is He Yours?" and "Nobody Else But Jesus." Robert nodded and began to sing—and he did not stop singing for Baptist congregants for the next sixty-seven years.[16]

Campbell, one of gospel music's shining lights, had been writing hymns and serving as music director for the National Baptists since 1916. She co-edited *Gospel Pearls*, one of the most popular and respected hymnals in American history.[17] She taught, sang, and played piano, so she knew talent when she heard it. Campbell cultivated and encouraged Bradley, urging him to go on the road for the Baptists; from that moment on, he toured with various quartets, including the Good Will Singers, until well after meeting and studying with Charles Faulkner Bryan.[18]

Bradley was not mistaken when he detected an air of refinement about the Bryans. Only four years after he and Bradley met at the McMinnville revival, Bryan went on to become Tennessee's most distinguished composer. In 1942 Bryan was the first Tennessee composer whose work was premiered by a large professional symphony orchestra and, in 1945, the first Tennessee composer to win a Guggenheim fellowship.[19]

A native of McMinnville, Bryan was the second son of a middle-class family who financed his way through the Nashville Conservatory of Music using the capital from an insurance policy.[20] Bryan, who studied piano and voice, performed regularly in Nashville throughout his four years at the conservatory, helping defray the expense of private higher education. He directed an elementary school orchestra, sang on WSM radio's "Rise and Shine" morning program and ushered at the Ryman Auditorium; he even held odd jobs in construction, food service, and, in his senior year, worked for room and board as a mother's helper. Bryan was always conscious of the fact that he chose an unusual and challenging career path, particularly during the Depression. He graduated from the conservatory in 1934 with a bachelor's degree in public school music, and the next year secured a teaching position—in fact, the only such teaching position—in the music division at Tennessee Polytechnic Institute (TPI) in Cookeville, forty-two miles north of his hometown.[21]

At TPI, between 1935 and 1939, Bryan collected a cadre of devoted students, young men and women he corresponded with for the rest of his life. He taught everything—voice, most instruments, music education, appreciation, and history.[22] To help make ends meet, he gave private lessons, charging seventy-five cents a session;[23] any instrument he did not already know how to play, he mastered quickly, staying one lesson ahead of his pupils.[24] He directed the Glee Club, assembled a modest student symphony orchestra, and even served as a booking agent, finding performance opportunities for his students throughout Middle Tennessee.[25]

Bryan also collected folk music. Early upon his arrival at TPI, where the Tennessee Folklore Society had just been formed under the direction of Dr. T.J. Farr, he learned that—far from being too casual a subject for scholarly work—folk songs were the stuff from which careers could be made. As a child, he loved the music of the people who lived in the hills surrounding his hometown. But he was classically trained; his ambition, increasingly,

The Bryan Student Orchestra. Credit: Charles Faulkner Bryan collection, Tennessee Tech Archives.

was to write symphonic music. It became apparent, soon after joining the TPI faculty, that there might be a way to combine those two passions.[26]

Bryan married Edith Hillis in 1936, two years before meeting J. Robert Bradley at the revival in McMinnville. He remained at TPI until the end of the 1938–1939 academic year, when Nashville's Peabody College offered him a graduate fellowship. Bryan ended his time at TPI with the premiere of his first opera, *Rebel Academy*, but not before beginning formal voice lessons with his new protégée, Bradley.[27]

During the week Bradley and his fellow revivalists camped in McMinnville in the summer of 1938, he and Bryan met every morning for a voice lesson. When the tour pulled up stakes, Bryan offered to continue their lessons, but it would not be easy. Bradley could not afford to leave the road long enough to study, but he was determined. He had found what he had been looking for (whether consciously or unconsciously) all his life—a way to move into a new, more exalted, realm of professional musicianship. So while he left McMinnville in August with his fellow musicians, he remembered Bryan's offer and stewed over it for months.[28] By that November, he was ready to make the leap. From his temporary home in Chattanooga, he wrote Bryan at TPI:

> Dear Sir–I owe you an apology that words cannot express. I know that you think that I am not grateful for your kind offer which was to benefit myself. I am planning to curtail all my plans and come and study with you commencing with the New Year–that is, if you have a place for me. I do appreciate all the kindnesses that you have offered to me and I wish to thank you in advance for what I hope for you to do for me. Please let me know at your earliest date possible your decision. Yours Very Anxiously Waiting For A Reply. . .[29]

Bryan and fellow faculty member, T.J. Farr, drove to the bus station to pick him up.[30] In his 1939 financial ledger, Bryan recorded a seventy-five cent fee for a "taxi and Negro guide" to take Bradley to his new temporary home, the household of minister, possibly Lee Gibson, in a predominantly black neighborhood in West Cookeville.[31] Off and on for the next few months, Bradley worked odd jobs around town to pay his room and board, studied reading and writing with Edith Bryan during the day, and went to Bryan's studio on the TPI campus at night for voice lessons.[32]

In 1939, Tennessee was still fifteen years away from a school board decision favoring integration; it would not be until 1964 that the first black students enrolled at TPI. Bryan and Bradley engaged in more than voice lessons; they were quite literally breaking the law.[33] The formally enrolled students knew it, too. It was impossible to hide—not just because Bradley was a large black man walking into and out of an academic hall on an all-white public campus, but because his singing was so distinctive. Most students had likely never heard anything like it, not live, anyway. One of Bryan's white students, H.S. Barnes, said there was no mistaking Bradley's presence because "his voice was so big"—so big, in fact, that it attracted the attention of the college administration.[34]

There are differing stories about how the path was smoothed for Bradley's presence on campus. One version has TPI President Q.M. Smith walking into Bryan's studio unexpectedly one evening, listening to Bradley sing and assuring both teacher and student that there would be no trouble as a result of the arrangement; Bradley remembered the incident this way.[35] But it was also possible, according to H.S. Barnes, that Bryan had quietly approached the president beforehand to ask permission to teach Bradley after hours and that it was granted based on Bryan's winning personality and popularity among students. Regardless, Bradley's music lessons continued off and on until Bryan left TPI for the engagement at Peabody in Nashville.[36]

Bradley, needing regular employment to support himself and to help his family, returned to the road periodically. In February 1939, he wrote:

> Mr. Bryan, God knows how I can thank you for what you done for me. I know that don't put no money in your pocket but some day I hope to pay you in a big way. Everyone who heard me sing before I came to you say I sing better than ever, so you can see that God is in the plane and I know we can't fall. I want to come back to Cookeville and learn some more about songs if it is the Lord's will. Write as soon as you can, From your friend, J. Robert Bradley.[37]

When Bryan moved on to Peabody, Bradley followed. Whenever he could afford to leave the road, he spent time in Nashville, walking from the YMCA over to the Peabody campus every day for lessons.[38]

In between studies with Bryan, he often despaired, aching to continue to make progress but unable to afford to leave the revival circuit. In October 1939, Bradley wrote from Toledo, Ohio:

> My way looks so dark right now. . . . I have no friends but Him . . . I know he will make a way for me. I want to come down . . . soon if it is the Lord's will, if I can make some money to pay my

> room and board. I had it bad. My mother took sick and it took every dime I had. Now I don't know what to do. I am up here singing in a revival but not making no money but I have helped save seven souls. If you can tell me what to do I will thank you.[39]

Throughout his career with the National Baptist Convention, it was common for various members of the organization to contribute to Bradley's living expenses. His most faithful patron, the convention's executive secretary, Dr. Arthur Melvin Townsend, sent him money for decades, subsidizing Bradley's inadequate salary.[40]

A few weeks after Bradley wrote to Bryan about his desire to go back to Tennessee for more studies, he wrote again, saying that another patron had withdrawn her support of him:

> Mr. Bryan, will you write Miss Ray and see if she will still help me ... say something good about me (smile). She is mad with me. She gave me $150.00 four months ago and then my mother took sick and you know I was gone to help my mother, she is all I got in this world, so I spent the money and she thought I gave it to some girl. But God in heaven, no, I didn't and I hope you don't feel like that because I did pay the doctor's bill.[41]

In November and December, having moved to Detroit, Bradley wrote again that his only hope in life was to resume his studies with Bryan. By now, having been on the road for nearly seven years, Bradley had experienced the triumphs and tribulations of singing sacred music professionally. He believed Bryan could be his salvation and take him to the next level of musicianship. Bryan, however, did not know any such thing; in fact, by the early 1940s, he was sure he had taught Bradley everything he could, and that the man's remarkable voice could only reach new heights with another, more experienced teacher.[42]

Bryan was also caught up in a rapid advance of his own career, which was moving in unexpected, but welcome, directions. While at Peabody, at just twenty-nine years old, he was offered the directorship of the Tennessee Music Project, a branch of President Franklin Delano Roosevelt's Works Progress Administration (WPA). He abandoned his graduate fellowship for the 1939–1940 academic year in order to take the position, which allowed him to develop ways to give unemployed Tennessee musicians opportunities in education and performance. It also indulged his growing inclination to promote folk music and American composers .[43] It was becoming a passion, this insistence on collecting the music of the people; Bryan heard great beauty in both the lyrics and music of folk songs, in all their manifestations: from simple children's ditties like "Skip to m'Lou" to ballads and field songs, but most especially the sacred music of the hills—the spirituals of both white and black people.

There was a distinction to be made between white spirituals and so-called Negro spirituals, but no one was really certain what it was. This created a new field of scholarship, and Bryan found himself deep in the middle of it, not only academically, but as a musician and composer. For his graduate thesis at Peabody, he wrote *White Spiritual Symphony*, an ethereal and complex orchestration that includes strains of what is commonly acknowledged as the most often-sung spiritual by either race, "Amazing Grace."[44] *White Spiritual Symphony* fully expressed Bryan's inclination to blend the vernacular with the cultivated, but he was not the first composer to do so. Folk songs of all varieties and nationalities had long been motifs in symphonic music, England's Ralph Vaughan Williams being perhaps the most well-known of the great composers who dedicated much of his career to collecting folk music and then incorporating it into new orchestral music.[45]

Bryan graduated from Peabody in 1940, about the same time that the Tennessee Music Project dissolved. He moved up the WPA ranks, being promoted to section chief and then regional head of the Public Activities Program. When that assignment ended in 1942, he moved into the Office of Civilian Defense for the duration of World War II.[46]

Bryan and Bradley continued their correspondence during this time frame, while Bradley toured as a member of the Good Will Singers. In 1942 and 1943, Bradley sent the Bryans postcards and letters from across the country: from Tulsa, Oklahoma; Shreveport, Louisiana; Pensacola, Florida; New York City; and Los Alamos, New Mexico:[47]

> Dear Mrs. Bryan–love to you and to all of the family. This finds me doing fine. For the last two years I have been doing quite a bit of work among the white churches in the U.S. I am trying to make friends with our white brothers and sisters. I believe the world is going to be saved by the people of God. And I know the Negro and the White can get along if we all give it a try. . . I am having a ball out here. The people are going out of their way to make my stay a fine one. This is the home of the Atom! Dr. and Mrs. Oppenheimer came to church to hear me sing Sunday morning and they are real nice people. On the 3rd of May, I will be in Miami, Fla., as guest soloist for the Board Meeting of the Baptist World Alliance. And on Sept. 1st, I am sailing for

> Europe. May the good Lord keep his eyes on you and yours always, Love, J. Robert Bradley. P.S. Not making much money but I am happy. There is no money in church work.[48]

The life of an itinerant musician is never easy, and it was particularly hard for black gospel singers in Jim Crow America.[49] Bradley, like so many of his fellow singers, stayed in friends' guest rooms, YMCAs, the backseats of cars and vans, because hotel accommodations were either unavailable or too expensive for them.[50] He jumped at the chance for steadier work when offered the position of director of the Gospel Choir at Olivet Baptist Church in Chicago, but even then, Bradley figured out ways to progress in his studies.[51] In February 1942, Bryan wrote another of his TPI and Peabody students, H.S. Barnes, now a private in the U.S. Army stationed at Fort Jackson, South Carolina: "J. Robert Bradley spent three months in Nashville on a leave of absence from his Chicago church. While here, we worked out several recitals. He was singing much better than I have ever heard him and I really think that he is going to be one of our most outstanding Negro singers. I made several phonograph records of him so that you can hear him when you come to see us."[52]

Bryan and another Bradley admirer, Louis Nicholas, found a more experienced voice teacher for Bradley in Metropolitan Opera singer Edyth Walker. She made her professional debut in Berlin in 1894 and sang in the Vienna Opera from 1895 to 1903 before returning to New York.[53] Walker, by now retired and living in a Manhattan apartment where she gave private lessons, had tutored the renowned Marian Anderson and Blanche Thebom. Both were idols of Bradley's who reached a higher pinnacle of success for black classical singers of the day than anyone thought possible. Bradley quickly grew enamored of Walker, despite the former diva's stern approach. She used a walking cane, and when Bradley forgot to roll his Rs, she smacked him with it, hard, and he sang the phrase again, getting it right the next time.[54]

Bryan returned to academic studies having won admission to Yale University. Due to the strength of *White Spiritual Symphony* and *Ballad of the Harp Weaver*, renowned German composer Paul Hindemith had agreed to take him on for a year.[55] On his way to New Haven, Connecticut, in September 1945, Bryan spent a day with Bradley. He wrote his wife that:

> . . . the train was about an hour late arriving in NY, and I began to worry about Robert knowing where to meet me. When I went up the first flight of steps there he was, so excited he could hardly talk. We checked my black bag and then caught a subway

> out to see Miss Walker. She was giving a lesson but stopped everything to talk to Robert's teacher. She really thinks he has the finest voice in NY and is all out to help him in every way. He has an official coach and sings for her every few days. She charges $20 per lesson but Robert is getting along with whatever money he can get. He really is in good hands and will have an opportunity to do a lot. He took me to Harlem and you should see his room. It is one of the nicest I have seen and in one of the finest sections of Harlem. He only pays $8 per week. He got it through friends at the Y.M.C.A. The people there spoke highly of him. He spoke to a lot of people he met and seems to have made a lot of friends. We went over his whole plan and it seems good. He is going to night school near his place of living. About four o'clock (I had not had lunch) we went to a very nice place. They all know Robert and they were looking for us. They had flowers on the table and since it was early in the evening we were the only ones. We had very special spaghetti and 2 pork chops each and a lot of other stuff along with it. Robert ordered it all and it was very good.[56]

For a time, the correspondence between Bryan and Bradley appears to have ceased. Both men were busier than ever, and both were destined for Carnegie Hall. Bryan went first. Robert Shaw and the Julliard Chorus and Orchestra premiered Bryan's *Bell Witch Cantata* at Carnegie in April 1947.[57] Bradley attended the performance, as did the Bryans. He wrote to them afterward that "the Bell Witch was more than great. I can only say keep up the good work for the Lord has done something great for you. He gave you a talent to write great music. Keep it up my friend. Your place will be a high one in this big world."[58]

Bradley's debut at Carnegie Hall was likely due at least in part to Edyth Walker, who had been teaching him the art songs of Franz Lizst, Frederic Chopin, and Robert Schumann. She taught Bradley German, Italian, and French, so that he did not simply sing the lyrics but understood them, interpreting them as meaningfully as hymns and spirituals.[59]

On the heels of Bradley's Carnegie Hall debut, a recital was arranged for him back home, at Nashville's War Memorial Auditorium in October 1951. Bradley split the program between the classics, including George Frideric Handel, Wolfgang Amadeus Mozart, Felix Mendelssohn, and Franz Schubert, and traditional hymns "He Knows Just How Much You Can Bear," and spirituals like "Dere's a Man Going Round," and "Goin' to Ride in de Chariot."[60]

The program was unusual. The concert stage was rarely the setting for performances of spirituals, particularly spirituals sung in a cultivated manner, as well as spirituals and hymns accompanying the same program containing European art songs. At the end of the War Memorial recital, one of Bradley's most dedicated supporters, Dr. A.M. Townsend of the National Baptist Convention, approached the stage and demanded an encore: his own arrangement of "Amazing Grace."[61]

Townsend likely felt he had the right to make claims on Bradley. After Bradley's Carnegie Hall debut, he had not asked the singer to continue his studies, but instead had insisted that Bradley come home to the church, to be the standard bearer (and by proxy, salesman) of the *Baptist Standard Hymnal.* On both occasions, Townsend in effect, demanded a return on his investment of all the years he personally supplemented Bradley's income as a National Baptist musician.[62]

Bradley made good on his vow to come home to the church, but in the meantime, he was as determined as ever to continue to learn classical music, the kind of music performed by his idols, Marian Anderson, Paul Robeson, and Roland Hayes. This was not only Bradley's personal ambition; it had been Bryan's directive, too—to go out and share this music with the world.[63]

Mahalia Jackson, arguably the world's finest gospel singer, often made fun of Bradley's ambitions. The two were roommates during Bradley's stint as choir director at the Olivet Baptist Church of Chicago, and they remained friends for the rest of Jackson's life. She told him he would never make the kind of money she enjoyed as a result of her recordings and live appearances. But for Bradley, it was rarely about the money. It was about acceptance and the continual ascension from the Memphis slums. As long as he had a roof over his head and plenty to eat, that was enough.[64]

In 1950 Edyth Walker died at age eighty-three.[65] Bradley was cast adrift. He floundered for a time before latching onto pianist and composer Lawrence Brown, who had accompanied Paul Robeson for years, most notably in England.[66] As he studied with Brown, Bradley began to consider a more formal approach to education. He wrote Bryan again seeking help:

> Dear Friend: It has been sometime since I have heard from you and your family, but we understand each other, we are working in the great field of the Arts which requires all of our time. I hope that you will be pleased at my trying for the Marian Anderson Scholarship. I would appreciate a letter of recommendation from you and the head of the Musical Dept. of Peabody College. I would like to have two copies of each letter, as I am

> also trying for the Thebom Scholarship. I will have to have these recommendations by the 29th of May. I hope this isn't rushing you too much. But you see I have just received the applications.[67]

Bryan, who had not heard from his pupil in some time, responded immediately with a brief note and this recommendation:

> J. Robert Bradley has one of the rarest voices I have ever heard. It was my privilege to work with him for many months and to receive at firsthand a knowledge of his wonderful concept of music, his intense zeal for the art, and his desire to contribute to music in general throughout the country. I have always felt that Mr. Bradley should receive one of the top scholarship awards as he has every qualification usually desired by these worthy foundations. To speak further of his vocal endowments, I need only to say, listen to several of his spirituals. He sings them far better than anyone I have ever heard except the very few who have been fortunate enough to gain world recognition.[68]

It is unclear whether Bradley applied for these or any other scholarships in America. Lawrence Brown was grooming him for a more ambitious endeavor: studies at London's Trinity College, and in August 1952, Bradley set sail onboard the *Queen Elizabeth.* He spent the next four years steadily building a career that eclipsed almost all his previous achievements or anything any African American singer short of Jackson, Anderson, Hayes, or Robeson had managed.[69]

Bradley studied with several teachers at Trinity, including Roger Quilter, whose hymns Bradley had performed in Nashville the previous autumn. The talent agent S.A. Gorlinsky, whose stable included Arturo Toscanini of the Philharmonia Orchestra, heard Bradley in an audition and offered to represent him. Bradley sang for the BBC and, still attached to the National Baptists, summered throughout Europe, performing in Baptist churches from Scotland to Scandinavia.[70]

Meanwhile, back home, Bryan's love affair with folk music deepened. As always, his adoration of the spirituals and other folk music of both races informed his symphonic compositions. Well before his *Bell Witch Cantata* premiered in Carnegie Hall, Bryan performed on the road singing folk songs, playing a dulcimer, and lecturing on the validity and beauty of the "people's music." The dulcimer was a forever-passion with Bryan, who made a similar instrument from a turtle shell and empty coffee can while a youngster. It seemed like an "old-timey," primitive instrument, but no one

Robert Bradley. Credit: Charles Faulkner Bryan collection, Tennessee Tech Archives.

really knew its origins. Bryan made it his mission to research the history of the dulcimer, a common instrument in the Upper Cumberland of his youth.[71]

In 1954, Charles and Edith Bryan decided to make the trip of their dreams, a European tour. At age forty-two Charles had never managed to leave the States, working far too hard and for too little money to afford such an extravagance. The Bryans combined work with pleasure, creating an itinerary that included stops in the Netherlands, France, and elsewhere, places Charles believed held clues to the dulcimer's origins. They included London in their itinerary so they could visit Bradley.[72] On June 10, 1954, Edith wrote their son Charles Jr., and the rest of the family about their adventures:

> This has been a most unusual day–We were up early and ate breakfast. Then Robert Bradley called–we told him we were going to see the Queen in "The Trouping of the Colors," so he said for us to wait and he would come get us. In a little while he drove up in a taxi with his arms loaded with beautiful flowers, which he had sent up to my room. We went down to the Palace and were able to get a place where we saw the parade. First we saw the Queen Mother, Princess Margaret and the children ride out of the palace in an open carriage. Then the guards and then the Queen riding on her horse and waving to all the people. We

> waited outside the Palace and at 1 o'clock the family returned and Charles took some pictures. Robert would hold Charles up on a wall so that he could get a better picture. . . When all of this was over Robert took us to a most elegant place to eat, and I don't know when I have tasted more delicious food. Everyone in the place knew him and came to the table to meet "his (Robert's) first teacher." Robert asked about all of you and especially wanted to know about the children. He is doing VERY well here. He is now living at the home of a Lord somebody (I have forgotten the name). He brought us back to the hotel and now we are waiting to hear from him to see if he has gotten tickets to a play in which one of his friends has a role.[73]

Bradley had, indeed, gotten those tickets. In his diary, Bryan, also wrote about the events of the day:

> This was a wonderful day. We call it Robert's day. He called for us in taxi at hotel with huge bouquet. We rushed down to Whitehead where we watched the Trouping of the Colors, Queen Elizabeth's birthday. It was a wonderful experience. I made about 14 color shots with Robert raising me up above the crowd. Robert then took us to La Boheme restaurant for superb meal. Then to hotel. Went to show at night. Robert got box seats to "The King and I." It was great. Back stage afterwards and met in dressing room Muriel Smith, one of the stars. She autographed program for Betty.[74]

None of them would ever forget this day—and not just because it was such a sweet reunion. June 10, 1954, was to be the last day Bradley and Bryan saw each other.

Charles Bryan was not well, and no one knew for sure what was wrong. For several years, he suffered inexplicable illnesses—sudden swelling around one of his eyes, debilitating headaches, heart palpitations. He had, in fact, been born with a heart murmur; that is what kept him home during World War II. Doctors ruled out allergies, brain cancer, endocarditis, yet still he suffered.[75]

Through it all, he and Edith soldiered on. He slowed his pace, taking on a professorship at a private school in Alabama at a much higher salary and less burdensome workload; that was what allowed him the luxury of extending his performance schedule and eventually making the European excursion. Year after year went by, he never got well, but he rarely let his physical ailment interrupt his career.[76]

In 1953, he completed one of his last great works, the symphonic *Birmingham Suite*. Bryan's biographer, Carolyn Livingston, believes that the composition was Bryan's commentary on civil rights in this country, a movement steadily building momentum since the integration of the military in 1948. As in his *White Spiritual Symphony* of 1940, where Bryan quoted "Amazing Grace," the *Birmingham Suite* referenced white and black spirituals. The second movement, incorporating black spirituals, is bracketed by movements containing fragments of white spirituals. It is no accident, says Livingston, that the music of black America finds itself surrounded by the music of the majority[77]

Meanwhile, across the Atlantic, if Bradley felt overcome by race relations, he never let on, at least not in writing. By now, his Trinity teachers expected Bradley to make his professional debut, and this typically occurred at London's Royal Festival Hall. It was an expensive proposition, however, renting a hall of that size and caliber. Bradley could not begin to pay for it himself. Even though he had gained an English patron—A.E. Johnson, president of the Grundig Corporation—he needed help from his Baptist sponsors, too.[78] He wrote to Bryan in September for an intercession:

> Please look over my long delay in answering your kind letter to Dr. Townsend and to me, but I have been so upset, for as of now I have only received a cablegram from him saying he had received all of our letters and cables and that we would hear from him. That was four weeks ago. The time is going so fast. You know how it is. One cannot help from worrying. This is a very fine letter you wrote him, for which I am more than grateful. I am asking you and Mrs. Bryan to pray for me, for I have so much to do in such a little time. I will be so glad when it is all over, for I do want to see my Mother and Brother. I don't have no new news, only my friend is willing to help put the program over in a big way if we get the help we need from Dr. Townsend. You know yourself, Mr. Bryan, it takes a lot of money to put on a concert anywhere but more so in London. Please don't worry about me. I am going to the end if it takes my life. I will not give up.[79]

One of J. Robert Bradley's teachers, Frank Tittleton, also wrote to Bryan on his student's behalf:

> Forgive me for writing you this urgent letter. Robert received a note from the Dr. that he was sending him further finances some little time ago and up to date nothing has happened and things are somewhat embarrassing for Robert just when we have got

> a very good chance of getting him going in this country. Mr. Johnson is prepared to back him for a recital in the Festival Hall next year at the time of the Baptist gathering in London. S.A. Gorlinksy–a big London agent–heard Robert sing an audition in the Albert Hall and was very pleased with him and hopes to start him off on television and other things to follow, but owing to worrying about finances, it is difficult to get the best out of Robert, just when I am preparing him for these things. Can you possibly let the Dr. know how urgent the matter is. You will be pleased to know there is still great improvement in his voice since you heard him.[80]

The letter campaign proved to be successful. Bradley, nearly giddy with relief, wrote to Bryan on Oct. 27, 1954.

> Your letter of Oct. 20th was received and brought me great joy. I am happy to say that I have received a very fine letter from Dr. Townsend and a check for $1,000 and he said before time for the concert he would give the rest. I cannot tell you know grateful I am to you for all your kindness. May God bless you and your dear family always. I never will forget you as long as I live and will try to show you how grateful I am by doing my best for God and mankind. And I hope and pray how soon the day will come that I can do something nice for you. Here is some good news—I am singing for the Duchess of Kent next month for her charity organization. This is the beginning of my build-up for my concerts. This is not a bad break, is it?[81]

The debut at Royal Festival Hall was scheduled for July 17, 1955. On the heels of this performance, Bradley was slated to open the annual National Baptist Convention for the ten thousand members expected to arrive the next morning at the Royal Albert and Queen Victoria Hall.

Between these performances, still flush with the glory of his London debut and excellent reviews in the London papers, Bradley opened a letter from the Bryans, who were unable to return to London for the performances. The envelope contained a photo from Charles, congratulating Bradley on his London recitals. It also contained a letter from Edith, informing him that Charles had died on July 7, 1955.[82]

Nearly forty years later the Reverend Amos Jones Jr., helped Bradley assemble his memoirs. Jones wrote:

> It was the sorrow songs which propelled J. Robert Bradley into the hearts of the people of the world. Negro spirituals seemed to be especially tailored for him. They evolved from hearts terribly broken from some of life's harshest circumstances. Sickness, death and suffering; loneliness, rejection, and a feeling of abandonment; and injustice, oppression and dehumanization drove Black people of American Slavery to cry tears which flowed from a soul smitten with brokenness, pain, and anguish; a heart overwhelmed with grief, sickness and death. In his personal life, J. Robert experienced all of this [and] it enhanced his singing.[83]

Bradley went onstage to face his Baptist brethren, his face swollen from weeping, and he sang songs from his youth—hymns written by Miss Lucie Campbell—the same hymns his teacher and friend Charles Faulkner Bryan had revered and collected throughout his too-short adult life. Bradley never stopped singing them, even as an old man in retirement. In his eighties, he could still sing, confined to his small Nashville apartment, his voice nearly as strong and easily as poignant, because all those years ago, Charles Bryan had taught him how.[84]

Epilogue

Edith Bryan moved back to McMinnville and lived another forty years in the home of her father-in-law, Falconhurst, where she raised her son Charles "Charlie" Faulkner Bryan Jr.[85] She saw her late husband's work performed by the symphony orchestra named in his honor, the Bryan Symphony Orchestra at Tennessee Technological University, in the concert hall named in his honor, the Bryan Fine Arts Building. This was the campus, in the heart of the Tennessee Upper Cumberland, where Charles Bryan had taught voice lessons to the young Robert Bradley, in spite of any risk to reputation and career.[86]

Music is language, a bond among people of every background. It had certainly sparked the bond between Bryan and Bradley. Edith Bryan knew that her late husband's compositions were a reminder that beauty can be found in all types of music, sometimes where people might least expect it:

> When he became interested in the white spirituals, he wanted to share this music with as many people as possible, and he had the idea of putting them in symphonic form. Charles saw in the *White Spiritual Symphony* the primitive beauty of the folk

> people of the South, and he wanted to share this beauty with the world. He used these songs as thematic material. He'd go to the piano and say, 'What beauty there is in these old songs.' This music is the real heart of the people of the South.[87]

J. Robert Bradley went home to see his mother and brother shortly after his professional debut in London. After Miss Lucie Campbell's death in 1963, he took her place as music director of the National Baptist Convention, doing exactly what Bryan charged him to do: take his music to the world. On behalf of the church, Bradley sang at Billy Graham crusades, National Baptist revivals, and conventions held on five continents. He performed before presidents and kings, one of whom knighted him. He recorded gospel music on record labels including Apollo and Decca, and along the way, he earned the title "Mr. Baptist." Mahalia Jackson once said that after Bradley had sung "Amazing Grace," no one else need try. Bradley sang at Jackson's funeral, nearly causing a riot among the grief-stricken.[88]

When he retired, Bradley went home to his small one-bedroom apartment on Gay Street in Nashville—right across the street from where he had once stayed as a young man studying with Charles Faulkner Bryan at Peabody—and left only for doctor's appointments. He lived on a modest Social Security check, and people from his hometown church, Spruce Street Baptist, came to minister to him and to help him with meals and bathing.[89] In 2003, he explained the allure and significance of vernacular sacred music:

> Negro spirituals. Hymns. Gospel. The blues—they're part of our life; the world's made up of it. Gospel singing is just now coming into its own all over the world. We use it for baptizing and revivals. It's good news—that's what the gospel is. The spiritual was born of trials, tribulations, hunger, beatings, killings. Spirituals gave messages like "I couldn't hear nobody pray. Way down yonder by myself, I couldn't hear nobody pray." Songs like, "He Knows Just How Much You Can Bear." These songs brought us, the black people, through the Depression. We sang. They gave us strength. And even in dying, we would say, "When the saints go marching in, when the saints go marching in, Lord, I want to be in that number, when the saints go marching in." It gave us strength to move, to keep going.
>
> It has to come from the heart. Some days in the National Baptist Convention, I stood and sang for thirty thousand people. And when I opened a white school in Birmingham, Alabama, I said, 'Lord, I don't see nothing in here but salt. Where's the black

pepper?' When I got through singing, the president of the college—the man who gave the money to build the school had said no blacks, no Jews—when I got through singing that day, the president said, 'Mr. Bradley, from THIS day on, you'll see some pepper.'

There's no reason for it, but as I've said before, all nations and races have had slaves since the beginning of time. We're just one more group. But men have to respect men as human beings. If you're in trouble, if I can help you, I'll do it. I don't care what color you are. That's what Jesus was talking about. Help your brother, give him a piece of bread when he's hungry, give him a glass of water when it's hot.[90]

J. Robert Bradley died on May 3, 2007. He lived twice as long as his beloved Charles Faulkner Bryan. At Bradley's funeral, the congregation sang "Amazing Grace," the most popular English hymn in American churches—black and white alike.[91]

NOTES

1. Carolyn Livingston, *Charles Faulkner Bryan: His Life and Music* (Knoxville: University of Tennessee Press, 2003), pp. 33–34.
2. *Ibid.*
3. *Ibid.*
4. Amos Jones Jr., *I Have Always Been in the Hands of God: The Life Story of J. Robert Bradley* (Nashville: Townsend Press, 1993), p. 24
5. Edith Hillis Bryan, Interviewed by Bill Zechman for "The Life and Works of Charles Faulkner Bryan" radio production (McMinnville, Tennessee: Cumberland Valley Broadcasting Company, 1972). The recording available in the Charles Faulkner Bryan Collection of the Tennessee Technological University Archives in Cookeville, Tennessee.
6. Livingston, 34.
7. J. Robert Bradley, Personal interview with the author (Nashville, Tennessee: July 2, 2003).
8. *Ibid.*
9. Jones, 16.
10. Bradley interview, July, 2003.
11. Horace Clarence Boyer, *How Sweet the Sound: The Golden Age of Gospel* (Washington D.C.: Elliott & Clark Publishing, 1995), pp. 41–43.
12. Livingston, 261.
13. Boyer, 7–10, 18–19 and 41–43. The Revival or Camp Meeting Movement of 1800, which began at Cane Ridge in Logan County, Kentucky, just west of the northern reaches of the Upper Cumberland, contributed to a more enthusiastic, often

ecstatic, rendering of hymns. See Paul K. Conkin, *Cane Ridge: America's Pentecost* (Madison: University of Wisconsin Press, 1990).

14. Livingston, 66–68.
15. Jones, 9–14.
16. *Ibid.*, 41–44.
17. Boyer, 41–42, 138–139.
18. Jones, 47–48.
19. Livingston, 101, 117.
20. *Ibid.*, 6, 20.
21. *Ibid.*, 6, 21–22, 24, 29.
22. *Ibid.*, 31.
23. Charles Faulkner Bryan Collection (Cookeville: Tennessee Technological University Archives) RG 42, Box 28, Folder 6, 1939 account book.
24. Bryan interview.
25. Livingston, 31; and Bryan Collection (Box 16, Scrapbook of Charles Faulkner Bryan, 1932–1949). A *Nashville Banner* clipping described a December 1938 TPI Glee Club performance at Vanderbilt to air over WSM and WSIX. Led by Bryan, the chorus was to "contrast Negro and White Folk Spirituals." The program included Bach's "O Sacred Head" and Handel's "Hallelujah Chorus" from The Messiah, as well as "I Have a Mother in the Promised Land" and "Going Over Jordan." Members of the chorus included future Cookeville attorney H.S. Barnes and Captain William Lafayette Anderson, who sang in the special octette for the contrasting spirituals. Both men revered Bryan's legacy and considered him an inspiration.
26. Livingston, 59. "Minutes of the First Meeting of the Tennessee Folklore Society," T.J. Farr Papers, RG 59 (Cookeville, Tennessee: Tennessee Technological University Archives): pp. 1–4
27. Livingston, 31, 32, 39.
28. *Ibid.*, 34; Bradley interview, July, 2003.
29. Bryan Collection, Box 2, Folder 5.
30. Livingston, 34.
31. Bryan Collection, Box 28, Folder 6.
32. Livingston, 34–35.
33. Harvey G. Neufeldt and W. Calvin Dickinson, *The Search for Identity: A History of Tennessee Technological University, 1915–1985* (Memphis: Memphis State University Press, 1991): p. 128.
34. H.S. Barnes, Personal interview with the author (Cookeville, Tennessee: May 11, 2011).
35. Jones, 59.
36. Barnes interview.
37. Bryan Collection, Box 2, Folder 5.
38. J. Robert Bradley. Personal interviews with the author (Nashville, Tennessee: July 2003 and September 10, 2003).
39. Bryan Collection, Box 2, Folder 5.
40. Jones, 187.

41. Bryan Collection, Box 2, Folder 5.
42. *Ibid.*; Jones, 187.
43. Livingston, 46–51.
44. *Ibid.*, 41, 46–53 *passim*, 75; Bryan interview.
45. *Ibid.*, 60. Antonin Dvorak blended American folk songs into his *New World Symphony* while Aaron Copland used the Shaker hymn "Simple Gifts" as a recurring motif throughout *Appalachian Spring.*
46. Livingston, 46–53.
47. Bryan Collection, Box 2, Folder 7.
48. *Ibid.*
49. Boyer, 54–57.
50. Bradley interview, July 2003.
51. Jones, 76.
52. Bryan Collection, Box 2, Folder 6.
53. Michael Kennedy and Joyce Bourne Kennedy, eds., *Oxford Concise Dictionary of Music*, 5th ed. (Oxford, England: Oxford University Press, 2007), p. 801; Livingston, 310.
54. Jones, 88.
55. Livingston, 118. *Ballad of the Harp Weaver* was inspired by the eponymous poem by Edna St. Vincent Millay.
56. Bryan Collection, Box 3, Folder 2.
57. Livingston, 132.
58. Bryan Collection, Box 2, Folder 1. The legend of the Bell Witch originated in Adams, Tennessee, on the Lower Cumberland of Montgomery County, Tennessee. It concerned a scorned woman who haunted the home of John Bell and caused general mischief. Andrew Jackson, according to local lore, confronted her on one occasion.
59. Jones, 90-92.
60. *Ibid.*, 93–94.
61. *Ibid.*, 95.
62. *Ibid.*, 91.
63. *Ibid.*, 128.
64. *Ibid.*, 79; Bradley interview, July, 2003.
65. Kennedy and Bourne, 801.
66. Jones, 101–104.
67. Bryan Collection, Box 5, Folder 1.
68. *Ibid.*
69. Jones 105, 214.
70. *Ibid.*, 93–94, 111–115, 123–124.
71. Livingston, 9, 133, 180-184, 237.
72. *Ibid.*, 237.
73. Bryan Collection, Box 7, Folder 2.
74. Bryan Collection, Box 18, Folder 14, 1954 diary.
75. Livingston, 234–236.
76. *Ibid.*, 213.

77. *Ibid.*, 151–154.
78. Jones, 129–133.
79. Bryan Collection, Box 7, Folder 3.
80. *Ibid.*
81. *Ibid.*
82. Jones, 135.
83. *Ibid.*, 146.
84. *Ibid.*
85. Interview with Charles F. Bryan Jr. (Cookeville, Tennessee, October 5, 2013). Charlie Bryan has few memories of his father since he was a child when his father died. He has fond memories of his mother and his grandfather. They instilled in him a love of history that led him to become a Civil War scholar and pursue a PhD, and later serve as the executive director of the prestigious Virginia Historical Society.
86. Livingston, 240-247.
87. Bryan interview.
88. Jon Pareles, "J. Robert Bradley, 87, Charismatic Gospel Singer, Dies," *New York Times* (May 4, 2007); and Boyer, 144–145.
89. Bradley interview, July 2003.
90. Bradley interview, September 2003.
91. Program of J. Robert Bradley's "Homecoming Celebration," found online at: jrobertbradley.com/homecoming_celebration.html On the occasion of the 50th anniversary of the Bryan Symphony Orchestra the concert season ended with the first performance of the *The Bell Witch Cantata* since the death of Charles Faulkner Bryan.

15

"As Long as Your Money is Green"

John's Place and Race Relations in the Upper Cumberland

Michael E. Birdwell

Since the end of the Civil War, the history of race relations in the Upper Cumberland has been fraught with difficulties and prejudice. Over the intervening years a number of African Americans and their white counterparts have labored to improve relations between the communities. John Lee McClellan, an African American businessman, worked diligently to find common ground among the races and was the first black man elected to public office in Putnam County, Tennessee. His brother Ed established an African American café and grocery, originally known as Ed's Place in 1949, in the black community of Cookeville. He later sold the operation to John Lee. From its inception, Ed's/John's Place catered to an integrated clientele in spite of the fact that Cookeville and Putnam County were segregated by lingering Jim Crow statutes. Through his calm, deliberate demeanor, John Lee earned the respect of the larger white community. He acted as the unofficial liaison along the county's racial divide. Though John's Place seemed little more than a honky-tonk or beer joint to the uninformed, it played a significant role in the history of post-World War II Cookeville, Putnam County, Tennessee Technological University, and the Upper Cumberland.

In the antebellum period, the Upper Cumberland region primarily consisted of small subsistence farms tended by individual families. Planters were a rarity in the Upper Cumberland due to the irregular terrain and poor soil. Most slave holders owned fewer than ten slaves, and they primarily settled along river bottoms in Jackson, Smith, White, and Warren counties in Tennessee, where land was more fertile. As a result of this, the slave population of the Upper Cumberland was relatively small, especially when compared to the labor-intensive areas of the Central Basin west of the Eastern Highland Rim. Freed blacks, however, established a few self-sustaining communities such as Free Hill in Clay County and Free State in Jackson County. The African American population of the Upper

Cumberland remained small and relatively stable throughout the antebellum period. During Reconstruction some serious racial incidents occurred as frustrated ex-Confederates focused their anger on freedmen. Governor William G. "Parson" Brownlow declared martial law in Overton and Jackson Counties to suppress Ku Klux Klan (KKK) violence.

The rise of black leaders like John Lee McClellan was a long time coming. Antipathy toward African Americans permeated portions of the Tennessee Upper Cumberland, largely due to ignorance and the lack of opportunity to interact with black people. The period immediately following the Civil War up to the advent of World War I witnessed an alarming exodus of black citizens fleeing the Upper Cumberland. Many were forced out of their homes, while others considered it prudent to leave. When investigating the history of race relations on the Cumberland Plateau, one is struck by the insensitivity and hatred focused toward black people.

In the late nineteenth century civic boosters in Cumberland County published broadsides to attract businesses and individuals to relocate on the plateau and Highland Rim. S.C. Bishop, editor of the *Crossville Chronicle,* boasted that there was "Not a negro in the county, no mosquitoes and no malaria."[1] Cumberland County's deeply conservative and clannish Browntown Community hosted an active cell of the KKK into the late twentieth century. Billboards stationed along roadsides at each county line bordering Cumberland County warned black people to leave before nightfall or suffer the consequences. Likewise, other Upper Cumberland counties, like Scott and Morgan lying along the Kentucky border, were dotted with billboards advising African Americans to keep moving, though few ever ventured into either county.[2]

In the post-bellum period, several Upper Cumberland counties in Kentucky and Tennessee experienced what historian James Loewen identified as "The Great Retreat," where the African American populations dwindled to the point that some counties had no blacks living within their borders by the 1930s.[3] Jim Crow legislation, upheld by the U.S. Supreme Court in such cases as *U.S. v. Cruikshank* (1877), *Plessy v. Ferguson* (1896), *Williams v. Mississippi* (1898), *Berea College v. Kentucky* (1908), made life more difficult for African Americans in the Upper Cumberland. In an atmosphere where blacks were systematically deprived of their Thirteenth, Fourteenth, and Fifthteenth Amendment rights their future in the region looked bleak. In the Kentucky Upper Cumberland the black population in 1960 represented only 0.2 percent of what it had been in 1890. As Loewen observed, "Throughout the plateau this decline was forced."[4] Jim Crow legislation and physical intimidation prompted a number of African Americans to leave the region for fear of their lives. From 1877 forward the black population decreased precipitously. As late as 2011, several Upper Cumberland counties had not one black person living within their borders. In 1950 the African American population of the fourteen counties in the Tennessee Upper Cumberland numbered only 4,269. A decade later Putnam County's entire black population totaled only 528, less than two percent of the county's population. According to the 2000 census the black population of the Upper Cumberland dwindled to 3,858 out of a total population of 304,998.

Though historically small in number, the black community made significant contributions to the region's history and culture. John Lee McClellan traced his ancestors back to emancipated African Americans in the Free State community on the Cumberland River. By the mid 1930s, however, the McClellan family left for more hospitable treatment in West Cookeville.[5] Shortly after they left, Jackson County's black population disappeared completely. John Lee McClellan, who encountered racial prejudice and intimidation, pioneered modern race relations in the region, setting an example often emulated by his successors.[6]

John Lee McClellan was not the first Upper Cumberland pioneer for African American rights by any means. In sharp contrast to the implicit and explicit racism that permeated the region, acceptance and tolerance crop up in historic records. At Silver Point, Tennessee, in western Putnam County a black community thrived in spite of Jim Crow. There black and white people got along well. They helped each other at times of harvest and in times of trouble. Friendships transcended race.

Independent and self-sufficient, the black community at Silver Point came to the attention of the newly created Church of Christ. Organized in

John Lee McClellan.
Credit: Mary Alice McClellan.

1906, it grew out of tensions within the Disciples of Christ over a number of doctrinal issues, among them: ordination of ministers, purpose of baptism, instrumental music in worship, and congregational autonomy. A significant number of African Americans embraced the "Restoration Movement," associated with the Church of Christ. Three black former Disciples of Christ ministers—including the aptly named Alexander Campbell, Sam Womack, and the forceful, charismatic, one-armed G.P. (George Phillip) Bowser (1875–1950)—led the way in founding the Church of Christ among African Americans. It was Bowser, however, who had the greatest impact in the Upper Cumberland.

A native of Maury County, Tennessee, G.P. Bowser's father died when he was a child and his mother, Cherry Elizabeth Bowser, raised five children as a single parent. Lacking formal education, she was determined that her children would have one. She moved to Nashville and enrolled them in Walden University, a Freedman Aid school sponsored by the Methodist Church.[7] A highly intelligent student, Bowser mastered six languages by the time he graduated from college—English, French, German, Greek, Hebrew, and Latin. Destined to preach, he became an exhorter in the Methodist Church in 1893, and was ordained in 1895, serving his first congregation in Cleveland, Tennessee. His initial foray leading a congregation went poorly. Racial prejudice hindered his abilities to do what he considered necessary to be an effective pastor, and Bowser soon returned to Middle Tennessee.

In 1896 he suffered a personal tragedy when courting his future wife, Fannie Billips. While crossing adjoining train tracks, Bowser was struck by an oncoming train, which broke one leg in two places and severely mangled his left arm. The leg healed poorly and he walked with a permanent limp, while his arm had to be amputated above the elbow.[8]

For personal reasons, Bowser grew disheartened with the Methodist Church and abandoned the ministry. He drifted around looking for a more satisfying religious experience, and attended a number of other denominations, including Baptist and Disciples of Christ churches. He was baptized into the Disciples of Christ by immersion in 1897. Taking an active role in his adopted church, Bowser launched *The Christian Echo* in 1902, the first journal targeted at black members of the Disciples of Christ. He considered the periodical an effective means of connecting African American congregations. A successful forum for ideas and their expression, *The Christian Echo* weighed into the debates that resulted in the creation of the Church of Christ in 1906. After joining the Church of Christ, Bowser transformed *The Christian Echo* into the black equivalent of David Lipscomb's *Gospel Advocate*. In 1907, Bowser and Sam Womack established the first Church of

Christ-sponsored school for African American children on Jackson Street in Nashville. Though the school got off to a rocky start, it emboldened Bowser. He recognized the advantages an education afforded him and was determined to provide formal instruction to black children regardless of their financial situation. In an era of separate but unequal Bowser faced an uphill battle, but the school he and Womack established grew steadily. Through the school on Jackson Street Bowser developed a model that could be reproduced elsewhere.

Flush with the success of the Nashville school he and Womack moved their families to Silver Point in 1909, to establish the Putnam County Normal, Industrial, and Orphan School, commonly known as the Silver Point Christian Institute. It acted as a public, not private, school and the campus included dormitories for males and females, a dining hall, the Laurel Hill Church of Christ, and the office/print shop for *The Christian Echo.* Bowser quickly became well known and respected in Silver Point and Cookeville. An effective negotiator, he brokered a deal with Putnam County officials to provide a modicum of financial support for the school. He convinced commissioners that the Silver Point Christian Institute was necessary and provided a vital service to the county. They agreed to provide modest revenue for up to four months annually. Students from Silver Point and beyond received a classically-based education, supplemented with practical trade skills through hands-on activities.[9]

For Bowser, Silver Point presented the ideal location for his mission to educate African Americans and challenge the racial prejudice he had experienced in Cleveland and Nashville. As biographer Vernon Boyd observed:

> The residents of the community [Silver Point] were unusual in that there seemed to be several white people with a mild attitude toward race. . . In Silver Point, some whites, but not all, openly admitted that a black relative was their cousin or aunt, etc., and visited and socialized freely back and forth. This was in sharp contrast to the nearby town of Baxter which had very bitter opinions about blacks. . . . But in Silver Point the white people were tolerant and peaceful.[10]

Silver Point Christian Institute, in western Putnam County, lay between the Walton Road (current Highway 70) and the Tennessee Central Railway, the two main east-west arteries across the county. Wagons and trains stopped there frequently and black and white members of the Silver Point community often intermingled at area businesses or at the railroad siding.[11] Black people operated freely in the Silver Point community without fear of molestation, and set the tone for future race relations in Putnam County and the region.[12]

Bowser bristled at the injustices of Jim Crow. Like W.E.B. Du Bois—who once taught school at nearby Alexandria, Tennessee, before moving on to create the National Association for the Advancement of Colored People (NAACP)—Bowser believed that the key to success for African Americans and improving race relations lay in education. He encouraged students at Silver Point to be respectful and courteous, but to also stand up for their rights. Bowser, who refused to enter commercial establishments through the back door or in any way demean himself, found life comfortable in Silver Point.[13] He earned the respect of the black and white communities through his sincerity and conviction; everyone referred to him as "Brother Bowser."[14] The one-armed black man with a pronounced limp "never turned anyone away from school. People were never too old or too young for him to try to help them," and race simply was not an issue in Silver Point and some other parts of Putnam County.[15] The school prospered until adversely affected by World War I. The war siphoned off students, much needed materials, and people from the Silver Point community who went into service, or moved away to work in wartime industries. Bowser tendered his resignation in 1918, and moved to Louisville, Kentucky.[16] Even so, the educational experiment in Silver Point helped lay the foundation for the creation of Darwin School in Cookeville, which educated black children from several surrounding counties for many years.[17]

In the early days of the Civil Rights movement the attitudes of a number of people in the Upper Cumberland towards race relations took a turn for the worse. Esther Sharp Sanderson, who published *County Scott and Its Mountain Folk* in 1958, observed: "In general the people of Scott County did not want slaves, neither did they like the Negro. After the slaves were freed, most of them moved out of Scott County to sections where there were more Negroes." By the turn of the twentieth century only one black couple remained in the county and "with their passing. . . the people had built up an aversion to all outside Negroes—they did not intend for them to ever get a foothold in the county. . . There is not a colored family living in Scott County at the present time."[18] That attitude prevailed in Cumberland, Fentress, Jackson, Macon, Morgan, Pickett, and Van Buren counties for decades.

Sanderson illustrated the antipathy held toward African Americans. She noted that eight hundred black mining families lived at Coal Hill and Glen Mary in 1907 in Scott County. Violence erupted when a white man was shot and local residents focused their rage on the black communities. "Negroes were only given two weeks to liquidate their holdings and leave the county. When they left others were not allowed to come back."

In neighboring Morgan County, as in Cumberland County, a sign on the county line threatened: "*Nigger don't let the sun set on your head.* They rarely ever passed through; if they did they made haste to get through."[19]

Decades later when Martin Luther King Jr. and Ralph Abernathy traveled from Georgia to attend workshops at Myles Horton's Highlander Folk School in nearby Grundy County, Tennessee, in 1957, billboards and brochures condemned Horton and his school. Critics alleged that Horton was a Communist and his school a bastion of Marxist sedition. Horton, who studied at Union Theological Seminary under the noted scholar-philosopher Reinhold Neibuhr, took his mentor's belief in social justice to heart. Not only did Horton teach nonviolent civil disobedience, he promoted equality among the races, upending the years-long tradition of Jim Crow. Horton and his students fomented insurrection in the eyes of those whose pathological hatred was simply based on skin color. Animosities stirred up by such groups eventually led to the closing of Highlander, forcing Myles Horton to leave the Upper Cumberland and relocate at New Market, Tennessee.[20]

Similarly Fentress County, former home of John Clemons, father of Mark Twain and the birthplace of Alvin C. York, endures a checkered reputation when it comes to race. Dr. Carl Owens, an African American professor of curriculum and instruction at Tennessee Technological University (TTU), who was raised in Birmingham, Alabama, in the 1960s, was quite familiar with racial prejudice. Even he was not prepared for the way some people in the Upper Cumberland interacted with him. He was stunned when he visited Jamestown for the first time in the 1980s. Sent there to conduct a technology assessment of York Institute, Owens stopped at a local store en route. People in the store, many of whom had never seen a black person except on television, stared at him as if he were a creature from outer space. As he wandered through the store with all eyes on him, Owens noticed a T-shirt displayed on the wall with an image of several Klansmen in hoods and capes. The legend on the shirt read, "The original Boys in the Hood." Owens, horrified and somewhat bemused by the T-shirt, opted to commute from Cookeville everyday until the assessment was completed instead of spending a single night in Jamestown.[21]

The racial divide was obvious to anyone willing to observe. Most black people in Cookeville lived in a small community adjacent to Highway 70, derisively referred to as "Bush Town."[22] Cookeville accepted Jim Crow legislation, and the town was dotted with segregated waiting rooms, rest rooms, and drinking fountains. "Colored Only" signs marked areas where blacks could congregate, wait for a train, or other such things. Their public movements were severely limited. Most African Americans could not eat in the town's restaurants, in spite of the fact that many cooks who prepared the meals were black. In Putnam County blacks had few options when it came to employment. They worked as day laborers, field hands, custodians, and toiled at various forms of menial labor. The Drake Hotel's staff included a black butler, maid, and janitor. Black people worked in homes of prominent white citizens, doing laundry, cooking, cleaning, and providing manual labor. Many places were simply off-limits to black folk in Putnam County and its immediate environs. While the Princess Theatre allowed black patrons to attend movies, they were forced to enter through a separate doorway tucked in the alley adjacent to Church Street, and they were confined to seats in the balcony.[23]

Though black and white people got along to a degree across Putnam County—with the exception of Baxter—racial lines were clearly drawn. Black communities in Cookeville, Algood, and Silver Point represented quasi-self sufficient islands surrounded by a sea of white people. Out of necessity and with the aid of some sympathetic white citizens like Charles Darwin, they created their own outlets for entertainment, socialization, and business. Though most public social events centered around church activities, Putnam County's African American communities developed a number of secular organizations as well. They had their own annual county fair at Putnam County's Colored Fair Grounds.[24] The annual fair mirrored the White County fair with competitions, pageants, music, and rides. Blacks had their own youth baseball and adult softball leagues; John Lee McClellan sponsored a team every year until his death. Ball fields were located on the east side of Gibson Avenue directly across the street from John's Place.[25]

Within that context John's Place played an important role racially and culturally in the history of the Upper Cumberland region. Well-respected in the African American community, John Lee McClellan earned a reputation as an astute businessman and local civic leader. In addition to operating John's Place in Cookeville, he managed the Hooker Funeral Home in Algood. In those two capacities McClellan interacted with the larger white community daily.[26] He worked tirelessly with both the black and white populations to bring integration peacefully to Cookeville. After the historic African American Darwin School burned down in 1963, McClellan acted as the point man for the black community. Working closely with the Putnam County School Board, the mayor, and key business leaders, McClellan argued against rebuilding Darwin School. Largely due to his efforts Cookeville public schools desegregated without any serious racial incidents.[27]

John Lee McClellan made Putnam County history when he became the first African American elected to the Putnam County Court as a justice of the peace in 1968. As Robert Farley, a close friend, said, "Everybody knew

John McClellan."[28] Due to his inclusive attitudes John's Place became a popular integrated hangout, attracting scores of Tennessee Tech students and faculty from the mid-1960s until the 1990s, when competition from chain restaurants and other establishments caused a sharp decline in its clientele.

Ed McClellan's son, John "Shakey" McClellan, took over the business after John Lee McClellan died of cancer in 1973. Shakey often boasted: "John's Place did more for integration and the Civil Rights movement here [Cookeville and the surrounding region] than the politicians. Lots of people around here, you know Crossville or Jamestown, never saw a black man or woman till they came to John's. This place integrated the Upper Cumberland. Lots of people met their future wives or husbands here. Lots of friendships that remain began here. We put a lot of people—black and white, through Tennessee Tech."[29]

Originally known as Ed's Place, the business first belonged to John Lee McClellan's brother Ed. Constructed in 1949, by local contractors, the simple cinder block building originally served as the African American community's second grocery store on the outskirts of Cookeville's West Side.[30] In 1950, Ed applied for a license to sell packaged beer in his grocery. When he

Ed's Place. Credit: Steve Farley.

obtained the license, Ed partitioned the building into two businesses. The grocery store occupied the north side while a restaurant took up the south side of the structure. At that point, the beer license stipulated that alcoholic beer not be consumed on the premises. Three years later, on April 13, 1953, the Putnam County Beer Board revoked Ed McClellan's license. Though he had broken no laws, the Beer Board canceled his permit because of his building's proximity to Wright's Chapel Methodist Church, which was less than one thousand feet away.[31] To charge Ed with violation of the county ordinance after three years of successful operation smacked of duplicity. According to local lore in the black community, Putnam County sheriff Ernest Webster spearheaded the movement to revoke Ed's license, arguing that selling beer to African Americans created a "public menace."[32]

For the next four years Ed's Place operated as a restaurant and grocery store. Due to its location on Highway 70, Ed's restaurant flourished, serving meals to an integrated clientele from its inception. The quality of the food and the friendliness of the staff made Ed' Place a favorite restaurant for truck drivers and other business people passing through. Known for its down-home cooking, Ed's Place featured traditional southern fare such as fried chicken, fried catfish, meat loaf, pork chops, pig's feet, chili, back bone, beef stew, liver and onions, hamburgers, fried corn, turnip and collard greens, pinto beans, green beans, mashed potatoes, French fries, fried okra, corn bread, biscuits, cold cut sandwiches, fried apples, fried pies, a variety of cakes and cobblers, and sweet iced tea or fountain drinks. Ed enlisted the entire McClellan family and everyone worked in the restaurant. His son, Charles Edward, bused the tables and swept the floors. Ed's wife Mary Lou and his daughter Elizabeth ran the kitchen. With the help of Bea McClellan, Lilly B. Bohannon, and Naomi Hale the women prepared meals from scratch each day.[33]

Before the mantra of "Buy Local, Eat Local," most vegetables served at Ed's Place came from neighborhood gardens, and if anything came out of a can it was not processed and massed produced in a factory somewhere far away. Vegetables, fruit, sausage, and the like were canned by African American women from West Cookeville in their own home kitchens, and later served at Ed's Place. All of the meat came from neighboring farms and was cut to order at local butcher shops.[34]

As Robert Farley noted:

> From the beginning this was a place where black and white folk were welcome. Ed did that. We had workers, mill hands, coming here to eat. Lots of traffic came through here on Highway 70. We didn't have an Interstate. Lots of people stopped in here on

> their way from one place to another. Word got around about this place, you know. This place had a steady clientele for years. I've seen it packed wall to wall with people. . . It's had an impact, in a good way, for a lot of life.[35]

With loyal patrons increasing in number, local residents in West Cookeville urged Ed to try to secure a new license to sell packaged beer. Encouraged by their support Ed circulated a petition among his friends and neighbors in 1957, which he submitted to the Putnam County Beer Board. Realizing that the deck would be stacked against him if the only signatories were black, Ed solicited some powerful leaders from the larger white community who gladly endorsed his petition. Ed prepared and delivered a formal request to the Beer Board with a signed statement, asking them to restore his beer license. It said in part:

> I am the owner of the premises and will conduct the operation of the business personally. I have not been convicted of any violation of the liquor law or of any crime involving moral turpitude during my entire life, and if granted this limited permit, I would rigidly enforce the law. . . I do not operate a dance hall in connection with or adjacent to the building, neither do I rent cabins in connection with or adjacent to the said business. I will not permit drunks, loose women or lawless characters to congregate at my place of business. . . [If granted a license I] will operate my business so as not to interfere with the public health, safety or morals."[36]

At the same time members of the black community circulated a petition of their own, which they submitted to the Beer Board. Their complaint was more pointed. They urged the Beer Board to grant a new license to Ed McClellan and his brother John, allowing them to sell beer "in packaging only, none to be consumed on the premises."[37] Attesting to the upstanding character of the McClellan brothers, honest businessmen, and community leaders, the petitioners argued:

> We have our own churches and our own schools and so far as we know none of the colored race lives within the corporate limits of Cookeville, and due to this fact there is no public place in Putnam County where the colored race can procure their requirements and we feel that it is practically a matter of spite that their permits were revoked and they being the only colored

> people in Putnam County who handle beer, we deeply feel this is an injustice in being thus restricted, and that all the colored people in the whole immediate vicinity feel like they should have a right to this privilege and not be discriminated against because they are colored folks . . . we deeply feel the colored people should have in their immediate section the same rights and privileges as is granted to other citizens.[38]

Significantly, one who signed was the Reverend Jesse P. Miller, pastor of Wright's Chapel Methodist Church, which was across the parking lot from Ed's Place. The McClellan brothers received a new license to sell packaged beer in the store adjacent to the restaurant as a result of the aforementioned efforts and the support of certain individuals from the white community who worked behind the scenes, including Clarence Newman, Bethel Newport, and T.C. Huddleston. The brothers agreed to rename their business "John's Place," upon the receipt of the new license.[39] Ed's name continued to be associated with a business across the street, Ed's Dairy Mart. In the days before McDonald's and other fast food franchises opened south of Cookeville near Interstate 40, Ed's Dairy Mart represented Cookeville's version of affordable take out food. Unlike his former restaurant across the street, the Dairy Mart had no seats and people lined up at a window to get their hamburgers to go. Like Ed's Place, Ed's Dairy Mart was an integrated establishment from its inception, serving hamburgers, French fries, and milk shakes to people of all ages and races.[40]

When the beer license issued in 1957 was later renewed, it granted John Lee McClellan broader privileges. He received permission to open a bar on the premises in the early 1960s, making it one of the first taverns in Putnam County since World War II. During the Tennessee Maneuvers, Cookeville was a designated R&R (rest and relaxation) destination and thousands of troops poured into the town at the end of each week's exercises. In addition to establishing a USO at Menzie's Shoe Factory, the Cookeville City Commission amended its prohibition laws for the duration of the exercises. Cookeville movie theatres opened on Sunday for the first time in their history and "beer gardens opened and establishments such as Poppy's Billiards and the Fox Café on the West Side advertised: 'Cold Beer, 5 cents.'"[41] Local folklore incorrectly dates the creation of John's Place as concurrent with the Tennessee Maneuvers, which supposedly provided an R&R facility for African American troops.[42]

For black troops the local USO near the Cookeville train depot was off limits, as were most of the other recreational facilities. The black citizens of Cookeville fed and entertained black troops in their homes, churches, and

Exterior of John's Place. Credit: Michael E. Birdwell.

the Colored Fair Grounds and played sports with them at the Colored Ball Fields. They also used the Darwin School as a gathering place to socialize. The sight of black men in uniform filled the small African American community with pride, especially when they came from Cookeville.[43]

Once the maneuvers ended, however, "the Putnam County Beer Board voted to revoke the beer permits for all establishments in the county. It says it will issue no more."[44] After that action, the Putnam County Beer board looked at beer permits with a jaundiced eye, equating the consumption of alcohol with depravity and lassitude. The fact that Ed McClellan was granted a permit at all speaks to his esteem in the community. The cavalier attitude and capriciousness of the Putnam County Beer Board actually provided an opportunity for the McClellan brothers. In the April meeting the board rejected every request for permits that came before them. County Judge Tom Haile criticized their actions because the board members denied all requests "on the grounds that 'all beer places are nuisances.'" Haile cautioned the board, saying that newly passed legislation in Tennessee required "a specific reason when applications are rejected," and he predicted that "lawsuits will now result in more taverns here."[45] While Haile's prediction proved untrue, it did result in Ed's Place making the transition from a package store into a pub.

Determined to upgrade the business, John Lee and friends renovated the building shortly after receipt of the new license. The partition between the restaurant and grocery store was removed and a horseshoe bar, designed

"Sitting along the original bar." Credit: Steve Farley.

by John Lee, was installed in 1963. The bar's configuration made it easier for employees to serve customers, and for thirsty patrons to interact with each other. Several people commented that when John began selling beer for on-site consumption, "he was strict."[46] He instituted a policy demanding that people act appropriately. If someone got drunk or started causing trouble, John Lee had them removed from the premises; once ejected, they were banned for life. On a few occasions John Lee called the sheriff's office for assistance.

After John's Place became a tavern, John Lee cultivated a working relationship with the new sheriff, Bill Bilyeau. They became good friends, and if the sheriff had a problem with anyone in the black community, he engaged John Lee's assistance in the matter. John Lee addressed the situation and took care of the problem. He became, in essence, the de facto law enforcement official for the African American community in Cookeville. While he never used physical force, John Lee proved intimidating due to his physical size and his demeanor.[47]

Though John's Place continued to provide southern cooking, John Lee wanted to create a signature food item for his establishment in 1964 that could be prepared quickly and easily. With family members he devised a special recipe and took it to Foutch's Meats. James Foutch worked with McClellan to perfect and mass produce the "John Dog."[48] Though no longer made locally, the signature short, fat, hot dog in a deep-red casing, remains the staple dish at John's Place. Split lengthwise and steamed in beer, the dog is dressed with John's homemade relish that remains a closely guarded family secret. Served mild, hot, or hot-hot, John Dogs have been a local favorite for nearly fifty years. Shakey McClellan personally prepared the signature relish in all of its permutations every Saturday until shortly before his death. For the hot relish he cut up jalapenos and habaneros with a pair of scissors, mixing them with yellow mustard, minced dill pickles, and other ingredients.

Demand for the John Dog grew precipitously, prompting John Lee to install a drive-in window. Though lots of people loved John Dogs, some white folk did not want to be seen emerging from a black establishment or a business that sold beer. The drive-in window allowed those who frowned on drinking to buy the hot dogs they craved without fear of social stigma. John Dogs achieved a degree of world fame. Every time the Tech Rugby team travels abroad, John Dogs go with them, and they have been eaten throughout the United States, British Isles, and New Zealand. John Dogs continue to satisfy people's hunger and were recently featured at a fund raiser for Cookeville's PBS affiliate WCTE.[49] Shakey McClellan added his own signature dish to the John's menu when he created his own hot pickled egg recipe. Like the John Dog, its ingredients remain a closely guarded family secret.

Robert Farley agreed with Shakey that many students who came to Tennessee Tech from the Cumberland Plateau had little, if any, interaction with African Americans before moving to Cookeville. He argued, however, that "they might have seen their first black person in the cafeteria at Tech. All of the cooks at Tech were black until recently. The Gist family, the Gardenhires, the Woodses, they all fed Tech students for years."[50] He continued, "Yes, it's true. John's Place sure did allow blacks and whites to mingle and there never was a bit of trouble. . . Everybody was welcome here. We didn't care what color you were as long as your money was green . . . People could mix here and just be themselves. I can't recall a single episode of racial tension here, not one."[51]

In that respect, Cookeville differed tremendously from most of the Upper Cumberland. While the African American population was minuscule in the region, blacks tended to receive better treatment in Cookeville than other towns and villages in the Upper Cumberland. In an interview with Mark Dudney, Shakey McClellan, who was born in 1940, stated that race relations in Cookeville were "very good. . . we never had any racial problems, you know, as far as I know, when I was raised up. It's never been any problem at all, a lot like it is now."[52] As a child he endured the stigma of segregation, attending the all black Darwin School, which had dedicated teachers with outdated texts and equipment. He remembered not being allowed to walk in the front door of white-owned businesses, having to sit in the balcony of the Princess Theatre, and separate waiting rooms at the doctor's office. Yet, he was not bitter. In spite of the depredations he had a happy childhood, and he witnessed white people interacting with blacks in generally positive ways.[53]

When asked about his experiences elsewhere he noted that he experienced racial intolerance while in the army and stationed in Mount Clement, Michigan. His overall military experience was generally positive. The army had been integrated for over a decade when he went in, and his best friend in the service was a white man from Columbia, South Carolina. The racism he witnessed came from the civilian population, not his brothers in arms.[54]

In college at Austin Peay State University, Shakey was one of only two African Americans on the basketball team. Though he found Clarksville, Tennessee, agreeable, the two black men endured racist attitudes and epithets when traveling on the road. Because a restaurant in Smithville, Tennessee, refused to serve the two black students, Coach Ed Fisher and the team walked out, saying that they would not eat anywhere that refused to serve the whole team. Fisher's stance made a huge impression on Shakey in those early days of the Civil Rights movement.[55]

Until 1967, the unincorporated black community lay just west of Cookeville's city limits. Annexation by Cookeville proved to be beneficial to both the black and white communities. Bobby Davis, a Cookeville pharmacist, was mayor at the time and saw an opportunity to improve living conditions for the black neighborhood and update the local hospital's facilities. Thanks to President Lyndon Baines Johnson's Great Society, federal funds were available through his War on Poverty and other grant-in-aid programs. Roads in the black community were abysmal with many unpaved. Black residents had no sewer system. Most people got their water from wells, many of which were contaminated. "What was unusual about West Cookeville was that most of those people owned their own property," Davis said, so that procuring War on Poverty funds offered a real opportunity to improve their quality of life.[56] John Lee McClellan assisted Davis immensely as they moved forward. The city applied for a grant through the Model Cities Program and received the Hospital-West Cookeville Urban Renewal Grant, which made it possible to improve existing roads in West Cookeville, build new ones, and add sidewalks in that section of town for the first time. The grant connected the black community to the city's sewer system and provided fluoridated water through new water lines. Many took advantage of other new federal programs, which made it possible for many black families to renovate their homes or even build a new house on the same property. The overall result was a general improvement in the basic quality of life for the black community, whose health suffered for years due to the harsh conditions in which they lived. The program added to John Lee McClellan's visibility in both the black and white communities as a public-minded civic leader.[57] When West Cookeville was annexed John's Place became the first business that could legally sell beer within the city limits since World War II.

During the 1960s and 1970s John Lee and Shakey McClellan took a personal interest in Tennessee Tech. Shakey was the second African American who enrolled at TTU in 1964 who did not play sports.[58] Though he did not attend Tech on an athletic scholarship, Shakey was an ardent supporter of Golden Eagles athletic teams, and in 2009 he was posthumously inducted into Tennessee Tech's Sports Hall of Fame.[59] Russell Clarkson, who enrolled at TTU in 1964, said Shakey was the first black student he encountered in his life, and they had several classes together. Clarkson and Shakey became life-long friends. In 1972 Clarkson went to work for Estes "Rooster" Williams, owner of the local Budweiser Distributorship and later married Williams daughter. "We made deliveries to John's Place six days a week. It was the only place we stocked everyday, because they sold more beer than any other business we serviced."[60]

In those days, Clarkson said, John's had a variety of distinct clientele. The business opened at 7:00 a.m. and older black couples began filing into the place. They ordered breakfast, which consisted mainly of egg dishes and coffee. Some of the men ordered a quart of beer which they nursed for three hours. During that time they caught up on local gossip, talked about the world's problems, and simply enjoyed each others' company. After ten the clientele were integrated. There was generally a lull from ten to eleven. The time from eleven to one was generally a hectic time full of activity. The lunch crowd showed up inside and outside the building. Cars lined up to order sacks of John Dogs and chips at the drive-in window, while workers of various stripes gathered inside to eat lunch and visit. Then the second lull of the day transpired between one and three. Blue collar workers, both black and white, began showing up between three and five to have a beer and a snack before going home to supper. As the blue collar workers filed out the "suits started showing up," and professionals—doctors, lawyers, ministers, and professors—took their places at the bar or booths, remaining until 6:30 or 7:00 p.m. After seven and until closing time at midnight a different crowd, primarily Tech students and staff, took over. John's Place was popular with people from all walks of life and bridged the gap between the races and the social classes.[61]

Clarkson, who grew up in segregated Alabama, was amazed to see such easy interaction among blacks and whites. Clarkson noted that "there are still two places in most of Tennessee that remain segregated—churches and funeral homes; but not so in Cookeville. There are no black funeral homes, and black and white alike use the same undertakers. It's not unusual to see blacks and whites in churches or at funeral homes in Cookeville. That was new to me, and certainly is not the case in Jackson, Tennessee (where he currently resides)."[62]

Shakey McClellan made himself known in Cookeville. A huge black man with a gruff demeanor and huge Afro hair style, he stood out in the larger white community. He exuded confidence. He moved easily among the black and white community, and counted a number of powerful local leaders among his friends. Shakey, like his uncle John Lee, acted as the unofficial liaison between for the African American community for many years.

A fearless competitor Shakey earned a reputation as an excellent racquetball player, winning numerous local championships. He also taught a number of people how to play the game, coaching them for free. Shakey was reported to be the first African American to play tennis in Cookeville. He played exceptionally well and encouraged local black youths to pick up a sport then primarily played by white people. Prior to the creation of the Cookeville Community Center in the late 1960s, there were no public tennis courts in Cookeville, and Shakey played on the courts at TTU.[63] He supported Tech athletes in a number of ways and took a special interest in the tennis team, often volunteering his time to assist the coaches. Anne Klein recalled that the McClellans financially supported numerous Tech students through employment, personal loans (often at no interest), and outright monetary gifts.[64]

The relationship between John's Place and Tennessee Tech is significant. Thousands of students and faculty visited John's over the years, including numerous TTU athletes who left Tech for professional careers, including Lonnie Warwick of the famed Minnesota Vikings' "Purple People Eaters," Larry Schreiber of the San Francisco 49ers, Jim Youngblood of the Los Angeles Rams, and Elois Grooms who played for the New Orleans Saints. Alumni of a certain age who visit Cookeville generally go to two places out of nostalgia: Ralph's Donuts and John's Place. Both establishments catered to the general population and TTU. When John's had to close at midnight prior to 1993, patrons often left John's and went directly to Ralph's. Each year at Homecoming, John's Place acts as the rendezvous point for hundreds of alumni. Mary Alice extends the size of the building by erecting a large tent for the overflow crowd, and serves barbecued ribs, pulled pork, pinto beans, and baked beans in addition to the usual John Dog and fried catfish.

Shakey told Mark F. Dudney that in the late 1960s through the late 1980s recruiters for various TTU athletic programs regularly visited John's Place. Shakey knew all of the coaches well, and they often came by his establishment at the end of the day to talk about sports, promising student athletes, and other topics. Shakey became acquainted with thousands of students over the years, and acted as a guardian for many of them, looking after them for the coaches. He kept a number of them in line and would not allow them to hang out at John's if they were there when they should either be studying or practicing their particular sport. Near the end of the interview Shakey said that numerous alumni told him, "If it hadn't been for John's, I wouldn't have come to Tennessee Tech. I mean I've had so many kids tell me that, years and years, and they're still telling me that. I think as far as racial problems, it's [John's Place] one of the spots that's really helped. Tech gets along with John's and John's gets along with Tech."[65]

Over the years numerous students and faculty convened at John's Place and engaged in serious discussions about a variety of academic topics. Others went there to simply enjoy a cold beer and a John Dog. Students advised each other about what classes to take or avoid, while professors talked about current research or university politics. As Dr. Homer Kemp, emeritus chair of the Tech English Department, observed "God only knows how many ideas for Master's Thesis or Grant Proposals were hatched at John's Place. Some were great ideas, and others were justifiably skewered, never to be mentioned again. John's provided a relaxed atmosphere where people could bounce ideas off each other and really hash them out."[66]

The Tech Rugby Club was started by TTU student Rick Knowles in the spring of 1976. John's Place acted as their club house from the beginning. Dr. David Narrie acted as the club's faculty sponsor. When TTU hosted rugby matches, the post game celebrations took place at John's Place. Narrie commented that when he first moved to Cookeville there were only two places for students to gather off campus, John's Place and Bud's Place. He fondly remembered students interacting with the local black population and there being no racial tension. Because Shakey ran a tight ship, and tolerated no nonsense, John's Place provided a safe venue for students and townspeople to mingle. John's Place continues to act as the official sponsor of the Tech Rugby Club.[67]

John's Place brought people of all types together, providing a venue for them to interact freely. Town and gown, black and white, rich and poor, found common ground at John's. For a region largely lacking in racial

Mary Alice McClellan. Credit: Hal Harder, Moose Creek Media.

diversity, John's Place initiated many individuals' first interaction with a person of color. Stereotypes were confronted head on, and John's Place helped folks see persons for who they were, not the color of their skin.[68]

Though John's Place fell into disrepair in recent years it has recently undergone a resurgence. Due to the efforts of the indefatigable Mary Alice McClellan, John's Place was listed on the National Register of Historic Places in January 2011 for its role in improving race relations in the Upper Cumberland. Once again people sit along the horseshoe bar munching happily on a John Dog and washing it down with a cold libation.

NOTES

1. From the files of W. Calvin Dickinson, author of *Cumberland County Tennessee, 1800–1985* (Cookeville: Tennessee Technological University, 1992). Until the creation of resort communities like Fairfield Glade, no African Americans lived in Cumberland County, and only a handful lived there in 2011.
2. Esther Sharp Sanderson, *County Scott and its Mountain Folk* (Nashville, Tennessee: Blue and Gray Press, 1958), pp. 185–186.
3. James W. Loewen, *Sundown Towns: A Hidden Dimension of American Racism* (New York: The New Press, 2005), pp. 47–89. Loewen argues that the Great Retreat was primarily a phenomenon of the Midwest and not the traditional South; however

due to its historically small black populations the Upper Cumberland fits within his framework. See pages 70–72.

4. Loewen, 72.
5. Morgan Dudney, Interview with author (Free State, Tennessee, May 29, 2011).
6. Wali R. Kharif, "Slavery, Freedom and Citizenship: African American Contributions to the Upper Cumberland," *Rural Life and Culture of the Upper Cumberland*, Michael E. Birdwell and W. Calvin Dickinson, eds. (Lexington: University Press of Kentucky, 2004), pp. 105–121; Randal Williams, "West End Church of Christ, National Register Nomination," (Cookeville, Tennessee: Upper Cumberland Development District, 2007), p. 83; Mary Jean DeLozier, *Putnam County, Tennessee, 1850–1970* (Nashville, Tennessee: McQuiddy Publishing, 1978), p. 324.
7. Walden University offered instruction from the primary grades through college-level classes.
8. R. Vernon Boyd, *Undying Dedication: The Story of G.P. Bowser* (Nashville: Gospel Advocate Co., 2001), pp. 16–22.
9. Boyd, 37–38. For those who could afford to board at the school the fee was six dollars per month. People who could not afford the expenditure were allowed to work in the print shop, the kitchen, or elsewhere. The school was also referred to as the Silver Point Christian College. Alexander Campbell and Sam Womack served on the board of directors. By 1916 the board was composed of nine men, four of whom were white.
10. G.P. Bowser, "Putnam County Normal, Industrial and Orphan School, Silver Point, Tennessee," *Gospel Advocate* 57 (July 29, 1915), pp. 1145–1167; Boyd, 33–34. Bowser was invited to be a guest minister in 1909 and blew the congregation away with his enthusiasm, intelligence, and charisma. They prevailed upon him to move the Nashville school to Putnam County.
11. Boyd, 34, 37–38.
12. *Ibid.*, 38.
13. Robert E. Hooper, *A Distinct People: A History of the Churches of Christ in the 20th Century* (Eugene, Oregon: Wipf and Stock Publishers, 2001), pp. 265–266. Bowser was involved in the creation of five African American schools during his career.
14. Boyd, 38. Because he was more highly educated than most in the Silver Point area, white people often came to him to enlist his aid in filling out paper work. During World War I, he helped white and black citizens complete a variety of things including conscientious objector forms.
15. *Ibid.*, 39.
16. *Ibid.*, 62–63; "Report of Silver Point Bible School for Negroes." *Gospel Advocate* 58 (August 9, 1917), p. 748; L.W. Lankford, "The School at Silver Point," *Gospel Advocate* 62 (January 15, 1920), p. 22. Bowser left Silver Point frustrated with white members of the board of directors and the lack of support from the white Churches of Christ. He went on to establish schools in Kentucky, Michigan, and Texas.
17. The Darwin School operated approximately three blocks from John's Place, and black children were bused to Cookeville from several counties because citizens from those counties refused to educate African Americans. See Wali Kharif, "Darwin School and Black Public Education: Cookeville in the Decade of the Brown Decision." *Tennessee Historical Quarterly* LVI (Spring 1997), 20–33.

18. Sanderson, 185–186.
19. *Ibid.*, 186.
20. Myles Horton, *The Long Haul: An Autobiography* (New York: Teacher's College Press, 1990).
21. Carl Owens, Personal Interview (Cookeville, Tennessee, May 26, 2011). Carl stated that when he first entered York Institute a student pointed at him, and shouted to his classmates, "Look! It's a coon!" Owens tried to buy the T-shirt but the proprietor would not sell it to him and told him to get out of his store.
22. Where the term "Bush Town," derived is unknown. That area west of Cookeville appears on some maps with the designation "Irby." Many blacks preferred to say that they resided in West Cookeville.
23. Robert Farley, Interviewed by Michael E. Birdwell, (Cookeville, Tennessee, October 12, 2009); hereafter Farley Interview. Farley noted that he hated the term Bush Town.
24. The Colored Fair Grounds were situated on the north side of Highway 70 on the property currently owned by the Farmers' Co-Op near John's Place.
25. *Ibid.*
26. Delozier, 324. Putnam County was unusual in the fact that there never was a funeral home specifically for African Americans. Black families used local, predominantly white funeral parlors and continue to do so.
27. Wali R. Kharif, "Darwin School and Black Public Education: Cookeville in the Decade of the Brown Decision." *Tennessee Historical Quarterly* LVI (Spring 1997), pp. 20–33; Wali R. Kharif "School Desegregation in Clinton and Cookeville, Tennessee." *Tennessee State of the Nation.* 2nd Ed. W. Calvin Dickinson and Larry H. Whiteaker, eds. (New York: American Heritage, 1995), pp. 233–242. The Darwin School taught African American children from several counties near Putnam and provided the only access to education for hundreds of children of color. The Darwin School was located approximately three blocks from where John's Place stands.
28. Farley interview. The Putnam County Court was the precursor of the County Commission.
29. Shakey McClellan interviewed by Michael E. Birdwell (Cookeville, Tennessee, June 21, 2008).
30. Farley Interview.
31. Ed McClellan, "State of Tennessee, County of Putnam: To the Beer Committee of Putnam County," (Cookeville, Tennessee, August 23, 1957), p. 1. Wright's Chapel had been Ed's Place's next door neighbor since the beginning of the business.
32. Farley Interview.
33. Mary Alice McClellan, Interviewed by Michael E. Birdwell (Cookeville, Tennessee, March 17, 2010); hereafter Mary Alice McClellan interview. Mary Alice McClellan recently began serving similar meals on Wednesday evenings. She allows her customers to choose the menu each preceding Wednesday, and prepares everything herself. John Dogs continue to be served daily, as do fried catfish, chicken wings, and hot pickled eggs. As Mary Alice said, "I do it all from scratch. Ain't nothing comes out of a can unless I canned it myself."

34. Farley Interview. All the people who worked in Ed's kitchen were African American.
35. Farley Interview.
36. Ed McClellan, "State of Tennessee, County of Putnam: To the Beer Committee of Putnam County," (Cookeville, Tennessee, August 23, 1957), p. 1.
37. "The Hon. Beer Board, Cookeville, Tennessee," (Cookeville, Tennessee, 1957), p. 1.
38. *Ibid.* The following people signed the petition: Herbert A. Verble, Billie Bohannon, Bobbie M. Hill, Isaac Carver, Betty L. McClellan, Radford Beasley, Jesse P. Miller, Nina Carver, William A. Howard, America Gipson, Butler Click, Robert Western, McHenry Myers, Bill Sadler, Louise Lancaster, Gerald Rawson, William Butler, Scott Hill, Charles Prigmore, Maron Prigmore, William Cartwright, Tom Pointer, Walter C. Buck, Evelyn Buck, Etta Robinson, Harry Burgess, Will Morford, Jim Bohannon, Leon Hale, Lee Allen Beaty, A.B. Carr, Naomi Carr, Bee Maddux, Morris Irby, William Lamberson, Connie L. Click, James A. Hayes, Alvin Montgomery, William Peake, Robert Farley, Tamella Hill, James A. Gist, James B. Goolsby, H.L. Goolsby, Ernest S. Cartwright, L.D. Western, Jerry Myers, Viola Bohannon, Mable Lancaster, Mary P. Roberts, Melvin Hardy, Alvin Hardy, Frank Peake, Agnes Stevens, and Melvin Carver.
39. Mary Alice McClellan Interview.
40. *Ibid.* Diane Birdwell Ragland remembered Ed's Dairy Mart fondly. She said that "as a child it was always a treat to go to Ed's Dairy Mart. The only other places like it, but not nearly as good, were the Dairy Queen franchise on Spring Street and the locally owned Tastee Freeze on South Jefferson. All hamburgers at Ed's were hand made from local beef they bought from Foutch's. They made the fries fresh daily; they weren't frozen. And you know, as a kid, I don't think it even dawned on me that it was a black-owned business. Everybody went there." Diane Birdwell Ragland, Interviewed by Michael E. Birdwell (Disputanta, Virginia, May 4, 2010).
41. G. Frank Burns, Kelly Sergio and Rex Bennett, "Somewhere in Tennessee: The Cumberland in Wartime, 1940–1947," *Rural Life and Culture of the Upper Cumberland*, Michael E. Birdwell and W. Calvin Dickinson, eds. (Lexington: University Press of Kentucky, 2004), pp. 239–241. See also William and Marilyn Brinker, "Not Exactly the Hollywood Canteen," (Cookeville, Tennessee: Tennessee Technological University, 1998) and Woody McMillin, *In the Presence of Soldiers: The 2nd Army Maneuvers and Other World War II Activity in Tennessee* (Nashville: Horton Heights Press, 2010).
42. John's Place was established in the heart of the black community.
43. Farley interview.
44. "Cookeville Commission Meeting," *Putnam County Herald* (April 12, 1945).
45. "Putnam County Beer Board," *Putnam County Herald* (April 11, 1961).
46. Farley Interview, Shakey McClellan Interview, Mary Alice McClellan Interview. John Edward Roberts Interview with Michael E. Birdwell (Cookeville, Tennessee, August 12, 2008).
47. Russell Clarkson, Interviewed by Michael E. Birdwell (Jackson, Tennessee, November 23, 2010); hereafter Clarkson Interview.

48. Foutch's Meats was established in 1910. They butchered and processed locally raised animals at their stockyard until the 1980s.
49. Mary Alice McClellan Interview; Farley Interview; WCTE "Blues and Brews" fundraiser, October 1, 2010; Dr. David Narrie, Interviewed by Michael E. Birdwell (Cookeville, Tennessee, November 16, 2010), hereafter Dr. Narrie Interview.
50. Farley Interview.
51. *Ibid.* Until TTU outsourced its Food Services to Chartwells, African Americans "ran the cafeteria. Margaret McClellan was a great pastry cook. Gladys Crawford was their boss. Thomas and Barbara Martin cooked for Tech students and faculty for over thirty years in addition to the families Mr. Farley mentioned." Mary Alice McClellan Interview.
52. Transcript of Shakey McClellan Interview with Mark F. Dudney (Cookeville, Tennessee, 30, 1990), p. 1.
53. *Ibid.*, 4–5
54. *Ibid.*, 2–4.
55. *Ibid.*, 5.
56. Bobby Davis, Interviewed by Michael E. Birdwell (Cookeville, Tennessee, November 17, 2010). Hereafter Davis Interview.
57. Davis Interview. The grant also made it possible to improve and enlarge Cookeville General Hospital. It provided more parking and called for the demolition of substandard housing near the hospital that threatened public health. Bobby Davis said that as far as he could recall no houses in West Cookeville faced demolition, because the citizens took pride in their homes in spite of the conditions they lived in. See also Laura E. Clemons, *The People's Hospital: A History of Cookeville Regional Medical Center, 1950–2010* (Cookeville, Tennessee: The Foundation of the Cookeville Regional Medical Center, 2010); Delozier, 324–5.
58. Harvey G. Neufeldt and W. Calvin Dickinson. *The Search for Identity: A History of Tennessee Technological University, 1915–1985* (Memphis: Memphis State University Press, 1991), p. 129. Shakey originally attended Austin Peay on a basketball scholarship, but transferred to TTU when the opportunity arose. Dudney Interview of Shakey McClellan, 2–3. Leona Lusk Officer was the first African American to attend TTU who did not play sports.
59. Shakey died in October, 2009 due to complications associated with diabetes, just weeks before he was inducted into the TTU Sports Hall of Fame. His funeral was attended by a capacity crowd that was in equal proportion black and white. People traveled to Cookeville from across the country, attesting to his high regard in Cookeville and throughout the Upper Cumberland.
60. Russell Clarkson, Interviewed by Michael E. Birdwell (Jackson, Tennessee, December 12, 2010). Hereafter Clarkson Interview.
61. Clarkson Interview.
62. *Ibid.*
63. Clarkson Interview.
64. Ann Klein, Interviewed by Michael E. Birdwell (Cookeville, Tennessee, November 13, 2010). Klein said that Shakey even hired tutors for some students.
65. Shakey McClellan Transcript, 7.

66. Dr. Homer Kemp, Interviewed by Michael E. Birdwell (Cookeville, Tennessee, August 14, 2009).
67. Dr. Narrie Interview.
68. In the 1980s the Reverend Jesse B. Garner, assistant pastor at First Presbyterian Church, often went to John's for lunch. When leaving the church he told the secretary that if anyone needed to find him he would be at busy at work at the "West Side Theological Office." Jesse B. Garner, Interviewed by Michael E. Birdwell (Philadelphia, Pennsylvania, December 18, 2010).

BIBILIOGRAPHY

African Americans

Baxter, David. "Reverand Walter R. Munday." Bowling Green, Kentucky: Western Kentucky University Folklife Archives, Kentucky Library, Unpublished Manuscript, April, 1992.

DeLozier, Mary Jean. *Putnam County, Tennessee, 1850–1970.* Cookeville, Tennessee: McQuiddy Publishing, 1979.

Foy, Don. "Rev. Leroy Jackson . . . Dies at 102." *Cookeville Herald Citizen* (Cookeville, Tennessee), December 9, 1993.

Hackett, Tracey. "Long-time Teachers Head Parade." *Cookeville Herald-Citizen* (Cookeville, Tennessee)November 30, 1997.

Hopson, Mary. *Siftings From Putnam County, Tennessee: Towns, Communities, People.* N.P., Diversified Graphics, 1991.

Johnson, Joshua. "Uncle Fount and His Four in Hand," Linda Branstetter, Kay Harbison, and Rita McMurtrey, eds. *Trails of Metcalfe County's Past,* Vol. 1. Summer Shade, Kentucky: Summer Shade Elementary School, 1991.

Judd, Cameron. "Dr. Shipley's Memories: A. [Abraham] Buck—A Man of History." *Cookeville Herald-Citizen,* (Cookeville, Tennessee) January 6, 1980.

Kharif, Wali R. "Darwin School and Black Public Education: Cookeville in the Decade of the Brown Decision." *Tennessee Historical Quarterly* LVI (Spring 1997.

Kharif, Wali R. "School Desegregation in Clinton and Cookeville, Tennessee." *Tennessee State of the Nation,* 3rd ed. W. Calvin Dickinson and Larry H. Whiteaker, eds. New York: American Heritage, 1995.

Kharif, Wali R. and Lynwood Montell. *Reminisces and Reflections: African Americans in the Kentucky-Tennessee Upper Cumberland Since the Civil War.* London, Kentucky: Janze Publications, 2005.

Mardis, Bill. "Rev. Munday Left His Seminary Sermon At Home." *Louisville Courier-Journal,* (February 27, 1933).

Newton, Jonathan. "Junk Yard Blues," *Celina,* Bowling Green: Western Kentucky University, 1985.

Peterson, Elizabeth and Tom Rankin, "Free Hill: A Sound Portrait of A Rural Afro-American Community," *Tennessee Folklore Society Bulletin* (1985).

Peterson, Elizabeth. "Trickster and Trader: Portrait of An Afro-American Entrepreneur." Bloomington: Indiana University, Unpublished Doctoral Dissertation, 1990.

Romaine, Anne. "In Memoriam: Robert 'Bud' Garrett (1916–1987)." *Tennessee Folklore Society Bulletin,* LIII:1 (1988).

Schmitzer, Jeanne Canella. "The Black Experience at Mammoth Cave, Edmonson County, Kentucky, 1838–1942." University of Central Florida: Unpublished Masters Thesis, 1996.

Sears, Bob. "Gentle Man of Dignity Left His Mark on Family, Community." *Pulaski News Journal* (Somerset, Kentucky) September 19, 1996.

Thompson, Kelly. "Johnnie Wheeler . . ., The First Black Person Elected to A County Office." *Putnam County Light,* (Cookeville, Tennessee) October 29, 1995.

Webb, Thomas G. *A Bicentennial History of DeKalb County, Tennessee.* Smithville: Bradley Printing Co, 1995.

Webb, Thomas G. "Town's Black Community Highly Respected." *Smithville Review,* (Smithville Tennessee) September 17, 1997.

American Indians

Adair, James. *The History of American Indians.* London: E. and C. Dilly, 1775.

Arnow, Harriette Simpson. *Seedtime on the Cumberland.* New York: Scribner, 1960.

Ball, Donald B. "Notes on a So-called 'Old Fort' Along the Caney Fork River in White County, Tennessee." *Ohio Valley Historical Archaeology* 24 (2010).

Barlow, Tim, ed. *The Life and Writing of Moses Fisk.* Collegedale, Tennessee: College Press, 1980.

Bentz, Charles Jr., Andrew Bradbury, Gary D. Crites, Charles H. Faulkner, Harry Lanham, and Michael W. Morris. *Archaeological Investigations at the Forbus Site (40FN122): An Unplowed Multi-Component Site in the Eastern Highland Rim of Tennessee.* Nashville: Tennessee Department of Transportation Environmental Planning Office Publications in Archeology No. 3, 1997.

Braun, E. Lucy. *Deciduous Forests of Eastern North America.* Philadelphia: Blakiston Co., 1950.

Cambron, James W. and David C. Hulse, *Handbook of Alabama Archaeology, Part I Point Types* Revised Edition. Archaeological Research Foundation of Alabama, 1975.

Carr, John. *Early Times in Middle Tennessee.* Nashville: E. Stevenson and F.A. Owen, 1857.

Clark, Jerry E. *The Shawnee.* Lexington: University of Press of Kentucky, 1977.

Corgan, James X. *Vertebrate Fossils of Tennessee.* Nashville: Tennessee Department of Environment and Conservation, Division of Geology, Bulletin 77, 1976.

Crothers, George M., Charles H. Faulkner, Jan Simek, Patty Jo Watson, and Robert C. Mainfort, eds. *The Woodland Southeast.* Tuscaloosa: University of Alabama Press, 2002.

Cumfer, Cynthia. *Separate Peoples, One Land: The Minds of Cherokees, Blacks, and Whites on the Tennessee Frontier.* Chapel Hill: University of North Carolina Press, 2007.

Des Jeans, Tom and Joseph L. Benthall. "A Lithic Based Prehistoric Cultural Chronology of the Upper Cumberland." *Tennessee Anthropologist* 19:2 (1994).

Dillehay, Thomas D. *The Settlement of the Americas.* New York: Basic Books, 2000.

Dupier, Charles Mayer, Jr. "Prehistoric Trails in the Upper Cumberland River Basin." *Filson Club History Quarterly* 74:4 (2000).

Ehle, John. *Trail of Tears: the Rise and Fall of the Cherokee Nation.* New York: Anchor Books, 1988.

Fagan, Brian M. *Ancient North America: The Archaeology of a Continent.* London: Thames and Hudson, 1991.

Faulkner, Charles H. "Four Thousand Years of Native American Cave Art in the Southern Appalachians." *Journal of Cave and Karst Studies* (December 1997).

Faulkner, Charles T. "Analysis of Desiccated Human Paleofeces from Big Bone Cave (40VB103), Van Buren County, Tennessee." Knoxville: University of Tennessee, Unpublished Master's Thesis, 1989.

Faulkner, Charles T. "Prehistoric Diet and Parasitic Infection in Tennessee: Evidence from Analysis of Dessicated Paleofeces." *American Antiquity* 56:4 (October 1991).

Fenneman, N.M. *Physiography of the Eastern United States.* New York: McGraw Hill, 1938.

Ferguson, Robert B., et al. "The Middle Cumberland Culture." Nashville: *Vanderbilt Publications in Archaeology,* No. 3., 1972.

Ferguson, Terry. "Lithic Analysis and the Discovery of Prehistoric Man-Land Relationships in the Uplands of the Big South Fork of the Tennessee Cumberland Plateau." Knoxville: University of Tennessee, Unpublished Doctoral Dissertation, 1989.

Finger, John R. *Tennessee Frontiers: Three Regions in Transition.* Bloomington: Indiana University Press, 2001.

Franklin, Jay D. "The Prehistory of Fentress County, Tennessee: An Archaeological Survey." Knoxville: University of Tennessee, Unpublished Doctoral Dissertation, 2002.

Fulcher, Richard Carlton. *1770–1790 Census of the Cumberland Settlements, Davidson, Sumner, and Tennessee Counties.* Brentwood, Tennessee: N.P., 1986.

Garrett, William R., ed. "Narrative of Capt. Hendly, his Defeat and Capture near Crab Orchard in 1793." *American History Magazine* 2 (1897).

Garrison, Tim Allen. *The Legal Ideology of Removal: The Southern Judiciary and the Sovereignty of Native American Nations.* Athens: University of Georgia Press, 2009.

Goodspeed's Histories of Cannon, Coffee, DeKalb, Warren and White Counties. Reprint. McMinnville, Tennessee: Ben Lomand Press, 1972.

Haile, Joshua. "Mounds on Flynn's Creek, Jackson County, Tennessee." *Smithsonian Institution Annual Report* (1881).

Haywood, John. *The Civil and Political History of Tennessee From Its Earliest Settlement up to the Year 1796.* Reprint. Nashville, Tennessee: Publishing House of the Methodist Episcopal Church, South, 1891.

Haywood, John. *Natural and Aboriginal History of Tennessee.* 1823. Reprint. Jackson, Tennessee: McCourt-Mercer Press, 1959.

Hogue, Albert R. *One Hundred Years in the Cumberland Mountains: Along the Continental Line.* McMinnville, Tennessee: Standard Printing Co., 1939.

Hudson, Charles. *The Southeastern Indians.* Knoxville: University of Tennessee Press, 1976.

Hudson, Charles. *Knights of Spain, Warriors of the Sun: Hernando De Soto and the South's Ancient Chiefdoms.* Athens: University of Georgia Press, 1997.

Jones, William S. "Tennessee Places: The Legacy of the Trail of Tears in Van Buren County." *Tennessee Historical Quarterly* 63:1 (2004).

Kehoe, Alice Beck. *America Before the European Invasions.* London: Pearson Education Books, 2002.

Lewis, Thomas N. and Madeline Kneberg. *Tribes That Slumber: Indians of the Tennessee Region*. Knoxville: University of Tennessee Press, 1958.

Luther, Edward T. *Our Restless Earth: The Geologic Regions of Tennessee*. Knoxville: University of Tennessee Press, 1977.

Malone, Henry Thompson. *Cherokees of the Old South: A People in Transition*. Athens: University of Georgia Press, 1956.

McClain, Walter S. *History of Putnam County, Tennessee*. Cookeville, Tennessee: Quimby Dyer and Co., 1925.

Mercer, Henry C. "The Finding of the Remains of the Fossil Sloth at Big Bone Cave, Tennessee in 1896." *American Philosophical Society Proceedings* 36 (1897).

Mooney, Richard H. "Archaeoastronomy in Tennessee: The Moonshadow Site and Indian Sunshrines of the Cumberland Plateau," *Tennessee Anthropologist*, XVIII: 1 (Spring 1992).

Moore, Michael C. and Kevin E. Smith, *Archaeological Expeditions of the Peabody Museum in Middle Tennessee, 1877–1884*. Nashville: Tennessee Department of Environment and Conservation, Division of Archaeology, Research Series No. 16, 2009.

Moore, Michael C. and Kevin E. Smith. *Archaeological Investigations at the Rutherford-Kaiser Site: A Mississippian Mound Center in Sumner County, Tennessee*. Nashville: Tennessee Department of Environment and Conservation, Division of Archaeology, Research Series No. 13, 2001.

Myer, William E. *Indian Trails of the Southeast*. Nashville, Tennessee: Blue and Gray Press, 1971.

Nance, Benjamin C. *The Trail of Tears in Tennessee: A Study of the Routes Used During the Cherokee Removal of 1838*. Nashville: Tennessee Department of Environment and Conservation, Division of Archaeology, 2001.

Perdue, Theda. *The Cherokee Nation and the Trail of Tears*. New York: Penguin, 2008.

Prehistory of the Middle Cumberland River Valley: the Hurricane Branch site, Jackson County, Tennessee. Lexington: University of Kentucky Department of Anthropology, 1984.

Ramsey, J.G.M. *Annals of Tennessee to the End of the Eighteenth Century*. Charleston, South Carolina: John Russell, 1853.

Safford, James M. "The Pelvis of a *Megalolynx* and Other Bones from Big Bone Cave, Tennessee." *Geological Society of America Bulletin* 3 (1892).

Satz, Ronald N. *Tennessee's Indian Peoples: From White Contact to Removal, 1540–1840* Knoxville: University of Tennessee Press, 1979.

Simek, Jan F. "The Sacred Darkness: Prehistoric Cave Art in Tennessee." *Tennessee Conservationist* (March/April 1997).

Simek, Jan F. and Alan Cressler. "On the Backs of Serpents: Prehistoric Cave Art in the Southeastern Woodlands." *Cave Archaeology of the Eastern Woodlands: Essays in Honor of Patty Jo Watson*. David H. Dye, ed. Knoxville: University of Tennessee Press, 2008.

Smith, Kevin E. and Emily L. Beahm, "Fortified Town at the Mouth of Dixon Creek" National Register of Historic Places Nomination Form. Murfreesboro: Middle Tennessee State University, January 31, 2010.

Smith, Samuel D. and Benjamin C. Nance, *An Archaeological Interpretation of the Site of Fort Blount, A 1790s Territorial Militia and Federal Military Post, Jackson County, Tennessee*. Nashville: Tennessee Department of Environment and Conservation, Division of Archaeology, Research Series No. 12, 2000.

Thornton, Russell. *The Cherokees: A Population History*. Lincoln: University of Nebraska Press, 1990.

Walthal, John A. "Rockshelters and Hunter-Gatherer Adaptation to the Pleistocene/Holocene Transition." *American Antiquity* 63:2 (April 1998).

Williams, Samuel Cole. *Early Travels in Tennessee*. Johnson City: Watauga Press, 1928.

Wirt, Alvin B. *The Upper Cumberland of Pioneer Times*. Washington, D.C., Privately Published, 1954.

J. Robert Bradley and Charles Faulkner Bryan

Boyer, Horace Clarence. *The Golden Age of Gospel*. Champagne/Urbana: University of Illinois Press, 2000.

Boyer, Horace Clarence. *How Sweet the Sound: The Golden Age of Gospel*. Washington D.C.: Elliott & Clark Publishing, 1995.

Bryan, Charles Faulkner. Unpublished Diaries. Cookeville, Tennessee: Tennessee Technological University Archives, Charles Faulkner Bryan Collection, RG 42.

Bryan, Edith Hillis. Interviewed by Bill Zechman for "The Life and Works of Charles Faulkner Bryan" Radio Production. McMinnville, Tennessee: Cumberland Valley Broadcasting Company, 1972.

Conkin, Paul. *Cane Ridge: America's Pentecost*. Madison: University of Wisconsin Press, 1990.

Darden, Bob. *People Get Ready! A New History of Black Gospel Music*. New York: Continuum, 2005.

Jones, Amos, Jr. *I Have Always Been in the Hands of God: The Life Story of J. Robert Bradley* Nashville: Townsend Press, 1993.

Jordan, Lewis Garrett. *Negro Baptist History U.S.A., 1750–1930*. West Berlin, New Jersey: Townsend Press, 1993.

Kennedy, Michael and Joyce Bourne Kennedy, eds. *Oxford Concise Dictionary of Music*. 5th ed. Oxford, England: Oxford University Press, 2007.

Livingston, Carolyn. *Charles Faulkner Bryan: His Life and Music*. Knoxville: University of Tennessee Press, 2003.

Neufeldt, Harvey G. and W. Calvin Dickinson. *The Search for Identity: A History of Tennessee Technological University, 1915–1985*. Memphis, Tennessee: Memphis State University Press, 1991.

Pareles, Jon. "J. Robert Bradley, 87, Charismatic Gospel Singer, Dies." *New York Times* (May 4, 2007).

Reagon, Bernice Johnson. *We'll Understand It Better By and By: Pioneering African American Gospel Composers*. Washington, D.C.: Smithsonian Institution, 1992.

Smith, Ralph Lee. *Appalachian Dulcimer Traditions*. Lanham, Maryland: Scarecrow Press, 2010.

Tennessee Folklore Society Papers, RG 59. Cookeville: Tennessee Technological University Archives.

John Catron

Alexander, Elizabeth Urban. *Notorious Woman: The Celebrated Case Of Myra Clark Gaines.* Baton Rouge: Louisiana State University Press, 2004.

Allen, Austin. "Jacksonian Jurisprudence and the Obscurity of Justice John Catron." *Vanderbilt Law Review* 62:2 (2009).

Allen, Austin. *Origins of the Dred Scott Case: Jacksonian Jurisprudence And the Supreme Court, 1837–1857.* Athens: University of Georgia Press, 2006.

Auchampaugh, Paul. "James Buchanan, the Court and the Dred Scott Case." *Tennessee Historical Magazine* IX: 4 (January 1926; issued Oct. 1928).

Bergeron, Paul. *Antebellum Politics in Tennessee.* Lexington: University Press of Kentucky, 1982.

Bergeron, Paul. "Tennessee's Response to the Nullification Crisis." *Journal of Southern History* 39: 1 (February 1973).

Benjamin R. Curtis to Ticknor, April 8, 1856, Benjamin R. Curtis, *Memoir of Benjamin Robbins Curtis.* Boston: Little, Brown, 1879.

Blair v. Pathkiller' Lessee, 2 Yerger 406, 10 Tenn. 361 (Knoxville, Tennessee, July 1830).

Boylston, James R. and Alan J. Wiener. *David Crockett in Congress: The Rise and Fall of the Poor Man's Friend.* New York: Bright Sky Press, 2009.

Brooks v. The State of Tennessee. 2 Yerger 482 (Cooper, ed.) 10 Tenn. 426 (Nashville, Tennessee, January 1831).

Brown, Theodore, Jr. "The Formative Period in the History of the Supreme Court in Tennessee, 1796–1835." *A History of the Tennessee Supreme Court.* John Ely, ed. Knoxville: University of Tennessee Press, 2002.

Caldwell, Joshua W. *Sketches of the Bench and Bar of Tennessee.* Knoxville, Tennessee: Ogden Brothers and Co. Printers, 1898.

Caldwell, Joshua W. *Studies in the Constitutional History of Tennessee.* 2nd ed. Cincinnati, Ohio: Robert Clark Co., 1907.

Carson, Hampton L. *The History of the Supreme Court of the United States; with Biographies.* Philadelphia, Pennsylvania: Ziegler and Co., 1902.

Catron, John. "Biographical Letter from Justice Catron, of the Supreme Court of the United States," *Portraits of Eminent Americans Now Living; Including President [Franklin] Pierce and His Cabinet with Biographical and Historical Memoirs of Their Lives and Actions.* John Livingston, ed. (London, U.K.: Sampson Low, Son, and Company, 1854.

Catron, John. "Biographical Letter." *Nashville Daily Union* (Thursday, June 1, 1865).

Catron, "Letter to the Judiciary Committee," reprinted in Robert H. White, ed., *Messages of the Governors of Tennessee, 1821–1835,* Vol. 2. Nashville: Tennessee Historical Commission, 1952.

Chandler, Walter S. "The Centenary of Associate Justice John Catron of the United States Supreme Court." *Tennessee Law Review,* 15 (December 1937–June 1938).

Cornet v Winton's Lessee, 2 Yerger 143, 10 Tenn. 129 (Knoxville, Tennessee, July 1826.

Cushman, Clare, ed. "John Catron, 1837–1865," *The Supreme Court Justices: Illustrated Biographies, 1789–1993.* Washington, D.C.: Supreme Court Historical Society, 1993).

Cutler, Wayne and James L. Rogers, II, eds. *Correspondence of James K. Polk: July–December 1845.* Knoxville: University of Tennessee Press, 2004.

Doe ex dem Mann and Hannah v. Wilson, 64 U.S. 457; 16 L. Ed. 584; 23 HOW 457 1 (Washington, D.C., May 4, 1860).

Dred Scot v Sandford, 60 U.S. 393, 407; 15 L. Ed. 691, 702; 19 Howard 393 (1857).

Dunlap, Boutwell. "Judge John Catron of the United States Supreme Court." *Virginia Magazine of History and Biography* 28 (1920).

Fehrenbacher, Don E. *The Dred Scott Case.* New York: Oxford University Press, 1978.

Fehrenbacher, Don E. *Slavery, Law, and Politics: The Dred Scott Case in Historical Perspective.* New York: Oxford University Press, 1981.

Fishers Negroes v. Dabbs, 6 Yerger 120, 14 Tenn. 78 (Cooper, ed., Nashville, Tennessee, 1834).

Foote, Henry S. *The Bench and Bar of the South and Southwest* (St. Louis, Missouri: Soule, Thomas and Wentworth, 1876.

Franklin, John Hope and Loren Schweninger. *In Search of the Promised Land: A Slave Family in the Old South.* New York: Oxford University Press, 2006.

Frierson, William L. "Some Incidents in the History of Tennessee's Court of Last Resort," *Proceedings of the Nineteenth Annual Meeting of the Bar Association of Tennessee Held at Lookout Mountain, Tennessee, July 18, 19, and 20, 1900.* Memphis, Tennessee: Paul & Neibert Printers and Publishers, 1900.

Frisby, Derek. "The Vortex to Secession: West Tennessee and the Rush to War," *Sister States/Enemy States: The Civil War in Kentucky and Tennessee.* Kent Dollar, Larry Whiteaker, and Calvin Dickinson, eds. Lexington: University Press of Kentucky, 2009.

"From Nashville: Judge Catron, of the Supreme Court, was Last Week Expelled from Nashville by the Vigilance Committee, because of his Refusal to Resign his Judgeship. He was Obliged to Leave his Wife in Nashville on Account of her Sickness." *New York Times* (August 14, 1861).

Garrison, Tim Allen. *The Legal Ideology of Removal: The Southern Judiciary and the Sovereignty of Native American Nations.* Athens: University of Georgia Press, 2009.

Gass, Edmund. "The Constitutional Opinions of Justice John Catron." *East Tennessee Society Publications* 8 (1936).

Gatell, Frank Otto. "John Catron." In *The Justices of the United States Supreme Court: Their Lives and Major Opinions*, Leon Friedman and Fred L. Israel, eds. ,1969. Reprint. New York: Chelsea House Publishers, 1997.

Gower, Herschel and Jack Allen, eds. *Pen and Sword: The Life and Journals of Randall W. McGavock, Colonel, C.S.A.* Nashville: Tennessee Historical Commission, 1959.

Grainger v. The State, 5 Yerger (Cooper, ed.) 458, 13 Tenn. 377 (Jackson March 1830).

Green, John W. *Lives of the Judges of the Supreme Court of Tennessee, 1796–1947.* Knoxville: Archer & Smith, 1947.

Guild, Josephus Conn. *Old Times in Tennessee with Historical, Personal, and Political Scraps and Sketches.* Nashville: Tavel, Eastman and Howell, 1878.

Hallum, John. *The Diary of an Old Lawyer: Scenes Behind the Curtain*. Nashville, Tennessee: Southwestern Publishing House, 1895.

Harding, Sidney L. *Crow Dog's Case*. New York: Cambridge University Press, 1994.

Harris v. Clarissa, 6 Yerg 227, 14 Tenn. 153 (Cooper, ed., Nashville, Tennessee 1834).

Hoobler, Jim. "Sally Thomas 1787–1850," *Civicscope Nashville*, http://www.civicscope.org/nashville-tn/SallyThomas

"How a Wife Made a Supreme Judge; Mrs. Catron Gets the Appointment from Andrew Jackson," *New York Times* (May 10, 1896).

Howington, Arthur F. "Not in the Condition of a Horse or an Ox: *Ford V. Ford*, the Law of Testamentary Manumission and the Tennessee Court's Recognition of Slave Humanity." *Tennessee Historical Quarterly* 34 (1975).

Howington, Arthur F. *What Sayeth the Law? The Treatment of Slaves and Free Blacks in the State and Local Courts of Tennessee*. New York: Garland, 1986.

Huebner, Timothy. "John Catron, Jacksonian Jurisprudence, and the Expansion of the South," *The Southern Judicial Tradition: State Judges and Sectional Distinctiveness, 1790–1890*. Athens: University of Georgia Press, 1999.

Huebner, Timothy S. *The Taney Court: Justices, Rulings, and Legacy*. ABC-CLIO, 2003.

Ingersoll, Henry Hulbert. "John Catron, 1781–1865," *Great American Lawyers; The Lives and Influence of Judges and Lawyers Who have Acquired Permanent National Reputations and have Developed Jurisprudence of the United States: A History of the Legal Profession in America*. William Draper Lewis, ed. Philadelphia, Pennsylvania: John C. Winston Company, 1907.

John Catron Papers, 1826–1865. Nashville: Tennessee State Library and Archives [TSLA], Small Collections, S-8. Ac. No. 79.

Jones, James B., Jr. "'The Reign of Terror of the Safety Committee has Passed Away Forever': A History of the Committees of Safety and Vigilance in West and Middle Tennessee, 1860–1862." *West Tennessee Historical Society Papers* LXIII (2009).

Laughlin, James. "Biographical Sketch of Justice Catron." *Tennessee Historical Magazine* 4 (1918).

Laughlin, S. H. "Sketches of Notable Men." *Tennessee Historical Magazine* 4 (1918).

Levy, Buddy. *American Legend: The Real-Life Adventures of David Crockett*. New York: Berkely Trade, 2006.

"Law Reports. . . Supreme Court–Chambers. A Missouri Judge on Treason. Charge of Judge Catron," *New York Times* (July 15, 1861).

Loftin v. Espy, 4Yerger 84, 12 Tenn 68 (Cooper, ed., Jackson, Tennessee 1833).

McGlasson, Cleo. "Pioneer Social Life in Overton County." *Tennessee Folklore Society Bulletin* 14:1 (March, 1948).

Marks, Albert S. "The Supreme Court of Tennessee," *The Green Bag: An Entertaining Magazine for Lawyers* 5 (1893).

Marsh, Lee and Delavan v Brooks, et al, 49 U.S. 223; 12 L. Ed. 1056; 8 Howard, 223 (Washington, D.C. February1850).

McConnell and Mayfield v. Mousepaine's Lessee, 2 Yerger 436, 10 Tenn, 387 (Knoxville, Tennessee, July 1830).

Mitchell v State, 13 Tenn. 340; 5 Yer. 340 (Cooper, ed.) (Sparta, Tennessee 1833).

Nash, A.E. Keir. "John Catron." *The Supreme Court Justices: A Biographical Dictionary.* Melvin I. Urofsky, ed. New York: Garland Publishing, 1994.

Newmeyer, William. *The Supreme Court Under Marshall and Taney.* Arlington Heights, Illinois: Harlan Davidson, 1968.

Ohio Life Insurance and Trust Co.v. Debolt, 57 U.S. 416, ; 14 L. Ed. 997; 16 Howard 416 (Washington City, May 24, 1854).

Phelps, Dawson L. and John T. Willett. "Iron Works Along the Natchez Trace." *Tennessee Historical Quarterly* 12:1 (March 1953).

Phillips, Harry. "The Courts," in *History of the Sixth Circuit.* Bicentennial Committee of the Judicial Conference of the United States 1976.

Remini, Robert. *Andrew Jackson and His Indian Wars.* New York: Penguin, 2002.

Reynolds, David S. *Waking Giant: America in the Age of Jackson.* New York: Harper Perennial, 2008.

"Southern News Through Louisville." *New York Times* (August 2, 1861).

The State v. Smith (Tenn. Cr. App., 612 S.W. 2d 493; Nashville, Tennessee, November 25, 1980).

The Supreme Court of the United States: Its Beginnings & Its Justices 1790–1991. Washington, DC: Library of Congress, 1992.

Swisher, Carl B. Swisher, *History of the Supreme Court of the United States.* Vol 5. New York: Macmillan, 1974.

Temple, Oliver P. *Notable Men of Tennessee form 1833 to 1875: Their Times and Their Contemporaries.* Mary B. Temple, ed. New York: The Cosmopolitan Press, 1912.

Tennessee v. Brown, 836 S.W.2d 530 (Knoxville, Tennessee,1992).

"What the Dred Scott Case Decided," *New York Times* (July 16, 1857).

White, Robert H. ed. *Messages of the Governors of Tennessee, 1821–1835.* Vol. 2. Nashville: Tennessee Historical Commission, 1952.

Whitman, Walt. "Song of Myself." *Leaves of Grass.* Boston, Massachusetts: Small, Maynard and Co., 1904.

Yerger, George S. Ed. *Calvin M. Smith v. the State of Tennessee* (Nashville, January, 1829) *Tennessee Reports of Cases Argued and Determined in the Supreme Court of Tennessee,* Vol. I. St. Louis, Missouri: G. I Jones and Co., 1876.

Yerger, George S. Ed. *Cornet v. Winston's Lessee* (Knoxville, July 1826) *Tennessee Reports of Cases Argued and Determined in the Supreme Court of Tennessee,* Vol. 2. St. Louis, Missouri: G.I. Jones and Co., 1876).

Yerger, George S. Ed. *The State v. Foreman* (Knoxville, July 1835), *Tennessee Reports of Cases Argued and Determined in the Supreme Court of Tennessee,* Vol. VIII (Columbia, Missouri: E.W. Stephens Publishing Co., 1912.

Cumberland River

"Account of Expenses." June, 1804. J.S. Bassett, ed. *Correspondence of Andrew Jackson,* 7 Vols. Washington, D.C.: USGPO, 1926–1935.

Allen, Michael. *Western Rivermen: Ohio and Mississippi Boatmen on the Myth of the Alligator Horse, 1763–1861.* Baton Rouge: Louisiana State University Press, 1990.

American Social History Productions. *Doing as They Can*. Wyckoff, New Jersey, 1987. VHS.

Baldwin, Leland. *The Keelboat Age on the Western Waters*. Pittsburgh: University of Pittsburgh Press, 1941.

Anderson, Douglas. "Old Times on the Upper Cumberland." *Nashville Banner*, (Nashville, Tennessee) 1925–1926.

Bedford, John R. "A Tour in 1807 Down the Cumberland, Ohio, and Mississippi Rivers from Nashville to New Orleans." *Tennessee History Magazine* 5(April 1919).

Brown, Arthur Aladine. *Lumbering on the Cumberland: A Romance Taken from Life*. Cincinnati, Ohio: The Lumber Worker Company, 1887.

Casseday, Ben. *The History of Louisville from its Earliest Settlement to 1852*. Louisville, Kentucky: Hull and Brother, 1852.

Clark, Thomas D. *The Rampaging Frontier: Manners and Humors of Pioneers of the South and Middle West*. Indianapolis, Indiana: Bobbs Merrill, 1939.

Douglas, Byrd. *Steamboating on the Cumberland*. Nashville, Tennessee: Parthenon Publishing, 1961.

Haites, Eric F., James Make, and Gary M. Walton. *Western River Transportation: The Era of Internal Development, 1810–1860*. Baltimore, Maryland: Johns Hopkins University Press, 1975.

Hunter, Louis C. *Steamboats on Western Rivers: An Economic and Technological History*. Cambridge, Massachusetts: Harvard University Press, 1949.

Keith, Jeannette. *Country People of the New South: Tennessee's Upper Cumberland*. Chapel Hill: University of North Carolina Press, 1995.

Knox, Jack. *Riverman*. Nashville, Tennessee: Abington Press, 1971.

Johnson, Leland. *Engineers on the Twin Rivers: A History of the U.S. Army Engineers Nashville District, 1769–1978*. Nashville, Tennessee: U.S. Army Corps of Engineers, 1978.

McCague, James. *The Cumberland*. New York: Holt McDougal, 1973.

Montell, W. Lynwood. *Don't Go Up Kettle Creek: Verbal Legacy of the Upper Cumberland* Knoxville: University of Tennessee Press, 1983.

O'Brien, Warren S. *Adventures Along the Cumberland*. New York: Vantage, 1963.

Paine, Anne. "Cumberland Once Busy. . . Colorful." *Nashville Tennessean* (January 27, 1985).

Parkinson, George P., Jr. and Brooks F. McCabe Jr. "Charles Ward and the *James V. Rumsey*: Regional Innovation in Steam Technology on the Western Rivers." *West Virginia History* 39 (January-April, 1978).

Phelps, Dawson A. "Travel on the Natchez Trace: A Study of its Economic Aspect." *Journal Mississippi History*, 15 (July 1953).

Robinson, Michael C. *History of Navigation of the Ohio River Basin*. [National Waterways Study NWS-83–5]. Washington, D.C.: USGPO, 1983.

Schreiber, Harry N. "The Ohio Flatboat Trade: Some Reconsiderations." David M. Ellis, ed. *The Frontier in American Development: Essays in Honor of Paul Wallace Gates*. Ithaca, New York: Cornell University Press, 1970).

Schulman, Steven A. "Logging in the Upper Cumberland: A Folk History." Bowling Green: Unpublished Master's Thesis, Western Kentucky University, 1973.

Schulman, Steven A. "The Lumber Industry of the Upper Cumberland River Valley." *Tennessee Historical Quarterly* 32 (1973).

Schulman, Stephen A. "Rafting Logs on the Upper Cumberland River." *Pioneer American* 6:1 (1974).

Schulman, Stephen A. "Reminiscence of Logging on the Cumberland." *Kentucky Folklore Record,* 18 (1972).

Smith, Winston. "Escar Olin Coe on the Upper Cumberland: Reminiscences of a River Pilot." *Kentucky Folklore Record* 20 (July-September 1974).

Subduing the Cumberland: A History of the "Old" Locks and Dams on the Cumberland River (Nashville, Tennessee: U.S. Army Corps of Engineers, N.D.)

Trevathan, Kim. *Coldhearted River: A Canoe Odyssey Down the Cumberland*. Knoxville: University of Tennessee Press, 2006.

Twain, Mark. *The Adventures of Huckleberry Finn*. Reprint. New York: Oxford, 1977.

Twain, Mark. *Life on the Mississippi*. (1874) Reprint. New York: 1986

Webb, George. "Peaceful Natives: Indians in the Upper Cumberland," in Calvin Dickinson, Larry Whiteaker, et al. (eds.). *Lend an Ear: Heritage of the Tennessee Upper Cumberland*. Lanham, Maryland: University Press of America, 1983.

Whitaker, Larry. "'The Enemy is my Brother': The Civil War in the Upper Cumberland." *Lend an Ear: Heritage of the Tennessee Upper Cumberland.* Lanham, Maryland: University Press of America, 1983

Wilkerson, S. "The Commerce of the West." *American Pioneer* 2 (March 1843).

Joe L. Evins

"A.J. Goodson, Postmaster." *Smithville Review,* (Smithville, Tennessee) May 20, 1901.

Aucoin, Brent J. "The Southern Manifesto and Southern Opposition to Desegregation." *Arkansas Historical Quarterly* 55: 2 (Summer 1996).

Badger, Tony. "Southerners Who Refused." *Historical Journal* 42: 2 (June 1999).

Balmer, Randall. *God in the White House: How Faith Shaped the Presidency From John F. Kennedy to George W. Bush*. New York: Harper Collins, 2008.

Balmer, Randall. "Jesus is Not a Republican." *Chronicle Review* (June 23, 2006).

Balmer, Randall. *Thy Kingdom Come: How the Religious Right Distorts the Faith and Threatens America*. Cambridge, Massachusetts; Basic Books, 2006.

Bartley, Numan V. *The Rise of Massive Resistance: Race and Politics in the South in the 1950's*. Baton Rouge: Louisiana State University Press, 1969.

Branscome, James. "Destroy to Save? Power to Move Mountains." *Environment* 17:6 (September 1975).

Burns, G. Frank. "Joe L Evins." Cookeville: Unpublished Manuscript, Tennessee Technological University Archives, Joe L. Evins Collection, Record Group 1.

Carter, Luther J. "Rep. Joe Evins: NSF and NASA Get a New Master of Finance." *Science* 155: 3764 (Feb. 17, 1967).

Clor, Harry, *On Moderation: Defending an Ancient Virtue in a Modern World*. Waco, Texas: Baylor University Press, 2008.

"Court's Ruling on Schools Called Abuse of Judiciary." *Nashville Tennessean* March 13, 1956.

"Evins Defends JFK in Pulpit." *New York Times* (October 21, 1960)

Evins, Joe L. *Congressional Record,*91st Congress, 2d session (October 1, 1970).

Evins, Joe L. *The Evins Family: A Genealogical Study*. Washington, D.C.: Joe L. Evins, 1938.

Evins, Joe L. *Understanding Congress*. New York: Clarkson N. Potter, 1963.

Freeman, S. David. "The Nine Lives of TVA." *Environment* 27:3 (April 1985).

Grantham, Dewey W. "Tennessee and Twentieth-Century American Politics." *Tennessee History: The Land, The People, The Culture*, Carroll Van West, ed. Knoxville: University of Tennessee Press, 1998.

Graves, Susan B. *Evins of Tennessee: Twenty-five Years in Congress*. New York: Popular Library, 1971.

"Joe Evins–Legend in His Own Time." *Cookeville Herald-Citizen* (October 18, 1966).

Lovett, Bobby L. *The Civil Rights Movement in Tennessee*. Knoxville: University of Tennessee Press, 2005.

Millet, Ann. "Joe L. Evins, Democratic Representative from Tennessee."

Representative Joe L. Evins Papers. Cookeville: Tennessee Technological University Archives, RG1.

Schrade, Brad and Anne Paine, "TVA Board Meets Behind Veil of Secrecy" and "Agency Created to be Run with Little Oversight," *NashvilleTennessean*, June 12, 2009.

"South's Political Battle Rages in Many Pulpits." *Washington Post* (October 24, 1960)

"Three Above Expediency." *Nashville Tennessean*, March 14, 1956.

Vineyard, Dale. "Congressional Committees on Small Business." *Midwest Journal of Political Science* 10: 3 (August 1966).

Webb, Thomas G. *A Bicentennial History of DeKalb County, Tennessee*. Smithville, Tennessee: Bradley Printing Co., 1995.

Webb, Thomas G. *DeKalb County*. Memphis: Memphis State University Press, 1986

West, Carroll Van, "Joseph Landon Evins, 1910–1984." *Tennessee Encyclopedia of History and Culture* (Nashville, Tennessee: Rutledge Hill Press, 1998).

Champ Ferguson

Austin, J.P. *The Blue and the Gray: Sketches of the Unwritten History of the Great American Civil War*. Atlanta, Georgia: Franklin Printing and Publishing, 1889.

Barra, Allen. "The Education of Little Fraud: How Did a Racist Speechwriter for George Wallace Turn into a 'Cherokee' Sage and Author of a Revered Multicultural Text? The Weird Tale of Asa ('Forrest') Carter." *Salon*, December 20, 2001. salon.com/2001/12/20/carter_6/

Brents, Major John A. *The Patriots and Guerillas of East Tennessee and Kentucky: The Sufferings of Patriots, Also the Experiences of the Author as an Officer in the Union Army, Including Sketches of Noted Guerillas and Distinguished Patriots*. New York: Henry Dexter Publishers, 1863.

Carter, Forrest. *The Outlaw Josey Wales*. New York: Dell, 1976.

Carter, Forrest. *Josey Wales: Two Novels*. Albuquerque: University of New Mexico Press, 1989.

Davis, William C. "The Massacre at Saltville." *Civil War Times Illustrated* (February 1971).

DeLozier, Mary Jean. "The Civil War and its Aftermath in Putnam County." *Tennessee Historical Quarterly* 36:2 (1977).

DeLozier, Mary Jean. "Civil War in Putnam County." *Tennessee Historical Quarterly.* 38. (1979).

Dixon, Thomas. *The Clansman*. New York: Grossett and Dunlap, 1905.

"Dr. Murfree Meets Champ Ferguson." *Rutherford County Historical Society* (Winter 1973).

Dudney, Betty Jane. "Civil War in White County, Tennessee, 1861–1865." Cookeville: Unpublished Master's Thesis, Tennessee Technological University, 1985.

Duke, Basil W. *History of Morgan's Cavalry.* Cincinnati: Miami Printing and Publishing Company, 1867.

Duke, Basil W. *The Civil War Remembrances of General Basil W. Duke, C.S.A.* New York: Cooper Square Press, 2001.

French, Philip. *Westerns: Aspects of a Movie Genre.* London: Carcanet Press, 2005.

Gilman, George S. *Edge: The Loner.* New York: Pinnacle Books, 1972.

Hale, J.D. *Champ Ferguson the Border Rebel, and Thief and Robber, and Murderer.* Cincinnati, Ohio: Self published, 1864.

Hale, J.D. *Champ Ferguson: A Sketch of the War in East Tennessee Detailing Some of the Leading Spirits of the Rebellion.* Cincinnati, Ohio: Self published, 1862.

Hale, J.D. *Sketches of Scenes in the Career of Champ Ferguson and his Lieutenant, With Champ's Confession, J. M. Hughs and the Ku Klux Klan.* N.P.: 1870.

Hell on Wheels. AMC TV, 2011.

Jones, James B., Jr. "Fevers Ran High: The Civil War in the Upper Cumberland." *Rural Life and Culture of the Upper Cumberland.* Michael E. Birdwell and W. Calvin Dickinson, eds. Lexington: University Press of Kentucky, 2004.

McDade, Arthur Butch. "The Civil War: Champ Ferguson, Guerrilla of the Upper Cumberland Plateau." *Tennessee Conservationist* 63:5 (September/October 1997).

McKnight, Brian. *Confederate Outlaw: Champ Ferguson and the Civil War in Appalachia.* Baton Rouge: Louisiana State University Press, 2011.

Miles, Nicholas Slayton. "I Do Not Want to be Buried in Such Soil as This: The Life and Trial of Confederate Guerrilla Champ Ferguson." Lexington: Unpublished Master's Thesis, University of Kentucky, 2005.

The Outlaw Josey Wales. Los Angeles, California: Warner Bros. DVD, 2011.

Ray, Robert B. *A Certain Tendency of the Hollywood Cinema,1930–1980.* New Jersey: Princeton University Press, 1985.

Ridley, Bromfield L. *Battles and Sketches of the Army of Tennessee.* Mexico, Missouri: Missouri Printing and Publishing Company, 1906.

Ridley, Bromfield L. "Champ Ferguson." *Confederate Veteran.* 7:10 (October 1899), 442.

Rogers, Elzia Guy (E.G.) *Memorable Historical Accounts of White County and Area.* Collegedale, Tennessee: The College Press, 1972.

Schickel, Richard. *Clint Eastwood: A Biography* (New York: Alfred A. Knopf, 1996.

Schickel, Richard. *D.W. Griffith: An America Life.* New York: Limelight Editions, 2004.

Sensing, Thurman. *Champ Ferguson: Confederate Guerilla.* Nashville: Vanderbilt University Press, 1942.

Sensing, Thurman. "The Fallacy of the Minimum Wage." *The Freeman: Ideas on Liberty* 10: 5 (May 1960).

Seraphim Falls. Los Angeles, California: Goldwyn Films, 2006.

Smith, Troy. "Don't You Beg and Don't You Dodge." *Civil War Times Illustrated* 40:6 (2001).

Smith, Troy. *Good Rebel Soil: The Champ Ferguson Story.* New York: Writer's Club Press, 2002.

Sproul, Mary Katherine. *A Civil War Diary.* Livingston, Tennessee: Overton County Historical Society, 2006.

Sutherland, Daniel. *Guerrillas, Partisans and Bushwhackers: Revisiting the American Civil War.* Chapel Hill: University of North Carolina Press, 2009.

Sutherland, Daniel. "Guerrilla Warfare, Democracy, and the Fate of the Confederacy," *Journal of Southern History* 68:2 (Spring, 2002).

Tarrant, Sergeant Estham. *The Wild Riders of the First Kentucky cavalry: A History of the Regiment, in the Great War of the Rebellion, 1861–1865: Pathetic Scenes, Amusing Incidents, and Thrilling Episodes; a Regimental Roster, Prison Life, Adventures, and Escapes.* Louisville, Kentucky: Press of R.H. Carothers, 1894.

Ward, Jason Morgan. *Defending White Democracy: The Making of a Segregationist Movement and the Remaking of Racial Politics, 1936–1965.* Chapel Hill: University of North Carolina Press, 2011.

White, Lucinda C. "Champ Ferguson: A Legacy of Blood." *Tennessee Folklore Society Bulletin* 44 (June 1978).

Folk Medicine

Bellar, Jim. *Red Boiling Springs The Tradition Lives.* Lafayette, Tennessee: Macon County Times Publishing Company, 1981.

Berliner, H.S. "A Larger Perspective on the Flexner Report." *International Journal of Health Service* 5 (1975).

Bolyard, Judith L. "Medicinal Plants and Home Remedies of Appalachia." *Economic Botany* 37:4 (1983).

Cavender, Anthony. "Folk Medical Uses of Plant Foods in Southern Appalachia, United States." *Journal of Ethnopharmacology* 108: 1, 3 (November 2006).

Cavender, Anthony. *Folk Medicine in Southern Appalachia.* Chapel Hill: University of North Carolina Press, 2003.

Cavender, Tony, ed. *A Folk Medical Lexicon of Southern Central Appalachia.* History of Medicine Society of Appalachia, Miscellaneous Paper No. 1. Johnson City: East Tennessee State University, 1990.

Clarke, James N. *To Those Seeking Homes and Health: Fentress County, Tennessee, Its Advantages.* Allardt: Self published, 1883.

Conley, Robert J. *Cherokee Medicine Man: The Life and Work of a Modern-Day Healer* Norman: University of Oklahoma Press, 2007.

Denning, Jeanette Keith. "A History of the Resort Business in Red Boiling Springs, Tennessee." Cookeville: Unpublished Master's Thesis, Tennessee Technological University, 1982.

Evans, E. Raymond, Clive Kileff and Karen Shelley. *Herbal Medicine: A Living Force in the Appalachians.* 1982.

Farr, T.J. "Folk Remedies." *Tennessee Folklore Society Bulletin* 1:3 (1935).

Farr, T.J. "Tennessee Superstitions and Beliefs." *Tennessee Folklore Society Bulletin* 1:2 (April, 1935).

Farr, T.J. "Survivals of Superstition in Tennessee." *Tennessee Folklore Society Bulletin* 21:1 (March, 1955).

Farr, T.J. "Tennessee Superstitions and Beliefs." *Tennessee Folklore Society Bulletin* 1:2 (April, 1935).

Gunn, John G. *Gunn's Domestic Medicine: Or Poor Man's Friend, In The Hours Of Affliction, Pain And Sickness* . Knoxville, Tennessee: 1830.

Heber, David. *PDR (Physicians Desk Reference) for Herbal Medicines.*4th ed. Montvale, New Jersey: Thomson Healthcare. 2007.

Helton, L.R. "Folk Medicine and Health Beliefs: An Appalachian Perspective." *Journal of Cultural Diversity* 3:4 (1996).

Howell, Patricia Kyritsi. *Medicinal Plants of Southern Appalachia.* Mountain City, Georgia: BotanosLogos, 2006.

Hufford, David. "Folk Healers." *Handbook of American Folklore.* Richard M. Dorson, ed. Bloomington: Indiana University Press, 1983.

Long, Grady M. "Folk Medicine in McMinn, Polk, Bradley and Meigs Counties, Tennessee, 1910–1927." *Tennessee Folklore Society Bulletin.* 28 (1962).

Lumpkin, Ben Gray. "Remedies." *Tennessee Folklore Society Bulletin* (1976).

Mahoney, James W. *The Cherokee physician, Or, Indian Guide to Health: Comprising a Brief View of Anatomy, With General Rules for Preserving Health Without the use of Medicines: The Diseases of the United States, With Their Symptoms, Causes, and Means of Prevention are Explained in Simple Terms: It Also Contains a Description of a Variety of Herbs and Roots, Many of Which are not Explained in any Other Book, the Medicinal Virtues of Which Have Hitherto Been Unknown to the Whites.* Chattanooga, Tennessee: 1846.

Marshall, Mary Louise. "Medicine in the Confederacy." New Orleans: 44th Annual Meeting of the Medical Library Association, New Orleans, May 7–9, 1942.

Melton, Callie Myers. *Folklore of the Upper Cumberland.* Self-Published, 2004.

Minton, Lee R. "An Early History of the Upper Cumberland Medical Society," *Journal of the Tennessee Medical Association* 65:2 (February, 1972).

Mooney, James. "Myths of the Cherokee and Sacred Formulas of the Cherokee." *Nineteenth Annual Report of the Bureau of American Ethnology 1897–98* Part I. (1900) and "The Sacred Formulas of the Cherokees," *Seventh Annual Report of the Bureau of Ethnology to the Secretary of the Smithsonian Institution, 1885–1886.* Washington, D.C.: Government Printing Office, Washington, 1891.

Mooney, James. *The Swimmer Manuscript: Cherokee Sacred Formulas and Medical Prescriptions.* Washington, D.C.: USGPO, 1932.

Mullins, G. "Herbs of the Southern Highlands and Their Medicinal Uses." *Kentucky Folklore Record* 18 (1973).

Pamplona-Roger, George D. *Foods and Their Healing Power.* Hagerstown, Maryland: Review and Herald Publishing Association, 2004.

Parr, Jerry S. "Folk Cures of Middle Tennessee." *Tennessee Folklore Society Bulletin* 28:1 (1962).

Roddy, Vernon. *Thousands to Cure: On the Early Story of Red Boiling Springs, Tennessee with Selected Supporting Materials.* Hartsville, Tennessee: Upper Country People Probe, 1991.

Rogers, E.G. (Elzia Guy). *Early Folk Medical Practices in Tennessee.* Murfreesboro, Tennessee: Mid-South Publishing, 1941.

Sharp, Sharon A. "Folk Medicine Practices: Women as Keepers and Carriers of Knowledge." *Women's International Studies Forum* 9:3 (1986).

Starfield, Barbara. "Medical Errors-A Leading Cause of Death." *Journal of the American Medical Association* 284:4 (July 26, 2000).

Stekert, Ellen J. "Focus for Conflict: Southern Mountain Medical Beliefs in Detroit." *The Urban Experience and Folk Tradition.* Paredes, Americo and Ellen J. Stekert, eds. Austin, Texas: University of Texas Press, 1971.

Thomas, Daniel Lindsey and Lucy B. *Kentucky Superstitions.* Princeton, New Jersey: Princeton University Press, 1920.

Waggoner, Tim. *Poor Man's Medicine Bag: Home Remedies and Helpful Hints.* Knoxville, Tennessee: The Kingdom Press, 1984.

Warner, John E. *Medicinal Plants of the Cumberland Plateau and Appalachian Mountains.* Warner Natural Herb Products, 1996.

Weiss, Harry B. and Howard R. Kemble. *The Great American Water Cure Craze: A History of Hydropathy in the United States.* Trenton, New Jersey: Past Times Press, 1967.

Wharton, May Cravath. *Doctor Woman of the Cumberlands.* Pleasant Hill: Uplands, 1953.

Wilkins, Thurman. *Cherokee Tragedy.* Norman: University of Oklahoma Press, 1989.

Cordell Hull and John Gore

Akins, Bill. "A Time of Testing: The Tennessee Career of Cordell Hull." *East Tennessee Historical Society's Publications* 54–55 (1982–1983).

Alligood, Leon. "Grateful Immigrant repays his Uncle Sam," *Nashville Tennessean,* (April 3, 2007.

"Aunt Polly Williams at Hotel," *Carthage Courier* (April 14, 1924).

Basso, H. "Jedge [*sic*] Hull." *New Republic* 102 (May 27, 1940).

Blake, Morgan. *Lawmakers and Public Men of Tennessee.* Nashville, Tennessee: Eagle Printing Co., 1915.

Cox, James N. "Hull Beat Cox Out of Girl; Lost Her to Kentuckian," *Carthage Courier,* (Carthage, Tennessee)May 2, 1940.

Crawford, W. H. and Cordell Hull. "We Shall Make the League an Issue." *Collier's* 72 (September 1, 1923).

Davenport, W. "Hull of the Hills." *Collier's* 105 (May 4, 1940).

"Deaths: Elijah Lee Dudney," *Jackson County Sentinel* (November 22, 1956).

Dickinson, W. Calvin, Michael E. Birdwell, and Homer D. Kemp, *Upper Cumberland Historic Architecture*. Franklin, Tennessee: Hillsboro Press, 2002.

Gellman, Irwin F. *Secret Affairs: FDR, Cordell Hull and Sumner Welles.* New York: Enigma Books, 2003.

"Gore Funeral Planned Today," *Nashville Tennessean*, February 23, 1939.

Grant, Philip A., Jr. "Tennesseans in the 63rdCongress, 1913–1915." *Tennessee Historical Quarterly* 29:3 (1970).

Green, John W. *Law and Lawyers: Sketches of the Federal Judges of Tennessee.* Jackson, Tennessee: McCowat-Mercer Press, 1950.

"Hill-Billy Cousin Cord." *New Republic* 104 (January 27, 1941).

Hinton, Harold B. *Cordell Hull: A Biography.* New York: Doubleday, Doran and Co., 1942.

Hixson, F. "Cord Hull: Tennessee Statesman." *Current History* 51 (1940).

Hull, Cordell. *The Memoirs of Cordell Hull.* 2 Vols. New York: Macmillan, 1948.

"Hulls of Tennessee Produced a Great Secretary of State." *Life* 8 (March 18, 1940).

John Gordon Gore biography, www.ca6.uscourts.gov

"Judge John J. Gore Dies After Heart Attack," *Nashville Tennessean,* February 22, 1939.

Keith, Jeannette. *Country People of the New South: Tennessee's Upper Cumberland.* Chapel Hill: University of North Carolina Press, 1995.

Larson, Erik. *In the Garden of Beasts: Love, Terror and an American Family in Hitler's Berlin.* New York: Broadway Books, 2012.

Ligon, L.A. "Hull Was Little Known When Appointed Judge at 32." *Carthage Courier,* (Carthage, Tennessee) May 2, 1940.

McGinness, H.B. "Hull's Outstanding Trait is his Plain, Simple Manner." *Carthage Courier,* (Carthage, Tennessee) May 2, 1940.

McKissack, Pat and Frederick McKissack, Jr. *Tennessee Trailblazers.* Brentwood, Tennessee: March Media, 1996.

Neese, Charles G. and Thomas A. Wiseman Jr., *Pen Sketches of the History and Judges of the Federal Court at Nashville, Tennessee: February 17, 1797 to February 17, 1988* (N.P: N.D.)

"Noted Lady Pays Tribute to Judge Gore and Gainesboro," *Jackson County Sentinel,* (Gainesboro, Tennessee) March 8, 1923.

"Our Picture Series No. 6: George Bancroft Murray," *Jackson County Sentinel,* (Gainesboro, Tennessee) February 2, 1899.

A Pictorial History of Jackson County, Tennessee. Paducah, Kentucky: Turner Publishing Company, 2001.

"Portrait: Cordell Hull." *Review of Reviews* 82 (December 1930.

"Portrait Unveiling Recalls Kindness of Judge Gore," *Nashville Tennessean,* (December 18, 1951).

Pratt, Julius. *Cordell Hull.* New York: Cooper Square, 1964.

Pruden, Caroline. "Tennessee and the Formative Years of the United Nations: A Case Study of Southern Opinion." *Tennessee Historical Quarterly* 52:1 (1993).

Randy, Clayton. *Sons of the South.* New York: The Fairfax Press, 1978.

"Scopes Fails to get Federal Injunction; State Trial Friday," *New York Times,* (July 7, 1925).

"St. Jude Donor Strives to Help a New Generation," January, 2006. www.stjude.org

Stanley, Judith M. "Cordell Hull and the Democratic Party Unity." *Tennessee Historical Quarterly* 32:2 (1973).

Tennessee Through Time: The Later Years. Salt Lake City: Gibbs Smith, 2008.

"TVA Clear," *Time* (January 31, 1938).

Upper Cumberland News, (Cookeville, Tennessee) March 8, 1923.

Webb, James. *Born Fighting: How the Scots-Irish Shaped America.* New York: Broadway Books, 2004.

Wyman, David S. *The Abandonment of the Jews: America and the Holocaust 1941–1945.* New York: The New Press, 2007.

Wyman, David S. *Paper Walls: American and the Refugee Crisis 1938–1941.* New York: Pantheon, 1985.

John's Place

Birdwell, Michael E. "Everybody's Welcome at John's Place." *Close Up: Public Television from the Upper Cumberland.* 26:1 (January-February, 2011).

Brinker, William J. and Marilyn. "Not Exactly the Hollywood Canteen." Cookeville, Tennessee: Tennessee Technological University, Unpublished Conference Paper, 1998.

Bowser, G.P. "Putnam County Normal, Industrial, and Orphan School, Silver Point, Tenn." *Gospel Advocate* 57 (1915).

Bowser, G.P. "Work Among the Colored People." *Gospel Advocate* 50 (1908).

Boyd, R. Vernon. *Undying Dedication: The Story of G.P. Bowser.* Nashville, Tennessee: Gospel Advocate Company, 1985.

Burns, G. Frank, Kelly Sergio, and Rex Bennett, "Somewhere in Tennessee: The Cumberland in Wartime, 1940–1947." *Rural Life and Culture of the Upper Cumberland.* Michael E. Birdwell and W. Calvin Dickinson, eds. Lexington: University Press of Kentucky, 2004.

Burton, A.M. "The Prospects and Needs of the Putnam County Industrial School for Negroes." *Gospel Advocate* 58 (February 10, 1916).

Campbell, Alexander. "Work Among the Colored People." *Gospel Advocate* 51 (2 December 1909).

Clemons, Laura E. *The People's Hospital: A History of Cookeville Regional Medical Center, 1950–2010.* Cookeville, Tennessee: The Foundation of the Cookeville Regional Medical Center 2010.

DeLozier, Mary Jean. *Putnam County, Tennessee, 1850–1970.* Nashville, Tennessee: McQuiddy Publishing, 1978.

Hooper, Robert E. *A Distinct People: A History of the Churches of Christ in the 20th Century.* Eugene, Oregon: Wipf and Stock Publishers, 2001.

Holt, Thelma M. *Life and Times of G.P. Bowser.* Nashville: Associated Publishing, 1964.

Horton, Myles. *The Long Haul: An Autobiography.* New York: Teacher's College Press, 1990.

Inscoe, John C. *Appalachians and Race: The Mountain South, From Slavery to Segregation* Lexington: University Press of Kentucky, 2001.

Kharif, Wali R. "Darwin School and Black Public Education: Cookeville in the Decade of the Brown Decision." *Tennessee Historical Quarterly* LVI (Spring 1997).

Kharif, Wali R. "School Desegregation in Clinton and Cookeville, Tennessee." *Tennessee State of the Nation.* 2nd ed. W. Calvin Dickinson and Larry H. Whiteaker, eds. (New York: American Heritage, 1995).

Kharif, Wali R. "School Integration in Cookeville 'Uneventful.'" *Cookeville Herald Citizen,* (Cookeville, Tennessee) September 6, 2004.

Kharif, Wali R. "Slavery, Freedom and Citizenship: African American Contributions to the Upper Cumberland," *Rural Life and Culture of the Upper Cumberland,* Michael E. Birdwell and W. Calvin Dickinson, eds. (Lexington: University Press of Kentucky, 2004).

Lankford, L.W. "The School at Silver Point," *Gospel Advocate* 62 (January 15, 1920).

Loewen, James. *Sundown Towns: A Hidden Dimension of American Racism.* New York: The New Press, 2005.

McClellan, Ed. "State of Tennessee, County of Putnam: To the Beer Committee of Putnam County." Cookeville, Tennessee: Petition in the collection of Mary Alice McClellan, August 23, 1957.

McMillin, Woody. *In the Presence of Soldiers: The 2nd Army Maneuvers and Other World War II Activity in Tennessee*. Nashville: Horton Heights Press, 2010.

Neufeldt, Harvey G. and W. Calvin Dickinson. *The Search for Identity: A History of Tennessee Technological University, 1915–1985*. Memphis: Memphis State University Press,1991.

Sanderson, Esther Sharp. *County Scott and its Mountain Folk*. Nashville, Tennessee: Blue and Gray Press, 1958.

"The Hon. Beer Board, Cookeville, Tennessee." Cookeville, Tennessee: Petition in the collection of Mary Alice McClellan, 1957.

Williams, Randal. "West End Church of Christ, National Register Nomination." Cookeville, Tennessee: Upper Cumberland Development District, 2007.

Kentucky Politics

Brents, Major John A. *The Patriots and Guerillas of East Tennessee and Kentucky: The Sufferings of Patriots, Also the Experiences of the Author as an Officer in the Union Army, Including Sketches of Noted Guerillas and Distingueshed Patriots*, New York: Henry Dexter Publishers, 1863.

Buchanan, Nancy. "W. Godfrey Hunter," Bowling Green, Kentucky: Unpublished paper written for Frances Richards, Western Kentucky State College, 1960.

Bush, Bryan S. *The Butcher Burbridge*. New York: Acclaim Press, 2008.

Coulter, E. Merton. *Civil War and Readjustment in Kentucky*. Gloucester, Massachusetts: Peter Smith Publishing, 1926.

Duke, Basil W. *History of Morgan's Cavalry*. Cincinnati: Miami Printing and Publishing Company, 1867.

Duke, Basil W. *The Civil War Remembrances of General Basil W. Duke, C.S.A.* New York: Cooper Square Press, 2001.

Harrison, Lowell, ed. *Kentucky's Governors*. Lexington: University Press of Kentucky, 2004.

Harrison, Lowell and James Klotter. *A New History of Kentucky*. Lexington: University Press of Kentucky, 1997.

Jillson, Willard Rouse. *Edwin P. Morrow, Kentuckian: A Contemporaneous Biographical Sketch*. Louisville, Kentucky: G.T. Dearing Printing Co., 1921.

Kennedy, Henry Clinton. *A Damphool in the Kentucky Legislature*. Chicago, Illinois: W.B. Conkey, Co., 1909.

Klotter, James. *Kentucky: Portrait in Paradox, 1900–1950*. Frankfort: Kentucky Historical Society, 1996.

Krebs, Albin. "John Sherman Cooper Dies at 89," *New York Times* (February 23, 1991).

Lucas, Marion B. *A History of Blacks in Kentucky: From Slavery to Segregation, 1760–1891*. Frankfort: Kentucky Historical Society, 1992.

McKnight, Brian. *Confederate Outlaw: Champ Ferguson and the Civil War in Appalachia*. Baton Rouge: Louisiana State University Press, 2011.

Marshall, Anne. *Creating a Confederate Kentucky: The Lost Cause and Civil War Memory in a Border State*. Chapel Hill: University of North Carolina Press, 2010.

Montell, W. Lynwood. *Upper Cumberland Country*. Oxford: University of Mississippi Press, 1993.

Shaler, Nathaniel Southgate. *Kentucky: A Pioneer Commonwealth*. New York: Houghton Miflin, 1884.

Schulman, Robert. *John Sherman Cooper, The Global Kentuckian*. Lexington: University Press of Kentucky, 1976.

Shannon, Jasper B. and Ruth McQuown. *Presidential Politics in Kentucky, 1824–1948*. Lexington: University Press of Kentucky, 1950.

Tapp, Hambleton. "Incidents in the Life of Frank Wolford, Colonel First Kentucky Union Cavalry." *Filson Club History Quarterly* 10 (April 1936).

Tapp, Hambleton, ed. *Union, The Civil War and John Tuttle: A Kentucky Captain's Account*. Frankfort: Kentucky Historical Society, 1980.

Tapp, Hambleton and James C. Klotter. *Kentucky: Decades of Discord, 1865–1900*. Frankfort: Kentucky Historical Society, 2008.

Tapp, Hambleton and James C. Klotter, eds. *The Union, the Civil War and John W. Tuttle: A Kentucky Captain's Account*. Frankfort: Kentucky Historical Society, 1980.

Tarrant, Sergeant Estham. *The Wild Riders of the First Kentucky Cavalry: A History of the Regiment, in the Great War of the Rebellion, 1861–1865: Pathetic Scenes, Amusing Incidents, and Thrilling Episodes; a Regimental Roster, Prison Life, Adventures, and Escapes*. Louisville, Kentucky: Press of R.H. Carothers, 1894.

Toplovich, Ann. "Cumberland River." *Tennessee Encyclopedia of History and Culture*. Nashville: Rutledge Hill Press, 1998.

Wells, Joseph William. *History of Cumberland County*. Standard Printing Co., 1947.

"Whittledycut." *Time* (July 5, 1954).

Moonshine

Alexander, Jerry L. *Where Have All Our Moonshiners Gone?* Seneca, South Carolina: Alex Press, 2006.

Allen, James. "Mountain Passes of the Cumberland." *Harper's New Monthly Magazine* 81 (September 1890).

Allen, James. "Through the Cumberland Gap on Horseback." *Harper's New Monthly Magazine* 73 (June 1886).

Alligood, Leon. "Moonshine Holds Spirited Past in State: Secret Stills Once Thrived in the Bible Belt." *Nashville Tennessean*, September 5, 1999.

Allison, Young E. "Moonshine Men." *Southern Bivouac* 5 (February 1887).

Argo, William Vincent, Sr. *No Place for Revenuers*. Washington, D.C.: Vantage Press, 1962.

Atkinson, George W. *After the Moonshiners by One of the Raiders: A Book of Thrilling yet Truthful Narratives*. Wheeling, West Virginia: Frew and Campbell Steam Book and Job Printers, 1881.

Baine, Donald. "Among the Moonshiners." *Dixie* 1 (August 1885).

Barton, Bruce. "Moonshiner's Judge." *The American Magazine* (n.d.).

Blythe, Samuel G. "Raiding Moonshiners." *Munsey's Magazine* 25 (June 1901).

Bradley, William Aspenwall. "The Folk Culture of the Kentucky Cumberlands." *The Dial* 64 (January 31, 1918).

Bradley, William Aspenwall. "Hobnobbing with Hillbillies." *Harpers* 133:787 (December 1915).

Brake, Patricia E. *Justice in the Valley: A Bicentennial Perspective of the United States District Court for the Eastern District of Tennessee.* Franklin, Tennessee: Hillsboro Press, 1998.

Boucherie, Anthony. *The Art of Making Whiskey So As to Obtain a Better, Purer, Cheaper and Greater Quantity of Spirit, From a Given Quantity of Grain.* Lexington, Kentucky: Worsley and Smith, 1819.

Burn, Harry T. "Tennessee is not a Hooch Paradise: Legislator Resents Articles Depicting State as National Habitat of the Moonshiner; Natives Like Other Folk and of Pure Anglo-Saxon Descent, He Says—Sterling-Towner Bill's Provisions Needed." *New York Times* (May 21, 1922).

"Campaign Against Moonshiners," *St. Louis Globe Democrat* (August 18, 1887).

Capshaw, Leigh. *Dixie University: Dixie College—A Historical Vignette.* Cookeville, Tennessee: Self-published, 1989.

Carr, Jess. *The Second Oldest Profession; An Informal History of Moonshining in America.* Englewood Cliffs, New Jersey: Prentice Hall, 1972.

"Causes of Feuds and Moonshining." *Literary Digest* 73 (April 22, 1922).

Cresswell, Stephen. *Mormons and Cowboys, Moonshiners and Klansmen: Federal Law Enforcement in the South and West, 1870–1893.* Tuscaloosa: University of Alabama Press, 1991.

Crutcher, Theophilus P. *Spurrier With the Wildcats and Moonshiners.* Nashville, Tennessee: University Press, 1895.

Dabney, Joseph Earl. *Mountain Spirits: A Chronicle of Corn Whiskey from King James's Ulster Plantation to America's Appalachians and the Moonshine Life.* Asheville, North Carolina: Bright Mountain Books, 1974.

Dabney, Joseph Earl. *More Mountain Spirits: The Continuing Chronicle of Moonshine Life and Corn Whiskey, Wines, Ciders & Beers in America's Appalachians.* Fairview, North Carolina: Bright Books, 1980.

Daniel, Fran. "This Isn't Your Grandaddy's Likker: Distillery Makes Catdaddy Carolina Moonshine and it's Legal." *Winston-Salem Journal* (June 17, 2006)

"A Defense of the Mountaineer," *Literary Digest* 44 (April 20,1912).

Douglas, Joseph C. "Caves and Moonshine: A New Area for Historical Inquiry." *Journal of Spelean History* 26.

Douglas, Joseph C. "Minerals, Moonshine and Misanthropes: The Historic Use of Caves in the Upper Cumberland." *Rural Life and Culture in the Upper Cumberland.* Michael E. Birdwell and W. Calvin Dickinson, eds. Lexington: University Press of Kentucky, 2004.

Douglas, Joseph C. "Miners and Moonshiners: Historical Industrial Use of Tennessee Caves." *Midcontinental Journal of Archaeology* 26 (2): 251-267.

Douglas, Joseph C. "Water, Milk, Whiskey and Wine: Historic Use of a Small Tennessee Cave in the First Half of the Twentieth Century." *Journal of Spelean History* 27:3 (2000).

Durand, Loyal, Jr. "Mountain Moonshining in East Tennessee." *Geographical Review* 46:2 (April 1956).

"East Tennessee Hooch Goes Legit in Nashville: Hank Jr. Backs Legendary Recipe." *Nashville Tennessean*, November 12, 2010)

Eller, Ronald. *Miners, Millhands, and Mountaineers: Industrialization of the Appalachian South, 1880–1930.* Knoxville: University of Tennessee Press, 1982.

"Five Distilleries Destroyed; One Day's Work of a Deputy Collector's Party in Tennessee. *New York Times*, October 17, 1878.

Fox, William P. "The Lost Art of Moonshining." *Saturday Evening Post* (March 26, 1966).

Guernsey, A. H. "Hunting for Stills." *Harper's Weekly* 11 (December 21, 1867).

Guernsey, A.H. "Illicit Distillation of Liquors." *Harper's Weekly* 11 (December 7, 1867).

Harder, Kelsie B. "The Jake Leg." *Tennessee Folklore Society Bulletin* 27:3 (September, 1961).

Harkin, Anthony. *Hillbilly: A Cultural History of an American Icon.* New York: Oxford University Press, 2005.

Hartt, Rollin Lynde. "Mountaineers: Our Own Lost Tribes." *Century* 95 (January 1918).

Hubbard, Leonidas. "The Moonshiner at Home." *Atlantic Monthly* 90 (August 1902).

Hull, Cordell. *Memoirs of Cordell Hull.* 2 Vols. Washington, D.C.: Hodder and Stoughton, 1948.

Jarrell, Todd. *Crank: Darkness on the Edge of Town*, PBS affiliate WCTE Cookeville, Tennessee: 2006. This is an incisive documentary about the plague of methamphetamine addiction in the Upper Cumberland in the early 2000s.

"Keeping Tennessee Dry." *Literary Digest* 47 (November 1, 1913).

Keith, Jeannette. *Country People of the New South: Tennessee's Upper Cumberland.* Chapel Hill: University of North Carolina Press, 1995.

Kelley, M. "From Mining to Moonshine." *Nation* 135 (October 26, 1932).

Kellner, Esther. *Moonshine.* Indianapolis: Bobbs-Merrill, 1971.

Kelsey, M. "From Mining to Moonshine." *Nation* 135 (October 26, 1932).

Kennedy, David M. *Over Here: The First World War and American Society.* New York: Oxford, 1980.

Kephart, Horace. Kephart, "The Mountain Moonshine I: Getting Acquainted." *Forest and Stream* (September 15, 1906).

Kephart, Horace. "The Mountain Moonshine II: Ways that are Dark." *Forest and Stream* (September 22, 1906).

Kephart, Horace. "The Mountain Moonshine III: A Leaf from the Past." *Forest and Stream* (October 20, 1906).

Kephart, Horace. "The Mountain Moonshine IV: The Revenue." *Forest and Stream* (November, 1906).

Kephart, Horace. "The Mountain Moonshine V: A Few Hard Facts." *Forest and Stream* (November 10, 1906).

"Killed by Moonshiners: Capt. James M. Davis Shot from an Ambush—Twenty Bullets in His Body." *New York Times* (March 14, 1882).

Licensed Beverage Industries, Inc. *Formula For Fraud: The Moonshine Menace in 1964.* (New York: Annual Report for the Licensed Beverage Industries, Inc., 1964.

"Local Happenings." *Putnam County Herald*, (Cookeville, Tennessee) April 26, 1903.

Looney, John. "Illicit Appalachian Crafts: From Mead to Meth." Antigua, Guatemala: Conference Paper Presented to the Benjamin Rush Society, January 27, 2012.

Love, Louanne Seagraves. "Murder, Mayhem and Moonshiners in the Upper Cumberland: The Assassination of Deputy U.S. Marshal Henry Seagraves." *The Upper Cumberland Researcher* 25:2 (Summer 2010).

Maurer, David W. "The Argot of the Moonshiner." *American Speech* 24:1 (February, 1949).

Maurer, David W. *Kentucky Moonshine*. Reprint. Lexington: University Press of Kentucky, 2003.

McClain, Walter S. *History of Putnam County, Tennessee*. Cookeville, Tennessee: Quimby Dyer and Co., 1925.

McWhiney, Grady. *Cracker Culture: Celtic Ways in the Old South*. Tuscaloosa: University of Alabama Press, 1988.

Merriman, Stony. *Midnight Moonshine Rendezvous: Secrets of Luke Alexander Denney's Moonshine Running Adventures (1930s-1960s)*. Smithville, Tennessee: M. Stone Pub., 1990.

Miller, Wilbur R. "The Revenue: Federal Law Enforcement in the Mountain South, 1870–1900." *Journal of Southern History* 55: 2 (May 1989): 195-216.

Miller, Wilbur R. *Revenuers and Moonshiners: Enforcing Federal Liquor Law in the Mountain South, 1865–1900*. Chapel Hill: University of North Carolina Press, 1991.

Montell, Lynwood. *Killings: Folk Justice in the Upper South*. Lexington: University Press of Kentucky, 1986.

"Moonshine in Tennessee: How the Illicit Distillers thrive in the South; A Few Gallons of Whisky Produced During the Year--the Farce Which has been Enacted in the Federal Courts--an Illiterate Crowd who are Trying to Make a Living by Breaking the Law. *New York Times* (February 2, 1880).

"Moonshine, is it Gone Forever?" *The Historical State of Tennessee News—Cumberland, Macon and Putnam County Areas* 30:39 (October 2010).

"Moonshine Land, Where Slackers and Deserters are Finding Refuge," *Scientific American* 86:2222 (August 3, 1918).

"Moonshine Quietly Gets a 21st Century Makeover: Sherman Owen's Moonshine Odyssey Started at 19 When he set out to Distill 'Ultra-Clean' Vodka." *West Virginia Gazette* (April 4, 2010).

"Moonshiners." *Harper's New Monthly Magazine* 58 (February 1879).

"Moonshiners Hide Out; Citizens of Overton Moving for the Suppression of Illicit Distilleries; The County Court Issues a Proclamation that Means Business." *Nashville Daily American* (October 26, 1878).

"Moonshiners' Judge." *The American Magazine* (n.d.).

"Moonshiners in Tennessee: A Prominent Churchman Captured for Making Illicit Whisky." *New York Times* (July 23, 1899).

Most Shocking: Moonshine Madness. Country Music Television (CMT), 2004.

Motlow v. State. Tennessee State Supreme Court, December Term, 1911: 557–594.

"On a Still-hunt for Stills." *Literary Digest* 59 (October 7, 1916).

Pendleton, Charles S. "Illicit Whiskey-Making." *Tennessee Folklore Society Bulletin* 12: 1 (March, 1946).

Price, Theodore H. and Richard Spillane, "The Commissioner of Internal Revenue as a Policeman: His Work in the Suppression of the Traffic in Moonshine Whisky, 'Dope,' and Counterfeit Butter." *The Outlook* 120 (November 27, 1918).

Pridemore, W. Francis. "How Doth the Busy Moonshiner! A One-time Operator of a West Virginia Still Ironically Considers a Growing Industry Which has Brought Affluence to Impoverished Communities." *North American Review* 228:1 (July, 1929).

Pridemore, W. Francis "What Prohibition has done for the Mountaineers." *Outlook* 146 (July 20, 1927).

"Prohibition in Kentucky." *New York Times* (August 5, 1907).

"A Raid on Moonshiners." *Literary Digest* 44 (May 4, 1912).

Rawls, Wendell, Jr., "Some Hard, Cold Facts about Moonshine Whisky." *Nashville Tennessean*, November 4, 1971.

Redman, Ben Ray. "In Moonshine Land." *New York Times*, June 19, 1921

Rohrbough, Malcolm J. *The Trans-Appalachian Frontier*. New York: Oxford University Press, 1977.

"The Sad Fate of Eliza Bleylock [*sic*]." *Harper's Weekly* (March 5, 1881).

"The Second Waterloo: Exciting Details of the Battle Between Davis' and Morgan's Men." *The Nashville Daily American*, (Nashville, Tennessee) (August 28, 1878).

Sennet, Stephen. "Along the Road in the Cumberlands." *The Mentor* 15 (July 1927).

Shrum, Shelia R. McCarter, Comp. *Bullets, Fire, Moonshine and the Bible: Life in Jackson County, Tennessee*. Lafayette, Tennessee: Ridge Runner Publications, 2004.

Sims, Lissa. "Local Distillers Bring New Respectability to an Age-old Illicit Kentucky Tradition." *Smiley Pete Publishing* (November 3, 2010). http://bizlex.com/2012/03/moonshine-reclaimed-2/

"Southern Highlanders Wake Up But Still Make Corn Likker." *Literary Digest* 65 (April 3, 1920).

Stewart, Bruce E. *Moonshiners and Prohibitionists: The Battle Over Alcohol in Southwest Appalachia*. Lexington: University Press of Kentucky, 2011.

Swafford, Thomas V. *Moonshine Man: The Life of Church Lester*. Pikeville, Tennessee: Printing Partners, 2007.

Swafford, Thomas V. *Whiskey Wars: The Life of Jim Hamilton*. Pikeville, Tennessee: Printing Partners, 2008.

"Tennessee: The Moonshiners," *Bangor (Maine) Daily Whig and Courier* (December 7, 1878).

"The Tennessee Moonshine Raids." *New York Times*, October 15, 1878.

"The Tennessee Revenue War. Gen Raum's Orders Growing Out of the TIMES' Dispatches—Force Enough to Stop Bloodshed Authorized." *New York Times*, August 28, 1878.

Tennessee v. Davis, 100 U.S. 257; 24 L. Ed. 648. Washington, D.C.: March1, 1880.

Tsai, Michelle. "Why is Moonshine Against the Law? You Can Make Your Own wine and Beer, Can't You?" *Slate*, October 18, 2007. slate.com/articles/news_and_politics/explainer/2007/10/why_is_moonshine_against_the_law.html

Waite, Campbell Waldo. *Among the Moonshiners*. Chicago: F. Tennyson Neely, 1899.

Waller, Altina. *Feud: Hatfields, McCoys, and Social Change in Appalachia, 1860–1900*. Chapel Hill: University of North Carolina Press, 1988.

Watman, Max. *Chasing the White Dog: An Amateur Outlaw's Adventures in Moonshine*. New York: Simon and Schuster, 2010.

"Ways of the Wicked: Arrest of Two Men for the Tennessee Moonshine Murders—Others Wanted." *Atchison (Kansas) Daily Globe* 2:423 (September 16, 1865).

West, Betsy Foster. "Francis Asbury's Travels in Tennessee." *Ansearchin' News* 34–36 (Spring, Summer, Fall 1987).

Williams, Edie Brown. "William Tyler: Judge, Jury and Executioner." *Cookeville Herald-Citizen*, (Cookeville, TN) (March 8, 2009).

Williamson, J.W. *Hillbillyland: What the Movies Did to the Mountains and What the Mountains Did to the Movies.* Chapel Hill: University of North Carolina Press, 1995.

Wilson, C.M. "Moonshiners." *Outlook* 150 (December 19, 1928).

Wilson, C.M. "Moonshing Becomes Respectable." *Outlook* 158 (May 20, 1931).

Wiltse, Henry M. *The Moonshiners.* Chattanooga, Tennessee: Chattanooga *Times,* 1895.

York, Max. "Moonshining Then and Now: Sometimes the Party Can Get Rough." *Nashville Tennessean Magazine,* July 7, 1968.

Upper Cumberland Medical Society and Physicians

Black Draught Advertisement. Pall Mall, Tennessee, Alvin C. York Papers, Chattanooga Medicine Files, Box 1, Folder 1, October 28, 1919.

Breen, William J. *Uncle Sam At Home: Civilian Mobilization, Wartime Federalism and the Council of National Defense.* West Port, Connecticut, Greenwood Press, 1984.

Clark, Thomas D. "The Farmer and His Almanac." Chattanooga, Tennessee: Bicentennial Library, Historical Collection Clipping File—Chattanooga Medicine Company.

Clemons, Laura E. *The People's Hospital: A History of Cookeville Regional Medical Center, 1950–2010.* Cookeville, Tennessee: The Foundation of the Cookeville Regional Medical Center, 2010.

Cunningham, Horace Herndon. *Doctors in Gray: The Confederate Medical Service.* Baton Rouge: Louisiana State University Press, 1993.

DeLozier, Mary Jean. *Putnam County, Tennessee, 1850–1970.* Nashville, Tennessee: McQuiddy Printing Co., 1979.

Davis, Louise. "Doctors Versus 'God's Will.'" *Nashville Tennessean,* June 13, 1971.

Denton, Mary Jo. "Dr. Thurman Shipley Remembers the Early Twentieth Century," *Cookeville Herald-Citizen,* (Cookeville, Tennessee) March 30, 1989.

Dudney, Robert Lee. "Personal Account." Free State, Tennessee: Unpublished reminiscence of his brush with death.

"Dr. Irvin Grote's Talk to Chattanooga Historical Association, 4/25/71." Chattanooga, Tennessee: Bicentennial Library, Historical Collection Clipping File—Chattanooga Medicine Company.

Garrett, Jacob. "Upper Cumberland Medical Society." Cookeville: Tennessee Technological University Library, Unpublished Student Paper in the Tennessee Room, 2008.

Eldridge, Robert L. and Mary. *Overton County, Tennessee: Bicentennial Echoes of the History of Overton County, 1976.* Livingston, Tennessee: Self-published, 1976.

Fletcher, James L. "Story of a Country Doctor and Banker," *Smith County Historical Society* 19:2 (Spring 2002)

Freeman, Frank R. *Gangrene and Glory: Medical Care during the American Civil War* Champagne-Urbana: University of Illinois Press, 2001.

Goodale, Dora Reed. "Forty Miles from a Hospital—In U.S.A.," *Missionary Review of the World* 60 (December 1937).

Huehls, Betty S. "Life in the Coal Towns of White County, Tennessee, 1882–1936." Cookeville: Tennessee Technological University, Unpublished Master's Thesis, 1983.

Kauffman, Maurice. *The Misadventures of an Appalachian Doctor.* Lexington, Kentucky: Capitol, 1982.

Minton, Lee R. "An Early History of the Upper Cumberland Medical Society," *Journal of the Tennessee Medical Association* 65:2 (February, 1972).

Montell, W. Lynwood. *Tales from Kentucky Doctors.* Lexington: University Press of Kentucky, 2008.

Moore, J. Thomas. *Dr. Tom: Memoirs of Dr. John Thomas Moore.* Nashville, Tennessee: Parthenon Press, 1957.

Myers, Pauline N. "Fighting the Will of God in the Kentucky Mountains," *Hygeia* (June, 1930).

Nolen, Jewel. *The History, Development, and Services of the Putnam County Health Department.* Cookeville, Tennessee: Putnam County Health Department Cooperating with the Putnam County Court, 1965.

O'Connell, Mary Rebecca "One Hundred Percent American," *Catholic World* 131 (May 1930).

Roberts-Moneyham Upper Cumberland Medical Society Collection. Cookeville, Tennessee: Tennessee Technological University Archives.

Rutkow, Ira. *Bleeding Blue and Gray: Civil War Surgery and the Evolution of American Medicine.* New York: Random House, 2005.

Sanderson, Esther Sharp. *County Scott and its Mountain Folk.* Nashville, Tennessee: Blue and Gray Press, 1958.

Shelton, Azariah. *Shelton's American Medicine: Or Improvement in Uniting His new Steam System and the old Practice of Medicine: In Which Doctors' Terms are Explained, and the Complaints of Men, Women and Children, are Treated in a Satisfactory manner; And Remedies Suited to all Climates, Constitutions and Circumstances of the American People; The Valuable Practice and Preparations of Dr. Isaac Wright, of Tennessee, are Fully Developed in This work; It Also Contains a Plain Description of the Whole Human frame: With General Rules for Preserving Health Without the use of Medicines; And a Choice Collection of Roots and Plants, not Explained in any Other Book; and the Practice is Made Perfectly Safe, Simple and Convenient to all Capacities, with but Little Expense.* Madisonville, Tennessee: Henderson and Johnson, 1834.

Shrum, Shelia R. McCarter, Comp. *Bullets, Fire, Moonshine and the Bible: Life in Jackson County, Tennessee.* Lafayette, Tennessee: Ridge Runner Publications, 2004.

Smith, Flavious Joseph Sr. *Enduring Memories: Growing up in Dry Valley, the Heart of the Upper Cumberland.* Cookeville, Tennessee: Self Published, 1984.

Wahler, Ken, Angela Wahler, and Salissa Wahler. "'Bad Roads and Blue Cohosh,' An Oral History of the Obed River Region, Tennessee (and McCreary Count Kentucky)." Wartburg, Tennessee: Unpublished Manuscript at the Obed National Scenic River, National Parks Services, N.D.

Wharton, May Cravath, *Doctor Woman of the Cumberlands.* Pleasant Hill: Uplands, 1953.

Young, William Byrd. "Our Family Tree." Bon Air, Tennessee: Unpublished Manuscript, ca. 1925.

May Cravath Wharton

Clemons, Laura E. *The People's Hospital: A History of Cookeville Regional Medical Center, 1950–2010*. Cookeville, Tennessee: The Foundation of the Cookeville Regional Medical Center, 2010.

Dickinson, W. Calvin. *Cumberland County*. Cookeville: Tennessee Technological University, 1992.

Dodge, Emma F. *History of Pleasant Hill*. Privately printed, 1938.

Dodge, Emma Florence, *Souvenir History of Pleasant Hill Academy*. Privately printed, 1924.

History and Culture. Nashville: Tennessee Historical Society, 1998.

History of Uplands: Cumberland Mountain Sanatorium, Pleasant Hill, Tennessee, 1920–1946 Printed history of Uplands, N.P., N.D.

Krechniak, Helen Bullard, and Joseph M. Krechniak, *Cumberland County's First Hundred Years*. Crossville: Centennial Committee, 1956.

"Organizational Meeting Minutes, Uplands Sanatorium, 1922–1954." Unpublished minutes of board meetings, Nashville, Tennessee: Tennessee State Library and Archives (TSLA), Pleasant Hill Collection.

Parker, Franklin, and Betty J. Parker. "May Cravath Wharton." *The Tennessee Encyclopedia of History and Culture*.

Pleasant Hill Collection. Nashville: Tennessee State Library and Archives.

Pleasant Hill Historical Society of the Cumberlands, *History By the Page*, 1976–2007.

Prosser, Margaret. "Uplands: Cumberland Mountain Hospital and Health Services," Unpublished typewritten report, 1940 in the Pleasant Hill Collection at TSLA.

Tretter, Evelyn K. "Doctor Woman." *Tennessee Conservationist* 54 (Nov–Dec 1988).

Wharton, May Cravath with Helen Bullard Krechniak. *Doctor Woman of the Cumberlands*. Pleasant Hill: Uplands, 1953.

Wharton, May Cravath. "Notebooks," Unpublished memoirs, 6 composition books, no page numbers. Nashville: TSLA, Pleasant Hill Collection.

Wharton Obituary, *Crossville Chronicle*, (Crossville, Tennessee) November 20, 1959.

Wright, E.M. *A People Without Consumption and Some Account of Their Country, the Cumberland Tableland*. Nashville: Tavel, Eastman & Howell, 1876.

Williams, Edie Brown. "Uplands: An Untold Story." Cookeville: Tennessee Technological University Archives, Unpublished Manuscript.

Dora Lee Wilder

Clemons, Laura E. *The People's Hospital: A History of the Cookeville Regional Medical Center* Cookeville, Tennessee: Foundation at Cookeville Regional Medical Center, 2010.

Dillard, John Roy. *Standing Stone, Tennessee: Monterey Early History*. Nashville, Tennessee: Harris Press, 1989.

Hale, Will T. and Dixon Merritt. *A History of Tennessee and Tennesseans: The Leaders and Representative Men in Commerce, Industry and Modern Activities*. Vol. 6. Chicago and New York: Lewis Publishing, 1913.

Lee, John, Jr. Brentwood, Tennessee, Personal papers related to Dora Lee in his possession, and email correspondence between him and W. Calvin Dickinson.

Rogers, Elzia Guy (E.G.). "Lore and Legend of the Upper Cumberlands: Dora Lee Wilder Pioneer Surgeon," *Cookeville Herald Citizen*, (Cookeville, Tennessee) January 28, 1964. Somers, Robert. *Southern States Since the War, 1870–1871*. London: Macmillan, 1871.

Wharton, May Cravath with Helen Bullard Krechniak. *Doctor Woman of the Cumberlands*. Pleasant Hill: Uplands, 1953.

Wilder, Dora Lee. "The Cure of Tuberculosis by the General Practioner [*sic*]." *Southern Medical Journal* (1910).

Wilder, Dora Lee. "The Physical Child Makes a Mental Man," (Cookeville: Tennessee Technological University (TTU) Archives, Unpublished Paper, N.D.

Wilder, Dora Lee. "The Woman in the Field of Medicine." Cookeville, Tennessee: (TTU) Archives, unpublished speech manuscript, N.D.

Williams, Samuel Cole. *General John T. Wilder, Commander of the Lightning Brigade* Bloomington: Indiana University Press, 1936.

Women

Arnow, Harriette Simpson. *Flowering of the Cumberland*. New York: Macmillan, 1963.

Arnow, Harriette Simpson. *The Dollmaker*. New York: Macmillan, 1954.

Arnow, Harriette Simpson. *Hunter's Horn*. New York: Macmillan, 1949.

Barlow, Timothy J. *The Life and Writings of Moses Fiske*. Collegedale: College Press, 1980.

Biggers, Jeff. *The United States of Appalachia: How Southern Mountaineers Brought Independence, Culture and Enlightenment to America*. Emeryville, California: Shoemaker and Hoard, 2006.

Cogswell, Robert. *Tradition: Tennessee Lives and Legacies*. Nashville: Tennessee Arts Commission, 2010.

Diary of Martha Moore Ballard (November 26, 1795) http://dohistory.org/diary/1795/11/17951123_txt.html?d=17951126

Dickinson, W. Calvin and Patrick D. Reagan. "Business, Labor, and the Blue Eagle: The Harriman Hosiery Mill Strike, 1933–1934." *Tennessee Historical Quarterly* LV:3 (Fall 1996).

Dickinson, W. Calvin. *The Walton Road: A Nineteenth Century Wilderness Highway in Tennessee*. Book Surge Publishing, 2007.

Eckley, Wilton. *Harriette Arnow*. New York: Twayne Publishers, 1974.

Faulkner, Charles H., and Carol K. Buckles, eds. *Glimpses of Southern Appalachian Folk Culture: Papers in Memory of Norbert F. Reidl*. Tennessee Anthropological Association, Miscellaneous Paper #3. Chattanooga, Tennessee: Tribute Press, 1978.

Finger, John R. *Tennessee Frontiers: Three Regions in Transition*. Bloomington: University of Indiana Press, 2001.

Gold Thwaites, Reuben., ed. *Travels West of the Alleghenies: Made in 1793–1796 by Andre Michaux, in 1802 by F.A. Michaux, and in 1803 by Thaddeus Mason Harris, M.A.* Cleveland, Ohio: Arthur H. Clark, Co., 1904.

Haywood, John. *The Civil and Political History of the State of Tennessee from its Settlement up to the Year 1796*. Nashville: W.H. Haywood, 1823.

Hughes, Richard T. *Reviving the Ancient Faith: The Story of the Churches of Christ in America*. Grand Rapids, Michigan: Eerdman's, 1996.

Ikard, Robert W. *Just for Fun: The Story of AAU Women's Basketball*. Fayetteville: University of Arkansas Press, 2005.

Keith, Jeannette. *Country People in the New South: Tennessee's Upper Cumberland*. Chapel Hill: University of North Carolina Press, 1995.

Marntz, Steve. "A Good Life Regretted." *The Sporting News* (March 4, 1996).

McBride, Robert M. and Dan M. Robison. "William Walton." *Biographical Directory of the Tennessee General Assembly, Vol. 1, 1796–1861*. Nashville: Tennessee Historical Commission.

McConnell, Deborah. "Lou Cretia Owen and the Old Hickory Munitions Plant During World War I." *Tennessee Historical Quarterly* (Summer 1999):128–139

McDowell, Amanda. *Fiddles in the Cumberland*. Lela McDowell Blankenship, ed. New York: Richard R. Smith, 1943.

"Memorial to Chief Justice D.L. Lansden, Supreme Court of Tennessee, February 12, 1925: Remarks of Hon. K.T. McConnico." *Reports of Cases Argued and Determined in the Supreme Court of Tennessee, 1924*. Vol. 150. Frank M. Thompson, ed. Columbia, Missouri: R.W. Stephens Publishing Co., 1925.

Michaux, Andre. "Journal of Andre Michaux, 1793–1796," *Philosophical Society Proceedings* (1889).

Montell, W. Lynwood. *Don't Go Up Kettle Creek: Verbal Legacy of the Upper Cumberland*. Knoxville: University of Tennessee Press, 1983.

Morris, Eastin. *The Tennessee Gazetteer*. 1834. Reprint. Nashville, 1971.

Puryear, Bill, Jack Masters, and Doug Drake. *Founding of the Cumberland Settlements, 1779–1804*. Vol. 1.

Rohrbough, Malcolm. *The Trans-Appalachian Frontier*. New York: Oxford, 1978.

Schroeder, Albert W., Jr., ed., "Writings of a Tennessee Unionist, Part 1," *Tennessee Historical Quarterly* (September 1960).

Shroeder, Albert W., Jr., ed., "Writings of a Tennessee Unionist, Concluded," *Tennessee Historical Quarterly* (September 1960).

Smith, Al. *Wordsmithing: My Life in Journalism*. Louisville, Kentucky: Pied Type Press, 2011.

Sproul, Mary Catherine. *A Civil War Diary*. Helen Roberts-Gayden, ed. Livingston, Tennessee: Privately Published, 1944.

Turner, Martha Billips. "The Demise of Mountain Life: Harriette Simpson Arnow's Analysis." (1991), *Border States On-Line Journal of the Kentucky-Tennessee American Studies Association*. http://spider.georgetowncollege.edu/htallant/border/bs8/turner.htm

Williams, Samuel Cole. *Early Travels in the Tennessee Country, 1540–1800*. Johnson City: The Watauga Press, 1928.

Manuscript Collections

Anderson, James Douglas (1867–1948) Papers–Addition 1 (1885–1940). Tennessee Historical Society Collections. Nashville: Tennessee State Library and Archives, THS Acc. No. 379.

Catron, John (1786–1865) Papers. Nashville: Tennessee State Library and Archives, Acc. Nos. 79; 97; 177.

Chattanooga Medicine Company Papers. Chattanooga, Tennessee: Bicentennial Library, Special Collections.

Douglas, Byrd Family Papers (1819–1968). Nashville: Tennessee State Library and Archives, Loc. VI-C-1v.

Epperson, Clara Cox Papers (1869–1937). Nashville: Tennessee State Library and Archives, Acc. No. 1991. 238.

Evins, Joe L. Collection. Cookeville, Tennessee: Tennessee Technological University Archives, RG 1.

Farr, T.J. Papers. Cookeville, Tennessee: Tennessee Technological University Archives, RG 59.

Laughlin, Samuel Hervey Papers, 1796–1850. Nashville: Tennessee State Library and Archives, THS 8.

Roberts-Moneyham Upper Cumberland Medical Society Collection. Cookeville, Tennessee: Tennessee Technological University Archives, RG 60.

Smith, Rutledge (1870–1962) and Graeme McGregor (1875–1949) Papers. Nashville: Tennessee State Library and Archives, Tennessee Historical Society Collections, THS RG 893.

Swisher, Carl Brent Collection of Research Materials Pertaining to Roger B. Taney. Washington, D.C.: Library of Congress, RG O4539.

York, Alvin C. Papers. Pall Mall, Tennessee: Sgt. Alvin C. York Historic Site.

CONTRIBUTORS

Michael Allen is a professor of history at the University of Washington at Tacoma. After serving in the Marine Corps as an artilleryman in Vietnam, Allen earned his BA at Central Washington State College, his MA from University of Montana, and his PhD from the University of Washington at Seattle. He taught at Tennessee Technological University (TTU), Deep Springs College in California, and Eastern Montana College. He was born and raised in Ellensburg, Washington. His six books include *Western Rivermen, 1763–1861: Ohio and Mississippi Boatmen and the Myth of the Alligator Horse* (LSU Press, 1990), *Rodeo Cowboys in the North American Imagination* (University of Nevada, 1998), *The Confederation Congress and Creation of the First American Trans-Appalachian Settlement Policy, 1783–1787* (Edwin Mellon, 2006) and the #1 Amazon.com and *New York Times* bestseller, *A Patriot's History of the United States: From Columbus's Great Discovery to the War on Terror* (Sentinel, 2004, coauthored with Larry Schweikart). He is currently working on a comprehensive history of the Ohio and Cumberland River watersheds.

Michael Birdwell is a professor of history at TTU and is the executive director of the Upper Cumberland Institute. He earned his BS and MA at TTU and his PhD at the University of Tennessee at Knoxville (UTK). A cultural historian, Birdwell has worked on over twenty documentary films and has published widely in the *Tennessee Historical Quarterly, Journal of the East Tennessee Historical Society, Film and History, Film/Literature Quarterly, The Columbia Companion to American History on Film,* among other journals. He is the author of *Celluloid Soldiers: Warner Bros. Campaign Against Nazism,* and is coeditor with W. Calvin Dickinson of *Upper Cumberland Historic Architecture* (Hillsboro Press, 2002) and *Rural Life and Culture of the Upper Cumberland* (University Press of Kentucky, 2004). He has a regular feature column in the Cookeville *Herald-Citizen* entitled "Cumberland Tales."

Laura Clemons is a graduate of TTU and learned her craft while serving as assistant news director at TTU. She is coeditor of *Practical Work: 100 Years of Dixie College and Tennessee Tech University* (2009) and author of *The People's Hospital, 1950–2010: A History of the Cookeville Regional Medical Center* (2010). She served as the executive director of the Bryan Symphony Orchestra and is currently spearheading the centennial celebration of Tennessee Technological University.

Al Cross has been director of the Institute for Rural Journalism and Community Issues at the University of Kentucky (UK) since 2004, where he is also an associate professor in the School of Journalism and Telecommunications. He reported for the *Louisville Courier-Journal* for twenty-six years, the last fifteen of those as its chief political writer. He continues to publish two political columns per month for the paper. A past president of the Society of Professional Journalists (2001–2002), he was inducted into the Kentucky Journalism Hall of Fame. He shared a Pulitzer Prize with other *Courier-Journal* staffers for their coverage of the nation's deadliest bus and drunk-driving crash. Cross has contributed to numerous books on Kentucky and politics and frequently speaks on those topics. He grew up in Albany, Kentucky and graduated from Western Kentucky University. After graduation he served as an editor and manager at weekly newspapers in Monticello, Leitchfield, and Russellville, Kentucky, before joining *The Courier-Journal* in 1978.

David Cross grew up in Albany, Kentucky, and graduated from Clinton County High School. He received his bachelors degree in history from Western Kentucky University, and he received a law degree from the University of Louisville Brandeis School of Law and began his legal career in the offices of Wilson & Smith, in Jamestown, Kentucky. He has practiced law in Albany since 1985 and was joined by his daughter in the practice in 2010. He has served as Clinton County Republican Party Chairman, as a delegate to the Republican National Convention, and as a current member of the Kentucky State Board of Elections.

W. Calvin Dickinson is professor emeritus of history at TTU. He earned his BA at Baylor University and his PhD at the University of North Carolina at Chapel Hill. He has published widely in a number of scholarly journals. He is the author, coauthor, or editor of the following: *Lend an Ear: Heritage of the Upper Cumberland; History of Morgan County, Tennessee in American History; Letters of Cornelius Tenure, Civil War Soldier; Cumberland County, Tennessee; Tennessee: State of the Nation; Tennessee Tales the Textbooks Don't Tell; History of Tennessee Tech University; Rural Life and Culture of the Upper Cumberland;* and *E is for Elvis,* among other works.

Janey Dudney earned her BA in English at TTU and two MAs, one in English and the other in history. She taught both English and history at TTU, and her soon to be published master's thesis, *Civil War in White County, Tennessee, 1861–1865,* is already highly renowned. Her husband, E. Morgan Dudney, practiced as a physician in Jackson County for over thirty years.

Mark Dudney, a native of Jackson County, Tennessee, earned his bachelors degree in history and political science at TTU and went on to pursue a law degree at the Nashville School of Law. He has contributed numerous articles to such publications as *Tennessee Living Magazine, The Cumberland Business Journal,* WCTE's *Close Up* magazine, and the ongoing series edited by W. Calvin Dickinson and Michael Birdwell for the Cookeville *Herald-Citizen,* "Cumberland Tales." He works as a public historian at the Upper Cumberland Development District where he continues to discover the rich history of the region.

Mary A. Evins earned her PhD from the University of Chicago and is an associate professor of history in the Center for Historic Preservation and the History Department at Middle Tennessee State University, where she coordinates the American Democracy Project, dedicated to civic learning and engagement. She has published numerous essays about women's history and is currently engaged in research about gender, women's work, and women's history in Tennessee and the U.S. She is the editor of *Tennessee Women in the Progressive Era: Toward the Public Sphere in the New South* (University of Tennessee Press, 2013).

Wali R. Kharif earned his BA, MA, and PhD from Florida State University and is a professor of history at TTU. He has published eight book chapters, eight scholarly articles, and numerous other writings. Among his works is *Reminiscences and Reflections: African Americans in the Kentucky-Tennessee Upper Cumberland Since the Civil War,* which was coauthored with W. Lynwood Montell.

John Nisbet III was born and raised in a north Alabama town named after Andrew Jackson, in a county named after John C. Calhoun (originally after Thomas Hart Benton) that his family started in 1830 having "bought" the land from Creek Indian Chief Ladiga and later (in 1836) bought more land that had suddenly become available from the United States government. Nisbet went to a Presbyterian college in Memphis, Tennessee, originally named "Southwestern." He graduated from the St. Louis School of Law and has practiced as an assistant attorney general, assistant district attorney, and assistant public defender. He was indoctrinated to be the family historian (and possessor of all things irrelevant in his extended birth family) and is currently devoting much of his time to the pursuit of legal history in the Upper Cumberland.

Troy Smith is an Upper Cumberland native from White County, Tennessee. Smith earned his BA in history at TTU and his PhD at the University of Illinois. Smith's dissertation, *Race, Slavery and Nation in Indian Territory, 1830–1866,* was selected as a finalist for the prestigious C. Vann Woodward award. In addition to being a professional historian, Smith is an accomplished novelist, storyteller, and short story writer who has won numerous accolades, including the coveted Silver Spur Award for Western fiction. He is an assistant professor of history at TTU.

After earning her BA in English and anthropology at the University of Tennessee at Knoxville, **Ann Toplovich** worked as a historic preservation specialist at the Tennessee Historical Commission. Currently executive director of the Tennessee Historical Society, Toplovich has been involved in both academic and public history throughout her career. She has served on numerous boards pertaining to public history, managed dozens of grant projects, and assisted in the publication of dozens of works dedicated to Tennessee history. Though not native to the Upper Cumberland, she and her husband have owned a home in Jackson County for decades, and they consider the region to be their real home. Her publications include "Marriage, Mayhem, and Presidential Politics: The Robards Jackson Backcountry Scandal," "Life at the Hermitage," and "The Tennessee Historical Society at 150: Tennessee History 'Just and True.'"

Opless Walker earned his BS and doctorate of pharmacy at the University of Tennessee at Memphis. He has taught numerous courses in clinical pharmacology, psychopharmacology, drugs and behavioral science, and he acted as pharmacy preceptor at UT Memphis, Mercer University, and Lipscomb University. He acts as head pharmacist at the Cookeville Regional Medical Center. An avid researcher, he has long been interested in the history and folklore of the region, and he formerly published a magazine devoted to its history, *The Standing Stone Press*.

Randal D. Williams earned his BS and MA at TTU and conducted additional graduate work at Miami University of Ohio. His educational background focused on history, anthropology, and sociolinguistics. He has worked as a field archaeologist with the Tennessee Division of Archaeology and taught numerous courses at TTU. He is the co-owner of Kwill Consultants and is working on numerous public history projects.

INDEX

Entries in **boldface** refer to illustrations.

www.ingramcontent.com/pod-product-compliance
Lightning Source LLC
Chambersburg PA
CBHW020242120726
47904CB00001B/62

* 9 7 8 1 6 2 1 9 0 3 7 1 0 *